RANDOM
HOUSE
WEBSTER'S

MEDICAL
SPELL CHECKER

RANDOM
HOUSE
WEBSTER'S

MEDICAL
SPELL CHECKER

RANDOM HOUSE
NEW YORK

CONTENTS

STAFF

Project Editor: Enid Pearsons
Contributing Editors: Barbara Ann Kipfer, Bonny Hart
Editorial Staff: Georgia S. Maas, Lisbeth Dyer
Database Manager: Constance A. Baboukis
Director of Production: Patricia W. Ehresmann
Editorial Director: Wendalyn Nichols
Publisher: Charles M. Levine

HOW TO USE THIS BOOK

When to Use a Spell Checker

Dictionaries offer a wealth of information about words. They tell you how words are spelled, how many syllables they have, and what they mean. They tell you how to say the words, where those words come from, where they fit into the grammar of the language, and when you ought to be cautious about using them. Some dictionaries even include information of the kind one finds in a thesaurus—lists of words that mean approximately the same thing. Larger dictionaries may also feature illustrations, maps, and other graphic materials.

But with all the information that dictionaries make available, research shows that the most common use people make of dictionaries is simply to check spellings. However, if you want to look up a spelling quickly, or find out where to break a word at the end of a line, the most convenient reference to use may not be a large standard dictionary at all, but a specialized book like the *Random House Webster's Medical Spell Checker*, a small, handy "speller-divider" dedicated to the vocabulary used in the field of medicine.

Contents

This spell checker has some 40,000 entries drawn from diverse medical fields, including anatomy, medicine, pathology, pharmacy, dentistry, and alternative medicine. These entries include up-to-date new terms that have burst into the public consciousness only recently: terms like bovine spongiform encephalopathy (mad cow disease), Evista (a brand name for raloxifene, a so-called "designer estrogen"), and cochlear implant (a controversial early treatment for a form of deafness). In addition, the book contains many relevant terms from the common vocabulary which are seen and heard frequently in medical contexts. This range of terms is presented in a single alphabetical list.

An appendix at the back of the book gives addresses for useful World Wide Web sites in the field of medicine, together with brief descriptions of their contents.

Word Division

The *Random House Medical Spell Checker* not only provides spellings for a vast number of difficult technical terms, but divides them into syllables. This can help users of the *Medical Spell Checker* in at least two ways: it can aid them in figuring out pronunciations, and it can show where best to divide a word at the end of a line. In fact, unlike most similar books, this one clearly distinguishes between those syllable divisions that may appropriately be used for end-of-line hyphenation and those that, preferably, should not be.

Symbols Used in this Book to Show Word Breaks

Word breaks, or syllable divisions, that are acceptable when a word must be hyphenated at the end of a line are indicated by a solid bullet, • , as in ab•sorb. Word breaks that are less acceptable (or not at all so) for use at the end of a line are indicated by a hollow bullet, ◦ , as in a◦buse. A hyphen also indicates a preferred division point, whether the hyphen is part of a word's spelling (lying-in) or is used to show the beginning of a shortened inflected form (-duced, -ducing).

Rules for Word Division

Like many sets of rules, preferences, and prohibitions, those that apply to word division exist in a graded continuum; some violations of the rules are worse than others. Here are some general guidelines about word division, with hints about which ones are important to follow, as against those that may be relaxed if the need arises.

- Do not ever divide a one-syllable word: ache. This includes past tenses like ached and breathed, which should never be split before the -ed ending.

- A syllable consisting of a single letter should never begin or end a line: the word a◦brad•ant should not be divided after the initial a, leaving a- at the end of a line. Similarly, the word cau•ter◦y should not be divided before the final -y, because that would mean that y alone had to begin a line.

- Word segments like -ceous, -scious, -tion, and -tious should not be divided: de•vo•lu•tion•ist (not -tio∘nist).

- It is best not to divide a word of five letters or less: ce∘cum should not be divided, but its variant spelling cae•cum may be.

- Hyphenated compounds should preferably be divided after the hyphen. If the first portion of the compound is a single letter, however, as in C-sec•tion, while it is best not to divide the word at all, an end-of-line division after C-sec- is less confusing than one after the initial C-.

Note that although we have shown permissible syllable breaks within the individual words that form hyphenated compounds, these division points should be used only if it is difficult or impossible to break after the hyphen.

- It is preferable not to divide before the final two letters of a word:

  am•pli∘fy (divide as am-plify, not ampli-fy)

  ki•net∘ic (divide as ki-netic, not kinet-ic)

  me•di∘um (divide as me-dium, not medi-um)

- Within a word, the general rule is to divide after rather than before a single vowel that is, a vowel between two consonants:

  ker∘a•to•sis (divide as kera-tosis, not ker-atosis)

  em∘i•gra•tion (divide as emi-gration, not em-igration)

- However, there are exceptions to this rule when strict adherence to it might result in mispronunciation of the portion of a word left at the end of the line. In the following words, division after what looks like a silent *e* would make a reader pronounce the previous vowel as if it were "long."

gen•e∘sis (divide as gen-esis, not gene-sis)

op•tom•e∘try (divide as optom-etry, not optome-try)

- In the following examples, the words are best divided so as to avert a misleading pronunciation of the letters *c* and *g*.

tox•ic∘i∘ty (divide as tox-icity, not toxic-ity)

ly•sog∘e∘ny (divide as ly-sogeny, not lysog-eny)

These rules mean that sometimes, even a word of more than five letters cannot be divided (for example, glos∘sa). But on the whole, such rules are worth following. While some of them may seem arbitrary, they exist so as to make reading easier. The fundamental idea behind rules of syllabification is to avoid forcing readers to retrace their steps in order to comprehend what they have just read.

RANDOM
HOUSE
WEBSTER'S

MEDICAL
SPELL CHECKER

A band
a∘bac∘te∘ri∘al
a∘ba∘sia
a∘ba∘sia trep∘i∘dans
a∘ba∘sic
ab•ax∘i∘al
Ab∘be con∘dens•er
Ab∘bo-Pac *Trademark.*
Ab•bo•ki•nase *Trademark.*
Ab•der•hal•den re•ac•tion
ab•do•men
ab•dom∘i∘nal
abdominal a∘or∘ta
abdominal cav∘i∘ty
abdominal flap
abdominal re•flex
abdominal re•gion
abdominal ring
ab•dom∘i•nal∘ly
ab•dom∘i•no•pel•vic
ab•dom∘i•no•per∘i•ne∘al
abdominoperineal re•sec•tion
ab•dom∘i•no•plas∘ty, *n., pl.*
  -ties.
ab•dom∘i•nous
ab•duce, *v.,* -duced, -duc•ing.
ab•du•cens, *n., pl.* -cen•tes.
ab•du•cens nerve
ab•du•cent
ab•duct
ab•duc•tion
ab•duc•tor
abductor dig∘i∘ti min∘i∘mi
abductor digiti quin∘ti nerve
  en•trap•ment
abductor hal•lu•cis
abductor pol•li•cis bre•vis
abductor pollicis lon•gus
A∘begg's rule

ab•em•bry•on∘ic
a∘ber•rant clone
ab•er•ra•tion
ab•er•ra•tion∘al
a∘bey•ance
ab∘i•ence
ab∘i•ent
ab•ies
a∘bi∘o∘gen•e∘sis
a∘bi∘o∘gen•e∘sist
a∘bi∘o∘gen∘ic
a∘bi∘o∘gen∘i•cal∘ly
a∘bi•og∘e∘nist
a∘bi∘o•log∘i∘cal
a∘bi∘o•log∘i∘cal∘ly
a∘bi•ot∘ic
a∘bi•ot∘i∘cal∘ly
a∘bi∘o•troph∘ic
a∘bi•ot•ro•phy
ab•lac•ta•tion
a∘blas•te•mic
a∘blas•tin
ab•late, *v.,* -lat∘ed, -lat•ing.
a∘bla•ti∘o pla•cen•tae
ab•la•tion
ab•lu•tion
a∘blu•tion•ar∘y
ab•nor•mal
abnormal psy∘chol∘o∘gy
ab•nor•mal∘i∘ty, *n., pl.* -ties.
ab•nor•mal∘ly
ABO sys•tem
ab∘o•ma∘sal
ab∘o•ma∘si•tis
ab∘o•ma•sum, *n., pl.* -ma∘sa.
ab•o∘rad
ab•o∘ral∘ly
a∘bort, *v.,* -bort∘ed,
  -bort•ing.

a○bort○er
a○bor○ti○cide
a○bor○ti○fa○cient
a○bor○tion
abortion-on-de○mand
abortion pill
a○bor○tion○ist
a○bor○tive
a○bor○tus, *n., pl.* -tus○es.
a○bou○li○a
a○bou○lic
a○bra○chi○a
a○brad○ant
a○brade, *v.,* -brad○ed, -brad○
  ing.
a○bra○sion
a○bra○sive
a○bra○sive○ness
ab○re○act
ab○re○ac○tion
ab○re○ac○tive
a○bro○si○a
ab○rup○ti○o pla○cen○tae
ab○scess
ab○scessed
ab○sces○sus flat○u○o○sus
abscessus per de○cu○bi○tum
ab○scis○sion
ab○sco○pal
ab○sence
ab○sinth
ab○sinthe
ab○sin○thin
ab○sin○thism
ab○sin○this○mic
ab○sin○thi○um
ab○sin○thol
ab○so○lute
absolute al○co○hol
absolute re○frac○to○ry
  pe○ri○od
ab○sorb

ab○sorb○a○ble
ab○sorb○ance
ab○sorb○an○cy
ab○sorbed
ab○sorb○e○fa○cient
ab○sorb○en○cy, *n., pl.* -cies.
ab○sorb○ent
absorbent cot○ton
ab○sorb○er
ab○sorp○ti○om○e○ter
ab○sorp○ti○o○met○ric
ab○sorp○tion
absorption co○ef○fi○cient
absorption spec○trum
ab○sorp○tive
ab○sorp○tiv○i○ty
ab○stain
ab○stain○er
ab○ster○gent
ab○sti○nence or ab○sti○nen○cy
abstinence syn○drome
ab○sti○nent
ab○sti○nent○ly
ab○stract
abstract at○ti○tude
ab○stract○er
ab○strac○tor
a○bu○li○a
a○bu○lic
a○bu○sa○ble
a○buse, *v.,* -bused,
  -bus○ing.
a○bus○er
a○but○ment
ac○a○dem○ic skills dis○or○der
a○cal○cu○li○a
a○can○thi○on
A○can○tho○ceph○a○la
a○can○tho○ceph○a○lan
A○can○tho○chei○lo○ne○ma
Acanthocheilonema per○stans
a○can○tho○cyte

a•can•thoid
ac•an•thol•y•sis, *n., pl.* -ses.
acantholysis bul•lo•sa
ac•an•tho•ma, *n., pl.* -mas,
  -ma•ta.
acanthoma ad•e•noi•des
acanthoma cys•ti•cum
ac•an•tho•sis
acanthosis ni•gri•cans
a•can•thot•ic
a•cap•ni•a
a•cap•ni•al
a•car•di•a•cus a•ceph•a•lus
acardiacus a•mor•phus
acardiacus an•ceps
a•car•di•ous
ac•a•ri•a•sis, *n. pl.* -ses.
a•car•i•cid•al
a•car•i•cide
ac•a•rid
Ac•a•ri•na
ac•a•rine
ac•a•ri•no•sis
ac•a•ro•der•ma•ti•tis
acarodermatitis ur•ti•car•i•
  oi•des
ac•a•rol•o•gist
ac•a•rol•o•gy
ac•a•ro•pho•bi•a
ac•a•rus, *n., pl.* -ri.
Acarus fol•lic•u•lo•rum
Acarus sca•bi•ei
a•cat•a•la•si•a
ac•a•thi•sia
a•cau•dal
a•cau•date
ac•cel•er•ate, *v.,* -at•ed,
  -at•ing.
ac•cel•er•a•tion
acceleration of grav•i•ty
ac•cel•er•a•tive
ac•cel•er•a•tor

accelerator glob•u•lin
accelerator nerve
ac•cel•er•a•to•ry
ac•cel•er•oin
ac•cel•er•om•e•ter
ac•cept
ac•cep•tor
ac•ces•so•ri•ous, *n., pl.* -ri•i.
accessorius ad flex•o•rem
  dig•i•to•rum pro•fun•dum
ac•ces•so•ry
accessory hem•i•a•zy•gos
  vein
accessory nerve
accessory ol•i•va•ry
  nu•cle•ous
accessory pan•cre•at•ic duct
ac•ci•dent
accident-prone
ac•ci•den•tal
accidental death
accidental in•ju•ry
ac•ci•den•tal•ly
ac•cli•mate, *v.,* -mat•ed,
  -mat•ing.
ac•cli•ma•tion
ac•cli•ma•ti•za•tion
ac•cli•ma•tize, *v.,* -tized,
  -tiz•ing.
ac•com•mo•da•tion
ac•com•mo•da•tive
ac•com•mo•date, *v.,* -dat•ed,
  -dat•ing.
ac•couche•ment
accouchement force
ac•cou•cheur
ac•cou•cheuse
ac•cre•ti•o cor•dis
ac•cre•tion
ac•cre•tion•ar•y
Ac•cu•pril *Trademark.*
Ac•cur•bron *Trademark.*

Ac•cu•tane *Trademark.*
Ace *Trademark.*
Ace band•age *Trademark.*
ACE in•hib•i•tor
a•cel•lu•lar
a•cen•tric
a•ce•pha•lia
a•ce•phal•ic
a•ceph•a•lo•cyst
a•ceph•a•lous
a•ceph•a•lus, *n., pl.*
-li.
ac•er•o•o•la
a•cer•vu•lus, *n., pl.* -vu•li.
acervulus ce•re•bri
a•ces•cent
a•ces•o•dyne
a•ce•ta
ac•e•tab•u•lar
acetabular notch
ac•e•tab•u•lo•plas•ty, *n., pl.*
-ties.
ac•e•tab•u•lum, *n., pl.*
ac•e•tal
ac•et•al•de•hyde
ac•et•am•ide
a•ce•ta•min•o•phen
Acetaminophen/
Co•deine *Trademark.*
ac•et•an•o•i•lid
ac•et•an•o•i•lide
ac•et•ar•sol
ac•et•ar•sone
ac•e•tate
ac•et•o•a•zol•o•a•mide
a•cet•e•onyl
a•cet•oic
acetic ac•id
acetic an•hy•dride
a•cet•o•i•fi•ca•tion
a•ce•ti•fi•er
a•ce•ti•fy, *v.,* -fied, -fy•ing.

ac•e•tim•e•ter
ac•e•tin
a•ce•to•a•ce•tate
a•ce•to•a•cet•oic acid
a•ce•to•bac•ter
a•ce•to•dol•u•ble
a•ce•to•hex•a•mide
a•ce•to•in
ac•e•tol•y•sis, *n., pl.* -ses.
a•ce•to•me•roc•tol
ac•e•tom•e•ter
a•ce•to•mor•phine
a•ce•to•naph•thone
ac•e•tone
acetone bod•y
ac•e•to•ne•mi•a
ac•e•to•ne•mic
ac•e•ton•ic
ac•e•to•ni•trile
ac•e•to•nu•ri•a
a•ce•to•phe•net•i•din
a•ce•to•phe•none
a•ce•tous
ac•e•tract
a•ce•tum, *n., pl.* -ta.
a•ce•tyl
acetyl CoA
acetyl co•en•zyme A
a•cet•o•y•lase
a•cet•o•y•late, *v.,* -lat•ed,
-lat•ing.
a•cet•o•y•la•tion
a•cet•o•y•la•tive
a•ce•tyl•cho•line
a•ce•tyl•cho•lin•es•ter•ase
a•ce•tyl•cho•lin•oic
a•ce•tyl•cys•te•ine
a•cet•o•y•lene
a•cet•o•y•len•oic
a•cet•yl•meth•yl•car•bi•nol
a•cet•yl•phen•yl•hy•dra•
zine

a○ce○tyl○sa○lic○y○late
a○ce○tyl○sal○i○cyl○ic ac○id
a○ce○tyl○trans○fer○ase
Ac•glob○u•lin
ach○a•la•sia
ache, n., v., ached, ach•ing.
a○che•mat○o○graph
Aches-N-Pain *Trademark.*
ach○i○er
ach○i•est
a○chieve•ment age
achievement test
A○chil•le○a
a○chil•le•ine
A○chil•les re•flex
Achilles or A○chil•les'
  ten•don
ach○i•ness
a○chi•ral
a○chlor•hy•dri○a
a○chlor•hy•dric
a○cho•li○a
a○chol○ic
ach○o○lous
ach○o•lu•ri○a
ach○o•lu•ric
a○chon•dro•pla•sia
a○chon•dro•plas•tic
A○cho•ri○on
a○chro•a•cyte
a○chro○ma
a○chro•ma•cyte
ach•ro•ma•sia
ach•ro•mat
ach•ro•mat○ic
achromatic fig•ure
achromatic lens
ach•ro•mat○i•cal○ly
a○chro•ma•tic○i○ty
a○chro•ma•tin
a○chro•ma•tism

a○chro•ma•tize, v., -tized,
  -tiz○ing.
a○chro•mat○o•cyte
a○chro•ma•tol○y•sis
a○chro•mat○o•phil
a○chro•mat○o•phil○i○a
a○chro•ma•top•si○a
a○chro•mi○a
achromia cu○tis
achromia par○a•sit○i○ca
a○chro•mic
a○chro•mo•bac•ter
a○chro•mo•trich○i○a
Ach•ro•my•cin *Trademark.*
Achromycin V *Trademark.*
ach○y
a○chyl○i○a
achylia gas•tri○ca
achylia pan•cre•at○i○ca
a○chy•lous
Aci-Jel *Trademark.*
a○cic○u•lar
ac○id
acid-base bal•ance
acid dye
acid-fast
acid-fast•ness
acid fuch•sin
acid funch•sine
ac○id•head
acid phos•pha•tase
acid pre•cip○i•ta•tion
acid rain
ac○i•de•mi○a
a○cid○ic
a○cid○i•fi•a•ble
a○cid○i•fi•ca•tion
a○cid○i•fi○er
a○cid•i○fy, v., -fied, -fy•ing.
ac○i•dim•e○ter
ac○i•di•met•ric
ac○i•dim•e○try

a○cid○i○ty
ac○i○do●gen○ic
a○cid○o●phil
a○cid○o●phile
ac○i○do●phil○i○a
a○cid○o●phil○ic or ac○i●doph○i●lous
ac○i○doph○i●lus milk
ac○i○do●sis
ac○i○dot○ic
a○cid○o○u●late, *v.*, -lat○ed, -lat○ing.
a○cid○o○u●lous
ac○i●du○ri○a
ac○i●du●ric
ac○i●dyl
ac○i●nar
a○cin○ic
ac○i●nose
ac○i●nous
ac○i●nus, *n., pl.* -ni.
ack○ee
ac●la●sis, *n., pl.* -ses.
a○clas●tic
Ac●lo●vate *Trademark.*
ac●me
ac●mes●the●sia
ac○ne
acne ro●sa●ce○a
acne ur●ti●ca○ta
acne vul●gar○is
ac○ned
Ac●ne●derm *Trademark.*
ac●ne●form
ac●ne●gen○ic
ac●ne●i●form
ac●ni●tis
Ac●no●mel *Trademark.*
Ac○o●can●ther○a
a○coe●lo●mate
a○co●ine
a○con○i●tase

ac○o●nite
ac○o●nit○ic ac○id
a○con○i●tine
A○co●ni●tum
a○cou●me●ter
a○cous○ma, *n., pl.* -mas, -ma○ta.
a○cous○tic
acoustic me●a●tus
acoustic mi●cro●scope
acoustic mi●cros●co○py
acoustic nerve
acoustic neu●ro○ma
acoustic re●flex
acoustic tu●ber●cle
a○cous○ti●cal
a○cous○tics
ac●quire, *v.*, -quired, -quir●ing.
ac●quired
acquired char●ac○ter
acquired im●mune de●fi●cien○cy syn●drome
acquired im●mu●ni○ty
ac●quir○ing
ac●ral
a○cra●ni○a
ac○rid
ac●ri●dine
acridine or●ange
ac●rid○ly
ac●ri●fla●vine
ac●ro●blast
ac●ro●cen●tric
ac●ro●ce●pha●li○a
ac●ro●ce●phal○ic
ac●ro●ceph○a●lo●syn●dac●ty○ly
ac●ro●ceph○a●lous
ac●ro●ceph○a○ly
ac●ro●chor●don
ac●ro●cy○a●no●sis
ac●ro●cy●a●not○ic

ac•ro•der•ma•ti•tis
acrodermatitis chron•i•ca
 a•troph•i•cans
acrodermatitis con•tin•u•a
acrodermatitis en•ter•o•
 path•i•ca
acrodermatitis hi•e•ma•lis
acrodermatitis pus•tu•lo•sa
 per•stans
ac•ro•dy•ni•a
ac•ro•dyn•ic
ac•ro•ge•ri•a
ac•ro•ker•a•to•sis
acrokeratosis ver•ru•ci•for•
 mis
a•cro•le•in
ac•ro•me•gal•ic
ac•ro•meg•a•loid
ac•ro•meg•a•ly
a•cro•mi•al
acromial proc•ess
ac•ro•mic•ri•a
ac•ro•mi•o•cla•vic•u•lar
acromioclavicular joint
a•cro•mi•on
a•cro•mi•o•nec•to•my
ac•ro•pach•y
ac•ro•par•es•the•si•a
a•crop•o•a•thy
ac•ro•phobe
ac•ro•pho•bi•a
ac•ro•pho•bic
ac•ro•scler•o•der•ma
ac•ro•scle•ro•sis
ac•ro•so•mal
ac•ro•some
ac•ryl•al•de•hyde
ac•ry•late
a•cryl•ic
acrylic ac•id
acrylic res•in
ac•ry•lo•ni•trile

act
act out
Ac•tae•a
Ac•ta•hist *Trademark.*
ACTH
Ac•thar *Trademark.*
Ac•ti•bine *Trademark.*
Ac•ti•cort *Trademark.*
Ac•ti•dil *Trademark.*
Ac•ti•do•es-Aq•ua *Trademark.*
Ac•ti•dose *Trademark.*
Ac•ti•fed *Trademark.*
Ac•ti•gall *Trademark.*
ac•tin
act•ing out
ac•tin•ic
actinic ray
ac•tin•i•cal•ly
ac•tin•ism
ac•tin•i•um
Ac•tin-N *Trademark.*
ac•ti•no•bac•il•lo•sis
ac•ti•no•ba•cil•lus, *n., pl.* -li.
Actinobacillus lig•ni•e•re•si•i
Actinobacillus mal•le•i
ac•ti•no•chem•is•try
ac•ti•no•der•ma•ti•tis
ac•tin•o•graph
ac•ti•nol•o•gy
ac•ti•nom•e•ter
ac•ti•no•met•ric
ac•ti•nom•e•try
ac•ti•no•my•ces, *n., pl.* -ces.
Actinomyces bo•vis
Actinomyces is•ra•e•li•i
Actinomyces naes•lun•di•i
Ac•ti•no•my•ce•ta•ce•ae
ac•ti•no•my•ce•tal
ac•ti•no•my•ce•ta•les
ac•ti•no•my•cete
ac•ti•no•mycetin

ac•ti•no•my•ce•tous
ac•ti•no•my•cin
actinomycin D
ac•ti•no•my•co•ma, *n.*, *pl.*
  -mas, -ma•ta.
ac•ti•no•my•co•sis
ac•ti•no•my•cot•ic
ac•ti•non
ac•ti•no•phage
ac•ti•no•phy•to•sis, *n.*, *pl.*
  -ses.
ac•ti•no•spec•ta•cin
ac•ti•no•ther•a•py
ac•tion
action po•ten•tial
Ac•ti•vase *Trademark.*
ac•ti•vat•ed char•coal
ac•ti•va•tor
ac•tive
active im•mu•ni•ty
active trans•port
ac•tive•ly
ac•tiv•i•ties of dai•ly liv•ing
ac•tiv•i•ty, *n.*, *pl.* -ties.
ac•to•my•o•sin
ac•tu•al cau•ter•y
actual neu•ro•sis
Ac•u•ar•i•a
a•cu•i•ty
a•cu•le•ate
a•cu•mi•nate
ac•u•pres•sure
ac•u•pres•sur•ist
ac•u•punc•ture
acupuncture point
ac•u•punc•tur•ist
ac•u•sec•tor
a•cute
acute ab•do•men
acute al•co•hol•ism
acute dis•sem•i•nat•ed
  en•ceph•a•lo•my•e•li•tis

acute moun•tain sick•ness
acute nec•ro•tiz•ing gin•gi•
  vi•tis
acute on•set
acute yel•low at•ro•phy
a•cute•ly
a•cute•ness
Ac•u•trim *Trademark.*
a•cy•a•not•ic
a•cyc•lic
a•cy•clo•vir
ac•yl
ac•yl•al
A•cyl•a•nid *Trademark.*
ac•y•lase
ac•y•late, *v.*, -lat•ed, -lat•ing.
ac•y•la•tion
a•cys•tic
ad lib
a•dac•tyl•i•a
a•dac•ty•lous
Ad•a•gen *Trademark.*
Ad•a•lat *Trademark.*
Adalat CC *Trademark.*
ad•a•man•tine
ad•a•man•ti•no•ma, *n.*, *pl.*
  -mas, -ma•ta.
ad•a•man•ti•nom•a•tous
ad•a•man•to•blast
ad•a•man•to•blas•to•ma, *n.*,
  pl. -mas, -ma•ta.
Ad•am's ap•ple
Ad•ams-Stokes at•tack
Adams-Stokes dis•ease
Adams-Stokes syn•drome
ad•ams•ite
A•dan•so•ni•a dig•i•ta•ta
Ad•a•pin *Trademark.*
a•dapt
ad•ap•ta•tion
ad•ap•ta•tion•al
ad•ap•ta•tion•al•ly

a○dapt○er
adapter RNA
a○dap•tive
adaptive be•hav•ior scales
adaptive ra•di•a•tion
a○dap•tive•ly
a○dap•tive•ness
ad•ap•tom•e○ter
ad•ap•tom•e○try
a○dap•tor
adaptor RNA
ad•ax○i○al
ad•der
ad•dict
ad•dic•tion
ad•dic•tive
ad•dic•tive•ness
Ad•dis count
Ad•di•son's a○ne•mi•a
Ad•di•so•ni○an
addisonian a○ne•mi•a
Ad•di•son's disease
ad•di•tive•ly
ad•di•tiv○i○ty, *n., pl.* -ties.
ad•du•cent
ad•duct
ad•duc•tion
ad•duc•tive
ad•duc•tor
adductor bre○vis
adductor ca•nal syn•drome
adductor hal•lu•cis
adductor lon•gus
adductor longus ten•di•ni•tis
adductor mag•nus
adductor pol•li•cis
adductor tu•ber•cle
ad•e○nase
a○den•drit○ic
a○denoi•form
ad•e○nine

ad•e○ni•tis
ad•e○no•ac•an•tho○ma, *n.,*
  pl. -mas, -ma○ta.
ad•e○no•car•ci•no○ma, *n., pl.*
  -mas, -ma○ta.
ad•e○no•car•ci•nom○a•tous
A○den○o○card *Trademark.*
ad•e○no•cys•to○ma, *n., pl.*
  -mas, -ma○ta.
adenocystoma
  lym•pho•ma•to•sum
ad•e○no•fi•bro○ma, *n., pl.*
  -mas, -ma○ta.
ad•e○no•hy•poph○y•se○al
ad•e○no•hy•po•phys○i○al
ad•e○no•hy•poph○y•sis, *n.,*
  pl. -ses.
ad•e○noid
ad•e○noi•dal
ad•e○noid•ec•to•my, *n., pl.*
  -mies.
ad•e○noid•ism
ad•e○noid○i•tis
ad•e○no•lym•pho•cele
ad•e○no•lym•pho○ma, *n., pl.*
  -mas, -ma○ta.
ad•e○no○ma, *n., pl.* -mas,
  -ma○ta.
adenoma de•stru•ens
adenoma ma•lig•num
adenoma se•ba•ce○um
adenoma sub•stan•ti○ae
  cor•ti•ca•lis su•pra•re•na•
  lis
adenoma su•do•rip○a•rum
ad•e○no•ma•toid
ad•e○no•ma•to•sis, *n., pl.*
  -ses.
ad•e○nom○a•tous
ad•e○no•mere
ad•e○no•my○o○ma, *n., pl.*
  -mas, -ma○ta.

ad•e•no•my•o•sis
ad•e•no•neu•ral
ad•e•nop•a•thy
a•den•o•sine
adenosine di•phos•phate
adenosine mon•o•phos•phate
adenosine phos•phate
adenosine tri•phos•phate
ad•e•no•sis
ad•e•no•tome
ad•e•not•o•my, *n.*, *pl.* -mies.
ad•e•no•vi•ral
ad•e•no•vi•rus, *n.*, *pl.*
-rus•es.
ad•e•onyl
adenyl cy•clase
a•den•y•late cyclase
ad•e•nyl•ic ac•id
ad•eps
adeps la•nae, *n.*, *pl.* ad•i•pes
la•nae.
ad•here, *v.*, -hered, -her•ing.
ad•her•ence
ad•he•si•o in•ter•tha•
lam•i•ca
ad•he•sion•al
ad•he•sive
adhesive per•i•car•di•tis
adhesive tape
ad•he•sive•ly
ad•i•ac•tin•ic
a•di•a•do•cho•ki•ne•sis, *n.*,
pl. -ses.
a•di•a•do•ko•ki•ne•sis, *n.*,
pl. -ses.
Ad•i•an•tum
a•di•a•ther•man•cy
ad•i•ence
ad•i•ent
A•din•i•o•da
a•din•i•dan
Ad•i•pex-P *Trademark*

a•diph•e•nine
a•dip•ic ac•id
ad•i•po•cere
ad•i•poc•er•ous
ad•i•po•cyte
ad•i•po•gen•e•sis
ad•i•po•ge•net•ic
ad•i•po•ne•cro•sis ne•o•na•
to•rum
adiponecrosis sub•cu•ta•ne•
an•e•o•na•to•rum
ad•i•pose
adipose tis•sue
ad•i•pose•ness
ad•i•po•sis
adiposis cer•e•o•bra•lis
adiposis dol•o•o•ro•sa
adiposis he•pat•i•ca
adiposis or•cha•lis
adiposis tu•be•ro•sa sim•plex
ad•i•pos•i•ty
ad•i•po•so•gen•i•tal
dys•tro•phy
Ad•i•post *Trademark.*
a•dip•si•a
ad•i•tus, *n.*, *pl.* -tus, -tus•es.
ad•junct
ad•junc•tive
ad•junc•tive•ly
ad•just
ad•just•a•bil•i•ty
ad•just•a•ble
ad•just•ive
ad•just•ment
adjustment dis•or•der
ad•just•men•tal
ad•ju•vant
Ad•le•ri•an
ad lib•i•tum
ad•max•il•lar•y
ad•mi•nic•u•lum lin•e•o•ae
al•bae

ad•min•is•ter
ad•min•is•tra•tion
ad•nex○a, *n., pl., sing.*
 -nex○um.
adnexa oc○u○li
adnexa u○ter○i
ad•nex○al
ad•nex○i•tis
ad•o•les•cence
ad•o•les•cent
ad○o•les•cent○ly
a○don○is
a○don○i•tol
a○dop•tion stud○y
ad○o•ral
ad•re•nal
adrenal gland
ad•re•nal•ec•to•mized
ad•re•nal•ec•to○my, *n.. pl.*
 -mies.
A○dren•al○in *Trademark.*
a○dren○o•a○line
ad•re•nal○i•ne•mi○a
ad•re•nal○ly
ad•re•nal•one
ad•ren•ar•che
ad•ren•er•gen
ad•ren•er•gic
ad•ren•er•gi•cal○ly
ad•ren•ine a○rab○i•no•side
a○dre•no•chrome
a○dre•no•cor•ti•cal
a○dre•no•cor•ti•coid
a○dre•no•cor•ti•co•mi○
 met○ic
a○dre•no•cor•ti•co•ster•oid
a○dre•no•cor•ti•co•troph○in
a○dre•no•cor•ti•co•trop○ic or
 a○dre•no•cor•ti•co•
 troph○ic
adrenocorticotropic hor•mone

a○dre•no•gen○i•tal
 syn•drome
a○dre•no•glo•mer•u•lo•
 trop○in
a○dre•no•lyt○ic
a○dre•no•me•dul•lar•y
a○dre•no•pause
a○dre•no•re•cep•tor
ad•re•nos•ter•one
a○dre•no•sym•pa•thet○ic
a○dre•no•troph○ic
a○dre•no•trop○ic
A○dri○a•my○cin
Adriamycin PFS *Trademark.*
Adriamycin RDF *Trademark.*
ad•sorb
ad•sorb•a•bil○i•ty
ad•sorb•a•ble
ad•sorb•ate
ad•sorb•ent
ad•sorp•tion
ad•sorp•tive
a○dult
adult-on○set di○a•be•tes
adult-onset o○be•si○ty
a○dul•ter•ant
a○dul•ter•ate, *v.,* -at○ed,
 -at○ing.
a○dul•ter○a•tion
a○dul•ter○a•tor
a○dult•hood
ad•vance di•rec•tive
ad•vance•ment
advancement flap
ad•ven•ti•tia
ad•ven•ti•tial
ad•ven•ti•tious
adventitious cyst
ad•ven•ti•tious○ly
ad•verse e○vent
adverse re○ac•tion
Ad•vil *Trademark.*

a•dy•na•mi•a
adynamia ep•i•sod•i•ca
  he•red•i•tar•i•a
a•dy•nam•ic
A•e•des ae•gyp•ti
ae•goph•o•ny, *n.*, *pl.* -nies.
ae•lu•ro•phobe
ae•lu•ro•pho•bi•a
aer•ate, *v.*, -at•ed, -at•ing.
aer•a•tion
aer•a•tor
aer•e•ole
ae•rif•er•ous
aer•o•bac•ter
Aerobacter aer•og•e•nes
aer•obe
aer•o•bic
aer•o•bi•cal•ly
aer•o•bics
Aer•o•bid *Trademark.*
aer•o•bi•o•log•i•cal
aer•o•bi•o•log•i•cal•ly
aer•o•bi•ol•o•gy
aer•o•bi•o•scope
aer•o•bi•o•sis
aer•o•bi•ot•ic
aer•o•bi•ot•i•cal•ly
aer•o•cele
Aer•o•Cham•ber *Trademark.*
aer•o•don•tal•gia
aer•o•don•tal•gic
aer•o•don•tia
aer•o•dy•nam•ic
aer•o•dy•nam•i•cal
aer•o•dy•nam•i•cal•ly
aer•o•dy•nam•i•cist
aer•o•dy•nam•ics
aer•o•em•bo•lism
aer•o•em•phy•se•ma
aer•o•gel
aer•og•e•nous
aer•og•e•nous•ly

Aer•o•late *Trademark.*
Aerolate III *Trademark.*
Aerolate JR *Trademark.*
Aerolate SR *Trademark.*
Aer•o•lone *Trademark.*
aer•o•med•i•cal
aer•o•med•i•cine
aer•om•e•ter
aer•o•neu•ro•sis
aer•o-o•ti•tis
aero-otitis me•di•a
aer•o•pause
aer•o•pha•gi•a
aer•oph•a•gy
aer•o•pho•bi•a
aer•o•pho•bic
aer•o•phore
aer•o•plank•ton
aer•o•scope
Aer•o•seb-Dex *Trademark*
Aeroseb-HC *Trademark.*
aer•o•si•nus•o•i•tis
aer•o•sol
aer•o•sol•i•za•tion
aer•o•sol•ize, *v.*, -ized,
  -iz•ing.
aer•o•sol•iz•er
aer•o•space med•i•cine
Aer•o•spo•rin *Trademark.*
aer•o•tax•is
aer•o•ther•a•peu•tics
aer•o•ther•a•py
aer•o•ti•tis
aer•o•to•nom•e•ter
aer•ot•ro•pism
Aes•cu•la•pi•an
Aesculapian staff
Aes•cu•la•pi•us
aes•cu•le•tin
aes•cu•lin
aes•the•sia
aes•thet•ics

aes•ti•val
aes•ti•vate
aes•ti•va•tion
ae•ti•ol•o•gy, *n., pl.* -gies.
ae•ti•o•por•phy•rin
a•fe-brile
af•fect
af•fec•tion
af•fec•tive
affective dis•or•der
af•fec•tive•ly
af•fec•tiv•i•ty
af•fer•ent
af•fer•ent•ly
af•fin•i•ty, *n., pl.* -ties.
af•flux
a•fi•bri•no•ge•ne•mi•a
af•la•tox•in
Af•ri•can horse sick•ness
African sleep•ing sick•ness
African try•pan•o•so•mi•a•sis
Af•ri•can•ized bee
Africanized hon•ey•bee
Af•rin *Trademark.*
Af•ri•nol *Trademark.*
Af•tate *Trademark.*
af•ter•birth
af•ter•brain
af•ter•care
af•ter•cat•a•ract
af•ter•damp
af•ter•dis•charge
af•ter•ef•fect
af•ter•im•age
af•ter•load
af•ter•pain
af•ter•po•ten•tial
af•ter•sen•sa•tion
af•ter•taste
af•ter•vi•sion
af•to•sa

a•ga•lac•ti•a
agalactia con•ta•gi•o•sa
a•ga•lac•tic
ag•a•mete
a•gam•ic
a•gam•i•cal•ly
a•gam•ma•glob•u•li•ne•mi•a
ag•a•mog•o•ny, *n., pl.* -nies.
Ag•a•mo•mer•mis
a•ga•mont
a•gan•gli•on•ic
a•gar
ag•a•ric
Ag•a•ri•ca•ce•ae
a•gar•i•cin
A•gar•i•cus
agaricus mus•car•i•us
ag•a•rose
a•gas•tric
a•ga•ve
Agave a•mer•i•ca•na
age, *n., v.,* aged, ag•ing or age•ing.
age of con•sent
a•gen•e•sis or a•ge•ne•sia
a•ge•net•ic
a•gen•tial
a•gen•i•tal•ism
a•ge•nize, *v.,* -nized, -niz•ing.
a•gent
Agent Or•ange
a•gen•tum ntir•oi•cum
a•geu•si•a
a•geu•sic
ag•er
agger na•si
ag•glom•er•ate, *v.,* -ated, -at•ing.
ag•glom•er•a•tion
ag•glu•ti•na•bil•i•ty
ag•glu•tin•a•ble

ag•glu•ti•nant
ag•glu•ti•nate, *v.*, -nat○ed,
  -nat○ing.
ag•glu•ti•na•tion
agglutination test
ag•glu•ti•na•tive
ag•glu•ti•nin
ag•glu•tin○o•gen
ag•glu•tin○o•gen○ic
ag•glu•tin•oid
ag•glu•tin○o•scope
ag•gre•gate
ag•gres•sin
ag•gres•sion
ag•gres•sive
ag•gres•sive•ly
ag•gres•sive•ness
ag•gres•siv○i○ty
ag•gres•sor
ag○i•ta•ted de•pres•sion
ag○i•ta•tion
ag○i•ta•tion○al
ag○i•to•pha•sia
Ag•kis•tro•don con•tor•trix
Agkistrodon pis•civ○o•rus
a○glo•mer○u•lar
a○glos•si○a
a○glu•con
a○glu•cone
a○gly•con
a○gly•cone
ag•ma•tine
ag•mi•nate
ag•mi•nat○ed
ag•nail
ag•na•thi○a
ag•na•thus
ag•no•gen○ic
ag•no•sia
ag•nos•ter○ol
ag○nus cas•tus
ag○o•nal

ag○o•nist
ag○o•nis•tic or ag○o•nis•ti•
  cal
ag○o•nis•ti•cal○ly
a○go•ny, *n., pl.* -nies.
ag○o•ra•phobe
ag○o•ra•pho•bic
ag○o•ra•pho•bi○ac
a○gou•ti
a○gram•ma•tism
a○gran○u•lo•cyte
a○gran○u•lo•cyt○ic an•gi○na
a○gran○u•lo•cy•to•sis
a○graph○i○a
a○graph○ic
Ag•ro•bac•te•ri○um tu•me•
  fa•ciens
Ag•ro•py•ron
a○gryp•ni○a
a○gue
aich•mo•pho•bi○a
aid
aid sta•tion
aide
aid•man, *n., pl.* -men.
AIDS
AIDS vi○rus
AIDS-re•lat○ed com•plex
ail
ai•lan•thus
ail•ment
ai•lu•ro•phobe
ai•lu•ro•pho•bi○a
ai•lu•ro•pho•bic
ain•hum
air bends
air cell
air em•bo•lism
air hunger
air sac
Air•bra•sive *Trademark.*
air•sick

air•sick•ness
air•way
aj∘o•wan oil
a∘kar∘y•ote
a∘ka•thi∘sia
a∘kee
a∘ki•ne∘si iro∘i•dis
a∘ki•ne•sia
akinesia al•ger∘a
akinesia am∘nes•ti∘ca
a∘ki•ne•sis
a∘ki•net∘ic
A∘kin∘e•ton *Trademark.*
Ak•ri∘nol *Trademark.*
a∘la•li∘a
a∘la na∘si, *n., pl.* a∘lae na∘si.
al∘a•nine
alanine a∘mi•no•trans•fer•ase
al∘a•nyl
a∘lar
alar car•ti•lage
alar lig∘a•ment
a∘larm re•ac•tion
a∘las•trim
al∘ba
Al•ba•lon *Trademark.*
Al•ba•my•cin *Trademark.*
al•ba•spi•din
al•be∘do
Al•bers-Schon•berg dis•ease
al•bin∘ic
al•bi•nism
al•bi•nis•mus cir•cum•scrip•tus
albinismus to•ta•lis
albinismus u∘ni•ver•sa•lis
al•bi•nis•tic
al•bi∘no, *n., pl.* -nos.
al•bi•no•ism
al•bi•not∘ic
al•bo•ci•ner•e∘ous

al•bu•gin•e∘a
albuginea oc∘u∘li
albuginea o∘var∘i∘i
albuginea pe∘nis
albuginea tes•tis
al•bu•men
al•bu•min
Al•bu•mi•nar *Trademark.*
al•bu•min•ate
al•bu•min•oid
a∘lbu•mi•nom•e∘ter
al•bu•mi•nous or al•bu•mi•nose
al•bu•mi•nu•ri∘a
al•bu•mi•nu•ric
al•bu•mose
al•bu•mo•su•ri∘a
Al•bu•mo•tope *Trademark.*
Al•bu•te∘in *Trademark.*
Al•bu•ter∘ol *Trademark.*
Albuterol Aer∘o∘sol *Trademark.*
Al•caine *Trademark.*
al•ca•lig∘e∘nes
al•cap•ton
al•cap•ton∘u•ri∘a
al•cap•ton∘u•ric
al•che•mist
al•che•mis•tic
al•che•mis•ti•cal
al•che∘my, *n., pl.* -mies.
Al•cock's ca•nal
al•co•gel
al•co•hol
al•co•hol•ate
al•co•hol∘ic
alcoholic fer•men•ta•tion
al•co•hol∘i•cal∘ly
al•co•hol•ism
al•co•hol•ist
al•co•hol∘i•za•tion

al•co•hol•ize, *v.*, -ized,
  -iz•ing.
al•co•hol•om•e•ter
al•co•hol•om•e•try
al•co•hol•o•phil•i•a
al•co•hol•y•sis
al•co•sol
al•cur•one
al•cur•on•ic
Al•dac•ta•zide *Trademark.*
Al•dac•tone *Trademark.*
al•de•hyde
al•de•hyd•ic
al•der buck•thorn
al•do•bi•u•ron•ic ac•id
Al•do•clor *Trademark.*
al•do•hex•ose
al•dol
al•do•lase
Al•do•met *Trademark.*
al•don•ic ac•id
Al•do•ril *Trademark.*
al•dose
al•do•side
al•do•ste•rone
al•do•ster•on•ism
al•dox•ime
al•drin
a•lec•i•thal
a•lem•bic
a•lem•mal
A•len•dro•nate
A•le•tris
a•leu•ke•mi•a
a•leu•ke•mic
aleukemic leu•ke•mi•a
A•leve *Trademark.*
Al•ex•an•der tech•nique
Al•ex•an•dri•an sen•na
a•lex•i•a
a•lex•ic
a•lex•in

a•lex•ine
a•lex•in•ic
a•lex•o•i•phar•mic
a•lex•i•thy•mi•a
Al•fen•ta *Trademark.*
Al•fer•on N *Trademark.*
al•ga, *n., pl.* al•gae.
Al•gae
al•gae•cide
al•gal
al•gas
al•ge•don•ic
al•ge•si•a
al•ge•sic
al•ge•sim•e•ter
al•ge•sim•e•try
al•get•ic
al•gi•cid•al
al•gi•cide
al•gid
al•gin
al•gi•nate
al•gin•ic ac•id
al•go•dys•tro•phy
al•go•gen•ic
al•goid
al•go•lag•ni•a
al•go•lag•ni•ac
al•go•lag•nic
al•go•lag•nist
al•go•log•i•cal
al•go•log•i•cal•ly
al•gol•o•gist
al•gol•o•gy
al•gom•e•ter
al•go•met•ric al•go•met•ri•
  cal.
al•go•met•ri•cal•ly
al•gom•e•try
al•go•phil•i•a
al•goph•i•list
al•go•pho•bi•a

al•gor
algor mor•tis
al•i•cy•clic
al•ien•ate, *v.*, -at•ed, -at•ing.
al•ien•a•tion
al•ien•ist
al•i•es•ter•ase
al•i•form
al•i•ment
al•i•men•ta•ry
alimentary ca•nal
alimentary sys•tem
al•i•men•ta•tion
al•i•men•to•ther•a•py
Al•i•men•tum *Trademark.*
al•i•na•sal
a•lin•oi•dine
al•i•phat•ic
al•i•quot
al•i•sphe•noid
a•live
a•liz•a•rin
a•liz•a•rine
Al•ka-Mints *Trademark.*
Alka-Selt•zer *Trademark.*
al•ka•le•mi•a
al•ka•les•cence
al•ka•les•cent
al•ka•li, *n.*, *pl.* -lis, -lies.
alkali dis•ease
alkali re•serve
al•ka•li•fy, *v.*, -fied, -fy•ing.
al•ka•lim•e•ter
al•ka•lim•e•try
al•ka•line
alkaline earth
alkaline-earth met•al
alkaline phos•pha•tase
al•ka•lin•i•ty
al•ka•lin•i•za•tion
al•ka•lin•ize, *v.*, -ized, -iz•ing.

al•ka•li•za•tion
al•ka•lize, *v.*, -lized, -liz•ing.
al•ka•liz•er
al•ka•loid
al•ka•loi•dal
al•ka•lo•sis
al•ka•lot•ic
al•kane
al•ka•net
al•kan•nin
al•kap•ton
al•kap•ton•u•ri•a
al•ka•ver•vir
al•kene
Al•ke•ran *Trademark.*
al•kox•y
al•kyl
al•kyl•a•mine
al•kyl•ate, *v.*, -at•ed, -at•ing.
al•kyl•a•tion
all-or-none
all-or-none law
all-or-noth•ing
al•lan•to•cho•ri•on
al•lan•to•ic
allantoic ves•i•cle
al•lan•toid
al•lan•to•is, *n.*, *pl.* -i•des.
All•bee C *Trademark.*
al•lele
al•lel•ic
al•lel•ism
al•le•lo•ca•tal•y•sis
al•le•lo•cat•a•lyst
al•le•lo•cat•a•lyt•ic
al•le•lo•morph
al•le•lo•mor•phic
al•le•lo•mor•phism
Al•lent *Trademark.*
Al•le•rest *Trademark.*
Al•ler•fed *Trademark.*

al•ler•gen
al•ler•gic
allergic rhi•ni•tis
al•ler•ge•nic•i•ty
al•ler•gic en•ceph○a•lo•my•
e•li•tis
al•ler•gin
al•ler•gist
al•ler•gi•za•tion
al•ler•gol○o○gy
al•ler•gy, n., pl. -gies.
Al•les•che•ri○a boy•di○i
al•leth•rin
al•le•vi•ate, v., -at○ed,
-at•ing.
al•le•vi•a•tion
al•le•vi•a•tive
al•li•cin
al•lied health per•son•nel
al•li•ga•tion
al•liin
al•li○um
allium ce○pa
allium cepa eu○phra•sia
of•fi•ci•na•lis
al○lo•an•ti•bod○y, n., pl. -ies.
al○lo•an•ti•gen
al○lo•an•ti•gen○ic
al○lo•bar•bi•tal
al○lo•bar•bi•tone
al○lo•chei•ri○a
al○lo•chi•ri○a
al○lo•cor•tex
al○lo•der•ma•nys•sus
al○lo•e○rot○ic
al○lo•e○rot○i•cism
al○lo•er○o•tism
al○lo•ge•ne○ic
al○lo•graft
al○lo•im•mune
al○lo•i○so•leu•cine
al○lo•met•ric

al•lom•e○try
al○lo•morph
al○lo•mor•phic
al○lo•mor•phism
al○lo•path or al•lop○a•thist
al○lo•path○ic
al○lo•path○i•cal○ly
al•lop○a•thy
al○lo•phe•nic
al○lo•plas•tic
al○lo•plas•tic•i○ty
al○lo•plas○ty, n., pl. -ties.
al○lo•pol○y•ploid
al○lo•pol○y•ploi○dy
al○lo•psy•chic
al○lo•pu•ri•nol
al•lose
al○lo•some
al○lo•ster○ic
al○lo•ster○i•cal○ly
al○lo•ster○ism
al○lo•ster○y
al○lo•tet•ra•ploid
al○lo•tet•ra•ploi○dy
al○lo•trans•plant
al○lo•trans•plan•ta•tion
al○lo•trope
al○lo•troph○ic
al○lo•trop○ic
al○lo•trop○i•cal○ly
al•lot•ro○py
al○lo•type
al○lo•typ○ic
al○lo○typ○i•cal○ly
al○lo•ty○py
al•lox○an
al•lox○a•zine
al○loy
al○lo•zyme
al○lo•zy•mic
all•spice

allspice oil
al•lyl
allyl i∘so•thi•o•cy•a•nate
al•lyl•a∘mine
al•lyl∘ic
al•lyl•thi•o•u•re∘a
al•mond
almond oil
al•mon∘er
al∘oe
aloe ver••∘a
al•oe•em∘o•din
al∘o•et∘ic
a∘lo•gia
al∘o∘in
al∘o•pe•ci∘a
alopecia ar∘e•a∘ta
al∘o•pe•cic
al∘pha
alpha-1-an•ti•tryp•sin
alpha-a∘dre•no•cep•tor
alpha-a∘dre•no•re•cep•tor
alpha-a∘mi∘no ac∘id
alpha block∘er or alpha-block∘er
alpha cell
alpha glob∘u•lin
alpha-hel∘i•cal
alpha he∘lix
alpha he•mol∘y•sis
alpha-hy•poph∘a•mine
Alpha Ker∘i *Trademark.*
alpha-ke•to•glu•tar∘ic ac∘id
alpha-lip∘o•pro•tein
alpha-naph•thol
alpha-naph•thyl•thi•o•u•re∘a
alpha par•ti•cle
Alpha Plus *Trademark.*
alpha ray
alpha recep•tor or al∘pha•re•cep•tor

alpha rhythm
alpha-to•coph•er∘ol
alpha wave
alpha-ad•ren•er•gic
alpha-block•ing
Al•pha•caine *Trademark.*
Alphacaine HCL *Trademark.*
Al•pha•derm *Trademark.*
Al•pha•drol *Trademark.*
alpha-fe•to•pro•tein
Al•pha•trex *Trademark.*
Al•praz∘o•lam
al•pren∘o•lol
Al•ra•mu•cil *Trademark.*
al•ser•ox∘y•lon
Al•sto•ni∘a
al•sto•nine
Al•tace *Trademark.*
al∘ter, *v.,* -tered, -ter•ing.
al•ter•ant
al•ter•a∘tive
al•tered state of con•scious•ness
Al•ter•na *Trademark.*
Al•ter•na•GEL *Trademark.*
Al•ter•nar∘i∘a
al•ter•nate host
al•ter•nat•ing per•so•nal∘i•ty
alternating psy•cho•sis
al•ter•na•tion of gen•er∘a•tions
al•ter•na•tive med∘i•cine
al•thae∘a
al•the∘a
al•ti•tude sick•ness
Alt•mann's gran•ules
al•tri•gen•der•ism
al•trose
Al∘u-Cap *Trademark.*
Al∘u•drox *Trademark.*
al∘um

a○lu•men, *n.*, *pl.* -mens,
-mi○na.
alumina a○lu•mi•num
al○u•min○i○um
aluminum
aluminum chlo•ride
aluminum hy•drox•ide
aluminum ox•ide
aluminum sul•fate
Al○u•pent *Trademark.*
Al○u•rate *Trademark.*
Al○u-Tab *Trademark.*
al•ve○o•lar
alveolar arch
alveolar ar•ter•y
alveolar ca•nals
alveolar ducts
alveolar in•dex
alveolar point
alveolar proc•ess
al○ve•o•lar○ly
al○ve•o•late
al○ve•o•la•tion
al•ve○o•lec•to○my, *n.*, *pl.*
-mies.
al○ve•o○li den•ta•les
man•dib○u•lae
alveoli dentales max•il•lae
alveoli pul•mo•nis
alveoli pu•lmo•num
al•ve○o•li•tis
al•ve○o•lo•con•dyl○e○an
al•ve○o•lo•na•sal
al•ve○o•lo•plas○ty, *n.*, *pl.*
-ties.
al•ve○o•lus, *n.*, *pl.* -li.
al•ve○o•plas○ty, *n.*, *pl.* -ties.
al•ve○us, *n.*, *pl.* -ve○i.
alveus hip•po•cam○pi
Alz•hei•mer's di•sease
a○maas
am○a•cri○nal

am○a•crine
amacrine cell
a○mal•gam
a○mal•ga•mate, *v.*, -mat○ed,
-mat○ing.
a○mal•ga•ma•tion
a○mal•ga•ma•tor
a○man•din
am○a•ni○ota
Amanita mus•car○i○a
Amanita phal•loi•des
am○a•ni•tin
a○man•ta•dine
am○a•ranth
Am○a•ran•thus
am○a•roid
a○mas•ti○a
a○math○o•pho•bi○a
am•au•ro•sis
amaurosis fu•gax
amaurosis par•ti•a•lis fu•gax
am•au•rot○ic
amaurotic fam○i•ly id○i•o○cy
amaurotic idiocy
a○max○o•pho•bi○a
Am•be•nyl *Trademark.*
Ambenyl-D *Trademark.*
am○ber
am•ber•gris
am•bi•dex•ter○i○ty
am•bi•dex•trous
am•bi•dex•trous○ly
am•bi•dex•trous•ness
Am•bi○en
am•bi•ent
am•bi•lat•er○al
am•bi•lat•er•al○i○ty
am•bi•lat•er•al○ly
am•bi•o•pi○a
am•bi•sex•u○al
am•bi•sex•u•al○i○ty

am•bi•ten•den•cy, *n., pl.*
 -cies.
am•biv∘a•lence
am•biv∘a•len∘cy
am•biv∘a•lent
am•biv∘a•lent∘ly
am•bi•ver•sion
am•bi•ver•sive
am•bi•vert
am•bly•chro•mat∘ic
Am•bly•om∘ma
am•bly•ope
am•bly∘o∘pi∘a
amblyopia al•bi•nis•mus
amblyopia ex a∘nop•si∘a
am•bly•op∘ic
am•bly∘o•scope
am∘bo
am•bo•cep•tor
Am•bo•dryl *Trademark.*
am∘bon, *n., pl.* -bo•nes.
am∘bos
Am•bro•si•a
am•bu•lance
am•bu•lant
am•bu•late, *v.,* -lat•ed, -lat•
 ing.
am•bu•la•tion
am•bu•la•to•ri∘ly
am•bu•la•to∘ry
am•by•sto∘ma
a∘me∘ba, *n., pl.* -bas, -bae.
a∘me•ba•cid∘al
a∘me•ba•cide
am•e∘bi•a•sis
a∘me•bic
amebic ab•scess
amebic dys•en•ter∘y
a∘me•bi•cid∘al
a∘me•bi•cide
a∘me•bi•form
a∘me•bo•cyte

a∘me•boid
am•e∘bu∘la, *n., pl.* -las.
a∘mei∘o•sis
a∘mei•ot∘ic
a∘mel∘a•not∘ic
am•e∘lo•blast
am•e∘lo•blas•tic
am•e∘lo•blas•to∘ma, *n., pl.*
 -mas, -ma∘ta.
am•e∘lo•den•tin∘al
am•e∘lo•gen•e∘sis, *n., pl.*
 -ses.
amelogenesis im•per•fec∘ta
am•e∘lus, *n., pl.* -li.
a∘men•or•rhe∘a ✓
a∘men•or•rhe∘al
a∘men•or•rhe∘ic
am•ent
a∘men•tia
A∘mer∘i•caine *Trademark.*
A∘mer∘i•can cock•roach
American dog tick
American gin•seng
American hel•le•bore
American sto•rax
American try•pan∘o•so•mi•
 a•sis
am•e∘ri•ci∘um
Ames test
a∘meth∘o•caine
am•e∘thop•ter∘in
am•e∘trope
am•e∘tro•pi∘a
am•e∘tro∘pic
am∘i•an•thoid
Am∘i•car *Trademark.*
am∘i•dase
Am∘i•date *Trademark.*
am∘ide
a∘mid∘ic
am∘i•dine
a∘mi∘do

am·i·done
a·mi·do·py·rine
am·i·dox·ime
Am·i·kin *Trademark.*
am·i·lo·ride
a·mim·i·a
am·i·nate, *v.*, -nat·ed, -nat·ing.
am·i·na·tion
am·in·a·zin
am·in·a·zine
a·mine
Am·i·ness *Trademark.*
am·ni·o, *n.*, *pl.* -os.
a·mi·no
amino ac·id
Amino-Cerv *Trademark.*
Amino Min D *Trademark.*
amino ni·tro·gen
Amino Zn *Trademark.*
a·mi·no·a·ce·tic ac·id
a·mi·no·ac·i·de·mi·a
a·mi·no·ac·id·u·ri·a
a·mi·no·ben·zo·ate
a·mi·no·ben·zo·ic acid
a·mi·no·glu·te·thi·mide
a·mi·no·gly·co·side
a·mi·no·lete
am·i·nol·y·sis, *n.*, *pl.* -ses.
a·mi·no·lyt·ic
a·mi·no·mine
a·mi·no·pep·ti·dase
am·i·noph·er·ase
a·mi·no·phyl·line
a·mi·no·plex
am·i·nop·ter·oin
a·mi·no·py·rine
a·mi·no·sal·i·cyl·ic acid
a·mi·no·sta·sis
A·mi·no·syn II *Trademark.*
a·mi·no·tate
a·mi·no·thi·a·zole

a·mi·no·trans·fer·ase
a·mi·no·vi·rox
Am·i·nox·in *Trademark.*
am·i·o·dar·one
Am·i·paque *Trademark.*
am·i·to·sis
am·i·tot·ic
am·i·tot·i·cal·ly
Am·i·tril *Trademark.*
am·i·trip·ty·line
Am·lo·di·pine
am·me·ter
am·mo·ni·a
ammonia al·um
ammonia wa·ter
am·mo·ni·ac
am·o·mo·ni·a·cal
am·mo·ni·ate, *v.*, -at·ed, -at·ing.
am·mo·ni·a·tion
am·mon·i·fi·ca·tion
am·mo·ni·fy, *v.*, -fied, -fy·ing.
am·mo·ni·um
ammonium al·um
ammonium car·bo·nate
ammonium chlo·ride
ammonium hy·drox·ide
ammonium ni·trate
ammonium phos·phate
ammonium sul·fate
am·mo·nol·y·sis, *n.*, *pl.* -ses.
am·mo·no·lyt·ic
am·ne·si·ac
am·nes·tic
Am·nes·tro·gen *Trademark.*
am·ni·o·cen·te·sis, *n* , *pl* -ses.
am·ni·o·gen·e·o·sis, *n.*, *pl.* -ses.
am·ni·og·ra·phy, *n.*, *pl* -phies.

am•ni○on, *n.*, *pl.* -ni•ons,
-ni○a.
am•ni•o•scope
am•ni•os•co○py, *n.*, *pl.* -pies.
Am•ni•o○ta
am•ni•o○te
am•ni•ot○ic
amniotic band
amniotic cav○i○ty
amniotic flu○id
amniotic fold
am•ni•ot○o○my, *n.*, *pl.* -mies.
am○o•bar•bi•tal
am○o•di•a•quin
am○o•di•a•quine
a○moe○ba, *n.*, *pl.* -bas, -bae.
am•oe•bi•a•sis
amoebiasis cu•tis
a○moe○bic
A○moe•bo•tae•ni○a
a○mok
a○mor in•sa•nus
amor les•bi•cus
amor sui
a○mor•phin•ism
a○mor•phous
a○mor•phus, *n.*, *pl* -phi.
a○mor•phus○es
A○mox○i•cil•lin/Clav○u•lan•
ate
A○mox○il *Trademark.*
am•per•age
am•pere
am•phet○a•mine
am○phi•ar•thro•di○al
am○phi•ar•thro•sis
am○phi•as•ter
am○phi•as•tral
Am•phib○i○a
am•phib○i○an
am○phi•blas•tic
am○phi•bol○ic

am○phi•cen•tric
am○phi•col
am○phi•cra•ni○a
am○phi•dip•loid
am○phi•di•ploi○dy, *n.*, *pl.*
-dies.
am○phi•mic•tic
am○phi•mic•ti•cal○ly
am○phi•mix○is, *n.*, *pl.* -mix○es.
am○phi•ox○us
am○phi•path
am○phi•path○ic
am○phi•phile
am○phi•phil○ic
am○phi•ploid
am○phi•ploi○dy
am○phi•sto•ma•ta
am○phi•stome
am•phit•ri•chous
Am•pho•jel *Trademark.*
am•pho•lyte
am•pho•lyt○ic
am•pho•phil
am•pho•phil○ic
am•phoph○i•lous
am•phor○ic
am•pho•ric○i○ty
am•pho•ter○ic
am•pho•ter○i•cin
amphotericin B
am•phot•er○ism
am•pi•cil•lin
am•plex○us
am•pli•fi•ca•tion
am•pli•fi○er
amp•li○fy, *v.*, -fied, -fy•ing.
am•pli•tude
amplitude of ac•com•mo•da•
tion
am•pule or
am○pul or am•poule
am•pul○la, *n.*, *pl.* -lae.

ampulla of Va•ter
am•pul•lae mem•bra•na•
  ce○ae
ampullae os•se○ae
am•pul•lar
am•pul•la○ry
am•pul•lu○la, *n., pl.* -lae.
am•pu•tate, *v.,* -tat○ed, -tat•
  ing.
am•pu•ta•tion
amputation neu•ro○ma
am•pu•tee
am•ox○i•cil•lin
a○muck
a○mu•sia
a○my•e•li○a
a○my•e•lin○ic
a○my•e•lon○ic
a○myg•da○la, *n., pl.* -lae.
a○myg•da•lase
a○myg•da•lec•to•mized
a○myg•da•lec•to○my, *n., pl.*
  -mies.
a○myg•da•lin
a○myg•da•line
a○myg•da•loid
amygdaloid bod○y
amygdaloid nu•cle○us
a○myg•da•lot○o○my, *n., pl.*
  -mies.
am○yl
amyl ac○e○tate
amyl al•co•hol
amyl ni•trite
amyl ni•tro•sum
am○y•la•ceous
am○yl•ase
am○yl•ene
am○y•lo•bar•bi•tone
am○y•lo•dex•trin
am○y•loid
amyloid de•gen•er○a•tion

am○y•loi•do•sis, *n., pl.* -ses.
amyloidosis cu○tis
am○y•lol○y•sis
am○y•lo•lyt○ic
am○y•lo•pec•tin
am○y•lo•plast
am○y•lop•sin
am○y•lose
am○y•lum
a○my•o•pla•sia con•gen○i•ta
a○my○o•stat○ic
a○my○o•to•ni○a
amyotonia con•gen○i○ta
a○my○o•tro•phi○a, *n., pl.* -as.
amyotrophia spi•na•lis
  pro•gres•si○va
a○my○o•troph○ic lat•eral
  scle•ro•sis
am○y•ot•ro•phy
Am○y•tal
an○a
Ana-Kit *Trademark.*
an○a•bae○na
a○nab○a•sine
an○a•bi•o•sis
an○a•bi•ot○ic
an•a•bol○ic
a○nab○o•lin
a○nab○o•lism
a○nab○o•lite
an○a•cid○i○ty
An○a•cin *Trademark.*
Anacin-3 *Trademark.*
an○a•cli•sis
an○a•clit○ic
anaclitic de•pres•sion
an○a•crot○ic
a○nac•ro•tism
an○a•cul•ture
An○a•drol-50 *Trademark.*
a○nae•mi○a
a○nae•mic

a○nae•mi•cal○ly
an•aer•obe
an•aer○o•bic
an•aer○o•bi•cal○ly
an•aer○o•bi•o•sis
an•aes•the•sia
an•aes•the•si•ol○o○gy
an•aes•thet○ic
an•aes•the•tist
an•aes•the•tize, *vt*, -tized, -tiz•ing.
A○naf•ra•nil *Trademark.*
an○a•gen
a○nal
anal ca○nal
anal e○rot○ic
anal e○rot○i•cism
anal sa•dism
anal sa•dis•tic
anal sphinc•ter
anal verge
an○a•lep•tic
an•al•ge•sia al•ger○a
analgesia do•lo•ro○sa
an•al•ge•sic
an•al•get○ic
a○nal○i○ty, *n.*, *pl.* -ties.
an•al•ler•gic
a○nal○ly
an○a•log
a○nal○o•gous
an○a•logue
a○nal○o•gy, *n.*, *pl.* -gies.
A○nal•pram-HC *Trademark.*
a○nal○y•sand
a○nal○y•sis, *n.*, *pl.* -ses.
analysis of var○i•ance
an○a•lyst
an○a•lyte
an○a•lyt○ic
analytic psy○chol○o○gy
an○a•lyt○i•cal

an○a•lyt○i•cal○ly
an○a•lyze, *v.*, -lyzed, -lyz•ing.
an○a•lyz○er
an•am•ne•sis, *n.*, *pl.* -ses.
an•am•nes•tic
an•am•nes•ti•cal○ly
A○nam•ni○a
an•am•ni•on○ic
An•am•ni•o○ta
an•am•ni○ote
an○a•mor•pho•sis, *n.*, *pl.* -ses.
an•an○a•sta•sia
an•an•cas•tic
an•an•kas•tic
a○naph○a•lan•ti•a•sis
an○a•phase
an○a•pha•sic
an•aph○o○ret○ic
an•aph•ro•di•sia
an•aph•ro•dis•i○ac
an○a•phy•lac•tic
anaphylactic shock
an○a•phy•lac•ti•cal○ly
an○a•phy•lac•to•gen
an○a•phy•lac•to•gen○ic
an○a•phy•lac•toid
an○a•phy•la•tox○in
an○a•phy•lax○is
an○a•pla•sia
an○a•plas○ma, *n.*, *pl.* -ma○ta, -mas.
An○a•plas•ma•ta•ce○ae
an○a•plas•mo•sis, *n.*, *pl.* -ses.
an○a•plas•tic
an○a•plas•tol○o○gist
an○a•plas•tol○o○gy
An○a•prox *Trademark.*
an○a•rith•mi○a
an•ar•thri○a
anarthria cen•tra•lis
anarthria let○e○ra•lis
an○a•sar•ca

an‧a‧sar‧cous
An‧a‧spaz *Trademark.*
an‧a‧stal‧sis, *n., pl.* -ses.
an‧a‧state
an‧as‧tig‧mat
an‧as‧tig‧mat‧ic
a‧nas‧to‧mose, *v.,* -mosed,
 -mos‧ing.
a‧nas‧to‧mo‧sis, *n., pl.* -ses.
anastomosis ar‧te‧ri‧o‧ve‧
 no‧sa
a‧nas‧to‧mot‧ic
a‧nas‧tral
an‧a‧tom‧i‧cal *or* an‧a‧
 tom‧ic
anatomical dead space
anatomical po‧si‧tion
an‧a‧tom‧i‧cal‧ly
an‧a‧tom‧i‧co‧path‧o‧
 log‧ic
an‧a‧tom‧i‧co‧path‧o‧
 log‧i‧cal
a‧nat‧o‧mist
a‧nat‧o‧mize, *v.,* -mized,
 -miz‧ing.
a‧nat‧o‧my, *n., pl.* -mies.
an‧a‧tox‧in
An‧a‧tuss *Trademark.*
an‧au‧di‧a
an‧au‧tog‧e‧nous
An‧a‧var *Trademark.*
An‧be‧sol *Trademark.*
An‧cef *Trademark.*
an‧chor, *v.,* -chored, -chor‧ing.
an‧chor‧age
an‧chy‧lose
an‧chy‧lo‧sis
an‧chy‧lo‧sto‧mi‧a‧sis, *n.,*
 pl. -ses.
an‧chy‧lot‧ic
An‧co‧bon *Trademark.*
an‧co‧nal

an‧co‧ne‧al
an‧co‧ne‧us in‧ter‧nus
An‧cy‧los‧to‧ma
Ancylostoma a‧mer‧i‧ca‧num
Ancylostoma bra‧zil‧iense
Ancylostoma can‧i‧num
Ancylostoma du‧od‧e‧na‧le
An‧cy‧los‧to‧mat‧oi‧dae
an‧cy‧lo‧stome
an‧cy‧roid
An‧dro‧di‧ol *Trademark.*
an‧dro‧ga‧mone
an‧dro‧gen
an‧dro‧ge‧net‧ic
an‧dro‧gen‧ic
an‧drog‧e‧nous
an‧dro‧gyne
an‧drog‧y‧nism
an‧drog‧y‧nous
an‧drog‧y‧ony
An‧droid *Trademark.*
an‧drom‧e‧da
an‧drom‧e‧do‧tox‧in
an‧dro‧mi‧met‧ic
an‧dro‧pho‧bi‧a
an‧dro‧pho‧bic
an‧dro‧stane
an‧dro‧stene‧di‧one
an‧dros‧ter‧one
A‧nec‧tine *Trademark.*
an‧e‧lec‧tro‧ton‧ic
an‧e‧lec‧trot‧o‧nus
a‧ne‧mi‧a
anemia pseu‧do‧leu‧ke‧
 mi‧ca
anemia pseudoleukemica
 in‧fan‧tum
a‧ne‧mic
a‧ne‧mi‧cal‧ly
a‧nem‧o‧one
a‧nem‧o‧nin
an‧en‧ce‧pha‧li‧a

an•en•ce•phal•ic
an•en•ceph•a•ly
an•en•ter•ous
a•neph•ric
a•ner•gic
an•e•roid
aneroid ba•rom•e•ter
A•nes•ta•con *Trademark.*
an•es•the•sia
anesthesia do•lo•ro•sa
A•nes•the•sin
an•es•the•si•ol•o•gist
an•es•the•si•ol•o•gy
an•es•thet•ic
an•es•thet•i•cal•ly
an•es•the•tist
an•es•the•ti•za•tion
an•es•the•tize, *v.,*
  -tized, -tiz•ing.
an•es•trous
an•es•trus
an•e•thole
an•eu•rin
an•eu•rine
an•eu•ris•mal
a•neu•ro•gen•ic
an•eu•rysm *or* an•eu•rism
an•eu•rys•mal
an•eu•rys•mal•ly
An•ex•si•a *Trademark.*
an•gel dust
an•gel•ic ac•id
an•gel•i•ca
angelica root
an•gen•e•sis, *n., pl.* -ses.
an•gi•i•tis, *n., pl.* an•gi•i•ti•
  des.
an•gi•na
angina pec•to•ris
an•gi•nal
an•gi•noid
an•gi•nose

an•gi•nous
An•gi•o-Con•ray *Trademark.*
an•gi•o•blast
an•gi•o•blas•tic
an•gi•o•car•di•o•gram
an•gi•o•car•di•o•graph•ic
an•gi•o•car•di•og•ra•phy,
  n., pl. -phies.
an•gi•o•cho•li•tis
an•gi•o•cyst
an•gi•o•e•de•ma, *n., pl.*
  -mas, -ma•ta.
an•gi•o•gen•e•sis, *n., pl.*
  -ses.
an•gi•o•gen•ic
an•gi•o•gram
an•gi•o•graph•ic
an•gi•o•graph•i•cal•ly
an•gi•og•ra•phy, *n., pl.*
  -phies.
an•gi•oid
an•gi•o•ker•a•to•ma, *n., pl.*
  -mas, -ma•ta.
angiokeratoma cor•po•ris
  dif•fu•sum
angiokeratoma corporis
  diffusum u•ni•ver•sa•le
angiokeratoma For•dyce
angiokeratoma Mi•bel•li
an•gi•ol•o•gy
an•gi•o•ma, *n., pl.* -mas,
  -ma•ta.
angioma in•fec•ti•o•sum
angioma se•nile
angioma ser•pi•gi•no•sum
an•gi•o•ma•to•sis, *n., pl.*
  -ses.
angiomatosis ret•i•nae
an•gi•om•a•tous
an•gi•o•neu•rot•ic e•de•ma
an•gi•op•a•thy, *n., pl.* -thies.

an•gi∘o•pha•co•ma•to•sis ret∘i•nae et cer∘e•bel∘li
an•gi∘o•plas∘ty, *n., pl.* -ties.
an•gi∘o•sar•co∘ma, *n., pl.* -mas, -ma∘ta.
an•gi∘o•sco•to∘ma, *n., pl.* -mas, -ma∘ta.
an∘gi∘o•sco•tom•e∘try
an∘gi∘o•spasm
an∘gi∘o•spas•tic
an∘gi∘o•sperm
an∘gi∘o•sper•mous
an•gi•os•to∘my, *n., pl.* -mies.
an•gi∘o•ten•sin
angiotensin con•vert•ing en∘zyme
angiotensin I
angiotensin II
an∘gi∘o•ten•si•nase
an∘gi∘o•ten•sin∘o•gen
an∘gi∘o•ton∘ic
an∘gi∘o•to•nin
an•gle
angle of de•pres•sion
angle of el∘e•va•tion
angle of in•ci•dence
angle of re•flec•tion
angle of re•frac•tion
angle of the jaw
angle of the man•di•ble
an•gle•ber∘ry, *n., pl.* -ries.
an•gled
an•gor an∘i∘mi
angor noc•tur•nus
angor oc∘u•lar∘is
angor pec•to•ris
an•gos•tu∘ra bark
ang•strom
angstrom u∘nit
An•guil•lu∘la
an•gu•lar
angular ap•er•ture

angular ar•ter∘y
angular gy∘rus
angular vein
an•gu•lar∘ly
an•gu•late, *v.,* -lat∘ed, -lat•ing.
an•gu•la•tion
an•gu•lus, *n., pl.* -gu∘li.
an•he•do•ni∘a
an•he•don∘ic
an•hi•dro•sis
an•hi•drot∘ic
an•hy•drase
an•hy•drate, *v.,* -drat∘ed, -drat•ing.
an•hy•dra•tion
an•hy•dre•mi∘a
an•hy•dre•mic
an•hy•dride
an•hy•dro•hy•drox∘y•pro•ges•ter•one
An•hy•dron *Trademark.*
an•hy•dro•sis
an•hy•drot∘ic
an•hy•drous
an•ic•ter∘ic
an∘i•dro•sis or an•hi•dro•sis
an∘i•drot∘ic
an•ile
an∘i•lide
an∘i•linc•tus
an∘i•line
aniline blue
aniline dye
an∘i•lin•gus
an∘i•lin•ism
a∘nil∘i∘ty
an•til∘y•sis, *n., pl.* -ses.
an∘i•o∘ma, *n., pl.* -mas.
an∘i•mal
animal heat
animal king•dom

animal mag•net•ism
animal mod•el
animal pole
animal pro•tein fac•tor
animal psy•chol∘o•gy
animal starch
an∘i•mal•cule
an∘i•mal•cu•lum, *n., pl.*
-cu∘la.
an∘i•mate
an∘i•mat∘ed
an∘i•ma•tion
an∘i•ma•tism
an∘i•ma•tis•tic
an∘i•mism
an∘i•mist
an∘i•mis•tic
an∘i•mus
an∘i•on
an∘i•on∘ic
an∘i•on∘i•cal∘ly
an∘i•on∘o•trop∘ic
an∘i•rid∘i∘a
an•ise
anise oil
an∘i•seed
aniseed oil
an∘i•sei•ko•ni∘a
an∘i•sei•kon∘ic
an•ise•seed
an∘i•so•co•ri∘a
an∘i•so•cy•to•sis
an∘i•so•cy•tot∘ic
an∘i•sog∘a•mous or an∘i•so•
gam∘ic
an∘i•sog•a∘my
an∘i•so•me•tro•pi∘a
an∘i•so•me•trop∘ic
an∘i•so•trop∘ic
an•i∘sot•ro•pism, *n., pl.*
-pisms.
an•i∘sot•ro∘py

an∘kle
ankle im•pinge•ment
syn•drome
ankle jerk
ankle joint
an•kle•bone
an•ky•lose, *v.,* -losed, -los•
ing.
an•ky•los•ing spon•dy•li•tis
an•ky•lo•sis, *n., pl.* -ses.
An•ky•los•to∘ma
an•ky•lo•stome
an•ky•lo•sto•mi∘a•sis
An•ky•lo•sto•mum
an•ky•lot∘ic
an•ky•roid
an•la∘ge, *n., pl.* -gen, -ges.
an•nat∘to
an•neal
an•neal∘er
an•nec•tent
annectent gy∘ri
an•ne•lid
An•nel∘oi∘da
an•nel∘oi•dan
an•nex∘a
an•nu•lar
annular lig∘a•ment
an•nu•larsyph∘i•lid
an•nu•lus, *n., pl.* -li, -lus∘es.
annulus fi•bro•sus
a∘no•ci•as•so•ci•a•tion
a∘no•ci•a•tion
a∘nod∘al
a∘nod•al∘ly
an•ode
a∘nod∘ic
a∘nod∘i•cal∘ly
an∘o•don•tia
an∘o•dyne
an∘o•dyn∘i∘a
an∘o•dyn•ous

an○o•e•sia
an○o○e•sis, *n.*, *pl.* -ses.
an•oes•trous
an•oes•trus
an○o•gen○i•tal
a○noi○a
a○nom○a•lo•scope
a○nom○a•lous
a○nom○a○ly, *n.*, *pl.* -lies.
an○o•mer
an○o•mer○ic
a○no•mi○a
a○nom○ic
anomic a○pha•sia
an○o•mie
an○o•my
an○o•nych○i○a
a○non•y○ma, *n.*, *pl.* -mae, -mas.
an○o•op•si○a
a○noph•e○les, *n.*, *pl.* -les.
a○noph•el○i•cide
a○noph•e○line
a○noph○e•lism
an•oph•thal•mi○a
an•oph•thal•mic
an•oph•thal•mos
an○o•pi○a
an○o•plas○ty, *n.*, *pl.* -ties.
An•op•lo•ceph○a○la
An•op•lo•ceph○a•lid
An•op•lo•ce•phal○i•dae
An○o•plu○ra
an•op•si○a
an•or•chism
an○o•rec•tal
an○o•rec•tic or an•o•ret○ic
anorectic bing○er
an○o•rex○i○a
anorexia ner•vo○sa
an○o•rex○i•ant
an○o•rex○ic

an○o•rex○i•gen○ic
an•or•gan○ic
an•or•tho•pi○a
an○o•scope
an○o•scop○ic
a○nos•co○py, *n.*, *pl.* -pies.
an•os•mat○ic an•os•mic
an•os•mi○a
an•os•phra•si○a
an•os•phre•si○a
an○o•tia
an○o•vag○i•nal
an•ov○u•lant
an•ov○u•la•tion
an•ov○u•la•to○ry or an•ov○u•lar
an•ox•e○mi○a
an•ox•e○mic
an•ox○i○a
an•ox○ic
an○sa, *n.*, *pl.* -sae.
ansa cer•vi•ca•lis
ansa hy•po•glos○si
ansa sub•cla•vi○a
an•sae ner•vi spi•na•lis
ansae ner•vo•rum spi•na•li○um
An•said *Trademark.*
an•si•form
An•spor *Trademark.*
an•a○bol○ic ster•oid
anabolic steroid poi•soning
Ant○a•buse *Trademark.*
ant•ac○id
an•tag○o○nism
an•tag○o○nist
an•tag○o○nis•tic
an•tag○o○nis•ti•cal○ly
an•tag○o○nize, *v.*, -nized, -niz•ing.
an•te•bra•chi○al

an•te•bra•chi∘um, *n., pl.*
-chi∘a.
an•te•car•di∘um
an•te•cor∘nu, *n., pl.* -nu∘a.
an•te•cu•bi•tal
antecubital fos∘sa
an•te•flex•ion
an•te•grade
an•te•hy•po•phy•sis, *n., pl.*
-ses.
an•te•mor•tem
an•te•na•tal∘ly
an•te•par
an•te•par•tum
an•te•ri∘o∘gram
an•te•ri∘or
anterior ce•re•bral ar•ter∘y
anterior cham•ber
anterior cho•roid artery
anterior cho•roi•dal artery
anterior col•umn
anterior com•mis•sure
anterior com•mu•ni•cat•ing
artery
anterior cor•ti•co•spi•nal
tract
anterior cra•ni∘al fos∘sa
anterior cru•ci•ate lig∘a•ment
anterior cru•ral nerve
anterior draw•er test
anterior fa•cial vein
anterior fon•ta•nel
anterior fon•ta•nelle
anterior fos∘sa
anterior fu•nic∘u•lus
anterior gray col•umn
anterior horn
anterior hu•mer∘al cir•cum•
flex artery
anterior in•fe•ri∘or cer∘e•
bel•lar artery
anterior inferior il∘i∘ac spine

anterior in•ter•cos•tal
artery
anterior jug∘u•lar vein
anterior lin•gual gland
anterior lobe
anterior me•di∘an fis•sure
anterior na∘sal spine
anterior pil•lar of the fau•ces
anterior pi•tu∘i•tar∘y
anterior root
anterior sac•ro•coc•cyg∘e∘al
mus•cle
anterior sca•lene
anterior spi•nal artery
anterior spi•no•cer∘e•bel•lar
tract
anterior spi•no•tha•lam∘ic
tract
anterior su•pe•ri∘or il∘i∘ac
spine
anterior syn•ech∘i∘a
anterior tem•po•ral artery
anterior tib∘i∘al artery
anterior tibial nerve
anterior tibial vein
anterior tri•an•gle
anterior ul∘nar re•cur•rent artery
an•te•ri∘or∘i∘ty
an•te•ri∘or∘ly
an•ter∘o∘grade
an∘ter∘o•in•fe•ri∘or
an∘ter∘o•in•fe•ri∘or∘ly
an∘ter∘o•lat•er∘al
an∘ter∘o•lat•er∘al∘ly
an∘ter∘o•me•di∘al
an∘ter∘o•pos•te•ri∘or
an∘ter∘o•pos•te•ri∘or∘ly
an∘ter∘o•su•pe•ri∘or
an∘ter∘o•su•pe•ri∘or∘ly
an•te•ver•sion
an•te•vert

ant•he•lix
an•thel•min•thic
ant•hel•min•tic
an•tho•cy•an
an•tho•cy•o•a•nin
An•thra-Derm *Trademark.*
an•thra•cene
an•thra•coid
an•thra•co•sil•i•co•sis
an•thra•co•sis
an•thra•cot•ic
an•thra•cy•cline
an•thra•lin
An•thra•mine *Trademark.*
an•thra•nil•ate
an•thra•nil•ic ac•id
an•thra•qui•none
an•thra•sil•i•co•sis
an•thrax, *n., pl.* -thra•ces.
an•throne
an•thro•po•gen•e•sis
an•thro•po•ge•net•ic
an•thro•po•gen•ic
an•thro•pog•e•ny
an•thro•pog•ra•phy
an•thro•poid
anthropoid ape
An•thro•poi•de•a
an•thro•poi•de•an
an•thro•po•log•i•cal
an•thro•po•log•i•cal•ly
an•thro•pol•o•gist
an•thro•pol•o•gy
an•thro•pom•e•ter
an•thro•po•met•ric
an•thro•pom•e•try
an•thro•po•mor•phic
an•thro•po•mor•phi•cal•ly
an•thro•po•mor•phism
an•thro•poph•a•gous
an•thro•poph•a•gy

an•thro•po•phil•ic
an•thro•poph•oi•lous
an•thro•po•pho•bi•a
an•ti•a•bor•tion
an•ti•a•bor•tion•ist
an•ti•ac•id
an•ti•ad•ren•er•gic
an•ti•ag•gres•sin
an•ti•ag•gres•sion
an•ti•al•ler•gen•ic
an•ti•al•ler•gic
an•ti•an•a•phy•lax•is
an•ti•an•dro•gen
an•ti•an•dro•gen•ic
an•ti•a•one•mic
antianemic fac•tor
an•ti•an•gi•nal
an•ti•an•ti•bod•y, *n., pl.*
-bod•ies.
an•ti•anx•i•e•ty
an•ti•car•cin•o•gen•ic
an•ti•ar•rhyth•mic
an•ti•arth•rit•ic
an•ti•bac•te•ri•al
an•ti•bi•o•sis
an•ti•bi•ot•ic
an•ti•bi•ot•i•cal•ly
an•ti•bod•y, *n., pl.* -bod•ies.
antibody-me•di•at•ed im•
mu•ni•ty
an•ti•bra•chi•al
an•ti•bra•chi•um, *n., pl.*
-chi•a.
an•ti•can•cer
an•ti•car•cin•o•gen
an•ti•car•di•um, *n., pl.* -di•a.
an•ti•car•ies
an•ti•cat•a•lyst
an•ti•ca•thex•is, *n., pl.*
-thex•es.
an•ti•cath•ode
an•ti•cho•lin•er•gic

an•ti•cho•lin•es •ter•ase
an•tic•i•pate, *v.*, -pat∘ed, -pat•ing.
an•tic•i•pa•tion
an∘ti•clot•ting
an∘ti•cne•mi∘on
an∘ti•co•ag•u•lant
an∘ti•co•ag∘u•late, *v.*, -lat∘ed, -lat•ing.
an∘ti•co•ag∘u•la•tion
an∘ti•co•ag∘u•la•to∘ry
an∘ti•co•ag∘u•lin
an∘ti•co•don
an∘ti•com•ple•ment
an∘ti•com•ple•men•ta∘ry
an∘ti•con•vul•sant
an∘ti•con•vul•sive
an∘ti•cus
an∘ti•de•pres•sant or an∘ti•de•pres•sive
an∘ti•di∘a•bet∘ic
an∘ti•di•ar•rhe∘al
an∘ti•di∘u•re•sis
an∘ti•di∘u•ret∘ic
antidiuretic hor•mone
an∘ti•dot∘al
an∘ti•dot∘al∘ly
an∘ti•dote, *n., v.*, -dot∘ed, -dot•ing.
an∘ti•drom∘ic
an∘ti•drom∘i•cal∘ly
an∘ti•dys•en•ter∘ic
an∘ti•eo•met∘ic
an∘ti•eo•met∘i•cal∘ly
an∘ti•en•zyme
an∘ti•es•tro•gen
an∘ti•es•tro•gen∘ic
an∘ti•fer•til∘i•ty
an∘ti•fi•bril•la•to∘ry
an∘ti•fi•bri•no•ly•sin
an∘ti•fi•bri•no•lyt∘ic
an∘ti•flat∘u•lent

an∘ti•fluor∘oi•da•tion•ist
an∘ti•fun•gal
an∘ti-G suit
an∘ti•gen
an∘ti•ge•ne•mi∘a
an∘ti•gen∘ic de•ter•mi•nant
an∘ti•gen∘i•cal∘ly
an∘ti•ge•nic∘i∘ty
an∘ti•ges•ta•tion∘al drug
an∘ti•glob•u•lin
an∘ti•go•nad∘o•trop∘ic
an∘ti•go•nad∘o•trop∘in
an∘ti•grav∘i∘ty suit
an∘ti•he•lix, *n., pl.* -hel∘i•ces, -he•lix∘es.
an∘ti•he•mo•phil∘ic fac•tor
an∘ti•hem•or•rhag∘ic
an∘ti•hi•drot∘ic
an∘ti•his•ta•mine
an∘ti•his•ta•min∘ic
an∘ti•hor•mone
an∘ti•hu•man
an∘ti•hy•per•lip∘oi•dem∘ic
an∘ti•hy•per•ten•sion
an∘ti•hy•per•ten•sive
an∘ti•id∘oi•o•type
an∘ti•id∘oi•o•typ∘ic
an∘ti•im•mu•no•glob∘u•lin
an•ti-in•fec•tive
an•ti-in•flam•ma•to∘ry, *adj., n., pl.* -ries.
an•ti-in•su•lin
an∘ti•ke•to•gen•e∘sis, *n., pl.* -ses.
an∘ti•leu•ke•mi∘a
an∘ti•leu•ke•mic
An∘ti•lir∘oi∘um *Trademark.*
an∘ti•lu•et∘ic
an∘ti•lym•pho•cyte glob∘u•lin
antilymphocyte se∘rum

an·ti·lym·pho·cyt·ic globu-
lin
antilymphocytic serum
an·ti·ly·sin
an·ti·ma·lar·i·al
an·ti·mere
an·ti·met·a·bol·ic
an·ti·me·tab·o·lite
an·ti·mi·cro·bi·al
an·ti·mi·cro·bic
An·ti·minth *Trademark.*
an·ti·mi·tot·ic
an·ti·mon·ic
an·ti·mo·nide
an·ti·mo·nil·i·al
an·ti·mo·ni·ous
an·ti·mo·ni·um cru·dum
antimonium tar·tar·i·cum
an·ti·mo·ony
antimony po·tas·si·um tar·
trate
an·ti·mo·nyl
an·ti·mus·ca·rin·ic
an·ti·mu·ta·gen·ic
an·ti·my·cin A
an·ti·my·cot·ic
an·ti·ne·o·plas·tic
an·ti·neu·rit·ic
an·ti·no·i·on
an·ti·no·ci·cep·tive
an·ti·nu·cle·ar
an·ti·oes·tro·gen
an·ti·ox·i·dant
an·ti·par·al·lel
an·ti·par·a·sit·ic
an·ti·par·kin·son
an·ti·par·kin·so·ni·an
an·ti·pa·thet·ic
an·ti·path·ic
an·tip·a·thy
an·ti·pe·ri·od·ic

an·ti·per·i·stal·sis, *n., pl.*
-ses.
an·ti·per·i·stal·tic
an·ti·per·spi·rant
an·ti·phlo·gis·tic
an·ti·ep·o·i·lep·tic
an·ti·plas·min
an·ti·plas·tic
an·ti·plate·let
an·ti·pneu·mo·coc·cal
an·ti·pneu·mo·coc·cic
an·ti·pneu·mo·coc·cus
an·ti·pode, *n., pl.* -tip·o·o·des.
an·ti·pol·lu·tion
an·ti·pol·lu·tion·ist
an·ti·pro·te·ase
an·ti·pro·throm·bin
an·ti·pro·to·zo·al
an·ti·pru·rit·ic
an·ti·pseu·do·mo·nal
an·ti·psy·chot·ic
an·ti·py·re·sis
an·ti·py·ret·ic
an·ti·py·rin
an·ti·py·rine
an·ti·ra·chit·ic
an·ti·tra·gus, *n., pl.* -tra·gi.
an·ti·ren·nin
an·ti·re·tic·u·lar cy·to·
tox·ic se·rum
an·ti·rheu·mat·ic
an·ti·ri·cin
an·ti·schis·to·so·mal
an·ti·schiz·o·o·phren·ic
an·ti·scor·bu·tic
an·ti·se·cre·to·ry
an·ti·sense
an·ti·sep·sis
an·ti·sep·tic
an·ti·sep·ti·cal·ly
an·ti·sep·ti·cize, *v.,* -cized,
-ciz·ing.

an○ti•se•rum, *n., pl.* -rums,
  -ra.
an○ti•sex
an○ti•sex○u○al
an○ti•si•al○a•gog○ic
an○ti•si•der○ic
an○ti•so•cial
an○ti•spas•mod○ic
an○ti•sperm
an○ti•strep•to•coc•cal
an○ti•strep•to•coc•cic
an○ti•strep•to•ki•nase
an○ti•strep•to•ly•sin
an○ti•syph○i•lit○ic
an○ti•the•nar
an○ti•throm•bic
an○ti•throm•bin
an○ti•throm•bo•plas•tin
an○ti•throm•bot○ic
an○ti•thy○roid
an○ti•tox○ic
an○ti•tox○in
an○ti•tox○i•no•gen○ic
an○ti•trag○i•cus, *n., pl.* -ci.
an○ti•try•pan○o○so•mal
an○ti•try•pan○o○some
an○ti•tryp•sin
an○ti•tryp•tic
an○ti•tu•ber•cu•lar
an○ti•tu•ber•cu•lo○sis
an○ti•tu•ber•cu•lous
an○ti•tu•mor
an○ti•tu•mor○al
an○ti•tus•sive
an○ti•ty•phoid
an○ti•ul•cer
an○ti•ven○in or an○ti•ven○om
An○ti•vert *Trademark.*
an○ti•vi○ral
an○ti•vi•ta•min
an○ti•vivsec•tion
an○ti•viv○i•sec•tion•ist

an○ti•xe○roph•thal•mic
an○ti•zy•mot○ic
an•tral
an•trec•to•my, *n., pl.* -mies.
An•tre•nyl *Trademark.*
An•tro•col *Trademark.*
an•trorse
an•trorse○ly
an•tro•scope
an•tros•to•my, *n., pl.* -mies.
an•trot○o○my, *n., pl.* -mies.
an•trum, *n., pl.* -tra.
antrum car○di•a•cum
antrum mas•toid•e○um
antrum of High•more
antrum py•lo•ri•cum
antrum tym•pan○i•cum
ANTU
An•tu•rane *Trademark.*
a○nu•cle•ate
a○nu•cle•at○ed
an○u○li fi•bro○si cor•dis
an○u•lus fi•bro•sus
an•u•re○sis
an•u•ret○ic
an•u○ri○a
an•u○ric
a○nus, *n., pl.* -nus○es.
anus vag○i•na•lis
anus ves○i•ca•lis
anus vul•vo•vag○i•na•lis
An○u•sol-HC *Trademark.*
an○vil
anx•i•e•tas pre•se•nil○us
anxietas tib○i•ar○um
anx○i○e○ty, *n., pl.* -ties.
anxiety dis•or•der
anxiety e○quiv○a•lent
anxiety hys•ter○i○a
anxiety re•ac•tion
anx○i○o•lyt○ic

anx•ious
a∘or∘ta, *n., pl.* -tas, -tae.
aorta ab•dom∘i•na•lis
aorta as•cend•ens
aorta des•cend•ens
aorta of Val•sal∘va
aorta tho•ra•ca•lis
aorta tho•ra•ci∘ca
a∘or•tal
a∘or•tic
aortic arch
aortic hi•a•tus
aortic in•suf•fi•cien•cy
aortic mur•mur
aortic re•gurg∘i•ta•tion
aortic rup•ture
aortic si∘nus
aortic sten∘o•sis
aortic valve
a∘or•ti•co•pul•mo•nar∘y
a∘or•ti•co•re•nal
a∘or•ti•tis
a∘or•to•cor∘o•nar∘y
a∘or•to•gram
a∘or•to•graph∘ic
a∘or•tog•ra•phy, *n., pl.*
  -phies.
a∘or•to•il∘i∘ac
a∘or•to•pul•mo•nar∘y
  win•dow
a∘or•to•sub•cla•vi∘an
a∘par∘a•lyt∘ic
Ap∘a•tate *Trademark.*
ap∘a•thet∘ic
ap∘a•thet∘i•cal∘ly
ap∘a•thy, *n., pl.* -thies.
ap∘a•tite
ape
a∘per∘i•ent
a∘pe•ri•od∘ic
a∘per∘i•stal•sis, *n., pl.* -ses.
a∘per∘i•tive

ap•er•tom•e∘ter
a∘per•tu∘ra, *n., pl.* -rae.
ap•er•ture
a∘pex, *n., pl.* -pex∘es,
  -pi∘ces.
a∘pex•car•di•og∘ra•phy, *n.*
  pl. -phies.
Ap∘gar score
a∘pha•gia
aphagia al•ge∘ra
a∘pha•ki∘a
a∘pha•kic
a∘pha•sia
a∘pha•si∘ac
a∘pha•sic
a∘pha•si∘ol∘o∘gist
a∘pha•si∘ol∘o∘gy
A∘phas•mid∘i∘a
a∘phe•mi∘a
a∘pher•e∘sis
aph•e∘ret∘ic
a∘pho•ni∘a
aphonia par∘a•no•i∘ca
a∘phon∘ic
a∘phos•pho•ro•sis
a∘phra•sia
a∘phra•sic
aph•ro•di•sia
aph•ro•dis∘i•ac
Aph•ro•dyne *Trademark.*
aph•tha, *n., pl.* -thae.
aphtha ep∘i•zo∘o•ot∘i∘ca
aphtha ser•pens
aph•thic
aph•thoid
aph•thon•gia
aph•tho•sis, *n., pl.* -ses.
aph•thous
aphthous fe•ver
aphthous stom∘a•ti•tis
a∘pi•cal
apical den•tal lig∘a•ment

apical fo•ra•men
a•pi•cal•ly
a•pi•ces
ap•i•ci•tis
a•pi•co•ec•to•my, *n., pl.*
  -mies.
ap•i•col•y•sis
A•pis mel•lif•er•a
apis mel•lif•oi•ca
A•pi•um
Apium grav•e•o•lens
a•pla•cen•tal
a•pla•nat•ic
a•pla•nat•i•cal•ly
a•plan•o•a•tism
a•pla•sia
aplasia ax•i•a•lis ex•tra•cor•
  ti•ca•lis con•gen•i•ta
a•plas•tic
aplastic a•ne•mi•a
Ap•li•sol *Trademark.*
Ap•li•test *Trademark.*
ap•ne•a
apnea va•gi
apnea ve•ra
ap•ne•ic
ap•neu•sis, *n., pl.* -ses.
ap•neus•tic
a•po E
ap•o•car•te•re•sis, *n., pl.*
  -ses.
a•po•chro•mat•ic
ap•o•crine
Ap•o•cy•num
ap•o•dal
ap•o•dous
ap•o•en•zyme
ap•o•fer•ri•tin
a•pog•a•mous
a•pog•a•my
a•po•lar
ap•o•li•po•pro•tein

ap•o•mict
ap•o•mic•tic
ap•o•mic•ti•cal•ly
ap•o•mix•is, *n., pl.* -mix•es.
ap•o•mor•phine or ap•o•
  mor•phin
ap•o•neu•ro•sis, *n., pl.* -ses.
aponeurosis ep•i•cra•ni•a•lis
aponeurosis lin•guae
aponeurosis mus•cu•li•bi•
  cip•i•tis bra•chi•oi
aponeurosis pal•ma•ris
aponeurosis plan•ta•ris
ap•o•neu•rot•ic
a•po•ni•a
ap•o•phys•e•al
ap•o•phy•sis, *n., pl.* -ses.
ap•o•phy•si•tis
ap•o•plec•tic or ap•o•plec•
  ti•cal
ap•o•plec•ti•cal•ly
ap•o•plec•ti•form
ap•o•plex•y
ap•o•pro•tein
a•poth•e•o•car•ies' meas•ure
apothecaries' weight
a•poth•e•o•car•y, *n., pl.* -car•
  ies.
ap•ox•e•sis
ap•o•zem
ap•o•ze•ma
ap•o•zy•mase
ap•pa•ra•tus, *n., pl.* -tus•es,
  -tus.
apparatus di•ges•to•ri•us
apparatus lac•ri•ma•lis
apparatus res•pi•ra•to•ri•us
apparatus u•ro•gen•i•ta•lis
ap•par•ent
apparent mo•tion
ap•pear
ap•pear•ance

Ap•pe•con *Trademark.*
ap•pend•age
ap•pen•dec•to•my, *n., pl.*
-mies.
ap•pen•di•cal
ap•pen•di•ce•al
ap•pen•di•cec•to•my, *n., pl.*
-mies.
ap•pen•di•ces ep•i•plo•i•cae
appendices ve•sic•u•lo•sae
ep•o•o•pho•ri
ap•pen•di•cial
ap•pen•di•ci•tis
appendicitis ob•lit•er•ans
ap•pen•di•cos•to•my, *n., pl.*
-mies.
ap•pen•dic•u•lar
ap•pen•dix, *n., pl.* -dix•es,
-di•ces.
ap•per•ceive, *v.,* -ceived,
-ceiv•ing.
ap•per•cep•tion
ap•per•cep•tive
ap•per•so•na•tion
ap•pe•stat
ap•pe•tite
ap•pe•ti•tion
ap•pet•oi•tive
ap•pla•nate
ap•pla•na•tion
applanation to•nom•e•ter
ap•ple
ap•pli•ance
ap•pli•ca•tion
ap•pl•ica•tor
ap•plied
ap•ply, *v.,* -plied, -ply•ing.
ap•po•sa•bil•i•ty
ap•pos•a•ble
ap•pose, *v.,* -posed, -pos•ing.
ap•po•si•tion
ap•po•si•tion•al

ap•proach
approach-approach con•flict
approach-a•void•ance
conflict
ap•prox•i•mal
ap•prox•i•mate, *v.,* -mat•ed,
-mat•ing.
ap•prox•i•ma•tion
a•prac•tic
a•prax•i•a
a•prax•ic
A•pres•a•zide *Trademark.*
A•pres•o•line *Trademark.*
ap•ri•cot-ker•nel oil
a•proc•tous
a•pron
ap•ros•ex•i•a
aprosexia na•sal•is
ap•ro•so•pus
a•pro•tin•in
ap•sel•a•phe•sia
ap•tha
ap•ti•tude
aptitude test
ap•ty•a•lism
ap•y•rase
a•py•ret•ic
a•py•rex•i•a, *n., pl.* -as.
a•py•rex•i•al
a•py•rex•y, *n., pl.* -rex•ies.
a•qua, *n., pl.* a•quae, a•quas.
aqua pu•ra
aqua re•gia
aqua vi•tae
Aq•ua•Me•phy•ton *Trade-mark.*
Aq•ua•nil *Trademark.*
Aq•ua•phor *Trademark.*
Aq•ua•phyl•lin *Trademark.*
Aq•ua•Tar *Trademark.*
Aq•ua•ten•sen *Trademark.*
a•quat•ic

aq•ue•duct
aqueduct of Fal•lo•pi•us
aqueduct of Syl•vi•us
aq•ue•duc•tus ce•re•bri
aqueductus coch•le•ae
aqueductus ves•tib•u•li
a•que•ous
aqueous flare
aqueous hu•mor
aq•ui•fer
a•quos•i•ty
ar•a-A *Trademark.*
ar•a•ban
a•rab•i•nose
a•rab•i•nos•ic
ar•a•bin•o•side
a•rab•i•tol
ar•a•chid•ic ac•id
ar•a•chi•do•nate
ar•a•chi•don•ic ac•id
ar•a•chis oil
a•rach•nid
A•rach•ni•da
a•rach•nid•ism
a•rach•ni•tis
a•rach•no•dac•ty•ly
a•rach•noid
arachnoid gran•u•la•tion
a•rach•noi•dal
a•rach•noi•de•a
arachnoidea en•ceph•a•li
arachnoidea spi•na•lis
a•rach•noid•ism
a•rach•noi•di•tis
arachnoiditis os•si•fi•cans
a•rach•no•ly•sin
Ar•a•len *Trademark.*
a•ra•li•a
Aralia rac•e•mo•sa
Ar•a•mine *Trademark.*
a•ra•ro•ba, *n., pl.* -bas.

ar•bor
ar•bo•res•cent
ar•bor•i•za•tion
ar•bo•rize, *v.,* -rized, -riz•ing.
ar•bor•vi•tae cer•e•bel•i
ar•bo•vi•rol•o•gist
ar•bo•vi•rol•o•gy
ar•bo•vi•rus, *n., pl.* -rus•es.
ar•bu•tin
Ar•bu•tus
ar•cade
Ar•car•i•dae
arch
arch of Cor•ti
arch of the a•or•ta
arch of the fau•ces
ar•chae•bac•te•ri•a or ar•chae•o•bac•te•ri•a, *n., pl., sing.,* -ri•um.
ar•cha•ic
arch•en•ceph•a•lon, *n., pl.* -lons, -la.
arch•en•ter•ic
ar•che•type
arch•en•ter•on, *n., pl.* -ter•a.
ar•che•spo•ri•al
ar•che•spo•ri•um, *n., pl.* -ri•a.
ar•che•typ•al
ar•che•typ•i•cal
ar•chi•a•ter
ar•chi•carp
ar•chil
ar•chi•pal•li•um
ar•chi•tec•ton•ic
ar•chi•tec•ton•ics
ar•chi•tec•tur•al
ar•chi•tec•tur•al•ly
ar•chi•tec•ture
ar•ci•form
Ar•co-Lase *Trademark.*
arc•to•staph•y•los

ar•cu•a•ole, *n., pl.* -li•a.
ar•cu•ate
arcuate ar•ter•y
arcuate lig•a•ment
arcuate nu•cle•us
arcuate po•plit•e•al
  lig•a•ment
arcuate vein
ar•cu•a•tion
ar•cus, *n., pl.* -cus.
ar•cus•se•nil•is
ar•dor urina
ardor u•ri•nae
ardor ven•tric•u•li
Ar•du•an *Trademark.*
ar•e•a
area o•pa•ca
area pel•lu•ci•da
area plac•en•ta•lis
area pos•tre•ma
area vas•cu•lo•sa
a•re•ca
a•re•co•line
a•re•flex•i•a
a•re•flex•ic
a•re•gen•er•a•tive
a•re•na•ceous
a•re•na•tion
ar•en•a•vi•rus, *n., pl.* -rus•es.
a•re•o•la, *n., pl.* -lae, -las.
areola mam•mae
areola pap•il•lar•is
a•re•o•lar
areolar tis•sue
a•re•o•late
a•re•o•la•tion
a•re•o•met•ric
a•re•o•met•ri•cal
a•re•o•met•ri•cal•ly
Ar•fo•nad *Trademark.*
Ar•gas
Argas per•si•cus

ar•ga•sid
Ar•gas•oi•dae
ar•gen•taf•fin
argentaffin cell
ar•gen•taf•fine
argentaffine cell
ar•gen•taf•fin•i•ty, *n., pl.*
  -ties.
ar•gen•taf•fin•o•o•ma, *n., pl.*
  -mas, -ma•ta.
ar•gen•tic
ar•gen•to•phil
ar•gen•to•phile
ar•gen•to•phil•ic
ar•gen•tous
ar•gen•tum
argentum ni•tri•cum
ar•gi•nase
ar•gi•nine
ar•gon
Ar•gyll Rob•ert•son pu•pil
ar•gyr•i•a
Ar•gy•rol
ar•gy•ro•phil
ar•gy•ro•phile
ar•gy•ro•phil•i•a
ar•gy•ro•phil•ic
ar•gy•roph•oi•lous
ar•gy•ro•sis
a•ri•bo•fla•vi•no•sis
A•ris•to•cort *Trademark.*
A•ris•to•lo•chi•a
Aristolochia re•tic•u•la•ta
Aristolochia ser•pen•tar•i•a
A•ris•to•span *Trademark.*
a•rith•mo•ma•ni•a
Ar•li•din *Trademark.*
arm
ar•ma•men•tar•i•um, *n., pl.*
  -tar•i•a.
ar•med
arm•pit

A•rneth in•dex
ar•ni•ca
arnica mon•tan•a
a•ro•ma•ther•a•py
ar•o•mat•ic
aromatic am•mo•ni•a spir•it
aromatic bit•ters
a•ro•ma•ti•za•tion
a•ro•ma•tize, v., -tized, -tiz•ing.
a•rous•al
a•rouse, v., a•roused, a•rous•ing.
ar•rec•tor, n., pl. -to•res, -tors.
arrector pi•li mus•cle
ar•rest
ar•rest•ment
ar•rhe•no•blas•to•ma, n., pl. -mas, -ma•ta.
ar•rhe•no•to•ky, n., pl. -kies.
ar•rhyth•mi•a
ar•rhyth•mic or ar•rhyth•mi•cal
ar•rhyth•mi•cal•ly
ar•row•root
ar•sa•nil•ic ac•id
ar•se•nate
ar•se•nic
arsenic ac•id
arsenic tri•ox•ide
ar•sen•i•cal
ar•sen•i•cal•ism
ar•sen•i•cum al•bum
ar•se•nide
ar•se•ni•ous
arsenious ac•id
arsenious ox•ide
ar•se•nite
ar•se•ni•um
ar•sen•iu•ret•ed
ar•sen•iu•ret•ted

ar•se•no•ther•a•py
ar•se•nous
ar•se•nox•ide
ar•sine
ar•so•ni•um
ars•phen•a•mine
Ar•tane *Trademark.*
ar•te•fact
ar•te•fac•tu•al
ar•te•mi•sia
ar•te•re•nol
ar•te•ri•a, n., pl. -ri•ae.
ar•te•ri•al
ar•te•ri•al•i•za•tion
ar•te•ri•al•ize, v., -ized, -iz•ing.
ar•te•ri•al•ly
ar•te•ri•o•cap•il•lar•y
ar•te•ri•o•gram
ar•te•ri•o•graph•ic
ar•te•ri•o•graph•i•cal•ly
ar•te•ri•og•ra•phy, n., pl. -phies.
ar•te•ri•o•la, n., pl. -ri•o•lae.
ar•te•ri•o•lar
ar•te•ri•ole
ar•te•ri•o•li•tis
ar•te•ri•o•lo•ne•cro•sis
ar•te•ri•o•lop•a•thy, n., pl. -thies.
ar•te•ri•o•lu•mi•nal
ar•te•ri•o•mes•en•ter•ic
ar•te•ri•op•a•thy, n., pl. -thies.
ar•te•ri•or•rha•phy, n., pl. -phies.
ar•te•ri•o•scle•ro•sis
arteriosclerosis ob•lit•er•ans
ar•te•ri•o•scle•rot•ic
ar•te•ri•o•si•nus•oi•dal
ar•te•ri•o•spasm
ar•te•ri•o•spas•tic

ar•te•ri•ot•o•o•my, *n., pl.*
  -mies.
ar•te•ri•o•ve•nous
arteriovenous
  mal•for•ma•tion
ar•te•ri•ot•ic
ar•te•ri•tis
arteritis de•for•mans
arteritis ob•lit•er•ans
ar•ter•o•y, *n., pl.* -ter•ies.
ar•thral
ar•thral•gia
arthralgia hys•ter•o•i•ca
arthralgia sat•ur•ni•o•na
ar•thral•gic
arth•rec•to•o•my, *n., pl.* -mies.
ar•thrit•ic
ar•thrit•o•i•cal•ly
ar•thri•tis
arthritis de•for•mans
arthritis fun•go•sa
arthritis u•ore•thrit•o•i•ca
arth•ro•cen•te•o•sis, *n., pl.* -ses.
ar•throd•e•o•sis, *n., pl.* -ses.
arth•ro•di•o•a, *n., pl.* -di•o•ae.
ar•thro•di•al
ar•throd•o•ic
ar•thro•dys•pla•sia
ar•throg•o•e•o•nous
ar•thro•gram
ar•thro•graph•o•ic
ar•throg•ra•phy, *n., pl.*
  -phies.
ar•thro•gry•po•sis
arthrogryposis mul•ti•plex
arthrogryposis multiplex
  con•gen•o•i•ta
ar•throl•o•o•gy
ar•throl•o•y•sis
ar•throm•e•o•ter
ar•thro•path•o•ic
ar•thro•po•a•thy

ar•thro•plas•o•ty, *n., pl.* -ties.
ar•thro•pod
Ar•throp•o•o•da
ar•throp•o•o•dan
ar•thro•scle•ro•sis
ar•thro•scope
ar•thro•scop•o•ic
ar•thros•co•o•py
ar•thro•sis
ar•thro•spore
ar•throt•o•o•my, *n., pl.* -mies.
Ar•thus phe•nom•e•o•non
ar•tic•o•u•lar
articular cap•sule
articular car•ti•lage
articular disk
articular la•mel•o•la
articular proc•ess
ar•tic•o•u•late, *v.,* -lat•o•ed,
  -lat•ing.
ar•tic•o•u•lat•o•ed joint
ar•tic•o•u•la•tion
ar•tic•o•u•la•tor
ar•tic•o•u•la•to•o•ry
ar•ti•fact
ar•ti•fac•ti•tious
ar•ti•fac•tu•al
ar•ti•fi•cial
artificial gene
artificial in•sem•o•i•na•tion
artificial kid•ney
artificial res•pir•o•a•tion
ar•ti•fi•cial•o•ly
ar•ti•o•o•dac•tyl
Ar•ti•o•o•dac•ty•o•la
ar•ti•o•o•dac•ty•lous
ar•y•ep•o•i•glot•tic
ar•oyl
ar•y•te•no•ep•o•i•glot•tic
ar•y•te•no•ep•o•i•glot•tid•
  e•o•an
ar•y•te•noid

ar•y•te•noid•ec•to•my
ar•y•ten•oi•do•pex•y, *n., pl.*
-pex•ies.
as•a•fet•oi•da
as•a•foet•oi•da
a•sa•rum
as•bes•tos
as•bes•to•sis
as•bes•tus
As•bron G *Trademark.*
as•ca•ri•a•sis
as•ca•ri•cid•al
as•ca•ri•cide
as•ca•rid
as•car•oi•des
As•ca•rid•oi•a
as•ca•ri•di•a•sis, *n., pl.* -ses.
As•ca•rid•oi•dae
as•ca•rid•oi•o•sis
as•ca•ri•do•sis
as•ca•ris, *n., pl.* -car•oi•des.
Ascaris e•quo•rum
Ascaris lum•bri•coi•des
Ascaris meg•a•lo•ceph•a•la
Ascaris mys•tax
Ascaris su•um
As•ca•rops
as•cend
as•cend•ing a•or•ta
ascending co•lon
ascending lum•bar vein
ascending pal•a•tine ar•ter•y
Asc•hel•min•thes
Asch•heim-Zon•dek test
Asch•off bod•y
as•ci•tes
ascites ad•i•po•sus
ascites chy•lo•sus
ascites sac•ca•tus
ascites vag•i•na•lis
ascites vul•ga•tior
as•cit•ic

as•cle•pi•as
as•co•carp
as•co•car•pic
as•co•go•ni•um, *n., pl.* -ni•a.
as•co•my•cete
As•co•my•ce•tes
as•co•my•ce•tous
a•scor•bate
a•scor•bic ac•id
as•co•spore
as•co•spor•ic
as•co•spo•rog•e•nous
A•scrip•tin A/D *Trademark.*
as•cus, *n., pl.* as•ci.
A•sen•din *Trademark.*
a•sep•sis
a•sep•tic
a•sep•ti•cal•ly
a•sex•u•al
asexual gen•er•a•tion
asexual re•pro•duc•tion
a•sex•u•al•i•ty
a•sex•u•al•i•za•tion
a•sex•u•al•ly
ash
A•sian in•flu•en•za
A•si•at•ic chol•er•a
a•sleep
a•so•cial
as•par•a•gi•nase
as•par•a•gine
as•pa•rag•i•nyl
as•par•a•gus
as•par•tame
as•par•tase
as•par•tate
as•par•tic ac•id
as•par•to•ki•nase
as•par•tyl
a•spe•cif•ic
as•pect

as•per•gil•lin
as•per•gil•lo•sis, *n., pl.* -ses.
as•per•gil•lus, *n., pl.* -li.
a•sper•ma•tism
a•sper•mi•a
a•sper•mic
as•per•tame
a•spher•ic
a•spher•oi•cal
as•phyx•i•a
asphyxia liv•i•da
asphyxia ne•o•na•to•rum
asphyxia pal•li•da
as•phyx•i•al
as•phyx•i•ant
as•phyx•i•ate, *v.,* -at•ed,
  -at•ing.
as•phyx•i•a•tion
as•phyx•i•a•tor
as•pi•di•nol
as•pid•i•um, *n., pl.* -pid•i•a.
as•pi•do•sper•ma
as•pi•do•sper•mine
as•pi•rate, *v.,* -rat•ed,
  -rat•ing.
as•pi•ra•tion
as•pi•ra•tion•al
as•pi•ra•tor
as•pir•a•to•ry
as•pi•rin, *n., pl.* -rin, -rins.
As•pis cor•nu•tus
as•po•ro•gen•ic
as•po•rog•e•nous
as•po•rous
as•por•u•late
as•sas•sin bug
as•say, *v.,* -sayed, -say•ing.
as•say•a•ble
as•say•er
as•ser•tive•ness train•ing
as•sim•i•la•ble

as•sim•i•late, *v.,* -lat•ed,
  -lat•ing.
as•sim•i•la•tion
as•sim•i•la•tive
as•sim•i•la•to•ry
as•sist
as•sis•tant
as•so•ci•ate, *v.,* -at•ed,
  -at•ing.
as•so•ci•a•tion
as•so•ci•a•tion•ism
as•so•ci•a•tion•ist
as•so•ci•a•tion•is•t•ic
as•so•ci•a•tive
as•so•nance
a•sta•sia
astasia-a•ba•sia
a•stat•ic
as•ta•tine
as•ter
a•ster•o•e•og•no•sis
as•te•ri•on, *n., pl.* -ri•a.
a•ster•nal
as•te•ro•coc•cus, *n., pl.* -ci.
as•ter•oid
as•the•ni•a
asthenia cru•rum par•es•
  thet•i•ca
asthenia pig•men•to•sa
asthenia u•ni•ver•sa•lis
  con•gen•i•ta
as•then•ic
as•the•no•co•ri•a
as•the•no•pi•a
as•the•nop•ic
asth•ma
asth•mat•ic
asth•mo•gen•ic
as•tig•mat•ic
as•tig•mat•i•cal•ly
a•stig•ma•tism
as•tig•ma•tom•e•ter

a○stig•mi○a
as•tig•mom•e○ter
as•tig•mom•e○try
a○stig•mo•scope
a○stom○a•tous
a○sto•mi○a
a○sto•mous
as•trag○a•lar
as•trag○a•lec•to○my, *n., pl.*
  -mies.
as•trag○a•lus, *n., pl.* -li,
  -lus○es.
as•tral
As•tra•morph *Trademark.*
a○stric•tion
as•tringe, *v.,* -tringed, -tring•
  ing.
as•trin•gen○cy
as•trin•gent
as•trin•gent○ly
as○tro•bi•o•log○i•cal
as○tro•bi•ol○o○gy
as○tro•blast
as•tro•blas•to○ma, *n., pl.*
  -mas, -ma○ta.
as•tro•cyte
as•tro•cyt○ic
as•tro•cy•to○ma, *n., pl.,* -mas,
  -ma○ta.
astrocytoma gi•gan•to•cel•
  lu•la○re
as•troid
as○tro•sphere
a○syl•la•bi○a
a○sy•lum
a○sym•bo•li○a
a○sym•met•ri•cal
a○sym•me•try
a○symp•to•mat○ic
a○symp•to•mat○i•cal○ly
a○syn•ap•sis, *n., pl.,* -ses.
a○syn•cli•tism

a○syn•de•sis, *n., pl.* -ses.
a○sy•ner•gi○a
a○sy•ner•gic
a○syn•er○gy, *n., pl.* -gies.
a○sys•tem•at○ic
a○sys•to○le
a○sys•tol○ic
At○a•brine *Trademark.*
a○tac•tic
at○a•rac•tic
At○a•rax *Trademark.*
at○a•rax○i○a
at○a•rax○ic
a○tav○ic
at○a•vism
at○a•vis•tic
a○tax○a•pha•sia
a○tax○i○a
ataxia cor•dis
a○tax•i•a•gram
a○tax•i•a•graph
a○tax•i•a•pha•sia
a○tax○ic
a○tax○y, *n., pl.* tax•-ies.
at••o•lec•ta•sis
at•e•lec•tat○ic
a○te•li•o•sis
a○te•li•ot○ic
A○ten○o•lol
a○the○li○a
ath•er•ec•to○my, *n., pl.* -mies.
a○ther•man○cy, *n., pl.* -cies.
a•ther•ma○nous
a○ther•mic
ath•er○o•gen•e○sis, *n., pl.*
  -ses.
ath•er○o•gen○ic
ath•er○o○ma, *n., pl.* -mas,
  -ma○ta.
ath•er○o•ma•to•sis
ath•er•om○a•tous
ath•er○o•scle•ro•sis

ath•er○o•scle•rot○ic
ath•er○o•scle•rot○i•cal○ly
ath○e•toid
ath○e•to•sic
ath○e•to•sis, *n.*, *pl.* -ses.
ath○e•tot○ic
ath•lete's foot
a○threp•si○a
a○threp•tic
ath•ro•cyte
ath•ro•cy•to•sis
A○throm•bin-K *Trademark.*
a○thy•re○o•sis
a○thy•ro•sis
At○i•van *Trademark.*
at•lan•tad
at•lan•to•ax○i○al
at•lan•to•oc•cip○i•tal
at○las
al•lan•to○in
at○loid
at•mol○y•sis, *n.*, *pl.* -ses.
at•mom•e○ter
at•mos•phere
AT•na○tiv An○ti•throm•bin III
  Trademark.
a○to•cia
at○om
at○om○ic
at○o•mic○i○ty
at○o•mism
at○o•mis•tic
at•om○i•za•tion
at○o•mize, *v.*, -mized, -miz•
  ing.
at•om○iz○er
at○o•nic○i○ty
a○to•ni○a
a○ton○ic
at○o○ny or a○to•ni○a
at○o•pen
a○top○ic

a○top•og•no•si○a
a○to•pog•no•sis
at○o○py, *n.*, *pl.* -pies.
a○tox○ic
A○trac-Tain *Trademark.*
a○tre•mi○a
a○tre•sia
atresia a○ni vag○i•na•lis
atresia fol•lic○u○li
atresia o○fit○er
atresia vul•vae
a○tre•sic
a○tret○ic
a○tri○al
atrial fib•ril•la•tion ✓
atrial na•tri○u•ret○ic
  fac•tor
atrial sep•tal de•fect
atrial sep•tum
a○trich○i○a
at•ri•cho•sis
at•ri•chous
a○tri○o•sep•to•pex○y, *n.*, *pl.*
  -pex•ies.
a○tri○o•ven•tric○u•l ar
atrioventricular bun•dle
atrioventricular node
a○tri○um, *n.*, *pl.* a○tri○a,
  a○tri○ums.
At•ro•hist L.A. *Trademark*
At•ro•mid-S *Trademark.*
A○tro○pa
a○tro•phi○a
a○troph○ic
a○tro•pho•der•ma
atrophoderma re•tic○u•la•
  tum
atrophoderma ver•mic○u•
  lar○is
at•ro•phy, *v.*, -phied, -phy•
  ing.
at•ro•pine

at•ro•pin○i•za•tion

at•ro•pin•ize, *v.*, -ized, -iz•ing.

at•ro•scine

At•ro•vent *Trademark*

at•tach•ment

at○tar

at•tend•ing

at•ten•tion def○i•cit dis•or•der

attention deficit hy•per•ac•tiv○i○ty disorder

at•ten•u•ate, *v.*, -at○ed, -at•ing.

at•ten•u○a•tion

At•ten•u•vax *Trademark.*

at•ti•co•an•trot○o○my, *n., pl.* -mies.

at•ti•co•mas•toid

at•ti•cot○o○my, *n., pl.* -mies.

at•ti•tude

at•ti•tu•di•nal

at•trac•tion

at•tri•tion

a○typ○i○a

a○typ○i•cal

a○typ•ism

Auch•me•ro•my○ia lu•te•o○la

au•dile

au•di○o○gen○ic

au•di○o•gram

au•di○o•log○i•cal

au•di•ol○o○gist

au•di•ol○o○gy

au•di•om•e○ter

au•di○o•met•ric

au•di○o•met•ri•cal○ly

au•di•om••e○trist

au•di•om••e○try

au•di○o○vis○u○al

au•di•tion

au•di•tive

au•di•to•ri•al○ly

au•di•to•ri○ly

au•di•to○ry

au•di•to○ry nerve

Auer•bach's plex○us

Aug•men•tin *Trademark.*

au○la, *n., pl.* au○las, au○lae.

au○ra, *n., pl.* au○ras. au○rae.

aura asth•mat○i○ca

aura cur•so•ri○a

aura hys•ter○i○ca

au○ral

Au•ral•gan *Trademark.*

au•ral○ly

Au•re○o•my•cin *Trademark.*

au○ric

au•ri•cle

au•ri•cled

au•ric○u○la, *n., pl.* -ric○u•las, -ric○u•lae.

auricula a○tri○i

auricula cor•dis

auricula dex•tra

auricula sin•is•tra

au•ric○u•lar

auricular he•ma•to○ma

au•ric○u•lar○e, *n., pl.* -ric○u•lar○i○a.

au•ric○u•lar○ly

au•ric○u•late

au•ric○u•lo•tem•po•ral

au•ric○u•lo•ven•tric○u•lar

au•ri•form

au○rin

au○ris dex•tra

auris ex•ter○na

auris in•ter○na

auris me○di○a

auris sin•is•tra

au•ro•thi○o•glu•cose

au○rum

aurum me•tal•li•cum
aus•cul•tate, *v.*, -tat•ed, -tat•
  ing.
aus•cul•ta•tion
aus•cul•ta•tive or aus•cul•
  ta•to•ry
aus•cul•ta•tor
aus•cul•ta•to•ry
aus•ten•it•ic
au•ta•coid
au•ta•coi•dal
au•te•cious
au•tism
autism pau•vre
au•tist
au•tis•tic
au•tis•ti•cal•ly
au•to•ag•glu•ti•na•tion
au•to•ag•glu•tin•nin
au•to•a•nal•y•sis
au•to•an•ti•bod•y, *n., pl.*
  -bod•ies.
au•to•an•ti•gen
au•to•ca•tal•y•sis, *n., pl.*
  -ses.
au•to•cat•a•lyt•ic
au•to•cat•a•lyt•i•cal•ly
au•toch•tho•nism
au•toch•tho•nous or au•
  toch•tho•nal
au•toch•tho•ny
au•to•cla•va•ble
au•to•clave
au•to•cy•tol•y•sis
au•to•di•ges•tion
au•to•e•cious
au•to•e•rot•ic
au•to•e•rot•i•cism
au•to•er•o•tism
au•to•gam•ic
au•tog•a•mous
au•tog•a•my

au•to•gen•e•o•sis, *n., pl.* -ses.
au•to•ge•net•ic
au•to•gen•ic
au•tog•e•nous
au•tog•e•nous•ly
au•tog•no•sis, *n., pl.* -ses.
au•to•graft
au•to•he•mol•y•sis, *n., pl.*
  -ses.
au•to•he•mo•ther•a•py
au•to•hyp•no•sis
au•to•hyp•not•ic
au•to•im•mune
autoimmune dis•ease
au•to•im•mu•ni•ty
au•to•im•mu•ni•za•tion
au•to•im•mu•nize, *v.*, -nized,
  -niz•ing.
au•to•in•fec•tion
au•to•i•noc•u•la•ble
au•to•in•oc•u•la•tion
au•to•in•tox•i•ca•tion
au•to•ki•ne•sis
au•to•ki•net•ic
au•tol•o•gous
autologous bone mar•row
  trans•plant
au•tol•y•sate
au•to•ly•sin
au•tol•y•sis
au•to•lyt•ic
au•to•lyze, *v.*, -lyzed,
  -lyz•ing.
au•to•ma•nip•u•la•tion
au•to•ma•nip•u•la•tive
au•to•mat•ic writ•ing
au•to•mat•i•cal•ly,
au•to•ma•tic•i•ty
au•tom•a•tism
au•to•mat•o•graph
au•to•mix•is, *n., pl.* -mix•es.
au•tom•ne•sia

au•to•my•so•pho•bi•a
au•to•nom•ic
autonomic a•rous•al dis•or•der
autonomic nerv•ous sys•tem
au•ton•o•mous
au•ton•o•my, *n., pl.* -mies.
au•to•ox•i•da•tion
au•to•pha•gia
au•to•phag•ic
au•toph•a•gy
au•to•pho•bi•a
au•to•plas•tic,
Au•to•plex T *Trademark.*
au•to•ploid
au•to•ploi•dy
au•to•pol•y•ploid
au•to•pol•y•ploi•dy
au•top•sist
au•top•sy, *n., pl.* -sies, *v.,* -sied, -sy•ing.
au•to•ra•di•o•gram
au•to•ra•di•og•ra•phy, *n. pl.* -phies.
au•to•reg•u•la•tion
au•to•reg•u•la•tive
au•to•reg•u•la•to•ry
au•to•scope
au•to•sen•si•ti•za•tion
au•to•se•rum
au•to•sex•ing
au•to•site
au•to•so•mal
au•to•some
au•to•sug•gest•i•ble
au•to•sug•ges•tion
au•to•tel•ic
au•to•tet•ra•ploi•dy
au•to•ther•a•py
au•tot•o•mize, *v.,* -mized, -miz•ing.
au•tot•o•my, *n., pl.* -mies.

au•to•tox•e•mi•a
au•to•tox•ic
au•to•tox•in
au•to•trans•fu•sion
au•to•trans•plant
au•to•trans•plan•ta•tion
au•to•troph
au•to•troph•ic
au•to•ox•i•da•tion
aux•an•o•gram
aux•an•o•graph•ic
aux•a•nog•ra•phy, *n., pl.* -phies.
aux•e•o•sis
aux•et•o•ic
aux•in
aux•o•chrome
aux•o•cyte
aux•o•drome
aux•o•ton•ic
aux•o•troph
aux•o•troph•ic
aux•ot•ro•phy
a•val•vu•lar
a•vas•cu•lar
A•ve•o•na
avena sa•ti•va
a•ven•in
a•ven•ine
a•ver•sion ther•a•py
a•ver•sive
aversive con•di•tion•ing
a•ver•sive•ly
a•vi•an
a•vi•an•ize, *v.,* -ized, -iz•ing.
a•vi•a•tion med•i•cine
av•i•din
a•vir•u•lence
a•vir•u•lent
a•vi•ta•min•o•sis
a•vi•ta•min•ot•ic
A•vo•ga•dro's con•stant

A•vo•ga•dro's num•ber
a•void•ance
a•void•ant
avoidant per•son•al•i•ty dis•or•der
av•oir•du•pois
a•vulse, *v.,* a•vulsed, a•vuls•ing.
a•vul•sion
a•xen•ic
a•xen•i•cal•ly
ax•i•al
axial skel•e•ton
Ax•id *Trademark.*
ax•il
ax•ile
ax•il•la, *n., pl.* -lae.
ax•il•lar
ax•il•lar•y
ax•is, *n., pl.* ax•es.
ax•ite
ax•o•den•drite
ax•om•e•ter
ax•on
ax•on•al
ax•one
ax•o•neme
ax•o•nom•e•ter
ax•o•plasm
ax•o•style
Ax•sa•in *Trademark.*
A•yer•za's dis•ease

Ay•ges•tin *Trademark.*
a•yur•ve•dic med•i•cine
A•zac•tam *Trademark.*
az•a•ser•ine
az•a•thi•o•prine
Az•done *Trademark.*
az•e•la•ic
a•ze•ot•rope
az•ide
a•zi•do•thy•mi•dine
A•zith•ro•my•cin
Az•lin *Trademark.*
Az•ma•cort *Trademark.*
A•zo Gan•ta•nol *Trademark.*
Azo Gan•tri•sin *Trademark.*
a•zo•ic
az•o•o•lit•min
a•zo•o•sper•mi•a
az•o•o•pro•tein
az•o•o•sul•fa•mide
az•o•ote
az•o•o•te•mi•a
az•o•o•te•mic
az•oth
az•o•o•to•bac•ter
az•o•o•tom•e•ter
az•o•o•tu•ri•a
A•zul•fi•dine *Trademark.*
az•o•ure
a•ozy•gos
a•ozy•gous

B

B com•plex
B lymph•o•o•cyte
bab•bitt met•al
Bab•cock test
ba•be•sia, *n., pl.* -sias.
Babesia bi•gem•i•na
Babesia bo•vis

Babesia ca•nis
Babesia eq•ui
Babesia o•vis
bab•e•o•si•a•sis
Ba•be•si•i•dae
ba•be•si•o•sis
Ba•bin•ski re•flex

Babinski sign
Ba•bin•ski's re•flex
Babinski's sign
bac•cate
Bac•i•guent *Trademark.*
Ba•cil•la•ce•ae
ba•cil•lar
bac•il•lar•y or bacillar
bac•il•le•mi•a
ba•cil•li•form
ba•cil•lo•sis
bac•il•lu•ri•a
ba•cil•lus, *n., pl.* -cil•li.
bacillus Cal•mette-Gué•rin
bac•i•tra•cin
back
back•ache
back•bone
back•cross
back•ground lev•el
back•pack pal•sy
bac•te•re•mi•a
bac•te•re•mic
bac•te•ri•a, *n., pl., sing.* -te•ri•um.
bac•te•ri•ae•mi•a
bac•te•ri•al
bac•te•ri•al•ly
bac•te•ri•cid•al
bac•te•ri•cid•al•ly
bac•te•ri•cide
bac•ter•i•cid•in
bac•ter•id
bac•te•ri•e•mi•a
bac•te•ri•um, *n., pl.* -ri•a.
bac•ter•in
bac•te•ri•o•chlo•ro•phyll
bac•te•ri•o•cid•al
bac•te•ri•o•cid•in
bac•te•ri•o•cin
bac•te•ri•o•gen•ic
bac•te•ri•og•e•nous

bac•te•ri•oid
bac•te•ri•ol
bac•te•ri•o•log•ic
bac•te•ri•o•log•i•cal
bac•te•ri•o•log•i•cal•ly
bac•te•ri•ol•o•gist
bac•te•ri•ol•o•gy
bac•te•ri•ol•y•sin
bac•te•ri•ol•y•sis
bac•te•ri•o•lyt•ic
bac•te•ri•o•phage
bac•te•ri•o•phag•ic or bac•te•ri•oph•a•gous
bac•te•ri•oph•a•gy
bac•te•ri•o•sis, *n., pl.* -ses.
bac•te•ri•o•sta•sis
bac•te•ri•o•stat
bac•te•ri•o•stat•ic
bac•te•ri•o•stat•i•cal•ly
bac•te•ri•o•tox•in
bac•te•ri•o•trop•ic
bac•te•ri•ot•ro•pin
bac•te•ri•um
bac•te•ri•u•ri•a or bac•ter•u•ri•a
bac•te•roid or bac•te•roi•dal
bac•te•rize, *v.,* -rized, -riz•ing.
bac•ter•oid
bac•ter•oi•des
Bacteroides cor•ro•dens
Bacteroides frag•i•lis
Bacteroides fun•dil•oi•for•mis
Bacteroides mel•a•ni•no•gen•i•cus
Bacteroides pneu•mo•sin•tes
Bac•tine *Trademark.*
Bac•to•cill *Trademark.*
Bac•trim *Trademark.*
Bact•ro•ban *Trademark.*
bac•u•lum, *n., pl.* -lums, bac•u•la.
bag of wa•ters

bag•as•so•sis
Bain•bridge re•flex
bak•ers' yeast
bak•ing so•da
ba•lan•ic
Bal○a•ni•tes
bal○a•ni•tis
balanitis xe•rot○i○ca ob•lit•er•ans
bal○a•no•pos•thi•tis
bal•an•tid•i•al
bal•an•ti•di•a•sis
bal•an•tid○ic
bal•an•tid○i•o•sis
bal•an•tid○i○um, *n.*, *pl.* -tid○i○a.
Bal•an•tidium co○li
bald•ness
ball-and-sock○et
ball-and-socket joint
bal•ling gun
balling i○ron
balling scale
bal•lism
bal•lis•mus
bal•lis•tic stretch•ing
bal•lis•to•car•di○o•gram
bal•lis•to•car•di○o•graph
bal•lis•to•car•di○og•ra•phy
bal•loon an•gi○o•plas○ty
balloon cells
bal•lot•ta•ble
bal•lotte•ment
Bal•mex *Trademark.*
bal•ne•a•tion
Bal•ne○ol *Trademark.*
bal•ne○o•log○ic or bal•ne○o•log○i•cal
bal•ne•ol○o•gist
bal•ne•ol○o•gy
bal•ne○o•ther○a○a•peu•tics
bal•ne○o•ther○a○py

Bal•ne•tar *Trademark.*
bal•ne•ol○o○gy
bal•sam
bal•sam○ic
ba○nal
Ban•cap HC *Trademark.*
band•age, *n.*, *v.*, -aged, -ag•ing.
Band-Aid
ban○dy-leg
ban○dy-leg•ged
bane
bang
Bang's dis•ease
Ban•thine *Trademark.*
Ban•ti's dis•ease
Banti's syn•drome
bant•ing
bant•ing•ism
bap•tis○ta tinc•to○ri○a
bar•ag•no•sis
Bá•rány chair
barb
bar○ba am○a•ril○la
barb•al•o○in
bar•ber○ory, *n.*, *pl.* -ries.
bar•ber's itch
bar•bi•tal
bar•bi•tone
bar•bi•tu•rate
bar•bi•tu•ric
barbituric ac○id
bar•bi•tur•ism
bar•bone
bar•bu○la hir○ci
bare•foot
bar•es•the•sia
bar○i•at•ric
bar○i•a•tri•cian
bar○i•at•rics
bar○ic
ba•ril○la

bar∘i∘um
barium sul•fate
barium x-ray
bar∘o•cep•tor
bar•og•no•sis
bar∘o•graph
bar∘o•graph∘ic
bar∘o•met•ro•graph
bar∘o•phil∘ic
bar∘o•re•cep•tor
bar∘o•scope
Ba•ros∘ma
bar∘o•stat
bar∘o•tax∘is, *n., pl.* -tax∘es.
bar∘o•ti•tis
barotitis ex•ter∘na
barotitis me∘dia
bar∘o•trau∘ma, *n., pl.* -ma∘ta, -mas.
Barr bod∘y
bar•ren
bar•tho•lin∘i•tis, *n., pl.* -lin∘i•tes.
Bar•tho•lin's gland
Bar•to∘nel∘la
Bar•to∘nel∘la•ce∘ae
bar•ton•el•lo•sis
bar∘ye
bar∘y•la•li∘a
bar∘y∘ta
ba•sad
ba∘sal
basal cell
basal cell car•ci•no∘ma
basal gang•li∘on
basal met∘a•bol∘ic rate
ba∘sal me•tab∘o•lism
ba•sa•lis, *n., pl.* -les.
Ba•sal•jel *Trademark.*
ba•sal∘ly
base
base pair

Ba•se•dow's dis•ease
base•line
base•ment
base-pair•ing
base•plate
ba•sic∘i∘ty
ba•si•cra•ni∘al
ba•sid•i∘al
Ba•sid•i∘o•my•ce•tes
ba•sid•i∘o•my•ce•tous
ba•sid•i∘o•spore
ba•sid∘i∘um, *n., pl.* -i∘a.
ba•si•fa•cial
ba•si•hy∘al
ba•si•hy•oid
bas∘i•lar or bas∘i•lar∘y
bas∘i•lar∘is cra•ni∘i
ba•si•oc•cip∘i•tal
ba•si∘on
ba•sip∘e•tal
ba•si•sphe•noid
ba•si•sphe•noid∘al
ba•si•tem•po•ral
ba•si•ver•te•bral
ba•so•cyte
ba•so•phil
ba•so•phile
ba•so•phil∘i∘a
ba•so•phil∘ic
ba•soph∘i•lous
bas•so•rin
bath
bath•mo•trop∘ic
ba•trach∘o∘tox∘in
bat•tered
bat•tle fa•tigue
bat∘yl
Bau∘me scale
bay•ber∘ry, *n., pl.* -ries.
bdel•li∘um
Bdel•lo•nys•sus ba•co∘ti

bdel•lo•vi•bri∘o, *n., pl.*
  -bri∘os.
beak∘er
bean•ase
Bean∘o *Trademark.*
bear•ber∘ry
Beau's lines
be•bee•rine
Bech•ter•ew's nu•cle∘us
Be•clo•meth∘a•sone
Be•clo•vent *Trademark.*
Be•co•nase *Trademark.*
Beconase AQ *Trademark.*
Bec•que•rel ray
Bec•ton Dik•in•son
bed•bug
bed•lam
bed•pan
bed•side
bed•so•ni∘a, *n., pl.* -ni∘ae.
Bedsonia psit•ta∘ci
bed•sore
bed•wet•ting
Bee•lith *Trademark.*
Beer's law
bees•wax
be•hav•ior
behavior mod∘i•fi•ca•tion
behavior ther∘a∘py
be•hav•ior∘al
be•hav•ior•al∘ly
be•hav•ior•ism
be•hav•ior∘ist
be•hav•ior∘is•tic
be•hav•ior∘is•ti•cal∘ly
be•hen∘ic
bej∘el
bel
belch
be•lem•noid
Bell-O-Ge∘sic *Trademark.*
bel•la•don∘na

Bel•ler•gal-S *Trademark.*
Bel•li•ni's duct
Bellini's tu•bule
bel•lows
Bell's pal∘sy
bel∘ly, *n., pl.* -lies.
belly but•ton
bel∘ly•ache
bem∘e•gride
Ben-Gay *Trademark.*
Be•na•cus gris•cus
Ben∘a•dryl *Trademark.*
Bence-Jones pro•tein
bend
Ben•der Ge•stalt test
bends
ben∘e
Ben∘e•dict's test
Ben∘e•mid *Trademark.*
be•nign
ben∘ne
Ben∘o•quin *Trademark.*
ben•to•nite
Ben•tyl *Trademark.*
ben∘ny, *n., pl.* -nies.
Ben∘y•lin *Trademark.*
Ben•zac *Trademark.*
Ben•za•gel
ben•zal•de•hyde
ben•zal•ko•ni•um
Ben•za•my•cin *Trademark.*
ben•zan•thra•cene
Ben•ze•drex *Trademark.*
Ben•ze•drine
ben•zene
ben•zes•trol
ben•zi•dine
ben•zi•mi•da•zole
ben•zin
ben•zine
ben•zo•ate

ben•zo•caine
ben•zo•di•az•e•pine
ben•zo•ic
benzoic ac•id
ben•zo•i•cum ac•i•dum
ben•zo•in
ben•zol
ben•zo•py•rene
ben•zo•qui•none
ben•zo•sul•fi•mide
ben•zo•yl
benz•py•rene
benz•py•rin•i•um
ben•zyl
ben•zyl•ic
ben•zyl•i•dene
ben•zyl•pen•i•cil•lin
bep•ri•dil
ber•ba•mine
ber•be•rine
ber•be•rois
berd•ache
ber•ga•mot
ber•gap•ten
ber•gap•tene
ber•i-ber•i
ber•i•ber•i
ber•i•ber•ic
ber•ke•li•um
Ber•lin blue
Be•roc•ca Trademark.
ber•serk
Ber•ti•el•la mu•cro•na•ta
Bertiella stu•de•ori
Ber•tin's col•umn
Be•ru•bi•gen Trademark.
be•ryl•li•o•sis
be•ryl•li•um
ber•yl•lo•sis
bes•ti•al•i•ty
be•ta block•er or be•ta-block•er

beta-block•ing
beta car•o•tene
beta cell
beta glob•u•lin
beta-ox•i•da•tion
beta re•cep•tor or beta-re•cep•tor
beta rhythm
beta waves
Beta-2 Trademark.
beta-ad•ren•er•gic
be•ta•cism
Be•ta•dine Trademark.
be•ta•ine
Be•ta•pen-VK Trademark.
Be•ta•trex Trademark.
be•ta•tron
be•tel
Be•top•tic Trademark.
Bet•u•la
bet•u•lin
bet•u•li•nol
be•tween•brain
Betz cell
be•zoar
bhang
bi•ar•tic•u•lar
bi•au•ric•u•lar
Bi•a•vax Trademark.
Bi•ax•in Susp Trademark.
bib•li•o•clast
bib•li•o•klept
bib•li•o•klep•to•ma•ni•a
bib•li•o•ma•ni•a
bib•li•o•ther•a•peu•tic
bib•li•o•ther•a•pist
bib•li•o•ther•a•py
bib•u•lous
bi•cam•er•al
bi•cap•su•lar
bi•car•bo•nate
bicarbonate of so•da

bi•cau•dal
bi•cau•date
bi•cel•lu•lar
bi•ceps, *n., pl.* -ceps, -ceps•es.
bi•chlo•ride
bi•chro•mate
bi•cil•i•ate
Bi•cil•lin *Trademark.*
bi•cip•i•tal
Bi•cit•ra *Trademark.*
BiCNU *Trademark.*
bi•con•cave
bi•con•vex
bi•cor•nate
bi•cor•nu•ate
bi•cor•nu•ous
bi•cus•pid
bicuspid valve
b.i.d.
Bid•der's gan•gli•on
Bidder's or•gan
bi•det
Bie•brich scar•let
Bier•mer's a•ne•mi•a
Biermer's dis•ease
bi•fid
bi•flag•el•late
bi•fo•cal
bi•fo•rate
bi•fur•cate
bi•fur•cat•ed
bi•fur•ca•tion
big toe
bi•gem•i•nal
bi•gem•i•ny
big•head
bi•lat•er•al
bilateral sym•met•ry
bi•lat•er•al•ism
bi•lay•er
bile

bile ac•id
bile salt
Bi•lex•yme *Trademark.*
bil•har•zi•a, *n., pl.* -zi•as.
bil•har•zi•a•sis
bil•har•zi•o•sis
bil•i•cy•an•in
bil•i•fi•ca•tion
bil•i•fus•cin
bil•i•hu•min
bil•i•neu•rine
bil•ious
bil•ious•ly
bil•ious•ness
bil•i•ru•bin
bil•i•ru•bi•nae•mi•a
bil•i•ru•bi•ne•mi•a
bil•i•ru•bi•nu•ri•a
bil•i•ar•y
bil•i•u•ri•a
bil•i•ver•din
Bil•i•vist *Trademark.*
bi•lo•bate or bi•lo•bat•ed,
   bi•lobed
bi•lob•u•lar
bi•loc•u•lar
bi•loc•u•late
Bil•o•paque *Trademark.*
bi•loph•o•dont
Bil•tri•cide *Trademark.*
bi•man•u•al
bi•man•u•al•ly
bi•mas•toid
bim•bri•ate
bi•mod•al
bi•mo•lec•u•lar
bi•na•ry, *n., pl.* -ries.
bin•au•ral
Bi•net age
Binet-Si•mon test
Binet-Simon scale
binge-purge syn•drome

bin•i•o•dide
bi•noc•u•lar
bi•no•mi•al
bin•ov•u•lar
bin•ox•ide
bi•nu•cle•ar
bi•nu•cle•ate
bi•nu•cle•o•late
bi∘o•a∘cous•ti•cal
bi∘o•a∘cous•tics
bi∘o•ac•tive
bi∘o•ac•tiv∘i•ty
bi∘o•as•say, *n., v.,* **-sayed,**
  -say•ing.
bi∘o•as•tro•nau•ti•cal
bi∘o•as•tro•nau•tics
bi∘o•au•to•graph
bi∘o•au•to•graph∘ic
bi∘o•au•tog•ra•phy
bi∘o•a•vail∘a•bil∘i•ty
bi∘o•a•vail∘a•ble
bi∘o•cat∘a•lyst
Bi∘o•cef *Trademark.*
bi∘o•ce•no•sis, *n., pl.* **-ses.**
bi∘o•chem∘i•cal
biochemical ox∘y•gen de•
  mand
bi∘o•chem∘i•cal∘ly
bi∘o•chem∘ist
bi∘o•chem•is•try
bi∘o•chip
bi∘o•cid∘al
bi∘o•cide
bi∘o•clean
bi∘o•cli•ma•tol•o∘gy
bi∘o•coe•no•sis, *n., pl.* **-ses.**
bi∘o•col•loid
bi∘o•com•pat∘i•bil∘i•ty
bi∘o•com•pat∘i•ble
bi∘o•con•trol
bi∘o•cor•ro•sion
bi∘o•cy•tin

bi∘o•de•grad∘a•bil∘i•ty
bi∘o•de•grad∘a•ble
bi∘o•deg•ra•da•tion
bi∘o•de•grade, *v.,* **-grad∘ed,**
  -grad•ing.
bi∘o•dy•nam∘ic
bi∘o•dy•nam∘ics
bi∘o•e∘col•o∘gy
bi∘o•e•lec•tric
bi∘o•e•lec•tri•cal
bi∘o•e•lec•tric∘i•ty
bi∘o•e•lect•ro•gen•e∘sis, *n.,*
  pl. **-e∘ses.**
bi∘o•e•lec•tron∘ic
bi∘o•e•lec•tron∘ics
bi∘o•en•er•get∘ics
bi∘o•en•gi•neer
bi∘o•en•gi•neer•ing
bi∘o•en•vi•ron•men•tal
bi∘o•e•quiv∘a•lence or bi∘o•
  e•quiv∘a•len•cy
bi∘o•e•quiv∘a•lent
bi∘o•eth∘i•cal
bi∘o•eth∘i•cist
bi∘o•eth∘ics
bi∘o•feed•back
bi∘o•fla•vo•noid
bi∘o•gen•e∘sis or bi•og∘e•ny
bi∘o•ge•net∘ic
bi∘o•ge•net∘i•cal∘ly
bi∘o•ge•net∘i•cist
bi∘o•ge•net∘ics
bi∘o•gen∘ic
bi∘o•geo•chem∘i•cal
bi∘o•geo•chem•is•try
bi∘o•haz∘ard
bi∘o•haz∘ard•ous
bi∘o•in•stru•men•ta•tion
Bi∘o•jec•tor
bi∘o•ki•net∘ics
bi∘o•log∘ic
bi∘o•log∘i•cal

biological clock
biological con•trol
biological mon•i•tor•ing
biological ox•y•gen de•mand
biological par•ent
biological rhythm
bi∘o•log∘i•cal∘ly
bi•ol∘o•gist
bi•ol∘o•gy
bi∘o•lu•mi•nes•cence
bi•ol∘y•sis
bi∘o•lyt∘ic
bi∘o•ma•te•ri∘al
bi∘o•math∘e•mat•ics
bi∘o•me•chan∘i•cal
bi∘o•me•chan∘i•cal∘ly
bi∘o•me•chan•ics
bi∘o•med∘i•cal
bi∘o•med∘i•cine
bi•om•e∘ter
bi∘o•met•ric
bi∘o•met•ri•cal∘ly
bi∘o•me•tri•cian or bi∘o•
    met•ri• cist
bi∘o•met•rics
bi•om•e∘try
bi∘o•mi•cro•scope
bi∘o•mi•cros•co•py, *n.*, *pl.*
    -pies.
Bi∘o•mox *Trademark.*
bi•on∘ics
bi∘o•nom•ics
bi•on∘o•my, *n.*, *pl.* -mies.
bi∘o•or•gan∘ic
bi•oph∘a•gous
bi•oph∘a•gy
bi∘o•phore
bi∘o•pho•tom•e∘ter
bi∘o•phys•ics
bi∘o•phys∘i•og•ra•phy, *n.*,
    pl. -phies.
bi∘o•plasm

bi∘o•plas•mic
bi∘o•pol∘y•mer
bi∘o•proc•ess
bi•op∘sy, *n.*, *pl.* -sies, *v.*, -sied,
    -sy•ing.
bi∘o•psy•chol∘o∘gy
bi•or•bi∘tal
bi∘o•re•ac∘tor
bi∘o•re•search
bi∘o•rhythm
bi∘o•rhyth•mic
bi∘o•rhyth•mic∘i∘ty
bi∘os, *n.*, *pl.* bi∘oi, bi∘o•ses.
bi∘o•safe∘ty
bi∘o•sat•el•lite
bi∘o•sci•ence
bi∘o•sci•en•tist
Bi∘o•scrub *Trademark.*
bi∘o•sen•sor
bi∘o•sphere
bi∘o•stat•is•ti•cian
bi∘o•sta•tis•tics
bi∘o•syn•the•sis
bi∘o•syn•thet∘ic
bi∘o•tech•ni•cal
bi•o•tech•no•log∘i•cal
bi∘o•tech•nol∘o•gist
bi∘o•tech•nol∘o∘gy
bi∘o•te•lem•e∘ter
bi∘o•tel•e∘met•ric
bi∘o•te•lem•e∘try
bi•ot∘ic or bi•ot∘i•cal
bi∘o•tin
Biotin Forte *Trademark.*
bi∘o•trans•for•ma•tion
bi∘o•tron
bi∘o•type
bi∘o•typ∘ic
bi•ov∘u•lar
bi•pa•ren•tal
bi•pa•ri•e•tal
bip∘a•rous

bi•ped
bi•ped•al
bi•pen•ni•form
bi•phen•yl
Bi•phet•o•a•mine *Trademark.*
bi•po•lar
bipolar dis•or•der
bi•po•ten•ti•al•i•ty
bi•ra•mose
bi•ra•mous
bird fan•ci•er's lung
bi•re•frac•tive
bi•re•frin•gent
bi•ro•ta•tion
birth ca•nal
birth cer•tif•i•cate
birth con•trol
birth-con•trol pill
birth de•fect
birth pang
birth par•ent
birth•ing
birth•mark
birth•weight
bis•cuit
bi•sex•u•al
bi•sex•u•al•ism
bi•sex•u•al•ly
bis•fe•ri•ous
bish•op
bis•hy•drox•y•cou•ma•rin
bis•muth
bis•muth•al
bis•muth•yl
Bi•so•pro•lol/HCTZ
bis•tou•ry, *n., pl.* -ries.
bis•tra•tal
bi•sul•fate
bi•sul•fide
bi•sul•fite
bi•tar•trate

bi•tem•po•ral
bite•wing
Bi•otis ga•bon•o•i•ca
Bitis lach•e•o•sis
Bitis na•si•cor•nis
bi•on•o•ic
bi•on•o•i•cal•o•ly
Bi•tot's spots
bi•tro•chan•ter•o•ic
bit•ter mel•on
bit•ters
bi•u•ret
bi•va•lence
bi•va•len•cy, *n., pl.* -cies.
bi•va•lent
bi•ven•ter
bi•ven•tral
bix•in
bi•zy•go•mat•ic
black-and-blue
black co•hosh
Black Death
black eye
black lung
black vom•it
black•head
black•leg
black•out
black•wa•ter
blackwater fe•ver
blad•der
bladder worm
blain
Bla•lock-Taus•sig op•er•a•
   tion
blast
blast cell
blas•te•o•ma, *n., pl.* -mas,
   -ma•ta.
blas•te•mat•ic
blas•te•mic
blas•tic

blas•tin

blas•to•coel

blas•to•coele

blas•to•coel∘ic

blas•to•cyst

blas•to•cyte

blas•to•derm

blas•to•der•mic

blas•to•disc

blas•to•disk

blas•to•gen•e∘sis

blas•to•gen∘ic

blas•to∘ma, *n., pl.* -mas, -ma∘ta.

blas•to•mere

blas•to•mer∘ic

Blas•to•my•ces

Blastomyces bra•sil•i•en•sis

Blastomyces der•ma•ti•ti•dis

blas•to•my•cete

Blas•to•my•ce•tes

blas•to•my•cet∘ic

blas•to•my•co•sis

blas•to•my•cot∘ic

blas•to•neu•ro•pore

blas•toph•tho•ri∘a, *n., pl.* -ri• as.

blas•toph•thor∘ic

blas•toph•tho∘ry, *n., pl.* -ries.

blas•top∘o•ral

blas•to•pore

blas•to•por∘ic

blas•to•sphere

blas•to•spher∘ic

blas•to•spore

blas•tot∘o∘my, *n., pl.* -mies.

blas•tu∘la, *n., pl.* -las, -lae.

blas•tu•lar

blas•tu•la•tion

Bla•tel∘la ger•man∘i∘ca

Blat∘ta

Blaud's pill

blear-eyed

blear∘y, *adj.,* blear∘i∘er, blear∘i•est.

bleary-eyed

bleb

bleb∘by

bleed, *v.,* bled, bleed•ing.

bleed∘er

Blem•E∘rase *Trademark.*

blem•ish

blend•ing in•her∘i•tance

blen•noid

blen•nor•rhe∘a

blen•nor•rhe∘al

blen•nor•rhoe∘a

blen•nor•rhoe∘al

Ble•nox∘an *Trademark.*

Bleph-10 *Trademark.*

Bleph-30 *Trademark.*

bleph∘a•ral

bleph∘a•rism

bleph∘a•rit∘ic

bleph∘a•ri•tis

blepharitis an•gu•lar∘is

blepharitis cil∘i•ar∘is

blepharitis gan•grae•no∘sa

blepharitis par∘a•sit∘i∘ca

blepharitis sim•plex

blepharitis squa•mo∘sa

blepharitis ul•ce•ro∘sa

bleph∘a•ro•con•junc•ti•vi• tis

bleph∘a•ro•plast

bleph∘a•ro•plas•tic

bleph∘a•ro•plas∘ty, *n., pl.* -ties.

bleph∘a•ro•spasm

bleph∘a•ro•stat

blind

blind gut

blind loop syn•drome

blind spot

blind∘ly
blind•ness
Blinx *Trademark.*
blis•ter
blis•ter∘y
bloat
Bl∘o∘cad•ren *Trademark.*
block
block•ade
block∘er
blood
blood bank
blood-brain bar•ri∘er
blood cell
blood count
blood dop•ing
blood fluke
blood group
blood heat
blood plas∘ma
blood plate•let
blood poi•son•ing
blood pres•sure
blood se∘rum
blood sug∘ar
blood test
blood trans•fu•sion
blood type
blood typ•ing
blood ves•sel
blood•less
blood•let•ter
blood•let•ting
blood•line
blood•mo•bile
blood•root
blood•shot
blood•stream
blood•suck∘er
blood•worm
blotch

blow•fly, *n., pl.* -flies.
blow•pipe
Blu•bo∘ro *Trademark.*
blue ba∘by
blue dev•ils
blue mold
blue•tongue
Bo•dan•sky u∘nit
bod∘i∘ly
Bo•do
bod∘y bur•den
body fat
body image
body lan•guage
body louse
body mass in∘dex
body wall
Boeck's dis•ease
Boeck's sar•coid
Bohr the∘o∘ry
boil
bol•dine
Bol•lin•ger body
bo•lom•e∘ter
bo•lus, *n., pl.* -lus∘es.
bond•ing
bone
bone•let
bone•set•ter
Bo•nine *Trademark.*
Bon•tril *Trademark.*
bon∘y prom∘i•nenc∘es
Bo•oph∘i•lus
Boophilus an•nu•la•tus
boost∘er
bo•rac∘ic
bor•age
bo•rate
bo•rat∘ed
bo•rax
bor•bo•ryg•mat∘ic

bor•bo•ryg•mic

bor•bo•ryg•mus, *n.*, *pl.* -rug∘mi.

bor•bo•ryg•my, *n.*, *pl.* -mies.

bor•der•line per•son•al∘i•ty dis•or•der

Bor∘det-Gen∘gou ba•cil•lus

Bordet-Gengou test

Bor•de•tel∘la bron•chi•sep•ti∘ca

Bordetella par∘a•per•tus•sis

Bordetella per•tus•sis

bo∘ric

boric ac∘id

bor•nane

bor•ne∘ol

bo∘ron

Bor•rel bod∘y

Bor•re•li∘a

Borrelia buc•cale

Borrelia dut•to•ni∘i

Borrelia nov∘yi

Borrelia re•cur•ren•tis

Borrelia re•frin•gens

Borrelia vin•cen•ti∘i

boss

bos•se•lat∘ed

bot

bo•tan∘i•cal

botch

bot•fly, *n.*, *pl.* -flies.

Both•ri∘o•ceph∘a•lus

both•ri∘um, *n.*, *pl.* -ri∘a, -ri•ums.

Both•rops al•ter•na∘ta

Bothrops a∘trox

Bothrops ja•ra•ra∘ca

Bothrops neu•wie•di∘i

Bothrops num•mi•fer

bot•ry•oid

bot•ry∘o•my•co∘sis

bot•ry•o•my•cot∘ic

bot•tle

bot∘u•lin

bot∘u•li∘nal

bot∘u•li•nus or bot∘u•li•num, *n.*, *pl.* -nus∘es, -nums.

bot∘u•lism

bou•gie

bou•gie•nage

bou•gi•nage

bouil•lon

Bouin's fluid

Bouin's so•lu•tion

bou•lim∘i∘a

bou•quet

bou•ton

bouton de•bis•kra

bouton do•ri•ent

bou•ton•niere

bou•ton ter•mi•nal, *n.*, *pl.* -mi•naux.

Bo•vic∘o∘la

bo•vine

bovine growth hor•mone

bovine spon•gi•form en•ceph∘a•lop∘a•thy

bow∘el

bowel move•ment

bow•el•less

Bow•en's dis•ease

bow•leg

bow•leg•ged

bow•leg•ged•ness

Bow•man's cap•sule

Bowman's glands

Bowman's mem•brane

Boyle's law

brace

brace•let

bra•chi•al

bra•chi•al•gia

bra•chi•ate, *v.*, -at∘ed, -at•ing.

bra•chi•a•tion
bra•chi•um, *n., pl.* bra•chi•a.
brach•y•ce•phal•ic or
 brach•y•ceph•a•lous
brach•y•ceph•a•lism
brach•y•ceph•a•ly
brach•y•dac•tyl•i•a, *n., pl.*
 -tyl•i•as.
brach•y•dac•tyl•ous
brach•y•dac•ty•ly, *n., pl.* -lies.
brach•y•dont
brach•y•fa•cial
brach•y•o•dont
brach•y•ther•a•py
brach•y•u•ran•ic
Brad•ford frame
brad•sot
brad•y•car•di•a
brad•y•car•dic
br•ady•crot•ic
brad•y•kin•in
brad•y•ki•ne•sia
brad•y•ki•net•ic
bra•dyp•ne•a
braille
brain
brain e•lec•tri•cal ac•tiv•i•ty
 map•ping
brain fe•ver
brain stem
brain wave
brain•case
brain-dead or brain•dead
brain death
brain•pan
brain•sick
brain•stem
brain•wash
bran•chi•a, *n., pl.* -chi•ae.
bran•chi•al
bran•chi•og•e•nous
bran•chi•o•mere

bran•chi•om•er•ism
brash
brax•y, *n., pl.* -ies.
bray•er•a
braze, *v.,* brazed, braz•ing.
break, *v.,* broke, bro•ken,
 break•ing.
break•bone fe•ver
break•down
break•through
breast
breast•bone
breast-feed, *v.,* -fed, -feed•ing.
breath
breath test
Breath•a•lyz•er
breath an•a•lyz•er
breathe, *v.,* breathed, breath•
 ing.
breech
breech de•liv•e•ry
breed, *n., v.,* bred, breed•ing.
breed•er
Bree•zee *Trademark.*
breg•ma, *n., pl.* -ma•ta.
breg•mat•ic
brei
Breth•aire *Trademark.*
Breth•an•cer *Trademark.*
Breth•ine *Trademark.*
Bre•tyl•i•um *Trademark.*
Bret•y•lol *Trademark.*
Brev•i•bloc *Trademark.*
Brev•i•con *Trademark.*
Brev•i•tal *Trademark.*
Brex•in L.A. *Trademark.*
Bric•a•nyl *Trademark.*
bridge
bridge•work
Bright's dis•ease
Brill's dis•ease
brim•stone

Bri•nell hard•ness
Brinell num•ber
bris•ket
Bris•ta•my•cin *Trademark.*
bris•tle
Brit•ish an•ti-lew•is•ite
British ther•mal u•nit
broad-spec•trum
Bro•ca scale
Bro•ca's a•pha•sia
Broca's ar•ea
Broca's con•vo•lu•tion
Broca's gy•rus
Broca's point
Brod•mann ar•e•a
Brod•mann's area
broke
bro•ken
bro•mac•e•tone
Bro•ma•rest DX *Trademark.*
Bro•mase *Trademark.*
bro•mate
brom•cre•sol
bro•me•lin
Brom•fed *Trademark.*
Bromfed-DM *Trademark.*
Bromfed-PD *Trademark.*
brom•hi•dro•sis
bro•mic
bro•mide
bro•mi•dro•sis
bro•mine
bro•min•ism
bro•mism
bro•mo, *n., pl.* -mos.
bro•mo•ac•e•tone
bro•mo•ben•zyl
bro•mo•cre•sol
bro•mo•form
bro•mo•phe•nol
bro•mo•u•ra•cil

brom•phe•nol
Bromp•ton cock•tail
bron•chi•al
bronchial asth•ma
bronchial pneu•mo•nia
bronchial tube
bron•chi•al•ly
bron•chi•ec•ta•sia
bron•chi•ec•ta•sis
bron•chi•o•gen•ic
bron•chi•o•lar
bron•chi•ole
bron•chi•ol•i•tis
bronchiolitis fi•bro•sa ob•lit•er•ans
bronchiolitis obliterans
bron•chi•o•lus, *n., pl.* -chi•o•li.
bron•chit•ic
bron•chi•tis
bronchitis con•vul•si•va
bron•chi•um, *n., pl.* -chi•a.
bron•cho•cele
bron•cho•con•stric•tor
bron•cho•di•la•tor
bron•cho•e•de•ma, *n., pl.* -mas, -ma•ta.
bron•cho•gen•ic
bron•cho•gram
bron•cho•graph•ic
bron•chog•ra•phy, *n., pl.* -phies.
Bron•cho•late *Trademark.*
bron•cho•lith
bron•choph•o•o•ny, *n., pl.* -nies.
bron•cho•pneu•mo•nia
bron•cho•pul•mo•nar•y
bron•chor•rhe•a
bron•cho•scope
bron•cho•scop•ic
bron•chos•co•pist

bron•chos•co∘py, *n., pl.* -pies.
bron∘cho•spasm
bron∘cho•spas•tic
bron∘cho•spi•rom•e∘try
bron•cho•sten∘o∘sis, *n., pl.*
   -ses.
bron•chot∘o∘my, *n., pl.* -mies.
bron•chus, *n., pl.* -chi.
Bron•keph•rine *Trademark.*
Bron•ko•dyl *Trademark.*
Bron•ko•lix∘ir *Trademark.*
Bron•kom•e∘ter *Trademark.*
Bron•ko•sol/Bron•kom•e∘ter
   Trademark.
Bron•ko•tabs *Trademark.*
bron•to•pho•bi∘a
bronze di∘a•be•tes
broth
broth∘y
brown fat
brown lung
bru•cel∘ola, *n., pl.* -cel•lae,
   -cel•las.
Brucella a∘bor•tus
Brucella mel∘i•ten•sis
Brucella suis
Brucella tu•la•ren•sis
Bru•cel∘la•ce∘ae
bru•cel•ler•gen
bru•cel•ler•gin
bru•cel•lin
bru•cel•lo•sis
bru•cine
Bru•gia ma•la∘yi
bruise
bruit
Brun•ner's gland
Brunn's mem•brane
brush•ite
brux•ism
brux∘o∘ma•ni∘a
bry∘o∘ni∘a

bu•bo, *n., pl.* -boes.
bu•boed
bu•bo•nal•gia
bu•bon∘ic
bubonic plague
bu•bon∘o•cele
buc∘ca
buc∘cal
buc•cal∘oly
buc•ci•na•tor
buc∘co•ax•i∘al
buc∘co•cer•vi•cal
buc∘co•clu•sal
buc∘co•dis•tal
buc∘co•gin•gi•val
buc•cu∘la, *n., pl.* -cu•lae.
Büch•ner fun•nel
bu•chu
buck-toothed
buck•bean
buck•thorn
buck•tooth, *n., pl.* -teeth.
Bu•cla•din-S *Trademark.*
Buer•ger's dis•ease
bu∘fa•gin
buff∘er
Buf•fer∘in *Trademark.*
buf∘fy coat
bu∘fo•gen∘in
Bu•fon∘i•dae
bu∘fo•ta•lin
bu∘fo•ten•ine
bu•fo•tox∘in
build•ing sick•ness
bul•bar
bul•bo•cap•nine
bul•bo•cav•er•no•sus, *n., pl.*
   -no∘si.
bul•bo•u•re•thral
bul•bous
bul•bus, *n., pl.* bul∘bi.
bu•lim∘o•a•rex∘i∘a

bu•lim•a•rex○ic
bu•lim○i○a
bu•lim○ic
bulk
bull neck
bul○la, *n., pl.* bul•lae.
bul•late
bul•lat○ed
bull•necked
bull•nose
bul•lock
bul•lose
bul•lous
bullous pem•phi•goid
Bu•mex *Trademark.*
Bu•mi•nate *Trademark.*
bun•dle of His
Bun•ga•rus can•di•dus
Bungarus fas•ci•a•tus
bu•no•dont
Bu•nos•to•mum
Bun•sen burn○er
bun•ion
buph•thal•mi○a
buph•thal•mos
Bu•pre○nex *Trademark.*
bur
bur•dock
bu•rette or bu○ret
Bur•kitt or Bur•kitt's lym•
  pho○ma
Burkitt or Burkitt's tu•mor
burn
burn•out
burr
bur○sa, *n., pl.* -sae, -sas.
bur•sal
bur•sec•to○my, *n., pl.* -mies.
bur•si•tis
bur•su○la, *n., pl.* -su•lae.

bush bor•der
Bu•Spar *Trademark.*
Bu•spi•rone
bu•sul•fan
Bu○ta-Barb *Trademark.*
bu•ta•caine
bu•tane
bu•ta•no○ic
bu•ta•nol
Bu•ta•zol○i•din *Trademark.*
bute
Bu•te•sin *Trademark.*
Bu•ti•sol *Trademark.*
bu•to•py•ro•nox○yl
but•ter
but•ter•fat
but•ter•fly, *n., pl.* -flies.
butterfly band•age
but•ter•milk
but•ter•nut
but•tock
but•tocks
but•ton•hole
bu○tyl
butyl hy•drox○y•ben•zo•ate
butyl par○a•hy•drox○y•ben•
  zo•ate
bu•tyl•am•ine
bu•tyl•ate
bu•tyl•at○ed hy•drox○y•
  an○i○sole
butylated hy•drox○y•tol○u•
  ene
bu•ty•ra•ceous
bu•ty•rate
bu•tyr○ic
bu•ty•rom•e○ter
bu•ty•rous
bu•tyr○yl
by•pass or by-pass
bys•si•no•sis

caa○pi
Cab○ot ring
Cab•ot's ring
cac•cal
ca•chec•tic or ca•chec•ti•cal, ca•chex○ic
ca•chet
ca•chex○i○a or ca•chex○y
cachexia ex•oph•thal•mi•ca
cachexia hy•po•phys•i•o• pri○va
cachexia stru•mi•pri•va
cachexia thy•ro•pri•va
cach•in•nate, v., -nat○ed, -nat•ing.
cach•in•na•tion
ca•chou, n., pl. -chous.
cac○o•de•mo•ni○a
cac○o•de•mon○o•ma•ni○a
cac○o•dyl
cac○o•dyl•ate
cac○o•dyl○ic
cac○o•ë•thes
ca•co•gen•e○sis, n., pl. -e○ses.
cac○o•gen○ic
cac○o•gen○ics
ca•cu•mi•nal
ca•dav○er
ca•dav•er○ic
ca•dav•er•ine
ca•dav•er•ous
ca•dav•er•ous○ly
cad•mi○um
ca•du•ce○an
ca•du•ce○us, n., pl. -ce○i.
cae○cal
cae•cum, n., pl. cae○ca.
cae•no•gen•e○sis

cae•no•ge•net○ic
cae•sar•e○an
cae•sar•i○an
cae•si○um
cafe-au-lait spot
Ca•fer•got
caf•fe○ic
caf•feine
caf•fein○ic
caf•fe○ol
caf•fe○one
ca•hin○ca
ca•in○ca
cais•son dis•ease
caj○a•put
caj○e•put
caj○e•pu•tol
caj○u•put
caj○u•pu•tol
Cal-Bid Trademark.
Cal-Plus Trademark.
cal○a•mine
cal○a•mus, n., pl. cal•a○mi.
calamus scrip•to•ri○us
Ca○lan Trademark.
Calan SR Trademark.
cal•ca•ne○al or cal•ca•ne○an
calcaneal a○poph○y•si•tis
cal•ca•ne○o•cu○boid
cal•ca•ne○o•dyn○i○a
cal•ca•ne○um, n., pl. -ne○a.
cal•ca•ne○us, n., pl. -ne○i.
cal•car, n., pl. -car○ia.
calcar a○vis, n., pl. cal•car○i○a a○vi○um.
cal•car○e○a car•bon○i○ca
calcarea pic•ra○ta
cal•car•e○ous
cal•car•e○ous○ly

cal•car•e•ous•ness
cal•ca•rine
cal•car•i•ous
cal•ces
Cal•cet *Trademark.*
Cal•ci-Chew *Trademark.*
Cal•ci-Mix *Trademark.*
Cal•ci•bind *Trademark.*
cal•cic
cal•ci•co•sis
Cal•ci•drine *Trademark.*
cal•cif•er•ol
cal•cif•er•ous
cal•cif•ic
cal•ci•fi•ca•tion
cal•ci•fy, *v.,* -fied,
  -fy•ing.
Cal•ci•mar *Trademark.*
cal•cim•e•ter
cal•ci•na•tion
cal•cine, *v.,* cal•cined, cal•cin•
  ing.
cal•ci•no•sis
Cal•cip•a•rine *Trademark.*
cal•ci•pe•ni•a
cal•ci•phy•lac•tic
cal•ci•phy•lac•ti•cal•ly
cal•ci•phy•lax•is
cal•cite
cal•ci•to•nin
cal•cit•ri•ol
cal•ci•um
calcium block•er
calcium phos•phate
calcium pro•pi•o•nate
cal•co•sphae•rite
cal•co•sphe•rite
cal•cu•lo•sis, *n., pl.* -ses.
cal•cu•lous
cal•cu•lus, *n., pl..* -cu•li,
  -lus•es.
Cal•de•CORT *Trademark.*

Cal•de•rol *Trademark.*
Cal•de•sene *Trademark.*
ca•le•fa•cient
Ca•lel-D *Trademark.*
ca•len•du•la
ca•len•du•lin
cal•en•ture
calf
cal•i•ber
cal•i•brate, *v.,* -brat•ed,
  -brat•ing.
cal•i•brat•er
cal•i•bra•tion
cal•i•bra•tor
cal•i•bre
cal•i•ce•al
cal•i•per
cal•i•sa•ya bark
cal•is•then•ics
ca•lix
cal•li•per
Cal•liph•o•ra
Calliphora vom•i•to•ri•a
cal•li•pho•rid
Cal•li•pho•ri•dae
cal•liph•o•rine
Cal•li•tro•ga
cal•lo•sal
cal•lose
cal•los•i•ty, *n., pl.* -ties.
cal•lo•sum, *n., pl.* -lo•sa.
cal•lous
cal•lus, *n., pl.* -lus•es.
calm•a•tive
cal•mod•u•lin
cal•o•mel
ca•lor
ca•lo•res•cence
ca•lo•res•cent
ca•lor•ic
cal•o•rie or cal•o•ry, *n., pl.*
  -ries.

ca•lor•i•fa•cient
cal•o•rif•ic
cal•o•rif•i•cal•ly
ca•lor•i•gen•ic
cal•o•rim•e•ter
ca•lor•i•met•ric
ca•lor•i•met•ri•cal
ca•lor•i•met•ri•cal•ly
cal•o•rim•e•try
cal•o•o•ry, *n., pl.* -ries.
Cal•pho•san *Trademark.*
Cal•trate *Trademark.*
ca•lum•ba
cal•var•i•a
cal•var•i•al
cal•var•i•um, *n., pl.* -var•i•a.
cal•vi•ties, *n., pl.* cal•vi•ties.
calx
ca•ly•ce•al
ca•ly•ces re•na•les
calyces renales ma•jo•res
calyces renales mi•no•res
ca•ly•coi•nal
cal•y•cine
cal•y•cle
ca•ly•cou•late
ca•lyc•u•lus, *n., pl.* -lyc•u•li.
Ca•lym•ma•to•bac•te•ri•oum
ca•lyx, *n., pl.* ca•ly•xes,
  ca•ly•ces.
Ca•o•ma
Ca•ma•lox
cam•bo•gia
cam•er•a lu•ci•da, *n., pl.*
  -er•as, -er•ae.
camera ob•scu•ra, *n., pl.*
  -er•as, -er•ae.
cam•oi•sole
cam•o•mile
Cam•o•quin *Trademark.*
cAMP
cam•phane

cam•phene
cam•phor
cam•pho•ra•ceous
cam•phor•ate, *v.,*
  -at•ed, -at•ing.
cam•phor•ic
cam•phor ice
cam•pim•e•ter
camp•to•cor•mi•a
Cam•py•lo•bac•ter co•li
Campylobacter fe•tus
Campylobacter je•ju•ni
can•a•dine
ca•nal
ca•na•les dip•lo•i•ci
canales pal•a•ti•ni
can•a•lic•u•lar
can•a•lic•u•la•tion
can•a•lic•u•li den•ta•les
canaliculi vas•cu•lo•si
can•a•lic•u•li•za•tion
can•a•lic•u•lus, *n., pl.*
  -lic•u•li.
canaliculus chor•dae
  tym•pa•ni
canaliculus coch•le•ae
canaliculus lac•ri•ma•lis
canaliculus mas•toid•e•ous
canaliculus tym•pan•i•cus
can•a•line
ca•na•lis, *n., pl.* -les.
can•al•i•za•tion
can•al•ize, *v.,* -lized, -liz•ing.
can•a•va•lin
can•a•va•nine
can•cel•late or can•cel•lat•ed
can•cel•lous
can•cel•lus, *n., pl.* -li.
can•cer
cancer gene
can•cer•ate
can•cer•i•gen•ic

can•cer•i•za•tion
can•cer•o•o•cid•al
can•cer•o•o•gen•ic
can•cer•ol•o•o•gist
can•cer•ol•o•o•gy
can•cer•o•lyt•ic
can•cer•o•pho•bi•a
can•cer•ous
can•cer•ous•ly
can•cer•pho•bi•a
can•croid
can•crum na•si
cancrum o•o•ris, n., pl. can•cra o•ris.
cancrum pu•den•di
can•de•ola
can•di•ci•din
Can•di•oda al•bi•cans
candida can•di•di•a•sis, n., pl. -ses.
can•di•di•a•sis, n., pl. -ses.
can•ody strip•er
ca•nic•o•o•la fe•ver
Can•oi•dae
ca•nine
ca•nin•i•form
Ca•nis
ca•ni•ti•es, n., pl. ca•ni•ti•es.
canities un•gui•um
can•ker
can•ker•ous
can•na•bic
can•na•bi•di•ol
can•na•bin
can•nab•i•noid
can•nab•i•nol
can•na•bis
can•na•bism
can•non bone
can•nu•la, n., pl. -las, -lae.
can•nu•lar
can•nu•late

can•nu•la•tion
can•thal
can•thar•oi•dal
can•thar•oi•date
can•thar•oi•de•an
can•tha•rid•i•o•an
can•thar•oi•din
can•thar•oi•dism
can•thar•oi•dize, v., -dized, -diz•ing.
can•thar•ois, n., pl. -thar•oi•des.
Cantharis ves•oi•ca•to•ri•oa
Can•tha•rone Trademark.
can•thus, n., pl. -thi.
Can•til Trademark.
can•ou•ola, n., pl. -las, -lae.
caout•chouc
ca•pac•oi•tance
ca•pac•oi•tate, v., -tat•ed, -tat•ing.
ca•pac•oi•ta•tion
ca•pac•oi•ta•tive
ca•pac•oi•tive
ca•pac•oi•tor
ca•pac•oi•ty, n., pl. -ties.
Cap•o•a•stat Trademark.
ca•pe•line
cap•il•la•rec•ta•sia
cap•il•lar•oi•oa
Capillaria ae•roph•oi•la
Capillaria he•pat•oi•ca
Capillaria phil•ip•pi•nen•sis
cap•il•la•ri•a•sis, n., pl. -ses.
cap•il•lar•oid
cap•il•lar•oi•o•sis
cap•il•lar•oi•ty, n., pl. -ties.
cap•il•lar•o•o•scope
cap•il•la•ros•co•o•py, n., pl -pies.
cap•il•lar•o•y, n., pl. -lar•ies.
cap•il•li•cul•ture
ca•pil•lus, n., pl. -li.

cap∘i∘ta
cap∘i∘tate
cap∘i∘tel•lum, *n., pl.* -tel∘la.
Cap∘i∘trol *Trademark.*
ca•pit∘u•lar
ca•pit∘u•lum, *n., pl.* -pit•u∘la.
cap•let
ca•pon∘i•za•tion
ca•pon•ize, *v.,*
  -nized, -niz•ing.
Cap∘o•ten *Trademark.*
Cap∘o•zide *Trademark.*
cap•rate
cap•ric
cap•rin
cap•ro•ate
ca•pro∘ic
cap•ro∘in
cap•ro∘yl
cap•ry•late
ca•pryl∘ic
cap•sa•i•cin
cap•si•cum
capsicum an•nu∘um
cap•sid
cap•sid∘al
cap•so•mere
cap•su∘la, *n., pl.* -lae.
cap•su•lar
cap•su•late
cap•su•lat∘ed
cap•su•la•tion
cap•sule
cap•to•pril
ca∘put, *n., pl.* ca•pi∘ta.
caput mor•tu∘um, *n., pl.* capita mor•tu∘a.
caput suc•ce•da•ne∘um, *n.,*
  pl. capita suc•ce•da•ne∘a.
Car∘a•fate *Trademark.*
car∘a•geen
car∘at

ca•ra∘te
car•ba•chol
car•ba•mate
Car•bam•az∘e•pine *Trade-*
  mark.
car•bam∘ic
car•bam•ide
carb•a•mi∘no
car•bam•o∘yl
car•ba•myl
car•bar•sone
car•bar∘yl
car•ba•zide
car•ba•zole
car•ba•zot∘ic
car•ben∘o•cil•lin
carb•he•mo•glo•bin
car•bide
car•bi•nol
car∘bo, *n., pl.* -bos.
car∘bo•ben•zox∘y
car∘bo•ben•zyl•ox∘y
Car∘bo•caine *Trademark.*
car∘bo•cy•clic
car∘bo•he•mo•glo•bin
car∘bo•hy•drase
car∘bo•hy•drate
car∘bo•hy•drat∘u•ri∘a
car•bo•late, *v.,* -lat∘ed,
  -lat•ing.
car∘bol•fuch•sin
car•bol∘ic
car∘bo•line
car∘bo•lize, *v.,* -lized, -liz•ing.
car•bo•load
car•bo•load•ing
car•bol•xy•lene
car∘bo•my•cin
car•bon cy•cle
carbon di•ox•ide
carbon mon•ox•ide

car•bo•nate, v., -nat○ed,
-nat○ing.
car•bon○ic
car•bon○i•za•tion
car•bo•nize, v., -niz○ed,
-niz○ing.
car•bo•nyl
car•bo•plat○in
car•box○y•he•mo•glo•bin
car•box○yl
car•box•yl•ase
car•box○y•late, v., -lat○ed,
-lat•ing.
car•box○y•la•tion
car•box○y•yl○ic
car•box○y•meth○yl
car•box○y•pep•ti•dase
car•bro•mal
car•bun•cle
car•bun•cled
car•bun•cu•lar
car•bun•cu•lo•sis, n., pl. -ses.
car•bu•ret, v., -ret○ed or -ret•
ted, -ret•ing or -ret•ting.
car•ce○ag
car•cin○o•gen
car•ci•no•gen•e○sis
car•ci•no•gen○ic
car•ci•no•ge•nic○i○ty
car•ci•noid
car•ci•no•lyt○ic
car•ci•no○ma, n., pl. -mas,
-ma○ta.
carcinoma in si○tu
car•ci•no•ma•toid
car•ci•no•ma•to•sis
car•ci•no•ma•tous
car•ci•no•sar•co○ma, n., pl.
-mas, -ma○ta.
car•ci•no•sis
car•da•mom
car•da•mon

car•da•mum
Car•dene Trademark.
car•di○a, n., pl. -di○ae, -di○as.
cardia ven•tric•u○li
car•di○ac
cardiac ar•rest
cardiac cy•cle
cardiac mus•cle
car•di•al•gi○a
car•di•ec•to○my, n., pl. -mies.
Car•di•late Trademark.
car○di○o•ac•cel•er○a•tion
car○di○o•dy•nam○ic
car○di○o•dy•nam•ics
car○di○o•gen○ic
Car•di•og•ra•fin Trademark.
car○di○o•gram
car○di○o•graph
car○di•og•ra•pher
car○di○o•graph○ic
car○di•og•ra•phy
car○di○o•he•pat○ic
car○di○oid
car○di○o•in•hib○i•to○ry
car○di○o•ki•net○ic
car○di○o•lip○in
Car•di○o•lite Trademark.
car○di○o•log○ic or car○di○o•
log○i•cal
car○di•ol○o○gist
car○di•ol○o○gy
car○di•ol○y•sis
car○di○o•meg○a○ly, n., pl.
-lies.
car○di○om•e○ter
car○di○o•met•ric
car○di○om•e○try
car○di○o•my•op○a•thy
car○di○o•path
car○di•op○a•thy
car○di○o•per○i•car○di○o•
pex○y, n., pl. -ies.

car•di∘o•per∘i•car∘di•tis
car∘di∘o•pho•bi∘a
car∘di∘o•plas•ty, *n., pl.* -ties.
car∘di∘o•ple•gia
car∘di∘o•pneu•mat∘ic
car∘di∘o•pul•mo•nar∘y
  by•pass ma•chine
Car∘di∘o•quin *Trademark.*
car∘di∘o•re•nal
car∘di∘o•res•pi•ra•to∘ry
car∘di•or•rha•phy, *n., pl.*
 -phies.
car∘di∘o•scope
car∘di∘o•spasm
car∘di∘o•spas•tic
car∘di∘o•ta•chom•e∘ter
Car∘di∘o•tec *Trademark.*
car∘di∘o•ther∘a∘py
car∘di•ot∘o•my, *n., pl.* -mies.
car∘di∘o•ton∘ic
car∘di∘o•tox∘ic
car∘di∘o•vas•cu•lar
car∘di∘o•ver•sion
car•dit∘ic
car•di•tis
Car•di•zem *Trademark.*
Cardizem CD *Trademark.*
Cardizem SR *Trademark.*
Car•du∘ra *Trademark.*
care•giv∘er
Car∘i•o•ca
car•ies, *n., pl.* -ies.
caries sic∘ca
ca•ri∘na, *n., pl.* -nas, -nae.
carina for•ni•cis
carina na∘si
carina tra•che∘ae
carina u∘re•thra•lis
carina vag∘i•nae
car∘i•nate
car∘i•nat∘ed
car∘i•o•gen∘ic

Car∘i•so•pro•dol
car∘i•ous
car•ma•lum
car•min∘a•tive
car•mine
car•min∘ic
Car•mol *Trademark.*
car•nas•si∘al
car•ni•fi•ca•tion
car•ni•tive
Car•ni•tor *Trademark.*
Car•niv∘o∘ra
car•ni•vore
car•niv∘o∘rous
car•no•sine
car∘ob
car∘o•ten•ae•mi∘a
car∘o•tene or car∘o•tin
Carotene-E *Trademark.*
car∘o•ten•e•mi∘a
ca•rot•e∘noid or ca•rot∘i•
 noid
car∘o•te•no•sis
ca•rot∘ic
ca•rot∘i•co•tym•pan∘ic
ca•rot∘id
carotid si∘nus
ca•rot∘id•al
car∘o•tin
car∘o•tin•e•mi∘a
ca•rot∘i•noid
car∘o•to•dyn∘i•a
car•paine
car•pal
carpal tun•nel syn•drome
car•pale
car•pec•to∘my, *n., pl.* -mies.
car•pho•lo•gi∘a, *n., pl.* -gi∘as.
car•phol∘o∘gy
car•pi•tis
car∘po•met∘a•car•pal
car∘po•ped∘al

Car•pu•ject *Trademark.*
car•pus, *n., pl.* car•pi.
car•ra•geen
car•ra•gee•nan or car•ra•gee•nin
car•ra•gheen
car•ra•ghee•nin
car•ri•er
Car•ri•on's dis•ease
car•ron oil
car•sick
car•sick•ness
Car•te•sian
Car•tha•mus
car•ti•lage
car•ti•la•gin•e•ous
car•ti•lag•oi•noid
car•ti•lag•oi•nous
Car•trol *Trademark.*
Car•um
car•un•cle
ca•run•cu•la, *n., pl.* -cu•lae.
caruncula hy•me•na•les
caruncula lac•ri•ma•lis
caruncula sub•lin•gua•lis
car•va•crol
carv•er
carv•ing
cas•cade
cas•car•a
cascara a•mar•ga
cascara sa•gra•da
cas•ca•ril•la
case
case con•trol stud•y
ca•se•ate, *v.,* -at•ed, -at•ing.
ca•se•a•tion
case•book
ca•sein
ca•sein•ate
ca•sein•o•gen
ca•se•ous

Cas•i•mi•ro•a ed•u•lis
casque
cas•sette
cas•sia
cast
Cas•ta•ne•a
Cas•tel•la•ni Paint *Trademark.*
Castellani's paint
Cas•tile soap
cast•ing
cas•tor
castor oil
cas•trate, *v.,* -trat•ed, -trat•ing.
cas•tra•tion
cas•tra•tor
cas•u•al•ty, *n., pl.* -ties.
cas•u•is•tics
CAT scan
CAT scan•ner
cat•a•bi•o•sis
cat•a•bi•ot•ic
cat•a•bol•ic
cat•a•bol•oi•cal•ly
ca•tab•o•lism
ca•tab•o•lite
ca•tab•o•lize, *v.,* -lized, -liz•ing.
cat•a•chro•ma•sis
cat•a•di•op•tric
cat•a•di•op•tri•cal
cat•a•gen•e•osis, *n., pl.* -e•oses.
cat•a•ge•net•ic
cat•a•lase
cat•a•lat•ic
cat•a•lep•sy or cat•a•lep•sis
cat•a•lep•tic
cat•a•lep•ti•cal•ly
cat•a•lep•toid
cat•a•lo•gia
ca•tal•y•sis, *n., pl.* -ses.
cat•a•lyst

cat○a•lyt○ic
cat○a•lyt○i•cal○ly
cat○a•lyze, *n., pl.* -lyzed,
　-lyz•ing.
cat○a•lyz○er
cat○a•me•ni•a
cat○a•me•ni•al
cat○a•mite
cat•am•ne•sis, *n., pl.* -ses.
cat•am•nes○tic
cat○a•pha•sia
cat○a•pho•re•sis, *n., pl.* -ses.
cat○a•pho•ret○ic
cat○a•pho•ret○i•cal○ly
cat○a•phor○ic
cat○a•pla•sia
cat○a•plasm
cat○a•plas•tic
cat○a•plec•tic
cat○a•plex○y, *n., pl.* -ies.
Cat○a•pres *Trademark.*
cat○a•ract
cat○a•rac○ta co•ro•nar○i○a
cataracta neu•ro•der•
　mat○i○ca
cat○a•rac•tal
cat○a•rac•tous
ca•tar•hine
ca•tar○i○a
ca•tarrh
ca•tarrh○al
catarrhal deaf•ness
ca•tar•rhal○ly
Cat○ar•rhi○na
cat•ar•rhine
cat•ar•rhin•i○an
ca•tarrh•ous
ca•tas•ta•sis, *n., pl.* -ses.
ca•tas•tate
cat○a•stat○ic
cat○a•ther•mom•e○ter
cat○a•to•ni○a

cat○a•ton○ic
cat•e○chin
cat•e○chol
cat•e○chol○a•mine
cat•e○chu
cat•e○lec•tro•ton○ic
cat•e○lec•tro•to•nus
Cat•e○mine *Trademark.*
cat•e○nate, *v.,* -nat○ed,
　-nat•ing.
cat•e○noid
ca•ten○u•late
cat•gut
Cath○a
ca•thar•sis, *n., pl.* -ses.
ca•thar•tic
ca•thect
ca•thec•tic
ca•thep•sin
ca•thep•tic
cath•e○ter
cath•e○ter○i•za•tion
cath•e○ter•ize, *v.,* -ized,
　-iz•ing.
ca•thex○is, *n., pl.* -thex○es.
cath○ode
ca•thod○ic
ca•thod○i•cal○ly
ca•thol○i•con
cat•i○on
cat•i○on○ic
cat•i○on○i•cal○ly
cat•nip
ca•top•tric
ca•top•tri•cal
ca•top•tri•cal○ly
cat-scratch fe○ver
cat•ta○lo, *n., pl.* -ta•loes,
　-ta•los.
cat•te○ry, *n., pl.* -ries.
cau○da, *n., pl.* cau•dae.
cau•dad

cau•da e•qui•na, *n., pl.*
  cau•dae e•qui•nae.
cauda hel•oi•cis, *n., pl.*
  cadae hel•oi•cis.
cau•dal
cau•dal•ly
cau•date
cau•dat•ed
cau•da•tion
cau•da•to•len•tic•u•lar
caul
cau•li•flow•er
cauliflower ear
cau•sal•gi•a
cau•sal•gic
caus•tic
caus•ti•cum
cau•ter
cau•ter•ant
cau•ter•oi•za•tion
cau•ter•ize, *v.*, -ized, -iz•ing.
cau•ter•y, *n., pl.* -ter•ies.
ca•va
ca•val
cav•al•ry bone
cav•a•scope
cav•ern
cav•er•no•ma, *n., pl.* -mas,
  -ma•ta.
cav•er•nos•to•my, *n., pl.*
  -mies.
cav•er•nous
Ca•vi•a
Ca•vi•i•dae
cav•oi•tar•y
cav•oi•tas gle•noid•a•lis
cavitas pul•pae
cav•oi•tate, *v.*, -tat•ed,
  -tat•ing.
cav•oi•ta•tion
cav•oi•ty, *n., pl.* -ties.
ca•vum, *n., pl.* ca•va.

ca•vy, *n., pl.* •vies.
CD an•ti•gens
ce•ba•dil•la
ce•cal
ce•cec•to•my, *n., pl.* -mies.
ce•ci•tis
Ce•clor *Trademark.*
ce•co•pex•y, *n., pl.* -ies.
ce•co•pli•ca•tion
ce•cop•to•sis
ce•cor•rha•phy, *n., pl.* -phies.
ce•co•sig•moid•os•to•my, *n.,*
  pl. -mies.
ce•cos•to•my, *n., pl.* -mies.
ce•cum, *n., pl.* ce•ca.
cecum cu•pu•la•re
cecum ves•tib•u•la•re
ce•dar•wood
Ce•dil•a•nid-D *Trademark.*
Cee•NU *Trademark.*
Cef•a•clor
Cef•a•drox•il
Cef•a•dyl *Trademark.*
Ce•fix•ime
Cef•oi•zox *Trademark.*
Cef•oo•bid *Trademark.*
Ce•fol *Trademark.*
Cef•oo•tan *Trademark.*
Cef•pro•zil
Cef•tin *Trademark.*
Ce•fu•rox•ime
Cef•zil *Trademark.*
ce•la•tion
ce•len•ter•on
cel•er•oy
Ce•les•tone *Trademark.*
ce•li•ac
celiac dis•ease
ce•li•o•col•pot•oo•my, *n., pl.*
  -mies.
ce•li•o•en•ter•ot•oo•my, *n.,*
  pl. -mies.

centrosomic

ce•li•os•co•opy, *n., pl.* -pies.
ce•li•ot•o•omy, *n., pl.* -mies.
cell
cell bi•ol•o•o•gy
cell cy•cle
cell fu•sion
cell of Clau•di•ous
cell of Cor•ti
cel•la, *n., pl.* cel•lae.
cel•lif•ou•gal
cel•lip•e•otal
cell-me•di•at•ed im•mu•ni•ty
cel•lo•bi•ose
cel•loi•din
cel•lose
cel•lu•o•la, *n., pl.* -lu•lae.
cel•lu•lar
cellular res•pi•ra•tion
cel•lu•lar•o•i•oty, *n., pl.* -ties.
cel•lu•lase
cel•lule
cel•lu•lif•ou•gal
cel•lu•lin
cel•lu•lip•e•otal
cel•lu•lite
cel•lu•li•tis
cel•lu•lo•lyt•ic
cel•lu•lo•san
cel•lu•lose
cel•lu•los•ic
ce•lom
ce•lom•ic
Ce•lon•tin *Trademark.*
Cel•si•ous
ce•ment
ce•men•ta•tion
ce•men•ti•cle
ce•men•ti•fi•ca•tion
ce•men•tite
ce•men•to•blast
ce•men•to•ma, *n., pl.* -mas, -ma•ota.
ce•men•tum, *n., pl.* -men•ota.
ce•nes•the•sia
ce•no•gen•e•osis
ce•no•ge•net•oic
ce•no•site
cen•sor
cen•sor•ship
cen•ter
cen•te•sis, *n., pl.* -ses.
cen•oti•bar
cen•oti•grade
cen•oti•gram
cen•oti•li•ter
cen•oti•me•ter
cen•oti•nor•mal
cen•oti•pede
cen•oti•poise
cen•oti•stoke
cen•trad
cen•tral
central nerv•ous sys•tem
Cen•trax *Trademark.*
cen•tric
cen•trif•ou•gal
cen•trif•ou•gal•i•za•tion
cen•trif•ou•gal•ize, *v.,* -ized, -iz•ing.
cen•trif•ou•gal•oly
cen•trif•ou•ga•tion
cen•tri•fuge, *v.,* -fuged, -fug•ing.
cen•tri•ole
cen•trip•e•otal
cen•trip•e•otal•oly
cen•tro•lec•oi•thal
cen•tro•mere
cen•tro•mer•oic
cen•tro•plasm
cen•tro•some
cen•tro•som•oic

cen•tro•sphere
Cen•trum *Trademark.*
centrum me•di•a•num
centrum o•va•le
centrum sem•i•o•va•le
centrum ten•din•e•um
centrum tendineum
  pe•rin•e•i
Cen•tru•roi•des
Ce•o-Two *Trademark.*
Cē•pa•col *Trademark.*
CE•PA•STAT *Trademark.*
ceph•a•e•line
Ceph•a•e•lis
ceph•a•lad
ceph•a•lal•gia
ce•pha•le•a at•to•ni•ta
ceph•a•lex•in
ceph•al•he•ma•to•ma, *n., pl.*
  -mas, -ma•ta.
ceph•al•hy•dro•cele
ce•phal•ic
cephalic in•dex
ce•phal•i•cal•ly
ceph•a•lin
ceph•a•li•za•tion
ceph•a•lo•cau•dal
ceph•a•lo•cele
ceph•a•lo•cen•te•sis, *n., pl.*
  -ses.
ceph•a•lo•gy•ric
ceph•a•lo•he•ma•to•cele
ceph•a•lo•me•ni•a
ceph•a•lo•lom•e•ter
ceph•a•lo•met•ric
ceph•a•lom•e•try
ceph•a•lop•a•gus
  oc•cip•i•ta•lis
cephalopagus pa•ri•e•ta•lis
ceph•a•lop•a•thy, *n., pl.*
  -thies.
ceph•a•lo•pel•vic

ceph•a•lo•pha•ryn•ge•ous
ceph•a•lor•i•dine
ceph•a•lo•spo•rin
ceph•a•lo•spo•ri•um
ce•phal•o•thin
ceph•a•lo•tho•rac•ic
ceph•a•lot•o•my, *n., pl.*
  -mies.
ceph•a•lo•tribe
ceph•a•lo•trip•o•sy, *n., pl.* -sies.
Ceph•u•lac *Trademark.*
ce•ra
ce•ra•ceous
Ce•ra•sus
ce•rate
cer•a•tin
cer•a•ti•tis
cer•a•to•con•junc•ti•vi•tis
Cer•a•toph•yl•lus
cer•a•tose
cer•car•i•a, *n., pl.* -i•ae.
cer•car•i•al
cer•car•i•an
cer•clage
Cer•co•mo•nas
Cer•co•pi•the•cus
cer•cus, *n., pl.* cer•ci.
cere, *v.,* cered, cer•ing.
ce•re•a flex•i•bil•i•tas
ce•re•al
cer•e•bel•lar
cer•e•bel•lo•ru•bral
cer•e•bel•lo•ru•bro•spi•nal
cer•e•bel•lo•spi•nal
cer•e•bel•lum, *n., pl.*
  -bel•lums, -bel•la.
ce•re•bral
cerebral cor•tex
cerebral hem•is•phere
cerebral hem•or•rhage
cerebral pal•sied
cerebral pal•sy

ce•re•bral○ly
ce•re•bral•pal•sied
cer○e•brate, *v.*, -brat○ed,
  -brat•ing.
cer○e•bra•tion
ce•re•bri•form
cer○e•brif○u•gal
cer○e•brip•e○tal
ce•re•broid
ce•re•bro•me•dul•lar○y
cer•e○bron○ic
ce○re•bro•scle•ro•sis
ce•re•brose
ce○re•bro•side
ce○re•bro•spi○nal
cerebrospinal flu○id
cerebrospinal men•in•gi•tis
ce○re•bro•to•ni○a
ce○re•bro•vas•cu○lar
cerebrovascular ac•ci•dent
ce•re•brum, *n., pl.* -brums,
  -bra.
cere•cloth
cere•ment
Ce•ren•kov ra•di•a•tion
cer•e○sin
cer•e○sine
Ce•re○us
ce○ri○a
ce•ri○um
ce•roid
Ce•rose-DM *Trademark.*
ce•rot○ic
cer•ti•fi○a•ble
cer•ti•fi•ca•tion
cer•ti○fy, *v.*, -fied, -fy•ing.
Ce•ru•bi•dine *Trademark.*
cer○u•lo•plas•min
ce•ru•men
Ce•ru•men•ex *Trademark.*
ce•ru•mi•nal
ce•ru•mi•no•sis

ce•ru•mi•nous
ce•ruse
cer•vi•cal
cervical cap
cer•vi•cec•to○my, *n., pl.*
  -mies.
cer•vi•ci•tis
cer○vi○co•buc•cal
cer○vi○co•dyn○i○a
cer○vi○co•fa•cial
cer○vi○co•la•bi○al
cer○vi○co•lin•gual
cer○vi○co•ves○i•cal
cer•vix, *n., pl.*
  cer•vix○es, cer•vi•ces.
cervix den•tis
cervix ob•sti○pa
cervix u○ter○i
cervix ves○i•cae
cer•vix•u•ter○i
ce○ryl
Ce•sar○e•an or Ce•sar○i•an
ce•sar•i○an
ce•si○um
Ces•to○da
ces•to•dan
ces•tode
ces•to•di•a•sis, *n., pl.* -ses.
ces•toid
Ces•toi•de○a
ces•toi•de○an
Ce•ta•caine *Trademark.*
ce•ta•ce○um
Ce•ta•phil *Trademark.*
Ce•tir○i○zine
Ce•trar○i○a
ce○tyl
cetyl ce•ty•late
cetyl pal•mi•tate
Ce•tyl•cide *Trademark.*
ce•tyl•py•ri•din○i○um
ce•va•dil○la

ce•va•dine
Ce○vi-Bid *Trademark.*
Ce○vi-Fer *Trademark.*
ce•vi•tam○ic ac○id
ceys•sa•tite
Cha•ber•tia
chae○ta, *n., pl.* chae•tae.
chae•tal
Cha•gas' dis•ease
cha•go○ma, *n., pl.* -mas,
    -ma○ta.
Chai-Hu
cha•la○za, *n., pl.* -la•zae,
    -la•zas.
cha•la•zi○on, *n., pl.* -zi○a.
chal•cone
chal•co○sis
chal○i•co•sis
chal•kone
chalk•stone
chal•lenge, *n., v.,* -lenged,
    -leng•ing, *adj.*
chal•one
cha•lyb•e○ate
Cham•ber•land fil•ter
cham○o•mile
chan•cre
chancre re○dux
chan•cri•form
chan•croid
chan•croi•dal
chan•crous
change of life
chan•nel, *v.,* -neled *or* -nelled,
    -nel•ing *or* -nel•ling.
char•ac•ter
character dis•or•der
char•ac•ter○i•za•tion
char•ac•ter○o•log○ic
char•ac•ter○o•log○i•cal
char•ac•ter○o•log○i•cal○ly
char•ac•ter•ol○o•gist

char•ac•ter•ol○o○o•gy
cha•ras
char•bon
char•coal
Char•cot joint
Charcot-Ma○rie-Tooth
    dis•ease
char•la•tan
char•la•tan•ism
Charles's law
char•ley horse
char•ta, *n., pl.* char•tae.
chart•ing
char•tu○la, *n., pl.* -tu•lae.
Chas•tek pa•ral○y•sis
chaul•mau•gra
chaul•moo•gra
chaul•mu•gra
check•bite
check•er•ber•ry, *n., pl.* -ries.
check•up
cheek
cheek•bone
chei•lec•to○my, *n., pl.* -mies.
chei•lec•tro•pi○on
chei•li•tis
cheilitis ac•tin○i•ca
cheilitis ex•fo•li•a•ti○va
cheilitis glan•du•lar○is
cheilitis ve•ne•na○ta
chei•lo•plas○ty, *n., pl.* -ties.
chei•los•chi○sis, *n., pl.* -ses.
chei•lo•sis
chei•rog•no○my
chei•rol○o○gy
chei•ro•meg○a○ly
chei•ro•plas○ty
chei•ro•pom•pho•lyx
chei•ro•spasm
che•late
che•la•tion
che•la•tor

che•lic•er•o•a, *n., pl.* -er•ae.
Chel•i•do•ni•um
chel•i•ped
che•loid
Che•lo•ni•a
che•lo•ni•an
chem•i•cal
chem•i•cal•ly
chem•i•lu•mi•nes•cence
che•mise
chem•ist
chem•is•try, *n., pl.* -tries.
che•mo
che•mo•au•to•troph
che•mo•au•to•troph•ic
che•mo•au•to•troph•i•cal•ly
che•mo•au•tot•ro•phy, *n., pl.*
  -phies.
che•mo•dec•to•ma, *n., pl.*
  -mas, -ma•ta.
che•mo•dif•fer•en•ti•a•tion
che•mo•ki•ne•sis, *n., pl.* -ses.
che•mo•ki•net•ic
che•mo•pro•phy•lac•tic
che•mo•pro•phy•lax•is
che•mo•re•cep•tion
che•mo•re•cep•tive
che•mo•re•cep•tiv•i•ty, *n.,*
  pl. -ties.
che•mo•re•cep•tor
che•mo•re•flex
che•mo•re•sist•ance
che•mo•sen•si•tive
che•mo•sen•si•tiv•i•ty, *n.,*
  pl. -ties.
che•mo•sen•so•ry
che•mo•sis, *n., pl.* -ses.
che•mos•mo•sis
che•mos•mot•ic
che•mo•ster•oi•lant
che•mo•ster•oi•li•za•tion

che•mo•ster•oi•lize, *v.,* -lized,
  -liz•ing.
che•mo•sur•ger•y
che•mo•sur•gi•cal
che•mo•syn•the•sis
che•mo•syn•thet•ic
che•mo•syn•thet•i•cal•ly
che•mo•tac•tic
che•mo•tac•ti•cal•ly
che•mo•tax•is, *n., pl.* -tax•es.
che•mo•tax•o•nom•i•cal•ly
che•mo•tax•on•o•mist
che•mo•tax•o•nom•ic
che•mo•tax•y, *n., pl.* -ies.
che•mo•ther•a•peu•tic
che•mo•ther•a•peu•ti•cal
che•mo•ther•a•peu•ti•cal•ly
che•mo•ther•a•peu•tics
che•mo•ther•a•pist
che•mo•ther•a•py
che•mot•ic
che•mo•troph
che•mo•troph•ic
che•mo•trop•ic
che•mot•ro•pism
Chem•strip *Trademark.*
che•no•de•ox•y•chol•ic
Che•no•po•di•um
Cher•a•col *Trademark.*
Che•ren•kov ra•di•a•tion
Che•ren•kov•ra•di•a•tion
chest
che•von
Cheyne-Stokes breath•ing
Cheyne-Stokes res•pi•ra•tion
chi•asm
chi•as•o ma or chi•asm *n., pl.*.
  -as•mas, -as•ma•ta or -asms.
chi•as•mat•ic
chi•as•ma•type
chi•as•ma•typ•y
chick•en breast

chicken pox
chicken-breast∘ed
chicken-breast•ed•ness
chick•en•pox or chick•en pox
chig•ger
chi•goe
chil•blain, *n.*, *pl.* chil•blains.
chil•blained
child•bear•ing
child•bed
childbed fe∘ver
child•birth
child•hood
chi•lec•tro•pi∘on
chi•li•tis
Chi•lo•mas•tix
Chi•lop∘o∘da
chi•lop∘o∘dan
chi•lop∘o•dous
chi•mae∘ra
chi•me∘ra, *n.*, *pl.* -ras.
chi•me•rism
chim•pan•zee
chi•myl
chi•na•crin
chi•na•crine
chin•bone
chinch
chin•cho∘na
chin•co∘na
chine
Chi•nese-res•taur•ant
  syn•drome
chin•i•o•fon
chin∘o•line
chin-ster•num-heart
  syn•drome
chin-up
chi•o•na•blep•si∘a
chip•blow∘er
chi•rog•no∘my
chi•rol∘o∘gy

chi∘ro•meg∘a∘ly
chi∘ro•plas∘ty
chi∘ro•po•di∘al
chi•rop∘o∘dist
chi•rop∘o∘dy
chi∘ro•prac•tic
chi∘ro•prac•tor
chi∘ro•prax∘is, *n.*, *pl.*
  -prax∘es.
chi∘ro•spasm
chla•myd∘i∘a, *n.*, *pl.*
  -myd∘i•ae.
Chlamydia psit•ta∘ci
Chlamydia tra•cho•mat∘is
Chlam∘y•di•a•ce∘ae
chlam∘y•do•mo•nas
chla•myd∘o•spore
chla•myd∘o•spor∘ic
chlo•as•ma grav∘i•da•rum
chloasma he•pat∘o∘i∘cum
chloasma u∘ter∘i•num
Chlor-3 *Trademark.*
chlor•ac∘ne
chlo•rae•mi∘a
Chlor∘o•a•fed *Trademark.*
chlo•ral
chlor∘a•lose
chlor•am•bu•cil
chlo•ra•mine
chlo•ram•phen∘i•col
chlo•ra•nae•mi∘a
chlo•ra•ne•mi∘a
chlo•ra•ne•mic
Chlo•ra•sep•tic *Trademark.*
chlor•bu•ta•nol
chlor•bu•tol
chlor•cy•cl•izine
chlor•dan
chlor•dane
chlor•di•az•e∘pox•ide
chlo•re•mi∘a
Chlo•re•si∘um *Trademark.*

chlor•gua•nide
chlor•hy•dri•a
chlo•ride
chlo•ri•nate, *v.* -nat•ed,
 -nat•ing.
chlo•ri•na•tion
chlo•ri•na•tor
chlo•rine
chlor•me•ro•drin
chlo•ro•az•o•din
chlo•ro•bu•ta•nol
chlo•ro•form
chlo•ro•for•mic
chlo•ro•gua•nide
chlo•ro•leu•kae•mi•a
chlo•ro•leu•ke•mi•a
chlo•ro•ma, *n., pl.* -mas,
 -ma•ta.
chlo•rom•a•tous
chlo•ro•meth•ane
Chlo•ro•my•ce•tin *Trademark.*
chlo•ro•phane
chlo•ro•phe•nol
chlo•ro•phe•no•thane
chlo•ro•phyll or chlo•ro•phyl
chlo•ro•pi•a
chlo•ro•pic•rin
Chlo•rop•i•dae
chlo•ro•pro•caine
chlo•rop•si•a
Chlo•rop•tic *Trademark.*
chlo•ro•quine
chlo•ro•sis
chlo•ro•then
chlo•ro•thi•a•zide
chlo•ro•thy•mol
chlo•rot•ic
chlo•rot•i•cal•ly
chlo•rous
chlor•phe•nol
chlor•pic•rin
chlor•prom•a•zine

chlor•pro•pa•mide
chlor•tet•ra•cy•cline
Chlor-Tri•me•ton *Trademark.*
cho•a•ona, *n., pl.* -a•nae.
cho•a•nate
Cho•an•o•tae•ni•a
Cho•lac *Trademark.*
cho•lae•mi•a
cho•la•gog•ic
cho•la•gogue
cho•lan•gi•ec•ta•sis, *n., pl.*
 -ses.
cho•lan•gi•o•gas•tros•
 to•my, *n., pl.* -mies.
chol•an•gi•o•gram
chol•an•gi•o•graph•ic
chol•an•gi•og•ra•phy
chol•an•gi•ole
chol•an•gi•o•lit•ic
cho•lan•gi•o•li•tis, *n., pl.*
 -lit•o•i•des.
cho•lan•gi•o•ma, *n., pl.* -mas,
 -ma•ta.
cho•lan•gi•os•to•my, *n., pl.*
 -mies.
cho•lan•gi•ot•o•my, *n., pl.*
 -mies.
cho•lan•gi•tis, *n., pl.*
 -git•o•i•des.
chol•an•threne
chol•as•o•ma
cho•late
Cho•le•brine
cho•le•cal•cif•er•ol
cho•le•cyst
cho•le•cys•ta•gogue
cho•le•cys•tec•ta•sia
cho•le•cys•tec•to•my, *n., pl*
 -mies.
cho•le•cys•tic
cho•le•cys•tis
cho•le•cys•ti•tis

cho•le•cys•to•du•o•de•nos•to•my, *n., pl.* -mies.

cho•le•cys•to•gas•tros•to•my, *n., pl.* -mies.

cho•le•cys•to•gram

cho•le•cys•to•graph•ic

cho•le•cys•tog•ra•phy, *n., pl.* -phies.

cho•le•cys•to•ki•nin

cho•le•cys•to•pex•y, *n., pl.* -ies.

cho•le•cys•tos•to•my, *n., pl.* -mies.

cho•le•cys•tot•o•my, *n., pl.* -mies.

cho•le•doch

cho•le•do•chal

cho•le•do•chi•tis

cho•led•o•cho•li•thi•a•sis

cho•led•o•cho•li•thot•o•my, *n., pl.* -mies.

cho•led•o•chos•to•my, *n , pl.* -mies.

cho•led•o•chus, *n., pl.* -chi.

Cho•le•dyl *Trademark.*

cho•le•glo•bin

cho•le•oic

cho•le•lith

cho•le•li•thi•a•sis

cho•lem•e•osis

cho•le•mi•a

cho•lem•ic

cho•le•poi•e•sis

cho•le•poi•et•ic

chol•er•a

cholera in•fan•tum

cholera mor•bus

cholera nos•tras

cholera sic•ca

cholera sid•er•ans

cholera vib•ri•o

chol•e•ra•ic

cho•le•re•sis, *n., pl.* -ses.

chol•e•ret•ic

cho•ler•ic

chol•er•oi•form

chol•er•oid

chol•er•rha•gia

cho•le•sta•sis

cho•le•stat•ic

cho•les•te•a•to•ma, *n., pl.* -mas, -ma•ta.

cho•les•ter•ae•mi•a

cho•les•ter•e•mi•a

cho•les•ter•oic

cho•les•ter•ol

cho•les•ter•o•lae•mi•a

cho•les•ter•o•le•mi•a

cho•les•ter•o•sis

cho•lic ac•id

cho•line

cho•lin•er•gic

cho•lin•es•ter•ase

cho•li•no•lyt•ic

chol•oi•no•mi•met•ic

Cho•log•ra•fin *Trademark.*

Cho•lox•in *Trademark.*

chol•ou•ri•a

Chol•oy•bar *Trademark.*

chon•dral

chon•drec•to•my, *n., pl.* -mies.

chon•dri•fi•ca•tion

chon•dri•fy, *v.,* -dri•fied, -dri•fy•ing.

chon•drin

chon•dri•tis

chon•dro•blast

chon•dro•blas•tic

chon•dro•clast

chon•dro•cos•tal

chon•dro•cra•ni•um, *n., pl.* -ni•ums, -ni•a.

chon•dro•cyte

chon○dro•dys•pla•sia
chon○dro•dys•tro•phi○a, *n., pl.* -phi○as.
chon○dro•dys•troph○ic
chon○dro•dys•tro•phy
chon○dro•gen•e○sis, *n., pl.* -e○ses.
chon○dro•ge•net○ic
chon○dro•gen○ic
chon○drog•e•nous
chon○dro•glos•sus, *n., pl.* -glos○si.
chon•droid
chon○dro•i•tin
chon•drol○o○gy
chon•dro•ma, *n., pl.* -mas, -ma○ta.
chon○dro•ma•la•cia
chon○dro•ma•tous
chon○dro•mu•coid
chon○dro•os•te○o•dys•tro•phy
chon•drop○a•thy
chon○dro•pha•ryn•ge○us, *n., pl.* -ge○i.
chon○dro•phyte
chon○dro•plast
chon○dro•plas○ty, *n., pl* -ties.
chon○dro•sar•co○ma, *n., pl.* -mas, -ma○ta.
chondrosarcoma myx○o•ma•to○des
chon○dro•sis
chon○dro•skel•e○ton
chon○dro•ster•nal
chon○dro•tome
chon•drot○o○my, *n., pl.* -mies.
chon•drox○i•phoid
chon•drus, *n., pl.* -dri.
Cho•part's joint
chor○da, *n., pl.* -dae.
chorda ten•din○e○a

chor•dae ten•din•e○ae
chordae Wil•lis•i○i
chor•dal
chor○da•mes○o•derm
chor○da•mes○o•der•mal
chorda ten•din•e○a, *n., pl.* -e○ae.
chor•dee
chor•di•tis
chorditis fi•bri•no○sa
chorditis no•do○sa
chorditis tu•be•ro○sa
chor•do○ma, *n., pl.* -mas, -ma○ta.
chor•do•mes○o•derm
chor•do•mes○o•der•mal
chor•dot○o○my, *n., pl.* -mies.
cho•re○a
chorea grav○i•da•rum
chorea in•sa•ni○ens
chorea nu•tans
cho•re○al
cho•re•at○ic
cho•re○ic
choreic a○bra•sia
cho•re•i•form
cho•re•o•ath•e○toid
cho•re•o•ath•e○to•sis
cho•re•o•ath•e○tot○ic
cho•re○oid
cho•ri○al
cho○ri○o•al•lan•to○ic
cho○ri○o•al•lan•toid
cho○ri○o•al•lan•to○is, *n., pl.* -to○i•des.
cho○ri○o•car•ci•no○ma, *n., pl.* -mas, -ma○ta.
cho○ri○o•cele
cho○ri○o•ep○i•the•li○o○ma, *n., pl.* -mas, -ma○ta.
cho○ri○o•ep○i•the•li•om•a•tous

cho•ri•oid
cho•ri•oi•di•tis
cho•ri•oo•ma, *n., pl.* -mas, -ma∘ta.
cho∘ri∘o•men•in•gi•tis, *n., pl.* -git∘i•des.
cho•ri•on
cho•ri•on•ep∘i•the•li∘o•ma, *n., pl.* -mas, -ma∘ta.
cho•ri•on∘ic
chorionic go•nad∘o•tro•pin
chorionic vil•lus
chorionic villus sam•pling
Cho•ri•op•tes
cho•ri•op•tic
cho∘ri∘o•ret∘i•ni•tis, *n., pl.* -nit∘i•des.
cho•roid
choroid coat
cho•roi•dal
cho•roi•di•tis
cho•roi•do•cyc•li•tis
cho•roi•do•i•ri•tis
cho•roi•do•ret∘i•ni•tis, *n., pl.* -nit∘i•des.
Christ•mas dis•ease
chro•maf•fin
chro•maf•fine
chro•maf•fi•no∘ma, *n., pl.* -mas, -ma∘ta.
Chro•ma•gen *Trademark.*
chro•mag•tog∘e∘nous
chro•ma•phil
chro•mat∘ic
chromatic a∘ber•ra•tion
chro•mat∘i•cal∘ly
chro•ma•tid
chro•ma•tin
chro•ma•tin∘ic
chro•ma•tism
chro∘mat∘o•gram
chro∘mat∘o•graph

chro∘mat∘o•graph∘ic
chro∘mat∘o•graph∘i•cal∘ly
chro•ma•tog•ra•phy, *n., pl.* -phies.
chro•ma•toid
chro•ma•tol∘y•sis
chro•mat∘o•lyt∘ic
chro•ma•tom•e•ter
chro•ma•top•a∘thy, *n., pl.* -ies.
chro•mat∘o•phil
chro•mat∘o•phile
chro•mat∘o•phil∘i∘a
chro•mat∘o•phore
chro•mat∘o•phor∘ic
chro•ma•toph∘o∘rous
chro•ma•top•si∘a
chrom•es•the•sia
chrom•hi•dro•sis
chro•mi•dro•sis
chro•mi∘um
chro∘mo•bac•te•ri∘um, *n., pl.* -te•ri∘a.
chro•mo•blast
chro•mo•blas•to•my•co•sis
chro•mo•cyte
chro•mo•gen
chro∘mo•gen•e∘sis, *n., pl.* -e∘ses.
chro•mo•gen∘ic
chro•mo•mere
chro•mo•mer∘ic
chro•mo•ne∘ma, *n., pl.* -ma∘ta.
chro•mo•ne•mat∘ic
chro•mo•phil
chro•mo•phile
chro•mo•philic
chro•moph•i∘ly
chro∘mo•phobe *or* chro∘mo•pho•bic
chro∘mo•pro•tein

chro•mo•scope
chro•mo•scop∘ic
chro•mos•co∘py, *n., pl.* -pies.
chro•mo•so•mal
chro•mo•so•mal∘ly
chro•mo•some
chro•mo•so•mic
chro•mo•ther∘a∘py
chro•mo•trich•i∘al
chro•nax∘ie or chro•nax∘y
chro•nax∘im•e∘ter
chro•nax∘i•met•ric
chro•nax•im•e∘try
chron∘ic
chronic fa•tigue syn•drome
chronic ob•struc•tive pul•mo•nar∘y dis•ease
chron∘i•cal∘ly
chro•nic∘i∘ty
chron∘o•bi∘o•log∘i∘cal
chron∘o•bi•ol∘o∘gist
chron∘o•bi•ol∘o∘gy
chron∘o•trop∘ic
chro•not•ro∘pism
Chron∘u•lac *Trademark.*
chrys∘a•ro•bin
chry•si∘a•sis, *n., pl.* -ses.
Chrys∘o•my∘a
Chrys∘o•my∘ia
Chrysomyia bez•zi•a∘na
Chrys•ops
chrys∘o•ther∘a∘py
chy•lan•gi∘o∘ma, *n., pl.* -mas, -ma∘ta.
chyle
chy•le•mi∘a
chy•li•fac•tion
chy•li•fac•tive
chy•lif•er•ous
chy•li•fi•ca•tion
chy•li•form
chy∘lo•cele

chy∘lo•cyst
chy∘lo•mi•cron
chy∘lo•po•et∘ic
chy∘lo•poi∘e•sis
chy∘lo•poi•et∘ic
chy•lor•rhe∘a
chy∘lo•sis
chy∘lo•tho•rax, *n., pl.* -rax∘es, -ra•ces.
chy•lous
chy•lu•ri∘a
chyme
chy•mi•fi•ca•tion
chy•mo•pa•pa∘in
chy•mo•tryp•sin
chy•mo•tryp•sin∘o∘gen
chy•mo•tryp•tic
chy•mous
Cib∘a•lith-S *Trademark.*
cic∘a•tri•cial
ci•cat•ri•cose
cic∘a•trix or cic•a•trice *n., pl.* cic∘a•tri•ces.
cic∘a•tri•zant
cic∘a•tri•za•tion
cic∘a•trize, *v.,* -trized, -triz•ing.
cic∘u•tox∘in
cil∘i∘a, *n., pl., sing.* -i∘um.
cil∘i•ar∘y
ciliary bod∘y
ciliary mus•cle
ciliary proc•ess
Cil•i•a∘ta
cil•i•ate
cil•i•at∘ed
Cil•i•oph∘o∘ora
cil•i•oph∘o∘ran
cil•i•o•scle•ral
cil∘i∘um, *n., pl.* cil∘i∘a.
cil•lo•sis
ci•met∘i•dine

ci•mex, *n., pl.* ci•mi•ces.

Cimex he•mip•te•rus

Cimex lec•tu•lar•i•ous

Cimex ro•tun•da•tus

ci•mi•cif•u•oga ra•ce•mo•sa

cim•i•co•sis

cin•cho•na

cin•chon•i•dine

cin•cho•nine

cin•cho•nism

cin•chon•ize, *v.,* -ized, -iz•ing.

cin•cho•phen

cin•e•an•gi•o•car•di•o•graph•ic

cin•e•an•gi•o•car•di•og•ra•phy, *n., pl.* -phies.

cin•e•an•gi•o•graph•ic

cin•e•an•gi•og•ra•phy, *n., pl.* -phies.

cin•e•fluor•o•graph•ic

cin•e•fluo•rog•ra•phy, *n., pl.* -phies.

cin•e•omat•ics

cin•e•omat•o•graph

cin•e•omat•o•graph•ic

cin•e•omat•o•graph•i•cal•ly

cin•e•ma•tog•ra•phy, *n., pl.* -phies.

cin•e•mi•cro•graph•ic

cin•e•mi•crog•ra•pher

cin•e•mi•crog•ra•phy

cin•e•ol

cin•e•ole

cin•e•oplas•tic

cin•e•oplas•ty

cin•e•ora•di•og•ra•phy, *n., pl.* -phies.

cin•e•ore•a

cin•e•ore•al

cin•e•orin

cin•e•oroent•ge•nog•ra•phy, *n., pl.* -phies.

ci•ne•sis

ci•ne•to•plast

cin•gu•lec•to•my, *n., pl.* -mies.

cin•gu•lum, *n., pl.* -gu•la.

Cin•o•bac *Trademark.*

ci•on

Cip•ro *Trademark.*

Cip•ro•flox•a•cin *Trademark.*

cir•ca•di•an

cir•ca•di•an•ly

circ•an•nu•al

cir•ci•nate

cir•cle of Wil•lis

cir•cu•late, *v.,* -lat•ed, -lat•ing.

cir•cu•la•tion

cir•cu•la•to•ry

circulatory sys•tem

cir•cu•lus, *n., pl.* -cu•li.

cir•cum•a•onal

cir•cum•ar•tic•u•lar

cir•cum•cise, *v.,* -cised, -cis•ing.

cir•cum•cis•er

cir•cum•ci•sion

cir•cum•cor•ne•al

cir•cum•duc•tion

cir•cum•fer•en•ti•a ar•tic•u•lar•is ra•di•oi

circumferentia articularis ul•nae

cir•cum•flex

cir•cum•in•su•lar

cir•cum•len•tal

cir•cum•o•ral

cir•cum•val•late

cir•cum•vas•cu•lar

cir•rhosed

cir•rho•sis

cir•rhot•ic

cir•rus, *n., pl.* cir•ori.

cir•sec•to∘my, *n., pl.* -mies.
cir•soid
Cis∘a•pride
cis•plat∘in or cis•plat∘i•num
cis•tern
cis•ter∘na, *n., pl.* -nae.
cisterna chy∘li, *n., pl.* -ter•nae
  chy∘li.
cisternae sub•a∘rach•noi•da•
  les
cisternae sub•a∘rach•noi•de•
  a•les
cis•ter•nal
cisterna mag∘na, *n., pl.*
  cisternae mag•nae.
cis•tron
cis•tron∘ic
Cit∘a•nest *Trademark.*
Cit•ra•cal *Trademark.*
cit•ric ac∘id
citric acid cy∘cle
cit•ri•nin
Cit•ro•bac•ter a∘mal∘o•
  nat∘i•cus
Citrobacter freun•di∘i
Cit•ro•lith *Trademark.*
cit•ro•nel∘la
cit•rul•line
Clad∘o∘spo•ri∘um
Claf∘o∘ran *Trademark.*
clair•voy•ance
clair•voy•an∘cy
clang•ing
clap
clar∘i•fi•a•ble
cla•rif∘i•cant
clar∘i•fi•ca•tion
clar∘i•fi∘er
clar•i∘fy, *v.,* -fied, -fy•ing.
Cla•rith•ro•my•cin
Clar∘i•tin *Trademark.*
Claritin D *Trademark.*

Clarke's col•umn
Clarke's nu•cle∘us
clas•mat∘o∘cyte
clas•mat∘o∘cyt∘ic
clas•ma•to•sis
clas•tic
clas•si•cal con•di•tion•ing
clas•si•fi•ca•tion
clas•si∘fy, *v.,* -si•fied, -si•fy•
  ing.
clath•rate
clath•ra•tion
clau•di•ca•tion
claus•tro•phobe
claus•tro•pho•bi∘a
claus•tro•pho•bi∘ac
claus•tro•pho•bic
claus•trum, *n., pl.* -tra.
cla∘va, *n., pl.* cla•vae.
cla•va•cin
cla•val
cla•vat
cla•vat∘ed
cla•vate∘ly
cla•va•tion
clav∘i•cle
cla•vic•u∘la, *n., pl.* -vic∘u•lae.
cla•vic•u∘lar
cla•vus, *n., pl.* cla∘vi.
Clay•ton gas
Clear Eyes *Trademark.*
Clear∘a•sil *Trademark.*
cleav•age
cleft lip
cleft pal•ate
clei•do•cos•tal
clei•do•cra•ni∘al
Cle•o•cin *Trademark.*
cle∘oid
clep•to•ma•ni∘a
clep•to•ma•ni∘ac
cli•mac•te•ri∘al

cli•mac•ter•ic
cli•mac•ter•i•cal•ly
cli•mac•te•ri•um, *n.*, *pl.* -a.
cli•ma•to•ther•a•py
cli•max
clin•ic
clin•i•cal
clinical di•ag•no•sis
clinical psy•chol•o•gist
clinical psy•chol•o•gy
clinical ther•mom•e•ter
clinical tri•al
clin•i•cal•ly
cli•ni•cian
clin•i•co•path•o•log•ic
clin•i•co•path•o•log•i•cal
cli•noid
cli•nom•e•ter
cli•no•met•ric
cli•no•met•ri•cal
cli•nom•e•try
Clin•o•ril *Trademark.*
Clis•tin *Trademark.*
clit•i•on, *n.*, *pl.* clit•i•a.
clit•o•ral
cli•tor•ic
clit•o•rid•e•an
clit•o•ri•dec•to•my, *n.*, *pl.*
  -mies.
clit•o•ri•di•tis
clit•o•ris, *n.*, *pl.* clit•o•ris•es,
  cli•to•ri•des.
clit•o•ri•tis
cli•vus, *n.*, *pl.* cli•vi.
clivus mon•tic•u•li
clo•a•ca, *n.*, *pl.* -cae.
clo•a•cal
clo•a•ci•tis
Clo•fi•brate *Trademark.*
Clo•mid *Trademark.*
clo•mi•phene
clon•al

Clo•naz•e•pam
clone, *n.*, *v.*, cloned, clon•ing.
clon•ic
clo•nic•i•ty
clon•i•dine
clo•nism
clo•nor•chi•a•sis
clo•nor•chi•o•sis
Clo•nor•chis
Clonorchis si•nen•sis
clo•nus, *n.*, *pl.* -nus•es.
Clor•pac•tin *Trademark.*
closed-an•gle glau•co•ma
clos•trid•i•al
clos•trid•i•an
clos•trid•i•um, *n.*, *pl.* -i•a.
clot, *n.*, *v.*, clot•ted, clot•ting.
Clo•tri•mox•a•zole/Bet•a•
  meth•a•sone
clox•a•cil•lin
Clox•a•pen *Trademark.*
Clo•za•ril *Trademark.*
club•foot, *n.*, *pl.* -feet.
club•foot•ed
club•hand
clump
clu•ne•al
clu•pe•in
clu•pe•ine
clus•ter head•ache
clut•ter•ing
cly•sis, *n.*, *pl.* -ses.
clys•ma, *n.*, *pl.* -ma•ta.
clys•ter
cne•mi•al
cne•mis, *n.*, *pl.* cnem•i•des.
cni•do•blast
co•ac•er•vate
co•ac•er•va•tion
co•ac•tive strat•e•gy
co•ad•ap•ta•tion
co•ad•ap•ta•tion•al

co•ad•ap•ta•tion•al○ly
co•a•dapt○ed
Co•Ad•vil *Trademark.*
co•ag○u•la•bil○i•ty, *n., pl.* -ties.
co•ag○u•la•ble
co•ag○u•lant
co•ag○u•lase
co•ag○u•late, *v.,* -lat○ed, -lat•ing.
co•ag○u•la•tion
co•ag○u•la•tive
co•ag○u•la•tor
co•ag○u•la•to○ry
co•ag○u•lin
co•ag○u•lom•e○ter
co•ag○u•lum, *n., pl.* -ag○u•la.
co•apt
co•ap•ta•tion
co•arct
co•arc•tate
co•arc•ta•tion
coarctation of the a○or○ta
co•at
coat pro•tein
co•bal○a•min or co•bal○a•mine
co•balt
cobalt 60
co○ca
co•caine
co•cain•ism
co•cain○i•za•tion
co•cain•ize, *v.,* -ized, -iz•ing.
co•car•box○y•lase
coc•cal
coc○ci
coc•cic
Coc•cid○i○a
coc•cid○i○al
Coc•cid○i•oi•des
coc•cid○i•oi•din

coc•cid○i•oi•do•my•co•sis
coc•cid○i○o○my•co•sis
coc•cid○i•o•sis
coc•cid○i•o•stat
coc•cid○i•um, *n., pl.* -cid○i•a.
coc•ci•gen○ic
coc•co•bac○il•lar○y
coc•co•ba•cil•lus, *n., pl.* -cil○li.
coc•co•gen○ic
coc•coid or coc•coi•dal
coc•cous
coc•cus, *n., pl.* coc○ci.
coc•cy•al•gia
coc•cy•dyn○i○a
coc•cyg○e○al
coc•cy•gec•to○my, *n., pl.* -mies.
coc•cyg•e○us, *n., pl.* -cyg○e○i.
coc•cy•go•dyn○i○a
coc•cyx, *n., pl.* coc•cy•ges.
coch○i•ne○al
coch•le○a, *n., pl.* -le○ae, -le○as.
coch•le○ar
cochlear im•plant
coch•le•a○re
coch•le•ar○i•form
coch•le•o•ves•tib○u•lar
Coch•li○o•my○i○a
Cochliomyia a○mer○i•ca○na
Cochliomyia hom○i•ni•vo•rax
Cochliomyia ma•ce•lar○i•a
coch•ro•mat○o○graph
co•chro•ma•tog•ra•phy, *n., pl.* -phies.
co•cid○i○an
co•cid○i•oi•dal
co•con•scious
co•con•scious•ness
code, *n., v.,* cod○ed, cod•ing.
code blue

co•de•hy•drog•e•nase
co•deine
co•de•pend•ence
co•de•pend•en•cy
co•de•pend•ent
cod•er
co•dex, *n.*, *pl.* co•di•ces.
Co•dic•le•ar DH *Trademark.*
Co•di•mal DH *Trademark.*
Codimal DM *Trademark.*
Codimal PH *Trademark.*
Codimal-L.A. *Trademark.*
cod-liv•er oil
co•dom•i•nance
co•dom•i•nant
co•don
Coe•len•ter•a•ta
coe•len•ter•ate
coe•len•ter•on, *n.*, *pl.* -ter•a.
coe•li•ac
coe•lom, *n.*, *pl.* -loms, -lo•ma•ta.
coe•lom•ic
coe•nes•the•sia
coe•no•cyte
coe•no•cyt•ic
coe•no•gen•e•sis
coe•no•ge•net•ic
coe•nu•ri•sis, *n.*, *pl.* -ses.
coe•nu•ro•sis
coe•nu•rus, *n.*, *pl.* -ri.
co•en•zy•mat•ic
co•en•zy•mat•i•cal•ly
co•en•zyme
coenzyme Q10
co•fac•tor
cof•fee•a tos•ta
Co•gen•tin *Trademark.*
Co-Ge•sic *Trademark.*
cog•ni•tion
cog•ni•tive
cognitive dis•so•nance

cognitive ther•a•py
cog•ni•tive•ly
cog•ni•tiv•i•ty
Cohn•heim's ar•e•a
co•ho•ba
co•hort
cohort stud•y
coil
co•oi•tal
co•oi•tion
co•oi•tion•al
co•oi•to•pho•bi•a
co•oi•tus
coitus in•ter•rup•tus
coitus res•er•va•tus
coke, *n.*, *v.*, coked, cok•ing.
co•ola nut
Co•lace *Trademark.*
co•la•mine
Col•BEN•E•MID *Traemark.*
col•chi•cine
col•chi•cum
colchicum au•tum•na•le
cold
cold sore
cold-blood•ed or cold•blood•ed
cold-blood•ed•ly
cold-blood•ed•ness
co•lec•to•my, *n.*, *pl.* -mies.
co•oles fem•oi•ni•nus
Co•les•tid *Trademark.*
co•les•ti•pol
co•oli
co•li•bac•il•le•mi•a
co•li•bac•il•lu•ri•a
col•oic
co•li•cin
co•li•cine
co•li•cin•o•gen•ic
col•oi•cin•o•ge•nic•i•ty, *n.*,
    pl. -ties.

col•i•ci•nog•e•ony
col•ick•y
col•i•form
col•i•phage
co•lis•tin
co•lit•ic
co•li•tis
colitis cys•ti•ca pro•fun•da
colitis cystica su•per•fi•ci•a•lis
colitis pol•y•po•sa
colitis ul•cer•a•ti•va
col•la•gen
col•lag•e•nase
col•la•gen•ic
col•la•gen•o•lyt•ic
col•la•gen•o•sis
col•lag•e•nous
col•lapse, *v.*, -lapsed, -laps•ing.
col•laps•i•ble
col•lar•bone
col•lat•er•al
collateral cir•cu•la•tion
col•lec•tive un•con•scious
co•lec•to•my, *n.*, *pl.* -mies.
Col•les's frac•ture
col•li•mate, *v.*, -mat•ed, -mat•ing.
col•li•ma•tion
col•li•ma•tor
col•li•qua•tion
col•li•qua•tive
col•lo•di•on
collodion ba•by
col•lo•di•um
col•loid
col•loi•dal
col•loi•dal•ly
col•lum, *n.*, *pl.* col•la.
col•lu•nar•i•um, *n.*, *pl.* -nar•i•a.

col•lu•to•ri•um, *n.*, *pl.* -ri•a.
col•lyr•i•um, *n.*, *pl.* -lyr•i•a, -lyr•i•ums.
Col•lyr•i•um Fresh *Trademark.*
colo•o•bo•ma, *n.*, *pl.* -ma•ta.
coloboma au•ris
coloboma pal•pe•brae
colo•o•bom•a•tous
Col•o•Care *Trademark.*
colo•o•col•ic
co•lo•co•los•to•my, *n.*, *pl.* -mies.
colo•o•cynth
co•lom•bo
co•lon, *n.*, *pl.* -lons, co•la.
colon as•cend•ens
colon des•cend•ens
colon sig•moi•de•um
colon trans•ver•sum
co•lon•ic
co•lon•o•scope
co•lon•os•co•py, *n.*, *pl.* -pies.
colo•o•ny, *n.*, *pl.* -nies.
colony stim•u•lat•ing fac•tor
co•lo•pex•y, *n.*, *pl.* -ies.
co•lo•proc•tos•to•my, *n.*, *pl.* -mies.
col•or blind•ness
col•or-blind
col•or•im•e•ter
col•or•im•e•try
Col•o•Screen *Trademark.*
co•lo•sig•moid•os•to•my, *n.*, *pl.* -mies.
co•los•to•my, *n.*, *pl.* -mies.
co•los•tral
co•los•tric
co•los•trous
co•los•trum
co•lot•o•o•my, *n.*, *pl.* -mies.
col•pal•gia
col•pa•tre•sia

col•pec•ta•sia

col•pec•to•my, _n._, _pl._ -mies.

col•pi•tis

col•po•cele

col•po•clei•sis, _n._, _pl._ -ses.

col•po•da, _n._, _pl._ -das.

col•po•per•oi•ne•o•plas•ty, _n._, _pl._ -ties.

col•po•pex•y, _n._, _pl._ -ies.

col•po•plas•ty, _n._, _pl._ -ties.

col•por•rha•phy, _n._, _pl._ -phies.

col•po•scope

col•po•scop•ic

col•pos•co•py, _n._, _pl._ -pies.

col•po•stat

col•pot•o•my, _n._, _pl._ -mies.

col•u•mel•o•la, _n._, _pl._ -mel•lae.

columella au•ris

col•u•mel•lar

col•u•mel•late

col•umn of Ber•tin

co•lum•na, _n._, _pl._ -lum•nae.

col•lum•nae a•na•les

columnae car•ne•o•ae

columnae gris•e•o•ae

columnae rec•ta•les

columnae re•na•les

columnae ru•ga•rum

col•um•nar

Co•ly-My•cin M _Trademark._

Coly-Mycin S _Trademark._

col•lyr•oi•oum, _n._, _pl._. -i•oa. -i• ums.

Co•lyte _Trademark._

co•ma, _n._, _pl._ -mas.

com•a•tose

com•a•tose•ly

com•bat fa•tigue

Com•bi•pres _Trademark._

com•e•do, _n._, _pl._ com•e•dos, com•e•do•nes.

com•e•do•car•ci•no•ma, _n._, _pl._ -mas, -ma•ta.

co•mes, _n._, _pl._ com•i•tes.

Com•hist LA _Trademark._

com•mi•nute, _v._, -nut•ed, -nut•ing.

com•mi•nu•tion

com•mis•su•ra, _n._, _pl._ -su•rae.

com•mis•su•ral

com•mis•sure

com•mis•sur•ot•o•o•my, _n._, _pl._ -mies.

com•mit•ment

com•mon cold

com•mo•tio

commotio ce•re•bri

commotio ret•i•nae

commotio spi•na•lis

com•mu•ni•ca•bil•i•ty

com•mu•ni•ca•ble

com•mu•ni•ca•ble•ness

com•mu•ni•ca•bly

co•mor•bid

co•mor•bid•i•ty

com•pac•ta

com•par•o•a•scope

com•par•o•o•scope

com•pat•i•bil•i•ty

com•pat•i•ble

Com•pa•zine _Trademark._

com•pen•sate, _v._, -sat•ed, -sat•ing.

com•pen•sat•ing•ly

com•pen•sa•tion

com•pen•sa•tion•al

com•pen•sa•tive

com•pen•sa•tor

com•pen•sa•to•ry

com•pe•tence

com•pe•ten•cy, _n._, _pl._ -cies.

com•pe•tent

com•pet•i•tive

com•ple•ment
complement fix○a•tion
com•ple•men•ta•ri•ness
com•ple•men•ta•ry
Com•plete *Trademark.*
complete blood count
complete re•sponse
com•plex
Complex-Cho *Trademark.*
com•plex•ion
com•plex○ion○al
com•plex•ioned
com•plex○ly
com•plex•ness
com•plex○us, *n., pl.* -plex○us.
com•pli•ance, *n., pl.* -ances.
com•pli•an○cy, *n., pl.* -cies.
com•pli•cate, *v.,* -cat○ed, -cat•
   ing.
com•pli•ca•tion
com•pli•ca•tive
com•pos men•tis
com•pound Q
compound frac•ture
com•press
com•pres•sion
com•pres•sor
com•pro•mised
com•pul•sion
com•pul•sions
com•pul•sive
com•pul•sive○ly
com•pul•sive•ness
com•put•ed tom•og•ra•phy
computed tomography scan
com•put•er-as•sist•ed tom•
   og•ra•phy
com•put•er•ized ax○i○al
   tom•og•ra•phy
Com•trex *Trademark.*
co•nal•bu•min
co•nar○i○um, *n., pl.* -nar○i○a.

co•na•tion
co•na•tion○al
con○a•tive
con•ca•nav○a•lin
con•cave
con•cav○i○ty, *n., pl.* -ties.
con•ca•vo-con•cave
concavo-con•vex
con•ceive, *v.,* -ceived, -ceiv•
   ing.
con•cen•trate, *v.,* -trat○ed,
   -trat•ing.
con•cen•tra•tion
con•cep•tion
con•cep•tive
Con•cep•trol *Trademark.*
con•cep•tus, *n., pl.* -tus○es.
con•cha, *n., pl.* -chae.
con•chi•tis
con•choi•dal
con•choi•dal○ly
con•cho•tome
con•cord•ance
con•cre•ment
con•cres•cence
con•cres•cent
con•cre•ti○o cor•dis
concretio per○i•car•di○i
con•cre•tion
con•cre•tion•ar○y
con•cuss
con•cus•sion
con•cus•sive
con•cus•sive○ly
con•di•tion
con•di•tion○al
con•di•tion•al○ly
con•di•tioned
conditioned re•sponse
con•di•tion•ing
con•dom
con•duct dis•or•der

con•duc•tion
con•duc•tion•al
con•duc•tiv∘i∘ty, *n., pl.* **-ties.**
con•duc•tor
con•du•ran∘go
con•dy•lar
con•dy•lar•thro••sis
con•dyle
con•dyl•ec•to∘my, *n., pl.*
  -mies.
con•dyl∘o∘i∘on
con•dy•loid
con•dy•lo∘o•ma, *n., pl.* **-mas,**
  -ma∘ta.
con•dy•lom∘a•tous
con•dy•lot∘o∘my, *n., pl.*
  -mies.
cone
con•fab∘u•late, *v.,* **-lat∘ed,**
  -lat•ing.
con•fab∘u•la•tion
con•fab∘u•la•tor
con•fec•ti∘o, *n., pl.* **-ti∘o•nes.**
con•fec•tion
con•fer•tus
con•fig∘u•ra•tion
con•fig∘u•ra•tion∘al
con•fig∘u•ra•tion•al∘ly
con•fig∘u•ra•tive
con•fine•ment
con•flict
con•for•ma•tion∘al
con•for•ma•tion•al∘ly
con•fu•sion
con•fu•sion∘al
cong
con•geal
con•ge•la•tion
con•gen∘i•tal
con•gen∘i•tal∘ly
Con•ges•pi•rin *Trademark.*
con•gest

Con•ges•tac *Trademark.*
con•gest∘i•ble
con•ges•tion
con•ges•tive
congestive heart fail•ure
con•gi∘ous, *n., pl.* **-gi∘i.**
con•glo•bate
con•glo•ba•tion
con•glom•er•ate, *v.,* **-at∘ed,**
  -at•ing.
con•glom•er∘a•tion
con•glu•ti•nant
con•glu•ti•nate, *v.,* **-nat∘ed,**
  -nat•ing.
con•glu•ti•na•tion
con•glu•ti•nin
con•hy•drine
co∘ni ep∘i•did∘y•mi•dis
coni tu•bu•lo∘si
co•nid•i∘al
co•nid•i∘o•phore
co•nid•i∘oph∘o•rous
co•nid•i∘o•spore
co•nid∘i∘um, *n., pl.* **-nid∘i∘a.**
co•nine
co•ni•ol∘o∘gy
co•ni•om•e∘ter
co•ni∘um
co∘ni•za•tion
con•ju•ga•ble
con•ju•ga•bly
con•ju•gal
con•ju•gal∘i∘ty
con•ju•gal∘ly
con•ju•gant
con•ju•ga∘ta, *n., pl.* **-ga•tae.**
con•ju•gate, *v.,* **-gat∘ed, -gat•**
  ing.
Con•ju•gat∘ed Es•tro•gens
  Trademark.
conjugated pro•tein
con•ju•ga•tion

con•ju•ga•tive
con•ju•ga•tor
con•junc•ti•va, *n., pl.* -vas,
 -vae.
con•junc•ti•val
con•junc•ti•vi•tis
con•nect∘er
con•nec•tive
connective tis•sue
con•nec•tor
con•nex∘us in•ter•ten•din•
 e∘us
connexus
 in•ter•tha•lam∘i•cus
co•noid
co•noi•dal
con•qui•nine
Con•ray *Trademark.*
con•san•guin•e∘ous or
 con•san•guine
con•san•guin•e∘ous∘ly
con•san•guin∘i∘ty
con•scious
con•scious∘ly
con•scious•ness
consciousness-rais•ing
con•sen•su∘al
con•sen•su•al∘ly
con•serve
con•sol∘i•date, *v.,* -dat∘ed,
 -dat•ing.
con•sol∘i•da•tion
con•sol∘i•da•tive
con•so•lute
Con•stant-T *Trademark.*
Con•sti•lac *Trademark.*
con•sti•pate, *v.,* -pat∘ed,
 -pat•ing.
con•sti•pa•tion
con•sti•tu•tion
con•sti•tu•tion∘al
con•strict

con•stric•tion
con•stric•tor
constrictor ra•di•cis pe•nis
constrictor vag∘i•nae
con•sult
con•sul•tant
con•sul•ta•tion
con•sum•ma•to∘ry
con•sump•tion
con•sump•tive
con•sump•tive∘ly
Con•tac *Trademark*
con•tact *Trademark.*
contact lens
con•tac•tant
con•tact∘ee
con•tac•tu∘al
con•tac•tu•al∘ly
con•ta•gion
con•ta•gious
con•ta•gious∘ly
con•ta•gious•ness
con•ta•gi∘um, *n., pl.* -gi∘a.
con•tam∘i•nant
con•tam∘i•nate, *v.,* -nat∘ed,
 -nat•ing.
con•tam∘i•na•tion
con•ti•gu∘i•ty, *n., pl.* -ties.
con•tig•u•ous
con•tig•u•ous∘ly
con•tig•u•ous•ness
con•ti•nence or
 con•ti•nen∘cy
con•ti•nent
con•ti•nent∘ly
con•tra•cep•tion
con•tra•cep•tive
con•tract
con•tract∘i•bil∘i∘ty, *n., pl.*
 -ties.
con•trac•tile
con•trac•til∘i∘ty, *n., pl.* -ties.

con•trac•tion
con•trac•tion∘al
con•trac•tive
con•trac•tive∘ly
con•trac•tive•ness
con•trac•tor
con•tract-re∘lax stretch•ing
con•trac•ture
con•trac•tured
con•tra•in•di•cant
con•tra•in•di•cate, v.,
 -cat∘ed, -cat•ing.
con•tra•in•di•ca•tion
con•tra•in•dic•a•tive
con•tra•lat•er•al
con•trast me•di∘um
con•tra•stim∘u•lant
con•tre•coup
con•trec•ta•tion
con•trol, v., -trolled, -trol•
 ling•
control group
con•trol•la•ble
con•trolled ex•per∘i•ment
controlled sub•stance
controlled-re•lease
con•tuse, v., -tused, -tus•ing.
con•tu•sion
con•tu•sioned
con•tu•sive
Co∘nus
conus ar•te•ri∘o•sus, n., pl.
 co∘ni ar∘te•ri∘o∘si.
con•va•lesce, v., -lesced,
 -lesc•ing.
con•va•les•cence
con•va•les•cent
con•vec•tion
con•vec•tive
con•ver•gence
con•ver•gent
con•ver•sion

con•ver•sion∘al
con•ver•sion•ar∘y
con•vex
con•vex∘i∘ty, n., pl. -ties.
con•vex∘o-con•cave
convexo-con•vex
con•vo•lute, v., -lut∘ed,
 -lut•ing.
con•vo•lut∘ed tu•bule
con•vo•lute∘ly
con•vo•lu•tion
con•vol•vu•lin
con•vol•vu•lus, n., pl. -lus∘es,
 -vu∘li.
con•vul•sant
con•vulse, v., -vulsed,
 -vuls•ing.
con•vuls•ed∘ly
con•vul•sion
con•vul•sion•ar∘y
con•vul•sive
con•vul•sive∘ly
Coo•ley's a∘ne•mi∘a
Cooley's dis•ease
Coo•lidge tube
Coo∘pe•ri∘a
coo•pe•rid
Coo•per's lig∘a•ment
co∘or•di•na•tion
co∘os•si•fi•ca•tion
co∘os•si•fy, v., -fied, -fy•ing.
coo•tie
co•pa•i∘ba
Co•pe•po∘da
co•pol∘y•mer
co•pol∘y•mer∘ic
co•pol∘y•mer•i•za•tion
co•po∘ly•mer•ize, v., -ized,
 -iz•ing.
cop•per
cop•per∘as
cop•per•head

Cop•per•tone *Trademark.*
cop•rem•e∘sis, *n., pl.* **-ses.**
cop∘ro•lag•ni∘a
cop∘ro•lag•nist
cop∘ro•la•li∘a
cop∘ro•lith
cop•rol∘o∘gy
cop∘ro•pha•gia
cop∘ro•phag∘ic
cop∘roph∘a•gist
cop∘roph∘a•gous
cop•roph•a∘gy
cop∘ro•phil∘i∘a
cop∘ro•phil∘i∘ac
cop∘ro•phil∘ic
co•proph∘i•lism
cop∘ro•pho•bi∘a
cop∘ro•por•phy•rin
cop∘ros•ta•nol
cop∘ros•te•rol
cop•u∘ola, *n., pl.* **cop∘u•las,**
  cop∘u•lae.
cop∘u•late, *v.,* **-lat∘ed,**
  -lat∘ing.
cop∘u•la•tion
cop∘u•la•to∘ry
co∘quille
cor pul•mo•na∘le, *n., pl.*
  cor•di∘a pul•mo•na•li∘a.
cor∘a•cid∘i∘um, *n., pl.*
  -cid∘i∘a.
cor∘a•co•bra•chi∘a•lis, *n., pl.*
  -les.
coracobrachialis bre•vis
coracobrachialis su•pe•ri∘or
co•ra•co•hu•mer∘al
co•ra•coid
co•ral•lin
co•ral•line
cord blood
Cor•da•rone *Trademark.*
cor•date

cor•date∘ly
cor•dec•to•my, *n., pl.* **-mies.**
cor•dial
cor•di•form
cor•di•tis
cor•don sa∘ni•taire
cor•do•pex∘y, *n., pl.* **-ies.**
cor•dot∘o∘my, *n., pl.* **-mies.**
Cor•dran *Trademark.*
Cordran SP *Trademark.*
Cordran-N *Trademark.*
cor•ec•ta•sis, *n., pl.* **-ses.**
co•rec•to•pi∘a
cor∘e•di•al∘y•sis
co•rel∘y•sis
co•re•om•e∘ter
co•re•pres•sor
co•res•te•no∘ma
Cor•gard *Trademark.*
Co•ri•ci•din *Trademark.*
co•ri∘um, *n., pl.* **co•ri∘a.**
corn
corn sug∘ar
cor•ne∘a, *n., pl.* **-ne∘as.**
cornea gut•ta∘ta
cor•ne∘al
cor•ne•i•tis
cor•ne∘o•bleph∘a•ron
cor•ne∘ous
cor•ne∘um, *n., pl.* **-ne∘a.**
cor•nic∘u•late
cor•nic∘u•lum
cor•ni•fi•ca∘tion
cor•ni∘fy, *v.,* **-fied, -fy•ing.**
cor∘nu, *n., pl.* **cor•nu∘a.**
corn•u∘al
co∘ro∘na
corona ra∘di∘a∘ta, *n., pl.* **co•**
  ro∘nae ra∘di∘a•tae.
cor∘o∘nal
cor∘o∘na∘le

cor•o•nar•y, *adj., n., pl*
-nar•ies.
coronary ar•ter•y
coronary artery by•pass graft
coronary artery bypass
sur•ger•y
coronary artery dis•ease
coronary bypass
coronary heart disease
coronary oc•clu•sion
coronary si•nus
coronary throm•bo•sis
coronary vein
coronary-care u•nit
co•ro•na•vi•rus, *n., pl.*
-rus•es.
cor•o•ner
cor•o•ner•ship
cor•o•net
co•ro•ni•on, *n., pl.* -ni•a.
cor•o•ni•tis
cor•o•noid
cor•po•re•al
cor•po•re•al•ly
corps•man, *n., pl.* -men.
cor•pu•lence
cor•pu•len•cy
cor•pu•lent
cor•pus, *n., pl.* -po•ra.
corpus al•bi•cans, *n., pl.* corpora al•bi•can•ti•a.
corpus cal•lo•sum, *n., pl.* corpora cal•lo•sa.
corpus ca•ver•no•sum, *n., pl.*
corpora ca•ver•no•sa.
corpus de•lic•ti, *n., pl.* corpora
de•lic•ti.
corpus lu•te•um, *n., pl.* corpora lu•te•a.
corpus stri•a•tum, *n., pl.* corpora stri•a•ta.
cor•pus•cle

corpuscle of Has•sal
corpuscle of Has•sall
corpuscle of Herbst
corpuscle of Krause
corpuscle of Va•ter
cor•pus•cu•lar
Cor•rec•tol *Trademark.*
cor•re•spond•ence
cor•re•spond•ing
Cor•ri•gan pulse
cor•ri•gent
cor•rode, *v.,* -rod•ed,-rod•ing.
cor•ro•sion
cor•ro•sive
cor•ro•sive•ly
cor•ro•sive•ness
cor•ru•ga•tor
corrugator cu•ti•sa•ni
corrugator su•per•cil•i•i
Cort-Dome *Trademark.*
Cort•aid *Trademark.*
Cor•tef *Trademark.*
Cort•en•e•ma *Trademark.*
cor•tex, *n., pl.* -ti•ces.
cor•tex•one
cor•ti•cal
cor•ti•cal•ly
cor•ti•cate
cor•ti•cif•u•gal
cor•ti•cip•e•tal
cor•ti•co•af•fer•ent
cor•ti•co•ef•fer•ent
cor•ti•coid
cor•ti•co•spi•nal
cor•ti•co•ster•oid
cor•ti•cos•ter•one
cor•ti•co•tha•lam•ic
cor•ti•co•tro•phin
cor•ti•co•tro•pin
corticotropin re•leas•ing
fac•tor
Cor•ti•foam *Trademark.*

cor•tin
Cor•ti's gan•gli•on
Corti's or•gan
cor•ti•sol
cor•ti•sone
Cor•ti•spo•rin *Trademark*
Cor•tone *Trademark.*
Cor•tril *Trademark.*
Cort•ro•syn *Trademark.*
co•run•dum
co•rus•ca•tion
co•ry•da•lis
cor•y•ne•bac•te•ri•a•ce•ae
cor•y•ne•bac•te•ri•al
cor•y•ne•bac•te•ri•um, *n.,*
pl. -ri•a.
co•ryn•e•form
co•ry•zal
co•ry•za
Cor•zide *Trademark.*
Cos•me•gen
cos•me•sis
cos•met•ic
cos•met•i•cal•ly
cos•me•ti•cian
cos•ta, *n., pl.* cos•tae.
costa fluc•tu•an•tes
costa spu•ri•ae
costa ver•ae
cos•tal
cos•tal•gia
cos•tate
cos•tec•to•my, *n., pl.* -mies.
cos•tive
cos•tive•ly
cos•tive•ness
cos•to•cen•tral
cos•to•chon•dral
cos•to•cla•vic•u•lar
cos•to•co•ra•coid
cos•to•scap•u•lar
cos•to•tome

cos•to•trans•verse
cos•to•trans•ver•sec•to•my,
n., pl. -mies.
cos•to•ver•te•bral
cos•to•xi•phoid
co•tar•nine
Co•ta•zym *Trademark.*
Cotazym-S *Trademark.*
co•trans•duc•tion
Co•trim *Trademark.*
cot•oy•loid
cough drop
cough syr•up
Cou•ma•din *Trademark.*
cou•ma•phos
cou•ma•rin
coun•sel, *v.,* -seled or -selled,
-sel•ing or -sel•ling.
coun•sel•ing
coun•sel•lor
coun•se•lor
coun•ter•con•di•tion•ing
coun•ter•cur•rent
coun•ter•ir•ri•tant
coun•ter•ir•ri•ta•tion
coun•ter•o•pen•ing
coun•ter•pho•bi•a
coun•ter•pho•bic
coun•ter•pul•sa•tion
coun•ter•punc•ture
coun•ter•shock
coun•ter•stain
coun•ter•trac•tion
coun•ter•trans•fer•ence
course
court plas•ter
cou•vade
co•va•lent
cov•er glass
cov•er•slip
cow hock
cow-hocked

cow•age
Cow•dri○a
cow•hage
cow•per○i•tis
Cow•per's gland
cow•pox
cox○a, *n., pl.* cox○ae.
coxa ad•duc○ta
coxa flex○a
coxa mag○na
coxa pla○na
coxa val○ga
coxa va○ra
cox○al
cox•al•gi○a or cox•al•gy
cox•al•gic
cox•al•gy, *n., pl.* **-gies.**
Cox•i•el○la
Coxiella bur•net•i•i
cox○i•tis, *n., pl.* cox•it○i•des.
coxitis cot○y•loi•de○a
cox○o•fem○o•ral
cox•sack•ie•vi•rus or Cox•
sack○ie vi○rus, *n., pl.*
-rus○es.
Co•zaar
crab
crab louse
crack
crack•les
cra○dle
cradle cap
cramp
cra•ni○al
cranial in•dex
cranial nerve
cra•ni•al○ly
Cra•ni•a○ta
cra•ni•ate
cra•ni•ec•to○my, *n., pl.* **-mies.**
cra○ni○o•cele
cra○ni○o•ce•re•bral
cra•ni•oc•la•sis, *n., pl.* **-ses.**
cra○ni○o•fa•cial
cra○ni○o•graph
cra○ni○o•log○i•cal
cra○ni○o•log○i•cal○ly
cra•ni•ol○o•gist
cra•ni•ol○o•gy
cra•ni•om•e○ter
cra○ni○o•met•ric or cra○ni○o•
met•ri•cal
cra•ni•om•et•ri•cal○ly
cra•ni•om•e○trist
cra•ni•om•e○try
cra•ni•op○a•gus, *n., pl.* **-gi.**
craniopagus fron•ta•lis
craniopagus oc•cip○i•ta•lis
craniopagus par○o•a•sit○i•cus
craniopagus pa•ri•e•ta•lis
cra•ni•op○a•thy, *n., pl.* **-thies.**
cra○ni○o•pha•ryn•ge○al
cra○ni○o•pha•ryn•gi•o○ma,
n., pl. **-mas, -ma○ta.**
cra○ni○o•phore
cra○ni○o•plas○ty, *n., pl.* **-ties.**
cra○ni○o•ra•chis•chi•sis, *n.,*
pl. **-ses.**
cra○ni○o•sa•cral
cra•ni•os○chi•sis, *n., pl.* **-ses.**
cra•ni•os○co•py, *n., pl.* **-pies.**
cra○ni○o•spi•nal
cra○ni○o•ste•no•sis, *n., pl.*
-ses.
cra○ni○o•syn•os•to•sis
cra○ni○o•ta•bes
cra○ni○o•tome
cra•ni•ot○o○my, *n., pl.* **-mies.**
cra•ni•um, *n., pl.* **-ni•ums,**
-ni○a.
cranium bif○i•dum
cranium cer•e•bra○le
cranium vis•ce•ra○le
crap○u•lence

crap○u•lent
crap○u•lous
crash
crash cart
cra•sis, *n., pl.* -ses.
cra•ter
craw-craw
C-re•ac•tive
C-reactive pro•tein
cre○a•tine
creatine phos•phate
cre•at○i•nine
cre•at○i•nu•ri○a
creche
cre•mains
cre•mas•ter
cre•mas•te•ri○al
cre•mas•ter○ic
cre•mate, *v.,* -mat○ed,
   -mat•ing.
cre•ma•tion
cre•ma•to•ri○um, *n., pl.* -ums,
   -a.
cre•ma•to○ry, *n., pl.* -ries.
creme
cre○na, *n., pl.* -nae.
crena a○ni
crena clu•ni○um
cre•nate
cre•nat○ed
cre•na•tion
cre•no•cyte
Cre○on *Trademark.*
cre•oph•a○gy
cre•o•sol
cre•o•sote
crep○i•tant
crep○i•ta•tion
crep○i•tus
cre•pus•cu•lar
cres•cent
cres•cen•tic

cres•co•graph
cre•sol
cre○ta
cre•tin
cre•tin•ism
cre•ti•noid
cre•tin•ous
Creutz•feldt-Ja•kob dis•ease
crev•ice
cre•vic○u•lar
cri du chat syn•drome
crib death
crib•ber
crib•bing
crib•rate
crib•ra•tion
crib•ri•form
cri•cet○oid
Cri•cet○oi•dae
cri•ce•tine
Cri•cet○u•lus
Cri•ce•tus
crick
cri•co•ar○y•te•noid
cri•coid
crim○i•nol○o○gy
crin○o•gen○ic
crip•ple, *v.t.* -pled, -pl•ing.
cri•sis, *n., pl.* -ses.
cris•pa•tion
cris•pa•tu○ra ten•di•num
cris○ta, *n., pl.* cris•tae.
crista a○cus•ti○ca, *n., pl.*
   cris•tae a○cus•ti○cae.
cristae cu○tis
cristae ma•tri•cis un•guis
cristae sa•cra•les
   ar•tic○u•la•res
cristae sacrales lat•er○a•les
crith
cri•thid○i○a
cri•thid○i•form

crit○i•cal
crit○i•cal○ly
crock
cro•cus, *n.*, *pl.* -es.
Crohn's dis•ease
cross-fir•ing
cross match•ing
cross re•ac•tion
cross-re•ac•tive
cross train•ing
cross•a○bil○i○ty, *n.*, *pl.* -ties.
cross-eye
cross-eyed
cross-fer•tile
cross-fer•til○i•za•tion
cross-fer•til•ize, *v.*, -lized, -liz•
  ing.
cross•ing o•ver
cross•o○ver
cross-re•ac•tiv○i○ty, *n.*, *pl.*
  -ties.
cross-ster•ile
cross-ste•ril○i○ty
cross-tol•er•ance
cross•way
cro•ta•lid
Cro•tal○i•dae
cro•ta•lin
cro•ta•line
cro•tal•ism
Cro•ta•lus
cro•taph•i○on
crotch
cro•tin
cro•ton
croton oil
croton tig•li○um
cro•ton○ic
cro•to•nyl
croup
croup•ous
croup○y, *adj.* -i○er, -i•est.

cru•ces pi•lo•rum
cru•ci•ble
Cru○ex *Trademark.*
crup•per
cru○ra am•pul•lar○i○a
crura ant•he•li•cis
crura os•se○a
cru•ral
crus, *n.* cru•ris, *pl.* cru○ra.
crus○ta, *n.*, *pl.* crus•tae.
crusta lac•te○a
Crus•ta•ce○a
crus•ta•ce○an
crus•tal
crutch
Crutch•field tongs
crux, *n.*, *pl.* -es, cru•ces.
cry•an•es•the•sia
cry○o○bi○o○logo○i•cal
cry○o○bi•o○logo○i•cal○ly
cry○o○bi•ol○o○gist
cry○o○bi•ol○o○gy
cry○o•gen
cry○o○gen○ic
cry○o○gen○i•cal○ly
cry○o○gen○ics
cry○og•e○nist
cry○o○glob○u•lin
cry○o○glob○u•li○ne•mi○a
cry○o•hy•drate
cry•om•e○ter
cry•on○ic
cry•on○ics
cry○o○phil○ic
cry○o•pre•cip○i•tate
cry○o•pre•cip○i•ta•tion
cry○o•pres•er•va•tion
cry○o•probe
cry○o•pro•tect•ant
cry○o•pro•tec•tive
cry○o•scope

culicosis

cry○o•scop○ic
cry○o•scop○i•cal
cry•os○co○py
cry○o•stat
cry○o•sur•geon
cry○o•sur•ger○y
cry○o•sur•gi•cal
cry○o•ther○a○py
crypt
crypt of Lie•ber•kühn
crypt of Mor•gag○ni
crypt•aes•the•sia
crypt○es•the•sia
cryp•tic
cryp•ti•cal○ly
cryp•ti•tis
cryp○to•bi○o•sis, *n., pl.* -ses.
cryp○to•coc•co•sis
cryp○to•coc•cus, *n., pl.*
  -coc•ci.
cryptococcus ne○o•for•mans
cryp○to•crys•tal•line
cryp○to•gam
cryp○to•ga•mi○a
cryp○to•gam○ic
cryp•tog○a•mous
cryp○to•ge•net○ic
cryp○to•gen○ic
cryp○to•lith
cryp○to•men•or•rhe○a
cryp•tom•ne•sia
cryp•tom•ne•sic
cryp○to•pine
cryp○to•pyr•role
cryp•tor•chi•dism or cryp•
  tor○chism
cryp•tor•chis
cryp•tor•chid
cryp○to•spo•ri•di○o•sis
cryp○to•xan•thin
cryp○to•zo○ite
cryp○to•zy•gous

crys•tal, *n., adj., v.,* -taled,
  -tal•ing. -talled, -tal•ling.
crys•tal•lin
crys•tal•line
crystalline lens
crys•tal•lite
crys•tal•li•za•tion
crys•tal•lo•gram
crys•tal•lo•graph○ic
crys•tal•lo•graph○i•cal
crys•tal•log•ra•phy, *n., pl.*
  -phies.
crys•tal•loid
crys•tal•loi•dal
crys•tal•lu•r○ia
Crys•to•dig○in *Trademark.*
C-sec•tion
CT scan
CT scan•ner
Cte•no•ce•phal○i•des
cu•beb
cu•bi•tal
cu•bi•tus, *n., pl.* -bi○ti.
cubitus val•gus
cubitus va○rus
cu•boid
cu•boi•dal
cu•cum•ber
cud•bear
cue
cuff
cui•rass
cul-de-sac, *n., pl.* culs-de-sac.
cul•do•cen•te•sis, *n., pl.* -ses.
cul•do•scop○ic
cul•dos•co○py, *n., pl.* -pies.
Cu•lex
Culex fat○i•gans
Culex pip•iens
Cu•lic○i•dae
cu•li•cide
cu•li•co•sis, *n., pl.* -ses.

cul•men, *n., pl.* -s, -mi∘na.
cul•ti•vate, *v.,* -vat∘ed, -vat•ing.
cul•ti•va•tion
cul•ture
culture me•di∘um
cu•ma•rin
cu•mu•la•tive
cu•mu•lus, *n., pl.* -li.
cumulus o∘oph•o•rus
cumulus o∘vig•er∘us
cumulus pro•lig∘er∘us
cu•ne•ate
cu•ne•at∘ed
cu•ne•i•form
cu•ne•o•cu•boid
cu•ne•o•na•vic∘u•lar
cu•ne∘ous, *n., pl.* -ne∘i.
cu•nic∘u•lus, *n., pl.* -li.
cun•ni•linc•tus
cun•ni•lin•guism
cun•ni•lin•gus or cun•ni•
   linc•tus
cun•nus, *n., pl.* -ni.
cu•po∘la
cup•ping
cupping glass
cu•pre•ine
cu•pric
Cu•prim∘i•ne *Trademark.*
cup•rum a∘cet∘i•cum
cuprum me•tal•li•cum
cu•pu∘la, *n., pl.* -lae.
cupula coch•le∘ae
cupula cris•tae am•pul•lar∘is
cupula op•ti∘ca
cupula pleu•rae
cur•a•ble
cu•ra∘re or cu•ra∘ri
cu•ra•ri•form
cu•ra•rine
cu•ra•ri•za•tion

cu•ra•rize, *v.,* -rized, -riz•ing.
cur∘a•tive
cur∘a•tive•ly
cur•cu∘ma
cure, *n., v.,* cured, cur•ing.
cu∘ret
cu•ret•ment
cu•ret•tage
cu•rette, *n., v.,* -ret•ted, -ret•
   ting.
cu•rette•ment
cu∘rie
cu•rine
cu•ri∘um
Cur•re•tab *Trademark.*
cur•va•tu∘ra ven•tric∘u•li
   ma•jor
curvatura ventriculi mi•nor
cur•va•ture
Cush•ing's dis•ease
Cushing's syn•drome
cush•ion
cus•pate
cus•pat∘ed
cus•pid
cus•pi•date
cus•pi•dat∘ed
cus•to•di∘al
cu•ta•ne∘ous
cu•ta•ne•ous∘ly
cut•down
Cu•te•reb∘ra
Cu•te•reb•rid
Cu•te•reb•ri•dae
Cu•te•reb•rine
cu•ti•cle
cu•tic∘u∘la, *n., pl.* -lae.
cuticula den•tis
cu•tic∘u•lar
cu•tic∘u•lar∘i•za•tion
cu•tic∘u•lar•ized
cu•tin

cu○tis, *n., pl.* cu○tes.
cutis an•se•ri○na
cutis lax○a
cutis mar•mo•ra○ta
cutis an•se•ri○na, *n., pl.*
  cu○tes an•se•ri○nae.
cutis ve○ra, *n., pl.* cutes
  ve○rae.
cu•vette
cy•an○a•mid
cy•an○a•mide
cy○a•nate
cy•an•hy•drin
cy•an○ic
cy○a•nide or cy○a•nid
cy•an○i•din
cy•an•meth•e○mo•glo•bin
cy○a•no•a•ce○tic
cy○a•no•ac○ry•late
cy○a•no•co•bal○a•min
cy•an○o•gen
cy○a•no•gen•e○sis, *n., pl.*
  -e○ses.
cy○a•no•ge•net○ic
cy○a•no•gen○ic
cy○a•no•hydrin
cy○a•no•met•he•mo•glo•bin
cy•an○o•phil
cy○an○o•phile
cy○an○o•phil○ic
cy○a•noph○i•lous
cy○a•no•phy•ce○ae
cy○a•no•sed
cy○a•no•sis
cy○a•not○ic
cy○a•nu•ric
cy•as○o•ma
cy•ber•cul•tur○al
cy•ber•cul•ture
cy•ber•nat○ed
cy•ber•na•tion
cy•ber•net○ic

cy•ber•net○i•cal
cy•ber•net○i•cal○ly
cy•ber•ne•ti•cian
cy•ber•net○i•cist
cy•ber•net○ics
cy•borg
cy•ca•sin
cy•cla•mate
cy•cla•men eu•ro•pae○um
cy•cla•min
Cy•cla•pen-W *Trademark.*
cy•clar•thro•sis, *n., pl.* -ses.
cy•clase
cy•claz○o•cine
cy•clic
cyclic AMP
cyclic GMP
cy•clic○i•ty
cy•cli•cot○o•my, *n., pl.* -mies.
cy•cli•tis
cyc•li•tol
Cy○clo•ben•za•prine
Cy○clo•cort *Trademark.*
cy•clo•di•al○y•sis, *n., pl.* -ses.
cy•clo•di○a•ther○my
cy•clo•gram
Cy○clo•gyl *Trademark.*
cy•clo•hex○i•mide
cy•cloid
cy•cloi•dal
cy•cloi•dal○ly
Cy•clo•par *Trademark.*
cy•clo•pho•ri○a
cy•clo•phos•pha•mide
Cy○clo•phyl•lid○e○a
cy•clo•phyl•lid•e○an
cy•clo•pi○a
cy•clo•ple•gi○a
cy•clo•ple•gic
cy•clo•pro•pane
cy•clops, *n., pl.* -clo•pes.

cy○clo○py
cy○clo•se•rine
cy○clo•sis, *n., pl.* -ses.
cy○clo•spo•rine or cy○clo•
  spo•rin
Cy○clo•sto•ma○ta
cy○clo•sto•mate
cy○clo•stom○a•tous
cy○clo•stome
Cy○clo•sto○mi
cy○clo•thyme
cy○clo•thy•mi○a
cy○clo•thy•mic
cy○clo•tome
cy•clot○o○my, *n., pl.* -mies.
Cy•crin *Trademark.*
Cy•do○ni○a
cy•e○sis, *n., pl.* -ses.
Cy•klock○a•pron *Trademark.*
Cy•lert *Trademark.*
cyl•in•droid
cyl•in•dro○ma, *n., pl.* -mas,
  -ma○ta.
cyl•in•dru•ro○ia
cy•ma•rin
cy•ma•rose
cym○ba, *n., pl.* -bae.
cym•bo•ce•phal○ic
cym•bo•ceph○a•lous
cym•bo•ceph○a•ly, *n., pl.*
  -lies.
cy•mo•graph
cy•nan•thro○py, *n., pl.* -pies.
cy•no•ceph○a•lus, *n., pl.* -li.
cy•no•mol•gus, *n., pl.* -gi.
Cy•prin○i•dae
cy•pro•hep•ta•dine
cy•pro•ter•one
cyr•tom•e○ter
cyr•to○sis, *n., pl.* -ses.
Cys
cyst

cyst•ad•e○no•car•ci•no○ma,
  n., pl. -mas, -ma○ta.
cyst•ad•e○no○ma, *n., pl.* -mas,
  -ma○ta.
cys•tal•gia
cys•ta•mine
cys•ta•thi○o•nine
cys•te•a•mine
cys•tec•ta•sia
cys•tec•to○my, *n., pl.* -mies.
cys•te○ic
cys•te•in○ic
cys•te•ine
cys•tic
cystic fi•bro•sis
cys•ti•cer•co•sis
cys•ti•cer•cus, *n., pl.* -cer○ci.
cys•tig○er•ous
cys•tine
cys•ti•no•sis
cys•ti•nu•ri○a
cys•ti•tis
cystitis cys•ti○ca
cystitis em•phy•se•ma•to○sa
cystitis fol•lic○u•lar○is
cystitis glan•du•lar○is
Cy○sto-Con○ray *Trademark.*
cys○to•cele
cys○to•fi•bro○ma pap•il•
  la○re
cys○to•gram
cys•tog○ra•phy, *n , pl.* -phies.
cyst•oid
cys○to•lith
cys○to•li•thi•a•sis
cys○to•lith○ic
cys○to○ma, *n., pl.* -mas,
  -ma○ta.
cys•tom•e○ter
cys○to•met•ro•gram
cys○to•pex○y, *n., pl.* -ies.
cys○to•plas○ty, *n., pl.* -ties.

cytoplastic

cys•to•py•e•li•tis

cys•to•py•e•log•ra•phy, *n., pl.* -phies.

cys•to•py•o•e•lo•ne•phri•tis

cys•tor•rha•phy, *n., pl.* -phies.

cys•to•sar•co•ma, *n., pl.* -mas, -ma•ta.

cystosarcoma phyl•lo•des

cystosarcoma phyl•loi•des

cys•to•scope

cys•to•scop•ic

cys•tos•co•pist

cys•tos•co•py, *n., pl.* -pies.

Cys•to•spaz *Trademark.*

Cystospaz M *Trademark.*

cys•to•sto•my, *n., pl.* -mies.

cys•to•tome

cys•tot•o•my, *n., pl.* -mies.

cys•to•u•re•ter•oi•tis

cys•to•u•reth•ro•gram

cys•tous

Cy•ta•dren *Trademark.*

cy•ti•dine

cy•to•ar•chi•tec•ton•ic

cy•to•ar•chi•tec•ton•ics

cy•to•ar•chi•tec•tur•al

cy•to•ar•chi•tec•ture

cy•to•chem•oi•cal

cy•to•chem•is•try

cy•to•chrome

cy•to•cid•al

cy•to•di•ag•no•sis, *n., pl.* -ses.

cy•to•dif•fer•en•ti•a•tion

cy•to•ge•net•oic

cy•to•ge•net•oi•cal

cy•to•ge•net•oi•cal•ly

cy•to•ge•net•oi•cist

cy•to•ge•net•oics

cy•to•kine

cy•to•ki•ne•sis

cy•to•ki•net•oic

cy•to•ki•nin

cy•to•log•oic

cy•to•log•oi•cal

cy•to•log•oi•cal•ly

cy•tol•o•o•gist

cy•tol•o•o•gy

cy•to•lymph

cy•tol•y•sin

cy•tol•y•sis

cy•to•lyt•oic

cy•to•me•gal•oic

cy•to•meg•a•lo•vi•rus, *n., pl.* -rus•es.

cy•to•meg•a•oly or cy•to•me•ga•li•a

Cy•to•mel *Trademark.*

cy•to•mem•brane

cy•tom•e•ter

cy•to•mor•pho•log•oi•cal

cy•to•mor•phol•o•o•gy

cy•ton

cy•to•path•oic

cy•to•path•o•gen•oic

cy•to•path•o•ge•nic•oi•ty, *n. pl.* -ties.

cy•to•pa•thol•o•o•gy

cy•to•pe•ni•a

cy•to•phag•oic

cy•toph•o•a•gous

cy•toph•a•ogy

cy•to•phil

cy•to•phil•oic

cy•to•pho•tom•e•ter

cy•to•pho•to•met•ric

cy•to•pho•to•met•ri•cal

cy•to•pho•to•met•ri•cal•ly

cy•to•pho•tom•e•otry

cy•to•plasm

cy•to•plas•mic

cy•to•plas•mi•cal•ly

cy•to•plast

cy•to•plas•tic

cy•to•py•ge
cy•tor•rhyc•tes, *n., pl.*
  cy•tor•rhyc•tes.
cy•to•ryc•tes
Cy•to•sar-U *Trademark.*
cy•to•sine
cytosine ar∘a•bin∘o•side
cy•to•skel•e∘tal
cy•to•skel•e∘ton
cy•to•sol
cy•to•sol∘ic
cy•to•some
cy•to•stat∘ic
cy•to•stat∘i•cal∘ly

cy•to•tax•on•o∘my, *n., pl.*
  -mies.
Cy•to•tec *Trademark.*
cy∘to•tech
cy•to•tech•nol∘o∘gist
cy•to•tech•nol∘o∘gy
cy•to•tox∘ic
cytotoxic T cell
cy•to•tox•ic∘i∘ty
cy•to•tox∘in
cy•to•troph∘o•blast
cy•to•trop∘ic
cy•tot•ro•pism
Cy•to•vene *Trademark.*
cy•to•vi•rin
Cy•tox∘an *Trademark.*

D

D and C
da•boi∘a
dac∘ry•ad•e•ni•tis
dac∘ry•a•gogue
dac∘ry∘o•ad•e∘nal•gia
dac∘ry∘o•ad•e∘ni•tis
dac∘ry∘o•blen•nor•rhe∘a
dac∘ry∘o•cyst
dac∘ry∘o•cys•tec•to∘my,
  n., pl. -mies.
dac∘ry∘o•cys•ti•tis
dac∘ry∘o•cys•to•blen•nor•
  re∘a
dac∘ry∘o•cys•to•cele
dac∘ry∘o•cys•to•rhi•nos•
  to∘my, *n., pl.* -mies.
dac∘ry∘o•cys•to•tome
dac∘ry∘o•cys•to•tot∘o∘my, *n.,*
  pl. -mies.
dac∘ry∘o•lith
dac∘ry∘o•lith∘i•a•sis
dac∘ry•o∘ma, *n., pl.* -mas,
  -ma∘ta.
dac∘ry•on, *n., pl.* dac∘ry∘a.

dac∘ry•ops
dac∘ry∘or•rhe∘a
dac∘ry∘o•so•le•ni•tis
dac∘ry∘o•ste•no•sis, *n., pl.*
  -ses.
dac∘ry∘o•syr•inx, *n., pl.* -sy•
  rin•ges, -syr•inx∘es.
dac•tyl
dac•tyl•ion
dac•ty•li•tis
dactylitis syph∘i•lit∘i∘ca
dac•ty•lo•gram
dac•ty•lo•graph
dac•ty•log•ra•pher
dac•ty•lo•graph∘ic
dac•ty•log•ra•phy, *n., pl.*
  -phies.
dac•ty•lol∘o∘gy
dac•ty•lo•scop∘ic
dac•ty•los•co•pist
dac•ty•los•co•py, *n., pl.* -pies.
dac•ty•lo•sym•phy•sis
dac•ty•lus, *n., pl.* dac•ty∘li.
dah•lin

Da•la•lone D.P. *Trademark.*
Dal•gan *Trademark.*
Dal•ler°gy *Trademark.*
Dal•mane *Trademark.*
dal•ton•ic
dal•ton•ism
Dam○a•son-P *Trademark.*
dance
dan•de•li○on root
dan•druff
dan•druff○y
Dan○ex *Trademark.*
Dan○o•crine *Trademark.*
Dan•tri○um *Trademark.*
Da•nysz ef•fect
Danysz phe•nom•e○non
dap•pen dish
dappen glass
dap•sone
Dar○a•nide *Trademark.*
Dar○a•prim *Trademark.*
Dar•bid *Trademark.*
Dar○i•con *Trademark.*
dark a•dap•ta•tion
dark-a•dapt•ed
dark•field
D'Ar•son○val cur•rent
dar•tos
dar•trous
Dar•vo•cet-N *Trademark.*
Darvocet-N 100 *Trademark.*
Dar•von *Trademark.*
Darvon-N *Trademark.*
Das○y•proc○ta
das○y•proc•tid
das○y•proc•tine
Das○y•pus
Da•tril *Trademark.*
da•tu○ra
da•tu○ric
dauer•schlaf

daugh•ter
dau•no•my•cin
day blind•ness
Day•a•lets *Trademark.*
Day•pro
de•a•cid○i•fi•ca•tion
de•a•cid•i•fy, *v.,* -fied, -fy•
　ing.
dead leg
dead space
dead○ly night•shade
deaf-mute
deaf-mut•ism
de•af•fer•en•ta•tion
deaf•ness
de•al•co•hol○i•za•tion
De•a•pril-ST *Trademark.*
de•ar•te•ri•al○i•za•tion
death
death ben○e•fit
death cer•tif○i•cate
death in•stinct
death rat•tle
death wish
de•bil○i•tant
de•bil○i○ty, *n., pl.* -ties.
de•bride, *v.,* -brid○ed, -brid•
　ing.
de•bride•ment
Deb•ri•san *Trademark.*
Deb•rox *Trademark.*
de•bulk
Dec○a-Du○rab○o•lin *Trade-*
　mark.
Dec○a•derm *Trademark.*
Dec○a•dron *Trademark.*
de•cal•ci•fi•ca•tion
de•cal•ci•fi○er
de•cal•ci•fy, *v.,* -fied, -fy•ing.
de•cal•vant
de•ca•me•tho•ni○um

de•cap•i•tate, v., -tat○ed,
  -tat•ing.
de•cap○i•ta•tion
de•cap○i•ta•tor
Dec○a•pryn Trademark.
de•cap•su•late, v., -lat○ed,
  -lat•ing.
de•cap•su•la•tion
de•car•bon○i•za•tion
de•car•bon•ize, v., -ized, -iz•
  ing.
de•car•box○y•lase
de•car•box○y•late
de•car•box○y•la•tion
Dec○a•spray Trademark.
de•cay
de•cer○e•brate, v.t., -brat○ed,
  -brat•ing.
de•cer○e•bra•tion
de•chlo•ri•da•tion
de•chlor○i•nate, v., -nat○ed,
  -nat•ing.
de•chlo•ri•na•tion
de•chlo•ru•ra•tion
De•cho•lin Trademark.
dec○i•bel
de•cid○u○a, n., pl. -u○as, -u•
  ae.
de•cid•u○al
de•cid•u•ate
de•cid•u•a•tion
de•cid•u•i•tis
de•cid•u○o○ma, n. pl. -mas,
  -ma○ta.
de•cid•u○o○sis, n., pl. -ses.
de•cid•u•ous
de•cip•a○ra, n., pl. -as, -ae.
dec•li•na•tion
de•clive
Dec•lo•my•cin Trademark.
de•coct
de•coc•tion

de•coc•tum, n., pl. -ta.
de•col•late, v., -lat○ed, -lat•
  ing.
de•col•la•tion
de•col•or○a•tion
de•col•or○i•za•tion
de•com•pen•sate, v., -sat○ed,
  -sat•ing.
de•com•pen•sa•tion
de•com•pose, v., -posed,
  -pos•ing.
de•com•po•si•tion
de•com•press
de•com•pres•sion
decompression cham•ber
decompression sick•ness
de•com•pres•sive
De•con○a•mine SR Trademark.
de•con•di•tion
de•con•gest
de•con•ges•tant
de•con•ges•tion
de•con•ges•tive
De•con•sal Trademark.
de•con•tam○i•nate, v.,
  -nat○ed, -nat•ing.
de•con•tam○i•na•tion
de•cor•ti•cate, v., -cat○ed,
  -cat•ing.
de•cor•ti•ca•tion
de•cor•ti•ca•tor
de•cu•ba•tion
de•cu•bi•tal
de•cu•bi•tus, n., pl. -ti.
decubitus ul○cer
de•cur•rent
de•cus•sate
de•cus•sa•tion
de•den•ti•tion
de•dif•fer•en•ti•ate, v.,
  -at○ed, -at•ing.
de•dif•fer•en•ti•a•tion

deep ve•nous throm•bo•sis

deer•fly

de•fat, *v.*, de•fat•ted, de•fat•ting.

def•e○cate, *v.*, -cat○ed, -cat•ing.

def•e○ca•tion

de•fect

de•fem○i•na•tion

de•fense

defense mech•an•ism

de•fen•sive

de•fen•sive•ly

de•fen•sive•ness

def•er•ens

def•er•ent

def•er•en•tec•to•my, *n., pl.* -mies.

def•er•en•tial

def•er•en•ti•tis

de•fer•ves•cence

de•fer•ves•cent

de•fi•bril•late, *v.*, -lat○ed, -lat•ing.

de•fi•bril•la•tion

de•fi•bril•la•tive

de•fi•bril•la•tor

de•fi•bril•la•to○ry

de•fi•bri•nate, *v.*, -nat○ed, -nat•ing.

de•fi•bri•na•tion

de•fi•cien○cy, *n., pl.* -cies.

deficiency dis•ease

de•fi•cient

de•fin○i•tive ther○a○py

de•flec•tion

de•flo•ra•tion

de•flo•res•cence

de•flu•vi○um

defluvium cap•il•lo•rum

defluvium un•gui○um

de•flux•ion

de•for•ma•tion

de•formed

de•form○i○ty, *n., pl.* -ties.

de•gan•gli•o•nate

de•gen•er○a○cy, *n., pl.* -cies.

de•gen•er•ate, *n., v.*, -at○ed, -at•ing.

de•gen•er○a•tion

de•gen•er○a•tive

degenerative joint dis•ease

de•glov•ing

de•glu•ti•tion

de•glu•ti•tious

deg•ra•da•tion

deg•ra•da•tion○al

deg•ra•da•tive

de•gran•u•la•tion

de•gus•ta•tion

de•his•cence

de•hu•mid○i•fi•ca•tion

de•hu•mid○i•fi○er

de•hu•mid•i○fy, *v.*, -fied, -fy•ing.

de•hy•dra•ce•tic

de•hy•drant

de•hy•drase

de•hy•dra•tase

de•hy•drate, *v.*, -drat○ed, -drat•ing.

de•hy•dra•tion

de•hy•dra•tor

de○hy○dro•a•ce•tic

de○hy○dro•as•cor•bic

de○hy○dro•chlo•ri•nase

de○hy○dro•chlo•ri•nate

de○hy○dro•chlo•ri•na•tion

de○hy○dro•cho•late

de○hy○dro•cho•les•ter•ol

de○hy○dro•chol○ic

de○hy○dro•cor•ti•cos•ter•one

de•hy•dro•epi•an•dros•ter•one

de•hy•dro•gen•ase

de•hy•drog•e•na•tion

de•hy•dro•gen•ize, v., -ized, -iz•ing.

de•hy•dro•iso•an•dros•ter•one

de•hyp•no•tize, v., -tized, -tiz•ing.

Dei•ters' cell

Deiters' nu•cle•ous

de•ja vu

deja vue

de•jec•ta

de•jec•tion

de•lac•ta•tion

De•la•lu•tin *Trademark.*

de•lam•i•na•tion

Del•a•tes•tryl *Trademark.*

de•layed hy•per•sen•si•tiv•i•ty

delayed mus•cle sore•ness

de•lead

Del•es•tro•gen *Trademark.*

del•e•te•ri•ous

de•le•tion

Del•fen *Trademark.*

de•lim•i•ta•tion

de•lin•quen•cy, n., pl. -cies.

de•lin•quent

del•i•quesce, v., -quesced, -quesc•ing.

del•i•ques•cence

del•i•ques•cent

de•liq•ui•um an•i•mi

de•lir•i•ant

de•lir•i•fa•cient

de•lir•i•ous

de•lir•i•ous•ly

de•lir•i•ous•ness

de•lir•i•um, n., pl. -ums, -lir•i•a.

delirium cor•dis

delirium gran•di•o•sum

delirium mite

delirium mus•si•tans

delirium tre•mens

del•i•tes•cence, n., pl. -scen•ces.

del•i•tes•cen•cy

de•liv•er

de•liv•er•y, n., pl. -ies.

del•le

del•o•mor•phic

del•o•mor•phous

de•louse, v., -loused, -lous•ing.

del•phi•nine

Del•ta-Cor•tef *Trademark.*

delta hep•a•ti•tis

delta rhythm

delta vi•rus

delta wave

Del•ta•lin *Trademark.*

Del•ta•sone *Trademark.*

del•toid

del•toi•de•ous, n., pl. -de•i.

delts

de•lu•sion

de•lu•sion•al or de•lu•sion•ar•y

de•mas•cu•lin•i•za•tion

de•mas•cu•li•nize, v., -nized, -niz•ing.

Dem•a•zin *Trademark.*

dem•e•car•i•um

de•ment•ed

de•men•tia

dementia par•a•lyt•i•ca

dementia prae•cox

dementia pu•gi•lis•ti•ca

de•men•tial

Dem•e•rol *Trademark.*
De•mi-Re•gro•ton *Trademark.*
dem•oi•lune
demilune of Gia•nuz•zi
demilune of Hei•den•hain
de•min•er•al•oi•za•tion
dem•oi•pen•ni•form
Dem•o•dex fol•lic•u•lo•rum
de•mog•ra•phy, *n., pl.* -phies.
de•mo•ni•ac
de•mo•ni•a•cal
de•mor•phi•ni•za•tion
Dem•ser *Trademark.*
de•mul•cent
Dem•ou•len *Trademark.*
Demulen 1/35 *Trademark.*
de•my•oe•li•nate, *v.,* -nat•ed,
 -nat•ing.
de•my•e•oli•na•tion
de•my•e•olin•oi•za•tion
de•nar•co•tize, *v.,* -tized, -tiz•
 ing.
de•na•tur•ant
de•na•tur•oa•tion
de•na•ture, *v.,* -tured, -tur•
 ing.
den•dri•form
den•drite
den•drit•ic
den•droid
den•dron, *n., pl.* -drons, -dra.
de•ner•vate, *v.,* -vat•ed, -vat•
 ing.
de•ner•va•tion
den•gue
de•ni•al
den•oi•da•tion
Den•o•rex *Trademark.*
dens, *n., pl.* den•tes.
dens e•pis•tro•phe•i
dens in•den•te
dens se•ro•ti•nus

den•sim•e•ter
den•si•tom•e•ter
den•si•tom•e•try
den•tal
dental car•ies
dental floss
dental hy•gien•ist
dental pulp
dental tech•ni•cian
den•tal•gia
den•tal•oi•ty
den•tal•oly
den•tate
den•tat•ed
den•ta•tion
den•tia prae•cox
dentia tar•oda
den•ti•cle
den•tic•ou•late
den•tic•ou•lat•ed
den•ti•form
den•ti•frice
den•tig•er•ous
den•ti•la•bi•al
den•ti•lin•gual
den•tin or den•tine
den•tin•al
den•ti•no•gen•e•sis, *n., pl.*
 -e•ses.
den•ti•noid
den•ti•no•ma, *n., pl.* -mas,
 -ma•ta.
den•tip•oa•rous
den•tist
den•tist•ory
den•ti•tion
den•to•al•ve•o•lar
den•toid
den•tu•lous
den•ture
de•nu•cle•at•ed
de•nu•da•tion

de•nude, *v.*, -nud○ed, -nud•
ing.
de•ob•stru•ent
de•on•tol○o•gy
de•or•sum•duc•tion
de•or•sum•ver•gence
de•os•si•fi•ca•tion
de•ox○i•da•tion
de•ox○i•di•za•tion
de•ox○i•dize, *v.*, -dized, -diz•
ing.
de○ox○y•cho○late
de○ox○y•chol○ic
de○ox○y•cor•ti•cos•ter•one
de○ox○y•cor•tone
de○ox○y•gen•ate, *v.*, -nat○ed,
-nat•ing.
de○ox○y•ge•na•tion
de○ox○y•ri•bo•nu•cle•ase
de○ox○y•ri•bo•nu•cle○ic
deoxyribonucleic ac○id
de•ox○y•ri•bo•nu•cle•
o○pro•tein
de○ox○y•ri•bo•nu•cle•o•side
de○ox○y•ri•bo•nu•cle•o•tide
de○ox○y•ri•bose
Dep○a•kene *Trademark.*
Dep○a•kote *Trademark.*
de•pan•cre○a•tize, *v.*, -tized,
-tiz•ing.
De○pen *Trademark.*
de•pend•ence
de•per•son•al○i•za•tion
depersonalization dis•or•der
de•per•son•al•ize, *v.*, -ized,
-iz•ing.
de•phos•pho•ryl○a•tion
de•pig•men•ta•tion
dep○i•late
dep○i•la•tion
de•pil○a•to○ry, *adj.*, *n.*, *pl.*
-ries.

de•plu•ma•tion
Dep○o-Es•tra•di○ol *Trademark.*
Depo-Med•rol *Trademark.*
Depo-Pro•ve○ra *Trademark.*
Depo-Tes•tos•ter•one *Trademark.*
de•po•lar○i•za•tion
de•po•lar•ize, *v.*, -ized, -iz•
ing.
de•pol○y•mer•ase
Dep○o•nit NTG *Trademark.*
de•pres•sant
de•pressed
de•pres•sing
de•pres•sion
de•pres•sive
de•pres•sive○ly
de•pres•sive•ness
de•pres•sor
dep•ri•va•tion
Dep•rol *Trademark.*
depth per•cep•tion
depth psy•chol○o•gy
de•pu•li•za•tion
de•pu•rant
depu•u•rate, *v.*, -rat○ed, -rat•
ing.
de•pu•ra•tion
de•re•al○i•za•tion
de•re•ism
de•re•is•tic
der•en•ceph○a•lus, *n.*, *pl.* -li.
der•en•ceph○a•ly, *n.*, *pl.* -lies.
de•re•press
de•re•pres•sion
Der○i•fil *Trademark.*
derm○a•bra•sion
Der•ma•cen•tor
Dermacentor an•der•so○ni
Dermacentor var•i•a•bil○is
Der•ma•ide *Trademark.*

der•mal
der•ma•my•i•a•sis
Der•ma•nys•sus
Dermanyssus a◦vi◦um
Dermanyssus gal•li•nae
der•ma•tal•gia
der•mat◦ic
der•ma•ti•tis
Der•ma•to•bi◦a
der◦mat◦o◦cel•lu◦li•tis
der◦mat◦o◦cha•la•sis, *n., pl.*
  -ses.
der◦mat◦o◦co•ni◦o•sis
der◦mat◦o◦cra•ni◦um, *n., pl.*
  -ums, -i◦a.
der◦mat◦o◦cyst
der◦mat◦o◦fi•bro◦ma, *n., pl.*
  -mas, -ma◦ta.
der◦mat◦o◦fi•bro•sar•
  co◦ma, *n., pl.* -mas, -ma◦ta.
der◦mat◦o◦glyph◦ic
der◦mat◦o◦glyph•ics
der◦mat◦o◦graph
der•ma•tog◦ra•phy, *n., pl.*
  -phies.
der◦mat◦o◦het•er◦o◦plas◦ty,
  n., pl. -ties.
der◦mat◦o◦his◦tol◦o◦gy
der•ma•toid
der◦mat◦o◦log◦i•cal or
  der◦ma•to•log◦ic
der◦ma•tol◦o◦gist
der◦ma•tol◦o◦gy
der◦ma•tol◦y•sis, *n., pl.* -ses.
der◦mat◦o◦meg◦a◦ly, *n., pl.*
  -lies.
der◦mat◦o◦mere
der•ma•tom◦ic or der•ma•
  to•mal
der◦mat◦o◦mu•co◦so•my◦o◦
  si•tis, *n., pl.* -si•tes, -sit◦i•
  des.

der◦mat◦o◦my•ces, *n., pl.*
  -ce•tes.
der◦mat◦o◦my•co•sis
der◦mat◦o◦my◦o◦ma, *n., pl.*
  -mas, -ma◦ta.
der◦mat◦o◦my◦o◦si•tis, *n.,*
  pl. -tis◦es, -sit◦i•des.
der◦mat◦o◦neu•ro•sis, *n., pl.*
  -ses.
der◦mat◦o◦path◦i◦a, *n., pl.*
  -ias.
der◦mat◦o◦path◦ic
der◦mat◦o◦pa•thol◦o◦gy
der•ma•top◦a•thy, *n., pl.*
  -thies.
der◦mat◦o◦phi•li•a•sis, *n., pl.*
  -ses.
der◦mat◦o◦phyte
der◦mat◦o◦phyt◦ic
der◦mat◦o◦phy•tid
der◦mat◦o◦phy•to•sis
der◦mat◦o◦plas•tic
der◦mat◦o◦plas◦ty, *n., pl.*
  -ties.
der◦mat◦o◦pol◦y•neu•ri•tis,
  n., pl. -tis◦es, -rit•i•des.
der◦mat◦or•rha•gia
der◦mat◦o◦scle•ro•sis
der•ma•tos•co◦py, *n., pl.*
  -pies.
der•ma•to•sis, *n., pl.* -to•ses.
dermatosis pap◦u•lo•sa•ni•
  gra
der◦mat◦o◦ther◦a◦py
der◦mat◦oth•la•sia
der◦mat◦o◦trop◦ic
der◦mat◦o◦zo◦on, *n., pl.*
  -zo◦a.
der◦mat◦o◦zo◦o◦no•sis
der•mic
der•mis
der◦mo•blast

der•mo•graph∘i∘a
dermographia al∘ba
dermographia ru∘bra
der•mog•ra•phism
der•mog•ra•phy, n., pl.
-phies.
der•moid
der•moi•dal
der•moid•ec•to∘my, n., pl.
-mies.
Der∘mo•late Trademark.
der∘mo•li•po∘ma, n., pl.
-mas, -ma∘ta.
der•mop∘a•thy, n., pl. -thies.
der∘mo•phle•bi•tis
Der∘mo•plast Trademark.
der∘mo•skel∘e•ton
der∘mo•ste•no•sis, n., pl.
-ses.
der∘mo•sto•sis, n., pl. -ses.
der∘mo•syph∘i∘lop∘a•thy
der∘mo•trop∘ic
de•ro•did∘y•mus
der•ren•ga•de∘ra
des•ce•me•ti•tis
des•ce•met∘o•cele
Des•ce•met's mem•brane
des•cend•ens cer•vi•cis
descendens hy•po•glos∘si
de•scend•ing co∘lon
des•cen•sus
Des∘e•nex Trademark.
de•sen•si•ti•za•tion
de•sen•si•tize, v., -tized, -tiz•
ing.
de•sen•si•tiz∘er
des•ert fe∘ver
de∘sex
de•sex∘u•al•ize, v., -ized, -iz•
ing.
Des•fer∘al Trademark.
des•ic•cant

des•ic•cate, v., -cat∘ed, -cat•
ing.
des•ic•ca•tion
des•ic•ca•tive
des•ic•ca•tor
des•ic•ca•to∘ry
de•sign•er drug
designer gene
des∘i•pra•mine
Des∘i•tin Trademark.
des•mo•cra•ni∘um, n., pl.
-ums, -a.
des•moid
des•moids
des•mo•lase
des•mo•pla•sia
des•mo•plas•tic
des•mo•some
des•mot∘o∘my, n., pl. -mies.
Des∘o•gen
Des∘o•ges•trel/Eth∘i•nyl Es•
tra•di∘ol
Des•Ow∘en Trademark.
des•ox∘y•cor•ti•cos•ter•one
Des•ox∘yn Trademark.
Des•pec Trademark.
des•qua•mate, v., -mat∘ed,
-mat•ing.
des•qua•ma•tio in•sen•
sib∘i•lis
desquamatio ne•o•na•to•rum
des•qua•ma•tion
des•qua•ma•tive
des•qua•ma•to∘ry
Des•quam-E Trademark.
Desquam-X Trademark.
de•stain
des•thi•o•bi•o•tin
des•tru∘do
Des∘y•rel Trademark.
de•tec•tion lim∘it
de•ter•gent

de•te•ri•o•rate, *v.*, -rat∘ed, -rat∘ing.
de•te•ri•o•ra•tion
de•ter•mi•nant
de•ter•mi•nate
de•ter•mi•na•tion
de•ter•mi•na•tive
de•ter•mine, *v.*, -mined, -min•ing.
de•ter•min•ism
de•ter•sive
de•tor•sion
de∘tox
de•tox∘i•cant
de•tox∘i•cate, *v.*, -cat∘ed, -cat∘ing.
de•tox∘i•ca•tion
de•tox∘i•ca•tor
de•tox∘i•fi•ca•tion or de•tox∘i•ca•tion
de•tox∘i•fi∘er
de•tox∘i•fy, *v.*, -fied, -fy•ing.
de•tri∘tal
de•tri∘tion
de•tri•tus, *n., pl.* de•tri•tus.
de•tru•sor
detrusor u∘ri•nae
detrusor ves∘i•cae
de•tu•ba•tion
de•tu•mes•cence
de•tu•mes•cent
deu•ter•o•a•nom•a•lous
deu•ter•o•a•nom∘a•ly, *n., pl.* -lies.
deu•ter•o•a•nope
deu•ter•o•a•no•pia
deu•ter•an•op∘ic
deu•te•ri∘um
deu•ter•on
deu•ter•op∘a•thy, *n., pl.* -thies.
deu•ter∘o•pro•te•ose

deu•ter•ot∘o∘oky, *n., pl.* -kies.
deu•ter∘o•tox∘in
deu•tom•er•ite
deu•to•plasm
deu•to•plas•mic
deu•to-plas∘mol∘y•sis
de•vas•cu•lar∘i•za•tion
de•vel∘op, *v.*, -oped, -op•ing.
de•vel•op•a•bil∘i•ty
de•vel•op•a∘ble
dev•il's grip, *n., pl.* dev•il's grips.
de•vi∘om•e∘ter
dev∘o∘lu•tion
dev∘o∘lu•tion•ar∘y
dev∘o∘lu•tion∘ist
dew•claw
dew•lap
dew•lapped
de•worm
dex∘a•meth∘a•sone
Dex•e∘drine *Trademark.*
dex•fen•flur∘a•mine
dex•ter
dex•trad
dex•tral
dex•tral∘i∘ty
dex•tral∘ly
dex•tran
dex•tra•nase
dex•trase
dex•trau•ral
dex•trin or dex•trine
dex•tri•no•gen∘ic
dex•tri•nu∘ri∘a
dex∘tro•am•phet∘a•mine
dex∘tro•car•di∘a
dex∘tro•car•di∘al
dex∘tro•car•di•o•gram
dex∘tro•ce•re•bral
dex•troc•u•lar
dex•troc•u•lar∘i∘ty

dex∘tro•duc•tion
dex∘tro•glu•cose
dex∘tro•man∘u•al
dex•trop•e∘dal
dex∘tro•po•si•tion
dex∘tro•ro•ta∘ry
dex∘tro•ro•ta•tion
dex∘tro•ro•ta•to∘ry or
  dex∘tro•ro•ta∘ry
dex•trose
dex∘tro•sin•is•tral
dex∘tro•su∘ri∘a
dex∘tro•tor•sion
dex∘tro•ver•sion
Di-Gel *Trademark.*
Di∘a•Be∘ta *Trademark.*
di∘a•be•tes
diabetes de•cip•i•ens
diabetes in•sip∘i•dus
diabetes mel•li•tus
di∘a•bet∘ic
diabetic co∘ma
diabetic ret∘i•nop∘a•thy
di∘a•be•to•gen∘ic
Di∘ab∘i•nese *Trademark.*
di•a•ce•tyl•mor•phine
di∘a•cla•si∘a, *n., pl.* -as.
di∘a•cla•sis, *n., pl.* -ses.
di∘a•coele
diad
di∘a•der•mal
di∘a•der•mat∘ic
di∘a•der•mic
di•ad∘ic
di•ad∘o∘cho•ki•ne•sia
di•ad∘o•cho•ki•ne•sis, *n., pl.*
  -ses.
di•ad∘o•cho•ki•net∘ic
di•ad∘o•ko•ki•ne•sia
di•ag•nos•a•ble
di•ag•nose, *v.,* -nosed, -nos•
  ing.

di•ag•nose•a•ble
di•ag•no•sis, *n., pl.* -ses.
diagnosis by ex•clu•sion
di•ag•nos•tic
diagnostic re•lat•ed groups
di•ag•nos•ti•cal∘ly
di•ag•nos•ti•cian
di•ag•nos•tics
di∘a•ki•ne•sis, *n., pl.* -ses.
Di∘a•lose *Trademark.*
di∘a•ly•sance
di∘a•ly•sate
di•al∘y•sis, *n., pl.* -ses.
di∘a•lyt∘ic
di∘a•lyt∘i•cal∘ly
di∘a•lyz•a∘bil∘i•ty
di∘a•lyz•a∘ble
di∘a•ly•zate
di∘a•ly•za•tion
di∘a•lyze, *v.,* -lyzed, -lyz∘ing.
di∘a•lyz∘er or di•al∘y•za•tor
Di∘a•mox *Trademark.*
di∘a•pe•de•sis
di∘a•pe•det∘ic
di•a•per
di∘a•pha•nom•e∘ter
di∘a•phan∘o•met•ric
di∘a•phan∘o•scope
di•aph∘a•nos•co∘py, *n., pl.*
  -pies.
di•aph∘o•rase
di∘a•pho•re•sis
di∘a•pho•ret∘ic
di∘a•phragm
di∘a•phrag•ma pel•vis
diaphragma sel•lae
diaphragma u∘ro•gen∘i•ta∘le
di∘a•phrag•mat∘ic
di∘a•phys∘e∘al
di•aph∘y•sec•to∘my, *n., pl.*
  -mies.
di∘a•phys∘i∘al

di•aph•y•sis, *n., pl.* -ses.
Di•a•pid *Trademark.*
di•a•plas•tic
di•a•poph•y•sis, *n., pl.* -ses.
di•ar•rhe•a
di•ar•rhe•al
di•ar•rhe•ic
di•ar•rhet•ic
di•ar•rhoe•a
di•ar•rhoe•al
di•ar•rhoe•ic
di•ar•thric
di•ar•thro•di•al
di•ar•thro•sis, *n., pl.* -ses.
di•ar•tic•u•lar
di•as•chi•sis, *n., pl.* -ses.
di•a•scope
di•a•scop•ic
di•as•co•py, *n., pl.* -pies.
di•a•stal•sis
di•a•stase
di•as•ta•sis, *n., pl.* -ses.
di•a•stat•ic or di•a•sta•sic
di•a•steo•ma, *n., pl.* -ma•ta.
di•a•ste•mat•ic
di•a•ste•mat•o•o•my•e•li•a
di•as•to•le
di•as•tol•ic
di•a•tax•i•a
di•a•ther•mic
di•a•ther•mo•co•ag•oulation
di•a•ther•my or di•a•ther•mi•a
di•ath•e•o•sis, *n., pl.* -ses.
di•a•thet•ic
di•a•ax•on
di•a•ax•one
di•a•ax•on•ic
di•a•az•e•opam
di•a•zine
Di•ben•zy•line *Trademark.*
Di•bo•thri•o•ceph•o•a•lus

di•bu•caine
Di•cal-D *Trademark.*
di•cen•tric
di•ceph•o•a•lus, *n., pl.* -li.
di•chlo•ra•mine
di•chlor•eth•o•yl
di•chlor•hy•drin
di•chlo•ro•ben•zene
di•chlo•ro•di•eth•o•yl sul•fide
di•chlo•ro•di•fluor•o•o•meth•ane
di•chlo•ro•eth•o•yl
di•chlo•ro•hy•drin
di•chlo•ro•phen•ar•sine
di•chlo•ro•phen•ox•y•a•ce•tic
di•cho•gam•ic
di•chog•o•a•mous
di•chog•o•a•my, *n., pl.* -mies.
di•cho•ri•al
di•cho•ri•on•o•ic
di•chot•ic
di•chot•i•cal•o•ly
di•chot•o•o•mous rea•son•ing
di•chro•ic
di•chro•ism
di•chro•it•o•ic
di•chro•mat
di•chro•mate
di•chro•mat•o•ic
di•chro•ma•tip•si•a
di•chro•ma•tism
di•chro•mic
di•chro•mo•phil
Dick test
di•cli•dot•o•o•my, *n., pl.* -mies.
Di•clof•o•e•nac
di•clo•fe•nac so•di•um
di•co•phane
di•cou•ma•rin
Di•cro•coe•li•um
Dicrocoelium den•drit•o•i•cum

di•cro•tal
di•crot•ic
di•cro•tism
di•cro•tous
Dic•ty•o•cau•lus
di•cu•ma•rol
Di•cu•rin *Trademark.*
Di•cy•clo•mine
di•dac•tyl
di•dac•ty•le
di•dac•tyl•ism
di•dac•tyl•ous
di•del•phic
Di•del•phis
Di•drex *Trademark.*
Di•dro•nel *Trademark.*
did•y•mi•tis
di•dym•i•um
di•el
di•el•drin
di•en•ce•phal•ic
di•en•ceph•a•lon, *n., pl.*
-lons, -ceph•a•la.
die•ner
die•nes•trol
die•noes•trol
Di•en•ta•moe•ba
Dientamoeba frag•i•lis
di•er•e•o•sis, *n., pl.* -ses.
di•es•ter
di•es•trous
di•es•tru•al
di•es•trum
di•es•trus
di•et
di•e•tar•i•ly
di•e•tar•y, *adj., n., pl.* -tar•
ies.
di•et•er
di•e•tet•ic
di•e•tet•i•cal•ly
di•e•tet•ics

di•eth•yl•am•ide
di•eth•yl•a•mine
di•eth•yl•car•bam•a•zine
di•eth•o•y•lene
di•eth•yl•stil•bes•trol
diethylstilbestrol di•pro•pi•o•
nate
di•e•ti•tian or di•e•ti•cian
Dietl's cri•sis
di•et•o•o•ther•a•py
dif•fer•en•tial
differential as•so•ci•a•tion
differential di•agn•o•sis
dif•fer•en•tial•ly
dif•fer•en•ti•ate, *v.,* -at•ed,
-at•ing.
dif•fer•en•ti•a•tion
dif•flu•ence
dif•flu•ent
dif•frac•tion
dif•fu•sate
dif•fuse, *v.,* -fused, -fus•ing.
dif•fu•si•ble
dif•fu•sion
Dif•lu•can *Trademark.*
dif•lu•ence
di•ga•met•ic
di•gas•tric
Di•ge•ne•a
di•ge•ne•ous
di•gen•e•sis, *n., pl.* -e•ses.
di•ge•net•ic
di•gest
di•gest•ant
di•gest•ed•ly
di•gest•ed•ness
di•gest•er
di•gest•i•bil•i•ty
di•gest•i•ble
di•gest•i•bly
di•ges•tion
di•ges•tion•al

di•ges•tive
digestive gland
digestive sys•tem
di•ges•tive•ly
di•ges•tive•ness
Di•ges•tol *Trademark.*
Dig•oi•bind *Trademark.*
dig•oi•lan•oid
dig•oi•lan•ide
dig•it
dig•it•al
dig•oi•tal•gia par•es•
　thet•oi•ca
dig•oi•tal•oin
dig•oi•tal•ois
digitalis pur•pu•re•a
dig•oi•tal•oi•za•tion
dig•oi•tal•ize, *v.,* -ized, -iz•ing.
dig•it•al•oly
dig•oi•tal•ose
dig•oi•tate
dig•oi•tat•ed
dig•oi•tate•ly
dig•oi•ta•tion
dig•oi•ti ma•nus
digiti pe•dis
dig•oi•ti•grade
dig•oi•to•nin
dig•oi•tox•oi•gen•in
dig•oi•tox•in
dig•oi•tox•ose
dig•its
di•gi•tus, *n., pl.* -ti.
di•glos•si•a
dig•ox•in
di•hy•brid
di•hy•brid•ism
di•hy•drate
di•hy•dro•er•go•cor•nine
di•hy•dro•er•got•am•ine
di•hy•dro•mor•phi•none
di•hy•dro•strep•to•my•cin

di•hy•dro•ta•chys•ter•ol
di•hy•drox•y•a•lu•mi•num
di•hy•drox•y•phen•yl•al•oa•
　nine
di•i•o•do•hy•drox•y•quin
di•i•o•do•hy•drox•y•
　quin•o•o•line
di•i•so•pro•pyl•fluor•o•
　phos•phate
di•lac•er•a•tion
Dil•a•cor XR
Di•lan•tin *Trademark.*
Dilantin In•fa•tabs *Trademark.*
Dilantin Kap•seals *Trademark.*
Dilantin-30 *Trademark.*
Dilantin-SR *Trademark.*
dil•oa•ta•tion
dil•oa•ta•tion•al
dil•oa•ta•tor
dil•lat•ed car•di•o•o•my•op•a•
　thy
dil•oa•ta•tion or di•la•tion
di•la•tor
dilator ir•oi•dis
dilator na•ris
dilator pu•pil•lae
dilator tu•bae
Di•lau•did *Trademark.*
Dilaudid H-P *Trademark.*
Di•lor *Trademark.*
dil•ti•oa•zem
Di•ma•col *Trademark.*
di•men•hy•dri•nate
Di•me•tane *Trademark.*
Dimetane-DC *Trademark.*
Dimetane-DX *Trademark.*
Di•me•tapp *Trademark.*
Dimetapp-DM *Trademark.*
di•meth•yl phthal•ate
dimethyl sulf•ox•ide
di•meth•yl•ni•tros•a•mine

di•meth•yl•sul•fox•ide
di•meth•yl•tryp•ta•mine
di•meth•yl•tu•bo•cu•ra•rine
di•me•tri•a
di•mor•phic
di•mor•phism
di•mor•phous
di•ni•tro•or•thoc•re•sol
di•ni•tr•ophe•nol
di•nu•cle•o•tide
Di•oc•to•phy•ma
Di•oc•to•phyme
di•o•es•trous
di•o•es•tru•al
di•o•es•trum
di•o•es•trus
Di•on•o•sil *Trademark.*
di•op•ter
di•op•tom•e•ter
di•op•tric
di•op•tri•cal•oly
di•op•trics
di•op•try, *n., pl.* -tries.
di•ose
di•os•ge•nin
di•ot•ic
di•ov•ou•lar
di•ox•ane
di•ox•ide
di•ox•in
di•pen•tene
di•pep•ti•dase
di•pep•tide
Di•pet•a•lo•ne•ma
di•phen•an
di•phen•hy•dra•mine
di•phen•yl•a•mine
di•phen•yl•chlor•ar•sine
di•phen•yl•chlo•ro•ar•sine
di•phen•yl•hy•dan•to•in
di•phos•gene

di•phos•phate
di•phos•pho•gly•ce•ric
di•phos•pho•py•ri•dine nu•cle•o•tide
di•phos•pho•thi•a•min
di•phos•pho•thi•a•mine
diph•the•ri•a
diph•the•ri•al
diph•the•ri•an
diph•the•ri•a•phor
diph•ther•oic
diph•the•rin
diph•the•rit•oic
diph•the•ri•tis
diph•the•roid
diph•the•ro•tox•in
di•phyl•lo•both•ri•a•sis
Di•phyl•lo•both•ri•i•dae
Di•phyl•lo•both•ri•ºum
di•phy•o•dont
dip•la•cu•sis, *n., pl.* -ses.
di•ple•gia
di•ple•gic
dip•lo•al•bu•mi•nu•ri•a
dip•lo•ba•cil•lus, *n., pl.* -li.
dip•lo•blas•tic
dip•lo•car•di•a
dip•lo•coc•cal
dip•lo•coc•cic
dip•lo•coc•coid
dip•lo•coc•cus, *n., pl.* -coc•ci.
dip•lo•co•ri•a
dip•lo•e
dip•lo•etic
dip•lo•gen•e•sis, *pl.* -e•ses.
dip•lo•ic
dip•loid
dip•loi•dic
dip•loi•dy
dip•lo•mate
dip•lo•neu•ral
dip•lont

Disipal

di•plo•pi•a
di•plop•ic
dip•lo•sis, *n., pl.* -ses.
dip○lo•some
dip○lo•tene
di•pole
di•po○tas•si○um
Dip•ri•van *Trademark.*
Dip•ro•lene *Trademark.*
Dip•ro•sone *Trademark.*
dip•ro•so•pus
diprosopus dir•rhi•nus
diprosopus par○a•sit○i•cus
dip•so•ma•ni○a
dip•so•ma•ni○ac
dip•so•ma•ni•a•cal
Dip•ter○yx
di•pus
di•py•gus
dipygus par○a•sit○i•cus
dipygus tet•ra•pus
dipygus tri•pus
Di•py•lid○i○um
di•pyr•id○a•mole
Di•qui•nol *Trademark.*
di•rhin○ic
Di•ro•fi•lar○i○a
dis•a○bil○i○ty, *n., pl.* -ties.
dis•a○ble, *v.,* -bled, -bling.
dis•a○ble•ment
di•sac•char○i•dase
di•sac•cha•ride
dis•ag•gre•ga•tion
Dis•al•cid *Trademark.*
dis•ar•ti•cu•late, *v.,* -lat•ed,
 -lat•ing.
dis•ar•tic○u•la•tion
dis•as•sim○i•late, *v.,* -lat•ed,
 -lat•ing.
dis•as•sim○i•la•tion
dis•as•sim○i•la•tive
disc

dis•charge
dis•ci•form
dis•cis•sion
dis•co•blas•tic
dis•co•blas•tu○la, *n., pl.* -las,
 -lae.
dis•co•gas•tru○la, *n., pl.* -las,
 -lae.
dis•cog•ra•phy, *n., pl.* -phies.
dis•coid
dis•cop○a•thy, *n., pl.* -thies.
dis•co•pla•cen○ta, *n., pl.* -tas,
 -tae.
dis•co•pla•cen•tal
dis•cus, *n., pl.* dis•cus○es,
 dis○ci.
discus pro•lig○er○us
dis•cu•ti•ent
dis•ease
dis•eased
dis•e○qui•li•bri•um, *n., pl.*
 -ums, -i○a.
dis•func•tion
dis•gen○ic
dis•in•fect
dis•in•fect•ant
dis•in•fec•tion
dis•in•fest
dis•in•fest•ant
dis•in•fes•ta•tion
dis•in•hi•bi•tion
dis•in•sec•tion
dis•in•ser•tion
dis•in•te•grate, *v.,* -grat○ed,
 -grat•ing.
dis•in•te•gra•tion
dis•in•te•gra•tive
dis•in•tox○i•cate, *v.,* -cat-ed,
 -cat•ing.
dis•in•tox○i•ca•tion
dis•in•vag○i•na•tion
Dis○i•pal *Trademark.*

dis•joint○ed
disk
disk•like
dis•lo•cate, *v.*, -cat○ed, -cat•
  ing.
dis•lo•ca•tion
dis•mem•ber
dis•mem•ber•ment
di•so•di•um cro•mog•ly•cate
disodium e○dath○a•mil
disodium e○de•tate
Dis○o•nate *Trademark.*
Dis○o•phrol *Trademark.*
di•so•pyr○a•mide
dis•or•der
dis•or•gan○i•za•tion
dis•or•ga•nize, *v.*, -nized,
  -niz•ing.
dis•or•gan○ized
  schiz○o•phren○i○a
dis•o○ri•ent
dis•o○ri•en•ta•tion
dis•pen•sa○ry, *n., pl.* -ries.
dis•pen•sa•to○ry, *n., pl.* -ries.
dis•pense, *v.*, -pensed, -pens•
  ing.
dis•per○my, *n., pl.* -mies.
dis•per•sant
di•spi○rem
di•spi•reme
dis•place, *v.*, -placed, -plac•
  ing.
dis•place•ment
dis•sect
dis•sec•tion
dis•sec•tor
dis•sem○i•nat○ed
dis•sep○i•ment
dis•sep○i•men•tal
dis•sim○i•late, *v.*, -lat○ed,
  -lat•ing.
dis•sim○i•la•tion

dis•sim○u•late, *v.*, -lat○ed,
  -lat•ing.
dis•sim○u•la•tion
dis•so•ci•ant
dis•so•ci•ate, *v.*, -at○ed, -at•
  ing.
dis•so•ci•a•tion
dis•so•ci•a•tive
dissociative dis•or•der
dissociative i○den•ti○ty dis•
  or•der
dis•so•lu•tion
dis•solve, *v.*, -solved, -solv•
  ing.
dis•so•nance
dis•tad
dis•tal
dis•tem•per
dis•tem•per○oid
dis•ten•si•bil○i○ty, *n., pl.*
  -ties.
dis•ten•si•ble
dis•ten•tion or dis•ten•sion
dis•tich○i○a
dis•til•late
dis•til•la•tion
dis•to•clu•sion
Dis•to○ma
dis•to•ma•to•sis, *n., pl.* -ses.
dis•to•mi•a•sis, *n., pl.* -ses.
Dis•to•mum
dis•to•oc○clu•sal
dis•tor•tion
dis•trac•ti•bil○i○ty
dis•trac•tion
dis•trac•tive
dis•trib•ute, *v.*, -ut○ed, -ut•
  ing.
dis•tri•bu•tion
dis•turb
dis•turb•ance
dis•turbed

di•sul•fate
di•sul•fide
di•sul•fi•ram
dith•ra•nol
Di•tro•pan *Trademark.*
Di•u•car•din *Trademark.*
Di•u•lo *Trademark.*
Di•u•pres *Trademark.*
di•u•re•sis
di•u•ret•ic
Di•u•ril *Trademark.*
Di•u•ten•sen-R *Trademark.*
di•va•ga•tion
di•va•lent
Di•val•pro•ex
di•var•i•ca•tion
di•ver•gence
di•ver•gent
di•ver•tic•u•lar
di•ver•tic•u•lec•to•my, *n., pl.*
-mies.
di•ver•tic•u•li•tis
di•ver•tic•u•lo•sis
di•ver•tic•u•lum, *n., pl.*
-tic•u•la.
diverticulum il•e•i
div•i-div•i, *n., pl.* -div•i-div•is.
di•vi•sion
di•vulse, *v.,* -vulsed, -vuls•ing.
di•vul•sion
di•vul•sor
di•zy•gos•i•ty
di•zy•got•ic *or* di•zy•gous
diz•zi•ness
diz•zy, *adj.,* -zi•er, -zi•est.
djen•kol•ic
DNAase
Dnase
Doan's Pills *Trademark.*
Do•bell's so•lu•tion
Dob•u•trex *Trademark.*
Do•ca *Trademark.*

doc•i•ma•si•a
do•ci•mas•tic
doc•i•ma•sy, *n., pl.* -sies.
doc•o•sa•hex•a•e•no•ic
ac•id
do•co•sa•no•ic
doc•tor
doc•trine
do•dec•a•no•ic
dog•ma•tist
dog•tooth
dol
Do•la•cet *Trademark.*
Do•lene *Trademark.*
dol•i•cho•ce•phal•ic
dol•i•cho•ceph•a•lism
dol•i•cho•ceph•a•lous
dol•i•cho•ceph•a•ly, *n., pl.*
-lies.
dol•i•cho•cra•ni•al
dol•i•cho•cra•ny, *n., pl.* -nies.
dol•i•cho•fa•cial
dol•i•cho•pel•lic
dol•i•cho•pro•sop•ic
dol•i•cho•u•ran•ic
Do•lo•bid *Trademark.*
Dol•o•phine *Trademark.*
do•lor
dolor cap•i•tis
dolor cox•ae
dolor va•gus
do•lo•rif•ic
do•lo•rim•e•try
Dome•bo•ro *Trademark.*
dom•i•nance
dom•i•nant
dom•i•na•tor
Don Juan•ism
Don•a•tus•sin *Trademark.*
do•nee
Don•na•gel *Trademark.*
Donnagel-PG *Trademark.*

don•nan e•qui•lib•ri•um
Don•na•tal *Trademark.*
Don•na•zyme *Trademark.*
do∘nor
do•nor•ship
Don∘o•van bod∘y
do∘pa
do•pa•mine
do•pa•mi•ner•gic
Do∘par *Trademark.*
dop•ing
Dop•pler ef•fect
Doppler shift
Do•pram *Trademark.*
Do∘ral *Trademark.*
do•ra•pho•bi∘a
Dor•col *Trademark.*
Do•ri•den *Trademark.*
dor•man∘cy
dor•mant
dor•nase
do•ro•ma•ni∘a
dor•sad
dor•sal
dorsal lip
dor•sal•gia
dor•sa•lis, *n., pl.* -les.
dorsalis pe∘dis
dor•sal∘ly
dor•si•duct
dor•si•flex
dor•si•flex•ion
dor•si•flex∘or
dor•si•lat•er•al
dor•si•lum•bar
dor•si•spi∘nal
dor•so•ceph∘a•lad
dor•so•lat•er•al
dor•so•lum•bar
dor•so•lum•ber
dor•so•ven•trad

dor•so•ven•tral
dor•so•ven•tral∘ly
dor•sum, *n., pl.* dor∘sa.
dorsum lin•guae
dorsum ma•nus
dorsum na∘si
dorsum pe∘dis
dorsum sel•lae
Do•ryx *Trademark.*
Dor•zol∘a•mide
dos•age
dose, *n., v.,* dosed, dos•ing.
dose•me•ter
dose-re•sponse curve
dos•im•e∘ter
dos∘i•met•ric
do•sim•e∘try
do∘sis cu•ra•ti∘va
dosis ef•fi•cax
dosis re•frac∘ta
dosis tol•er•a∘ta
dou•ble bind
double he∘lix
double vi•sion
double-blind
double-joint∘ed
dou•blet
douche, *n., v.,* douched, douch•ing.
douche bag
doug•la•si•tis
dou•rine
Do•ver's pow•der
dove•tail
Down
down∘er
Down's syn•drome
down•stream
Dox∘a•zo∘sin
Dox∘i•dan *Trademark.*
dox∘o•ru•bi•cin
Dox∘y•chel *Trademark.*

ductus deferens

Dox○y•cy•cline
Doxycycline Hy•clate
dox•yl○a•mine
drachm
drac•on•ti•a•sis, *n., pl.* -ses.
dra•cun•cu•li•a•sis
dra•cun•cu•lo•sis
Dra•cun•cu•lus
drag•ée
drag•on's blood
drain•age
Dram○a•mine *Trademark.*
drap•e○to•ma•ni○a
dras•tic
draw, *v.,* drew, drawn, draw•ing.
draw○a•ble
draw•sheet
dream•work
drench
drep○a•no•cyte
drep○a•no•cy•to•sis, *n., pl.*
-ses.
dress
Drin•ker res•pi•ra•tor
drip
Dris•dol *Trademark.*
Dris•tan *Trademark.*
Drith○o-Scalp *Trademark.*
Drith○o•creme *Trademark.*
Drix○o•ral *Trademark.*
Drize *Trademark.*
Drol•ban *Trademark.*
dro•mo•graph
dro•mo•ma•ni○a
dro•mo•trop○ic
dro•nab○i•nol
drop
drop•let
drop•per
drop•si•cal
drop•si•cal○ly

drop•sied
drop○sy
dros○er○a ro•tun•di•fo•li○a
dro•soph○i•la
drug, *n., v.,* drugged, drug•ging.
drug e○rup•tion
drug hol○i•day
drug•fast
drug•gist
drug•mak○er
drug•store
drum•head
drunk•ard
drunk○en
drunk•en○ly
drunk•en•ness
drunk•om•e○ter
druse, *n., pl.* dru•sen.
dry eye
dry-nurse, *v.,* -nursed, -nurs•ing.
Dry•sol *Trademark.*
d.t.'s or D.T.'s
Du Bois-Rey•mond's law
Du Bois-Reymond's prin•ci•ple
du•al•ism
Du•boi•sia
Du•chenne-Erb pa•ral○y•sis
duck•foot○ed
Du•crey's ba•cil•lus
duct
duc•tal
duc•til○i○ty, *n., pl.* -ties.
duct•less
ductless gland
duc•tule
duc•tus, *n., pl.* duc•tus.
ductus ar•te•ri○o•sis
ductus ar•te•ri○o•sus
ductus cho•led○o•chus
ductus def•er•ens

ductus ve•no•sus
Duf°fy an•ti•gen
Duffy fac•tor
dul•cam•a•ra
dul•ci•tol
Dul•co•lax *Trademark.*
Du•long and Pet•it's law
dum•my, *n., pl.* -mies, *adj.*
dump•ing syn•drome
Du°o-Med°i•ha•ler *Trade-mark.*
Du°o•Cet *Trademark.*
du°o•de•nal
duodenal ul°cer
du°o•de•nec•to•my, *n., pl.* -mies.
du°o•de•ni•tis
du°o•de•no•en•ter•os•to•my, *n., pl.* -mies.
du°o•de•nor•rha•phy, *n., pl.* -phies.
du°o•de•nos•co°py, *n., pl.* -pies.
du°o•de•num, *n., pl.* du°o•de°na, du•o•de•nums.
Du°o•DERM *Trademark.*
Du°o•film *Trademark.*
Du°o•plant *Trademark.*
Du•pha•lac *Trademark.*
du•plex
du•plic°i•tas
Du•puy•tren's con•trac•ture
Dupuytren's frac•ture
du°ra
Dura-Gest *Trademark.*
dura ma°ter
dura mater en•ceph°a•li
dura mater spi•na•lis
Dura-Tap *Trademark.*
Dura-Vent/A *Trademark.*
Dura-Vent/DA *Trademark.*
Du•ra•bo•lin *Trademark.*

Du•ra•cil•lin *Trademark.*
du°ral
Du•ra•morph *Trademark.*
Du•ra•nest *Trademark.*
du•ra•plas°ty, *n., pl.* -ties.
Du•ra•quin *Trademark.*
Du•ri•cef *Trademark.*
du•ri•tis
du•ro•ar•ach•ni•tis
Du•void *Trademark.*
dwarf, *n., pl.* dwarfs, dwarves.
dwarf•ism
dwarf•ness
dy°ad
dy•ad°ic
Dy•a•zide *Trademark.*
Dy•cill *Trademark.*
Dy•clone *Trademark.*
Dy•me•lor *Trademark.*
Dy•na•Circ *Trademark.*
dy•nam°ic spa•tial re•con•struc•tor
dy•nam°ics
dy•na•mo•gen•e°sis, *n., pl.* -e°ses.
dy•na•mo•gen°ic
dy•na•mog°e•nous
dy•na•mog°e•ny, *n., pl.* -nies.
dy•nam°o•graph
dy•na•mom•e°ter
dy•na•mo•met•ric
dy•na•mom•e°try
dy•na•mo•neure
dy•nam°o•scope
Dy•na•pen *Trademark.*
dy•na•therm
dyne
Dy•re•ni°um *Trademark.*
dys°a•cou•si°a, *n., pl.* -ias.
dys°a•cou•sis, *n., pl.* -ses.
dys•ad•ap•ta•tion
dys•an•ti•graph°i°a

dys•o•a•phia
dys•ap•ta•tion
dys•ar•te•ri•ot•o•o•ny
dys•ar•thri•a
dys•ar•thric
dys•arth•ro•sis, *n., pl.* **-ses.**
dys•au•to•no•mi•a
dys•au•to•nom•ic
dys•ba•rism
dys•ba•sia
dys•bu•li•a
dys•che•sia
dys•che•zia
dys•che•zic
dys•chir•oi•a
dys•chon•dro•pla•sia
dys•chroi•a
dys•chro•ma•tip•ic
dys•chro•ma•top•si•a
dys•chro•mi•a
dys•co•ri•a
dys•cra•sia
dys•cra•sial
dys•cras•ic or dys•crat•ic
dys•cri•nism
dys•di•a•do•cho•ki•ne•sia
dys•en•ter•ic
dys•en•ter•y
dys•er•gi•a
dys•er•gy
dys•es•the•sia
dys•es•thet•ic
dys•func•tion
dys•func•tion•al
dys•gen•e•sis, *n., pl.* **-e•ses.**
dys•gen•ic
dys•gen•ics
dys•ger•mi•no•ma, *n., pl.*
  -mas, -ma•ta.
dys•geu•sia
dys•gno•sia
dys•gon•ic

dys•graph•oi•a
dys•hi•dro•sis, *n., pl.* **-ses.**
dyskeratosis, *n., pl.* **-ses.**
dysker•oa•to•sis
  con•gen•oi•ota
dys•ker•oa•tot•oic
dys•ki•ne•sia
dys•ki•net•ic
dys•la•li•a
dys•lec•tic
dys•lex•oi•a
dys•lex•oi•oac
dys•lex•oic
dys•lo•gia
dys•men•or•rhe•a
dysmenorrhea in•ter•men•
  stru•a•lis
dys•men•or•rhe•al
dys•men•or•rhe•ic
dys•men•or•rhoe•a
dys•metr•oi•a
dys•mne•sia
dys•mor•phi•a
dys•mor•pho•pho•bi•a
dys•on•to•ge•net•ic
dys•os•mi•a
dys•os•to•sis, *n., pl.* **-ses.**
dysostosis clei•do•cra•
  ni•oa•lis
dysostosis mul•ti•ple
dys•pa•reu•ni•a
dys•pep•sia or dys•pep•sy
dys•pep•tic or dys•pep•ti•cal
dys•pep•ti•cal•ly
dys•pha•gia
dysphagia con•stric•ota
dysphagia glo•bo•sa
dysphagia lu•so•ri•a
dysphagia spas•ti•ca
dys•phag•ic
dys•pha•sia
dys•pha•sic

dys•phe•mi∘a
dys•pho•ni∘a
dysphonia spas•ti∘ca
dys•phon∘ic
dys•pho•ri∘a
dys•phor∘ic
dys•phra•sia
dys•pla•sia
dys•plas•tic
dysp•ne∘a
dysp•ne∘al
dysp•ne∘ic
dys•pnoe∘a
dys•pnoe∘ic
dys•prax∘i∘a
dys•pro•si∘um
dys•rhyth•mi∘a
dys•rhyth•mic
dys•se•ba•cia
dys•so•cial
dys•som•ni∘a
dys•sta•sia

dys•syn•er•gi∘a, *n., pl.* **-gi∘as.**
dys•syn•er•gic
dys•syn•er∘gy, *n., pl.* **-gies.**
dys•tax∘i∘a
dys•thy•mi∘a
dys•thy•mic
dysthymic dis•or•der
dys•to•ci∘a
dys•to•ci∘al
dys•to•ki∘a
dys•to•ni∘a
dystonia de•for•mans
dystonia mus•cu•lo•rum
dys•ton∘ic
dys•to•pi∘a
dys•tro•phi∘a, *n., pl.* **-as.**
dys•troph∘ic
dys•tro•phy or dys•tro•phi∘a
dys•u∘ri∘a
dys•u∘ric
Dy•tuss *Trademark.*

E

E. co∘li
ear
ear drops
ear pick
ear•ache
ear•drum
ear•lobe
ear•piece
ear•plug
ear•wax
Eas•prin *Trademark.*
eat•ing dis•or•der
E∘berth•el∘la
E∘bo∘la vi∘rus
e∘bri•e∘ty
e∘bul•lism

e∘bur den•tis
e∘bur•na•tion
e∘bur•ne•ous
e∘cau•date
ec•bol∘ic
ec•cen•tric
ec•cen•tri•cal∘ly
ec•chon•dro∘ma
ec•chy•mosed
ec•chy•mo•sis, *n., pl.* **-ses.**
ec•chy•mot∘ic
ec•co•pro•ti•co•phor∘ic
ec•crine
ec•cri•nol∘o∘gy
ec•cy•e∘sis, *n., pl.* **-ses.**
ec•de•mic

ec•dys•i•al
ec•dy•sis
ec•dy•sone
ec•go•nine
echoi•na•ce•a an•gus•ti•fo•li•a
ech•i•nate
ech•i•nat•ed
e•chi•no•coc•co•sis
Echoi•no•der•ma•ta
Ech•i•noi•de•a
Ech•i•no•rhyn•chus
e•chin•u•late
e•chin•u•lat•ed
Ech•is
echoo, *n., pl.* ech•oes.
echoo•car•di•o•gram
echoo•car•di•o•graph
echoo•en•ceph•a•lo•gram
echoo•en•ceph•a•lo•graph•ic
echoo•en•ceph•a•log•ra•phy
echoo•gram
echoo•ki•ne•sia, *n., pl.* -sias.
echoo•ki•ne•sis, *n., pl.* -ses.
echoo•la•li•a
echoo•lal•ic
echoo•lo•ca•tion
echoo•mim•oi•a
echoo•prax•oi•a
echoo•vi•rus, *n., pl.* -rus•es.
Eck fis•tu•la
ec•lamp•si•a
eclampsia grav•i•da•rum
eclampsia nu•tans
eclampsia ro•tans
ec•lamp•tic
ec•lec•tic
ec•lec•ti•cism
e•clipse
e•coid
e•co•phy•si•ol•o•gist

Ec•oo•trin *Trademark.*
ec•pho•ri•a, *n., pl.* -ri•as, -ri•ae.
ec•pho•rize, *v.* -rized, -riz•ing.
ec•sta•sy, *n., pl.* -sies.
ec•stat•ic
ec•tad
ec•tal
ec•ta•sia
ec•ta•sis, *n., pl.* -ses.
ec•tat•ic
ec•teth•moid
ec•teth•moi•dal
ec•thy•oma
ecthyma gan•gre•no•sum
ec•thy•ma•tous
ec•to•blast
ec•to•car•di•a
ec•to•cor•ne•a
ec•to•crine
ec•to•cyst
ec•to•derm
ec•to•der•mal
ec•to•der•mic
ec•to•der•moi•dal
ec•to•der•mo•sis
ec•to•en•tad
ec•to•eth•moid
ec•to•gen•ic
ec•tog•e•nous
ec•to•hor•mo•nal
ec•to•hor•mone
ec•to•loph
ec•to•mere
ec•to•mer•ic
ec•to•morph
ec•to•mor•phic
ec•to•morph•y
ec•to•par•a•site
ec•to•par•a•sit•ic
ec•to•phyte
ec•to•pi•a

ectopia cor•dis
ectopia len•tis
ectopia pu•pil•lae
ectopia re•nis
ectopia tes•tis
ec•top•ic
ectopic preg•nan•cy
ec•top•i•cal•ly
ec•to•pla•cen•tal
ec•to•plasm
ec•to•plas•mat•ic
ec•to•plas•mic
ec•to•steal
ec•tos•to•sis
ec•to•thrix
ec•to•zo•on, *n., pl.* **-zo•a.**
ec•tro•dac•tyl•i•a
ec•tro•dac•tyl•ism
ec•tro•dac•ty•ly, *n., pl.* **-lies.**
ec•tro•me•li•a
ec•tro•mel•ic
ec•tro•pi•on
ec•tro•pi•um
ec•ze•ma
ec•ze•ma•ti•za•tion
ec•zem•a•tous
E•dec•rin *Trademark.*
e•de•ma, *n., pl.* **-mas, -ma•ta.**
e•dem•a•tous
e•den•tate
e•den•tu•late
e•den•tu•lous
e•duct
e•duc•tion
ef•fect
ef•fec•tive dose
ef•fec•tor
ef•fem•i•na•tion
ef•fer•ent
ef•fer•ent•ly
ef•fer•vesce, *v.,* **-vesced,**
  -vesc•ing.

ef•fer•ves•cence
ef•fer•ves•cent
Ef•fex•or
ef•fleu•rage
ef•flo•resce, *v.,* **-resced, -resc•**
  ing.
ef•flo•res•cence
ef•flo•res•cent
ef•flu•vi•um, *n., pl.* **-vi•a.**
ef•fort throm•bo•sis
ef•fu•sion
Ef•u•dex *Trademark.*
e•gest
e•ges•ta
e•ges•tion
e•ges•tive
egg
e•go, *n., pl.* **e•gos.**
ego i•de•al
e•go•cen•tric
e•go•cen•tric•i•ty
e•go•dys•ton•ic
e•go•ism
e•go•ist
e•go•is•tic
e•go•is•ti•cal
e•go•is•ti•cal•ly
e•go•ma•ni•a
e•go•ma•ni•ac
e•go•ma•ni•a•cal
e•go•ma•ni•a•cal•ly
e•goph•o•ny, *n., pl.* **-nies.**
e•go•syn•ton•ic
e•go•syn•to•ny, *n., pl.* **-nies.**
e•go•tism
e•go•tist
e•go•tis•tic
e•go•tis•ti•cal
e•go•tis•ti•cal•ly
ehr•lich•i•o•sis
ei•co•sa•pen•ta•e•no•ic
  ac•id

ei•det•ic
Eijk•man test
ei•ko•nom•e•ter
Ei•me•ri•a
Ei•me•ri•i•dae
e•jac•u•late, *v.*, -lat•ed, -lat•ing.
e•jac•u•la•tion
e•jac•u•la•to•ry
ejaculatory duct
e•jec•ta
e•jec•tion frac•tion
e•jec•tor
e•lae•o•ste•ar•ic
e•lap•id
E•lap•i•dae
E•lase *Trademark.*
e•las•tase
e•las•ti•ca
e•las•tic•i•ty
e•las•tin
e•las•tom•e•ter
e•las•to•sis, *n., pl.* -ses.
elastosis se•nil•is
e•la•tion
El•a•vil *Trademark.*
el•bow
El•de•cort *Trademark.*
El•de•pryl *Trademark.*
El•der•caps *Trademark.*
El•der•ton•ic *Trademark.*
El•do•paque *Trademark.*
El•do•quin Forte *Trademark.*
E•lec•tra com•plex
e•lec•tro•bi•ol•o•gy
e•lec•tro•car•di•o•gram
e•lec•tro•car•di•o•graph
e•lec•tro•car•di•o•graph•ic
e•lec•tro•car•di•og•ra•phy
e•lec•tro•cau•ter•i•za•tion
e•lec•tro•cau•ter•y, *n., pl.* -ter•ies.

e•lec•tro•co•ag•u•la•tion
e•lec•tro•con•trac•til•i•ty, *n., pl.* -ties.
e•lec•tro•con•vul•sive
electroconvulsive ther•a•py
e•lec•tro•cor•ti•co•gram
e•lec•tro•cor•ti•co•graph•ic
e•lec•tro•cor•ti•co•graph•i•cal•ly
e•lec•tro•cute, *v.*, -cut•ed, -cut•ing.
e•lec•tro•cu•tion
e•lec•trode
e•lec•tro•der•mal
e•lec•tro•des•ic•ca•tion
e•lec•tro•di•al•y•sis, *n., pl.* -ses.
e•lec•tro•en•ceph•a•lo•gram
e•lec•tro•en•ceph•a•lo•graph
e•lec•tro•en•ceph•a•lo•graph•ic
e•lec•tro•en•ceph•a•log•ra•phy
e•lec•tro•en•dos•mose
e•lec•tro•en•dos•mo•sis, *n., pl.* -ses.
e•lec•tro•gen•e•osis, *n., pl.* -e•oses.
e•lec•tro•gen•ic
e•lec•tro•gram
e•lec•trog•ra•phy, *n., pl.* -phies.
e•lec•tro•hys•ter•o•graph
e•lec•tro•ky•mo•graph
e•lec•tro•ky•mog•ra•phy, *n., pl.* -phies.
e•lec•trol•o•gist
e•lec•trol•o•gy
e•lec•trol•y•sis
e•lec•tro•lyte

e•lec•tro•lyt•ic

e•lec•tro•lyze, *v.*, -lyzed, -lyz•ing.

e•lec•tro•mag•net

e•lec•tro•my○o•gram

e•lec•tro•my○o•graph

e•lec•tro•my○o•graph○ic

e•lec•tro•my○o•graph○i•cal○ly

e•lec•tro•my•og•ra•phy

e•lec•tron mi•cro•scope

electron trans•port

e•lec•tro•nar•co•sis

e•lec•tro•neg○a•tive

e•lec•tro•oc○u•lo•gram

e•lec•tro•oc○u•log•ra•phy, *n.*, *pl.* -phies.

e•lec•tro•os•mose, *n.*, *pl.* -mos○es.

e•lec•tro•os•mo•sis

e•lec•tro•pho•rese

e•lec•tro•pho•resed

e•lec•tro•pho•res•ing

e•lec•tro•pho•re•sis

e•lec•tro•pho•ret○ic

e•lec•tro•pho•re•to•gram

e•lec•tro•phren○ic

e•lec•tro•phys•i•o•log○i•cal

e•lec•tro•phys•i•ol○o•gist

e•lec•tro•phys•i•ol○o○gy

e•lec•tro•plex○y

e•lec•tro•pos○i•tive

e•lec•tro•ret○i•no•gram

e•lec•tro•ret○i•no•graph

e•lec•tro•ret○i•no•graph○ic

e•lec•tro•ret○i•nog•ra•phy

e•lec•tro•shock

e•lec•tro•sleep

e•lec•tro•sur•ger○y

e•lec•tro•tax○is

e•lec•tro•ther○a○py

e•lec•tro•tome

e•lec•tro•ton○ic

e•lec•trot○o○nus

e•lec•tro•tro•pism

e•lec•tu•ar○y, *n.*, *pl.* -ries.

el○e•doi•sin

El○e•mite *Trademark.*

el•e○o•ste○ar○ic

el•e○ophant man's dis•ease

el•e○ophan•ti•asis

elephantiasis neu•ro•ma•to○sa

elephantiasis nos•tras

el○e•va•tor

e○lim○i•nant

e•lim○i•nate, *v.*, -nat○ed, -nat•ing.

e○lim○i•na•tion

e○lim○i•na•tive

e○lix○ir

E○lix○o•phyl•lin *Trademark.*

el•lip•sis, *n.*, *pl.* el•lip•ses.

El○o•con *Trademark.*

El•spar *Trademark.*

el○u•ant

el○u•ate

el○u•ent

e○lute, *v.*, e○lut○ed, e○lut•ing.

e○lu•tion

e○ma•ci•ate, *v.*, -at○ed, -at•ing.

e○ma•ci•a•tion

em○a•na•tion

e○man•ci•pa•tion

e○man•si○omen•si○um

e○mas•cu•late, *v.*, -lat○ed, -lat•ing.

e○mas•cu•la•tion

e○mas•cu•la•tor

Em•ba•do•mo•nas

em•balm

em•balm○er

em•balm•ment

em•bar•rass
em•bar•rass•ment
em•bed, *v*, -bed•ded, -bed•
  ding.
em•be•li∘a
em•bo•la•li∘a
em•bo•le
em•bo•lec•to•my, *n.*, *pl.*
  -mies.
em•bol∘ic
em•bo•lism
em•bo•lis•mic
em•bo•li•za•tion
em•bo•lo•la•li∘a
em•bo•lo•phra•sia
em•bo•lus, *n.*, *pl.* -li.
em•bo∘ly, *n.*, *pl.* -lies.
em•bouche•ment
em•bra•sure
em•bro•cate, *v.*, -cat∘ed, -cat•
  ing.
em•bro•ca•tion
em•bry∘o, *n.*, *pl.* -os.
embryo trans•fer
em∘bry∘o•car∘di∘a
em∘bry∘o∘gen•e∘sis, *n.*, *pl.*
  -e∘ses.
em∘bry∘o∘ge•net∘ic
em∘bry∘o•gen∘ic
em•bry•og∘e∘ny or
  em∘bry∘o•gen•e∘sis
em•bry•oid
em∘bry∘o∘log∘i•cal∘ly
em•bry•ol∘o•gist
em•bry•ol∘o∘gy, *n.*, *pl.* -gies.
em•bry∘o∘ma, *n.*, *pl.* -mas,
  -ma∘ta.
em∘bry∘o∘nal
em∘bry∘o∘nate
em•bry•on∘ic
embryonic disk
embryonic mem•brane

em•bry•on∘i•cal∘ly
em•bry∘o∘path∘y, *n.*, *pl.*
  -thies.
em∘bry∘o∘phore
em∘bry∘o∘tome
em•bry∘ot∘o∘my, *n.*, *pl.*
  -mies.
em∘bry∘o•troph
em∘bry∘o•trophe
em∘bry∘ot∘ro•phy
Em∘cyt *Trademark.*
e∘mer•gen∘cy room
e∘mer•gi∘cen•ter
em•e∘osis
Em•ete-con *Trademark.*
e∘met∘ic
e∘met∘i•cal∘ly
em∘e∘tine
Em∘e∘trol *Trademark.*
em∘i•gra∘tion
em∘i•gra•tion∘al
Em∘i•nase *Trademark.*
em∘i•nence
em∘i•nen•tia
em•is•sar∘i∘um con•dy•loi•
  de∘um
emissarium mas•toi•de∘um
emissarium oc•cip∘i•ta∘le
emissarium pa•ri•e•ta∘le
e∘mis•sion
Em∘ko *Trademark.*
em•men∘a•gog∘ic
em•men∘a•gogue
em•me•trope
em•me•tro•pi∘a
em•me•trop∘ic
e∘mo•din
e∘mol•lience
e∘mol•lient
e∘mo•tion
e∘mo•tion∘al
em•pa•thet∘ic

em•path○ic
em•pa•thize, *v.*, -thized,
　-thiz•ing.
em•pa•thy
em•phy•se○ma
em•phy•sem○a•tous
em•phy•se•mic
em•pir○ic
em•pir○i•cal
em•pir○i•cal○ly
em•pir○i•cism
Em•pi○rin *Trademark.*
em•plas•tic
em•pros•thot○o•nos
emp○ty cal○o○rie
empty nest syn•drome
em•py○e•ma
empyema ne•ces•si•ta•tis
em•py○e•mic
em•py•reu○ma, *n.*, *pl* -ma○ta.
em•py•reu•mat○ic
em•py•reu•mat○i•cal
e○mul•gent
e○mul•si○ble
e○mul•si•fi○er
e○mul•si○fy, *v.*, -fied, -fy•ing.
e○mul•sin
e○mul•sion
e○mul•sive
e○mul•soid
E○mul•so○il *Trademark.*
e○munc•to○ry, *n.*, *pl.* -ries.
E○nal○o•a○pril
e○nam○el
en•an•them, *n.*, *pl.* -s.
en•an•the○ma, *n.*, *pl.* -ma○ta.
e○nan•them○a•tous
en•ar•thro•di○al
en•ar•thro•sis, *n.*, *pl.* -ses.
en•cai•nide
en•cap•su•lant

en•cap•su•late, *v.*, -lat○ed,
　-lat•ing.
en•cap•su•la•tion
en•cap•sule, *v.*, -suled, -sul•
　ing.
en•ceinte
en•ceph○a•lal•gia
en•ce•phal○ic
en•ceph○a•lit○ic
en•ceph○a•li○tis
encephalitis le•thar•gi○ca
encephalitis per•i•ax•i•a•lis
　con•cen•tri○ca
encephalitis periaxialis dif•
　fu○sa
en•ceph○a•li○to•gen○ic
en•ceph○a•li○tog•e○nous
en•ceph○a•lit○o•zo○on, *n.*, *pl.*
　-zo○a.
en•ceph○a•lo•cele
en•ceph○a•lo•coele
en•ceph○a•lo•gram
en•ceph○a•lo•graph
en•ceph○a•lo•graph○ic
en•ceph○a•log•ra•phy
en•ceph○a•loid
en•ceph○a•lo•ma•la•cia
en•ceph○a•lo•men•in•gi○tis,
　n., *pl.* -git○i•des.
en•ceph○a•lo•mere
en•ceph○a•lo•my•e○lit○ic
en•ceph○a•lo•my•e○li○tis
en•ceph○a•lon, *n.*, *pl.* -la.
en•ceph○a•lop○a•thy
en•ceph○a•lo•sis, *n.*, *pl.* -ses.
en•chon•dral
en•chon•dro○ma, *n.*, *pl.* -mas,
　-ma○ta.
en•clave
en•clit○ic
en•cop•re•sis
en•coun•ter group

en•crus•ta•tion
en•cyst
en•cys•ta•tion
en•cyst•ment
end or•gan
En∘dal-HD *Trademark.*
end•a•me•ba
end•a•moe•ba
end•a•or•ti•tis
end•ar•ter•ec•to•my, *n., pl*
  -mies.
end•ar•te•ri•al
end•ar•te•ri•tis
endarteritis de•for•mans
endarteritis ob•lit•er•ans
end•ar•te•ri•um, *n., pl.* -ri∘a.
end•au•ral
end•brain
en•dem∘ic
En∘dep *Trademark.*
end•er•gon∘ic
en•der•mic
en•der•mi•cal∘ly
en∘do•bi•ot∘ic
en∘do•blast
en∘do•blas•tic
en∘do•bron•chi∘al
en∘do•car•di•ac
en∘do•car•di∘al
en∘do•car•dit∘ic
en∘do•car•di•tis
endocarditis len∘ta
en∘do•car•di∘um, *n., pl.*
  -di∘a.
en∘do•cer•vi•cal
en∘do•cer•vi•ci•tis
en∘do•chon•dral
en∘do•cra•ni∘al
en∘do•cra•ni∘um, *n., pl.*
  -ni∘a.
en∘do•crine
endocrine gland

en∘do•crin∘ic
en∘do•crin∘o•log∘ic
en∘do•crin∘o•log∘i•cal
en∘do•cri•nol∘o∘gy
en∘do•crin∘o•path∘ic
en∘do•cri•nop∘a•thy, *n., pl.*
  -thies.
en∘doc•ri•nous
en∘do•cyst
en∘do•cyt∘ic or en∘do•cy•
  tot∘ic
en∘do•cy•to•sis
en∘do•derm
en∘do•der•mal
en∘do•der•mic
en∘do•don•tia
en∘do•don•tic
en∘do•don•ti•cal∘ly
en∘do•don•tics
en∘do•don•tist
en∘do•en•zyme
en∘do•e∘ryth•ro•cyt∘ic
en•dog∘a∘my, *n., pl.* -mies.
en∘do•gas•tric
en∘do•gen∘ic
en∘do•ge•nic∘i∘ty
en∘dog∘e∘nous
en∘dog∘e∘nous∘ly
en∘dog∘e∘ny or en∘do•gen•
  e∘sis
en•dog•nath∘i∘on
En∘do•li•max
Endolimax na∘na
en∘do•lymph
en∘do•lym•phat∘ic
en∘do•me•tri∘al
en∘do•me•tri∘o∘ma, *n., pl.*
  -mas, -ma∘ta.
en∘do•me•tri∘o•sis
en∘do•me•tri•tis
endometritis ex•fo•li•a•ti∘va

en•do•me•tri•um, *n., pl.*
-tri•a.
en•do•mi•to•sis
en•do•mix•is
en•do•morph
en•do•mor•phic
en•do•mor•phy
en•do•my•si•um, *n., pl.* -si•a.
en•do•neu•ri•um, *n., pl.*
-ri•a.
en•do•nu•cle•ase
en•do•par•a•site
en•do•par•a•sit•ic
en•do•par•a•sit•ism
en•do•pep•ti•dase
en•do•phle•bi•tis, *n., pl.*
-bit•i•des.
en•do•phyte
en•do•phyt•ic
en•do•plasm
en•do•plas•mic
endoplasmic re•tic•u•lum
en•do•plast
en•do•plas•tic
en•do•pol•y•ploid
en•do•pol•y•ploi•dy
en•do•ra•di•o•sonde
En•dor•phan *Trademark.*
En•dor•phe•nyl *Trademark.*
en•dor•phin
en•do•sarc
en•do•scope
en•do•scop•ic
en•do•scop•i•cal•ly
en•dos•co•pist
en•dos•co•py
en•do•sep•sis, *n., pl.* -ses.
en•do•skel•e•ton
en•dos•mom•e•ter
en•dos•mo•sis
en•dos•mot•ic
en•dos•mot•i•cal•ly

en•do•some
en•do•spore
en•do•ste•al
en•do•ste•i•tis
end•os•te•um, *n., pl.* -te•a.
en•do•sti•tis
en•dos•to•ma, *n., pl.* -mas,
-ma•ta.
en•do•the•li•al
en•do•the•li•o•cho•ri•al
en•do•the•li•o•cyte
en•do•the•li•o•oma, *n., pl.*
-mas, -ma•ta.
endothelioma an•gi•o•
mat•o•sum
endothelioma cap•i•tis
en•do•the•li•o•um, *n., pl.* -li•a.
en•do•ther•o•my, *n., pl.* -mies.
en•do•thrix, *n., pl.* -thri•ces.
en•do•tox•ic
en•do•tox•in
en•do•tra•che•al
en•do•ve•nous
En•du•ron *Trademark.*
En•du•ro•nyl *Trademark.*
Enduronyl For•te *Trademark.*
en•dy•o•ma
en•o•e•oma, *n., pl.* -mas.
en•er•get•ic
en•er•get•i•cal•ly
en•er•get•ics
en•er•gid
En•er•gix-B *Trademark.*
en•er•giz•er
en•er•o•gy, *n., pl.* -gies.
en•er•vate, *v.,* -vat•ed, -vat•
ing.
en•er•va•tion
en•globe, *v.,* -globed, -glob•
ing.
en•globe•ment

en•gorge, v., -gorged, -gorg•ing.
en•gorge•ment
en•graft
en•graf•ta•tion
en•graft•ment
en•gram
en•gramme
en•gram•mic
En•kaid Trademark.
en•keph•al•oin
en•large, v., -larged, -larg•ing.
en•large•ment
En•lon Trademark.
e•no•lase
e•no•li•za•tion
e•nol•o•gy
e•noph•thal•mos
e•noph•thal•mus
e•nor•gan•ic
e•nos•to•sis, n., pl. -ses.
En•o•vid Trademark.
en•rich
en•rich•ment
en•sheathe
en•si•form
En•sure Trademark.
en•tad
en•tal
ent•o•a•me•o•ba or ent•o•a•moe•o•ba, n., pl. -bae, -bas.
ent•am•e•bi•a•sis
ent•a•moe•o•ba
ent•am•oe•bi•a•sis
en•ter•al
en•te•ral•gia
en•ter•ec•to•my, n., pl. -mies.
en•ter•ic
enteric fe•ver
en•ter•oi•ti•dis
en•ter•oi•tis
enteritis cam•py•lo•bac•ter

enteritis ne•crot•oi•cans
en•ter•o•o•bac•te•ri•o•a, n., pl., sing. -te•ri•um.
En•ter•o•o•bac•te•ri•a•ce•ae
en•ter•o•o•bac•te•ri•al
en•ter•o•o•bac•te•ri•um, n., pl. -ri•a.
en•ter•o•o•bi•a•sis
En•ter•o•o•bi•ous
Enterobius ver•mic•u•lar•is
en•ter•o•cele
en•ter•o•o•coc•cus, n., pl. -coc•ci.
en•ter•o•o•coel
en•ter•o•o•coele
en•ter•o•o•coel•oic
en•ter•o•o•coel•ous
en•ter•o•o•co•li•tis
en•ter•o•o•cyst
en•ter•o•o•cys•to•cele
en•ter•o•o•en•te•ros•to•my, n., pl. -mies.
en•ter•o•o•gas•trone
en•ter•og•oe•o•nous
en•ter•o•o•hep•a•ti•tis
en•ter•o•o•ki•nase
en•ter•o•o•lith
en•ter•ol•o•y•sis
en•ter•on, n., pl. -ter•o•a.
en•ter•o•o•path•o•gen•ic
en•ter•op•o•a•thy, n., pl. -thies.
en•ter•o•o•pex•oy, n., pl. -ies.
en•ter•o•o•plas•o•ty, n., pl. -ties.
en•ter•op•to•sis, n., pl. -ses.
en•ter•op•tot•oic
en•ter•or•or•rha•gia
en•ter•or•or•rha•phy, n., pl. -phies.
en•ter•os•to•mal
en•ter•os•to•omy, n., pl. -mies.
en•ter•ot•o•omy, n., pl. -mies.

en•ter•o•o•tox•e•mi•a
en•ter•o•o•tox•in
en•ter•o•o•vi•ral
en•ter•o•o•vi•rus, *n., pl.*
  -rus•es.
en•ter•o•o•zo•a
en•ter•o•o•zo•an
En•tex *Trademark.*
Entex LA *Trademark.*
en•to•blast
en•to•coel
en•to•coele
en•to•cone
en•to•co•nid
en•to•cor•ne•a
en•to•derm
En•to•lase-HP *Trademark.*
en•to•mol•o•gy
En•to•moph•tho•ra
en•top•ic
en•to•plasm
en•top•tic
en•top•tos•co•py, *n., pl.*
  -pies.
en•to•ret•i•na
en•to•sarc
en•to•zo•a
en•to•zo•ic
en•to•zo•on, *n., pl.* -zo•a.
En•to•zyme *Trademark.*
en•tro•pi•on
En•tuss *Trademark.*
Entuss-D *Trademark.*
en•ty•py
e•nu•cle•ate, *adj., v.,* -at•ed,
  -at•ing.
e•nu•cle•a•tion
en•u•ore•sis
en•u•ret•ic
en•ven•o•ma•tion
en•ven•o•mi•za•tion
en•vi•ron•ment

en•vi•ron•men•tal
en•vi•ron•men•tal•ism
en•vi•ron•men•tal•ist
en•vi•ron•men•tal•ly
en•zo•ot•ic
en•zy•got•ic
en•zy•mat•ic or en•zy•mic
en•zy•mat•i•cal•ly or en•zy•
  mi•cal•ly
en•zyme
en•zy•mic
en•zy•mi•cal•ly
en•zy•mol•o•gist
en•zy•mol•o•gy
e•o•nism
e•o•sin or e•o•sine
e•o•sin•ic
e•o•sin•o•cyte
e•o•sin•o•pe•ni•a
e•o•sin•o•phil or e•o•sin•o•
  phile
e•o•sin•o•phil•i•a
e•o•sin•o•phil•ic or e•o•si•
  noph•i•lous or e•o•sin•o•
  phil
e•pac•tal
e•par•te•ri•al
e•pax•i•al
e•pax•on•ic
ep•en•ceph•o•a•lon, *n., pl.* -la.
e•open•dy•oma
e•open•dy•mal
ep•en•dy•mi•tis, *n., pl.* -mi•
  ti•des.
ep•en•dy•mo•ma, *n., pl.*
  -mas, -ma•ta.
ep•e•o•ryth•ro•zo•oon, *n., pl.*
  -zo•a.
ep•e•o•ryth•ro•zo•o•no•sis,
  n., pl. -ses.
e•ophe•bic
e•ophed•o•ra, *n., pl.* -ras.

e○phed•rine
e○phe•lis, *n., pl.* -li•des.
eph○i•dro•sis cru•en○ta
ephidrosis tinc○ta
ep○i•blast
ep○i•blas•tic
e○pib○o○ole, *n., pl.* -les.
ep○i•bol○ic
e○pib○o○oly, *n., pl.* -lies.
ep○i•can•thic
ep○i•can•thus, *n., pl.* -thi.
ep○i•car•di○a
ep○i•car•di○al
ep○i•car•di○um, *n., pl.* -di○a.
ep○i•chor•dal
ep○i•con•dyle
ep○i•con•dyl•i○an
ep○i•con•dyl○ic
ep○i•con•dy•li•tis
ep○i•co•ra•coid
ep○i•co•ra•coi•dal
ep○i•cra•ni○al
ep○i•cra•ni○um, *n., pl.* -ums,
  -ni○a.
ep○i•cri•sis, *n., pl.* -ses.
ep○i•crit○ic
ep○i•cys•ti•tis
ep○i•cyte
ep○i•dem○i•cal○ly
ep○i•de•mic○i○ty
ep○i•de•mi○o•log○ic
ep○i•de•mi○o•log○i•cal○ly
ep○i•de•mi○ol○o○gist
ep○i•de•mi○ol○o○gy
ep○i•derm
ep○i•der•mis
ep○i•der•mat○ic
ep○i•der•mic
ep○i•der•mi•cal○ly
ep○i•der•mi•dal○i○za•tion
ep○i•der•mi•za•tion
ep○i•der•moid

ep○i•der•moi•dal
ep○i•der•mol○y•sis, *n., pl.*
  -ses.
ep○i•der•mo•my•co•sis
Ep○i•der•mo•phy•ton
ep○i•der•mo•phy•to•sis
ep○i•did○oy•mal
ep○i•did○oy•mis, *n., pl.* -di•
  dym○i•des.
ep○i•did○oy•mi•tis
ep○i•du•ral
Ep○i•foam *Trademark.*
ep○i•fol•lic○u•li•tis
ep○i•gas•trae○um, *n., pl.*
  -trae○a.
ep○i•gas•tral
ep○i•gas•tri○al
ep○i•gas•tric
ep○i•gas•tri•cal
ep○i•gas•tri○um, *n., pl.* -tri○a.
ep○i•gas•tri○us par○o•a•sit○i•
  cus
ep○i•gen•e○sis, *n., pl.* -e○ses.
e•pig○e○onist
ep○i•ge•net○ic
ep○i•ge•net○i•cal○ly
ep○i•glot•tal
ep○i•glot•tic
ep○i•glot•tid•e○an
ep○i•glot•tis, *n., pl.* -tis○es,
  -ti•des.
ep○i•glot•ti•tis
ep○i•hy○al
ep○i•la•mel•lar
ep○i•late, *v.,* -lat○ed, -lat•ing.
ep○i•la•tion
ep○i•la•tor
ep○i•lem○a
ep○i•lem•mal
ep○i•lep•si○a ar•ith•
  met○oi○ca
epilepsia mi•tis

ep•i•lep•si•a par•ti•a•lis con•
 tin•u•a
epilepsia ver•tig•i•no•sa
ep•i•lep•sy
ep•i•lep•tic
ep•i•lep•ti•cal•ly
ep•i•lep•ti•form
ep•i•lep•to•gen•ic
ep•i•lep•toid
ep•i•loi•a
ep•i•mere
ep•i•mer•ic
ep•i•me•rite
ep•i•mor•pho•sis
ep•i•my•si•um, n., pl. -si•a.
ep•i•neph•rine or ep•i•neph•
 rin
ep•i•neu•ral
ep•i•neu•ri•um
ep•i•nych•i•um
ep•i•o•nych•i•um
ep•i•ot•ic
Ep•i•Pen Trademark.
ep•i•phar•ynx
ep•i•phe•nom•e•nal•ly
ep•i•phe•nom•e•nal•ism
ep•i•phe•nom•e•non, n., pl.
 -e•na, -nons.
e•piph•o•o•ra
e•piph•y•se•al
ep•i•phys•i•al
ep•i•phys•i•o•de•sis, n., pl.
 -ses.
ep•i•phys•i•ol•y•sis
e•piph•y•sis, n., pl. -ses.
epiphysis ce•re•bri
ep•i•phy•si•tis
e•pip•i•al
ep•i•plo•ic
ep•i•plo•on, n., pl. -lo•a.
ep•ip•ter•oic
ep•i•scle•ora

ep•i•scle•ral
e•pi•si•ot•o•omy, n., pl. -mies.
ep•i•so•mal
ep•i•so•mal•ly
ep•i•some
ep•i•spa•di•as
ep•i•spas•tic
e•pis•ta•sis, n., pl. -ses.
ep•i•stat•ic
ep•i•stax•is
e•pis•te•mo•phil•oi•a
e•pis•te•mo•phil•o•i•ac
ep•i•ster•nal
ep•i•ster•num, n., pl.
 -ster•na.
ep•i•stro•phe•us
ep•i•tax•oy, n., pl. -ies.
ep•i•ten•din•e•um
ep•i•thal•o•a•mus, n., pl. -mi.
ep•i•the•li•al
ep•i•the•li•al•oi•za•tion
ep•i•the•li•o•a•lize, v., -lized,
 -liz•ing.
ep•i•the•li•oid
ep•i•the•li•o•ma, n., pl. -mas,
 -ma•ta.
ep•i•the•li•om•a•tous
ep•i•the•li•um, n., pl. -li•
 ums, -li•a.
ep•i•the•li•za•tion
ep•i•the•lize, v., -lized, -liz•
 ing.
ep•i•tope
Ep•i•trate Trademark.
ep•i•trich•i•al
ep•i•trich•i•um, n., pl. -ums.
ep•i•troch•le•a
ep•i•troch•le•ar
ep•i•tu•ber•cu•lo•sis
ep•i•tym•pan•ic
ep•i•tym•pa•num, n., pl. -ni,
 -nums.

ep•oi•typh•li•tis

ep•oi•vag•oi•ni•tis

ep•oi•zo•oic

ep•oi•zo•ol•o•gy

ep•oi•zo•oon, *n., pl.* -zo•a.

ep•oi•zo•ot•oic

ep•oi•zo•ot•i•ol•o•gy

ep•oi•zo•o•tol•o•gy

Ep•oo•gen *Trademark.*

ep•o•nych•i•um

ep•o•oph•o•o•ron

ep•or•nit•oic

Ep•o•py/N *Trademark.*

Ep•som salt

Ep•stein-Barr vi•rus

e•pu•lis, *n., pl.* -li•des.

ep•u•loid

E•qua•ge•sic *Trademark.*

E•qua•ni *Trademark.*

e•qua•tion

e•qua•tion•al

e•qua•tion•al•ly

e•qua•tor

equator len•tis

e•qua•to•ri•al

e•qui•len•oin

e•qui•li•bri•um, *n., pl.* -ri•ums, -ri•a.

e•qui•lin

e•quine en•ceph•o•a•li•tis

e•qui•po•tent

e•quiv•o•a•lence

e•quiv•o•a•len•cy, *n., pl.* -cies.

e•quiv•o•a•lent

e•quiv•o•a•lent•ly

e•ra•sion

e•rec•tile

e•rec•til•oi•o•ty

e•rec•tion

e•rec•tor

er•e•o•ma•cau•sis

er•e•o•thism

er•e•o•this•mic

er•e•o•this•tic or er•e•o•thit•oic or e•reth•oic

Er•gam•oi•sol *Trademark.*

er•ga•sia

er•gas•tic

er•gas•to•plasm

er•o•go•cal•cif•er•ol

er•o•go•cor•nine

er•o•go•cris•tine

er•o•go•gen•oic

er•o•go•graph

er•o•go•graph•oic

er•o•got•ism

Er•o•go•mar *Trademark.*

er•o•gom•e•ter

er•o•go•met•ric

er•o•go•met•rine

er•o•go•nom•oic

er•o•go•nom•ics

er•o•gon•o•o•mist

er•o•go•no•vine

Er•o•go•stat *Trademark.*

er•o•gos•ter•ol

er•o•got

er•o•got•o•a•mine

er•o•go•ther•o•a•py

er•o•go•thi•o•ne•ine

er•o•go•ti•nine

er•o•go•tized

Er•o•go•trate Mal•o•e•ate *Trademark.*

er•i•o•o•dic•ty•oon

Er•len•mey•o•er flask

e•o•ro•gen•oic

e•o•rog•e•o•nous

E•o•ros, *n., pl.* -ro•tes.

e•o•rose

e•o•rose•o•ly

e•o•ro•sion

e•o•ro•sive

e•o•ro•sive•ness

e•ro•siv•i•ty, *n., pl.* -ties.
e•rot•ic
e•rot•i•cal
e•rot•i•cal•ly
e•rot•i•cism
e•rot•i•cist
e•rot•i•ci•za•tion
e•rot•i•ci•cize, *v.,* -cized, -ciz•
ing.
er•o•tism
er•o•ti•za•tion
er•o•tize, *v.,* -tized, -tiz•ing.
e•ro•to•gen•e•sis, *n., pl.*
-e•ses.
e•ro•to•gen•ic
e•ro•to•ma•ni•a
e•ro•to•ma•ni•ac
e•ro•to•man•ic
e•rot•o•path
er•o•top•a•thy
er•rat•ic
er•rhine
er•u•bes•cent
e•ru•cic
e•ruct
e•ruc•tate, *v.,* -tat•ed, -tat•
ing.
e•ruc•ta•tion
e•rup•tion
e•rup•tive
e•rup•tive•ly
e•rup•tiv•i•ty
Er•y-Tab *Trademark.*
ERYC *Trademark.*
Er•y•cette *Trademark.*
Er•y•Derm *Trademark.*
Er•y•gel *Trademark.*
Er•y•max *Trademark.*
Er•y•Ped *Trademark.*
Er•y•si•mum
er•y•sip•e•las
er•y•si•pel•a•tous

er•y•sip•e•loid
er•y•sip•e•loth•rix
er•y•the•ma
erythema in•fec•ti•o•sum
er•y•the•mal
er•y•them•a•tous or er•y•
the•mic
er•y•thor•bate
er•y•thor•bic
er•y•thrae•mi•a
er•y•thras•ma
er•yth•re•de•ma
er•y•thre•mi•a
er•yth•rism
er•y•thris•mal
er•yth•ris•tic
e•ryth•ri•tol
e•ryth•ro•blast
e•ryth•ro•blas•te•mi•a
e•ryth•ro•blas•tic
e•ryth•ro•blas•to•sis
erythroblastosis fe•ta•lis
erythroblastosis ne•o•na•to•
rum
e•ryth•ro•blas•tot•ic
E•ryth•ro•cin *Trademark.*
Erythrocin Ste•a•rate
e•ryth•ro•cru•o•rin
e•ryth•ro•cyte
e•ryth•ro•cy•the•mi•a
e•ryth•ro•my•cin
e•ryth•ro•cy•tom•e•ter
e•ryth•ro•cy•to•poi•e•sis
e•ryth•ro•cy•to•sis, *n., pl.*
-ses.
e•ryth•ro•der•ma
e•ryth•ro•der•mi•a
e•ryth•ro•dex•trin
e•ryth•ro•dex•trine
e•ryth•ro•gen•e•sis, *n., pl.*
-e•ses.
e•ryth•ro•gen•ic

e•ryth•ro•gone
e•ryth•ro•go•ni•um
e•ryth•roid
e•ryth•roi•dine
e•ryth•ro•leu•co•sis
e•ryth•ro•leu•ke•mi•a
e•ryth•ro•leu•ko•sis
e•ryth•ro•me•lal•gia
e•ryth•ron
e•ryth•ro•phage
e•ryth•ro•pha•gia
e•ryth•ro•phag•o•cy•to•sis, *n., pl.* -ses.
e•ryth•ro•phile
er•yth•roph•oi•lous
e•ryth•ro•phle•ine
e•ryth•ro•phore
er•yth•ro•pi•a
e•ryth•ro•pla•sia
e•ryth•ro•poi•e•sis
e•ryth•ro•poi•et•ic
e•ryth•ro•poi•e•tin
er•yth•rop•si•a
e•ryth•rose
er•yth•ru•lose
es•cape, *v.,* -caped, -cap•ing.
escape mech•a•nism
es•cap•ism
es•cap•ist
es•char
es•cha•rot•ic
Es•che•rich•i•a
Escherichia co•li
es•cu•le•tin
es•cu•lin
es•cutch•eon ✓
es•er•ine
Es•gic-Plus *Trademark.*
Es•oi•drix *Trademark.*
Es•oi•mil *Trademark.*
Es•ka•lith *Trademark.*
Eskalith CR *Trademark.*

Es•march ban•dage
e•sod•ic
e•soph•a•gal
e•soph•a•ge•al
e•soph•a•gi•tis ✓
e•soph•a•go•gas•tros•to•my, *n., pl.* -mies.
e•soph•a•go•scope
e•soph•a•gos•to•my ex•ter•na
esophagostomy in•ter•na
e•soph•a•gus, *n., pl.* -gi.
e•so•pho•ri•a
Es•o•té•ri•ca *Trademark.*
es•o•tro•pi•a
es•o•trop•ic
es•pun•di•a
es•sence
es•sen•tial
essential a•mi•no ac•id
essential fat•ty ac•ids
Es•tar Gel *Trademark.*
es•ter
es•ter•ase
es•ter•oi•fi•ca•tion
es•ter•oi•ofy, *v.,* -fied, -fy•ing.
es•the•sia
es•the•si•om•e•ter
es•the•si•om•e•try
es•the•si•o•phys•i•ol•o•gy
es•the•sis, *n., pl.* -ses.
es•thet•ics
es•thi•o•mene
Es•ti•nyl *Trademark.*
Es•trace *Trademark.*
Es•tra•derm *Trademark.*
es•tra•di•ol
Es•tra•du•rin *Trademark.*
es•tral
Es•tra•tab *Trademark.*
Es•tra•test *Trademark.*

es•trin
es•tri•ol
es•tro•gen•ic
es•tro•gen re•place•ment
 ther•a•py
es•tro•gen•ic•i•ty, *n., pl.*
 -ties.
es•trone
es•tro•pip•ate
es•trous
Es•tro•vis *Trademark.*
es•tru•al
es•trum
es•trus
e•tat la•cu•naire
etat ma•me•lonne
etat mar•bre
eth•am•bu•tol
Eth•a•mide *Trademark.*
e•tha•mi•van
E•tha•mo•lin *Trademark.*
eth•a•nol
eth•a•no•la•mine
e•ther
e•the•re•al
e•the•ri•al
e•ther•ic
e•ther•i•fi•ca•tion
e•ther•i•o•fy, *v.,* -fied, -fy•ing.
e•ther•i•za•tion
e•ther•ize, *v.,* -ized, -iz•ing.
eth•i•cal
eth•i•cal•i•ty
eth•i•cal•ly
eth•i•cal•ness
eth•ics
E•thi•o•dol *Trademark.*
e•thi•on•am•ide
e•this•ter•one
eth•moid
eth•moi•dal
eth•moi•di•tis

eth•mo•tur•bi•nal
Eth•mo•zine *Trademark.*
eth•no•phar•ma•co•log•ic
eth•no•phar•ma•
 co•log•i•cal
eth•no•phar•ma•col•o•gy
eth•o•hex•a•di•ol
e•thol•o•gy
eth•o•sux•i•mide
Eth•rane *Trademark.*
Eth•ril *Trademark.*
eth•yl
eth•y•lene
eth•y•lene•di•a•mine
eth•y•lene•di•a•mine•tet•
 ra•a•ce•tic
ethylenediaminetetraacetic
 ac•id
eth•yl•mor•phine
Eth•y•no•di•ol/Eth•i•nyl Es•
 tra•di•ol
e•ti•o•late, *v.,* -lat•ed, -lat•
 ing.
e•ti•o•la•tion
e•ti•o•log•ic
e•ti•o•log•i•cal
e•ti•ol•o•gist
e•ti•ol•o•gy, *n., pl.* -gies.
e•ti•o•path•o•gen•e•sis, *n.,*
 pl. -e•ses.
e•ti•o•por•phy•rin
E•to•do•lac
Et•ra•fon Forte *Trademark.*
Etrafon-A *Trademark.*
Eu•bac•te•ri•um
eu•caine
eu•ca•lyp•tol
eu•ca•lyp•tole
eu•ca•lyp•tus, *n., pl.* -ti.
eu•ca•tro•pine
Eu•ce•rin *Trademark.*
Eu•ces•to•da

eu•chro•mat•ic
eu•chro•ma•tin
eu•cra•sia
eu•di•om•e•ter
eu•gen•ic
eu•gen•i•cal
eu•gen•i•cal•ly
eu•gen•i•cist
eu•gen•ics
eu•gen•ism
eu•ge•nol
eu•gle•na, *n., pl.* -nas.
eu•gle•noid or eu•gle•na, *n., pl.* -noids or -nas.
eu•glob•u•lin
eu•gon•ic
eu•kar•y•ote
eu•kar•y•ot•ic
Eu•lex•in *Trademark.*
eu•mor•phic
eu•my•cete
Eu•my•ce•tes
eu•nuch
eu•nuch•ism
eu•nuch•oid
eu•nuch•oi•dal
eu•nuch•oid•ism
eu•pa•to•rin
eu•pa•to•ri•um
eu•pep•sia
eu•pep•tic
eu•phen•ic
eu•phen•ics
eu•pho•ri•a
eu•pho•ri•ant
eu•phor•ic
eu•pho•ri•cal•ly
eu•pho•ri•gen•ic
eu•plas•tic
eu•ploid
eu•ploi•dy
eup•ne•a

eup•no•es
eu•prax•i•a
Eu•rax *Trademark.*
Eu•ro•ti•a•les
eu•ry•ce•phal•ic
eu•ry•ceph•a•lous
eu•ryg•nath•ic
eu•ryg•na•thism
eu•ryg•gna•thous
eu•ry•on
eu•ry•so•mat•ic
eu•ry•some
eu•ry•so•mic
eu•sta•chian
Eustachian tube
eu•tec•tic
eu•tha•na•sia
eu•tha•na•si•ast
eu•tha•na•sic
eu•tha•nize, *v.,* -nized, -niz•ing.
eu•then•ics
eu•ther•mic
Eu•throid *Trademark.*
eu•thy•roid
eu•thy•roid•ism
eu•to•ci•a
Eu•to•nyl *Trademark.*
Eu•tron *Trademark.*
eu•troph•ic
eu•tro•phy
E•vac-Q-Kit *Trademark.*
Evac-Q-Kwik *Trademark.*
e•vac•u•ant
e•vac•u•ate, *v.,* -at•ed, -at•ing.
e•vac•u•a•tion
e•vac•u•a•tor
e•vag•i•na•ble
e•vag•i•nate, *v.,* -nat•ed, -nat•ing.
e•vag•i•na•tion

e○val•u•a○tion
ev○a•nes•cent
eve•ning prim•rose
e○ven•tra○tion
e○over•sion
ev○i•rate
ev○i•ra○tion
e○vis•cer•ate, v., -at○ed, -at•
  ing.
e○vis•cer○a○tion
E○vis○ta Trademark.
ev○o•ca•tion
ev○o•ca•tor
e○voked po○ten•tial
ev○o•lu○tion
e○vul•sion
ewe-neck
ewe-necked
Ew•ing's sar•co○ma
Ewing's tu•mor
ex•am○i•na○tion
ex•am•ine, v., -ined, -in•ing.
ex•am•in○er
ex•an•them
exanthem su•bi•tum
ex•an•the○ma, n., pl.
  -the•ma○ta, -the•mas.
ex•an•the•mat○ic
ex•an•them○a•tous
ex•ca•vate, v., -vat○ed, -vat•
  ing.
ex•ca•va○tio dis○ci
excavatio rec○to•u•te○ri○na
excavatio rec○to•ves○i•ca•lis
excavatio ves○i•cou•te○ri○na
ex•ca•va○tion
ex•ca•va•tor
Ex•ced•rin Trademark.
ex•cip•i•ent
ex•cis○a•ble
ex•cise, v., -cised, -cis•ing.
ex•ci○sion

ex•ci•sion○al
excisional bi○op○sy
ex•cit○a•bil○i○ty
ex•cit○a•ble
ex•cit○a•ble•ness
ex•cit○a•bly
ex•cit•ant
ex•ci•ta•tion
ex•ci•ta•to○ry
ex•cite, v., -cit○ed, -cit•ing.
ex•cite•ment
ex•ci•tor
ex•clave
ex•clu•sion
ex•clu•sion•ar○y
ex•co•ri•ate, v., -at○ed, -at•
  ing.
ex•co•ri•a○tion
ex•cre•ment
ex•cre•men•tal
ex•cre•men•ti○tious
ex•cre•men•tous
ex•cres•cence
ex•cres•cent
ex•cres•cent○ly
ex•cre○ta
ex•cre○tal
ex•crete, v., -cret○ed, -cret•
  ing.
ex•cret•er
ex•cre•tion
ex•cre•tive
ex•cre•to○ry
ex•cur•sion
ex•cys•ta•tion
ex•cyst•ment
Ex•el•derm Trademark.
ex•en•ter•ate, v., -at○ed, -at•
  ing.
ex•en•te•ra○tion
ex•er•cise in•ten•si○ty
exercise load

exercise stress test
ex•er•e•o•sis, *n., pl.* -ses.
ex•er•gon•ic
ex•flag•el•la•tion
ex•fo•li•ate, *v.,* -at•ed, -at•
  ing.
ex•fo•li•a•tion
ex•fo•li•a•tive
ex•hal•ant
ex•ha•la•tion
ex•hale, *v.,* -haled, -hal•ing.
ex•haust
ex•haus•tion
ex•hi•bi•tion•ism
ex•hi•bi•tion•ist
ex•hi•bi•tion•is•tic
ex•hil•o•a•rant
ex•hu•ma•tion
ex•hume, *v.,* -humed, -hum•
  ing.
ex•o•i•tus, *n., pl.* -tus.
ex•lamp•tic
Ex•na *Trademark.*
ex•o•o•cho•ri•on, *n., pl.* -ri•a.
ex•o•o•crine
exocrine gland
ex•o•o•cri•nol•o•o•gy
ex•o•o•cyt•o•ic
ex•o•o•cy•to•sis
ex•o•o•cy•tot•o•ic
ex•od•o•ic
ex•o•o•don•tia
ex•o•o•don•tist
ex•o•o•en•zyme
ex•o•o•e•ryth•ro•cyt•o•ic
ex•o•og•o•a•mous or ex•o•o•
  gam•o•ic
ex•og•o•a•my
ex•o•o•gas•tru•la
ex•og•e•o•nous
ex•o•on
ex•o•o•nu•cle•ase

ex•o•o•pep•ti•dase
ex•o•o•pho•ri•a
ex•oph•thal•mic
ex•oph•thal•mos or ex•oph•
  thal•mus or ex•oph•thal•
  mi•a
ex•o•o•phyt•o•ic
Ex•or•bin *Trademark.*
ex•o•o•skel•e•o•ton
ex•os•mo•o•sis
ex•os•mot•o•ic
ex•os•mot•o•i•cal•o•ly
ex•o•o•spore
ex•o•o•spo•ri•um, *n., pl.* -ri•o•a.
ex•os•to•sis, *n., pl.* -ses.
exostosis car•ti•la•gin•e•a
ex•o•o•ter•o•ic
ex•o•o•ter•o•i•cal•o•ly
ex•o•o•tox•o•ic
ex•o•o•tox•o•in
ex•o•o•tro•pi•a
ex•o•o•trop•o•ic
ex•pect•ant
ex•pec•to•rant
ex•pec•to•rate, *v.,* -rat•ed,
  -rat•ing.
ex•pec•to•ra•tion
ex•pec•to•ra•tor
ex•per•o•i•ment
ex•pi•ra•tion
ex•pi•ra•to•ry
ex•pire, *v.,* -pired, -pir•ing.
ex•plant
ex•plan•ta•tion
ex•plor•o•a•bil•o•i•ty
ex•plor•o•a•ble
ex•plo•ra•tion
ex•plo•ra•to•ry
ex•plore, *v.,* -plored, -plor•ing.

ex•plor∘er
ex•plor•ing∘ly
ex•plo•sion
ex•plo•sive per•son•al∘i∘ty
ex•pose, *v.*, -posed, -pos•ing.
ex•po•sure
exposure as•sess•ment
ex•press
ex•pres•sion
ex•pres•siv∘i∘ty
ex•san•gui•nate, *v.*, -nat∘ed, -nat•ing.
ex•san•gui•na•tion
ex•san•guine
ex•san•guin∘i∘ty
ex•scind
ex•sect
ex•sec•tion
Ex•sel *Trademark.*
ex•sic•cate, *v.*, -cat∘ed, -cat•ing.
ex•sic•ca•tion
ex•sic•co∘sis, *n.*, *pl.* -ses.
ex•stro•phy, *n.*, *pl.* -phies.
ex•tend•ed care
ex•tend∘er
Ex•ten•dryl *Trademark.*
ex•ten•sion
ex•ten•si∘ty
ex•ten•sor
ex•te•ri∘or
ex•te•ri•or∘i∘za•tion
ex•te•ri•or•ize, *v.*, -ized, -iz•ing.
ex•tern
ex•ter•nal
ex•ter•nal∘ly
ex•ter•o•cep•tive
ex•ter•o•cep•tor
ex•ter•o•fec•tive
ex•ti∘ma, *n.*, *pl.* -mae, -mas.
ex•tinc•tion

ex•tin•guish
ex•tir•pate, *v.*, -pat∘ed, -pat•ing.
ex•tir•pa•tion
ex•tor•sion
ex∘tra-ar•tic∘u•lar
ex∘tra•buc•cal
ex∘tra•bul•bar
ex∘tra•cap•su•lar
ex∘tra•cel•lu•lar
ex∘tra•chro•mo•so•mal
ex∘tra•cor•po•re∘al
ex∘tra•cor•po•re•al∘ly
ex∘tract•ant
ex∘trac•tion
ex∘trac•tive
ex∘trac•tor
ex∘tra•cys•tic
ex∘tra•du•ral
ex∘tra•em•bry•o•nal
ex∘tra•em•bry•on∘ic
extraembryonic mem•brane
ex∘tra•gen∘i•tal
ex∘tra•he•pat∘ic
ex∘tra•me•dul•lar∘y
ex∘tra•mi•to•chon•dri∘al
ex∘tra•mu•ral
ex∘tra•nu•cle∘ar
ex∘tra•oc∘u•lar
ex∘tra•py•ram∘i•dal
ex∘tra•re•nal
ex∘tra•sen•so∘ry
ex∘tra•sen•sor∘y per•cep•tion
ex∘tra•sys•to∘le, *n.*, *pl.* -les.
ex∘tra•sys•tol∘ic
ex∘tra•tu•bal
ex∘tra•u•ter•ine
ex∘tra•vag∘i•nal
ex∘trav∘a•sate, *v.*, -sat∘ed, -sat•ing.
ex∘trav∘a•sa•tion

ex•tra•vas•cu•lar
ex∘tra•ven•tric∘u•lar
ex∘tra•ver•sion
ex∘tra•ver•sive
ex∘tra•vert
ex∘tra•vert∘ed
ex•trem∘i∘ty, *n.*, *pl.* -ties.
ex•trin•sic
extrinsic fac•tor
ex∘tro•spec•tion
ex∘tro•ver•sion
ex∘tro•ver•sive
ex∘tro•vert
ex∘tro•vert∘ed
ex∘tro•ver•tive
ex•trude, *v.*, -trud∘ed, -trud•
    ing.
ex•tru•sion
ex•tu•bate, *v.*, -bat∘ed, -bat•
    ing.
ex•tu•ba•tion
ex∘u•date
ex∘u•da•tion
ex∘u•da•tive

ex∘ude, *v.*, -ud∘ed, -ud•ing.
ex∘u•vi∘ae
ex∘u•vi∘al
ex∘u•vi•ate, *v.*, -at∘ed, -at•
    ing.
ex∘u•vi•a•tion
eye
eye chart
eye doc•tor
eye tuck
eye•ball
eye•brow
eye•cup
ey•ed•ness
eye•drop•per
eye•drop•per•ful
eye•glass•es
eye•lash
eye•lid
eye•lift
eye•sight
eye•strain
eye•wash

F

fa•bel∘la, *n.*, *pl.* -lae.
Fa•bi•an∘a
fab•ri•ca•tion
Fab•ry's dis•ease
fab∘u•la•tion
face-lift•ing
face•bow
face-lift or face•lift
fac∘et
fa•cette
fa∘cia
fa•cial
facial nerve
fa•cially
fa•ci∘es, *n.*, *pl.* fa•ci∘es.

fa•cil∘i•ta•tion
fac•ti•tious
fac•tor
factor VIII
fac•to•ri∘al
Fac•trel *Trademark.*
fac•ul•ta•tive•ly
fae•cal
fae•ca•lith
fae•ces
fag∘o•py•rism
Fahr•en•heit
fail•ure
failure to thrive
faint

fa•lac•tan
fal•cate
fal•cial
fal•ci•form
fal•cu•ola
fal•cu•lar
Fal•lo•pi•an
fallopian or Fallopian tube
Fal•lot pen•tal•o•gy
Fallot tet•ral•o•gy
Fal•lot's tet•ral•o•gy
false preg•nan•cy
false-neg•a•tive
false-pos•i•tive
falx, *n., pl.* fal•ces.
falx ap•o•neu•rot•i•ca
falx cer•e•o•bel•oli
falx ce•re•bri
falx in•gui•na•lis
falx sep•ti
fames
fa•mil•i•al
fam•i•ly, *n., pl.* -lies.
family plan•ning
family prac•tice
family prac•ti•tion•er
family ther•a•py
Fa•mo•ti•dine
fa•mous fec•es test
fan•go
Fan•ni•a
Fan•si•dar *Trademark.*
fan•ta•size, *v.,* -sized, -siz•ing.
fan•tasm
fan•tast
fan•ta•sy, *n., pl.* -sies.
fan•tom
far•a•da•ic
fa•rad•ic
far•a•dism
far•a•di•za•tion

far•a•dize, *v.,* -dized, -diz•ing.
far•a•diz•er
far•cy
far•i•na•ceous
farm•er's lung
far-point
far•sight•ed
far•sight•ed•ness
fas•ci•a, *n., pl.* fas•ci•ae.
fas•ci•ae mus•cu•la•res
  bul•bi
fasciae musculares oc•u•oli
fasciae or•bi•ta•les
fas•cial
fas•ci•cle
fas•ci•cled
fas•cic•ou•lar
fas•cic•ou•late
fas•cic•ou•lat•ed
fas•cic•ou•la•tion
fas•cic•ou•lus, *n., pl.* -li.
fas•ci•ec•to•my, *n., pl.* -mies.
Fas•ci•o•o•la
fasciola ci•ne•re•o•a
fas•ci•o•lar
Fas•ci•o•loi•des
fas•ci•o•lop•si•a•sis, *n., pl.*
  -ses.
Fas•ci•o•lop•sis
fas•ci•o•lop•sis
fas•ci•i•tis
fas•tid•i•um
fas•tig•i•um, *n., pl.* -tig•i•
  ums, -tig•i•a.
Fas•tin *Trademark.*
fast•ness
fat cell
fa•tal
fa•tal•i•ty, *n., pl.* -ties.
fate map
fat•i•ga•bil•i•ty, *n., pl.* -ties.
fa•tig•a•ble

fa•tigu•a•ble
fa•tigue
fat-sol○u•ble
fat○ty, *adj.* -ti○er, -ti•est.
fatty ac○id
fau•ces
fau•cial
fa•ve○o•late
fa•ve○o•lus, *n., pl.* -li.
fav•ism
fa○vus, *n., pl.* -vus○es.
fe•bric○u○la
feb•ri•fa•cient
fe•brif○ic
fe•brif○u•gal
feb•ri•fuge
fe•brile
fe•bril○i○ty
feb•ris
fe○cal
fe•ca•lith
fe•ca•loid
fe○ces
Fech•ner's law
fec○u○la, *n., pl.* -lae.
fec○u•lent
fe•cun•date, *v.,* -dat○ed, -dat•
  ing.
fec•un•da•tion
fe•cun•di○ty
Fed○a•hist *Trademark.*
fee•ble•mind○ed
fee•ble-mind•ed•ness
feed•back
Feen-A-Mint *Trademark.*
Feh•ling so•lu•tion
Feh•ling's solution
Fel•dene
Fel○i•dae
fe•line
fel•late, *v.,* -lat○ed, -lat•ing.
fel•la•ti○o

fel•la•tion
fel•la•tor
feo•lo-de-se, *n., pl.* feo•lo○nes-
  de-se, fe•los-de-se.
fel○on
felt•work
fe•male
female con•dom
fem○i•nism
fem○i•ni•za•tion
fem○i•nize, *v.,* -nized, -niz•
  ing.
Fem○o•gen *Trademark.*
fem○o•ral
fem○o•ro•tib•i○al
Fem•stat *Trademark.*
fe○mur, *n., pl.* fe•murs,
  fem○o○ra.
Fe•ne•sin *Trademark.*
fe•nes•tra, *n., pl.* -trae.
fenestra coch•le○ae
fenestra o○va•lis
fenestra ro•tun○da
fenestra ves•tib○u○li
fe•nes•tral
fen•es•trate
fen•es•trat○ed
fen•es•tra•tion
fen•flur○a•mine
Fe•no•pro•fen *Trademark.*
fen/phen
Fen•ta•nyl *Trademark.*
fen○u•greek
Fe•o•sol *Trademark.*
Fe•o•stat *Trademark.*
Fer•an•cee *Trademark.*
Ferancee-HP *Trademark.*
fer•ment
fer•men•ta•tion
fer•men•ta•tive
Fer○o-Fol○ic-500 *Trademark.*
Fer○o-Grad-500 *Trademark.*

Fer○o-Grad○u•met *Trademark.*
Fer•ra•let *Trademark.*
fer•re•dox○in
fer•ric
fer○ri•he•mo•glo•bin
fer○ri•por•phy•rin
fer○ri•pro•to•por•phy•rin
fer○ri•tin
Fer○ro-Se•quels *Trademark*
fer○ro•por•phy•rin
fer○ro•pro•to•por•phy•rin
fer•rous
fer•ru•gin•e○ous
fer•ru•gi•nous
fer•rule
fer•rum phos•pho○i•cum
fer•tile
fer•tile○ly
fer•tile•ness
fer•til○i○ty
fer•ti•li•za•tion
fer•ti•lize, *v.,* -lized, -liz•ing.
fer•ti•li•zin
fes•cue foot
Fes•tal II *Trademark.*
fes•ter
fes•ti•nat•ing gait
fes•ti•na•tion
fes•toon
fe○tal
fetal al•co•hol syn•drome
fetal hy•dan•to○in syn•drome
fetal po•si•tion
fe•ta•tion
fet•ich
fet•ich•ism
fe•ti•cid○al
fe•ti•cide
fet•ish
fet•ish•ism
fet•lock

fe•tol○o•gist
fe•tol○o•gy
fe•tom•e•try
fe○tor
fetor ex○o○ore
fetor he•pat○i•cus
fe•to•scope
fe•to•scop○ic
fe•tos•co○py
Fe•trin *Trademark.*
fe•tus
fetus com•pres•sus
fetus cy•lin•dri•cus
fetus in•fe○tu
fetus pa•py•ra•ceus
Feul•gen re•ac•tion
fe○ver
fever blis•ter
Fe•ver•all *Trademark.*
fe•ver○ish
fe•ver•ous
fi○ber
fiber-op•tic
fiber op•tics
Fi•ber•all *Trademark.*
Fi•ber•Con *Trademark.*
Fi•ber•med *Trademark.*
fi•ber•scope
Fi•brad *Trademark.*
fi○bre
fi•bril
fi•bril○la, *n., pl.* -lae.
fib•ril•lar
fib•ril•lar○y
fi•bril•late, *v.,* -lat○ed, -lat•ing.
fi•bril•la•tion
fi•brin
fi•brin○o•gen
fi•bri•no•gen○o•pe○ni○a
fi•bri•noid
fi•bri•nol○y•sin

fi•bri•nol•y•sis, *n., pl.* -ses.
fi•bri•no•lyt•ic
fi•bri•no•pu•ru•lent
fi•brin•ous
fi•bro•ad•e•no•ma, *n., pl.* -mas, -ma•ta.
fi•bro•blast
fi•bro•blas•tic
fi•bro•car•ti•lage
fi•bro•car•ti•lag•oi•nous
fi•bro•car•ti•la•go ba•sa•lis
fibrocartilago na•vic•u•laris
fi•bro•cel•lu•lar
fi•bro•cys•tic
fi•bro•cyte
fi•bro•e•las•tic
fi•broid
fi•bro∘in
fi•bro∘ma, *n., pl.* -mas, -ma•ta.
fi•bro•ma•toid
fi•bro•ma•to•sis, *n., pl.* -ses.
fibromatosis gin•gi•vae
fi•brom∘a•tous
fi•bro•mus•cu•lar
fi•bro•my•al•gia
fi•bro•my•o∘ma, *n., pl.* -mas, -ma•ta.
fi•bro•my•o•si•tis
fi•bro•myx∘o∘ma, *n., pl.* -mas, -ma•ta.
fi•bro•pla•sia
fi•bro•plas•tic
fi•bro•sar•co•ma, *n., pl.* -mas, -ma•ta.
fibrosarcoma myx∘o•ma•to•des
fibrosarcoma phyl•lo•des
fi•brose
fi•bro•sis
fi•bro•si•tis
fi•brot∘ic

fi•brous
fi•brous•ly
fi•brous•ness
fib∘u•la, *n., pl.* -lae, -las.
fib∘u•lar
fib∘u•lo•cal•ca•ne•al
fi∘cin
field of vi•sion
fifth dis•ease
fight-or-flight re•sponse
fi•la•ceous
fil∘a•ment
fi∘lar
fi•lar∘i•a, *n., pl.* -lar∘i∘ae.
fi•lar∘i•al
fi•lar•i•a•sis, *n., pl.* -ses.
fi•lar∘i•cide
fil∘a•riid
Fi•lar•i•oi•de•a
fil∘i∘al
Fi•li•bon *Trademark.*
fi•lic∘ic
fi•li•form
fil•let
fill•ing
fil∘o•pod, *n., pl.* -pods.
fil∘o•po•di∘um, *n., pl.* -di∘a.
fil∘o•vi•rus, *n., pl.* -rus∘es.
fil•ter
fil•ter•a•bil•i•ty
fil•ter•a•ble
filterable vi•rus
fil•ter•a•ble•ness
fil•tra•ble
fil•trate, *v.,* -trat∘ed, -trat•ing.
fil•tra•tion
fil•trum
fi∘lum, *n., pl.* fi∘la.
fim•bri•a, *n., pl.* -bri∘ae.
fimbria hip•po•cam•pi
fimbria o•var•i•ca

fim•bri•at•ed
fim•bri•a•tion
fin•ger
fin•gered
fin•ger•nail
fin•ger•print
fin•ger•print•ing
fin•ger•tip
Fi•or•oi•cet *Trademark.*
Fi•or•oi•nal *Trademark.*
fire•bug
fire•damp
first aid
first-de•gree
first-degree burn
fish-scale dis•ease
fish•skin dis•ease
fis•sion
fis•sip○a•rous
fis•su○ra, *n., pl.* -rae.
fis•su•ral
fis•su•ra•tion
fis•sure, *v.,* -sured, -sur•ing.
fis•tu○la, *n., pl.* -las, -lae.
fis•tu•li•za○tion
fis•tu•lize, *v.,* -lized, -liz○ing.
fis•tu•lot○o○my, *n., pl.* -mies.
fis•tu•lous or fis•tu•lar, fis•
  tu•late
fix•ate, *v.,* -at○ed, -at•ing.
fix○a•tion
fix○a•tive
fixed i○de○a
fix•ing
fla•bel•lum, *n., pl.* -bel○la.
flac•cid
flac•cid○i○ty
fla•gel•lar
Flag○el•la○ta
Flag○el•la•tae
fla•gel•late, *v.,* -lat○ed, -lat•
  ing.

flag○el•la•tion
flag○el•lo•sis, *n., pl.* -ses.
fla•gel•lum, *n., pl.* -gel○la,
  -gel○lums.
Fla•gyl *Trademark.*
flash•back
flat•foot, *n., pl.* -feet.
flat•foot○ed
flat○u•lence
flat○u•len○cy
flat○u•lent
Flat○u•lex *Trademark.*
fla•tus, *n., pl.* -tus○es.
flat•worm
fla•va•none
fla•ve○do, *n., pl.* -dos.
fla•vi•an○ic
fla•vin
fla•vine
Fla•vo○bac•te•ri○um
fla•vone
fla•vo•noid
fla•vo•nol
fla•vo•pro•tein
fla•vor
Flax○e•dil *Trademark.*
flea-bit•ten
flea•bite
fle•cai•nide
flec•tion
Fleet *Trademark.*
flesh wound
Fletch•er•ism
fletch•er•ize, *v.,* -ized, -iz•ing.
flex
Flex•er○il *Trademark.*
flex•im•e•ter
flex•ion
flex○or
flex○u•ral
flex•ure
flight of i○de○as

Flint•stones *Trademark.*
floa•ta•tion
float•ing
floc, *v.*, flocced, floc•cing.
floc•cil•la•tion
floc•cose
floc•cu•lar
floc•cu•late, *v.*, -lat∘ed, -lat•ing.
floc•cu•la•tion
floc•cule
floc•cu•lence
floc•cu•lent
floc•cu•lus, *n.*, *pl.* -cu∘li.
floc∘il•la•tion
Flo•nase
flood•ing
flo∘ra, *n.*, *pl.* flo•ras, flo•rae.
Flo•rence flask
Flo•ri•nef *Trademark.*
Flor•one *Trademark.*
Flo•ro•pryl *Trademark.*
Flor•vite *Trademark.*
floss
flo•ta•tion
flow cy•tom•e∘ter
flow cy•tom•e∘try
flow•me•ter
Flox∘in
flu
Flu-I∘mune *Trademark.*
Flu•con∘a•zole
fluc•tu•ant
flu∘id
flu•id∘ex•tract
flu•id∘glyc∘er•ate
flu•id∘i∘ty, *n.*, *pl.* -ties.
flu•id∘ounce
flu•i•drachm
flu•i•dram
fluke
flu•mi∘na pi•lo∘rum

flu•o•cin∘o•lone
ac∘e∘to•nide
Flu•o•gen *Trademark.*
Flu•o•nid *Trademark.*
flu∘or
fluor al•bus
fluor•ap∘a•tite
fluo•rence
fluo•res•ce∘in
fluorescein an•gi•og•ra•phy
fluo•res•cence
fluorescence-ac•ti•vat∘ed cell
sort∘er
flu•o•res•cent
Flu•o•ri-Meth•ane *Trademark.*
fluoro•i•date, *v.*, -dat∘ed, -dat•ing.
fluoro•i•da•tion
fluo•ride
fluo•rid∘i•za•tion
fluoro•i•dize, *v.*, -dized, -diz•ing.
fluo•rim•e∘ter
fluo•rim•e∘try
fluoro•i•nate, *v.*, -nat∘ed, -nat•ing.
fluor•i•na•tion
fluor•ine
Fluoro•i•tab *Trademark.*
fluoro∘o•chrome
fluo•rog•ra•phy
fluo•rom•e∘ter
fluo•rom•e∘try
fluoro∘o•roent•gen•og•ra•phy, *n.*, *pl.* -phies.
fluoro∘o•scope, *n.*, *v.*, -scoped, -scop•ing.
fluoro∘o•scop∘ic
fluoro∘o•scop∘i•cal∘ly
flu•o•ros•co•pist
fluo•ros•co∘py
fluo•ro•sis

fluoro•o•u•ra•cil
flu•o•sil•i•cate
Flu•o•thane *Trademark.*
Flu•ox•e•tine *Trademark.*
flu•phen•a•zine
Flu•ress *Trademark.*
Flu•ro-Ethyl *Trademark.*
Flu•ror•plex *Trademark.*
Flu•ti•ca•sone
flut•ter
Flu•va•stat•in
flux
fly ag•a•ric
fly•belt
fo•cal
fo•cal•ize, *v.*, -ized, -iz•ing.
fo•cim•e•ter
fo•com•e•ter
fo•cus, *n., pl.* -cus•es, -ci.
foen•u•greek
foe•tal
foet•i•cide
foe•tor
foe•tus
fo•la•cin
fo•late
Fo•lex *Trademark.*
Fo•lex PFS *Trademark.*
Fo•ley cath•e•ter
fo•li•a•ceous
fo•li•ate
fol•ic
folic ac•id
fo•lie
folie à deux, *n., pl.* fo•lies à
deux.
folie de gran•deur, *n., pl.* fo-
lies de gran•deur.
fo•lin•ic
fo•li•ose
fo•li•ous
fo•li•um, *n., pl.* fo•li•a.

folk med•i•cine
fol•li•cle
follicle mite
follicle-stim•u•lat•ing hor•
mone
fol•lic•u•lar
fol•lic•u•late
fol•lic•u•lated
fol•lic•u•lin
fol•lic•u•li•tis
fol•lic•u•lo•ma, *n., pl.* -mas,
-ma•ta.
fol•lic•u•lus, *n., pl.* -lic•u•li.
folliculus lym•phat•i•cus
folliculus pi•li
fol•low-up
Fol•lu•te•in *Trademark.*
fo•lo•ri•met•ric
Fol•vite *Trademark.*
fo•ment
fo•men•ta•tion
fom•ites
Fon•tan op•er•a•tion
fon•ta•nel or fon•ta•nelle
food poi•son•ing
foot
foot-and-mouth dis•ease
foot•bath
foot•drop
foot•sore
foot•sore•ness
fo•ra•men, *n., pl.* -ram•i•na,
-ra•mens.
foramen mag•num
foramen o•va•le
fo•ram•i•nif•er•ous
Fo•rane *Trademark.*
for•bid•den clone
for•ceps, *n., pl.* -ceps, -ci•pes.
for•ci•pate
for•ci•pat•ed
for•ci•pi•al

for•ci•pres•sure
For•dyce dis•ease
fore•arm
fore•brain
fore•cons•cious
fore•fin•ger
fore•foot, *n., pl.* -feet.
fore•gut
fore•head
fore•leg
fore•limb
fore•milk
fo•ren•sic
forensic an•thro•pol∘o∘gy
forensic med∘i•cine
fo•ren•si•cal∘ly
fore•paw
fore•play
fore•pleas•ure
fore•skin
fore•stom•ach
fore•top
fore•wa•ters
for•mal•de•hyde
for•ma•lin
for•ma•lin•ize, *v.,* -ized, -iz•ing.
for•mate
for•ma•tion
form∘a•tive
form∘a•tive∘ly
form∘a•tive•ness
forme fruste, *n., pl.* **formes frustes.**
for•mic
formic ac∘id
for•mi•ca•tion
for•mo•lize, *v.,* -lized, -liz•ing.
for•mu∘la, *n., pl.* -las, -lae.
for•mu•lar∘y, *n., pl.* -lar•ies.
for•mu•la•tion
for•myl

for•ni•cal
for•ni•cate, *v.,* -cat∘ed, -cat•ing.
for•ni•ca•tion
for•ni•ca•tor
for•nix, *n., pl.* -ni•ces.
Fortaz
Fos∘a•max
Fosfree
Fos∘i•no•pril
fos∘sa, *n., pl.* fos•sae.
fos•sette
fos•su∘la, *n., pl.* -su•lae.
fos•su•late
Fo•to•tar *Trademark.*
fou•droy•ant
found∘er
four•chette
fo•ve∘a, *n., pl.* -ve∘ae.
fovea cen•tra•lis
fo•ve∘al
fo•ve•ate
fo•ve•at∘ed
fo•ve•a•tion
fo•ve•i•form
fo•ve∘o∘la, *n., pl.* -lae, -las.
foveola coc•cyg∘e∘a
foveola pal∘a•ti∘na
foveolae gas•tri•cae
foveolae gran∘u•la•res
fo•ve•o•lar
fo•ve•o•late
fox•glove
frac•tion•ate, *v.,* -at∘ed, -at•ing.
frac•tion•a•tion
frac•tur∘a•ble
frac•tur∘al
frac•ture, *n., v.,* -tured, -tur•ing.
fra•gile X syn•drome
frag∘i•li•tas crin∘i∘um

fragilitas os•si•um
fra•gil•i•ty
fra•gil•o•cyte
fra•gil•o•cy•to•sis
fraise
fram•be•sia
fram•boe•sia
frame•shift
frame•work
fran•ci•um
fra•ter•nal
fraternal twin
Fre•A•mine
freck•le
free-as•so•ci•ate, *v.*, -at•ed,
  -at•ing.
free as•so•ci•a•tion
free flap
free-float•ing
free-float•ing anx•i•e•ty
free-liv•ing
free rad•i•cal
free•base or free-base, *v.*,
  -based, -bas•ing.
free•bas•er
free•mar•tin
freeze-dry, *v.*, -dried, -dry•ing.
freeze-etch•ing
frem•i•tus, *n.*, *pl.* -tus.
fre•nal
fren•u•lum, *n.*, *pl.* fren•u•la.
fre•num, *n.*, *pl.* fre•na.
fren•zied
fren•zy, *n.*, *pl.* -zies.
fre•tum, *n.*, *pl.* fre•ta.
Freud•i•an
Freudian slip
Freud•i•an•ism
Freund's ad•ju•vant
fri•a•bil•i•ty, *n.*, *pl.* -ties.
fri•a•ble
fri•a•ble•ness

Fried•län•der's ba•cil•lus
Fried•man's test
Fried•reich's a•tax•i
Friedreich's dis•ease
frig•id
fri•gid•i•ty
frig•o•rif•ic
Fröh•lich's syn•drome
frons, *n.*, *pl.* fron•tes.
front•ad
fron•tal
frontal bone
frontal lobe
fron•ta•lis
front•al•ly
front•let
fron•to-oc•cip•i•tal
fron•to-pa•ri•e•tal
fron•to-tem•po•ral
frost•bit
frost•bite
frost•bit•ing
frost•bit•ten
frost•nip
frot•tage
fruc•to•san
fruc•tose
fruc•to•side
fru•giv•o•rous
frus•trate, *n.*, *pl.* -trat•ed,
  -trat•ing.
frus•tra•tion
fuch•sin
fuch•sine
fuch•sin•o•phil
fuch•sin•o•phil•ic
fu•cose
fu•cus ve•sic•u•lo•si•us
fu•gac•i•ty, *n.*, *pl.* -ties.
fu•gi•tive
fugue
Ful-Glo *Trademark.*

ful•crum, *n., pl.* -crums, -cra.
ful•gu•rant
ful•gu•rate, *v.,* -rat∘ed, -rat•ing.
ful•gu•ra•tion
full-blood∘ed
full•mouthed
ful•mi•nant
ful•mi•nate, *v.* -nat∘ed, -nat•ing.
Ful•vi•cin P/G *Trademark.*
Fulvicin-U/F *Trademark.*
fu•ma•gil•lin
fu•ma•rase
fu•ma•rate
fu•mar∘ic
fu•mi•ga•cin
func•ti∘o lae•sa
func•tion
func•tion∘al
functional MRI
func•tion•al•ism
func•tion•al•ist
func•tion•al•is∘tic
func•tion•al∘i∘ty
func•tion•al∘ly
fun∘dal
fun•da•ment
fun•dec•to∘my, *n., pl.* -mies.
'fun•dic
fun•do•scop∘ic
fun•dos•co∘py, *n., pl.* -pies.
fun•du•lus, *n., pl.* fun•du•lus.
fun•dus, *n., pl.* fun∘di.
fun•du•scop∘ic
fun•dus•co∘py, *n., pl.* -pies.
fun∘gal
fun•gate, *v.,* -gat∘ed, -gat•ing.
Fun∘gi Im•per•fec∘ti
Fungi-Nail *Trademark.*
fun•gi•cid∘al

fun•gi•cid•al∘ly
fun•gi•cide
fun•gi•cid∘in
fun•gi•form
fun•gi•stat∘ic
fun•gi•tox∘ic
fun•gi•tox•ic∘i∘ty, *n., pl.* -ties.
Fun•gi•zone *Trademark.*
fun•goid
Fungoid HC *Trademark.*
fun•gos•i∘ty, *n., pl.* -ties.
fun•gous
fun•gus, *n., pl.* fun∘gi, fun•gus∘es.
fu∘nic
fu•ni•cle
fu•nic∘u•lar
fu•nic∘u•li∘tis
fu•nic∘u•lus, *n., pl.* -nic∘u∘li.
fu∘nis
fun∘ny bone
Fu•ra•cin *Trademark.*
Fu•ra•dan•tin *Trademark.*
fu•ra•nose
fu•ra•zol∘i•done
fur∘ca or•bi•ta•lis
fur•cal
fur•co•ce•rous
fur•cu∘la, *n., pl.* -lae.
fur•fur
fur•fu•ra•ceous
fur•fur∘al
fur•fur∘yl
fu∘ror am∘a•to∘ri∘us
furor ep∘i•lep•ti•cus
furor gen∘i•ta•lis
Fu•ros∘e∘mide
Fu•rox•one *Trademark.*
fur•se•mide
fu•run•cle

fu•run•cu•lar or fu•run•cu•lous

fu•run•cu•loid

fu•run•cu•lo•sis

furunculosis o•ri•en•ta•lis

fu•run•cu•lous

fu•run•cu•lus, *n., pl.* -cu•li.

fu•sar○i○um, *n., pl.* -sar○i○a.

fu•si•form

fusiform an•eu•rysm

fusiform gy○rus

Fu•si•for•mis

fu•sion

fu•sion○al

fu•so•bac•te•ri•um, *n., pl.* -ri○a.

fu•so•cel•lu•lar

fu•so•spi•ro•che•tal

fus•ti•ga•tion

G

G ac○id

gad•fly, *n., pl.* -flies.

Gad○i•dae

gad○o○le○ic

Gad○us

gag, *v.,* gagged, gag•ging.

ga•lac•ta•gogue

ga•lac•tic

ga•lac•tin

ga○lac○to•cele

ga○lac○to•gogue

ga○lac○to•lip○id

ga○lac○to•lip•ide

ga○lac○to•lip○in

ga○lac○to•phore

ga○lac○to•pho•ri•tis

gal•ac•toph○o○rous

ga○lac○to•poi•e○sis

ga○lac○to•poi•et○ic

ga•lac○tor•rhe○a ✓

ga○lac○tor•rhoe○a

gal•ac•tos•a•mine

ga○lac○to•scope

ga○lac○tose

ga○lac○to•se•mi○a

ga○lac○to•se•mic

ga○lac○to•sid•ase

ga○lac○to•side

ga○lac○to•sis

ga○lac○to•su•ri○a

ga○lac○to•ther○a○py

gal•e○a

galea ap○o•neu•rot○i○ca

galea cap○i•tis

ga•len○ic

ga•len○i•cal

Ga•len•ism

gal○la

gal•la•mine

gal•late

gall•blad•der or gall blad•der

gal•le○in

gal•lic

Gal•li•for•mes

gal•li○um scan

gal•li•na•ceous

gal•li○um

gall•stone

ga•log○e○ton

gal•van○ic

galvanic skin re•sponse

gal•va•nism

gal•van•i•za•tion

gal•va•nize, *v.,* -nized, -niz•ing.

gal○va○no•cau•ter○y, *n., pl.* -ries.

gal•va•nom•e○ter

gal•va•no•sur•ger•y, *n., pl.*
-ries.
gal•va•no•tax•is, *n., pl.*
-tax•es.
gal•va•no•trop•ic
gal•va•not•ro•pism
gam•boge
ga•met•al
gam•e•tan•gi•um, *n., pl.*
-gi•a.
gam•ete
ga•met•ic
ga•met•i•cal•ly
ga•me•to•cide
ga•me•to•cyte
ga•me•to•gen•e•sis, *n., pl.*
-e•ses.
ga•me•to•gen•ic
gam•e•tog•e•nous
gam•e•tog•e•ny, *n., pl.* -tog•
e•nies.
ga•me•to•go•ni•um, *n., pl.*
-ni•a.
gam•e•tog•o•ny
gam•e•toid
ga•me•to•ki•net•ic
gam•ic
gam•ma-ben•zene hex•a•
chlo•ride
gamma cam•er•a
gamma glob•u•lin
gamma knife sur•ger•y
gamma-a•mi•no•bu•tyr•ic
ac•id
gam•ma•cism
gam•ma•cis•mus
Gam•mar *Trademark.*
Gammar-IV *Trademark.*
gam•o•gen•e•sis
gam•o•ge•net•ic or gam•o•
ge•net•i•cal
gam•o•ge•net•i•cal•ly

gam•one
gam•ont
Gam•o•phen *Trademark.*
Gam•u•lin Rh *Trademark.*
gan•gli•al
gan•gli•ar
gan•gli•ate
gan•gli•at•ed
gan•gli•form
gan•gli•o•blast
gan•gli•o•cyte
gan•gli•o•ma, *n., pl.* -mas,
-ma•ta.
gan•gli•on, *n., pl..* -gli•a. -gli•
ons.
gan•gli•o•nate
gan•gli•o•nat•ed
gan•gli•on•ec•to•my, *n., pl.*
-mies.
gan•gli•o•neu•ro•ma
gan•gli•on•ic
gan•gli•o•ni•tis
gan•gli•o•side
gan•gli•o•si•do•sis, *n., pl.*
-ses.
gan•go•sa
gan•grene, *n., v.,* -grened,
-gren•ing.
gan•gre•nous
gan•oja or gan•jah
Gan•ser syn•drome
Gan•ta•nol *Trademark.*
Gan•tri•sin *Trademark.*
gan•try, *n., pl.* -tries.
gape•worm
Gar•a•my•cin *Trademark.*
Gar•cin•i•a cam•bo•gi•a
Gard•ner's syn•drome
gar•get
gar•goyl•ism
gar•lic
gar•ru•li•ty

Gart•ner's duct
gas
gas gan•grene
gas•e•ous
gas•kin
gas•se•ri•an
gas•ter
Gas•ter•oph•i•lus
gas•tral
gas•tral•gia
gas•tral•gic
gas•trec•to•my, *n., pl.* -mies.
gas•tric
gastric bub•ble
gastric juice
gastric ul∘cer
gas•trin
gas•trit∘ic
gas•tri•tis
gas∘tro•a•ceph∘a•lus, *n., pl.*
  -pha∘li.
gas∘tro•a•nas•to•mo•sis, *n.,*
  pl. -ses.
gas∘tro•cele
gas•troc•ne•mi∘al
gas•troc•ne•mi∘an
gas•troc•ne•mi∘us, *n., pl.*
  -mi∘i.
gas∘tro•coel
gas∘tro•coele
gas∘tro•col∘ic
gas∘tro•co•lot∘o•my, *n., pl.*
  -mies.
Gas∘tro•crom *Trademark.*
gas∘tro•di•a•phane
gas∘tro•di∘a•pha•nos•co∘py,
  n., pl. -pies.
Gas∘tro•dis•coi•des
gas∘tro•du∘o•de•nal
gas∘tro•du∘o•de•ni∘tis
gas∘tro•du∘o•de•nos•to∘my,
  n., pl. -mies.

gas∘tro•en•ter∘ic
gas∘tro•en•ter•it∘ic
gas∘tro•en•ter•oi•tis
gas∘tro•en•ter∘o∘log∘ic or
  gas∘tro•en•ter∘o∘log∘i•cal.
gas∘tro•en•te•rol∘o•gist
gas∘tro•en•ter•ol∘o∘gy
gas∘tro•en•ter•op∘a•thy, *n.*
  pl. -thies.
gas∘tro•en•ter•os•to∘my, *n.,*
  pl. -mies.
gas∘tro•ep∘i•plo∘ic
gas∘tro•e•soph∘a•ge∘al
gastroesophageal re∘flux
  dis•ease
gas∘tro•e•soph∘a•gi•tis
gas∘tro•ga•vage
gas∘tro•gen∘ic
gas∘tro•graph
gas∘tro•he•pat∘ic
gas∘tro•in•tes•ti•nal
gas∘tro•je•ju•nos•to∘my, *n.*
  pl. -mies.
gas∘tro•la•vage
gas∘tro•li∘e•nal
gas∘tro•lith
gas•trol∘o∘gist
gas•trol∘o∘gy
gas•trol•y•sis
gas∘tro•pex∘y, *n., pl.* -ies.
Gas•troph∘i•lus
gas∘tro•pho∘tor
gas∘tro•phren∘ic
gas∘tro•plas∘ty, *n., pl.* -ties.
gas∘tro•pli•ca•tion
Gas•trop∘o•da
gas•trop∘o•dous
gas•trop•to•sis
gas•tror•rha•phy
gas•tros•chi•sis, *n., pl.* -ses.
gas∘tro•scope
gas∘tro•scop∘ic

gas•tros•co•py, *n., pl.* -pies.
Gas•tro•sed *Trademark.*
gas•tro•splen•ic
gas•tros•to•my, *n., pl.* -mies.
gas•tro•tom•ic
gas•trot•o•my, *n., pl.* -mies.
gas•tru•la, *n., pl.* -las, -lae.
gas•tru•lar
gas•tru•late, *v.,* -lat•ed, -lat•ing.
gas•tru•la•tion
Gas-X *Trademark.*
Gatch bed
gate•way drug
Gau•cher's dis•ease
gaul•the•ri•a
gaul•the•rin
gaunt•let
gauze
ga•vage
Gav•is•con *Trademark.*
geel•dik•kop
Gei•ger count•er
Geiger Mül•ler count•er
gel, *v.,* gelled, gel•ling.
gel e•lec•tro•phor•e•sis
gel•ate, *v.,* -at•ed, -at•ing.
gel•a•tin
gel•a•tine
gel•a•tin•i•za•tion
ge•lat•i•nize, *v.,* -nized, -niz•ing.
ge•lat•i•nous
ge•la•tion
ge•lose
Gel•pi•rin *Trademark.*
Gelpirin-CCF *Trademark.*
gel•se•mine
gel•sem•i•um sem•per•vir•ens
ge•mel•lus, *n., pl.* -mel•li, -mel•lus•es.

Gem•fi•bro•zil
gem•i•nate, *v.,* -nat•ed, -nat•ing.
gem•i•nate•ly
gem•i•na•tion
gem•i•nous
gem•ma, *n., pl.* gem•mae.
gem•mate
gem•ma•tion
gem•mu•la•tion
gem•mule
Gem•o•nil *Trademark.*
Gen-XENE *Trademark.*
ge•nal
gen•der
gender i•den•ti•ty
gender identity dis•or•der
gender role
gene
gene amp•li•fi•ca•tion
gene flow
gene fre•quen•cy
gene knock•out mouse
gene map
gene map•ping
gene pool
gene splic•ing
gene ther•a•py
gene trans•fer
ge•ne•al•o•gy, *n., pl.* -gies.
gen•er•al prac•ti•tion•er
gen•er•al•i•za•tion
gen•er•al•ized anx•i•e•ty dis•or•der
gen•er•a•tion
gen•er•a•tion•al
gen•er•a•tion•al•ly
gen•er•a•tive
gen•er•a•tively
ge•ner•ic
ge•ner•i•cal•ly
ge•net•ic

genetic code
genetic coun•sel•ing
genetic drift
genetic en•gi•neer
genetic en•gi•neer•ing
genetic fin•ger•print
genetic load
genetic map
genetic mark∘er
genetic screen•ing
genetic test•ing
ge•net∘i•cal∘ly
ge•net∘i•cist
ge•net∘ics
ge∘net∘o•troph∘ic
ge•ni∘al
gen∘ic
gen∘i•cal∘ly
ge•nic∘u•late
ge•nic∘u•lat∘ed
ge•nic∘u•late∘ly
ge•nic∘u•lum, *n., pl.* -nic•u∘la.
ge•ni∘o•glos•sus, *n., pl.* -glos∘si.
ge•ni∘o•hy•oid
ge•ni•on
ge•ni∘o•plas∘ty, *n., pl.* -ties.
gen∘i•tal
genital her•pes
genital warts
gen∘i•ta•li•a
gen∘i•tal∘ic or gen∘i•ta•li∘al
gen∘i•tal∘i•ty
gen∘i•tals
gen∘i•to•cru•ral
gen∘i•to•fem∘o•ral
gen∘i•to•u∘ri•nar∘y
ge•nius ep∘i•dem∘i•cus
genius mor∘bi
gen∘o•der•ma•to•sis
gen∘o•gram

ge•nom
ge•nome
ge•no•mic
genomic DNA
Ge•no∘ra 1/35
gen∘o•type
gen∘o•typ∘ic
gen∘o•typ∘i•cal
gen•o•typ∘i•cal∘ly
gen•ta•mi•cin
gen•tian
gen•ti•o•bi•ose
gen•ti•o•pic•rin
gen•tis∘ic
gen•ti•sin
ge•nu, *n., pl.* ge•nu∘a.
genu val•gum
genu var∘um
ge•nus, *n., pl.* gen•er∘a.
gen∘y•plas∘ty, *n., pl.* -ties.
Geo•cil•lin *Trademark.*
geo•med∘i•cine
geo•o•pa•thol∘o•gy
Geo•pen *Trademark.*
ge•o•pha•gia
ge•oph∘a•gism
ge•oph∘a•gy
Ge•oph∘i•lus
ge•o•tax∘is
ge•o•tax∘y, *n., pl.* -tax•ies.
ge•o•tri•cho•sis
ge•o•trop∘ic
ge•o•trop∘i•cal∘ly
ge•ot•ro•pism
ge•ran•i∘ol
ge•rat∘ic
ger∘a•tol∘o•gy
ger•bil
ger•bille
ger∘i•at•ric
ger∘i•a•tri•cian or ger∘i•at•rist

ger•oi•at•rics
ge•ri•at•rist
Ger•oi•med *Trademark.*
Ger•oi•plex-FS *Trademark.*
Ger•oi•ton•ic *Trademark.*
germ
germ cell
germ lay•er
germ plasm
germ the•o•o•ry
Ger•man mea•sles
ger•ma•nin
ger•ma•ni•um
germ•free
ger•mi•cid•al
ger•mi•cide
ger•mi•nal
germinal ves•oi•cle
ger•mi•no•o•ma
germ•like
germ•proof
ge•ro•der•o•ma
ge•ro•der•mi•a
ge•ron•tal
ge•ron•tic
ge•ron•to•log•o•i•cal
ger•on•tol•o•o•gist
ger•on•tol•o•o•gy
ge•oron•to•phil•o•i•a
ger•on•to•ther•o•a•py
ge•stalt, *n., pl.* -stalts, -stal•ten.
Gestalt psy•chol•o•o•gy
ges•tate, *v.,* -tat•ed, -tat•ing.
ges•ta•tion•al
gestational car•ri•er
ges•ta•tive
ges•to•sis, *n., pl.* -ses.
get•er•o•o•gen•ic
Gev•ra•bon *Trademark.*
Gev•ral T *Trademark.*
GI se•ries

gi•ant•ism
gi•ar•di•oa
gi•ar•di•a•sis
gi•ar•di•o•sis
gib•ber•el•lic
gib•ber•el•lin
gib•ber•ish
gib•bon
gib•bos•oi•ty
gib•bous
gib•bus
gib•lets
gi•gan•tism
gil•bert
gill•arch
gill cleft
gill slit
Gill•more nee•dles
gilt
Gim•ber•nat's lig•o•a•ment
gin•ger
gin•ger•nail
gin•gi•va, *n., pl.* -gi•vae.
gin•gi•val
gin•gi•vec•to•o•my, *n., pl.* -mies.
gin•gi•vi•tis
gin•gi•vo•la•bi•al
gin•gi•vo•plas•ty, *n., pl.* -ties.
gin•gi•vo•sto•ma•ti•tis, *n., pl.* -tit•oi•des, -ti•tis•es.
ging•ko
gin•gly•form
gin•gly•mo•ar•thro•di•a
gin•gly•mo•ar•thro•di•al
gin•gly•moid
gin•gly•mus, *n., pl.* -gly•omi.
gin•seng
Gi•rard re•a•gent
Gi•rard's re•a•gent
gir•dle
git•o•a•lin

gi•to•gen•in

gi•tox•i•gen•in

giz•zard

gla•bel•la, *n., pl.* -bel•lae.

gla•bel•lar

gla•bel•lum, *n., pl.* -bel•la.

glab•rous

glad•i•ate

glad•i•o•lus, *n., pl.* glad•i•o•o•li.

glair•y, *adj.* glair•i•er, glair•i•est.

gland

gland of Bar•tho•lin

glan•dered

glan•der•ous

glan•ders

glan•du•la, *n., pl.* -lae.

glan•du•lar

glandular fe•ver

glan•du•lous

glans, *n., pl.* glan•des.

glans cli•to•ri•dis

glans pe•o•nis

Gla•se•ri•an fis•sure

Glas•ser's dis•ease

glass•es

Glau•ber salt

Glau•ber's salt

glau•co•ma

glau•co•ma•to•cy•clit•ic

glau•co•ma•tous

Glea•son score

gleet

gleet•y, *adj.* gleet•i•er, gleet•i•est.

gle•no•hu•mer•al

gli•a

gli•a•cyte

gli•a•din

gli•al

glial cells

gli•o•blas•to•ma, *n., pl.* -mas, -ma•ta.

glioblastoma i•so•morphe

glioblastoma mul•ti•forme

gli•o•ma, *n., pl.* -mas, -ma•ta.

gli•o•ma•to•sis

gliomatosis ce•re•bri

gli•o•ma•tous

gli•o•sis

gli•o•tox•in

Glip•i•zide

Glis•son's cap•sule

Glo•bid•i•um

glo•bin

glo•bose

glo•bose•ly

glo•bos•i•ty

glob•ou•lar

glob•ule

glob•ou•lin

glo•bus hys•ter•i•cus

globus ma•jor ep•i•did•o•y•mi•dis

globus mi•nor epididymidis

globus pal•li•dus

glo•mal

glom•an•gi•o•o•ma, *n., pl.* -mas, -ma•ta.

glome

glo•mec•to•o•my, *n., pl.* -mies.

glom•er•ate

glo•mer•ou•lar

glo•mer•u•o•li re•nis

glo•mer•u•li•tis

glo•mer•u•lo•ne•phri•tis

glo•mer•u•lo•scle•ro•sis, *n., pl.* -ses.

glo•mer•u•lose

glo•mer•u•lus, *n., pl.* -li.

glo•mus, *n., pl.* glom•er•a, glo•mi.

glomus ca•rot•i•cum

glo•no•i•num
gloom bu•lim○i○a
glos○sa, *n., pl.* -sae, -sas.
glos•sal
glos•sal•gia
glos•san•thrax
glos•si○na
glos•sit○ic
glos•si○tis
glos○so•dy•na•mom•e○ter
glos○so•dynia
glossodynia ex•fo•li•a•ti○va
glos○so•graph
glos○so•hy○al
glos○so•kin•es•thet○ic
glos○so•la•li○a
glos•sol○o○gy
glos•so•pal○a•ti○nus, *n., pl.*
  -ti○ni.
glos•sop○a•thy, *n., pl.* -thies.
glos○so•pha•ryn•ge○al
glot•tal
glot•tic
glot•tis, *n., pl.* glot•tis○es,
  glot•ti○des.
glot•tol○o○gy
glu•ca•gon
glu•car○ic
Glu•cern *Trademark.*
glu•cide
glu○co•as•cor•bic
glu○co•cor•ti•coid
glu○co•ki•nase
glu○co•ki•nin
glu○co•lipid
glu○co•lipide
glu•col○y•sis, *n., pl.* -ses.
glu•co•ne○o○gen•e○sis
glu•con○ic
Glu○co•phage
glu○co•pro•tein
glu○co•py•ra•nose

glu•co•sa•mine
glu•co•san
glu•cose
glucose-1-phos•phate
glucose-6-phos•phate
glu○co•si•dase
glu○co•side
glu○co•sid○ic
glu○co•sid○i•cal○ly
glu○co•sone
glu○co•su•ri○a
Glu○co•trol *Trademark.*
Glucotrol XL *Trademark.*
glu•cu•ron○ic
glu•cu•ron○ic ac○id
glu•cu•ron○i•dase
glu•cu•ro•nide
glue ear
glu•ta•mate
glu•tam○ic
glutamic ac○id or glu•ta•
  min○ic ac○id
glu•ta•mi•nase
glu•ta•mine
glu•ta•min○ic
glu•ta•ral•de•hyde
glu•tar○ic
glu•ta•thi•one
glu•te○al
glu•te•lin
glu•ten
glu•ten○in
glu•ten•ous
glu•te○o•fem○o•ral
glu•teth○i•mide
glu•te○us, *n., pl.* -te○i.
gluteus max○i•mus, *n., pl.*
  glu•te○i max○i•mi.
gluteus me•di○us
gluteus min○i•mus
glu•ti•nous
Glu•to•fac *Trademak.*

Glu•tose *Trademak.*
Gly-Ox•ide
glyb○u•ride
gly•cae•mi○a
gly•can
gly•ce•mi○a
gly•ce•mic
glyc•er•al•de•hyde
glyc•er○ic
glyc•er•ide
glyc•er•id○ic
glyc•er○in
glyc•er•ine
glyc•er•ite
glyc•er○ol
glyc•er•o•phos•phate
glyc•er•op○hos•phor○ic
glyc•er•ose
gly•cine
gly•ci•nu•ri○a
gly•co○cho•late
gly•co•chol○ic
gly•co•coll
gly○co○cy•a•mine
gly•co•gen
gly•co•gen•e○sis, *n., pl.*
 -e○ses.
gly○co•ge•net○ic
gly○co•gen○ic
gly•co•ge•nol○y•sis, *n., pl.*
 -ses.
gly•cog○e○nous
gly•col
gly•col•al•de•hyde
gly•co•late
gly•col○ic
gly•co•lip○oid
gly•co•lip•ide
gly•col•lic
gly•col○y•sis
gly•co•lyt○ic
gly•co•lyt○i•cal○ly

gly•co•ne○o•gen•e○sis, *n., pl.*
 -e○ses.
gly○co•pep•tide
gly•co•pro•tein
gly○co•pty•a•lism
gly•cor•rhe○a
gly•cos○a•mi•no•gly•can
gly•co•si•a•li○a
gly•co•si•dase
gly•co•side
gly•co•sid○ic
gly•cos○u•ri○a
gly•cos○u•ric
gly•co•troph○ic
gly•co•trop○ic
glycou•re○sis, *n., pl.* -ses.
gly•cu•ron○ic
gly•cyr•rhiz○ic
gly•cyr•rhiz○in
Gly•nase Pres•tab
gl•yoxal
gly•ox○a•lase
gly•ox○a•line
gly•ox•yl○ic
gnath○al
gnath•al•gia
gnath○ic
gnath○i○on
Gnath•o•sto○ma
gna•thos•to•mi•a•sis
gno•to•bi•ol○o○gy
gno•to•bi•o•sis *or* gno•to•
 bi•ot○ics
gno•to•bi•ote
gno•to•bi•ot○ic
gno•to•bi•ot○i•cal○ly
gno•to•bi•ot○ics
Go○a pow•der
gob•let cell
goi•ter
goi•ter○o•gen○ic
goi•tre

goi•tro•gen
goi•tro•gen◦ic
goi•tro•ge•nic◦i◦ty, *n.*, *pl.*
  -ties.
goi•trous
Gol◦gi ap•pa•rat◦us
Golgi bod◦y
Golgi com•plex
Go•LYTE◦LY *Trademark.*
go◦mer
gom•pho•sis, *n.*, *pl.* -ses.
go◦nad
go•nad◦al
go•na•dec•to•mize, *v.*,
  -mized, -miz◦ing.
go•na•dec•to◦my, *n.*, *pl.*
  -mies.
go•na•di◦al
go•nad◦ic
go◦nad◦o•troph◦ic
go◦nad◦o•tro•phin
go◦nad◦o•trop◦ic
go•nad◦o•tro•pin
gonadotropin re•leas•ing
  hor•mone
go•nads o◦be•si◦ty
gon•o•duct
gon•al•gia
gon•ar•thro•cace
gon•ar•throt◦o◦my, *n.*, *pl.*
  -mies.
gon•e•cys•to•lith
gon•e◦poi•e◦sis
go•ni◦o•cra•ni•om•e◦try
go•ni•om•e◦ter
go•ni◦on, *n.*, *pl.* go•ni◦a.
go◦ni◦o•scope
go◦ni◦o•scop◦ic
go•ni•os◦co•py, *n.*, *pl.* -pies.
go•ni•tis
gon◦o•coc•cal
gon◦o•coc•cic

gon◦o•coc•coid
gon◦o•coc•cus, *n.*, *pl.* -coc◦ci.
gon◦o•cyte
gon◦o•duct
gon◦o•gen•e◦sis, *n.*, *pl.*
  -e◦ses.
go•nom•er◦y
gon◦o•phore
gon•or•rhe◦a
gon•or•rhe◦al
gon•or•rhe◦ic
gon•y•au•lax
Gooch cru•ci•ble
Gooch fil•ter
goof•ball
goose bumps
goose pim•ples
goose•flesh
gorge, *n.*, *pl.* gorged, gorg•
  ing.
gor•get
gork
gos•sy•pol
goun•dou, *n.*, *pl.* -dous.
gout
gout◦i•ness
gout◦y, *adj.* gout•i◦er,
  gout•i◦est.
Gow•ers's tract
Graaf◦i•an fol•li◦cle
gra•cil◦is
gra•di◦ent
Graf•fi◦an fol•li◦cle
graft
graft-ver•sus-host dis•ease
graft-versus-leu•ke•mi◦a ef•
  fect
Gra•ham's law
grain
gram
gram cal◦o◦rie
gram mo•lec◦u•lar weight

gram mol•e•cule
Gram-neg•a•tive
Gram-pos•i•tive
Gram stain
gram-var•i•a•ble
gram∘i•ci•din
gram∘i•niv∘o•rous
Gram's meth•od
Gram's so•lu•tion
Gram's stain
gra•na, *n.pl., sing.* gra•num.
gra•na•tum
grand mal
grand rounds
gran•di•ose
gran•di•os∘i∘ty
gran∘u•lar
gran∘u•late, *v.,* -lat∘ed, -lat•
   ing.
gran∘u•la•tion
gran•ule
Gran∘u•lex *Trademark.*
gran∘u•lo•blast
gran∘u•lo•blas•tic
gran∘u•lo•blas•to•sis
gran∘u•lo•cyte
granulocyte col•on∘y-stim∘u•
   lat∘ing factor
granulocyte-mac•ro•phage
   colony-stimulating factor
gran∘u•lo•cyt∘ic
gran∘u•lo•cy∘to•pe•ni∘a
gran∘u•lo•cy∘to•pe•nic
gran∘u•lo•cy•to•poi∘e-sis
gran∘u•lo•cy•to•sis
gran∘u•lo∘ma, *n., pl.* -mas,
   -ma∘ta.
granuloma in•gui•na∘le
granuloma py•o•gen∘i•cum
granuloma ve•ne•re∘um
gran∘u•lo•ma•to•sis
gran∘u•lom∘a•tous

gran∘u•lo•pe•ni∘a
gran∘u•lo•plas•tic
gran∘u•lo•poi∘e•sis
gran∘u•lo∘sa
gran∘u•lo•sis
gra•num, *n., pl.* gra∘na.
grape sug•ar
graph•ite
gra•phit∘ic
graph∘o•log∘i•cal
gra•phol∘o∘gy
graph∘o•mo•tor
graph∘or•rhe∘a
graph∘o•spasm
grat•tage
grav∘el
gravel-blind
Graves' dis•ease
grav∘id
grav∘i∘da, *n., pl.* -das, -dae.
gra•vid∘ic
gra•vid∘i•tas ex•am∘i•na•lis
graviditas ex∘o•cho•ri•a•li∘a
gra•vid∘i∘ty, *n., pl.* -ties.
grav•id•ness
grav∘i•do•car•di∘ac
gra•vim•e∘ter
grav∘i•met•ric
grav∘i•met•ri•cal
grav∘i•met•ri•cal∘ly
gra•vim•e∘try
grav∘i∘ty, *n., pl.* -ties.
gray
gray mat•ter
gray∘out
great•er o∘men•tum
green mon•key dis•ease
green soap
green tea
green•sick
green•sick•ness

green•stick frac•ture
gref•fo•tome
greg•o•a•loid
Greg•o•a•ri•na
greg•o•a•rine
greg•o•a•rin•o•i•an
Greg•o•a•rin•o•i•o•da
greg•o•a•ri•no•sis
Greg•o•o•ry's pow•der
grief
Gri•ful•vin **V** *Trademark.*
grin•de•li•a
grind•ing
grip•pal
grippe
Gris-PEG *Trademark.*
Gri•sac•tin *Trademark.*
gri•se•o•ful•vin
gris•tle
gro•cer's itch
gross a•nat•o•o•my
group dy•nam•ics
group prac•tice
group psy•cho•ther•a•py
group ther•a•py
grow, *v.,* grew, grown, grow•ing.
grow•ing pains
growth
growth fac•tor
growth hor•mone
growth hormone re•leas•ing fac•tor
gru•el
grume
gru•mous
gru•mous•ness
grunt•ing
gry•po•sis, *n., pl.* -ses.
gu•ai•o•ac
guai•a•col
guai•a•cum

Guai•fed *Trademark.*
Guai•fen•o•e•sin/Phen•yl•pro•pa•no•la•mine
Guaifenesin/PPA
Guai•tab *Trademark.*
gua•nase
gua•neth•o•i•dine
gua•ni•dine
gua•nine
gua•no•phore
gua•no•sine
guanosine mon•o•phos•phate
guanosine tri•phos•phate
gua•nyl•o•ic
guanylic ac•id
gua•ra•o•na
gu•ber•nac•u•lum, *n., pl.* -nac•u•la.
gubernaculum den•tis
gubernaculum tes•tis
Guil•lain-Bar•ré syn•drome
guil•lo•tine
guin•ea pig
guinea worm
gu•lar
gul•let
gu•lose
gum
gum ar•a•bic
gum•boil
gum•ma, *n., pl.* gum•mas, gum•ma•ta.
gum•ma•tous
gum•my, *adj.* -mi•er, -mi•est.
gur•ney, *n., pl.* -neys.
Gus•tase *Trademark.*
gus•ta•tion
gus•ta•tive
gus•ta•to•ri•al
gus•ta•to•ri•al•ly
gus•ta•to•ri•ly

gus•ta•to•ry
gut•ta, *n., pl.* -tae.
gutta-per•cha
gut•tate
gut•tie
gut•tu•ral
Gut•zeit test
Gym•ne•ma syl•ves•tre
gy•nan•drism
gy•nan•droid
gy•nan•dro•morph
gy•nan•dro•mor•phic
gy•nan•dro•morph•ism
gy•nan•dro•mor•phous
gy•nan•dro•mor•phy
gy•na•tre•sia
Gy•one-Lo•tri•min *Trademark.*
gy•ne•co•gen•ic
gy•ne•cog•ra•phy, *n., pl.*
  -phies.

gy•ne•coid
gy•ne•col
gy•ne•co•log•ic or gy•ne•
  co•log•i•cal.
gy•ne•col•o•gist
gy•ne•col•o•gy
gy•ne•co•mas•ti•a or gy•ne•
  co•mas•ty
gy•nog•a•mone
gy•no•gen•e•sis
Gy•nol II *Trademark.*
gyre
gy•rec•to•my, *n., pl.* -mies.
gyr•en•ceph•a•late
gyr•en•ce•phal•ic
gyr•en•ceph•a•lous
gy•rose
gy•ro•spasm
gy•rus, *n., pl.* gy•ri.

H

ha•be•u•o•la, *n., pl.* -lae.
hab•it-form•ing
ha•bit•u•ate, *v.,* -at•ed, -at•
  ing.
ha•bit•u•a•tion
hab•i•tus, *n., pl.* -tus.
hab•ro•ne•mi•a•sis
hae•mo•bar•ton•el•la, *n., pl.*
  -lae.
hair
hair im•plant
hair trans•plant
Hal•ci•on
half-life or half•life, *n., pl.*
  -lives.
hal•i•to•sis
hal•lu•ci•nate, *v.,* -nat•ed,
  -nat•ing.
hal•lu•ci•na•tion

hal•lu•ci•na•tive
hal•lu•ci•na•to•ry
hal•lu•ci•no•gen
hal•lu•ci•no•gen•ic
hal•lu•ci•no•sis
hal•lux, *n., pl.* hal•lu•ces.
ha•lo ef•fect
hal•o•bac•te•ri•a *n.pl., sing.*
  -te•ri•um
hal•o•per•i•dol
hal•o•thane
ham•ar•to•ma, *n., pl.* -mas,
  -ma•ta.
ha•ma•tum, *n., pl.* -ta, -tums.
ham•mer
ham•mer•toe
ham•string
ham•u•lus, *n., pl.* ham•u•li.
hand

hematein

hand•ed•ness
hang•nail
Han•sen's dis•ease
Hansen's ba•cil•lus
han•ta•vi•ral
han•ta•vi•rus, *n., pl.* -rus∘es.
hap•lo•don∘ty, *n., pl.* -ties.
hap•loid, *adj.* hap•loi∘dic.
hap•loi∘dy
hap•lol∘o∘gy
hap•lont
hap•tic sense
hard
hard pal•ate
hare•lip
hare•lipped
har•mo∘ny, *n., pl.* -nies.
haus•to•ri∘um, *n., pl.* -ri∘a.
haus•trum, *n., pl.* -tra.
haus•tus, *n., pl.* -tus.
Ha•ver•si∘an ca∘nal
Haw•thorne ef•fect
hay fe∘ver
head
health∘y, *adj.,* -i∘er, -i•est.
hear•ing aid
hearing-im•paired
heart
heart at•tack
heart block
heart dis•ease
heart fail•ure
heart mur•mur
heart•beat
heart•burn
heart-lung ma•chine
heat ex•haus•tion
heat pros•tra•tion
heat rash
heat shock pro•teins
heat•stroke

he•be•phre•ni∘a
he•be•phren∘ic
he•bet∘ic
hec•tic
he•don∘ics
heel spur
Heim•lich ma•neu•ver
He•La or He•la or he•la cell
Hel∘i•co•bac•ter pylo∘ri
he•li•o•sis, *n., pl.* -ses.
he•li∘o•tax∘is, *n., pl.* -tax∘es.
he•li∘o•ther∘a∘py
he∘lix, *n., pl.* hel∘i•ces, he•
lix∘es.
hel•minth
hel•min•thi•a•sis
hel•min•thic
hel•min•thol∘o∘gy
he•lo∘ma, *n., pl.* -mas, -ma∘ta.
he•lot∘o∘my, *n., pl* -mies.
help∘er T cell
he•ma•cy•tom•e∘ter
he•mag•glu•ti•nate, *v.,*
-nat∘ed, -nat∘ing.
he•mag•glu•ti•na•tion
he•mag•glu•tin∘a•tive
he•mag•glu•ti•nin
he∘mal
he•man•gi•ec•ta•sis, *n., pl.*
-ses.
he•man•gi∘o•blas•to∘ma, *n.,*
pl. -mas, -ma∘ta.
he•man•gi∘o•en•do•the•
li∘o∘ma, *n., pl.* -mas, -ma∘ta.
he•man•gi•o∘ma, *n., pl.* -mas,
-ma∘ta.
he•man•gi∘o•ma•to•sis
he•man•gi∘o•sar•co∘ma, *n.,*
pl. -mas, -ma∘ta.
he•ma•poi•e∘sis
he•mar•thro•sis, *n., pl.* -ses.
he•ma•te∘in

he•mat○ic
he•ma•tin or he•ma•tine
he•ma•tin○ic
he•mat○o•blast
he•mat○o•cele
he•mat○o•crit
he•ma•tog○e○nous
he•ma•to•log○ic or he•ma•to•log○i•cal, *adj.*
he•ma•tol○o•gist
he•ma•tol○o•gy
he•ma•to•lym•phan•gi○o○ma, *n., pl.* -mas, -ma○ta.
he•ma•tol○y•sis
he•ma•to•ma, *n., pl.* -mas, -ma○ta.
he•ma•to•my•e○li•tis, *n., pl.* -lit○i•des.
he•mat○o•poi○e•sis
he•mat○o•poi○et○ic stem cell
he•ma•to•sal•pinx, *n., pl.* -pin•ges.
he•ma•to•sis
he•ma•to•zo○on, *n., pl.* -zo○a.
he•ma•tu•ri○a
he•ma•tu•ric
heme
heme i•ron
hem•er○a•lo•pi○a
hem•er○a•lop○ic
hem○i•at•ro•phy
he○mic
hem○i•cen•trum, *n., pl.* -trums, -tra.
hem○i•cer•e○brum, *n., pl.* -brums, -bra.
hem○i•co•lec•to○my, *n., pl.* -mies.
hem○i•cra○ni○a
hem○i•dys•tro•phy

hem○i•glos•sec•to○my, *n., pl.* -mies.
hem○i•hy•per•tro•phy, *n., pl.* -phies.
hem○i•lam○i•nec•to○my, *n., pl.* -mies.
hem○i•lar•yn•gec•to○my, *n., pl.* -mies.
hem○i•man•dib○u•lec•to○my, *n., pl.* -mies.
he○min
hem○i•ne•phrec•to○my, *n., pl.* -mies.
hem○i•pa•re•sis, *n., pl.* -ses.
hem○i•pel•vec•to○my, *n., pl.* -mies.
hem○i•ple•gi○a
hem○i•ple•gic
hem○i•spher•ec•to○my, *n., pl.* -mies.
hem○i•tho•rax, *n., pl.* -rax○es, -rac○es.
he•mo•chro•ma•to•sis
he•mo•chro•ma•tot○ic
he•mo•co•ni•o•sis
he•mo•cy•tom•e○ter
he•mo•di•al○y•sis
he•mo•flag•el•late
he•mo•glo•bic
he•mo•glo•bin
he•mo•glo•bi•nom•e○try
he•mo•glo•bi•nop○a•thy, *n., pl.* -thies.
he•mo•glo•bin•ous
he•mo•glo•bi•nu•ri○a
he•mo•glo•bi•nu•ric
he•mol○y•sis
he•mo•lyt○ic
he•mo•lyze, *v.,* -lyzed, -lyz•ing.
he•mom•e○try
he•mop○a•thy, *n., pl.* -thies.

he•mo•per•i•car•di•um, *n.*, *pl.* -di•a.
he•mo•per•i•to•ne•um, *pl.* -ne•ums, -ne•a.
he•mo•phil•i•a
he•mo•phil•i•ac
he•mo•phil•ic
he•mo•pneu•mo•tho•rax, *n.*, *pl.* -rax•es, -ra•ces.
he•mo•poi•e•sis
he•mo•poi•et•ic
he•mop•ty•sis
hem•or•rhage, *n.*, *v.*, -rhaged, -rhag•ing.
hem•or•rhag•ic
hem•or•rhoid, *n.*
hem•or•rhoi•dal
hem•or•rhoid•ec•to•my, *n.*, *pl.* -mies.
he•mo•sal•pinx, *n.*, *pl.* -pin•ges.
he•mo•sid•er•o•sis, *n.*, *pl.* -ses.
he•mo•sta•sis or he•mo•sta•sia
he•mo•stat
he•mo•stat•ic
he•mo•tho•rax, *n.*, *pl.* -rax•es, -ra•ces.
he•mo•zo•on, *n.*, *pl.* -zo•a.
Hen•le's loop
hep•ar sul•phu•is cal•car•e•um
hep•a•rin•ize, *v.*, -ized, -iz•ing.
hep•a•tec•to•mize, *v.*, -mized, -miz•ing.
hep•a•tec•to•my, *n.*, *pl.* -mies.
he•pat•ic
he•pat•i•co•du•o•de•nos•to•my, *n.*, *pl.* -mies.

he•pat•i•co•li•thot•o•my, *n.*, *pl.* -mies.
hep•a•ti•tis
hepatitis del•ta
hepatitis non-A, non-B
hep•a•tize, *v.*, -tized, -tiz•ing.
hep•a•to•ma, *n.*, *pl.* -mas, -ma•ta.
hep•a•to•meg•a•ly
hep•a•top•a•thy, *n.*, *pl.* -thies.
hep•a•to•pex•y, *n.*, *pl.* -ies.
hep•a•tos•co•py, *n.*, *pl.* -pies.
hep•a•to•sple•no•meg•a•ly
hep•a•to•tox•ic•i•ty, *n.*, *pl.* -ties.
hep•a•rin
herb doc•tor
herb•al•ist
herd im•mu•ni•ty
he•red•oi•tar•i•an
he•red•oi•tar•i•an•ism
he•red•oi•tar•i•ly
he•red•oi•tar•i•ness
he•red•oi•tar•y
he•red•i•ty, *n.*, *pl.* -ties.
her•i•ta•bil•i•ty
her•maph•ro•dism
her•maph•ro•dite
her•maph•ro•dit•ic
her•maph•ro•dit•i•cal•ly
her•maph•ro•dit•ism
her•ni•a, *n.*, *pl.* -ni•as, -ni•ae.
her•ni•al
her•ni•ate, *v.*, -at•ed, -at•ing.
her•ni•at•ed disk
her•ni•a•tion
her•ni•or•rha•phy, *n.*, *pl.* -phies.
her•ni•ot•o•my, *n.*, *pl.* -mies.
her•o•in
her•pes

herpes gen•i•tal•is
herpes la•bi•al•is
herpes sim•plex
herpes•vi•rus, *n.*, *pl.* -rus•es.
herpes zos•ter
herpes zoster vi•rus
her•pet•ic
het•er•o•blas•ty
het•er•o•chro•mat•ic
het•er•o•chro•ma•tin
het•er•o•chro•ma•tism
het•er•o•chron•ism
het•er•och•ro•ny, *n.*, *pl.* -nies.
het•er•og•a•mous
het•er•og•a•my
het•er•o•ge•ne•i•ty
het•er•o•gen•e•sis, *n.*, *pl.* -e•ses.
het•er•og•o•ny
het•er•o•graft
het•er•o•lec•i•thal
het•er•ol•o•gous
het•er•ol•o•gy
het•er•ol•y•sis, *n.*, *pl.* -ses.
het•er•o•mor•pho•sis, *n.*, *pl.* -ses.
het•er•o•oph•e•my
het•er•o•phil
het•er•o•plas•tic
het•er•o•plas•ty, *n.*, *pl.* -ties.
het•er•o•ploi•dy
het•er•os•co•py, *n.*, *pl.* -pies.
het•er•o•sex•u•al
het•er•o•sex•u•al•i•ty
het•er•o•sis
het•er•o•tac•tic
het•er•o•tac•tous
het•er•o•tax•i•a, *n.*, *pl.* -tax•i•as.
het•er•o•tax•ic

het•er•o•tax•is or het•er•o•tax•i•a
het•er•o•tax•y
het•er•o•to•pi•a
het•er•ot•o•py
het•er•o•tri•cho•sis
het•er•o•tro•phy
het•er•o•zy•go•sis
het•er•o•zy•gos•i•ty
het•er•o•zy•gote
het•er•o•zy•gous or het•er•o•zy•got•ic
hex•a•meth•yl•ene•tet•ra•mine
hex•a•ploid
hex•a•ploi•dy
hex•o•ki•nase
hex•ose
hi•a•tus or hi•a•tal her•ni•a
hi•ber•nate, *v.*, -nat•ed, -nat•ing.
hic•cup or hic•cough *n.*, *v.*, -cuped or -cupped or -coughed, -cup•ing or -cup•ping or -cough•ing.
Hick•man cath•e•ter
hid•den hun•ger
hi•drad•e•no•ma, *n.*, *pl.* -mas, -ma•ta.
hi•dro•sis
hi•drot•ic
high al•ti•tude dis•or•der
high altitude pul•mo•nar•y e•de•ma
high blood pres•sure
high-den•si•ty li•po•pro•tein
hi•lum, *n.*, *pl.* hi•li.
hind•brain
hind•gut
hip
hip•bone
hip•po•cam•pal

hip•po•cam•pus, *n.*, *pl.*
  -cam•pi.
Hip•po•crat•ic oath
hip•pol•o•gy
hir•sut•ism
hir•u•din
hir•u•di•ni•a•sis
his•tam•i•nase
his•ta•mine
his•ta•min•ic
his•ti•dine
his•ti•o•cy•to•ma, *n.*, *pl.*
  -mas, -ma•ta.
his•ti•o•cy•to•sis, *n.*, *pl.* -ses.
his•to•chem•is•try, *n.*, *pl.*
  -tries.
his•to•chem•og•ra•phy, *n.*,
  pl. -phies.
his•to•com•pat•i•bility
his•to•com•pat•i•ble
his•to•gen•e•osis
his•to•ge•net•ic
his•to•ge•net•i•cal•ly
his•tog•e•ny, *n.*, *pl.* -tog•
  e•nies.
his•tol•o•gy
his•tol•y•sis
his•to•lyt•ic
his•tone
his•to•path•o•log•ic or his•
  to•path•o•log•i•cal
his•to•pa•thol•o•gist
his•to•pa•thol•o•gy
his•to•phys•i•o•log•i•cal
his•to•phys•i•ol•o•gy
his•to•plas•mo•sis
his•to•ry, *n.*, *pl.* -ries.
his•tri•on•ic per•son•al•i•ty
  dis•or•der
HIV pos•i•tive
hives
Hodg•kin's dis•ease

hol•an•dric
ho•lism
ho•list
ho•lis•tic med•i•cine
hol•o•blas•tic
ho•lo•blas•ti•cal•ly
hol•o•crine
hol•o•en•zyme
ho•log•a•mous
ho•log•a•my
hol•o•gram•ic brain the•o•ry
ho•log•ra•phy, *n.*, *pl.* -phies.
hol•o•gyn•ic
hol•o•mor•pho•sis, *n.*, *pl.*
  -ses.
hol•ox•en•ic
Hol•ter or holter mon•itor
ho•me•o•box gene
ho•me•o•path
ho•me•o•path•ic
ho•me•o•path•i•cal•ly
ho•me•op•a•thist
ho•me•op•a•thy
ho•me•o•sta•sis
ho•me•o•stat•ic
ho•me•o•stat•i•cal•ly
Ho•mo
ho•mog•a•mous
ho•mog•a•my, *n.*, *pl.* -mies.
ho•mo•gen•e•osis, *n.*, *pl.* -ses.
ho•mog•e•nize, *v.*, -nized,
  -niz•ing.
ho•mog•e•ny, *n.*, *pl.* -nies.
ho•mo•graft
ho•mo•lec•i•thal
ho•mo•log•i•cal or ho•mo•
  log•ic
ho•mo•log•i•cal•ly
ho•mol•o•gize, *v.*, -gized,
  -giz•ing.
ho•mol•o•gous
ho•mo•logue or ho•mo•log

ho•mol○o•gy, *n.*, *pl.* -gies.
ho•mol○y•sis, *n.*, *pl.* -ses.
ho•mo•phobe
ho•mo•pho•bi○a
ho•mo•pho•bic
ho•mo•sex○u○al
ho•mo•sex○u•al○i○ty
ho•mos•po○ry, *n.*, *pl.* -ries.
ho•mo•trans•plant
ho•mo•zy•go•sis, *n.*, *pl.* -ses.
ho•mo•zy•gos○i○ty
ho•mo•zy•gote
ho•mo•zy•gous or ho•mo•
  zy•got○ic
ho•mun•cu•lus, *n.*, *pl.* -cu○li.
hook•worm
hop•head
hor•de○o•lum, *n.*, *pl.* -de○
  o○la.
hor•mo•nal
hor•mone
hormone re•place•ment
  ther○a○py
hor•mon○ic
horse•rad•ish per•ox○i•dase
hos•pice
hos•pi•tal•ize, *v.*, -ized, -iz•
  ing.
host
host-spe•cif○ic
hot flash
hot spot or hot•spot
house•maid's knee
hu•man cho•ri•on○ic go•
  nad○o•tro•pin
Human Ge•nome Proj•ect
human gran○u•lo•cyt○ic ehr•
  lich○i○o•sis
human growth hor•mone
human mon○o○cyt○ic ehr•
  lich○i○o•sis
human pa•pil•lo•ma•vi•rus

human par•vo•vi•rus B19
human po•ten•tial move•
  ment
human re•la•tions
human T-cell lymph○o•tro•
  phic vi○rus
hu•mer○us, *n.*, *pl.* -mer○i.
hu•mid•i○fy, *v.*, -fied, -fy•ing.
hu•mid○i○ty, *n.*, *pl.* -ties.
hu•mor○al
hun•ger
Hun•ting•ton's cho•re○a
HY an•ti•gen
hy○a•line
hy•al○i•no•sis, *n.*, *pl.* -ses.
hy○a•loid
hyaloid mem•brane
hy○a•lu•ron○ic ac○id
hy○a•lu•ron○i•dase
hy•brid
hybrid vig○or
hy•brid•ism
hy•brid○i○ty
hy•brid•iz○a•ble
hy•brid•i•za•tion
hy•brid•ize, *v.*, -ized, -iz•ing.
hy•brid○o•ma, *n.*, *pl.* -mas.
hy•da•tid
hy•dat○i•do•sis
hy•drar•thro•sis
hy•dras•tis cana•den•sis
hy•drate, *v.*, -drat○ed, -drat•
  ing.
hy•dren•ceph○a•lus, *n.*, *pl.*
  -ceph•a○li.
hy•dren•ceph○a○ly, *n.*, *pl.*
  -lies.
hy•dro•cele
hy•dro•ce•phal○ic
hy•dro•ceph○a•lous
hy•dro•ceph○a•lus or hy•
  dro•ceph○a○ly

hy•dro•ceph•a•ly
hy•dro•chlo•ric ac•id
hy•dro•chlo•ro•thi•a•zide
hy•dro•chol•er•e•osis
hy•dro•co•done/a•ce•ta•min•o•phen
hy•dro•cor•ti•sone
hy•dro•cy•an•oic ac•oid
Hy•dro•di•u•ril *Trademark.*
hy•dro•gen
hydrogen per•ox•ide
hy•drog•e•o•nate, *v.*, -nat•ed, -nat•ing.
hy•dro•lase
hy•dro•lo•y•sis, *n.*, *pl.* -ses.
hy•dro•lyt•oic
hy•dro•lyz•a•ble
hy•dro•ly•za•tion
hy•dro•lyze, *v.*, -lyzed, -lyz•ing.
hy•dro•lyzed veg•e•ta•ble pro•tein
hy•dro•lyz•oer
hy•dro•men•in•gi•tis
hy•dro•me•ter
hy•dro•met•ric hy•dr o•met•ri•cal.
hy•drom•e•try
hy•dro•ne•phro•sis
hy•dro•path
hy•dro•path•oic or hy•dro•path•o•i•cal.
hy•drop•a•thist
hy•drop•a•thy
hy•dro•per•oi•car•di•um, *n.*, *pl.* -di•a.
hy•dro•per•oi•to•ne•um, *n.*, *pl.* -ne•ums, -ne•a.
hy•dro•phil•oic
hy•dro•pho•bi•a
hy•dro•pho•bic
hy•dro•pho•bic•oi•ty, *n.*, *pl.* -ties.
hy•dro•pneu•mo•tho•rax
hy•drops
hy•drop•osy
hy•dro•sal•pinx
hy•dro•tax•ois
hy•dro•ther•a•peu•tic
hy•dro•ther•a•peu•tics
hy•dro•ther•a•pist
hy•dro•ther•a•o•py
hy•dro•tho•rac•ic
hy•dro•tho•rax
hy•drox•oy ac•id
hy•drox•oy•bu•tyr•oic ac•oid
hy•drox•oy•chlo•ro•quine sul•fate
hy•drox•yl
hy•drox•yl•oic
hy•drox•oy•pro•line
hy•dro•zo•oon, *n.*, *pl.* -zo•a, -zo•ons.
hy•giene
hy•gi•en•oics
hy•gro•ma, *n.*, *pl.* -mas, -ma•ta.
hy•grom•e•try
hy•gro•sco•pic•oi•ty, *n.*, *pl.* -ties.
hy•men
hy•men•oal
hy•me•nop•ter•oon, *n.*, *pl.* -ter•a, -ons.
hy•men•ot•o•omy, *n.*, *pl.* -mies.
hy•o•gloss•sus, *n.*, *pl.* -glos•si.
hy•oid
hy•os•cine
hy•os•cy•a•mine
hy•os•cy•a•mus
hyoscyamus ni•ger
hyp•al•ge•si•a or hy•pal•gia

hyp•al•ge•sic
hype
hy•per•ac•id
hy•per•a•cid•i•ty
hy•per•ac•tive
hy•per•ac•tive•ly
hy•per•ac•tiv•i•ty
hy•per•ae•mi•a
hy•per•aes•the•sia
hy•per•al•ge•si•a or hy•pe
r•al•gi•a
hy•per•al•ge•sic
hy•per•al•get•ic
hy•per•al•i•men•ta•tion
hy•per•bar•ic
hyperbaric cham•ber
hy•per•brach•y•ceph•a•ly
hy•per•cal•ce•mi•a
hy•per•cap•ni•a
hy•per•ca•thex•is, n., pl.
-thex•es.
hy•per•ce•men•to•sis, n., pl.
-ses.
hy•per•cho•les•ter•ol•
e•mi•a or hy•per•cho•les•
ter•e•mi•a
hy•per•chro•ma•to•sis
hy•per•dip•loi•dy
hy•per•em•e•sis
hy•per•e•mi•a
hy•per•e•mic
hy•per•en•de•mic•i•ty, n.,
pl. -ties.
hy•per•er•o•gy, n., pl. -gies.
hy•per•es•the•sia
hy•per•es•thet•ic
hy•per•ex•cit•a•bil•i•ty
hy•per•func•tion
hy•per•func•tion•ing
hy•per•gly•ce•mi•a
hy•per•gly•ce•mic

hy•per•hi•dro•sis or hy•p
er•oi•dro•sis
hy•per•in•som•ni•a
hy•per•in•su•lin•ism
hy•per•ir•ri•ta•bil•i•ty
hy•per•ir•ri•ta•ble
hy•per•ka•le•mi•a
hy•per•ka•le•mic
hy•per•ker•a•to•sis, n., pl.
-ses.
hy•per•ker•a•tot•ic
hy•per•ki•ne•sia
hy•per•ki•ne•sis
hy•per•ki•net•ic
hy•per•li•pe•mi•a
hy•per•li•pe•mic
hy•per•lip•oi•de•mi•a
hy•per•lip•oi•de•mic
hy•per•lip•o•pro•tein•
e•mi•a
hy•per•met•a•mor•pho•sis
hy•perm•ne•sia
hy•perm•ne•sic
hy•per•ne•phro•ma, n., pl.
-mas, -ma•ta.
hy•per•o•o•pi•a
hy•per•op•ic
hy•per•os•mo•lar co•ma
hy•per•os•to•sis
hy•per•os•tot•ic
hy•per•par•a•thy•roid•ism
hy•per•per•oi•stal•sis, n., pl.
-ses.
hy•per•pha•gi•a
hy•per•phag•ic
hy•per•pi•tu•i•ta•rism
hy•per•pla•sia
hy•per•plas•tic
hyperplastic obe•sity
hy•per•ploid
hy•per•ploi•dy
hy•perp•ne•a

hy○per•po•lar•ize, *v.*, -ized,
  -iz•ing.
hy○per•pot•as•se•mi○a
hy○per•pot•as•se•mic
hy○per•py•ret○ic
hy○per•py•rex○i○a
hy○per•py•rex○i○al
hy○per•sen•si•tive
hy○per•sen•si•tive•ness
hy○per•sen•si•tiv○i○ty
hy○per•sen•si•tize, *v.*, -tized,
  -tiz•ing.
hy○per•sex•u○al
hy○per•sex○u•al○i○ty
hy○per•sex•u•al○ly
hy○per•sple•ni○a
hy○per•sple•nic
hy○per•splen•ism
hy○per•sus•cep•ti•bil○i○ty,
  n., *pl.* -ties.
hy○per•ten•sion
hy○per•ten•sive
hy○per•ther•mi○a
hy○per•ther•my
hy○per•thy•re○o•sis
hy○per•thy•roid
hy○per•thy•roid•ism
hy○per•thy•ro•sis
hy○per•to•ni○a, *n.*, *pl.* -ni○as.
hy○per•ton○ic
hy○per•to•nic○i○ty
hy○per•to○ny
hy○per•tri•cho•sis
hy○per•troph○ic
hypertrophic car•di○o•my•
  op○a•thy
hypertrophic o○be•si○ty
hy○per•tro•phy, *n.*, *pl.* -phies.
hy•per○u•ri•ce•mi○a
hy•per○u•ri•ce•mic
hy○per•ven•ti•late, *v.*,
  -lat○ed, -lat•ing.

hy○per•ven•ti•la•tion
hy○per•vi•ta•mi•no•sis, *n.*,
  pl. -ses.
hyp•es•the•sia
hyp•es•the•sic
hy○pha, *n.*, *pl.* -phae.
hy•phi•dro•sis
hy•pho•my•co•sis, *n.*, *pl.* -ses.
hyp•na•gog○ic
hyp•no•a○nal○y•sis, *n.*, *pl.*
  -ses.
hyp•no•an•a○lyt○ic
hyp•no•gen•e○sis, *n.*, *pl.* -ses.
hyp•no•ge•net○ic
hyp•noid
hyp•noi•dal
hyp•no•log○ic
hyp•no•log○i•cal
hyp•nol○o•gist
hyp•nol○o○gy
hyp•no•pho•bi○a, *n.*, *pl.*
  -bi○as.
hyp•no•pom•pic
hyp•no•sis, *n.*, *pl.* -ses.
hyp•no•ther○a•pist
hyp•no•ther○a○py
hyp•not○ic
hyp•not○i•cal○ly
hyp•no•tism
hyp•no•tist
hyp•no•tize, *v.*, -tized, -tiz•
  ing.
hy○po, *n.*, *pl.* -pos.
hy○po•a○cid○i○ty
hy○po•al•ler•gen○ic
hy○po•bar○ic
hy○po•blast
hy○po•blas•tic
hy○po•cal•ce•mi○a
hy○po•chon•dri○a
hy○po•chon•dri○ac
hy○po•chon•dri•a•cal○ly

hy•po•chon•dri•a•sis

hy•po•chon•dri○um, *n., pl.*
-dri○a.

hy•po•der•mic

hypodermic sy•ringe

hy•po•der•mi•cal○ly

hy•po•der•mo•cly•sis, *n., pl.*
-ses.

hy•po•di•ploi○dy

hy•po•er○gy

hy•po•gas•tri○um, *n., pl.*
-tri○a.

hy•po•gen•e○sis, *n., pl.* -ses.

hy•po•glos•sal

hypoglossal nerve

hy•po•glos•sus, *n., pl.*
-glos○si.

hy•po•glot•tis, *n., pl.* -tis•ses,
-glot•ti•des.

hy•po•gly•ce•mi○a

hy•po•gly•ce•mic

hy•po•hi•dro•sis

hy•po•ka•le•mi○a

hy•po•ka•le•mic

hy•po•ki•ne○sis, *n., pl.* -ses.

hy•po•mo•til○i○ty

hy•po•phar•ynx, *n., pl.*
-yn•ges, -ynx○es.

hy•po•phre•no•sis

hy•poph○y•se•al

hy•poph○y•sec•to•mize, *v.,*
-mized, -miz•ing.

hy•poph○y•sec•to○my, *n., pl*
-mies.

hy•poph○y•si○al

hy•poph○y•sis, *n., pl.* -ses.

hy○po•pi•tu○i•ta•rism

hy○po•pla•sia

hy○po•plas•tic

hy○po•plas○ty

hy○po•ploid

hy○po•ploi○dy

hy○po•py○on

hy•po•ri•bo•flav○i•no•sis,
n., pl. -ses.

hy•po•sen•si•tiv○i○ty

hy•po•sen•si•ti•za•tion

hy•po•sen•si•tize, *v.,* -tized,
-tiz•ing.

hy•po•sta•sis, *n., pl.* -ses.

hy•po•stat○ic

hy•po•stat○i•cal

hy•po•stat○i•cal○ly

hy•po•ten•sion

hy•po•ten•sive

hy•po•tha•lam○ic

hy•po•thal○a•mus, *n., pl.*
-thal•a○mi.

hy•poth○e○nar

hypothenar ham•mer syn•
drome

hy•po•ther•mi○a

hy•po•ther•mic

hy•poth○e○sis, *n., pl.* -e○ses.

hy•po•thy•roid

hy•po•thy•roid•ism

hy•po•to•ni○a, *n., pl.* -ni○as.

hy•po•ton○ic

hy•po•to•nic○i○ty, *n., pl.*
-ties.

hy•pot○o○ny

hy•po•tri•cho•sis

hy•pot•ro•phy, *n., pl.* -phies.

hy•po•tym•pa•num, *n., pl.*
-pa○na, -pa•nums.

hy•po•vi•ta•mi•no•sis

hy•pox•e•mi○a

hy•pox•e•mic

hy•pox○i○a

hy•pox○ic

hys•ter•ec•to•mize, *v.,*
-mized, -miz•ing.

hys•ter•ec•to○my, *n., pl.*
-mies.

hys•te•ri∘a
hys•ter•oi•cal
hysterical neur∘o•sis, con•
  ver•sion type
hys•ter∘o-ep∘i•lep∘sy
hys•ter∘o∘gen∘ic
hys•ter•og∘e∘ny
hys•ter•og•ra•phy, *n., pl.*
  -phies.
hys•ter•ol∘o∘gy
hys•ter•ol∘y•sis, *n., pl.* -ses.
hys•ter∘o-o∘o∘pho•rec•
  to∘my, *n., pl.* -mies.
hys•ter•o•pex∘y, *n., pl.* -pex•
  ies.
hys•ter•or•rha•phy, *n., pl.*
  -phies.
hys•ter•or•rhex∘is, *n., pl.*
  -rhex∘es.

hys•ter∘o•sal•pin•gec•
  to∘my, *n., pl.* -mies.
hys•ter∘o•sal•pin•gog•ra•
  phy, *n., pl.* -phies.
hys•ter∘o•sal•
  pin∘go-o∘o∘pho•rec•to∘my,
  n., pl. -mies.
hys•ter•os•co∘py, *n., pl.* -pies.
hys•ter∘o•sto•mat∘o∘my, *n.,
  pl.* -mies.
hys•ter•ot•e∘ly, *n., pl.* -lies.
hys•ter•ot∘o∘my, *n., pl.*
  -mies.
hys•ter∘o•tra•che•lec•
  to∘my, *n., pl.* -mies.
hys•ter∘o•tra•che•lor•rha•
  phy, *n., pl.* -phies.
hys•ter∘o•tra•che•lot∘o∘my,
  n., pl. -mies.

I J K

i∘at•ric
i∘at•ri•cal
i∘a•tro•chem•is•try
i∘at•ro•gen•e∘sis
i∘at•ro•gen∘ic
i∘a•tro•gen•ic∘i∘ty, *n., pl.*
  -ties.
i∘bu•pro•fen
ice
ice bag
ice pack
i∘chor
i∘chor•ous
ich•thy•ism
ich•thy•is•mus
ich•thy∘o∘sis, *n., pl.* -ses.
ich•thy•ot∘ic
ic•ter•ic
ic•ter∘i•cal
ic•ter∘us

ic∘tic
ic∘tus, *n., pl.* -tus∘es, -tus.
id
i∘dée fixe
i∘de∘a•li•za•tion
i∘den•ti•cal twin
i∘den•ti•fi•ca•tion
i∘den•ti∘fy, *v.,* -fied, -fy•ing.
i∘den•ti∘ty, *n., pl.* -ties.
i∘de∘o•mo∘tion
i∘de∘o•mo•tor
id∘i•oc•ra∘sy, *n., pl.* -sies.
id•i∘o∘cy, *n., pl.* -cies.
id∘i∘o•gen•e∘sis, *n., pl.* -ses.
id∘i∘o•path∘ic
id∘i∘o•path∘i•cal∘ly
id•i•op∘a•thy, *n., pl.* -thies.
id∘i∘o•syn•cra∘sy, *n., pl.* -sies.
id∘i∘o•syn•crat∘ic
id∘i•o•syn•crat∘i•cal∘ly

id∘i∘ot
idiot sa•vant, *n., pl.* id∘i∘ot
 sa•vants.
ig•na•ti∘a a∘ma∘ra
il∘e∘ac
il•e•al
il•e∘ec•to∘my, *n., pl.* -mies.
il∘e∘i∘tis, *n., pl.* -ti•des.
il∘e∘o•ce•cos•to∘my,, *n., pl.*
 -mies.
il∘e∘o•ce•cum, *n., pl.* -ce∘ca.
il∘e∘o•co•los•to∘my, *n., pl.*
 -mies.
il•e∘os•to∘my, *n., pl.* -mies.
il•e∘um, *n., pl.* -il∘e∘a.
il•e∘us
il•i∘ac
i∘li∘a•cus, *n., pl.* i∘li∘a∘ci.
il•i∘o•tib∘i∘al band
il∘i∘um, *n., pl.* il∘i∘a.
il•le•git∘i•ma∘cy, *n., pl.* -cies.
il•lu•sion
il•lu•sion∘al
il•lu•sion•ar∘y
im∘age
im•age∘ry, *n., pl.* -ries.
i∘mag•ine, *v.,* -ined, -in•ing.
im•ag∘ing
i∘ma∘go, *n., pl.* i∘ma•goes.
im•be•cile
im•be•cile∘ly
im•be•cil∘i∘ty, *n., pl.* -ties.
im∘bed, *v.,* -bed•ded, -bed•
 ding.
im•bibe, *v.,* -bibed, -bib•ing.
im•bri•cate, *v.,* -cat∘ed, -cat•
 ing.
i∘mid∘a•zole
im•ma•tu•ri∘ty
im•merse, *v.,* -mersed, -mers•
 ing.
im•mo•bil∘i∘ty

im•mo•bi•li•za•tion
im•mo•bi•lize, *v.,* -lized, liz•
 ing.
im•mo•bi•liz∘er
im•mor•tal∘i∘ty
im•mune
immune com•plex
immune re•sponse
im•mun∘i∘ty, *n., pl.* -ties.
im•mu•ni•za•tion
im•mu•nize, *v.,* -nized, -niz•
 ing.
im•mu•niz∘er
im•mu•no•as•say
im•mu•no•as•say∘a•ble
im•mu•no•bi∘o•log∘ic
im•mu•no•bi∘o•log∘i•cal
im•mu•no•bi•ol∘o•gist
im•mu•no•bi•ol∘o∘gy
im•mu•no•chem∘i•cal
im•mu•no•chem∘i•cal∘ly
im•mu•no•chem∘ist
im•mu•no•cy•to•chem•is•
 try, *n., pl.* -tries.
im•mu•no•de•fi•cien∘cy, *n.,*
 pl. -cies.
im•mu•no•de•fi•cient
im•mu•no•di•ag•no∘sis, *n.,*
 pl. -ses.
im•mu•no•dif•fu•sion
im•mu•no•e•lec•tro•pho•
 re•sis
im•mu•no•gen
im•mu•no•gen•e∘sis, *n., pl.*
 -ses.
im•mu•no•gen∘ic
im•mu•no•ge•nic∘i∘ty
im•mu•no•glob∘u•lin
im•mu•no•he•ma•to•log∘ic
im•mu•no•he•ma•to•log∘i•
 cal

im•mu•no•he•ma•tol○o•gy
im•mu•no•his•to•chem•is•try, *n., pl.* -tries.
im•mu•no•his•to•log○ic
im•mu•no•his•to•log○i•cal
im•mu•no•his•to•log○i•cal○ly
im•mu•no•his•tol○o○gy
im•mu•no•log○ic
im•mu•no•log○i•cal
im•mu•no•log○i•cal○ly
im•mu•nol○o•gist
im•mu•nol○o○gy
im•mu•no•path○o○log○ic
im•mu•no•path○o○log○i•cal
im•mu•no•path○o○log○i•cal○ly
im•mu•no•pa•thol○o•gist
im•mu•no•pa•thol○o○gy
im•mu•no•pre•cip○i•ta•tion
im•mu•no•re•ac•tiv○i•ty, *n., pl.* -ties.
im•mu•no•sup•press
im•mu•no•sup•pres•sion
im•mu•no•sup•pres•sive
im•mu•no•ther○a•peu•tic
im•mu•no•ther○a○py
im•mu•no•tox○in
im•per•me•a•bil○i•ty
im•pe•tig○i•nous
im•pe•ti○go
im•plant
im•plant○a•ble
im•plan•ta•tion
im•po•tence
im•po•ten○cy
im•po•tent
im•preg•na•ble
im•preg•nate, *v.,* -nat○ed, -nat•ing.
im•preg•na•tion
im•pulse

in u○ter○o
in vi○tro
in vitro fer•til○i•za•tion
in vi○vo
in•ac•ti•vate, *v.,* -vat○ed, -vat•ing.
in•ac•tiv○i•ty
in•ad•e○qua○cy, *n., pl.* -cies.
in•breathe, *v.,* -breathed, -breath•ing.
in•breed, *v.,* -bred, -breed•ing.
in•ca•pac○i•tate, *v.,* -tat○ed, -tat•ing.
in•car•cer•ate, *v.,* -at○ed, -at•ing.
in•cen•di•ar○y, *n., pl.* -ries.
in•ci•dence
in•cise, *v.,* -cised, -cis•ing.
in•cised
in•ci•sion
in•ci•sion○al
incisional bi•op○sy
in•ci•su○ra, *n., pl.* -rae.
in•ci•sure, *n., pl.* -sures.
in•com•pat○i•bil○i○ty, *n., pl.* -ties.
in•com•pat○i•ble
in•com•pat○i•bly
in•com•pe•ten○cy, *n., pl.* -cies.
in•con•ti•nence
in•con•ti•nen○cy
in•con•ti•nent
in•cu•bate, *v.,* -bat○ed, -bat•ing.
in•cu•ba•tion
in•cu•ba•tion○al
in•cu•ba•tor
in•cu•ba•to○ry
in•cu•bus, *n., pl.* -cu○bi.
in•cu•dal
in•cu•date

in•cus, *n., pl.* -cu•des.
in•dex, *n., pl.* in•dex•es, in•
di•ces.
In•di•an to•bac•co
in•di•can
in•di•cate, *v.,* -cat•ed, -cat•
ing.
in•di•ca•tion
in•di•ges•ti•bil•i•ty
in•di•ges•tion
in•di•go
in•do•lent
in•do•meth•a•cin
in•duce, *v.,* -duced, -duc•ing.
in•duc•er
in•duc•i•ble
in•duc•tion
in•duc•tive
in•duc•tive•ly
in•duc•tive•ness
in•duc•to•ther•o•my, *n., pl.*
-mies.
in•du•rate, *v.* -rat•ed, -rat•
ing.
in•du•ra•tion
in•du•ra•tive
in•du•si•um, *n., pl.* -si•a.
in•e•bri•ate, *v.,* -at•ed, -at•
ing.
in•e•bri•e•ty, *n., pl.* -ties.
in•ert
in•er•tia
in•ert•ly
in•ert•ness
in•fan•cy, *n., pl.* -cies.
in•fan•tile pa•ral•y•sis
in•fan•ti•lism
in•farct
in•farct•ed
in•farc•tion
in•fect
in•fec•tion

in•fec•tious
infectious hep•a•ti•tis
infectious mon•o•nu•cle•o•
sis
in•fec•tious•ly
in•fec•tious•ness
in•fec•tiv•i•ty, *n., pl.* -ties.
in•fe•cun•di•ty
in•fe•ri•or ve•na ca•va
in•fe•ri•or•i•ty *n. pl.* -ties.
inferiority com•plex
in•fer•tile
in•fer•til•i•ty
in•fil•trate, *v.,* -trat•ed, -trat•
ing.
in•fil•tra•tion
in•fil•tra•tive
in•fil•tra•tor
in•fir•ma•ry, *n., pl.* -ries.
in•fir•mi•ty, *n., pl.* -ties.
in•flame, *v.,* -flamed, -flam•
ing.
in•flam•ma•tion
in•flam•ma•to•ri•ly
in•flam•ma•to•ry
in•flu•en•za
in•flu•en•zal
in•formed con•sent
in•fra•di•an rhythm
in•fra•spi•na•tus, *n., pl.*
-na•ti.
in•fun•dib•u•lum, *n., pl.*
-dib•u•la.
in•fuse, *v.,* -fused, -fus•ing.
in•fu•sion
in•fu•so•ri•al
in•fu•so•ri•an
in•gest
in•gest•i•ble
in•ges•tion
in•ges•tive
in•glu•vies, *n., pl.* -vies.

in•grown
in•guen, *n., pl.* -gui•na.
in•gui•nal
in•hal•ant
in•ha•la•tor
in•hale, *v.,* -haled, -hal•ing.
in•her•i•ta•bil•i•ty
in•hib•in
in•hib•it
in•hib•it•ed
in•hi•bi•tion
in•hib•i•tive
in•hib•i•to•ry
in•ho•mo•ge•ne•i•ty
in•ject
in•ject•a•ble
in•jec•tion
in•jec•tor
in•jure, *v.,* -jured, -jur•ing.
in•ju•ry, *n., pl.* -ries.
ink•blot test
in•ner ear
in•ner•vate, *v.,* -vat•ed, -vat•
  ing.
in•ner•va•tion
in•nom•i•nate bone
in•oc•u•late, *v.,* -lat•ed, -lat•
  ing.
in•oc•u•la•tion
in•oc•u•la•tive
in•oc•u•la•tor
in•oc•u•lum, *n., pl.* -oc•u•la.
in•op•er•a•ble
in•os•cu•late, *v.,* -lat•ed, -lat•
  ing.
i•no•si•tol
i•no•trop•ic
in•sal•i•vate, *v.,* -vat•ed,
  -vat•ing.
in•sa•lu•bri•ty, *n., pl.* -ties.
in•sane
in•san•i•ty, *n., pl.* -ties.

in•se•cur•i•ty, *n., pl.* -ties.
in•sem•i•nate, *v.,* -nat•ed,
  -nat•ing.
in•sem•i•na•tion
in•sheathe, *v.,* -sheathed,
  -sheath•ing.
in•sight
in•so•la•tion
in•sol•u•bil•i•ty, *n., pl.* -ties.
in•sol•u•ble fi•ber
in•som•ni•a
in•som•ni•ac
in•som•ni•ous
in•spire, *v.,* -spired, -spir•ing.
in•spis•sate, *v.,* -sat•ed, -sat•
  ing.
in•sta•bil•i•ty, *n., pl.* -ties.
in•step
in•still, *v.,* -stilled, -still•ing.
in•stru•men•tar•i•um, *n., pl.*
  -tar•i•a.
in•suf•fi•cien•cy, *n., pl.* -cies.
in•suf•flate, *v.,* -flat•ed, -flat•
  ing.
in•suf•fla•tion
in•suf•fla•tor
in•su•la, *n., pl.* -lae.
in•su•late, *v.,* -lat•ed, -lat•
  ing.
in•su•lin
insulin-co•ma ther•a•py
insulin shock
in•sur•ance
in•sus•cep•ti•bil•i•ty
in•tact dil•a•ta•tion and ex•
  trac•tion
in•te•grate, *v.,* -grat•ed,
  -grat•ing.
in•te•gra•tion
in•teg•ri•ty
in•teg•u•ment
in•tel•lec•tu•al•i•za•tion

in•tel•lec•tu•al•ize, v., -ized,
-iz•ing.
in•ten•siv∘ist
in∘ter•breed, v., -bred,
-breed•ing.
in∘ter•ca•late, v., -lat∘ed,
-lat•ing.
in•ter•cel•lu•lar
in•ter•cos•tal
in•ter•cos•tal∘ly
in•ter•course
in•ter•cur•rence
in•ter•cur•rent
in∘ter•dig∘i•tate, v., -tat∘ed,
-tat•ing.
in•ter•fer•ence
in•ter•fe•ren•tial
in∘ter•fe•rom•e∘try
in•ter•fer•on
in•ter•fe•ron al∘pha
in∘ter•fer•til∘i∘ty
in∘ter•ki•ne•sis, n., pl. -ses.
in•ter•leu•kin
in∘ter•max•il•o•la, n., pl. -las,
-lae.
in•ter•mit•tence
in∘ter•mit•ten∘cy
in•ter•mit•tent
intermittent clau•di•ca•tion
in•ter•mit•tent∘ly
in•ter•mo•lec∘u•lar
in•tern
in•ter•nal med∘i•cine
in•ter•nal∘ize, v., -ized, -iz•
ing.
in•ter•na•tion∘al u∘nit
in•tern∘ist
in•ter∘o•cep•tive
interoceptive dis•turb•ance
in•ter∘o•cep•tor
in∘ter•os•se•ous
in•ter•phase

in•ter•po•late, v., -lat∘ed,
-lat•ing.
in•ter•sex
in•ter•sex•u∘al
in•ter•sex∘ou•al•ism
in∘ter•sex∘ou•al∘i∘ty, n., pl.
-ties.
in•ter•sex∘ou•al∘ly
in∘ter•spi•na•lis, n., pl. -les.
in∘ter•ste•ril∘i∘ty, n., pl. -ties.
in•ter•stice, n., pl. -sti•ces.
in∘ter•sti•tial
interstitial-cell-stim∘u•lat•ing
hor•mone
interstitial ra•di•o•a•tion
in•ter•sti•tial∘ly
in∘ter•sti•ti∘um, n., pl. -ti∘a.
in∘ter•tri∘go, n., pl. -gos.
in•ter•val train•ing
in•ter•ven•tion
in•ter•ver•te•bral
intervertebral disk
in•ter•ver•te•bral∘ly
in•tes•ti•nal
in•tes•ti•nal∘ly
in•tes•tine
in•ti∘ma, n., pl. -mae, -mas.
in•tox∘i•cate, v., -cat∘ed,
-cat•ing.
in•tox∘i•ca•tion
in∘tra•a•or•tic bal•loon
pump
in∘tra•cel•lu•lar
in∘tra•cel•lu•lar∘ly
in∘tra•cra•ni•al
in∘tra•cu•ta•ne•ous
intracutaneous test
in∘tra•cu•ta•ne•ous∘ly
in∘tra•der•mal
in∘tra•der•mal∘ly
in∘tra•der•mic
in∘tra•der•mi•cal∘ly

in•tra•mo•lec•u•lar
in•tra•oc•u•lar
in•tra•oc•u•lar lens
in•tra•oc•u•lar•ly
in•tra•psy•chic
in•tra•psy•chi•cal•ly
in•tra•u•ter•ine
intrauterine de•vice
in•trav◦a•sa•tion
in•tra•vas•cu•lar
in•tra•ve•nous
intravenous py◦e•lo•gram
intravenous py◦e•log•ra•phy
in•tra•ve•nous•ly
in•trin•sic fac•tor
in•troi•tus, *n., pl.* in•troi•tus.
in•tro•jec•tion
in•tron
in•tro•ver•sion
in•tro•ver•sive
in•tro•vert
in•tro•ver•tive
in•tu•bate, *v.,* -bat◦ed, -bat•
  ing.
in•tu•ba•tion
in•tu•mesce, *v.,* -mesced,
  -mesc◦ing.
in•tu•mes•cence
in•tu•mes•cent
in•tus•sus•cept
in•tus•sus•cep•tion
in•tus•sus•cep•tive
in•tus•sus•cep•tum, *n., pl.*
  -cep◦ta.
in•tus•sus•cip◦i•ens, *n., pl.*
  -cip◦i•en•tes.
in◦u•lase
in◦u•lin
in•vade, *v.,* -vad◦ed, -vad•ing.
in•vag◦i•nate, *v.,* -nat◦ed,
  -nat•ing.
in•vag◦i•na•tion

in•va•lid•ism
in•va•sion
in•va•sive
in•ver•sion
in•ver•sive
in•vert sug◦ar
in•vert•ase
in•ver•tin
in•ves•ti•ga•tion◦al new
  drug
in•vi◦a•bil◦i•ty
in•vi◦a•ble
in•vo•lu•crum, *n., pl.* -cra.
in•vol•un•tar◦i•ly
in•vol•un•tar◦i•ness
in•vol•un•tar◦y
in•vo•lu•tion
in•vo•lu•tion◦al
involutional mel•an•cho•li◦a
i◦o•dim•e•try
i◦o•di•nate, *v.,* -nat◦ed, -nat•
  ing.
i◦o•dine
i◦o•di•za•tion
i◦o•dize, *v.,* -dized, -diz•ing.
i◦o•diz◦er
i◦o•do•form
i◦o•dom•e•try
i◦o•dop•sin
i◦on•ize, *v.,* -ized, -iz•ing.
i◦on◦o•phore
i◦on•to•pho•re•sis, *n., pl.*
  -ses.
i◦on•to•pho•ret◦ic
ip•e◦cac
ip•e◦cac◦u•an◦ha
ir◦i•dec•to•mize, *v.,* -mized,
  -miz•ing.
ir◦i•dec•to◦my, *pl.* -mies.
ir◦i•do•cy•clec•to◦my
ir◦i•do•cys•tec•to◦my, *n., pl.*
  -mies.

ir•i•do•di•al•y•sis, *n., pl.*
 -ses.
ir•i•do•do•ne•sis, *n., pl.* -ses.
ir•i•dol•o•gist
ir•i•dol•o•gy, *n., pl.* -gies.
ir•i•do•scle•rot•o•my, *n., pl.*
 -mies.
i•ris, *n., pl.* i•ris•es, ir•i•des.
i•rit•ic
i•ri•tis
i•ron lung
iron-stor•age dis•ease
ir•ra•di•ate, *v.,* -at•ed, -at•
 ing.
ir•ra•di•a•tion
ir•ra•tion•al•o•i•ty, *n., pl.* -ties.
ir•re•duc•i•bil•i•ty, *n., pl.*
 -ties.
ir•reg•u•lar•i•ty, *n., pl.* -ties.
ir•ri•ga•ble
ir•ri•ga•bly
ir•ri•gate, *v.,* -gat•ed, -gat•
 ing.
ir•ri•ga•tion
ir•ri•ga•tion•al
ir•ri•ta•bil•i•ty, *n., pl.* -ties.
ir•ri•ta•ble
irritable bow•el syn•drome
ir•ri•ta•bly
ir•ri•tan•cy
ir•ri•tant
ir•ri•tate, *v.,* -tat•ed, -tat•ing.
ir•ri•ta•tion
ir•ri•ta•tive
ir•ri•ta•tive•ness
is•aux•e•sis
is•chae•mi•a
is•che•mi•a
is•che•mic
ischemic heart dis•ease
is•chi•o•coc•cyg•e•ous, *n., pl.*
 -cyg•e•i.

is•chi•om•e•olus, *n., pl.* -e•oli.
is•chi•op•a•gus, *n., pl.* -op•
 a•gi.
is•chi•um, *n., pl.* -chi•a.
is•olet of Lang•er•hans
i•so•ag•glu•ti•na•tion
i•so•an•ti•bod•y, *n., pl.* -ies.
i•so•cor•tex, *n., pl.* -ti•ces,
 -tex•es.
i•so•en•zyme
i•sog•o•a•mous
i•sog•a•omy
i•so•gen•e•sis, *n., pl.* -ses.
i•sog•e•onous
i•sog•e•ony
i•sog•o•ony, *n., pl.* -nies.
i•so•he•mol•y•sis
i•so•late, *v.,* -lat•ed, -lat•ing.
i•so•lette
i•so•leu•cine
i•som•er•ase
i•som•er•ize, *v.,* -ized, -iz•ing.
i•so•met•ric
isometric ex•er•cise
i•so•met•ri•cal•ly
i•so•me•tro•pi•a
i•so•mor•phic
i•so•mor•phism
i•so•ni•a•zid
i•sop•a•thy
i•so•pro•ter•e•onol
I•sop•tin *Trademark.*
I•sor•dil *Trademark.*
i•so•sor•bide
i•sos•po•o•ry, *n., pl.* -ries.
i•so•ton•ic
i•so•to•nic•i•ty
i•so•zyme
is•sue, *n., v.,* -sued, -su•ing.
isth•mec•to•my, *n., pl.* -mies.
IV, *n., pl.* IVs, IV's.
ix•o•di•a•sis

jac•ti•tate, *v.*, -tat∘ed, -tat•ing.

jake

Ja•kob-Creutz•feldt dis•ease

jaun•dice

jec∘o•rize, *v.*, -rized, -riz•ing.

je•ju•nal

je•ju•nec•to•my, *n.*, *pl.* -mies.

je•ju•no•co•los•to•my, *n.*, *pl.* -mies.

je•ju•no•il•e∘i•tis

je•ju•no•il•e∘os•to∘my, *n.*, *pl.* -mies.

je•ju•no•je•ju•nos•to∘my, *n.*, *pl.* -mies.

je•ju•nos•to∘my, *n.*, *pl.* -mies.

je•ju•not∘o∘my, *n.*, *pl.* -mies.

je•ju•num, *n.*, *pl.* -ju∘na.

jes•sa•mine

jet gun

jet lag or jet•lag

jet-lagged

jock itch

jog•ger's nip•ple

joint

jug∘u•lar

jug∘u•lum, *n.*, *pl.* jug•u∘la.

jump•ing gene

junc•tu∘ra, *n.*, *pl.* -rae.

Jung∘i∘an

jun•gle fe∘ver

ju•ve•nile-on∘set di∘a•be•tes

juvenile rheu•ma•toid arth•ri•tis

jux•ta•pose, *v.*, -posed, -pos•ing.

ka•ki•dro•sis

ka∘la-a∘zar

kal∘i bromatum

kali phos•phor∘i•cum

kal∘i∘um bi•chom∘i•cum

ka∘o∘li•no•sis

Ka•po∘si's sa•rco•ma

kar∘y•en•chy∘ma, *n.*, *pl.* -ma∘ta, -mas.

kar∘y∘o∘cla•sis

kar∘y•og•a∘my

kar∘y∘o•ki•ne•sis, *n.*, *pl.* -ses.

kar∘y∘o•kla•sis

kar∘y•ol∘o∘gy

kar∘y•ol∘y•sis

kar∘y∘o•mi•to•sis, *n.*, *pl.* -ses.

kar∘y•or•rhex∘is, *n.*, *pl.* -rhex∘es.

kar∘y∘o•sta•sis, *n.*, *pl.* -ses.

kar∘y∘o∘type

kar∘y∘o∘typ∘ic

kar∘y∘o∘typ∘i•cal

kar∘y∘o∘typ∘ing

ka•ta•chro•ma•sis, *n.*, *pl.* -ses.

Ka•wa•sa•ki's dis•ease

ke•loid

ke•loi•dal

ke•lo∘ma, *n.*, *pl.* -mas, -ma∘ta.

ker∘a•tec•to∘my, *n.*, *pl.* -mies.

ker∘a•tin

ker∘a•tin∘i•za•tion

ker∘a•tin•ize, *v.*, -ized, -iz•ing.

ke•rat∘i•nous

ker∘a•ti•tis, *n. pl.* -tit∘i•des.

ker∘a•to•ac•an•tho∘ma, *n.*, *pl.* -mas, -ma∘ta.

ker∘a•to•cen•te•sis, *n.*, *pl.* -ses.

ker∘a•to•chro•ma•to•sis, *n.*, *pl.* -ses.

ker∘a•to•gen•e∘sis, *n.*, *pl.* -ses.

ker∘a•to•hel•co•sis, *n.*, *pl.* -ses.

ker∘a•toid

ker∘a•tol∘y•sis

ker○a•to•lyt○ic

ker○a•to○ma, *n., pl.* **-mas,**
   -ma○ta.

ker○a•to•my•co○sis, *n., pl.*
   -ses.

ker○a•to•nyx○is, *n., pl.* **-es.**

ker○a•to•plas•tic

ker○a•to•plas○ty, *n., pl.* **-ties.**

ker○a•tor•rhex○is, *n., pl.*
   -rhex○es.

ker○a•tos•co○py, *n., pl.* **-pies.**

ker○a•to•sic

ker○a•to•sis, *n., pl.* **-ses.**

ker○a•tot○ic

ker○a•tot○o•my, *n., pl.* **-mies.**

ke•to•ac○i•do○sis

ke•to•con○a•zole

ke•to•gen•e○sis, *n., pl.*
   -e○ses.

ke•to•gen○ic di○et

ke•tol○y•sis, *n., pl.* **-ses.**

ke•tone bod○y

ke•to•nu•ri○a

ke•to•pro•fen

ke•tose

ke•to•sis

ke•tos•ter•oid

kid•ney, *n., pl.* **-neys.**

kid•ney stone

kill○er cell

kill○er T cell

kil○o•cal○o•rie

kil○o•gram

kin•aes•the•sis, *n., pl.* **-ses.**

ki•nase

kin•e○plas○ty, *n., pl.* **-ties.**

ki•ne•si•ol○o○gy

ki•ne•sis

ki•ne•si•ther○a○py

kin•es•the•sia

kin•es•the•sis, *n., pl.* **-ses.**

kin•es•thet○ic

ki•net○ic

ki•ne•to•nu•cle○us, *n., pl.*
   -cle○i, -cle•us○es.

kin•e○to•sis

ki○nin

ki•no•cen•trum, *n., pl.* **-trums,**
   -tra.

ki•ot○o○my, *n., pl.* **-mies.**

kjel•dahl•ize, *v.,* **-ized, -iz○ing.**

klep•to•ma•ni○a

Kline•fel•ter's syn•drome

knee

knee jerk

knee•cap

knock•out mouse

knuck○le

ko•ni○o•cor○tex, *n., pl.* **-ti•**
   ces.

ko•ni•ol○o○gy

Kor•sa•koff's syn•drome

krau•ro•sis

Krause's cor•puscle

Krebs cy•cle

ku○ru

kwash○i•or•kor

ky•mo•gram

ky•mo•graph

ky•mo•graph○ic

ky•mog•ra•phy, *n., pl.* **-phies.**

ky•pho•sco•li•o○sis

ky•pho•sis

ky•phot○ic

L-do∘pa
la∘bel, *n., v.,* -beled, -bel∙ing
   or -belled, -bel∙ling.
la∘bel∘er
la∘bi∘a ma∘jo∘ra, *n.pl., sing.*
   la∘bi∘um ma∘jus.
labia mi∙no∘ra, *n.pl., sing.* la-
   bium mi∘nus.
la∘bi∘al
la∘bi∘al∘i∘ty
la∘bi∘al∘ly
la∘bil∘i∘ty
la∘bi∘o∘plas∘ty, *n., pl.* -ties.
la∘bi∘um, *n., pl.* -bi∘a.
la∘bor
la∘bor∙ing∘ly
lab∘y∙rinth
lab∘y∙rin∙thec∙to∘my, *n., pl.*
   -mies.
lab∘y∙rin∙thi∙tis
lab∘y∙rin∙thot∘o∘my, *n., pl.*
   -mies.
lac∘er∙ate, *v.,* -at∘ed, -at∙ing.
lac∙er∘a∙tion
lach∙e∘osis mu∘tus
lach∙ry∙ma∙tor
lac∙ri∙mal
lacrimal bone
lacrimal gland
lac∙ri∙ma∙tion
lac∙ri∙ma∙tor
lac∙ri∙mot∘o∘my, *n., pl.* -mies.
lac∙tal∙bu∙min
lac∙tase
lac∙tate, *v.,* -tat∘ed, -tat∙ing.
lac∙tate de∙hy∙dro∙ge∙nase
lac∙ta∙tion
lac∙ta∙tion∘al
lac∙ta∙tion∘al∘ly

lac∙te∘al
lac∙te∙al∘ly
lac∙tic ac∘id
lac∙to∙ba∙cil∙lus, *n., pl.* -li.
lac∙to∙gen∙e∘sis, *n., pl.* -ses.
lac∙to∙gen∘ic
lac∙tor∙rhe∘a
lac∙tose
la∙cu∘na, *n., pl.* -nae, -nas.
la∘e∘trile
la∙ge∘na, *n., pl.* -nae.
lake, *v.,* laked, lak∙ing.
la∙lop∘a∙thy, *n., pl.* -thies.
La∙maze meth∘od
la∙mel∘la, *n., pl.* -las, -lae.
la∙mel∙lar
lamellar ex∙fo∙li∘a∙tion of
   the new∙born
lam∙i∘na, *n., pl.* -nas, -nae.
lamina cri∙bro∘sa, *n., pl.*
   lam∘i∙nae cri∙bro∙sae.
lamina pro∙pri∘a, *n., pl.* lami-
   nae pro∙pri∘ae.
lam∘i∙nar air flow u∙nit
lam∘i∙nate, *v.,* -nat∘ed, -nat∙
   ing.
lam∘i∙nec∙to∘my, *n., pl.*
   -mies.
lam∘i∙not∘o∘my, *n., pl.* -mies.
lance, *v.,* lanced, lanc∙ing.
lan∙cet
lan∙ci∙nat∘ing
Lang∙er∙hans' cells
la∙nu∘go
lap∘a∙ror∙rha∙phy
lap∘a∙ro∙scope
lap∘a∙ro∙scop∘ic
lap∘a∙ros∙co∙pist
lap∘a∙ros∙co∘py, *n., pl.* -pies.

lap•a•rot○o•my, *n.*, *pl.* -mies.
lap•sus lin•guae
large in•tes•tine
lar○va, *n.*, *pl.* -vas, -vae.
larva mi•grans, *n.*, *pl.* larvae mi•gran•tes.
la•ryn•gal
la•ryn•ge○al
la•ryn•ge•al○ly
lar•yn•gec•to•mize, *v.*, -mized, -miz•ing.
lar•yn•gec•to○my, *n.*, *pl.* -mies.
lar•yn•gis•mus, *n.*, *pl.* -mi.
laryngismus stri•du•lus, *n.*, *pl.* -gis○mi -du○li.
lar•yn•git○ic
lar•yn•gi•tis
la•ryn•go•log○ic
la•ryn•go•log○i•cal
lar•yn•gol○o•gist
lar•yn•gol○o○gy
la•ryn•go•pa•ral○y•sis
lar•yn•gop○a•thy, *n.*, *pl.* -thies.
la•ryn•go•phar•yn•gec•to○my, *n.*, *pl.* -mies.
la•ryn•go•phar•yn•gi•tis
la•ryn•go•phar•ynx, *n.*, *pl.* -pha•ryn•ges, -phar•ynx○es.
la•ryn•go•plas○ty, *n.*, *pl.* -ties.
la•ryn•go•rhi○nol○o○gy
la•ryn•go•scle•ro○ma, *n.*, *pl.* -mas, -ma○ta.
la•ryn•go•scope
la•ryn•go•scop○ic
la•ryn•gos•co•pist
lar•yn•gos•co○py, *n.*, *pl.* -pies.
la•ryn•go•ste•no•sis
lar•yn•gos•to•my, *n.*, *pl.* -mies.

lar•yn•got○o○my, *n.*, *pl.* -mies.
la•ryn•go•tra•che○o•bron•chi○tis
la•ryn•go•tra•che•ot○o○my, *n.*, *pl.* -mies.
la•ryn•go•xe•ro•sis
lar•ynx, *n.*, *pl.* la•ryn•ges, lar•ynx○es.
la○ser
La•six *Trademark.*
Las○sa fe○ver
la•ten○cy, *n.*, *pl.* -cies.
latency pe•ri○od
la•tent
latent pe•ri○od
la•tent○ly
lat•er•al○i○ty
lat•er•al○i•za○tion
lath○y•rism
lath○y•rit○ic
la•tis•si•mus dor○si, *n.*, *pl.* la•tis•si○mi do○rsi.
lats
lat•tice, *v.*, -ticed, -tic•ing.
lau•da•num
laugh•ing gas
la•vage
law of dom○i•nance
law of in•de•pend•ent as•sort•ment
law of seg•re•ga○tion
lax○a•tive
lax○a•tive○ly
lax○a•tive•ness
laz○ar
laz○a•ret
laz○a•rette
la•za•ret○to, *n.*, *pl.* -tos.
la○zy eye
lead col○ic
lead poi•son•ing

lead time
learned help•less•ness
learn•ing dis•a•bil∘i∘ty
learn•ing-dis•a•bled
lec∘i•thal
lec∘i•thic
lec∘i•thin
lec•tin
left ven•tri•cle
left ven•tric•u•lar as•sist
  de•vice
left ventricular e∘jec•tion
  frac•tion
leg
Legg-Cal•vé-Per•thes dis•ease
le•gion•naires' dis•ease
lei∘o•my∘o•fi•bro∘ma, *n., pl.*
  -mas, -ma∘ta.
lei∘o•my∘o•ma, *n., pl.* -mas,
  -ma∘ta.
lei∘o•my•om∘a•tous
lei∘o•my∘o•sar•co∘ma, *n., pl.*
  -mas, -ma∘ta.
leish•man∘i•a•sis
leish•man∘i•o•sis
lem•nis•cus, *n., pl.* -ci.
lens
lens•less
lens•like
len•tic•u∘la, *n., pl.* -las, -lae.
len•ti∘go, *n., pl.* -tig∘i•nes.
len•ti•vi•rus, *n., pl.* -rus∘es.
le•on•ti•a•sis
lep∘er
lep∘i•do•sis, *n., pl.* -ses.
lep∘o•thrix
lep•rol∘o•gy
lep•ro∘ma, *n., pl.* -mas,
  -ma∘ta.
lep•ro•sar∘i∘um, *n., pl.* -i•
  ums, -i∘a.
lep•ro∘sy

lep•rot∘ic
lep•rous
lep•rous∘ly
lep•rous•ness
lep•tin
lep∘to•ceph∘a•lus, *n., pl.* -li.
lep∘to•men•in•gi•tis
lep∘to•men•in•gop∘a•thy,
  n., pl. -thies.
lep∘to•men•inx, *n., pl.* -me•
  nin∘ges.
lep∘to•spi∘ra, *n., pl.* -rae, -ras.
lep∘to•spi•ro∘sis
lep•to•tene
le•sion
less∘er o∘men•tum
le•thal gene
le•thal∘i•ty
leth•ar∘gy
leu•cine
leu∘co•cyte
leu∘co•cy•to•poi•e∘sis
leu∘co•cy•to∘sis
leu∘co•der∘oma
leu∘co•en•ceph∘a•li•tis
leu•co∘ma
leu∘co•pe•ni∘a•leu•ko•cy•
  to∘pe•ni∘a
leu∘co•pla•ki∘a
leu∘co•pla•sia
leu∘co•poi•e∘sis
leu∘co•sis
leu∘co•tri•ene
leu•ke•mi∘a
leu•ke•mic
leu•ke•mo•gen•e∘sis, *n., pl.*
  -ses.
leu∘ko•blas•to•sis
leu∘ko•cyte
leu∘ko•cyt∘ic
leu∘ko•cy•to•gen•e∘sis, *n.,*
  pl. -ses.

leu○ko•cy•to•ly•sis
leu○ko•cy•to○ma, *n., pl.* -mas,
 -ma○ta.
leu○ko•cy•to•poi○e○sis
leu○ko•cy•to•sis
leu○ko•cy•tot○ic
leu○ko•der○ma
leu○ko•dys•tro•phy, *n., pl.*
 -phies.
leu○ko•en•ceph○a•li•tis
leu○ko•en•ceph○a•
 lop○a•thy, *n., pl.* -thies.
leu•ko○ma
leu•kop○a•thy, *n., pl.* -thies.
leu○ko•pe•de•sis
leu○ko•pe•ni○a
leu○ko•pe•nic
leu○ko•pla•ki○a
leu○ko•pla•sia
leu○ko•poi○e○sis
leu○ko•poi•et○ic
leu○ko•sar•co○ma, *n., pl.*
 -mas, -ma○ta.
leu○ko•sar•co•ma•to•sis
leu○ko•sis
leu•kot○o○my, *n., pl.* -mies.
leu○ko•tri•ene
le•va•tor
le•vo•do○pa
le•vo•ro•ta○ry
le•vo•ro•ta•to○ry
lev○u•lose
li•bid○i•nal
li•bid○i•nal○ly
li•bid○i•nize, *v.,* -nized, -niz•
 ing.
li•bi○do, *n., pl.* -dos.
Lib•ri○um
lice, *n., pl., sing.* **louse.**
li•chen
li•chen•ous
li•do•caine

li•en•cu•lus, *n., pl.* -li.
li•e○nog•ra•phy, *n., pl.*
 -phies.
li•e○nop○oa•thy, *n., pl.* -thies.
li•en•ter○y
li•en•un•cu•lus, *n., pl.* -cu○li.
life, *n., pl.* lives.
life-care
life cy•cle
life ex•pect•an○cy
life his•to○ry
life in•stinct
life span
life-sup•port
life•care
lig○a•ment
lig○a•men•to•pex○y, *n., pl.*
 -pex•ies.
lig○a•men•tum, *n., pl.* -ta.
ligamentum fla•vum, *n., pl.*
 lig○a•men○ta fla○va.
ligamentum nu•chae, *n., pl.*
 ligamenta nu•chae.
li•gand
li•gase
li•gate, *v.,* -gat○ed, -gat•ing.
li•ga•tion
lig○a•tive
lig○a•ture
light a○dap•ta•tion
light-a○dapt•ed
lig•num, *n., pl.* -nums, -na.
lig•u○la, *n., pl.* -lae,
 -las.
lim•bic sys•tem
li○men, *n., pl.* li•mens,
 lim○i○na.
lime•wa•ter
lim○i○na
lim○i•nal
lim•oph•thi•sis
lin○e○a, *n., pl.* lin○e○ae.

linea al○ba, *n., pl.* lineae
  al○bae.
lin•gua, *n., pl.* -guae.
lin•gual
lin•gual○ly
lin•gua•tu•lo•sis
lin•gu○la, *n., pl.* -lae.
lin○i•ment
link•age
linkage map
linked
li○pase
li○pec•to○my, *n., pl.* -mies.
li○pe•mi○a
li○pe•mic
lip○id
lipid bi•layer
lip•ide
lip○i•do•sis, *n., pl.* -ses.
li○po•chon•dro•dys•tro•phy,
  n., pl. -phies.
li○po•chrome
li○po•chro○mic
li○po•cyte
li○po•dys•tro•phy, *n., pl.*
  -phies.
li○po•fi•bro○ma, *n., pl.* -mas,
  -ma○ta.
li○po•fill•ing
li○po•gen•e○sis, *n., pl.* -ses.
li○po•gran○u•lo○ma, *n., pl.*
  -mas, -ma○ta.
lip•oid
li○poi•do•sis, *n., pl.* -ses.
li○po•lit○ic
li○pol○y•sis
li○po○ma, *n., pl.* -mas, -ma○ta.
li○po•ma•to•sis
li○pom○a•tous
li○po•phan•e○ro○sis
li○po•phil○ic
li○po•pol○y•sac•cha•ride

li○po•pro•tein
lipoprotein li•pase
li○po•sar•co○ma, *n., pl.* -mas,
  -ma○ta.
li•po•sis, *n., pl.* -ses.
li○po•so•mal
li○po•some
li○po•suc•tion
li○po•thy•mi○a
li○po•thy○my
li○po•trop○ic
li○po•tro•pin
li•pot○ro•pism
li•pox•e○ny, *n., pl.* -ies.
lis•sen•ceph○a•li○a
lis•sen•ceph○a○ly
lis•ter•el•lo•sis, *n., pl.* -ses.
lis•te•ri•a•sis, *n., pl.* -ses.
lis•ter○i•o•sis, *n., pl.* -ses.
lis•ter•ize, *v.,* -ized, -iz•ing.
li•thec•to○my, *n., pl.* -mies.
lith○i•a•sis
lith○i•um
lithium car•bo•nate
lith○o•di•al○y•sis
lith•ol○a•pax○y, *n., pl.* -ies.
lith•ol○o○gy
lith○o•ne•phri•tis
lith○o•ne•phrot○o○my, *n., pl.*
  -mies.
lith○o•tom○ic
lith○o•tom○i•cal
li•thot○o○mist
lith•ot○o○mize, *v.,* -mized,
  -miz•ing.
lith○ot○o○my, *n., pl.* -mies.
lith○o•trip○sy, *n., pl.* -sies.
lith○o•trip•ter
lith○o•trip•tic
li•thot•ri•tist
lith•ot•ri○ty
liv○er

liver spots
liv•er•ish
liv•er•ish•ness
li•vid•i•ty
liv•ing will
lo•ai•a•sis
lo•bar
lo•bec•to•my, *n.*, *pl.* -mies.
lo•bel•ia in•fla•ta
lo•bot•o•mist
lo•bot•o•mi•za•tion
lo•bot•o•mize, *v.*, -mized, -miz•ing.
lo•bot•o•my, *n.*, *pl.* -mies.
lob•u•lus, *n.*, *pl.* -li.
lo•bus, *n.*, *pl.* -bi.
lo•cal
local wide ex•ci•sion
lo•cal•ize, *v.*, -ized, -iz•ing.
lo•cal•ized
lo•cal•ly
lo•chi•a, *n.*, *pl.* -a.
lo•chi•os•che•sis
lo•ci, *n.*, *pl.*, *sing.* -cus.
lock•jaw
lo•co, *n.*, *pl.* -cos, -coes.
lo•co•ism
lo•co•mo•tor a•tax•i•a
loc•u•lus, *n.*, *pl.* -li.
lo•cum-ten•en•cy, *n.*, *pl.* -cies.
lo•cum ten•ens, *n.*, *pl.* lo•cum ten•en•tes.
lo•cus, *n.*, *pl.* -ci.
lo•gop•a•thy, *n.*, *pl.* -thies.
log•or•rhe•a
log•or•rhe•ic
lo•i•a•sis
loop
loop of Hen•le
Lo•pid *Trademark.*
Lo•pres•sor *Trademark.*

lo•ra•ze•pam
lor•do•sis
lor•dot•ic
lo•ti•o, *n.*, *pl.* -os.
lo•tion
Lou Gehr•ig's dis•ease
Louis-Bar syn•drome
louse, *n.*, *pl.* lice.
lous•y, *adj.*, lous•i•er, lous•i•est.
lo•va•stat•in
low blood pres•sure
low-den•si•ty lip•o•pro•tein
lu•cid dream•ing
lu•cid•i•ty
lu•es
lu•et•ic
lum•ba•go
lum•bar
lumbar punc•ture
lum•bo•co•los•to•my, *n.*, *pl.* -mies.
lum•bri•cal
lum•bri•cal•is, *n.*, *pl.* -cal•es.
lu•men, *n.*, *pl.* lu•mi•na, lu•mens.
Lu•mi•nal
lu•mi•nesce, *v.*, -nesced, -nes•cing.
lump•ec•to•my, *n.*, *pl.* -mies.
lump•y jaw
lu•na•cy, *n.*, *pl.* -cies.
lu•nar caus•tic
lu•na•re, *n.*, *pl.* -ri•a.
lu•na•tum, *n.*, *pl.* -na•ta.
lung
lung•wort
lu•nu•la, *n.*, *pl.* -lae.
lu•pous
lu•pus
lupus er•y•the•ma•to•sus
lupus vul•ga•ris

lu•te•al
lu•te•in
lu•te•in•ize, *v.*, -ized, -iz•ing.
lu•te•in•iz•ing hor•mone
lu•te•o•o•ma, *n., pl.* -mas, -ma•ta.
lu•te•o•o•troph•ic
lu•te•o•o•trop•ic
luteotropic hor•mone
lu•te•o•o•tro•pin
lux•ate, *v.*, -at•ed, -at•ing.
lux•a•tion
ly•can•thrope
ly•can•throp•ic
ly•can•thro•py
ly•co•pene
ly•co•pen•e•o•mi•a
ly•co•per•don•o•o•sis
ly•co•po•di•um clav•o•a•tum
ly•ing-in, *n., pl.* -ings-in, -ing-ins.
Lyme dis•ease
lymph
lymph node
lym•phad•e•o•nec•to•o•my, *n., pl.* -mies.
lym•phad•e•o•ni•tis
lym•phad•e•o•no•ma, *n., pl.* -mas, -ma•ta.
lym•phad•e•o•no•ma•to•sis
lym•phad•e•o•nop•o•a•thy, *n., pl.* -thies.
lym•phad•e•o•no•sis, *n., pl.* -ses.
lym•phan•gi•o•o•gram
lym•phan•gi•og•ra•phy

lym•phan•gi•o•o•ma, *n., pl.* -mas, -ma•ta.
lym•phan•gi•om•o•a•tous
lym•phat•ic
lymphatic sys•tem
lym•phat•o•i•cal•o•ly
lym•pho•cyte
lym•pho•cyt•ic
lym•pho•cy•to•sis
lym•pho•cy•tot•o•ic
lym•pho•gran•u•lo•o•ma, *n., pl.* -mas, -ma•ta.
lym•phog•ra•phy
lym•phoid
lym•pho•o•ma, *n., pl.* -mas, -ma•ta.
lym•pho•ma•toid
lym•pho•ma•to•sis
lym•pho•poi•e•sis
lym•pho•poi•et•ic
lym•pho•sar•co•ma
lym•pho•troph•ic
lyse, *v.*, lysed, lys•ing.
Ly•sen•ko•ism
lyser•gic ac•id di•eth•yl•am•ide
ly•o•sin
ly•sine
ly•o•sis
ly•so•gen
ly•so•gen•e•o•sis, *n., pl.* -ses.
ly•so•gen•ic
ly•so•ge•nic•i•o•ty
ly•sog•e•nize, *v.*, -nized, -niz•ing.
ly•sog•e•ony, *n., pl.* -nies.
ly•so•zyme

ma huang
mac•er•ate, *v.*, -at•ed, -at•
  ing.
mac•er•a•tion
mac•ren•ceph•a•ly
mac•ro•bi•ot•ic
mac•ro•bi•ot•i•cal•ly
mac•ro•bi•ot•ics
mac•ro•ce•phal•ic
mac•ro•ceph•a•lus, *n., pl.* -li.
mac•ro•ceph•a•ly
mac•ro•cyte
mac•ro•cyt•ic
mac•ro•cy•to•sis
mac•ro•gam•ete
mac•ro•glos•si•a
mac•rom•e•lus, *n., pl.* -li.
mac•ro•mere
mac•ro•mo•lec•u•lar
mac•ro•mol•e•cule
mac•ro•mu•tant
mac•ro•mu•ta•tion
mac•ro•nu•cle•us, *n., pl.*
  -cle•i, -cle•us•es.
mac•ro•nu•tri•ent
mac•ro•phage
mac•ro•phag•ic
mac•rop•si•a
mac•rop•sy
mac•u•la, *n., pl.* -lae, -las.
macula lu•te•a, *pl.*
  mac•u•lae lu•te•ae.
macula a•cu•sti•ca, *n., pl.*
  maculae a•cu•sti•cae.
mac•u•lar
macular de•gen•er•a•tion
mac•u•la•tion
mac•ule
mad cow dis•ease

mad•a•ro•sis
mad•u•ro•my•co•sis
mag•i•cal think•ing
mag•is•ter•y, *n., pl.* -ries.
mag•ne•sia
magnesia car•bon•i•ca
magnesia phos•phor•i•ca
mag•ne•sian
mag•net•ic res•o•nance im•
  ag•ing
magnetic resonance scan•ner
mag•net•ite
mag•ne•to•car•di•og•ra•
  phy, *n., pl.* -phies.
mag•ne•to•en•ceph•a•log•
  ra•phy
mag•ni•fy, *v.*, -fied, -fy•ing.
main•stream•ing
ma•jor af•fec•tive dis•or•
  ders
major his•to•com•
  pat•i•bil•i•ty com•plex
major tran•quil•iz•er
ma•la
mal•ab•sorp•tion
ma•la•cia
mal•a•coid
mal•a•cot•ic
mal•a•dy, *n., pl.* -dies.
ma•laise
ma•lar•i•a
ma•lar•i•al
ma•lar•i•an
ma•lar•i•ol•o•gy
ma•lar•i•o•ther•a•py, *n., pl.*
  -pies.
ma•lar•i•ous
mal•ax•ate, *v.*, -at•ed, -at•
  ing.

male
mal•for•ma•tion
mal•formed
mal•ic ac•id
ma•lig•nan•cy, *n., pl.* -cies.
ma•lig•nant
ma•lig•nant•ly
ma•lig•ni•ty
ma•lin•ger•ing
mal•le•o•lus, *n., pl.* -li.
mal•le•ot•o•my, *n., pl.* -mies.
mal•le•ous, *n., pl.* -le•i.
mal•nour•ished
mal•nu•tri•tion
mal•oc•clu•sion
Mal•pigh•i•an cor•pus•cle
mal•po•si•tion
mal•prac•tice
mal•prax•is
Mal•ta fe•ver
malt•ase
malt•ose
mal•um
ma•mil•la, *n., pl.* -lae.
mam•ma, *n., pl.* mam•mae.
mam•mal
mam•ma•plas•ty, *n., pl.* -ties.
mam•ma•ry
mammary gland
mam•mec•to•my, *n., pl.*
 -mies.
mam•mil•la, *n., pl.* -mil•lae.
mam•mil•li•plas•ty, *n., pl.*
 -ties.
mam•mi•tis
mam•mo•gram
mam•mog•ra•phy, *n., pl.*
 -phies.
mam•mo•plas•ty, *n., pl.* -ties.
mam•mot•o•my, *n., pl.* -mies.
man•o•met•ri•cal•ly
man•aged-care

man•di•ble
man•dib•u•lar
man•dib•u•late
mange
man•gy, *adj.* -gi•er, -gi•est.
ma•ni•a, *n., pl.* -as.
ma•ni•ac
man•ic
manic-de•pres•sive
manic dis•or•der
manic ep•i•sode
ma•nip•u•lat•a•ble
ma•nip•u•late, *v.,* -lat•ed,
 -lat•ing.
ma•nip•u•la•tion
ma•nip•u•la•to•ry
man•ni•tol
ma•nom•e•ter
man•o•met•ric
man•o•met•ri•cal
ma•nom•e•try
Man•toux test
man•u•al ther•a•py
ma•nu•bri•al
ma•nu•bri•um, *n., pl.* -bri•a,
 -bri•ums.
ma•nus, *n., pl.* -nus.
ma•ras•mic
ma•ras•moid
ma•ras•mus
Mar•burg dis•ease
Mar•fan syn•drome
mar•gin
mar•gi•nate, *v.,* -nat•ed,
 -nat•ing.
mar•gin•o•plas•ty, *n., pl.*
 -ties.
ma•ri•hua•na
ma•ri•jua•na
Mar•i•nol *Trademark.*
mark•er
marker gene

mar•row
mar•su•pi○a•lize, *v.*, -lized, -liz•ing.
mar•su•pi○um, *n.*, *pl.* -pi○a.
mas•cu•lin○i○ty
mas•cu•li•nize, *v.*, -nized, -niz•ing.
masked de•pres•sion
mask•ing
mas•och•ism
mas•och•ist
mas•och•is•tic
mas•och•is•ti•cal○ly
mas•se○ter
mas•so•ther○a○py, *n.*, *pl.* -pies.
MAST suit
mas•tal•gia
mas•tec•to○my, *n.*, *pl.* -mies.
mas•ter cell
mas•ti•cate, *v.*, -cat○ed, -cat•ing.
ma•stit○ic
mas•ti•tis
mas•to•cy•to○ma, *n.*, *pl.* -mas, -ma○ta.
mas•toid
mastoid proc•ess
mas•toi•dec•to○my, *n.*, *pl.* -mies.
mas•toi•di•tis
mas•toi•dot•o○my, *n.*, *pl.* -mies.
mas•top○a•thy, *n.*, *pl.* -thies.
mas•to•pex○y, *n.*, *pl.* -pex•ies.
mas•to•plas○ty, *n.*, *pl.* -ties.
mas•to•scir•rhus
mas•tot○o○my, *n.*, *pl.* -mies.
mas•tur•bate, *v.*, -bat○ed, -bat•ing.
mas•tur•ba•tion

mas•tur•ba•tion○al
ma•te•ri○a med○i○ca
ma•ter•ni○ty
ma•ti○co, *n.*, *pl.* -cos.
mat•ri•car○i○a
ma•trix, *n.*, *pl.* -tri•ces, -trix○es.
mat•ter
mat○u•rate, *v.*, -rat○ed, -rat•ing.
mat○u•ra•tion○al cri•sis
ma•ture, *v.*, -tured, -tur•ing.
ma•tur○i○ty
max•il○la, *n.*, *pl.* -lae, -las.
max•il•lar○y, *adj.*, *n.*, *pl.* -lar•ies.
max○i•mum, *n.*, *pl.* -ma, -mums.
Max•zide *Trademark.*
May ap○ple
mea•sles
meas○ly, *adj.*, -li○er, -li•est.
me○a•tal
me○a•tot○o○my, *n.*, *pl.* -mies.
me○a•tus, *n.*, *pl.* -tus○es, -tus.
mech•an•ism
mech○a•no•chem•is•try
mech○a•no•re•cep•tor
mech○a•no•ther○a○py, *n.*, *pl.* -pies.
me•co•ni○um
med
me○di○a, *n.*, *pl.* -ae.
me•di○an le•thal dose
me•di•as•ti○nal
me•di•as•ti•ni•tis
me•di•as•ti•no•per○i•car•di•tis
me•di•as•ti•nos•co○py, *n.*, *pl.* -pies.

me•di•as•ti•not•o•o•my, n., pl. -mies.

me•di•as•ti•num, n., pl. -na.

me•di•ate, v., -at∘ed, -at•ing.

med∘ic

med∘i•ca∘go sat∘i∘va

med∘i•cal

medical ex•am•in∘er

med∘i•cal∘ly

me•dic∘a•ment

med∘i•ca•men•tal

Med∘i•care

med∘i•cate, v., -cat∘ed, -cat•ing.

med∘i•ca•tion

me•dic∘i•nal

me•dic∘i•nal∘ly

med∘i•cine

med∘i•co, n., pl. -cos.

med∘i•co•le∘gal

med∘i•co•psy•chol∘o∘gy

med∘i•gap

me•di∘o•ne•cro•sis

Med•iter•ra•ne∘an fe∘ver

me•di∘um, n., pl. -di•ums, -di∘a.

me•di∘us, n., pl. me∘di∘i.

me•drox∘y•pro•ges•ter•one

me•dul∘la, n., pl. -las, -lae.

medulla ob•lon•ga∘ta, n., pl. -dul∘lae -ga•tas, -dul∘lae -ga•tae.

med•ul•lar∘y

medullary sheath

med•ul•lat∘ed

me•dul•lo•blas•to∘ma, n., pl. -mas, -ma∘ta.

Mees' lines

meg∘a•ceph∘a∘ly

meg∘a•dose

meg∘a•e∘soph∘a•gus, n., pl. -gi.

meg∘a•ga•mete

meg∘a•lo•blast

meg∘a•lo•blas•tic

meg∘a•lo•car•di∘a

meg∘a•lo•ceph∘a∘ly

meg∘a•lo•ma•ni∘a

meg∘a•lo•ma•ni∘ac

meg∘a•lo•ma•ni∘a•cal

meg•a•lo•man∘ic

meg∘a•spor∘o•gen•e∘sis, n., pl. -eses.

meg∘a•vi•ta•min

mei∘o•sis, n., pl. -ses.

mei•ot∘ic

mel

mel•an•cho•li∘a

mel•an•cho•li∘ac

mel•an•chol∘ic

mel•an•chol∘y, n., pl. -chol•ies.

me•lan∘ic

mel•a•nin

mel∘a•nize, v., -nized, -niz•ing.

mel∘a•no•blas•to∘ma, n., pl. -mas, -ma∘ta.

mel∘a•no•car•ci•no∘ma, n., pl. -mas, -ma∘ta.

me•lan∘o•cyte

melanocyte-stim∘u•lat•ing hor•mone

mel∘a•no•gen•e∘sis, n., pl. -ses.

mel∘a•noid

mel∘a•no∘ma, n., pl. -mas, -ma∘ta.

mel∘a•no•ma•to•sis

mel∘a•no•sis, n., pl. -ses.

mel∘a•not∘ic

mel∘a•to•nin

mel∘i•lo•tus of•fic∘i•nal∘is

mel∘i•oi•do•sis

mel○o•plas○ty, *n., pl.* -ties.
mem•bra○na, *n., pl.* -nae.
mem•brum, *n., pl.* -bra.
mem○o○ry, *n., pl.* -ries.
memory trace
men○a•di•one
men•ar•che
men•ar•che○al
men•ar•chi○al
Men•de•li○an
Men•del•ism
men•del•ize, *v.,* -ized, -iz•ing.
Men•del's law
Mé•nière's dis•ease
me•nin•ge○al
me•nin•ges, *n.pl., sing.* me•ninx.
me•nin•gi○o○ma, *n., pl.* -mas, -ma○ta.
me•nin•gism
me•nin•gis•mus
men•in•git○ic
me•nin•gi•tis
me•nin•go•coc•cal
me•nin•go•coc•cic
me•nin•go•coc•cus, *n., pl.* -coc○ci.
me•nin•go•en•ceph○a•li•tis
me•nin•go•en•ceph○a•lo•my○e•li•tis
me•nin•go•my○e○li•tis
me•nin•gop○a•thy, *n., pl.* -thies.
me•ninx, *n., pl.* me•nin•ges.
me•nis•cec•to○my, *n., pl.* -mies.
me•nis•coc○y•to•sis
me•nis•coid
me•nis•cus, *n., pl.* -nis○ci, -nis•cus○es.
men○o○pau•sal
men○o○pause

men•or•rha•gi○a
men•or•rhag○ic
men•or•rhe○a
men•or•rhe○al
men•or•rhe○ic
men•or•rhoe○a
me•no•tax○is
men•ses
men•stru○al
men•stru•ate, *v.,* -at○ed, -at•ing.
men•stru○a•tion
men•stru○um, *n., pl.* -stru•ums, -stru○a.
men•tal
mental age
mental health
mental ill•ness
mental re•tar•da•tion
men•ta•lis
men•tal○i○ty, *n., pl.* -ties.
men•tal○ly
men•ta•tion
men•tum, *n., pl.* men○ta.
me•per○i•dine
me•pro•ba•mate
mer•bro•min
mer•cu•ri○al
mer•cur•i○us cor•ro•si○vus
mercurius sol○u•bil○is
mercurius vi○vus
Mer•cu•ro•chrome
mer•cu•rous chlo•ride
mer•cu○ry, *n., pl.* -ries.
mer○cy kill•ing
mer○o•blas•tic
mer○o•blas•ti○cal○ly
mer○o•gen•e○sis, *n., pl.* -e○ses.
mer○o•gon○ic
me•rog○o•nous
me•rog○o○ny

me•rot○o○my, *n., pl.* -mies.

Mer•thi○o•late

me•sat○i•pel•lic

mes•cal

mescal but•ton

mes•ca•line

mes•en•ce•phal○ic

mes•en•ceph○a•lon, *n., pl.*
-ceph○a•lons, -ceph○a○la.

mes•en•chy•mal

mes•en•chym•a•tous

mes•en•chyme

mes•en•ter○ic

mes•en•ter○on, *n., pl.* -ter○a.

mes•en•ter•on○ic

mes•en•ter○y, *n., pl.* -ter•ies.

mes•mer•ize, *v.,* -ized, -iz•ing.

mes○o•ap•pen•dix, *n., pl.*
-dix○es, -di○ces.

mes○o•blast

mes○o•blas•te○ma, *n., pl.*
-mas, -ma○ta.

mes○o•blas•tic

mes○o•ce•cum, *n., pl.* -ce○ca.

mes○o•ceph○a○ly

mes○o•derm

mes○o•der•mal

mes○o•der•mic

mes○o•don○ty

mes○o•du○o○de•num, *n., pl.*
-de○na, -de•nums.

mes○o•e•soph○a○gus, *n., pl.*
-soph•a○gi.

mes○o•gas•tri○um, *n., pl.*
-tri○a.

mes•og•na•thy

mes○o•mere

mes○o•met•ri○um, *n., pl.*
-ri○a.

mes○o•mor•phic

mes○o•mor•phism

mes○o•mor•phy

mes○o•neph•ric

mes○o•neph•ron

mes○o•neph•ros, *n., pl.* -roi.

mes○o•phry○on, *n., pl.*
-phry○a.

mes○o•pros○o○py, *n., pl.*
-pies.

mes•or•chi○um, *n., pl.* -chi○a.

mes○o•sal•pinx, *n., pl.* -pin•
ges.

mes○o•ster•num, *n., pl.*
-ster○na.

mes○o•the•li○al

mes○o•the•li○o○ma, *n., pl.*
-mas, -ma○ta.

mes○o•the•li○um, *n., pl.* -li○a.

mes○o•var○i○um, *n., pl.*
-var○i○a.

mes•sen•ger RNA

met○a-a○nal○y•sis

me•tab•a•sis, *n., pl.* -ses.

met○a•bi○o•sis

met○a•bol○ic

met○a•bol○i•cal○ly

me•tab○o•lism

me•tab○o•lite

me•tab○o•liz○a•ble

me•tab○o•lize, *v.,* -lized, -liz•
ing.

met○a•car•pal

met○a•car•pus, *n., pl.* -pi.

met○a•cen•tric

met○a•cen•tric○i○ty

met○a•chro•ma•si○a, *n., pl.*
-si○as.

met○a•chro•ma○sy, *n., pl.*
-sies.

met○a•chro•mat○ic

met○a•chro•ma•tism

met○a•chro•sis

met○a•gen•e○sis, *n., pl.*
-e○ses.

met○a•mor•phose, *v.*,
-phosed, -phos○ing.
met○a•mor•pho•sis, *n., pl.*
-ses.
met○a•neph•ric
met○a•neph•ron, *n., pl.*
-neph○ra.
met○a•neph•ros, *n., pl.* -roi.
met○a•phase
met○a•phy•sis, *n., pl.* -ses.
met○a•pla•sia
met○a•plasm
met○a•plas•mic
met○a•plas•tic
met○a•poph○y•sis, *n., pl.* -ses.
me•tas•ta•sis, *n., pl.* -ses.
me•tas•ta•size, *v.*, -sized,
-siz•ing.
met○a•stat○ic
met○a•stat○i•cal○ly
met○a•tar•sal
met○a•tar•sal○ly
met○a•tar•sus, *n., pl.* -tar○si.
met○a•tro•phic
met•en•ce•phal○ic
met•en•ceph○a•lon, *n., pl.*
-ceph○a•lons, -ceph○a○la.
met•es•trus
meth○a•donemeth○a•don
meth•am•phet○a•mine
meth•an○o•gen
meth•an○o•gen○ic
meth•a○qua•lone
Meth•e○drine
met•he•mo•glo•bin
me•thi○o•nine
meth○o•trex○ate
meth○y•late, *v.*, -lat○ed, -lat•
ing.
meth•yl•do○pa
meth•yl•ene blue

methylene di•ox○y•am•
phet○a•mine
meth•yl•phen○i•date
meth•yl•tes•tos•ter•one
me•to•pro•lol
met○ra, *n., pl.* -rae.
me•tri•tis
met•ro•cys•to•sis
me•tro•cy•to•sis
met•ro•nid○a•zole
me•tro•pa•ral○y•sis
me•trop•a○thy, *n., pl.* -thies.
me•trop•to•sis
me•tror•rha•gi○a
me•tror•rhag○ic
me•tror•rhex○is, *n., pl.*
-rhex○es.
me•tro•sal•pin•gog•ra•phy,
n., pl. -phies.
me•tro•ste•no•sis
mex•il•e○tine
mho, *n., pl.* mhos.
mi•as○ma, *n., pl.* -mas,
-ma○ta.
mi•cel○la, *n., pl.* -lae.
mi•celle, *n., pl.* -celles.
mi•cren•ceph○a•lon, *n., pl.*
-ceph○a•la.
mi•cren•ceph○a○ly
mi○cro•a○nal○y•sis, *n., pl.*
-ses.
mi○cro•a○nat•o○my, *n., pl.*
-mies.
mi○cro•bac•te•ri○um, *n., pl.*
-ri○a.
mi•crobe
mi•cro•bi○al
mi•cro•bic
mi•cro•bi•cid○al
mi•cro•bi•cide
mi○cro•bi○o○log○ic
mi○cro•bi○o○log○i•cal

mi•cro•bi•ol•o•gist

mi•cro•bi•ol•o•gy

mi•cro•bi•on, *n.*, *pl.* -bi•a.

mi•cro•bi•o•sis

mi•cro•bo•dy, *n.*, *pl.* -dies.

mi•cro•cap•sule

mi•cro•cen•trum, *n.*, *pl.* -trums, -tra.

mi•cro•ce•phal•ic

mi•cro•ceph•a•lus, *n.*, *pl.* -a•li.

mi•cro•ceph•a•ly

mi•cro•chem•is•try

mi•cro•cin•e•ma•tog•ra•phy, *n.*, *pl.* -phies.

mi•cro•coc•cal

mi•cro•coc•cic

mi•cro•coc•cus, *n.*, *pl.* -coc•ci.

mi•cro•co•nid•i•um, *n.*, *pl.* -nid•i•a.

mi•cro•crys•tal•lin•i•ty, *n.*, *pl.* -ties.

mi•cro•cy•to•sis

mi•cro•dac•tyl•i•a

mic•ro•dac•ty•ly

mic•ro•drep•a•no•cy•to•sis

mi•cro•en•cap•su•late, *v.*, -lat•ed, -lat•ing.

mi•cro•en•ceph•a•ly

mi•cro•fi•lar•i•a, *n.*, *pl.* -lar•i•ae.

mi•cro•gam•ete

mi•cro•gram

mi•cro•graph•ic sur•gery

mi•crog•ra•phy, *n.*, *pl.* -phies.

mi•cro•in•ject

mi•cro•in•jec•tion

mi•cro•li•thi•a•sis

mi•crol•o•gy

mi•crom•e•o•lus, *n.*, *pl.* -e•o•li.

mi•cro•mere

mi•cro•me•tas•ta•sis

mi•cro•me•ter

mi•cro•mor•phol•o•gy

mi•cron, *n.*, *pl.* mi•crons, mi•cra.

Mi•cro•nase *Trademark.*

mi•cro•nu•cle•us, *n.*, *pl.* -cle•i, -cle•us•es.

mi•cro•nu•tri•ent

mi•cro•nych•i•a

mi•cro•or•gan•ic

mi•cro•or•gan•ism

mi•cro•or•gan•is•mal

mi•cro•pe•nis, *n.*, *pl.* -nes, -nis•es.

mi•cro•phage

mic•ro•phal•lus, *n.*, *pl.* -phal•li, -plal•lus•es.

mi•cro•pho•tog•ra•phy

mi•croph•thal•mos

mi•croph•thal•mus, *n.*, *pl.* -thal•mi.

mi•cro•pi•pet

mi•cro•pi•pette

mi•cro•probe

mi•crop•si•a

mi•crop•sy

mi•cro•pump

mi•cro•py•lar

mi•cro•pyle

mi•cro•ra•di•og•ra•phy, *n.*, *pl.* -phies.

mi•cros•co•py, *n.*, *pl.* -pies.

mi•cro•so•mal

mi•cro•some

mi•cro•spec•tro•pho•tom•e•try

mi•cro•spo•ro•sis

mi•cro•sto•mi•a

mi•cro•sto•mus, *n.*, *pl.* -sto•mi.

mi•cro•sur•geon

mi•cro•sur•ger•y, *n.*, *pl.* -ies.

mi○cro•sur•gi•cal

mi○cro•tome

mi○cro•tom○ic

mi•crot○o•mist

mi•crot○o•my, *n., pl.* -mies.

mi○cro•vil•lus, *n., pl.* -vil○li.

mi○cro•zo○o○on, *n., pl.* -zo○a.

mi•crur○gy

mic•tu•rate, *v.,* -rat○ed, -rat•ing.

mic•tu•ri•tion

mid•brain

mid•dle ear

mid•gut

mid•life cri•sis

mid•wife, *n., pl.* -wives.

mid•wif•er○y

mif•e○pris•tone

mi•graine

mi•grain•ous

mi•grate, *v.,* -grat○ed, -grat•ing.

mil•i•ar○i○a

mil•i•ar•ia ru○bra

mil•i•ar○y

mi•lieu, *n., pl.* -lieus, -lieux.

mil○i○um, *n., pl.* mil○i○a.

milk

milk fe○ver

milk leg

milk of mag•ne•sia

milk sick•ness

mil•li•gram

mil•li•mo•lar○i○ty, *n., pl.* -ties.

mi•me•sis, *pl.* -ses.

mim•ic, *v.,* mim•icked, mim•ick•ing.

mim•ic○ry, *n., pl.* -ries.

Min○a•ma○ta dis•ease

mind-al•tering

min•er○al

mineral oil

min•er•al○o○cor•ti•coid

min○i•mal brain dys•func•tion

min○i•pill

min•is•ter, *v.,* -tered, -ter•ing.

mi○nor tran•quil•iz○er

min•ox○i•dil

mi•o•sis, *n., pl.* -ses.

mi•ot○ic

mi•ra•cid○i○um, *n., pl.* -cid○i○a.

mir○a•cle drug

mis•an•dry

mis•an•thro○py

mis•car•riage

mis•car○ry, *v.,* -ried, -ry•ing.

mis•ci•bil○i○ty, *n., pl.* -ties.

mis•di•ag•nose, *v.,* -nosed, -nos•ing.

mis•di•ag•no○sis, *n., pl.* -ses.

mi•sog•a○my

mi•sog•y○ny

mi•sol○o○gy

mis○o•pros•tol

mis•tle•toe

mith•ri•date

mit○i•gate, *v.,* -gat○ed, -gat•ing.

mi•to•chon•dri○al

mi•to•chon•dri○on, *n., pl.* -dri○a.

mi•to•gen

mi•to•gen•e○sis, *n., pl.* -e○ses.

mi•to•gen○ic

mi•to•ge•nic○i○ty, *n., pl.* -ties.

mi•to•sis, *n., pl.* -ses.

mi•tot○ic

mi•tot○i•cal○ly

mi•tral in•suf•fi•cien○cy

mitral valve
mitral valve pro•lapse
mo•bil•i•ty
mo•bi•lize v., -lized, -liz•ing.
mo•dal•i•ty, n., pl. -ties.
mo•di•o•lus, n., pl. -di•o•li.
Mohs' mi•cro•graph•ic sur•
  ger•y
moi•e•ty, n., pl. -ties.
mo•lal•i•ty, n., pl. -ties.
mo•lar
mo•lar•i•ty
mold•y, adj. mold•i•er,
  mold•i•est.
mole
mo•lec•u•lar bi•ol•o•gy
molecular clock
molecular ge•net•ics
mo•li•men, n., pl. -lim•i•na.
mol•lus•cum, n., pl. -lus•ca.
molluscum con•ta•gi•o•sum,
  n., pl. mol•lus•ca con•ta•
  gi•o•sa.
mo•men•tum, n., pl. -tums,
  -men•ta.
mon•ar•thri•tis
mo•nas, n., pl. -na•des.
mon•ath•e•o•to•sis
mon•gol•ism
Mon•gol•oid
mo•nil•e•thrix
mo•nil•i•a
mon•i•li•a•sis
mon•o•a•mine
monoamine ox•i•dase
monoamine oxidase in•hib•i•
  tor
mon•o•ceph•a•lus, n., pl.
  -ceph•a•li.
mon•o•chro•ma•sy
mon•o•chro•mat•ic
mon•o•chro•mat•i•cal•ly

mon•o•chro•ma•tic•i•ty
mon•o•chro•ma•tism
mon•o•clo•nal
monoclonal an•ti•bod•y
mon•o•clo•nal•i•ty
mon•o•con•tam•i•nate, v.,
  -nat•ed, -nat•ing.
mo•noc•u•lus, n., pl. -noc•
  u•li.
mon•o•cyte
mon•o•cyt•ic
mon•o•cy•toid
mon•o•cy•to•sis
mon•o•dac•tyl•ism
mon•o•dac•ty•ly, n., pl. -lies.
mo•nog•a•my
mon•o•gen•e•osis, n., pl. -ses.
mon•o•gen•ic
mon•o•gen•i•cal•ly
mon•om•pha•lus, n., pl.
  -pha•li.
mon•o•neu•ri•tis
mon•o•nu•cle•ar
mon•o•nu•cle•ate
mon•o•nu•cle•o•sis
mon•o•pa•re•sis
mon•o•pho•bi•a, n., pl.
  -bi•as.
mon•o•phy•le•tism
mon•o•phy•le•ty, n., pl. -ties.
mon•o•ple•gi•a
mon•o•ple•gic
mon•o•ploid
mon•or•chis, n., pl. -chi•des.
mon•o•sac•cha•ride
mon•o•sex•u•al
mon•o•so•di•um glu•ta•
  mate
mon•o•some
mon•o•so•mic
mon•o•un•sat•u•rate
mon•o•un•sat•u•rat•ed

mon•o•zy•got•ic
mon•o•zy•gous
mons, *n., pl.* mon•tes.
mons pu•bis, *n., pl.* mon•tes pu•bis.
mons ve•ne•ris, *n., pl.* montes ve•ne•ris.
mon•stros•i•ty, *n., pl.* -ties.
mor•bid•i•ty
mor•bus, *n., pl.* mor•bi.
mor•i•bund
mor•i•ci•zine
morn•ing-af•ter pill
morning sick•ness
mo•ron, *n., pl.* -rons.
mo•ron•ic
Mo•ro re•flex
mor•phal•lax•is, *n., pl.* -lax•es.
mor•phe•a
mor•phi•a
mor•phine
mor•phin•ic
mor•phi•nize, *v.,* -nized, -niz•ing.
mor•pho•gen•e•sis, *n., pl.* -e•ses.
mor•pho•ge•net•ic
mor•pho•gen•ic
mor•phog•ra•phy, *n., pl.* -phies.
mor•phol•o•gy, *n., pl.* -gies.
mor•pho•phys•i•ol•o•gy
mor•pho•sis, *n., pl.* -ses.
mor•phot•ic
mor•tal•i•ty, *n., pl.* -ties.
mor•ti•fi•ca•tion
mor•ti•fy, *v.,* -fied, -fy•ing.
mor•tu•ar•y, *n., pl.* -ar•ies.
mor•u•la, *n., pl.* -las, -lae.
mor•u•lar
mo•sa•ic

mo•sa•i•cism
mos•qui•to, *n., pl.* -tos, -toes.
mo•til•i•ty
mo•tion sick•ness
mo•ti•vate, *v.,* -vat•ed, -vat•ing.
mo•to•neu•ron
mo•tor
motor cor•tex
motor end plate
motor ho•mun•cu•lus
motor neu•ron
mo•to•ri•um, *n., pl.* -ri•a.
Mo•trin *Trademark.*
moun•tain sick•ness
mouse, *n., pl.* mice.
mouth hun•ger
mouth-to-mouth re•sus•ci•ta•tion
move, *v.,* moved, mov•ing.
move•ment
mu
mu•cif•er•ous
mu•ci•fi•ca•tion
mu•cig•e•nous
mu•ci•lage
mu•ci•lag•i•nous
mu•cin
mu•ci•no•sis, *n., pl.* -ses.
mu•ci•nous
mu•co•en•ter•o•i•tis
mu•coid
mu•co•lyt•ic
mu•co•per•i•os•te•um, *n., pl.* -te•a.
mu•co•pol•y•sac•cha•ride
mu•co•pro•tein
mu•co•pu•ru•lent
mu•cor•my•co•sis, *n., pl.* -ses.
mu•co•sa, *n., pl.* -sae, -sas.
mu•co•sal
mu•cos•i•ty

mu•cous
mucous mem•brane
mu•co•vis•ci•do•sis
mu○cro, n., pl. -cro•nes, -cros.
mu○cus
mu•lat○to, n., pl. -tos, -toes.
mu•li•e•bri•ty
mul•tan•gu•lum, n., pl.
 -gu○la.
mul○ti•cel•lu•lar○i○ty
mul○ti•cen•tric○i○ty
mul•ti•com•pul•sive
mul○ti•fi•dus, n., pl. -fi○di.
mul•ti•fo•cal
mul•ti•gat•ed acquisi•tion
 scan
mul○ti•grav•i○da
mul•tip•a○ra
mul○ti•par○i○ty
mul•tip○a•rous
mul•ti•ple al•leles
multiple al•lel•ism
multiple fac•tors
multiple my•e○lo○ma
multiple per•son•al○i○ty dis•
 or○der
multiple scle•ro○sis
mul•ti•vi•ta•min
mum•mi○fy, n., pl. -fied, -fy•
 ing.
mumps
Munch•hau•sen's syn•drome
mur•mur
mus•cle
muscle dys•mor•phi○a
muscle fi○ber
muscle spin•dle
mus•cu•lar
muscular dys•tro•phy
mus•cu•lar○i○ty
mus•cu•lo○skel•e○tal
mus•cu•lus, n., pl. -cu○li.

mu•si•co•ther○a○py, n., pl.
 -pies.
mus•tard plas•ter
mu•ta•gen
mu•ta•gen•e○sis, n., pl.
 -e○ses.
mu•ta•ge•net○ic
mu•ta•gen○ic
mu•ta•gen○i•cal○ly
mu•ta•ge•nic○i○ty, n., pl.
 -ties.
mu•tant
mu•tate, v., -tat○ed, -tat•ing.
mu•ta•tion
mu•ta•tion○al
mu•ti•late, v., -lat○ed, -lat•
 ing.
mut•ism
muz•zle, v., -zled, -zling.
my•al•gi○a
my•al•gic
my•as•the•ni○a
myasthenia gra•vis
my•as•then○ic
my•ce•li○um, n., pl. -li○a.
my•ce•tis•mus, n., pl. -tis○mi.
my•ce•to○ma, n., pl. -mas,
 -ma○ta.
my•ce•to•ma•tous
my•co•bac•te•ri○o•sis, n., pl.
 -ses.
my•co•bac•te•ri○um, n., pl.
 -ri○a.
my•col○o○gy
my•co•plas○ma, n., pl. -mas,
 -ma○ta.
my•co•sis, n., pl. -ses.
my•cot○ic
my•co•tox•ic○i○ty, n., pl.
 -ties.
my•co•tox○i•co•sis
my•co•tox○in

my•co•vi•rus, *n.*, *pl.* -rus○es.
my•dri•a•sis
myd•ri•at○ic
my•ec•to•my, *n.*, *pl.* -mies.
my•e○lat•ro•phy
my•el•en•ce•phal○ic
my•e○len•ceph○a•lon, *n.*, *pl.*
  -ceph•a○la.
my•e○lin
myelin sheath
my•e○li•nat○ed
my•e○li•na•tion
my•e○lin○ic
my•e○lin•oi•za•tion
my•e○lin•oc•la•sis
my•e○lin•o○gen•e○sis, *n.*, *pl.*
  -e○ses.
my•e○li•nol○y•sis
my•e○li•no•sis
my•e○li•tis
my•e○lo•blas•to○ma, *n.*, *pl.*
  -mas, -ma○ta.
my•e○lo•blas•to•sis, *n.*, *pl.*
  -ses.
my•e○lo•cyte
my•e○lo•cyt○ic
my•e○lo•cy•to○ma, *n.*, *pl.*
  -mas, -ma○ta.
my•e○lo•cy•to•sis
my•e○lo•dys•pla•si○a
my•e○lo•dys•plas•tic
my•e○lo•en•ceph○a•li•tis
my•e○lo•fi•bro•sis
my•e○lo•gen•e○sis, *n.*, *pl.*
  -e○ses.
my•e○lo•gen○ic
my•e○log○e•nous
my•e○lo•gram, *n.*, *pl.* -grams.
my•e○log•ra•phy, *n.*, *pl.*
  -phies.
my•e○lo•li•po○ma, *n.*, *pl.*
  -mas, -ma○ta.

my○e○lo○ma, *n.*, *pl.* -mas,
  -ma○ta.
my○e○lo•ma•to•sis
my○e○lo•men•in•gi•tis
my○e○lo•neu•ri•tis
my○e○lo•pa•ral○y•sis
my○e○lo•path○ic
my•e○lop○a•thy, *n.*, *pl.* -thies.
my•e○loph•thi•sis
my○e○lo•plax, *n.*, *pl.* -plax○es,
  -pla○ces.
my○e○lo•poi•e○sis
my○e○lo•pro•lif•er○a•tive
my○e○lo•ra•dic○u•lop○a•thy,
  n., *pl.* -thies.
my○e○lo•sar•co○ma, *n.*, *pl.*
  -mas, -ma○ta.
my○e○los•chi•sis, *n.*, *pl.* -ses,
  -sises.
my○e○lo•sis, *pl.* -ses.
my○e○lo•spon•gi○um, *n.*, *pl.*
  -gi○a.
my○e○lo•sup•pres•sion
my○i•a•sis
my•lo•hy•oi•de○us, *n.*, *pl.*
  -de○i.
my○o•car•di○al
my○o•car•di○o•graph
my○o•car•di•op○a•thy, *n.*, *pl.*
  -thies.
my○o•car•di•tis
my○o•car•di○um, *n.*, *pl.* -di○a.
my○o•car•do•sis, *n.*, *pl.* -ses.
my○o•clon○ic
my•oc•lo•nus
my○o•com○a, *n.*, *pl.* -ma○ta,
  -mas.
my○o•dys•to•ni○a
my○o•dys•to○ny, *n.*, *pl.* -nies.
my○o•dys•tro•phy, *pl.* -phies.
my○o•e○de○ma, *n.*, *pl.* -mas,
  -ma○ta.

my○o•e○lec•tric
my○o•ep○i•the•li○o○ma, *n.*
  pl. -mas, -ma○ta.
my○o•fi•bro○ma, *n., pl.* -mas,
  -ma○ta.
my○o•fi•bro○sis
my○o•gen○ic
my○o•ge•nic○i○ty, *n., pl.* -ties.
my•o•glo•bin
my○o•graph
my•o•graph○ic
my•og○ra•phy, *n., pl.* -phies.
my○o•he•mo•glo•bin
my○o•lem○o○ma, *n., pl.* -mas,
  -ma○ta.
my○o•log○ic
my○o•log○i•cal
my•ol•o•gist
my○ol○o○gy
my○o○ma, *n., pl.* -mas, -ma○ta.
my•om○a•tous
my○o•mec•to○my, *n., pl.* -mies.
my○o•pa•ral○y•sis
my○o•pa•re•sis
my○o•path○ic
my•op○a•thy, *n., pl.* -thies.
my○o•per○i•car•di•tis
my○o•pi○a
my•op○ic
my○o•plas○ty, *n., pl.* -ties.
my○o•psy•cho•sis, *n., pl.* -ses.
my•or•rha•phy, *n., pl.* -phies.
my○o•sar•co○ma, *n., pl.* -mas,
  -ma○ta.
my○o•scle•ro•sis
my○o•sep•tum, *pl.* -sep○ta.
my○o•sin
my○o•sis, *n., pl.* -ses.
my○o•sit○ic
my○o•si•tis
my○o•te•not○o○my, *n., pl.*
  -mies.

my•ot○ic
my•ot○o○my, *n., pl.* -mies.
my○o•to•ni○a
my○o•ton○ic
my•ot•ro•phy
myr•in•gec•to○my, *n., pl.*
  -mies.
myr•in•gi○tis
my•rin•go•dec•to○my, *n., pl.*
  -mies.
my•rin•go•my•co•sis, *n., pl.*
  -ses.
my•rin•go•plas○ty, *n., pl.*
  -ties.
myr•in•got○o○my, *n., pl.*
  -mies.
myth○o•ma•ni○a
myth○o•ma•ni○ac
myx•ad•e○no○ma, *pl.* -mas,
  -ma○ta.
myx•e○de○ma, *n., pl.* -mas,
  -ma○ta.
myx•e○dem○a•tous
myx○o•chon•dro•fi•bro•sar•
  co○ma, *n., pl.* -mas, -ma○ta.
myx○o•chon•dro○ma, *n., pl.*
  -mas, -ma○ta.
myx○o•fi•bro○ma, *n., pl.*
  -mas, -ma○ta.
myx○o•fi•bro•sar•co○ma, *n.,*
  pl. -mas, -ma○ta.
myx○o•li•po○ma, *n., pl.* -mas,
  -ma○ta.
myx○o○ma, *n., pl.* -mas,
  -ma○ta.
myx○o•ma•to•sis
myx•om○a•tous
myx○o•neu•ro○ma, *n., pl.*
  -mas, -ma○ta.
myx○o•sar•co○ma, *pl.* -mas,
  -ma○ta.
myx○o•vi•rus, *n., pl.* -rus○es.

nae•vus, *n.*, *pl.* nae•vi.
nail
na•ive or na•ïve
na•ive•ly
na•ive•ness
nal•ox•one
nal•trex•one
nan•o•me•ter
nape
Nap•ro•syn *Trademark.*
na•prox•en
nar•cis•sism
nar•cis•sis•tic
narcissistic per•so•nal•i•ty
dis•or•der
nar•co•a•nal•y•sis
nar•co•di•ag•no•sis, *n.*, *pl.*
-ses.
nar•co•hyp•no•sis, *n.*, *pl.*
-ses.
nar•co•lep•sy
nar•co•lep•tic
nar•co•ma, *n.*, *pl.* -mas,
ma•ta.
nar•com•a•tous
nar•co•sis
nar•co•syn•the•sis, *n.*, *pl.*
-ses.
nar•co•ther•a•py, *n.*, *pl.*
-pies.
nar•cot•ic
nar•cot•i•cal•ly
nar•co•tize, *v.*, -tized, -tiz•ing.
nar•es, *n.pl.*, *sing.* nar•is.
nar•is, *n.*, *pl.* nar•es.
nar•row-an•gle glau•co•ma
na•sal
na•so•gas•tric tube
na•so•lac•ri•mal duct

na•so•pha•ryn•ge•al
na•so•phar•yn•gi•tis
na•so•phar•ynx, *n.*, *pl.* -pha•
ryn•ges, -phar•ynx•es.
na•sus, *n.*, *pl.* na•si.
na•tal•i•ty
na•tiv•ism
na•tiv•ist
na•tiv•is•tic
na•tri•u•re•sis
na•tri•u•ret•ic
nat•rum car•bon•i•cum
natrum mur•i•t•i•cum
natrum sul•phur•i•cum
nat•u•ral
natural child•birth
natural kill•er cell
na•tur•o•path
na•tur•o•path•ic
na•tur•op•a•thy
nau•se•a
nau•se•ant
nau•se•ate, *v.*, -at•ed, -at•
ing.
nau•se•at•ing
nau•se•at•ing•ly
nau•se•ous
nau•se•ous•ly
nau•se•ous•ness
na•vel
na•vic•u•lar
near-point
near•sight•ed
near•sight•ed•ness
ne•ar•thro•sis, *n.*, *pl.* -ses.
neb•u•la, *n.*, *pl.* -las, -lae.
neb•u•lize, *v.*, -lized, -liz•ing.
neck
nec•ro•bac•il•lo•sis

nec•ro•bi•o•sis
nec•ro•bi•ot•ic
ne•crol•o•gy, *n., pl.* -gies.
nec•ro•pha•gi•a
nec•ro•pha•gy
nec•ro•phile
nec•ro•phil•i•a
nec•ro•phil•i•ac
nec•ro•phil•ic
ne•croph•i•lism
nec•ro•pho•bi•a
nec•ro•pho•bic
nec•rop•sy, *n., pl.* -sies.
ne•crose, *v.,* -crosed, -cros•
  ing.
ne•cro•sis
ne•crot•ic
nec•ro•tize, *v.,* -tized,
  -tiz•ing.
ne•crot•o•my, *n., pl.* -mies.
nee•dle
needle bi•op•sy
ne•en•ceph•a•lon, *n., pl.*
  -ceph•a•la.
neg•a•tive
negative trans•fer
neg•a•tiv•ism
neg•a•tiv•ist
neg•a•tiv•is•tic
nem•a•tode
nem•a•to•di•a•sis
nem•a•tol•o•gy
Nem•bu•tal *Trademark.*
ne•o-Freu•di•an
neo-Sy•neph•rine
ne•o•cer•e•bel•lum, *n., pl.*
  -bel•lums, -bel•la.
ne•o•cor•tex, *n., pl.* -ti•ces,
  -tex•es.
ne•o•cor•ti•cal
ne•o•gen•e•sis, *n., pl.*
  -ses.

ne•o•log•ic
ne•o•log•i•cal
ne•o•log•i•cal•ly
ne•ol•o•gism
ne•ol•o•gis•tic
ne•ol•o•gize, *v.,* -gized, -giz•
  ing.
ne•ol•o•gy, *n., pl.* -gies.
ne•o•na•tal
ne•o•nate
ne•o•na•tol•o•gist
ne•o•na•tol•o•gy
ne•o•pal•li•um, *n., pl.* -li•a.
ne•o•pla•sia
ne•o•plasm
ne•o•plas•tic
ne•o•stig•mine
ne•o•stri•a•tum, *n., pl.*
  -stri•a•tums, -stri•a•ta.
ne•ot•e•ny
ne•o•thal•a•mus, *n., pl.*
  -thal•a•mi.
ne•o•vas•cu•lar•i•za•tion
neph•e•lom•e•try
ne•phrec•to•mize, *v.,* -mized,
  -miz•ing.
ne•phrec•to•my, *n., pl.*
  -mies.
ne•phrid•i•um, *n., pl.*
  -phrid•i•a.
ne•phrit•ic
ne•phri•tis
neph•ro•cal•ci•no•sis
neph•ro•li•thi•a•sis
neph•ro•li•thot•o•my, *n., pl.*
  -mies.
ne•phrol•o•gist
ne•phrol•o•gy
ne•phro•ma, *n., pl.* -mas,
  -ma•ta.
neph•ron
neph•ro•path•ic

ne•phrop•a•thy, *n., pl.*
-thies.
neph•ro•pex•y, *n., pl.* -pex•
ies.
neph•rop•to•sis
ne•phror•rha•phy, *n., pl.*
-phies.
neph•ro•scle•ro•sis, *n., pl.*
-ses.
ne•phro•sis, *n., pl.* -ses.
ne•phros•to•ma, *n., pl.*
-ma•ta.
neph•ro•stome, *n., pl.*
-stomes.
ne•phrot•ic
ne•phrot•o•my, *n., pl.*
-mies.
neph•ro•tox•ic•i•ty
nerve
nerve block
nerve cell
nerve cord
nerve fi•ber
nerve growth fac•tor
nerve im•pulse
nerve root clip•ping
ner•vos•i•ty, *n., pl.* -ties.
nerv•ous break•down
nervous sys•tem
ner•vus, *n., pl.* ner•vi.
ness•ler•ize, *v.,* -ized, -iz•ing.
net•tle rash
neu•ral
neural crest
neural tube
neural tube de•fect
neu•ral•gia
neu•ral•gic
neu•ral•ly
neu•ra•poph•y•sis, *n., pl.*
-ses.
neur•a•prax•i•a

neur•as•the•ni•a
neur•as•then•ic
neur•as•then•i•cal•ly
neu•rax•is, *n., pl.* -rax•es.
neu•rec•to•my, *n., pl.*
-mies.
neu•ri•lem•ma, *n., pl.* -mas.
neu•ri•lem•mal
neu•ri•lem•mo•ma, *n., pl.*
-mas, -ma•ta.
neu•ri•le•mo•ma, *n., pl.* -mas,
-ma•ta.
neu•ril•i•ty
neu•ri•no•ma, *n., pl.* -mas,
-ma•ta.
neu•rit•ic
neu•ri•tis
neu•ro•an•a•tom•ic
neu•ro•an•a•tom•i•cal
neu•ro•a•nat•o•mist
neu•ro•a•nat•o•my, *n., pl.*
-mies.
neu•ro•bi•ol•o•gy
neu•ro•bi•o•tax•is, *n., pl.*
-tax•es.
neu•ro•blas•to•ma, *n., pl.*
-mas, -ma•ta.
neu•ro•cen•trum, *n., pl.*
-trums, -tra.
neu•ro•chem•i•cal
neu•ro•chem•ist
neu•ro•chem•is•try
neu•ro•cra•ni•um, *n., pl.* -ni•
ums, -ni•a.
neu•ro•cy•to•ma, *n., pl.* -mas,
-ma•ta.
neu•ro•der•ma•ti•tis
neu•ro•en•do•crine
neu•ro•en•do•crin•o•
log•i•cal
neu•ro•en•do•cri•nol•o•gist
neu•ro•en•do•cri•nol•o•gy

neu·ro·ep·i·the·li·um, *n., pl.*
  -li·a.
neu·ro·fi·bril
neu·ro·fi·bril·la, *n., pl.* -lae.
neu·ro·fi·bril·lar
neu·ro·fi·bril·lar·y
neu·ro·fi·bro·ma, *n., pl.*
  -mas, -ma·ta.
neu·ro·fi·bro·ma·to·sis
neu·ro·gen·ic
neu·rog·e·nous
neu·rog·li·a
neu·rog·li·al
neu·ro·gli·o·ma, *n., pl.* -mas,
  -ma·ta.
neu·ro·gli·o·sis
neu·rog·ra·phy, *n., pl.* -phies.
neu·ro·hor·mo·nal
neu·ro·hor·mone
neu·ro·hy·poph·y·se·al
neu·ro·hy·poph·y·sis, *n., pl.*
  -ses.
neu·ro·im·mu·nol·o·gy
neu·ro·lep·tic
neu·ro·lin·guis·tics
neu·ro·log·i·cal
neu·ro·log·i·cal·ly
neu·rol·o·gist
neu·rol·o·gize, *v.,* -gized,
  -giz·ing.
neu·rol·o·gy
neu·ro·lym·pho·ma·to·sis
neu·rol·y·sis
neu·ro·ma, *n., pl.* -mas,
  -ma·ta.
neu·ro·ma·tous
neu·ro·mod·u·la·tor
neu·ro·mo·tor
neu·ro·mus·cu·lar
neu·ro·my·e·li·tis
neu·ron
neu·ron·al

neu·ron·o·pha·gi·a, *n., pl.*
  -gi·as.
neu·ro·noph·a·gy
neu·ro·path·ic
neu·ro·path·i·cal·ly
neu·ro·path·o·log·i·cal
neu·ro·pa·thol·o·gist
neu·ro·pa·thol·o·gy
neu·rop·a·thy, *n., pl.* -thies.
neu·ro·pep·tide
neu·ro·phar·ma·co·
  log·i·cal
neu·ro·phar·ma·col·o·gist
neu·ro·phar·ma·col·o·gy
neu·ro·phys·i·o·log·i·cal
neu·ro·phys·i·ol·o·gist
neu·ro·phys·i·ol·o·gy
neu·ro·po·di·um, *n., pl.*
  -di·a.
neu·ro·psy·chi·at·ric
neu·ro·psy·chi·a·trist
neu·ro·psy·chi·a·try
neu·ro·psy·chol·o·gy
neu·ro·ret·i·ni·tis
neu·ro·sci·ence
neu·ro·sci·en·tif·ic
neu·ro·sci·en·tist
neu·ro·sen·so·ry
neu·ro·sis, *n., pl.* -ses.
neu·ro·spon·gi·um, *n., pl.*
  -gi·a.
neu·ro·sur·geon
neu·ro·sur·ger·y, *n., pl.*
  -ger·ies.
neu·ro·sur·gi·cal
neu·rot·ic
neu·rot·i·cal·ly
neu·rot·i·cism
neu·rot·o·my, *n., pl.* -mies.
neu·ro·tox·ic
neu·ro·tox·ic·i·ty, *n., pl.*
  -ties.

neu∘ro•tox∘in
neu∘ro•trans•mis•sion
neu∘ro•trans•mit•ter
neu∘ro•trop∘ic
neu•ru∘la, *n., pl.* -las, -lae.
neu•ru∘lar
neu•ru∘la•tion
neu•tra•lize, *v.,* -lized, -liz•ing.
neu•tri∘no, *n., pl.* -nos.
neu•tro•pe•ni∘a
neu•tro•phil
neu•tro•phile
ne•void
ne∘vus, *n., pl.* ne∘vi.
nex∘us, *n., pl.* nex•us∘es, nex∘us.
ni∘a•cin
ni∘a•cin∘a•mide
nick
nic∘o∘tin∘a•mide
nicotinamide ad•e∘nine di•nu•cle∘o•tide
nic∘o∘tine
nic∘o∘tined
nic∘o∘tine•less
nic∘o∘tin∘ic
nicotinic ac∘id
nic∘o∘tin•ism
nic•tate, *v.,* -tat∘ed, -tat•ing.
nic•ti•tate, *v.,* -tat∘ed, -tat•ing.
ni∘dal
ni•da•tion
ni•dus, *n., pl.* ni∘di, -ni•dus∘es.
ni•fed∘i•pine
night blind•ness
night ter•ror
night•blind
night•shade
ni•sus, *n., pl.* ni•sus.

ni•tric ox∘ide
nit•ri∘cum ac∘i•dum
ni•tri∘fy, *v.,* -fied, -fy•ing.
ni•trite
ni•tro•gen
nitrogen bal•ance
nitrogen mus•tard
nitrogen nar•co∘sis
ni•trog•en•ase
ni•trog•en•ize, *v.,* -ized, -iz•ing.
ni•tro•glyc•er∘in
ni•tro•glyc•er•ine
ni•trous ox∘ide
no•car•di•o•sis, *n., pl.* -ses.
noc•tam•bu•lism
noc•tam•bu•list
noc•tu•ri∘a
noc•tur•nal e∘mis•sion
nod∘al in•volve•ment
node
no•dos∘i∘ty, *n., pl.* -ties.
nod∘u•lar
nod∘u•late, *v.,* -lat∘ed, -lat•ing.
nod•ule
nod∘u•lus, *n., pl.* nod•u∘li.
no∘dus, *n., pl.* no∘di.
no∘ma, *n., pl.* -mas.
non-A, non-B hep∘a•ti•tis
non•ad•dic•tive
non•com•pli•ance
non•com•pli•ant
non•com•ply•ing
non•gon∘o•coc•cal u∘re•thri•tis
non•heme i∘ron
non•in•va•sive
non•in•va•sive∘ly
non•pre•scrip•tion
non•self
non•sense

non•sen•si•cal
non•sen•si•cal○i•ty
non•sen•si•cal•ly
non•sen•si•cal•ness
non•ste•roi•dal
nonsteroidal an•ti•in•flam•ma•tor•y drug
non•vi○a•bil○i•ty
non•vi○a•ble
no•ol○o○gy
no○o•tro•pics
nor○a•dren○a•lin
nor○a•dren○a•line
nor•ep○i•neph•rine
nor•eth•in•drone
nor○ma, *n.*, *pl.* -mae.
nor•mal○cy
nor•mal○i•ty
nor•mal•ize, *v.*, -ized, -iz•ing.
nor•mer•gic
nor•mo•ten•sive
Nor•plant *Trademark.*
North•ern blot
Nor•wood pro•ce•dure
nose
nose job
nose•bleed
nos○o•co•mi○al
nos○o•gen•e○sis, *n.*, *pl.* -e○ses.
no•sog○ra•pher
nos○o•graph○ic
nos○o•graph○i•cal
nos○o•graph○i•cal○ly
no•sog•ra•phy
nos○o•log○i•cal
no•sol○o○gist
no•sol○o○gy
nos○o•phil○i○a
nos•trum
no•to•chord
no•to•chord○al

No•vo•caine *Trademark.*
nox○a, *n.*, *pl.* nox○ae.
nu•bil○i•ty
nu○cha, *n.*, *pl.* -chae.
nu•cle○ar mag○net○ic res○o○nance
nuclear med○i•cine
nu•cle•ase
nu•cle○ic ac○id
nu•cle○o•cap•sid
nu•cle•oid
nu•cle○o•lus, *n.*, *pl.* -cle○o○li.
nu•cle○o•pro•tein
nu•cle○o•side
nu•cle○o•some
nu•cle○o•tide
nu•cle○us, *n.*, *pl.* -cle○i, -cle○us○es.
nucleus dor•sa○lis, *n.*, *pl.* nuclei dor•sa○les.
nucleus pul•po○sus, *n.*, *pl.* nuclei pul•po○si.
nu•clide
nude mouse
nul•li•grav•i○da
nul•lip•a○ra
nul•li•par○i•ty
nul•lip○a•rous
nurse
nurse-prac•ti•tion○er
nurs•er○y, *n.*, *pl.* -er•ies.
nurse's aide
nu•tri•ent
nu•tri•ment
nu•tri•men•tal
nu•tri•tion
nu•tri•tion○al
nu•tri•tion•al○ly
nu•tri•tion•ar○y
nu•tri•tion•ist
nu•tri•tious
nu•tri•tious○ly

nu•tri•tious•ness
nu•tri•tive
nu•tri•tive•ly
nu•tri•tive•ness
nux vom•i•ca, *n., pl.* nux
  vom•i•ca.
nyc•ta•lo•pi•a
nyc•ta•lop•ic

nym•pha, *n., pl.* -phae.
nym•pho•lep•sy, *n., pl.* -sies.
nym•pho•ma•ni•a
nym•pho•ma•ni•ac
nym•pho•ma•ni•a•cal
nys•tag•mic
nys•tag•mus
nyx•is, *n., pl.* nyx•es.

O

ob•ce•ca•tion
ob•dor•mi•tion
ob•duc•tion
o•be•li•ac
o•be•li•al
o•be•li•on, *n., pl.* -li•a.
o•be•si•ty
o•bex
ob•fus•cate, *v.,* -cat•ed, -cat•
  ing.
ob•fus•ca•tion
ob•fus•ca•to•ry
ob-gyn or ob/gyn
ob•ject
ob•jec•tive
ob•jec•tive•ly
ob•li•gate
ob•lig•a•to•ri•ly
o•blig•a•to•ry
o•blique
o•bliq•ui•ty, *n., pl.* -ties.
o•blit•er•ate, *v.,* -at•ed, -at•
  ing.
o•blit•e•ra•tion
o•blit•e•ra•tive
ob•li•ves•cence
ob•lon•ga•ta, *n., pl.* -tas, -tae.
ob•lon•ga•tal
ob•mu•tes•cence
ob•nu•bi•la•tion

ob•ses•sion
ob•ses•sion•al
ob•ses•sions
ob•ses•sive
obsessive-com•pul•sive
obsessive-compulsive dis•or•
  der
ob•ses•sive•ly
ob•ses•sive•ness
ob•so•lete
ob•stet•ric
ob•stet•ri•cal
ob•stet•ri•cal•ly
ob•ste•tri•cian
ob•stet•rics
ob•sti•na•cy
ob•sti•pate, *v.,* -pat•ed, -pat•
  ing.
ob•sti•pa•tion
ob•struc•tion
ob•struc•tive
ob•struc•tive•ness
ob•stru•ent
ob•tund
ob•tund•ent
ob•tu•rate, *v.,* -rat•ed, -rat•
  ing.
ob•tu•ra•tion
ob•tu•ra•tor
ob•tu•sion
oc•cip•i•tal

occipital bone
occipital lobe
oc•cip∘i•ta•lis
oc•cip∘i•tal∘ly
oc∘cip∘i∘to•fron•tal
oc∘cip∘i∘to•fron•ta•lis
oc∘cip∘i∘to•mas•toid
oc∘cip∘i∘to•pa•ri•e∘tal
oc•ci•put, *n.*, *pl.* -ci•puts,
    -cip•i∘ta.
oc•clude, *v.*, -clud∘ed, -clud•
    ing.
Oc•clu•sal *Trademark.*
Occlusal-HP *Trademark.*
oc•clu•si∘o pu•pil•lae
oc•clu•sion
oc•clu•sive
oc•clu•som•e∘ter
Oc•cu•coat *Trademark.*
oc•cult
occult frac•ture
oc•cult∘ly
oc•cult•ness
oc•cu•pa•tion
oc•cu•pa•tion∘al
occupational ther∘a•pist
occupational ther∘a∘py
oc•cu•pa•tion•al∘ly
o∘cel•lar
o∘cel•lus, *n.*, *pl.* o∘cel∘li.
och•lo•pho•bi∘a
och•lo•pho•bist
och•ra•tox∘in
och•ro•no•sis, *n.*, *pl.* -ses.
och•ro•not∘ic
oc•tad
oc∘ta•dec∘a•di•e∘no∘ic
oc•ta•dec∘a•no•ic
oc•ta•dec∘e•no∘ic
oc∘ta•meth•yl py•ro•phos•
    phor∘a•mide
Oc•ta•mide PFS *Trademark.*

oc•ta•no∘ic
oc•ta•pep•tide
oc•ta•va•lent
oc•to•ge•nar•i∘an
oc•to•roon
oc•tose
Oc∘u•Clear
oc∘u•lar
oc∘u•list
oc∘u•lo•gy•ral
oc∘ul∘o∘gy•ric
oc∘u•lo•mo•tor
oculomotor nerve
oc∘u•lo•my•co•sis, *n.*, *pl.*
    -ses.
oc∘u•lus, *n.*, *pl.* oc•u∘li.
OD, *n.*, *pl.* ODs, OD's, *v.*, OD'd,
    ODed, OD'•ing.
o∘dax•es•mus
Od•di's sphinc•ter
o∘don•tal•gia
o∘don•tal•gic
o∘don•tec•to∘my, *n.*, *pl.*
    -mies.
o∘don•ti•a•sis
o∘don•ti•tis
o∘don•to•blast
o∘don•to•blas•tic
o∘don∘to•cele
o∘don∘to•clast
o∘don•to•gen∘ic
o∘don•to•graph
o∘don•tog•ra•phy, *n.*, *pl.*
    -phies.
o∘don•toid
o∘don∘to•log∘i•cal
o∘don•tol•o∘gist
o∘don•tol∘o∘gy
o∘don∘to•loxia
o∘don•to∘ma, *n.*, *pl.* -mas,
    -ma∘ta.
o∘don∘top•ri•sis

o•don•to•sis, *n., pl.* -ses.
o•don•tot•o•o•my, *n., pl.* -mies.
o•dor•ant
o•dor•if•er•ous
o•dor•if•er•ous•ly
o•dor•if•er•ous•ness
o•dor•im•e•ter
o•dor•im•e•try
o•dor•i•phore
oe•coid
oe•de•o•ma, *n., pl.* -ma•ta.
oed•i•pal
Oed•i•pe•an
Oed•i•pus
Oedipus com•plex
oe•nol•o•o•gy
oe•soph•o•a•ge•al
Oe•soph•o•a•go•sto•mum
oe•soph•o•a•gus, *n., pl.*
  -soph•a•o•gi.
oes•tra•di•ol
oes•tral
oes•trid
oes•trin
oes•trin•es•trin•o•i•za•tion
oes•tri•ol
oes•tro•gen
oes•tro•gen•ic
oes•trone
oes•trous
oes•tru•o•al
oes•trum
Oes•trus
off-la•o•bel
of•fal
of•fi•cial
of•fic•oi•nal
of•fic•oi•nal•ly
O•floxoa•cin
O•gen *Trademark.*
ohm•am•me•o•ter
ohm•meter

o•id•o•i•o•o•my•co•sis, *n., pl.*
  -ses.
o•id•o•i•um, *n., pl.* o•id•o•i•o•a.
oint•ment
old man's pem•phi•gus
o•le•ag•o•i•nous
o•le•an•der
o•le•an•do•my•cin
o•le•ate
o•lec•ra•nál
o•lec•ran•ar•thri•tis
o•lec•ra•non
o•le•fin
o•le•fine
o•le•fin•o•ic
o•le•oic
o•le•oin
o•le•o•o•mar•ga•rin
o•le•o•o•mar•ga•rine
o•le•om•e•o•ter
o•le•o•o•res•oin
o•le•o•o•sac•cha•rum, *n., pl.*
  -cha•ra.
o•le•o•o•tho•rax, *n., pl.*
  -rax•oes, -ra•ces.
o•le•o•o•vi•ta•min
O•les•tra
o•le•oum, *n., pl.* o•le•o•a.
oleum suc•ci•oni
o•le•oyl
ol•fac•tion
ol•fac•tol•o•o•gy
ol•fac•tom•e•o•ter
ol•o•fac•to•met•ric
ol•o•fac•to•met•ri•cal•o•ly
ol•fac•tom•e•o•try
ol•fac•to•o•ry, *adj., n., pl.* -ries.
olfactory bulb
olfactory fa•tigue
olfactory lobe
olfactory nerve
ol•fac•tron•ics

o∘lib∘a∘num
ol∘i∘ge∘mi∘a
ol∘i∘ge∘mic
ol∘i∘gid∘ic
ol∘i∘go∘chro∘me∘mi∘a
ol∘i∘go∘cy∘the∘mi∘a
ol∘i∘go∘cy∘them∘ic
ol∘i∘go∘dac∘tyl∘i∘a
ol∘i∘go∘dac∘ty∘ly
ol∘i∘go∘den∘dro∘cyte
ol∘i∘go∘den∘drog∘li∘a
ol∘i∘go∘den∘dro∘gli∘o∘oma,
  n., pl. -mas, -ma∘ta.
ol∘i∘go∘don∘tia
ol∘i∘go∘dy∘nam∘ic
ol∘i∘go∘gene
ol∘i∘go∘gen∘ic
ol∘i∘go∘hid∘ri∘a
ol∘i∘go∘hy∘dram∘ni∘os
ol∘i∘go∘lec∘i∘thal
ol∘i∘go∘men∘or∘rhe∘a ✓
ol∘i∘go∘mer
ol∘i∘go∘mer∘ic
ol∘i∘go∘mer∘i∘za∘tion
ol∘i∘go∘my∘cin
ol∘i∘go∘nu∘cle∘o∘tide
ol∘i∘go∘phre∘ni∘a
ol∘i∘go∘phren∘ic
ol∘i∘go∘py∘rene
ol∘i∘go∘sac∘cha∘ride
ol∘i∘go∘sper∘mat∘ic
ol∘i∘go∘sper∘mi∘a
ol∘i∘go∘trich∘i∘a
ol∘i∘go∘zo∘o∘sper∘mi∘a
ol∘i∘gu∘ri∘a
ol∘i∘va∘ory
ol∘ive
o∘lo∘li∘u∘qui
o∘ma∘si∘tis
o∘ma∘sum, *n., pl.* o∘ma∘sa.
o∘me∘ga-3 fat∘ty ac∘id
o∘men∘tal

o∘men∘tec∘to∘my, *n., pl.*
  -mies.
o∘men∘to∘pex∘y, *n., pl.* -pex∘
  ies.
o∘men∘tu∘lum, *n., pl.* -tu∘la.
o∘men∘tum, *n., pl.* o∘men∘ta,
  -o∘men∘tums.
omentum ma∘jus
omentum mi∘nus
O∘mep∘ra∘zole
om∘ma∘ti∘di∘um, *n., pl.* -di∘a.
om∘ni∘fo∘cal
Om∘ni∘paque *Trademark.*
Om∘ni∘pen *Trademark.*
Omnipen-N *Trademark.*
o∘mo∘dyn∘i∘a
o∘mo∘hy∘oid
om∘phal∘ic
om∘pha∘li∘tis
om∘pha∘lo∘mes∘en∘ter∘ic
om∘pha∘lo∘phle∘bi∘tis
om∘pha∘los, *n., pl.* -pha∘li.
o∘nan∘ism
o∘nan∘ist
o∘nan∘is∘tic
On∘cho∘cer∘ca
Onchocerca cae∘cu∘ti∘ens
Onchocerca vo∘lvu∘lus
on∘cho∘cer∘cal
on∘cho∘cer∘ci∘a∘sis
on∘cho∘cer∘co∘ma
on∘cho∘cer∘co∘sis, *n., pl.* -ses.
on∘cho∘sphere
on∘co∘cyte
on∘co∘cy∘to∘ma
on∘co∘gene
on∘co∘gen∘e∘osis, *n., pl.*
  -e∘oses.
on∘co∘ge∘net∘ic
on∘co∘gen∘ic
on∘co∘ge∘nic∘i∘ty
on∘cog∘e∘nous

on•co•graph
on•cog•ra•phy, *n., pl.* -phies.
on•co•log•ic
on•co•log•i•cal
on•col•o•gist
on•col•o•gy
on•col•y•sis
on•co•lyt•ic
on•co•me•la•ni•a
on•com•e•ter
on•cor•na•vi•rus, *n., pl.* -rus•es.
on•co•sphere
on•cot•o•my, *n., pl.* -mies.
on•co•vin
on•co•vi•rus
One-A-Day *Trademark.*
o•nei•ric
o•ni•o•ma•ni•a
o•ni•o•ma•ni•ac
o•ni•um
on•o•ma•tol•o•gy
on•o•mat•o•ma•ni•a
on•o•mat•o•poi•e•sis
on•to•gen•e•sis, *n., pl.* -e•ses.
on•to•ge•net•ic
on•to•ge•net•i•cal•ly
on•to•gen•ic
on•to•gen•i•cal•ly
on•tog•e•onist
on•tog•e•ony
on•tog•e•onyon•to•gen•e•sis
on•y•chaux•is, *n., pl.* -chaux•es.
on•y•chec•to•my, *n., pl.* -mies.
o•nych•oi•a
onychia cr•aquele
onychia la•ta
onychia ma•lig•ona
onychia punc•ta•ta

onychia sim•plex
on•y•chi•tis
on•y•cho•gry•po•sis
on•y•choid
on•y•chol•y•sis
on•y•cho•ma•de•sis
on•y•cho•ma•la•cia
on•y•cho•my•co•sis, *n., pl.* -ses.
on•y•cho•pha•gia
on•y•choph•a•gy
on•y•chor•rhex•is, *n., pl.* -rhex•es.
on•y•cho•schizo•i•a
on•y•cho•sis, *n., pl.* -ses.
on•yx
o•onyx•is
o•o•blast
o•o•cy•e•osis, *n., pl.* -ses.
o•o•cyst
o•o•cyte
o•o•gen•e•osis, *n., pl.* -e•oses.
o•o•ge•net•ic
o•o•go•ni•a
o•o•go•ni•um
o•o•kin•e•osis
o•o•ki•nete
o•o•ki•net•ic
o•o•lem•oma
o•o•pho•rec•to•mize, *v.,* -mized, -miz•ing.
o•o•pho•rec•to•my, *n., pl.* -mies.
o•o•pho•ri•tis
o•oph•o•ro•cys•tec•to•my, *n., pl.* -mies.
o•o•pho•ro•ma fol•lic•u•la•re
o•oph•o•ron
o•o•plasm
o•o•plas•mic
o•o•por•phy•rin

o○o•sperm
O○os•po○ra
o○o•spore
o○o•the○ca, *n.,* *pl.* -cae.
o○o•the○cal
o○o•tid
o○o•type
o○pac○i•fi•ca○tion
o○pac○i•fy, *v.,* -fied, -fy•ing.
o○pac○i○ty, *n.,* *pl.* -ties.
o○pal•es•cent
o○pei○do•scope
o○pen-an○gle glau•co○ma
o○pen frac•ture
o○pen-heart
open-heart sur•ger○y
op•er○a•bil○i○ty
op•er○a•ble
op•er○a•bly
op•er•ant
op•er○a•ate, *v.,* -at○ed, -at•ing.
op•er○a•tion
op•er○a•tive
op•er○a•tive○ly
op•er○a•tor
o○per•cu•lar
o○per•cu•late
o○per•cu•lat○e
o○per•cu•lum, *n.,* *pl.* -cu○la,
  -cu•lums.
operculum fron•ta○le
operculum il○e○i
operculum tem•po•ra○le
op•er○on
o○phi•a•sis
O○phid○i○a
o○phry○on
Oph○ry•o○sco•lec○i•dae
Op•hthaine *Trademark.*
oph•thal•mec•to○my, *n.,* *pl.*
  -mies.

oph•thal•men•ceph○a•lon,
  n., *pl.* -ceph•a○la.
oph•thal•mi○a
ophthalmia e○lec•tri○ca
ophthalmia ne○o•na•to•rum
ophthalmia ni•va•lis
ophthalmia no•do○sa
oph•thal•mic
oph○thal•mo•cen•te•sis
oph○thal•mo•di•a•stim•
  e○ter
oph○thal•mo•dy•na•mom•
  e○ter
oph○thal•mo•dyn○i○a
oph•thal•mo•graph
oph○thal•mo•leu•co•scope
oph○thal•mo•leu•ko•scope
oph•thal•mo•log○ic
oph•thal•mo•log○i•cal
oph•thal•mol○o•gist
oph•thal•mol○o○gy
oph○thal•mo•ma•la•cia
oph○thal•mom•e•ter
oph○thal•mom•e○try
oph○thal•mo•my•co•sis, *n.,*
  pl. -ses.
oph•thal•mop○a•thy, *n.,* *pl.*
  -thies.
oph○thal•mo•ple•gia
oph○thal•mo•ple•gic
oph○thal•mo•re•ac•tion
oph○thal•mor•rhex○is
oph•thal•mo•scope
oph•thal•mo•scop○ic
oph○thal•mo•scop○i•cal
oph•thal•mo•scop○i•cal○ly
oph•thal•mos•co○py, *n.,* *pl.*
  -pies.
oph•thal•mos•ta•sis, *n.,* *pl.*
  -ses.
oph○thal•mo•trope
oph○thal○mo•tro•pom•e○ter

Oph•thet•ic *Trademark.*
o•pi•ate
o•pi•oid
o•pis•the•nar
o•pis•thi•on, *n., pl.* -thi•a,
-thi•ons.
o•pis•tho•cra•ni•on
o•pis•thog•na•thism
o•pis•thorchiasis
o•pis•thorchis
o•pis•thotic
o•pis•tho•tonic
o•pis•tho•tonos
o•pi•um
o•po•bal•sam
o•po•bal•sa•mum
op•po•nens, *n., pl.* -nen•tes.
opponens pol•li•cis
op•por•tun•ist
op•por•tun•is•tic
op•por•tun•is•ti•cal•ly
op•po•si•tion•al de•fi•ant
dis•or•der
op•sin
op•son•ic
op•so•nin
op•so•nize, *v.,* -nized, -niz•
ing.
op•so•no•cy•to•phag•ic
op•tic
optic chi•as•ma
optic nerve
op•ti•cal
optical il•lu•sion
op•ti•cal•ly
op•ti•cian
op•ti•coel
op•ti•co•pu•pil•lar•y
Op•ti•crom *Trademark.*
op•tics
Op•ti•lets-500 *Trademark.*
Optilets-M-500 *Trademark.*

op•tim•e•ter
Op•ti•mine *Trademark.*
Op•ti•ray *Trademark.*
op•to•gram
op•to•ki•net•ic
op•tom•e•ter
op•to•met•ric
op•to•met•ri•cal
op•tom•e•trist
op•tom•e•try
op•to•type
o•ora
O•ora•base HCA *Trademark.*
o•orad
O•ora•graf•in *Trademark.*
o•oral
oral con•tra•cep•tive
oral her•pes
o•ora•le
o•oral•oi•ty
o•oral•ly
o•oral•o•o•gy, *n., pl.* -gies.
O•orap *Trademark.*
ora ser•ra•ota, *n.,*
pl. o•orae ser•ra•tae.
O•ora•zinc *Trademark.*
or•bic•u•lar
or•bic•u•lar•is, *n., pl.* -lar•es.
orbicularis oc•u•li
orbicularis o•oris
orbicularis pal•pe•bra•rum
or•bic•u•lar•i•oty
or•bic•u•lar•ly
or•bic•u•lus cil•i•a•ris
or•bit
or•bit•al
or•o•bio•to•sphe•noid
or•o•bio•to•sphe•noi•dal
or•ce•in
or•chec•to•my, *n., pl.* -mies.
or•chi•dec•to•my, *n., pl.*
-mies.

or•chi•do•pex•y, *n., pl.* -pex•
  ies.
or•chi•ec•to•my, *n., pl.* -mies.
or•chil
or•chi•o•pex•y, *n., pl.* -pex•
  ies.
or•chi•o•plas•ty, *n., pl.* -ties.
or•chit•ic
or•chi•tis
or•cin
or•ci•nol
or•der
or•der•ly, *n., pl.* -lies.
or•di•nate
o•rec•tic
O•ret•ic *Trademark.*
O•ret•i•cyl *Trademark.*
Or•e•ton *Trademark.*
o•rex•i•a
O•rex•in *Trademark.*
o•rex•is
or•gan
organ of Cor•ti
organ of Ja•cob•son
or•gan•el•la
or•gan•elle
or•gan•ic
organic brain syn•drome
or•gan•oi•cal•ly
or•gan•oi•cism
or•gan•oi•cist
or•gan•oi•cis•tic
or•ga•nic•oi•ty
Or•gan•oi•din *Trademark.*
or•gan•ism
or•gan•iz•er
or•ga•no•gel
or•ga•no•gen•e•sis, *n., pl.*
  -e•ses.
or•ga•no•ge•net•ic
or•ga•no•ge•net•i•cal•ly
or•ga•no•gen•ic

or•ga•nog•e•ony, *n., pl.* -nog•
  e•onies.
or•ga•no•graph•ic
or•ga•nog•ra•phy, *n., pl.*
  -phies.
or•ga•noid
or•ga•no•lep•tic
or•ga•no•lep•ti•cal•ly
or•ga•no•log•ic
or•ga•nol•o•gy
or•ga•no•mer•cu•ri•al
or•ga•no•me•tal•lic
or•ga•non
organon au•di•tous
organon gus•tus
organon ol•fac•tus
organon spi•ra•le
organon vi•sus
or•ga•no•og•i•cal
or•ga•no•phos•phate
or•ga•no•phos•pho•rus
or•ga•nos•co•py, *n., pl.* -pies.
or•ga•no•sol
or•ga•no•ther•a•peu•tic
or•ga•no•ther•a•py, *n., pl.*
  -pies.
or•ga•no•troph•ic
or•ga•no•trop•ic
or•ga•no•trop•i•cal•ly
or•ga•not•ro•pism
or•ga•not•ro•py
or•ga•num
organum gus•tus
organum ol•fac•tus
organum spi•ra•le
organum vi•sus
or•gasm
or•gas•mic
or•gas•tic
o•ri•en•ta•tion
o•ri•en•ta•tive
or•i•fice

or•i•fi•cial
or•i•ga•num
or•i•gin
Or•oi•mune *Trademark.*
Or•oi•nase *Trademark.*
O•ornade *Trademark.*
Or•onex *Trademark.*
Or•ni•dyl *Trademark.*
or•ni•ghu•ric
or•ni•thine
Or•ni•tho•do•ros
or•ni•tho•sis
o•ro•pha•ryn•ge•al
o•ro•phar•ynx, *n., pl.* -phar•
   yn•ges, -phar•ynx•es.
o•rot•ic
O•roy•a fe•ver
or•phan drug
Or•phen•ge•sic *Trademark.*
Or•tho *Trademark.*
Or•tho-Cept *Trademark.*
Ortho-Creme *Trademark.*
Ortho-Cy•clen *Trademark.*
Ortho Di•en•es•trol *Trade-*
   mark.
Ortho-Gy•nol *Trademark.*
Ortho-No•vum *Trademark.*
Ortho Tri-Cy•clen *Trademark.*
or•tho•ce•phal•ic
or•tho•ceph•a•lous
or•tho•ceph•a•ly
or•tho•chro•mat•ic
or•tho•clone
or•thoc•re•sol
or•tho•di•a•gram
or•tho•don•tia
or•tho•don•tic
or•tho•don•tics
or•tho•don•tist
or•tho•dro•mic
or•tho•gen•e•sis, *n., pl.*
   -e•ses.

or•tho•ge•net•ic
or•tho•ge•net•i•cal•ly
or•tho•gen•ic
or•tho•grade
or•thom•e•ter
or•tho•mo•lec•u•lar
orthomolecular treat•ment
or•tho•myx•o•vi•rus, *n., pl.*
   -rus•es.
or•tho•pae•dic
or•tho•pae•dics
or•tho•pae•dist
or•tho•pe•dic
or•tho•pe•di•cal•ly
or•tho•pe•dics
or•tho•pe•dist
or•tho•pho•ri•a
or•tho•phos•phate
or•thop•ne•a
or•thop•ne•ic
or•thop•noe•a
or•thop•noe•ic
or•tho•prax•y
or•tho•psy•chi•at•ric
or•tho•psy•chi•at•ri•cal
or•tho•psy•chi•a•trist
or•tho•psy•chi•a•try
or•thop•tic
or•thop•tics
or•thop•tist
or•tho•scope
or•tho•scop•ic
or•tho•sis, *n., pl.* -ses.
or•tho•stat•ic
or•tho•ster•e•o•scope
or•tho•ster•e•o•scop•ic
or•thot•ic
or•thot•ics
or•thot•ist
or•thot•o•nus
or•tho•topic
O•ru•dis *Trademark.*

Or•o•u•vail *Trademark.*
os¹, *n., pl.* os•sa. (bone)
os², *n., pl.* o•ra. (mouth)
os•a•zone
Os-Cal *Trademark.*
os cal•cis, *n., pl.* os•sa cal•cis.
os•cil•la•tion
os•cil•la•tor
os•cil•la•tor•y
os•cil•lo•gram
os•cil•lo•graph
os•cil•lo•graph•ic
os•cil•lo•graph•i•cal•ly
os•cil•log•ra•phy, *n., pl.*
  -phies.
os•cil•lom•e•ter
os•cil•lom•e•try
os•cil•lo•scope
os•cil•lo•scop•ic
os•cil•lo•scop•i•cal•ly
os•cine
Os•cin•o•i•dae
os cox•ae, *n., pl.* os•sa
  cox•ae.
os•cu•la•tion
os•cu•lum, *n., pl.* -cu•la.
os•mate
os•mat•ic
os•me•sis
os•mic
os•mics
os•mi•dro•sis
os•mi•o•phil
os•mi•o•phil•ic
os•mi•um
os•mol
os•mo•lal
os•mo•lal•i•ty
os•mo•lar
os•mo•lar•i•ty
Os•mo•lite *Trademark.*

os•mo•met•ric
os•mom•e•try
os•mo•phore
os•mo•phor•ic
os•mo•re•cep•tor
os•mo•reg•u•la•tion
os•mo•reg•u•la•tor
os•mo•reg•u•la•to•ry
os•mose, *v.,* -mosed, -mos•
  ing.
os•mo•sis
os•mot•ic
os•mot•i•cal•ly
o•so•mo•e•ter
os•phre•sis
os•phret•ic
os•sa
os•se•o•in
os•se•let
os•se•o•car•ti•lag•o•i•nous
os•se•ous
os•se•ous•ly
os•si•cle
os•sic•u•lar
os•si•cu•lec•to•my, *n., pl.*
  -mies.
os•si•cu•lot•o•my, *n., pl.*
  -mies.
os•si•cu•lum, *n., pl.* -cu•la.
os•sif•ic
os•si•fi•ca•tion
os•sif•i•ca•to•ry
os•si•fy, *v.,* -fied, -fy•ing.
os•tal•gia
os•te•al
os•tec•to•my, *n., pl.* -mies.
os•te•in
os•te•it•ic
os•te•i•tis
osteitis de•for•mans
osteitis fi•bro•sa
os•te•o•ar•thrit•ic

os○te○o•arth•ri•tis

os○te○o•ar•throp○a•thy, *n.*,
  pl. -thies.

os○te○o•ar•thro•sis

os○te○o•ar•throt○o•my, *n.*,
  pl. -mies.

os○te○o•blast

os○te○o•blas•tic

os○te○o•car•ti•lag○i•nous

os○te○o•chon•dral

os○te○o•chon•dri•tis

os○te○o•chon•dro•ma, *n.*, *pl.*
  -mas, -ma○ta.

os○te○o•chon•dro•ma•to•sis

os○te○o•chon•drop○a•thy, *n.*,
  pl. -thies.

os○te○o•chon•dro•sar•
  co○ma, *n.*, *pl.* -mas, -ma○ta.

os○te○o•chon•dro•sis, *n.*, *pl.*
  -ses.

os○te○o•chon•drot○ic

os○te○o•chon•drous

os•te•oc•la•sis

os○te○o•clast

os○te○o•clas•tic

os○te○o•com○ma

os○te○o•cra•ni○um, *n.*, *pl.*
  -ni•ums, -ni○a.

os○te○o•cyte

os○te○o•den•tin

os○te○o•den•tine

os○te○o•der•ma•tous

os○te○o•der•mous

os○te○o•dyn○i○a

os○te○o•dys•tro•phi○a

osteodystrophia de•for•mans

osteodystrophia fi•bro○sa

os○te○o•dys•troph○ic

os○te○o•dys•tro•phy, *n.*, *pl.*
  -phies.

os○te○o•fi•bro○ma, *n.*, *pl.*
  -mas, -ma○ta.

os○te○o•fi•bro•sis, *n.*, *pl.* -ses.

os○te○o•fi•brous

os○te○o•gen•e○sis, *n.*, *pl.*
  -ses.

osteogenesis im•per•fec○ta

osteogenesis imperfecta con•
  gen○i○ta

osteogenesis imperfecta cys•
  ti○ca

osteogenesis imperfecta
  tar○da

os○te○o•ge•net○ic

os○te○o•gen○ic

os•te•og○e○nous

os•te•og•ra•phy, *n.*, *pl.*
  -phies.

os•te•oid

os○te○o•log○ic

os○te○o•log○i•cal

os○te○o•log○i•cal○ly

os•te•ol○o○gist

os•te•ol○o○gy

os•te•ol○y•sis

os○te○o•lyt○ic

os•te•o○ma, *n.*, *pl.* -mas,
  -ma○ta.

osteoma cu•tis

osteoma du•rum

osteoma e○bur•ne○um

osteoma me•dul•la○re

osteoma spon•gi○o•sum

os○te○o•ma•la•cia

os○te○o•ma•la•cial

os○te○o•ma•lac○ic

os○te○o•ma•toid

os•te•om○a•tous

os○te○o•met•ric

os○te○o•met•ri•cal

os•te•om•e○try

os○te○o•my•e○lit○ic

os○te○o•my•e○li•tis

os•te•on

os•te•o○•ne•cro•sis

os•te○o•path

os•te○o•path○ic

os•te○o•path○i•cal○ly

os•te•op○o•a•thist

os•te•op○o•a•thy, *n., pl.* -thies.

os•te○o•pe○nia

os•te○o•per•i•o•sti•tis

os•te○o•pe•tro•sis, *n., pl.* -ses.

osteopetrosis gal•li•na•rum

osteopetrosis gen•er•al○i•sa○ta

os•te○o•pe•trot○ic

os•te○o•phage

os•te○o•pha•gia

os•te○o•phyte

os•te○o•phyt○ic

os•te○o•plast

os•te○o•plas•tic

os•te○o•plas○ty, *n., pl.* -ties.

os•te○o•po•ro•sis

os•te○o•po•rot○ic

os•te•op•sathy•ro•sis

os•te○o•ra•di○o•ne•cro•sis

os•te○o•sar•co•ma, *n., pl.* -mas, -ma○ta.

os•te○o•scle•ro•sis, *n., pl.* -ses.

os•te○o•scle•rot○ic

os•te○o•sis cu•tis

os•te○o•syn•the•sis, *n., pl.* -ses.

os•te○o•tome

os•te•ot○o•mist

os•te•ot○o•my, *n., pl.* -mies.

os•te○o•tribe

Os•ter•ta•gia

Os○ti-Derm *Trademark.*

os•ti○al

os•ti○um, *n., pl.* -ti○a.

ostium pri•mum

ostium se•cun•dum

os•to○my, *n., pl.* -mies.

o○ta•cous•tic

o○tal•gi○a

o○tal•gic

o○the•ma•to○ma

ot○ic

Otic Dome•bo○ro *Trademark.*

Otic Tri•des○i•lon *Trademark.*

o○tit○ic

o○ti•tis

otitis ex•ter○na

otitis me•di○a

otitis me○di○a

O○to•bi•ot○ic *Trademark.*

O○to•bi○us

o○to•ce•phal○ic

o○to•ceph○a•ly

o○to•co•ni○um, *n., pl.* -ni○a.

O○to•cort *Trademark.*

o○to•cyst

o○to•cys•tic

O○to•dec•tes

o○to•dec•tic

o○to•gen○ic

o○tog○e•nous

o○to•la•ryn•go•log○i•cal

o○to•lar•yn•gol○o•gist

o○to•lar•yn•gol○o•gy

o○to•lith

o○to•lith○ic

o○to•log○ic

o○to•log○i•cal

o○to•log○i•cal○ly

o○tol○o•gist

o○tol○o•gy

o○to•my•co•sis, *n., pl.* -ses.

o○to•my•cot○ic

o○to•plas○ty, *n., pl.* -ties.

o○to•rhi•no•la•ryn•go•log○i•cal

o‧to‧rhi‧no‧lar‧yn‧gol‧o‧gist

o‧to‧rhi‧no‧lar‧yn‧gol‧o‧gy

o‧tor‧rhe‧a

o‧tor‧rhoe‧a

o‧to‧sal‧pinx, *n.*, *pl.* -pin‧ges.

o‧to‧scle‧ro‧sis

o‧to‧scle‧rot‧ic

o‧to‧scope

o‧to‧scop‧ic

o‧tos‧co‧py, *n.*, *pl.* -pies.

o‧to‧sis

o‧tos‧te‧al

o‧tos‧te‧on

o‧tot‧o‧my, *n.*, *pl.* -mies.

o‧to‧tox‧ic

o‧to‧tox‧ic‧i‧ty, *n.*, *pl.* -ties.

O‧tri‧vin *Trademark.*

ou‧a‧bain

out-of-bod‧y

out-pa‧tient

out‧break

out‧pa‧tient

out‧pock‧et‧ing

o‧va

ov‧al‧bu‧min

o‧val‧o‧cyte

o‧val‧o‧cyt‧ic

o‧val‧o‧cy‧to‧sis

o‧var‧i‧al

o‧var‧i‧an

o‧var‧i‧ec‧to‧mize, *v.*, -mized, -miz‧ing.

o‧var‧i‧ec‧to‧my, *n.*, *pl.* -mies.

o‧var‧i‧o‧hys‧ter‧ec‧to‧my, *n.*, *pl.* -mies.

o‧var‧i‧ot‧o‧my, *n.*, *pl.* -mies.

o‧va‧ri‧tis

o‧va‧ry, *n.*, *pl.* -ries.

Ov‧con *Trademark.*

o‧ver-the-count‧er

o‧ver‧a‧chieve, *v.*, -a‧chieved, -a‧chiev‧ing.

o‧ver‧a‧chiev‧er

o‧ver‧bite

o‧ver‧com‧pen‧sate, *v.*, -sat‧ed, -sat‧ing.

o‧ver‧com‧pen‧sa‧tion

o‧ver‧cor‧rec‧tion

o‧ver‧dos‧age

o‧ver‧dose, *n.*, *v.*, -dosed, -dos‧ing.

o‧ver‧ex‧ten‧sion

o‧ver‧fa‧tigue

o‧ver‧fa‧tigued

o‧ver‧flow

o‧ver‧graft‧ing

o‧ver‧growth

o‧ver‧hang

o‧ver‧jet

o‧ver‧lap, *v.*, -lapped, -lap‧ping, *n.*

o‧ver‧lay, *v.*, -laid, -lay‧ing, *n.*

o‧ver‧nu‧tri‧tion

o‧ver‧pro‧duc‧tiv‧i‧ty

o‧ver‧reach‧ing

o‧ver‧re‧sponse

o‧ver‧sexed

o‧ver‧stain

o‧ver‧strain

o‧ver‧stress

o‧ver‧toe

o‧ver‧tone

o‧ver‧train‧ing syn‧drome

o‧ver‧trans‧fu‧sion

o‧ver‧ven‧ti‧la‧tion

o‧ver‧weight

o‧vi‧cid‧al

o‧vi‧du‧cal

o‧vi‧duct

o‧vi‧duc‧tal

o‧vi‧form

o○vi•gen•e○sis, *n., pl.* -ses.
o○vi•ge•net○ic
o○vig○er•ous
o○vi•na•tion
o○vip○a•rous
o○vip○a•rous○ly
o○vip○a•rous•ness
o○vi•pos○it
o○vi•po•si•tion
o○vi•po•si•tion•al
o○vi•pos○i•tor
o○vi•sac
o○vo•cyte
o○vo•fla•vin
o○vo•gen•e○sis, *n., pl.* -ses.
o○vo•mu•cin
o○vo•mu•coid
o○vo•plasm
o○vo•plas•mic
o○vo•tes•tic○u•lar
o○vo•tes•tis, *n., pl.* -tes.
o○vo•vi•tel•lin
o○vo•vi•vip○a•rous
o○vo•vi•vip○a•rous○ly
o○vo•vi•vip○a•rous•ness
Ov•ral *Trademark.*
Ov•rette *Trademark.*
ov○u•lar
o○vu•late, *v.,* -lat○ed, -lat•ing.
ov○u•la•tion
ov○u•la•to○ry
ov○ule
Ov○u•len *Trademark.*
o○vum, *n., pl.* o○va.
ovum tu•ber•cu•lo•sum
ox○a•cil•lin
ox○a•late
ox•al○ic
ox○a•lo○a•ce•tic ac○id
ox○a•lo•suc•cin○ic
ox○a•lu•ri○a

ox○a•lyl
ox○a•lyl•u•re○a
ox○a•mide
Ox○a•pro•zin
ox○a•ze•pam
ox•gall
ox○i•dant
ox○i•dase
ox○i•da•sic
ox○i•da•tion
oxidation-re•duc•tion
ox○i•da•tive
oxidative phos•pho•ryl○a•tion
ox○i•da•tive○ly
ox•ide
ox•id○ic
ox○i•di•za•tion
ox○i•dize, *v.,* -dized, -diz•ing.
ox○i•do-re•duc•tase
ox○i○do-re•duc•tase
ox•ime
ox•im•e○ter
ox○i•met•ric
ox•im•e○try
Ox○i•stat *Trademark.*
ox○o•ni○um
ox○o•phe•nar•sine
ox○o•tre•mo•rine
Ox•sor○a•len *Trademark.*
Oxsoralen-Ul○tra *Trademark.*
Ox○y Clean *Trademark.*
ox○y•a•can•thine
ox○y•ac○id
ox○y•bi○o•tin
ox○y•blep•si○a
ox○y•cal○o○rim•e○ter
ox○y•ce•phal○ic
ox○y•ceph○a•lous
ox○y•ceph○a○ly
ox○y•chlo•ride
ox○y•chro•mat○ic

ox•y•chro•ma•tin
ox•y•chro•ma•tin•ic
Ox•y•co•done/APAP
ox•y•gen
oxygen debt
oxygen mask
oxygen tent
ox•y•gen•ase
ox•y•gen•ate, *v.*, -at•ed, -at•ing.
ox•y•gen•a•tion
ox•y•gen•a•tor
ox•y•gen•ic
ox•y•gen•ic•i•ty
ox•y•gen•ize, *v.*, -iz•ed, -iz•ing.
ox•yg•e•nous
ox•y•he•mo•glo•bin
ox•y•hy•dro•gen
ox•y•mel
ox•y•my•o•glo•bin
ox•y•neu•rine
ox•yn•tic
ox•y•o•o•pi•a, *n.*, *pl.* -pi•as.
ox•y•phil
ox•y•phil•ic
ox•yph•i•lous
ox•y•pol•y•gel•a•tin
ox•y•some
Ox•y•spir•ou•ra
ox•y•tet•ra•cy•cline
ox•y•to•cia
ox•y•to•cic
ox•y•to•cin
ox•y•u•ri•a•sis
ox•y•u•ric
ox•y•uricide
ox•y•urid
Ox•y•uris
o•zae•na
o•ze•na
o•zoe•na
o•zon•a•tor
o•zone
o•zon•ide
o•zon•i•za•tion
o•zon•ize, *v.*, -ized, -iz•ing.
o•zon•iz•er
o•zo•nol•y•sis, *n.*, *pl.* -ses.
o•zos•to•mi•a

pab•u•lum
Pa•caps *Trademark.*
Pac•chi•o•ni•an bod•y
Pacchionian cor•pus•cle
pace•mak•er
pace•mak•ing
pach•y•a•cri•a
pach•y•ce•pha•li•a, *n.*, *pl.* -li•as.
pach•y•ceph•a•ly
pach•y•chei•li•a
pach•y•der•ma•tous
pach•y•der•mi•a
pach•y•der•mi•al
pach•y•lep•to•men•in•gi•tis
pach•y•men•in•gi•tis
pach•y•me•ninx, *n.*, *pl.* -me•nin•ges.
pach•y•o•nych•i•a
pachyonychia con•gen•i•ta
pach•y•per•i•to•ni•tis
pach•y•tene
Pa•cin•i•an cor•pus•cle
Pa•ci•ni's cor•pus•cle
pae•di•at•ric
pae•di•at•rics

pae•do•phil•i∘a
pa•ge∘toid
Pag•et's dis•ease
pa•go•pha•gi∘a
pain scale
pain thresh•old
pain•kill∘er
pain•kill•ing
paint•er's col∘ic
paired-as•so•ci•ate learn•ing
pa•ja•huel∘lo
pa•ja•ro•el∘lo
pal∘a•tal
pal•ate
pal∘a•tine
pal∘a•ti•tis
pal∘a∘to•glos•sal
pal∘a∘to•gram
pal∘a∘to•graph∘ic
pal∘a•tog•ra•phy, n., pl.
  -phies.
pal∘a∘to•max•il•lar∘y
pal∘a∘to•na•sal
pal∘a∘to•pha•ryn•ge∘al
pal∘a∘to•pha•ryn•ge∘us
pal∘a∘to•plas∘ty, n., pl. -ties.
pal∘a∘to•ple•gia
pal∘a•tor•rha•phy, n., pl.
  -phies.
pal∘a•tos•chi•sis
pa•la∘tum, n., pl. -la∘ta.
palatum du•rum
palatum fis•sum
palatum mo•bile
palatum mol∘le
palatum os•se∘um
pa•le•en•ceph∘a•lon, n., pl.
  -ceph•a∘la.
pa∘le∘o•cer∘e•bel•lar
pa∘le∘o•cer•e∘bel•lum, n., pl.
  -e∘bel•lums, -e∘bel•la.

pa∘le∘o•cor•tex, n., pl. -ti•
  ces.
pa∘le∘o•en•ceph∘a•lon, n.,
  pl. -ceph•a∘la.
pa∘le∘o•pal•li∘um, n., pl.
  -li∘a, -li•ums.
pa∘le∘o•stri•a•tal
pa∘le∘o•stri•a•tum, n., pl.
  -stri∘a∘ta.
pa∘le∘o•thal∘a•mus, n., pl.
  -thal•a∘mi.
pal∘i•ki•ne•sia
pal∘i•la•li∘a
pal•in•dro•mi∘a
pal•in•dro•mic
pal•in•dro•mi•cal∘ly
pal•la•di∘um
pal•lan•es•the•sia
pal•les•the•sia
pal•li∘al
pal•li•ate, v., -at∘ed, -at•ing.
pal•li•a∘tion
pal•li•a∘tive
pal•li•a∘tive∘ly
pal•li•a∘tor
pal•li∘dal
pal•li∘um, n., pl. -li∘a, -li•ums.
pal∘ma ma•nus
pal•mar
pal•mar∘is
pal•ma•ture
pal•mi•tate
pal•mit∘ic
pal•mod∘ic
pal•mo•spas•mus
pal•mus, n., pl. pal∘mi.
pal•pa•ble
pal•pate, v., -pat∘ed, -pat•ing.
pal•pa•tion
pal•pa•to∘ry
pal•pe•bra, n., pl. -brae.
pal•pe•bral

pal•pe•brate, *v.,* -brat•ed,
  -brat•ing.
pal•pe•bra•tion
pal•pi•tate, *v.,* -tated, -tating.
pal•pi•ta•tion
PALS *Trademark.*
pal•sied
pal•sy, *n., pl.* -sies.
pa•lu•dal
pal•u•dism
pam•a•quin
pam•a•quine
Pam•o•e•lor *Trademark.*
Pam•ine *Trademark.*
Pan•o•a•fil *Trademark.*
Panafil-White *Trademark.*
pan•ag•glu•ti•na•bil•i•ty, *n.,*
  pl. -ties.
pan•ag•glu•ti•na•ble
pa•nag•glu•ti•na•tion
Pan•al•ge•sic Gold *Trademark.*
pan•ar•ter•i•tis
pan•arth•ri•tis
pan•at•ro•phy, *n., pl.* -phies.
pan•car•di•tis
pan•co•lec•to•my, *n., pl.*
  -mies.
pan•cre•as
Pan•cre•ase *Trademark.*
Pancrease MT *Trademark.*
pan•cre•a•tec•to•mize, *v.,*
  -mized, -miz•ing.
pan•cre•a•tec•to•my, *n., pl.*
  -mies.
pan•cre•at•ic
pancreatic juice
pancreatic pol•y•pep•tide
pan•cre•at•i•co•du•o•de•
  nal
pan•cre•at•i•co•en•ter•
  os•to•my, *n., pl.* -mies.

pan•cre•at•i•co•gas•tros•
  to•my, *n., pl.* -mies.
pan•cre•at•i•co•je•ju•
  nos•to•my, *n., pl.* -mies.
pan•cre•o•a•tin
pan•cre•o•a•tism
pan•cre•o•a•ti•tis
pan•cre•a•tog•e•nous
pan•cre•at•o•lith
pan•cre•o•a•to•li•thot•o•o•my,
  n., pl. -mies.
pan•cre•o•a•tot•o•o•my, *n., pl.*
  -mies.
pan•cy•to•pe•ni•a
pan•cy•to•pe•nic
pan•dem•ic
pan•dic•u•la•tion
pan•en•do•scope
pan•en•do•scop•ic
pan•en•dos•co•py, *n., pl.*
  -pies.
Pan•he•ma•tin *Trademark.*
pan•hy•po•pi•tu•i•tar•ism
pan•hy•po•pi•tu•i•tar•y
pan•hys•ter•ec•to•my, *n., pl.*
  -mies.
pan•hys•ter•o•o•sal•pin•gec•
  to•my, *n., pl.* -mies.
pan•hys•ter•o•o•sal•pin•
  go•o•oph•o•o•rec•to•my, *n.,*
  pl. -mies.
pan•ic
panic at•tack
panic dis•or•der
pan•leu•co•pe•ni•a
pan•leu•ko•pe•ni•a
Pan•my•cin *Trademark.*
pan•my•e•lop•o•a•thy
pan•my•e•loph•thi•sis
pan•nic•u•li•tis
pan•nic•u•lus, *n., pl.* -nic•
  u•li.

pan•nus, *n., pl.* pan•ni.
pan•oph•thal•mi•tis
pan•op•tic
pan•op•ti•cal
pan•o•ti•tis
Pan•Ox•yl *Trademark.*
pan•scle•ro•sis, *n., pl.* -ses.
pan•sex•u•al
pan•sex•u•al•i•ty
pan•si•nus•i•tis
pan•sper•ma•tism
pan•sper•mi•a
Pan•stron•gy•lus ge•nic•u•
   la•tus
Panstrongylus me•gis•tus
pan•te•the•ine
Pan•to•paque *Trademark.*
Pan•to•pon *Trademark.*
pan•toth•e•nate
pan•to•then•ic
pantothenic ac•id
pan•trop•ic
pa•nus fau•ci•um
panus in•gui•na•lis
Pan•war•fin *Trademark.*
pan•zo•ot•ic
Pap smear
Pap test
pa•pa•in
Pa•pa•ni•co•laou test
Pap•a•ver
pa•pav•er•ine
pa•pil•la, *n., pl.* -lae.
pa•pil•la of Va•ter
pa•pil•lar
pap•il•lar•y
pap•il•late
pap•il•lat•ed
pap•il•lec•to•my, *n., pl.*
   -mies.
pa•pil•le•de•ma, *n., pl.* -mas,
   -ma•ta.

pap•il•lif•er•ous
pa•pil•li•form
pap•il•li•tis
pap•il•lo•e•de•ma, *n., pl.*
   -mas, -ma•ta.
pap•il•lo•ma, *n., pl.* -mas,
   -ma•ta.
papilloma cho•roi•de•um
pap•il•lo•ma•to•sis
pap•il•lo•ma•tous
pap•il•lo•ma•vi•rus, *n., pl.*
   -rus•es.
pap•il•lo•ret•o•i•ni•tis
pa•po•va•vi•rus, *n., pl.*
   -rus•es.
pap•pose
pap•pous
pap•pus, *n., pl.* pap•pi.
pap•u•lar
pap•u•la•tion
pap•ule
pap•u•lo•er•y•the•ma•tous
pap•u•lo•pus•tu•lar
pap•u•lose
pap•u•lo•squa•mous
pap•u•lo•ve•sic•u•lar
pap•y•ra•ceous
par•a
para-a•mi•no•ben•zo•ic
para-aminobenzoic ac•id
para-a•mi•no•hip•pu•ric
para-an•al•ge•sia
para-an•es•the•sia
par•a•bi•o•sis
par•a•bi•ot•ic
par•a•bi•ot•o•i•cal•ly
par•a•blep•si•a
par•a•blep•sis, *n., pl.* -ses.
par•a•blep•sy, *n., pl.* -sies.
par•a•bu•li•a
par•a•car•mine
Par•a•cel•si•an

par•o•a•cen•te•sis, *n., pl.* -ses.
paracentesis oc•u•o•li
par•o•a•cen•tral
par•o•a•chor•dal
par•o•a•co•li•tis
par•o•a•col•pi•tis
par•o•a•col•pi•um
par•o•a•cone
par•o•a•cu•si•o, *n., pl.* -si•os as.
paracusia du•pli•ca•ta
paracusia lo•ca•lis
paracusia ob•tu•sa
par•o•a•cu•sis, *n., pl.* -ses.
par•o•a•cys•tic
par•o•a•cys•ti•tis
par•o•a•cys•ti•um, *n., pl.* -ti•a.
par•o•a•den•tal
par•o•a•den•ti•tis
par•o•a•den•ti•um, *n., pl.* -ti•a.
par•o•a•den•to•sis
par•o•a•did•o•mis
Par•o•a•di•one *Trademark.*
par•o•a•dox•o•i•cal sleep
par•aes•the•sia
par•aes•thet•ic
par•af•fin
par•af•fine
par•af•fi•no•ma, *n., pl.* -mas, -ma•ta.
Par•o•a•flex *Trademark.*
Par•o•a•fon Forte *Trademark.*
par•o•a•gam•ma•cism
par•o•a•gam•ma•cis•mus, *n., pl.* -mus•es.
par•o•a•gan•gli•o•o•ma, *n., pl.* -mas, -ma•ta.
par•o•a•gan•gli•on, *n., pl.* -gli•o, -gli•ons.
paraganglion ca•rot•i•cum
paraganglion caroticum sar•co•o•ma

paraganglion ca•rot•i•cus tu•o mor
par•o•a•gan•gli•on•ic
Par•o•a•Gard *Trademark.*
par•o•a•geu•sia
par•ag•glu•ti•na•tion
par•o•a•glos•si•o
pa•rag•na•thus
par•o•a•gon•o•i•mi•a•sis
Par•o•a•gon•i•mus
par•o•a•graph•o•i•a
par•o•a•he•mo•phil•o•i•a
par•o•a•he•pat•o•ic
par•o•a•hor•mone
par•o•a•hor•mon•o•ic
par•o•a•hy•drox•o•y•ben•zo•ic
par•o•a•in•flu•en•o•za
par•o•a•ker•o•a•to•sis, *n., pl.* -ses.
parakeratosis gon•or•rhe•i•o•ca
parakeratosis scut•o•u•lar•o•is
parakeratosis var•i•e•ga•ta
par•o•a•ker•o•a•tot•o•ic
par•o•a•ki•ne•si•o, *n., pl.* -si•os as.
par•o•a•ki•ne•sis
par•o•a•ki•net•o•ic
par•o•a•la•li•o•a
par•o•a•lamb•da•cism
par•al•de•hyde
par•o•a•lex•o•i•a
par•o•a•lex•o•ic
par•o•a•la•ge•sia
par•al•ge•sic
par•o•a•lo•gia
par•o•a•lo•gism
par•o•a•ly•sant
pa•ral•o•y•sis, *n., pl.* -ses.
paralysis ag•o•i•tans
par•o•a•lyt•o•ic
par•o•a•lyt•o•i•cal

par•a•lyt•i•cal•ly
par•a•ly•zant
par•a•ly•za•tion
par•a•lyze, *v.*, -lyzed, -lyz•ing.
par•a•lyz•er
par•a•mas•ti•tis
par•a•mas•toid
par•a•me•ci•um, *n., pl.* -ci•a.
par•a•me•di•an
par•a•med•ic
par•a•med•i•cal
paramedical per•son•nel
par•a•me•ni•a
par•a•meth•a•di•one
par•a•me•tri•al
par•a•me•tri•tis
par•a•me•tri•um, *n., pl.*
  -tri•a.
par•a•mim•i•a
par•am•ne•sia
Par•am•phis•to•mum
par•a•mu•sia
par•a•my•lum
par•a•my•o•clo•nus mul•ti•
  plex
par•a•my•o•to•ni•a
par•a•myx•o•vi•rus, *n., pl.*
  -rus•es.
par•a•nee
par•a•neph•ric
par•a•ne•phri•tis
par•a•neu•ral
par•a•noi•a
par•a•noi•ac
par•a•no•ic
par•a•noid
par•a•no•mi•a
par•a•nor•mal
par•a•nor•mal•ly
par•a•nu•cle•ar
par•a•nu•cle•ous, *n., pl.* -cle•i,
  -cle•us•es.

par•a•ox•on
par•a•pan•cre•at•ic
par•a•pa•re•sis
par•a•pha•sia
par•a•pha•sic
par•a•phen•yl•ene•di•a•
  mine
par•a•phil•oi•a
par•a•phil•i•ac
par•a•phil•ic
par•a•phi•mo•sis
paraphimosis oc•u•li
par•a•pho•ni•a
paraphonia pu•be•rum
paraphonia pu•bes•cen•
  ti•um
par•a•phrasia
paraphrasia ve•sa•na
par•a•phre•ni•a
par•a•phren•ic
par•a•phys•e•al
par•a•phys•i•al
par•a•phy•sis, *n., pl.* -ses.
Par•a•plat•in *Trademark.*
par•a•ple•gi•a
par•a•ple•gic
par•ap•o•plex•y, *n., pl.* -ies.
par•a•prax•i•a
par•a•prax•is
par•a•proc•ti•tis
par•a•proc•ti•um, *n., pl.*
  -ti•a.
par•a•pro•tein
par•a•pro•tein•e•mi•a
par•a•pso•ri•a•sis
par•a•psy•cho•log•i•cal
par•a•psy•chol•o•gist
par•a•psy•chol•o•gy
par•a•rec•tal
par•a•ro•san•i•line
par•ar•thri•a
par•a•sa•cral

Par•a•sal
Par•a•scar•is
par•a•se•cre•tion
par•a•sex•u•al
par•a•sex•u•al•i•ty, *n., pl.*
  -ties.
par•a•sig•ma•tism
par•a•site
par•a•si•te•mi•a
par•a•sit•ic
par•a•sit•i•cal
par•a•sit•i•cal•ly
par•a•sit•i•cid•al
par•a•sit•i•cide
par•a•sit•i•cid•ic
par•a•sit•ism
par•a•sit•i•za•tion
par•a•sit•ize, *v.,* -ized, -iz•
  ing.
par•a•sit•o•o•gen•ic
par•a•sit•o•o•log•ic
par•a•sit•o•o•log•i•cal
par•a•sit•ol•o•o•gist
par•a•si•tol•o•o•gy
par•a•si•to•sis
par•a•sit•o•o•trop•ic
par•a•spa•di•as
par•a•ster•nal
par•a•ster•nal•ly
par•a•sym•pa•thet•ic
par•a•sym•pa•thet•i•co•mi•
  met•ic
par•a•sym•pa•tho•lyt•ic
par•a•sym•pa•tho•mi•
  met•ic
par•a•syph•o•i•lit•ic
Par•a•thar *Trademark.*
par•a•thi•on
par•a•thy•roid
parathyroid gland
parathyroid hor•mone
par•a•thy•roi•dal

par•a•thy•roi•dec•to•mized
par•a•thy•roi•dec•to•my, *n.,*
  pl. -mies.
par•a•thy•ro•pri•val
par•a•thy•ro•priv•ic
par•a•thy•ro•trop•ic
par•a•troph•ic
pa•rat•ro•phy, *n., pl.* -phies.
par•a•tu•ber•cu•lo•sis
par•a•tu•ber•cu•lous
par•a•ty•phoid
par•a•typ•ic
par•a•typ•i•cal
par•a•um•bil•i•cal
par•a•u•re•thral
par•a•vag•i•nal
par•a•vag•i•nal•ly
par•a•vag•i•ni•tis
par•a•ver•te•bral
par•a•ver•te•bral•ly
par•a•ves•i•cal
par•ax•i•al
par•ax•i•al•ly
Par-De•con *Trademark.*
par•ec•ta•si•a, *n., pl.* -si•as.
par•ec•ta•sis, *n., pl.* -ses.
par•e•gor•ic
pa•ren•chy•ma
pa•ren•chy•mal
par•en•chy•mat•ic
par•en•chy•ma•tous
par•en•chy•ma•tous•ly
par•en•chyme
par•en•chy•mous
pa•ren•tal
pa•ren•tal•ly
par•en•ter•al
par•en•ter•al•ly
Pa•re•pec•to•lin *Trademark.*
par•ep•oi•did•o•y•mis, *n., pl.*
  -did•o•y•mi•des.
par•er•ga•sia

pa•re•sis
par•es•the•sia
par•es•thet•ic
pa•ret•ic
pa•ret∘i•cal∘ly
Par-Glyc•er∘ol *Trademark.*
Par-Glycerol C *Trademark.*
Par-Glycerol DM *Trademark.*
par•gy•line
par•i∘es, *n., pl.* pa•ri∘e•tes.
pa•ri∘e•tal
parietal bone
parietal lobe
pa•ri•e•to-oc•cip∘i•tal
pa•ri•e•to•fron•tal
par∘i∘ty
par•kin•so•ni•an
par•kin•son•ism
Par•kin•son's dis•ease
Parkinson's syn•drome
Par•nate *Trademark.*
par•oc•cip∘i•tal
par∘o•don•tal
par∘o•don•ti•tis
par∘o•don•ti∘um
par∘o•mo•my•cin
par∘o•nir∘i∘a am•bu•lans
par∘o•nych∘i∘a
paronychia diph•the•rit∘i∘ca
par∘o•nych∘i∘al
par∘o•oph∘o∘ron
par•oph•thal•mi∘a
par∘o•rex∘i∘a
par•os•mi∘a
par•os•ti•tis
pa•rot∘ic
pa•rot∘id
pa•rot∘i•de∘an
pa•rot∘i•dec•to∘my, *n., pl.*
  -mies.
pa•rot∘i•di•tis
par∘o•tit∘ic

par∘o•ti∘tis
par•ous
par∘o•var•i∘an
par∘o•ovar∘i∘ot∘o∘my, *n., pl.*
  -mies.
par∘o•ovar∘i∘um, *n., pl.*
  -o∘var∘i∘a.
Par•ox∘e•tine
par•ox•ysm
par•ox•ys•mal
paroxysmal noc•tur•nal dysp•
  ne∘a
par•ox•ys•mal∘ly
par•ox•ys•mic
par•rot fe∘ver
pars ner•vo∘sa
Par•si∘dol *Trademark.*
par•the•no•gen•e∘sis, *n., pl.*
  -ses.
par•the•no•ge•net∘ic
par•the•no•ge•net∘i•cal∘ly
par•the•no•gen∘ic
par•tial-birth a∘bor•tion
partial re∘sponse
par•tu•ri•en∘cy
par•tu•ri•ent
par•tu•ri•fa•cient
par•tu•ri•tion
pa•ru•lis, *n., pl.* -li•des.
par•um•bil∘i•cal
par•vi•cel∘lu•lar
par∘ovo, *n., pl.* -vos.
Par•vo•bac•te•ri∘a•ce∘ae
par•vo•vi•rus, *n., pl.* -rus∘es.
par•vule
Pas•ka•li∘um *Trademark.*
pas•si•flo∘ra in•car•na∘ta
pas•sion-flow∘er
pas•sive ex•er•cise
passive im•mu•ni∘ty
passive smok•ing
pas•tern

Pas•teur ef•fect
Pasteur treat•ment
pas•teu•rel•la, *n.*, *pl.* -las, -lae.
pas•teu•rel•lo•sis
pas•teur•oi•za•tion
pas•teur•ize, *v.*, -ized, -iz•ing.
pas•teur•iz•er
pas•til
pas•tille
patch
patch test
pa•tel•la, *n.*, *pl.* -lae, -las.
pa•tel•lar
pat•el•lec•to•my, *n.*, *pl.* -mies.
pa•tel•li•form
pat•en•cy, *n.*, *pl.* -cies.
pa•tent
patent duc•tus ar•te•ri•o•sus
patent med•i•cine
pat•ent•ly
pa•ter•ni•ty
path
pa•thet•ic
Path•o•cil *Trademark.*
path•o•don•tia
path•o•gen
path•o•gene
path•o•gen•e•sis, *n.*, *pl.* -e•ses.
path•o•ge•net•ic
path•o•gen•ic
path•o•gen•i•cal•ly
path•o•ge•nic•i•ty
pa•thog•e•ny
pa•thog•no•mon•ic
path•og•no•mon•i•cal
path•og•no•mon•i•cal•ly
pa•thog•no•my, *n.*, *pl.* -mies.
path•o•log•ic
path•o•log•i•cal

path•o•log•i•cal•ly
pa•thol•o•gist
pa•thol•o•gy, *n.*, *pl.* -gies.
path•om•e•ter
path•o•mor•pho•log•ic
path•o•mor•pho•log•i•cal
path•o•mor•phol•o•gy, *n.*, *pl.* -gies.
path•o•neu•ro•sis, *n.*, *pl.* -ses.
path•o•phys•i•o•log•ic
path•o•phys•i•o•log•i•cal
path•o•phys•i•ol•o•gy
path•o•psy•chol•o•gy
pa•tho•sis, *n.*, *pl.* -ses.
path•way
pa•tient
pat•ri•lin•e•al
pat•ou•lin
pat•ou•lous
pat•ou•lous•ly
Pav•a•bid *Trademark.*
Pavabid HP *Trademark.*
Pav•lov pouch
Pav•lo•vi•an
Pavlovian con•di•tion•ing
pav•or
Pav•u•lon *Trademark.*
Pax•il *Trademark.*
Pax•i•pam *Trademark.*
Pa•zo *Trademark.*
pec•cant
pec•tase
pec•ten, *n.*, *pl.* -tens, -ti•nes.
pec•tic
pec•tin
pec•ti•nase
pec•tin•e•al
pec•tin•es•ter•ase
pec•tin•e•ous, *n.*, *pl.* -tin•e•i.
pec•to•ral
pectoral mus•cle

pec•to•ra•lis, *n., pl.* -les.
pec•to•ral•ly
pec•to•ril•o•quy
pec•tus, *n., pl.* -to•ra.
pectus caroi•na•tum
pectus ex•ca•va•tum
ped○al
Ped•a•meth *Trademark.*
ped•er•ast
ped•er•as•tic
ped•er•as•ti•cal•ly
ped•er•as○ty
Ped○i-Pro *Trademark.*
Pe•di•a•Care *Trademark.*
Pe•di•a•cof *Trademark.*
Pe•di•a•flor *Trademark.*
Pe•di•a•lyte *Trademark.*
Pe•di•a•my•cin *Trademark.*
Pe•di•a•pred *Trademark.*
Pe•di•a•Pro•fen *Trademark.*
Pe•di•a•Sure *Trademark.*
pe•di•at•ric
pe•di•a•tri•cian
pe•di•at•rics
pe•di•at•rist
Pe•di•a•zole *Trademark.*
Ped○i-Bo○ro *Trademark.*
ped○i•cel
ped○i•cel•late
ped○i•cel•lat○ed
ped○i•cle
ped○i•cled
pe•dic○u•lar
pe•dic○u•late
pe•dic○u•lat○ed
pe•dic○u•la•tion
pe•dic○u•li•cid○al
pe•dic○u•li•cide
Pe•dic○u•loi•des ven•tri•co•sus
pe•dic○u•lo•sis, *n., pl.* -ses.
pe•dic○u•lous

pe•dic○u•lus, *n., pl.* -dic•u○li, -dic○u•lus.
ped○i•cure
Ped○i-Dri *Trademark.*
Pe•di•Ot○ic *Trademark.*
pe○do•don○tia
pe○do•don•tic
pe○do•don•tics
pe○do•don•tist
pe○do•log○ic
pe○do•log○i•cal
pe•dol○o•gist
pe•dol○o○gy
pe•dom•e○ter
pe•do•phile
pe•do•phil○i○a
pe•do•phil○i○ac
pe•do•phil○ic
pe•dun•cle
pe•dun•cled
pe•dun•cu•lar
pe•dun•cu•late
pe•dun•cu•lat○ed
pe•dun•cu•la•tion
Ped•vaxHIB *Trademark.*
Peg○a•none *Trademark.*
pel•lag○ra
pel•lag•ra•gen○ic
pel•lag•ric
pel•la•grin
pel•la•groid
pel•la•grose
pel•lag•rous
pel•li•cle
pel•lic○u•lar
pel•mat○o○gram
pe○loid
pe•lo•ther○a○py
pel•vic
pelvic gir•dle
pelvic in•flam•ma•tor○y dis•ease

pel○vi•graph
pel•vim•e○ter
pel•vim•e○try
pel•vis, *n., pl.* -vis○es, -ves.
pel○vi•sa○cral
pel○vi•scope
pem○o•line
pem•phi•goid
pem•phi•gus, *n., pl.* -phi•gus○es, -phi○gi.
Pen○a•par-VK *Trademark.*
Pen•bri•tin-S *Trademark.*
Pen•e•cort *Trademark.*
pen•e○trance
Pen○e•trex *Trademark.*
pe•ni○al
pen○i•cil•la•mine
pen○i•cil•lin
pen○i•cil•li•nase
pen○i•cil•lin○ic
Pen○i•cil•lin VK *Trademark.*
pen○i•cil•li•o•sis, *n., pl.* -ses.
pen○i•cil•li○um, *n., pl.* -li○a.
pen○i•cil•lo○ic
pen○i•cil•lus, *n., pl.* -cil○li.
pe•nile
pe○nis, *n., pl.* pe•nis○es, pe○nes.
pen•nate
pen•nat○ed
pen•ny•weight
pen•ta•chlo•ro•phe•nol
pen○ta•dac○tyl
pen○ta•dac•tyl•ate
pen○ta•dac•tyl•ism
pen•tae•ryth•ri•tol tet•ra•ni○trate
pen○ta•gas•trin
pen•tal•o○gy
Pen•tam 300 *Trademark.*
pen•tam○i•dine
pen•tane

pen•ta•ploid
pen•ta•ploi○dy
Pen○ta•span *Trademark.*
pen•taz○o○cine
Pen•thrane *Trademark.*
Pen•tids *Trademark.*
pen•to•bar•bi•tal
pen○to•bar•bi•tone
pen•tose
pen•to•side
pen•to•su•ri○a
Pen•to•thal *Trademark.*
Pen•tox○i•fyl•line
Pen•trax *Trademark.*
pen•tyl•ene•tet•ra•zol
pe•○o•til•lo•ma•nia
pep pill
Pep•cid *Trademark.*
pep•si•gogue
pep•sin
pep•sin○o•gen
Pep•tav•lon *Trademark.*
pep•tic
peptic ul○cer
pep•ti•dase
pep•tide
peptide bond
pep•ti•do•gly•can
Pep•to-Bis•mol *Trademark.*
pep•tone
pep•ton○ic
pep•to•ni•za•tion
pep•to•nize, *v.,* -nized, -niz•ing.
pep•to•noid
pep•to•nu•ri○a
per an○um
per os
per pri○mam
per rec○tum
per○a•cet○ic
per•a•cute

per•cep•tion
Per•co•cet *Trademark.*
Per•co•dan *Trademark.*
Percodan-Dem○i *Trademark.*
Per•co•ge•sic *Trademark.*
per•co•la•tion
per•co•la•tor
Per•cor•ten *Trademark.*
per•cuss
per•cus•sion
per•cus•sion○al
per•cus•sor
per•cu•ta•ne•ous
percutaneous trans•lu•mi•nal cor○o•nar•y
per•cu•ta•ne•ous○ly
Per•di○um *Trademark.*
per•fec•tion•ism
per•fla•tion
per•fo•rans
per•fo•rate, *v.*, -rat○ed, -rat•ing.
per•fo•ra•tion
per•fo•ra•tor
per•fri•ca•tion
per•fu•sate
per•fuse, *v.*, -fused, -fus•ing.
per•fu•sion
perfusion im•ag•ing
per•fu•sive
Per•go•nal *Trademark.*
per○i•a•ci•nal
per○i•a•ci•nous
Per○i•ac•tin *Trademark.*
per○i•a•de•ni•tis
per○i•a•nal
per○i•an•gi○i•tis
per○i•an•gi•o•cho•li•tis
per○i•a•or•tal
per○i•a•or•tic
per○i•a•or•ti•tis
per○i•a•pi•cal

per○i•a•pi•cal○ly
per○i•ap•pen•di•citis
per○i•aq•ue•duc•tal gray ar○e○a
per○i•ar•te•ri○al
per○i•ar•te•ri•tis
per○i•arth•ri•tis
per○i•ar•tic•u•lar
per○i•au•ric○u•lar
per○i•ax•i○al
per○i•blast
per○i•blas•tic
per○i•bron•chi○al
per○i•bron•chi•tis
per○i•car•di•ec•to○my, *n., pl.* -mies.
per○i•car•di•ot○o○my, *n., pl.* -mies.
per○i•car•dit○ic
per○i•car•di•tis
pericarditis ob•lit•er•ans
per○i•car•di○um, *n., pl.* -di○a.
pericardium fi•bro•sum
pericardium se•ro•sum
per○i•car○y•on
per○i•ca•val
per○i•ce•cal
per○i•ce•ci•tis
per○i•cel•lu•lar
per○i•ce•men•tal
per○i•ce•men•ti•tis
per○i•ce•men•tum
per○i•cho•lan•gi•tis
per○i•chon•dral
per○i•chon•dri○al
per○i•chon•dri•tis
per○i•chon•dri○um, *n., pl.* -dri○a.
per○i•chord
per○i•chor•dal
Peri-Co•lace *Trademark.*
per○i•col○ic

per•i•co•li•tis
per•i•con•chal
per•i•cor•ne•al
per•i•coro•o•nal
per•i•coro•o•ni•tis
per•i•cra•ni•al
per•i•cra•ni•um, *n.*, *pl.* -ni•a.
per•i•cys•tic
per•i•cys•ti•tis
per•i•cys•ti•um, *n.*, *pl.* -ti•a.
per•i•cyte
per•i•cy•tial
per•i•den•dri•to•ic
per•i•den•tal
per•i•derm
per•i•der•mal
per•i•der•mic
per•i•des•mic
per•i•des•mi•um
Per•i•dex *Trademark.*
per•i•di•as•to•le
per•i•did•o•y•mis, *n.*, *pl.* -mi•des.
Per•i•din-C *Trademark.*
per•i•di•ver•tic•ou•li•tis
per•i•don•tia
per•i•don•tic
per•i•don•tics
per•i•don•tist
per•i•don•ti•tis
per•i•don•tol•o•gy
per•i•don•to•sis, *n.*, *pl.* -ses.
per•i•du•o•de•ni•tis
per•i•du•ral
per•i•en•ter•ic
per•i•en•ter•o•itis
per•i•en•ter•on
per•i•ep•en•dy•mal
per•i•epo•i•glot•tic
per•i•e•sopho•a•ge•al
per•i•e•sopho•a•gi•tis
per•i•fo•cal

per•i•fol•lic•ou•lar
per•i•fol•lic•ou•li•tis
per•i•gan•gli•tis
per•i•gas•tri•tis
per•i•glan•du•lar
per•i•glot•tic
per•i•glot•tis, *n.*, *pl.* -tis•es, -ti•des.
per•i•he•pat•ic
per•i•hepo•a•ti•tis
per•i•kar•y•al
per•i•kar•y•on
per•i•la•ryn•ge•al
per•i•lymph
per•i•lym•phat•ic
per•i•mas•ti•tis
pe•rim•e•ter
per•i•me•tri•tis
per•i•me•tri•um, *n.*, *pl.* -tri•a.
pe•rim•e•try, *n.*, *pl.* -e•tries.
per•i•my•e•oli•tis
per•i•my•lol•oy•sis
per•i•myo•o•si•tis
per•i•my•si•al
per•i•my•si•um, *n.*, *pl.* -si•a.
perimysium ex•ter•num
perimysium in•ter•num
per•i•na•tal
per•i•na•tal•oy
per•i•ne•al
per•i•ne•om•e•ter
per•i•neo•o•plas•ty, *n.*, *pl.* -ties.
per•i•ne•or•rha•phy, *n.*, *pl.* -phies.
per•i•ne•o•scro•tal
per•i•ne•ot•o•o•my, *n.*, *pl.* -mies.
per•i•ne•o•vag•i•nal
per•i•neph•ric
per•i•ne•phrit•ic
per•i•ne•phri•tis

per○i•neph•ri○um, *n., pl.*
  -ri○a.
per○i•ne○um, *n., pl.* -ne○a.
per○i•neu•ral
per○i•neu•ri○al
per○i•neu•ri•tis
per○i•neu•ri○um, *n., pl.* -ri○a.
per○i•nu•cle○ar
per○i•oc○u•lar
pe•ri○od
per○i•o•don•tal
periodontal dis•ease
per○i•o○don•tia
per○i•o•don•tic
per○i•o•don•tics
per○i•o•don•tist
per○i•o•don•ti•tis
per○i•o•don•ti○um, *n., pl.*
  -ti○a.
per○i•om•phal○ic
per○i•o•nych○i○a
per○i•o•nych○i○um, *n., pl.*
  -nych○i○a.
per○i•on○yx
per○i•o•o•pho•ri•tis
per○i•o•oph○o○ro•sal•pin•
  gi•tis
per○i•ople
per○i•op•lic
per○i•op•tom•e○try
per○i•o•ral
per○i•or•bit
per○i•or•bi•tal
per○i•or•bi•ti•tis
per○i•or•chi•tis
per○i•ost
per○i•os•te○al
per○i•os•te•al○y
per○i•os•te••o○ma, *n., pl.*
  -mas, -ma○ta.
per○i•os•te••o•phyte

per○i•os•te•ot○o○my, *n., pl.*
  -mies.
per○i•os•te○ous
per○i•os•te○um, *n., pl.* -te○a.
per○i•os•tit○ic
per○i•os•ti•tis
per○i•os•to○ma
per○i•os•to•sis, *n., pl.* -ses.
per○i•ot○ic
per○i•ov○u•lar
per○i•pan•cre○a•ti•tis
per○i•pap•il•lar○y
per○i•pha•ci•tis
per○i•pha•ryn•ge○al
per○iph•er○ad
pe•riph•er○al
peripheral nerv•ous sys•tem
peripheral vas•cu•lar dis•ease
peripheral vi•sion
per○iph•er•al○y
per•iph•er○a•phose
pe•riph•e○ry, *n., pl.* -ries.
per○i•phle•bi•tis
Per○i•pla•ne○ta
per○i•por•tal
per○i•proc•tal
per○i•proc•tic
per○i•proc•ti•tis
per○i•proc•tous
per○i•pros•tat○ic
per○i•pros•ta•ti•tis
per○i•py•le•phle•bi•tis
per○i•py•lor○ic
per○i•rec•tal
per○i•re○nal
per○i•rhi•nal
per○i•sal•pin•gi•tis
per○i•sal•pinx, *n., pl.* -pin•
  ges.
per○i•sig•moi•di•tis
per○i•sin○u•ous
per○i•si•nu•si•tis

per•o•i•sper•ma•ti•tis
per•o•i•splen•oic
per•o•i•sple•ni•tis
per•o•i•spon•dyl•oic
per•o•i•spon•dy•li•tis
per•o•i•stal•sis
per•o•i•stal•tic
per•o•i•stal•ti•cal•ly
per•o•i•staph•o•y•line
per•o•i•syn•o•o•vi•al
per•o•i•tec•to•o•my, *n.*, *pl.* -mies.
per•o•i•ten•din•e•oum, *n.*, *pl.*
  -din•e•a.
per•o•i•ten•di•ni•tis
peritendinitis cal•car•o•e•a
per•o•i•ten•on
per•o•i•ten•on•ti•tis
per•o•i•the•li•al
per•o•i•the•li•o•o•ma, *n.*, *pl.*
  -mas, -ma•ta.
per•o•i•the•li•oum, *n.*, *pl.* -li•a.
per•o•i•thy•roi•di•tis
Per•o•i•tin•oic *Trademark.*
pe•ri•to•o•my, *n.*, *pl.* -mies.
per•o•i•to•ne•al
per•o•i•to•ne•al•o•ly
per•o•i•to•ne•o•o•cen•te•sis, *n.*,
  pl. -ses.
per•o•i•to•ne•op•o•a•thy, *n.*, *pl.*
  -thies.
per•o•i•to•ne•o•per•o•i•car•
  di•al
per•o•i•to•ne•o•o•pex•oy, *n.*, *pl.*
  -ies.
per•o•i•to•ne•o•scope
per•o•i•to•ne•o•scop•ic
per•o•i•to•ne•os•co•pist
per•o•i•to•ne•os•co•opy, *n.*, *pl.*
  -pies.
per•o•i•to•ne•ot•o•o•my, *n.*, *pl.*
  -mies.

per•o•i•to•ne•oum, *n.*, *pl.* -ne•
  ums, -ne•o•a.
peritoneum pa•ri•e•ta•o•le
peritoneum vis•ce•ra•o•le
per•o•i•to•nit•al
per•o•i•to•nit•oic
per•o•i•to•ni•tis
per•o•i•to•nize, *v.*, -nized, -niz•
  ing.
per•o•i•ton•sil•lar
per•o•i•ton•sil•li•tis
per•o•i•tra•che•al
Per•o•i•trate *Trademark.*
Peritrate SA *Trademark.*
per•o•i•typh•lic
per•o•i•typh•li•tis
per•o•i•um•bil•o•i•cal
per•o•i•un•gu•al
per•o•i•u•re•ter•al
per•o•i•u•re•ter•oic
per•o•i•u•re•te•ri•tis
per•o•i•u•re•thral
per•o•i•u•ore•thri•tis
per•o•i•u•ter•ine
per•o•i•u•vu•lar
per•o•i•vas•cu•lar
per•o•i•vas•cu•li•tis
per•o•i•ve•nous
per•o•i•ver•te•bral
per•o•i•ves•o•i•cal
per•o•i•vis•cer•al
per•o•i•vis•ce•ri•tis
per•o•i•vi•tel•line
per•lèche
per•lin•gual
per•lin•gual•ly
Per•ma•pen *Trademark.*
Per•max *Trademark.*
per•me•ase
per•mis•sive
Per•mi•til *Trademark.*
per•ni•cious

pernicious a○ne•mi○a
per•ni○o, *n., pl.* -ni○o•nes.
per○o•bra•chi○us
per○o•chi•rus
per○o•cor•mus
per○o•dac•ty•lus, *n., pl.*
  -ty○li.
per○o•me•li○a
pe•rom•e○lus, *n., pl.* -e○li.
per○o•ne○al
per○o•ne○us, *n., pl.* -ne○i.
per○o•pus
per○o•ral
per○o•ral○ly
pe•ro○sis
pe•ro•so○mus, *n., pl.* -so○mi,
  -so○mus•es.
per○o•splanch•ni○a
per•os•se•ous
per•ot○ic
per•ox○i•dase
per•ox○i•so○mal
per•ox○i•some
per•ox○y•a•ce•tic
per•phen○a•zine
per•rec•tal
per•rec•tally
Per○sa-Gel *Trademark.*
Per•san•tine *Trademark.*
per•so○na, *n., pl.* -nae, -nas.
per•son•al○i○ty, *n., pl.* -ties.
personality dis•or•der
per•spi•ra•tion
per•spi•ra•to○ry
per•spire, *v.,* -spired, -spir•ing.
Per•to•frane *Trademark.*
per•tus•sal
per•tus•sis
per•ver•sion
per•vert○ed
per•vi•gil○i○um
pes, *n., pl.* pe○des.

pes•sa○ry, *n., pl.* -ries.
pes•ti•cid○al
pes•ti•cide
pes•tif•er•ous
pes•tif•er•ous○ly
pes•ti•lence
pes•ti•lent
pes•ti•len•tial
pes•ti•len•tial○ly
pes•tis
pes•tle
PET scan
PET scan•ner
pe•te•chi○a, *n., pl.* -chi○ae.
pe•te•chi○al
pe•te•chi•ate
pe•te•chi•a•tion
peth○i•dine
pet○i•o•late
pet○i•o•lat○ed
pet○i•ole
pe•ti○o•lus, *n., pl.* -ti○o○li.
petiolus ep○i•glot○i•dis
pe•tit mal
Pe○tri dish
pet•ri•fac•tion
pet•ri•fac•tive
pet•ri•fi•ca•tion
pet•ri○fy, *v.,* -fied, -fy•ing.
pet•ris•sage
pet○ro•la•tum
pe•tro•le○um
pet○ro•mas•toid
pet○ro-oc•cip○i○tal
pet○ro•pha•ryn•ge○us
pe•tro○sa, *n., pl.* -sae.
pet○ro•sal
pet○ro•si•tis
pet○ro•sphe•noid
pet○ro•squa•mous
pet○ro•tym•pan○ic

pe•trox•o•lin
Pey•e•ri○an gland
Pey•er's gland
Peyer's patch
pe•yo○te, *n., pl.* -tes.
pey•otl
Pey•ro•nie's dis•ease
Pfeif•fer's ba•cil•lus
Pfeiffer's in•flu•en○za
Pfi•zer•pen *Trademark.*
Pfizerpen-AS *Trademark.*
pH
phac○o•e•mul•si•fi•ca•tion
pha•co•er○y•sis
pha•col○y•sis
pha•com•e○ter
phac○o•scle•ro•sis, *n., pl.*
  -ses.
phage
phag○o•cyte
phag○o•cyt○ic
phagocytic in○dex
phag○o•cy•tize, *v.,* -tized,
  -tiz•ing.
phag○o•cy•tol○y•sis
pha○go•cy•tose, *v.,* -tosed,
  -tos•ing.
phag○o•cy•to•sis
phag○o•cy•tot○ic
pha○go•cy•toze, *v.,* -tozed,
  -toz•ing.
pha○go•dy•na•mom•e○ter
pha•gol○y•sis
pha○go•lyt○ic
pha○go•ma•ni○a
pha○go•some
phal○a•cro•sis
pha•lange
pha•lan•ge○al
phal•an•gec•to○my, *n., pl.*
  -mies.
pha•lan•gette

pha•lanx, *n., pl.* -lanx○es,
  -lan•ges.
phal•lic
phal•li•cal○ly
phal•loid
phal•loi•din
phal•loi•dine
phal•lus, *n., pl.* phal○li, phal•
  lus○es.
pha•ner○o•gam
Phan○e•ro•ga•mi○a
phan○e•ro•ge•net○ic
phan○e•ro•gen○ic
phan○e•ro•ma•ni○a
phan•er○o•sis
phan○e•ro•zo○ic
phan○e•ro•zo•ite
phan○e•ro•zo•it○ic
phan•tasm
phan•tas•ma•go•ri○a, *n., pl.*
  -ri○as.
phan•tas•ma•gor○ic
phan•tas•ma•gor○i•cal
phan•tast
phan•ta○sy
phan•tom
phantom limb pain
phar○ma•cal
phar○ma•ceu•tic
phar○ma•ceu•ti•cal
phar○ma•ceu•ti•cal○ly
phar○ma•ceu•tics
phar○ma•ceu•tist
phar○ma•cist
phar○ma•co•dy•nam○ic
phar○ma•co•dy•nam•i•cal○ly
phar○ma•co•dy•nam○ics
phar○ma•co•ge•net○ic
phar○ma•co•ge•net○ics
phar○ma•cog•no•sist
phar○ma•cog•nos•tic
phar○ma•cog•nos•ti•cal

phar·ma·cog·no·sy, *n.*, *pl.*
-sies.
phar·ma○co·ki·net·ics
phar·ma○co·log○ic
phar·ma○co·log○i·cal
phar·ma○co·log○i·cal○ly
phar·ma·col○o·gist
phar·ma·col○o·gy
phar·ma○co·pe·di○a
phar·ma○co·pe·dic
phar·ma○co·pe·dics
phar·ma○co·pe○ia
phar·ma○co·poe○ia
phar·ma○co·poe·ial
phar·ma○co·poe○ic
phar·ma○co·poe○ist
phar·ma○co·ther○a·peu·tic
phar·ma○co·ther○a·peu·tical
phar·ma○co·ther○a·peu·tics
phar·ma○co·ther○a○py, *n.*, *pl.*
-pies.
Phar·ma·Creme *Trademark.*
phar·ma○cy, *n.*, *pl.* -cies.
pha·ryn·gal
pha·ryn·ge○al
phar·yn·gec·to○my, *n.*, *pl.*
-mies.
phar·yn·gis·mus, *n.*, *pl.*
-gis○mi.
phar·yn·gi·tis
pharyngitis sic·ca
pha○ryn·go·cele
pha○ryn○go·ep○i·glot·tic
pha○ryn○go·e·soph○a·ge○al
pha○ryn○go·glos·sus, *n.*, *pl.*
-glos○si.
pha○ryn○go·lar·yn·gi·tis
pha○ryn○go·log○i·cal
pha·ryn·gol○o○gy
phar·yn·go·na·sal
pha○ryn○go·pal○a·tine
pha○ryn○go·rhi·ni·tis

pha○ryn○go·scope
pha○ryn○go·scop○ic
phar·yn·gos·co·pist
phar·yn·gos·co○py
pha○ryn○go·spasm
phar·yn·got○o○my, *n.*, *pl.*
-mies.
phar·yn·go·ton·sil·li·tis
phar·ynx, *n.*, *pl.* pha·ryn·ges,
phar·ynx○es.
phase-con·trast
pha·se○o·lin
Phas·mid○i○a
phas·mid·i○an
Pha·zyme *Trademark.*
phen○a·caine
Phen○a·Cal *Trademark.*
phen·ac○e○tin
phen○a·kis·to·scope
phen·an·threne
Phen○a·phen *Trademark.*
phe·nate
phe·naz○o·cine
phen○a·zone
phen·cy·cli·dine
phene
phen·el·zine
Phen·er·gan *Trademark.*
Phenergan-D *Trademark.*
Phenergan VC *Trademark.*
phe·neth○i·cil·lin
phe·net○i·dine
phen·for·min
phen·met·ra·zine
phe·no·bar·bi·tal
phe·no·bar·bi·tone
phe·no·cain
phe○no·coll
phe○no·cop○y, *n.*, *pl.* -ies.
phe·nol
phe○no·lase

phe•no•late, *v.*, -lat○ed, -lat•ing.
phe•nol○ic
phe○no•log○ic
phe○no•log○i•cal
phe○no•log○i•cal○ly
phe•nol○o•gist
phe•nol○o•gy
phe•nol•phthal•e○in
phe•nol•sul•fone•phthal•e○in
phe•nol•sul•fon•phthal•e○in
phe○no•thi○a•zine
phe○no•type
phe○no•typ○ic
phe○no•typ○i•cal
phe○no•typ○i•cal○ly
phe•nox○y
phe•nox○y•meth•yl•pen○i•cil•lin
phen•ter•mine
phen•tol○a•mine
Phen○u•rone
phen○yl
phen○yl•a•ce•tic
phen○yl•al○a•nine
phen○yl•bu•ta•zone
phen○yl•ene•di•a•mine
phen○yl•eph•rine
phen○yl•hy•dra•zine
phe•nyl○ic
phen○yl•ke•to•nu•ri○a
phen○yl•ke•to•nu•ric
phen○yl•mer•cu•ric
phen○yl•pro•pan•ol○a•mine
phen○yl•py•ru•vic
phen○yl•thi○o•car•ba•mide
phen○yl•thi•o•u•re○a
phen○y•to○in
phe○o•chrome
phe○o•chro•mo•blast

phe○o•chro•mo•blas•to•ma, *n., pl.* -mas, -ma○ta.
phe○o•chro•mo•cyte
phe○o•chro•mo•cy•to•blast
phe○o•chro•mo•cy•to•ma, *n., pl.* -mas, -ma○ta.
phe•ren•ta○sin
phi phe•nom•e○non
phi○al
Phi•a•loph○o•ra
phi•lo•pro•gen○i•tive
phil•ter
phil•tre
phil•trum, *n., pl.* -tra.
phi○mosed
phi•mo•sis
phi•mot○ic
pHi•so•Derm *Trademark.*
pHi•so•Hex *Trademark.*
phle•bec•to○my, *n., pl.* -mies.
phle•bit○ic
phle•bi•tis
phle•boc•ly•sis
phleb○o•gram
phleb○o•graph○ic
phle•bog•ra•phy, *n , pl.* -phies.
phleb•oid
phle•boi•dal
phleb○o•lith
phleb○o•li•thi•a•sis
phle•bol○o•gist
phle•bol○o•gy
phleb○o•scle•ro•sis, *n., pl.* -ses.
phleb○o•scle•rot○ic
phleb○o•throm•bo•sis
phleb○o•tom○ic
phleb○o•tom○i•cal
phleb○o•tom○i•cal○ly
phle•bot○o•mist

phle•bot○o•mize, v., -mized,
  -miz○ing.
phle•bot○o•mus, n., pl.
  -bot○o•mi, -bot○o•mus○es.
phle•bot○o•my, n., pl. -mies.
phlegm
phleg•ma•sia
phlegmasia al○ba do•lens
phleg•mat○ic
phleg•mat○i•cal
phleg•mat○i•cal○ly
phleg•mon
phleg•mon○ic
phleg•mo•nous
phleg•mo•nous○ly
phlo•gis○tic
phlo•go•ge•net○ic
phlo•go•gen○ic
phlo•gog○e○nous
phlo•re•tin
phlo•rhi•zin
phlo•rid•zin
phlo•ri•zin
phlor○o○o•glu•cin
phlor○o○o•glu•ci•nol
phlor•rhi•zin
phlox•ine
phlyc•te○na, n., pl. -nae.
phlyc•te•noid
phlyc•ten○u○u•la, n., pl. -lae.
phlyc•ten○u•lar
phlyc•ten•ule
pho•bi○a, n., pl. -bi•as.
pho•bi○ac
pho•bic
pho•bism
pho•co•me•li○a
pho•co•me•lic
pho•com••e○lus, n., pl. -e○li.
pho•ko•me•li○a
pho•nal
pho•nas•the•ni○a

pho•nate, v., -nat○ed, -nat•
  ing.
pho•na•tion
pho•na•to○ry
phon•au•to•graph
phon•au•to•graph○ic
phon•au•to•graph○i•cal○ly
phon•en•do•scope
pho•ni•at○ric
pho•nism
pho○no•car•di○o•gram
pho○no•car•di○o•graph
pho○no•car•di○o•graph○ic
pho○no•car•di○og•ra•phy, n.,
  pl. -phies.
pho○no•gram
pho○no•gram○ic
pho○no•gram○i•cal○ly
pho○no•gram•mic
pho○no•gram•mi•cal○ly
pho○no•log○ic
pho○no•log○i•cal
pho○no•log○i•cal○ly
pho•nol○o○gist
pho•nol○o○gy
pho○no•ma•ni○a
pho•nom•e○ter
pho○no•met•ric
pho•nom•e○try
pho○no•pho•bi○a
pho○no•phore
pho○no•pho•to•gram
pho○no•pho•to•graph
pho○no•pho•tog•ra•phy, n.,
  pl. -phies.
pho○no•re•cep•tion
pho○no•re•cep•tor
pho○no•scope
phor•ri○a
Phor•mi○a
pho•rom•e○ter
pho•ro•met•ric

pho•rom•e•try
Phos•Chol *Trademark.*
phose
Phos-Ex *Trademark.*
Phos-Flur *Trademark.*
phos•gene
phos•gen∘ic
phos•pha•gen
pHos-pHaid *Trademark.*
phos•pha•tase
phos•pha•tide
phos•pha•te•mi∘a
phos•phat∘ic
phos•pha•tide
phos•pha•tu•ri∘a
phos•pha•tu•ric
phos•phene
phos•phide
phos•phine
phos•phite
phos∘pho•ar•gi•nine
phos∘pho•cre•a∘tine
phos∘pho•di•es•ter•ase
phos∘pho•e•nol•py•ru•vate
phos∘pho•e•nol•py•ru•vic
phos∘pho•fruc•to•ki•nase
phos∘pho•glu•co•mu•tase
phos∘pho•glyc•er•al•de•hyde
phos∘pho•glyc•er•ate
phos∘pho•gly•cer∘ic
phos∘pho•ki•nase
Phos∘pho•line I∘o•dide *Trademark.*
phos∘pho•li•pase
phos•pho•lip∘id
phospholipid bi•lay∘er
phos∘pho•mo•lyb•dic
phos∘pho•mon•o•es•ter•ase
phos∘pho•ne•cro•sis
phos∘pho•ni•um
phos∘pho•pro•tein

phos∘pho•py•ru•vate
phos∘pho•py•ru•vic
phos•phor
phos•pho•rate, *v.,* -rat∘ed, -rat•ing.
phos•phore
phos•phor∘ic
phos•phor∘i•cum ac∘i•dum
phos•pho•rism
phos•pho•rize, *v.,* -rized, -riz•ing.
phos•phor•ol∘y•sis
phos•phor∘o•lyt∘ic
phos•pho•rous
phos•pho•rus
phos∘pho•ryl
phos•pho•ryl•ase
phos•pho•ry•late, *v.,* -lat∘ed, -lat•ing.
phos•pho•ryl∘a•tion
phos•pho•ryl∘a•tive
phos•pho•tung•state
phos•pho•tung•stic
phos•vi•tin
pho•tal•gia
phot∘ic
pho•tism
pho∘to•ag•ing
pho∘to•al•ler∘gy, *n., pl.* -gies.
pho∘to•bi•o•log∘ic
pho∘to•bi•o•log∘i•cal
pho∘to•bi•ol∘o∘gist
pho∘to•bi•ol∘o∘gy
pho∘to•bi•ot∘ic
pho∘to•ca•tal∘y•sis *pl.* -ses.
pho∘to•cat∘a•lyst
pho∘to•cat∘a•lyt∘ic
pho∘to•chem∘i•cal
pho∘to•chem∘i•cal∘ly
pho∘to•chem•ist
pho∘to•chem•is•try

pho‧to‧co‧ag‧u‧late, *v.*,
  -lat‧ed, -lat‧ing.
pho‧to‧co‧ag‧u‧la‧tion
pho‧to‧co‧ag‧u‧la‧tive
pho‧to‧co‧ag‧u‧la‧tor
pho‧to‧de‧com‧po‧si‧tion
pho‧to‧dy‧nam‧ic
pho‧to‧dy‧nam‧i‧cal‧ly
pho‧to‧e‧lec‧tric
pho‧to‧e‧lec‧tric‧i‧ty
pho‧to‧e‧lec‧tron
pho‧to‧fluo‧ro‧gram
pho‧to‧fluo‧ro‧graph‧ic
pho‧to‧fluo‧rog‧ra‧phy
pho‧to‧fluo‧ros‧co‧py, *n., pl.*
  -pies.
pho‧to‧gene
pho‧to‧gen‧ic
pho‧to‧gen‧i‧cal‧ly
pho‧to‧in‧duced
pho‧to‧in‧duc‧tion
pho‧to‧in‧duc‧tive
pho‧to‧ki‧ne‧sis
pho‧to‧ki‧net‧ic
pho‧to‧ky‧mo‧graph
pho‧to‧ky‧mo‧graph‧ic
pho‧to‧lu‧mi‧nes‧cence
pho‧to‧lu‧mi‧nes‧cent
pho‧tol‧y‧sis
pho‧to‧lyt‧ic
pho‧to‧lyt‧i‧cal‧ly
pho‧to‧lyze, *v.*, -lyzed, -lyz‧
  ing.
pho‧to‧mac‧ro‧graph
pho‧to‧mac‧ro‧graph‧ic
pho‧to‧ma‧crog‧ra‧phy
pho‧tom‧e‧ter
pho‧to‧met‧ric
pho‧to‧met‧ri‧cal
pho‧to‧met‧ri‧cal‧ly
pho‧tom‧e‧try
pho‧to‧mi‧cro‧gram

pho‧to‧mi‧cro‧graph
pho‧to‧mi‧crog‧ra‧pher
pho‧to‧mi‧cro‧graph‧ic
pho‧to‧mi‧cro‧graph‧ical
pho‧to‧mi‧cro‧graph‧i‧
  cal‧ly
pho‧to‧mi‧crog‧ra‧phy
pho‧ton
pho‧to‧neg‧a‧tive
pho‧ton‧o‧o‧sus, *n., pl.*
  -ton‧o‧o‧si.
pho‧to‧path‧ic
pho‧top‧a‧thy
pho‧to‧pe‧ri‧od
pho‧to‧pe‧ri‧od‧ic
pho‧to‧pe‧ri‧od‧i‧cal
pho‧to‧pe‧ri‧od‧i‧cal‧ly
pho‧to‧pe‧ri‧od‧ism
pho‧to‧phile
pho‧to‧phil‧ic
pho‧toph‧i‧lous
pho‧to‧pho‧bi‧a
pho‧to‧pho‧bic
pho‧to‧phore
pho‧to‧pho‧re‧sis
pho‧to‧phos‧pho‧ryl‧a‧tion
pho‧toph‧thal‧mi‧a
pho‧to‧pi‧a
pho‧to‧pic
Pho‧to‧plex *Trademark.*
pho‧to‧pos‧i‧tive
pho‧top‧si‧a
pho‧top‧tom‧e‧ter
pho‧to‧re‧ac‧tion
pho‧to‧re‧ac‧ti‧vat‧ing
pho‧to‧re‧ac‧ti‧va‧tion
pho‧to‧re‧cep‧tion
pho‧to‧re‧cep‧tive
pho‧to‧re‧cep‧tor
pho‧to‧re‧duc‧tion
pho‧to‧scan, *v.*, -scanned,
  -scan‧ning.

pho○to•scope
pho○to•sen•si•tive
pho○to•sen•si•tiv○i•ty
pho○to•sen•si•ti•za•tion
pho○to•sen•si•tize, *v.*, -tized,
-tiz○ing.
pho○to•sen•si•tiz○er
pho○to•shock
pho○to•sta•bil○i○ty
pho○to•sta•ble
pho○to•syn•the•sis, *n.*, *pl.*
-ses.
pho○to•syn•the•size, *v.*,
-sized, -siz•ing.
pho○to•syn•thet○ic
pho○to•syn•thet○i•cal○ly
pho○to•tac•tic
pho○to•tac•ti•cal○ly
pho○to•tax○is, *n.*, *pl.* -tax○es.
pho○to•tax○y, *n.*, *pl.* -tax•ies.
pho○to•ther○a○py, *n.*, *pl.*
-pies.
pho○to•ther•mal
pho○to•ther•mic
pho•tot○i•mer
pho•tot○o•nus
pho○to•tox○in
pho○to•troph○ic
pho○to•trop○ic
pho○to•trop○i•cal○ly
pho○to•tro•pism
phrag•mo•plast
phren
phren•as•the•ni○a
phren•em•phrax○is, *n.*, *pl.*
-phrax○es.
phre•net○ic
phre•net○i•cal
phren○ic
phren○i•cec•to○my, *n.*, *pl.*
-mies.
phren○i•cla•si○a, *n.*, *pl.* -si○as.

phren○i•cla•sis
phren○i•cot○o○my, *n.*, *pl.*
-mies.
Phren○i•lin *Trademark.*
Phrenilin Forte *Trademark.*
phren○o•car•di○a
phren○o•car•di○ac
phren○o•gas•tric
phren○o•glot•tic
phren○o•log○ic
phren○o•log○i•cal
phren○o•log○i•cal○ly
phre•nol○o○gist
phre•nol○o○gy
phren○o•ple•gia
phren○o•sin
phren○o•sin○ic
phren○o•sple•nic
phren○sy
phryn○in
phryn○o•der○ma
phthal•ate
phthal•e○in
phthal○ic
phthal○in
phthal○yl•sul•fa•thi•a•zole
phthi•o•col
phthi○o○ic
phthi○ri•a•sis
Phthir•i○us
phthis○ic
phthis○i•cal
phthis○i•cky
phthis○i•ol○o○gist
phthis○i•ol○o○gy
phthis○i○o•ther○a○py, *n.*, *pl.*
-pies.
phthi•sis
phthisis bul○bi
phthisis cor•ne○ae
phy○co•bil○in
phy○co•chrom

phy○co•chrome
phy○co•cy○an
phy○co•cy○a•nin
phy○co•e•ryth•rin
phy○co•my•cete
Phy○co•my•ce•tes
phy○co•my•ce•tous
phy○go•ga•lac•tic
Phyl○lo•con•tin
phyl○lo•por•phy•rin
phyl○lo•pyr•role
phyl•lo•qui•none
phy•log○e•onist
phy•log○e•ony
phy•lum, n., pl. phy○la.
phy○ma, n., pl. -mas, -ma○ta.
phy•mat○ic
phy•mat○or•rhy•sin
phy•ma•to•sis
phy•sa•lis
Phy•sa•lop•ter○a
phys○i•an•thro○py
phys○i•at•ric
phys○i•at•ri○cal
phys○i•at•rics
phy•si○a•trist
phy•si○a•try
phys○ic
phys○i•cal
physical ex○am○i•na•tion
physical med○i•cine
physical ther○a•pist
physical ther○a○py
phys○i•cal○i○ty, n., pl. -ties.
phy•si•cian
physician as•sis•tant
phy•si•cian○ly
phy•si•cian's di•rec•tive
phys○i•cist
phys○i•cky
phys○i•co•chem○i•cal

phys○i•co•chem○i•cal○ly
phys•ics
phys○i○o•gen○ic
phys○i•og•no•mic
phys○i•og•nom○i•cal
phys○i•og•nom○i•cal○ly
phys○i•og•no•mist
phys○i•og•no○my, n., pl.
  -mies.
phys○i○o•log○ic
phys○i○o•log○i•cal
physiological psy•chol○o○gy
phys○i○o•log○i•cal○ly
phys•i•ol○o•gist
phys○i•ol○o○gy
phys○i○o•path○o○log○ic
phys○i○o•path○o○log○i•cal
phys○i○o•pa•thol○o○gy
phys○i○o•psy•chic
phys○i○o•ther○a•peu•tic
phys○i○o•ther○a•peu•tics
phys○i○o•ther○a•pist
phys○i○o•ther○a○py, n., pl.
  -pies.
phy•sique
Phy○so•ceph○a•lus
phy○so•stig•ma
phy•so•stig•mine
phy•tal•bu•mose
phy•tase
phy○to•a•lex○in
phy○to•be•zoar
phy○to•chem○i•cal
phy○to•chem○i•cal○ly
phy○to•chem•ist
phy○to•chem•is•try
phy○to•chrome
Phy○to•flag○el•la○ta
phy○to•flu•ene
phy○to•gen•e○sis, n., pl.
  -e○ses.
phy○to•gen○ic

phy•to•hae•mag•glu•ti•nin
phy○to•he•mag•glu•ti•nin
phy○to•hor•mone
phy•toid
phy•tol
Phy○to•mas•ti•gi•na
phy○to•na•di•one
phy○to•par○a•site
phy○to•path○o•gen
phy○to•path○o•gen○ic
phy○to•path○o•log○ic
phy○to•path○o•log○i•cal
phy○to•pa•thol○o○gist
phy○to•pa•thol○o○gy
phy•toph○a•gous
phy•to•phar•ma•col○o○gy
phy•to•pneu•mo•co•ni•o•sis
phy•to•sis, *n.*, *pl.* -ses.
phy○to•ste•rol
phy○to•tox○ic
phy○to•tox•ic○i○ty, *n.*, *pl.*
phy○to•tox○in
phy•to•tron
phy•tyl
pi○a
pia ma○ter
pia mater en•ceph○a•li
pia mater spi•na•lis
pia-a•rach•noid
pia-a•rach•noi•dal
pi○al
pi○a•ma•tral
pi○an
pi•a•rach•noid
pi•block○to
pi•blok○to
pi○ca
pi•ceous
pi•chi
Pick's dis•ease
Pick•wick•i○an syn•drome

pic•nom•e○ter
pi•co•li•nate
pi•cor•na•vi•rus, *n.*, *pl.*
  -rus○es.
pic•rate
pic•ric
pic•ri•cum ac○i•dum
pic•ro•car•mine
pic•ro•po•do•phyl•lin
pic•ro•rhi○za
pic•ro•tin
pic•ro•tox○ic
pic•ro•tox○in
pic•ro•tox○i•nin
pic•ryl
pic•to•graph
pie•bald
pie•bald•ism
pie•dra
pi•e○zo•chem•is•try
pi•e•zom•e○ter
pi•e•zo•met•ric
pi•geon breast
pigeon-toed
pig•ment
pig•men•ta•tion
pig•men•to•phage
Pig•net in•dex
pig•weed
pi○lar
pi•la○ry
pi•las•ter
pi•las•tered
pile
pil•e•ous
piles
pi•le○us, *n.*, *pl.* pi•le○i.
pi○li an•nu•la○ti
pili in•car•na○ti
pili mul•ti•gem○i•ni
pili tac•ti•les
pili tor○ti

pi•li•be•zoar
pi•li•gan
pill
pil•lar
pil•let
pil•li∘on
pil•lu•lar
pil•lute
pi•lo•car•pi•dine
pi•lo•car•pine
pi•lo•car•pus
pi•lo•cys•tic
pi•lo•e∘rec•tion
pi•lo•ma•trix∘o∘ma, *n., pl.*
 -mas, -ma∘ta.
pi•lo•mo•tor
pi•lo•ni•dal
Pi•lo∘pine HS *Trademark.*
pi•lose
pi•lo•se•ba•ceous
pi•lo•sis
pi•los∘i∘ty
pil∘u•lar
pil•ule
pi•lus, *n., pl.* pi∘li.
pilus cu•nic∘u•la•tus
pilus in∘car•na•tus
Pi∘ma *Trademark.*
pi•me•lic
pim•ple, *v.,* -pled, -pling.
pim•ply
pin∘a•co•lone
pin•bone
pin•cers
pinched nerve
pin•e∘al
pineal gland
pin∘e∘a•lo∘ma, *n., pl.* -mas,
 -ma∘ta.
pin•ene
pin•guec∘u∘la, *n., pl.* -lae.
pink•eye

pin∘na, *n., pl.* -nae, -nas.
pin•nal
pin∘o•cy•to•sis
pin∘o•cy•tot∘ic
pin∘o•cy•tot∘i∘cal∘ly
pin∘ta
pin•tid
pin•to
pin•worm
pi•per∘o•a•zine
pi•per∘i•dine
pi•per•ine
pi•per∘o•caine
pi•per∘o•nal
pi•per•ox∘an
pi∘pet
pi•pette
Pip•ra•cil *Trademark.*
pip•sis∘se∘wa
pir∘i•form
pir∘i•for∘mis
Pir∘o•plas∘ma
pir∘o•plas∘mic
pir∘o•plas∘mo∘sis, *n., pl.* -ses.
pi•rox∘i•cam
Pir•quet re∘ac•tion
Pirquet test
pis•ci•cid∘al
pis•ci•cide
pis∘i•form
pitch•blende
pith∘e•coid
Pit∘o•cin *Trademark.*
Pi•tres•sin *Trademark.*
pit•ted ker∘a•tol∘y•sis
pi•tu•i•cyte
pi•tu•i∘ta, *n., pl.* -tae.
pi•tu•i•tar∘i∘um an•te•ri∘us
pituitarium pos•te•ri∘us
pituitarium to•tum
pi•tu∘i•tar∘y, *n., pl.* -ies.

pituitary gland
pit•o•y•ri•as○ic
pit•o•y•ri•a•sis
piv○ot
pla•ce○bo, *n., pl.* -bos.
placebo ef•fect
pla•cen○ta, *n., pl.* -tas, -tae.
placenta pre•vi•a, *n., pl.* pla•
 cen•tae pre•vi○ae.
pla•cen•tal
plac•en•ta•tion
plac○en•ti•tis
plac○en•tog•ra•phy, *n., pl.*
 -phies.
plac○en•to○ma, *n., pl.* -mas,
 -ma○ta.
Plac○i•dyl *Trademark.*
plac•ode
placque
pla•gi•o•ce•phal○ic
pla•gi•o•ceph○a•ly
plague
plan•chet
plan○i•gram
plan○i•graph
pla•nig•ra•phy, *n., pl.* -phies.
pla•nim•e○ter
plan○i•met•ric
pla•no•con•cave
pla•no•con•vex
Pla•nor•bis
plan•ta○go
plan•tar
plantar fas•ci○a
plantar fas•ci○i•tis
plan•ta•ris, *n., pl.* -res.
plan•ta•tion
plan•ti•grade
plan•u○la, *n., pl.* -lae.
pla•num, *n., pl.* pla○na.
planum tem•po•ra○le, *n., pl.*
 pla○na tem•po•ra•li○a.

plaque
Pla•que•nil *Trademark.*
Plaquenil Sul•fate *Trademark.*
plas○ma
plasma cell
plas○ma•blast
plas○ma•cyte
plas○ma•cy•toid
plas○ma•cy•to○ma, *n., pl.*
 -mas, -ma○ta.
plas○ma•cy•to•sis
plas○ma•gel
plas•mal
plas○ma•lem○ma
plas•mal○o•gen
plas○ma•pher•e○sis
Plasma-Plex *Trademark.*
plas○ma•sol
plas○ma•some
Plas○ma•te○in *Trademark.*
plas•mat○ic
plas○ma•tor•rhex○is, *n., pl.*
 -rhex○es.
plas•mic
plas•mi•cal○ly
plas•mid
plas•min
plas•min○o•gen
plas○mo•cy•to○ma, *n., pl.*
 -mas, -ma○ta.
plas○mo•des○ma, *n., pl.*
 -ma○ta.
plas○mo•di○al
plas○mo•di•a•sis
plas○mo•di•ate
plas•mod○ic
plas•mod○i•cide
plas○mo•di•o•sis, *n., pl.* -ses.
plas○mo•di•troph○o•blast
plas○mo•di○um, *n., pl.* -di○a.
plas•mog○a○my
plas•mol○y•sis

plas•mo•lyt•ic
plas•mo•lyt•i•cal•ly
plas•mo•lyz•a•bil•i•ty, *n., pl.*
  -ties.
plas•mo•lyz•a•ble
plas•mo•lyze, *v.,* -lyzed, -lyz•
  ing.
plas•mon
plas•mone
plas•mop•ty•sis
plas•mo•so•ma
plas•mo•some
plas•mot•o•my, *n., pl.* -mies.
plas•te•in
plas•ter
plaster of Par•is
plas•tic
plastic sur•geon
plastic sur•ger•y
plas•tic•i•ty, *n., pl.* -ties.
plas•ti•ciz•er
plas•tics
plas•tid
plas•tid•i•al
plas•tin
plas•tog•a•my
plas•to•qui•none
pla•teau, *n., pl.* -teaus, -teaux.
plate•let
platelet in•hib•i•tor
pla•tin•ic
Plat•i•nol *Trademark.*
Platinol-AQ *Trademark.*
plat•i•nous
plat•i•num
plat•ode
plat•y•ce•li•an
pla•tyc•oe•lous
plat•y•ce•phal•ic
plat•y•ceph•a•lous
plat•y•ceph•a•ly
plat•yc•ne•mi•a

plat•yc•ne•mic
plat•yc•ne•my, *n., pl.* -mies.
plat•y•coe•li•an
plat•y•coe•lous
plat•y•cra•ni•a
plat•y•hel•minth, *n., pl.*
  -minths.
Plat•y•hel•min•thes
plat•y•hel•min•thic
plat•y•hi•er•oic
plat•y•mer•oic
plat•y•o•ope
plat•y•o•pi•a
plat•y•op•ic
plat•y•pel•oic
plat•y•pel•lic
plat•y•pel•loid
plat•y•pel•ly, *n., pl.* -lies.
plat•y•po•di•a
plat•y•rhine
plat•y•rhin•i•an
plat•y•rhin•ic
plat•yr•rhine
plat•yr•rhin•i•an
plat•yr•rhi•ny, *n., pl.* -nies.
pla•tys•ma, *n., pl.* -ma•ta,
  -mas.
platysma my•oi•des
plat•y•sten•ce•phal•ic
plat•ys•ten•ceph•a•ly
pleas•ure cen•ter
pleasure prin•ci•ple
plec•tri•di•um, *n., pl.* -di•a.
pledg•et
Pleg•ine *Trademark.*
plei•o•mor•phic
plei•o•trop•ic
plei•o•trop•i•cal•ly
plei•ot•ro•pism
plei•ot•ro•py
ple•o•chro•ic
ple•och•ro•ism

ple•och•ro•ous
ple•o•cy•to•sis
ple•o•mas•ti•a
ple•o•mas•tic
ple•o•ma•zia
ple•o•mor•phic
ple•o•mor•phism
ple•o•mor•phous
ple•o•nasm
ple•o•nex•i•a
ple•oph•a•gous
ples•sor
pleth•o•ora
plethora ap•o•cop•ti•ca
pleth•o•ric
ple•thys•mo•gram
ple•thys•mo•graph
ple•thys•mo•graph•ic
ple•thys•mo•graph•i•cal•ly
pleth•ys•mog•ra•phy, *n., pl.*
  -phies.
pleu•ra, *n., pl.* -rae, -ras.
pleu•ral
pleural ef•fu•sion
pleur•a•poph•y•sis, *n., pl.*
  -ses.
pleu•ri•sy
pleu•rit•ic
pleu•ri•tis
pleu•ro•cen•trum, *n., pl.*
  -trums, -tra.
pleu•ro•dont
pleu•ro•dyn•i•a
pleu•ro•gen•ic
pleu•rog•e•nous
pleu•rol•y•sis
pleu•ro•per•i•car•di•tis
pleu•ro•per•i•to•ne•al
pleu•ro•pneu•mo•nia
pleuropneumonia-like or•gan•
  ism
pleu•ro•pneu•mon•ic

pleu•ro•pul•mo•nar•y
pleu•ro•thot•o•nos
pleu•ro•vis•cer•al
plex•al
plex•oi•form
plex•im•e•ter
plex•i•met•ric
plex•im•e•try
plex•or
plex•us, *n., pl.* plex•us•es,
  plex•us.
pli•ca, *n., pl.* pli•cae.
plica po•lon•i•ca, *n., pl.* plic•
  ae po•lon•i•cae.
pli•cae a•lar•es
plicae cir•cu•lar•es
pli•cal
pli•cate
pli•cate•ly
pli•cate•ness
pli•ca•tion
ploi•dy
plom•bage
plum•ba•gin
plum•ba•go
plum•bic
plum•bism
plum•bum
Plum•mer-Vin•son syn•drome
plu•mose
plum•per
plu•rig•lan•du•lar
plu•ri•loc•u•lar
plu•rip•a•ra
plu•rip•o•tent
plu•ri•po•ten•ti•al•i•ty, *n.,*
  pl. -ties.
plu•to•ma•ni•a
plu•to•nism
plu•to•ni•um
pneu•ma
pneu•mat•ic

pneu•mat•oi•cal•ly
pneu•mat•ics
pneu•ma•tism
pneu•ma•ti•za•tion
pneu•ma•tized
pneu•mat•o•cele
pneu•mat•o•gram
pneu•mat•o•graph
pneu•ma•tom•e•ter
pneu•ma•tom•e•try
pneu•ma•to•sis, *n., pl.* -ses.
pneu•ma•tu•ri•a
pneu•mec•to•my, *n., pl.*
-mies.
pneu∘mo•ba•cil•lus, *n., pl.*
-cil∘li.
pneu∘mo•cele
pneu∘mo•cen•te•sis, *n., pl.*
-ses.
pneu∘mo•coc•cal
pneu∘mo•coc•ce•mi∘a
pneu∘mo•coc•cic
pneu∘mo•coc•cus, *n., pl.*
-coc∘ci.
pneu∘mo•con∘i∘o•sis
Pneu∘mo•cys•tis ca•rin•i∘i
pneumocystis pneu∘mo•ni•a
pneu∘mo•en•ceph∘a•li•tis
pneu∘mo•en•ceph∘a•lo•
gram
pneu∘mo•en•ceph∘a•lo•
graph
pneu∘mo•en•ceph∘a•lo•
graph∘ic
pneu∘mo•en•ceph∘a•lo•
graph∘i•cal∘ly
pneu∘mo•en•ceph∘a•log•ra•
phy, *n., pl.* -phies.
pneu∘mo•en•ter•o•i•tis
pneu∘mo•gas•tric
pneu∘mo•gram
pneu∘mo•graph

pneu∘mo•graph∘ic
pneu∘mo•graph∘oi•cal∘ly
pneu∘mog•ra•phy, *n., pl.*
-phies.
pneu∘mo•he•mo•tho•rax, *n.,*
pl. -rax∘es, -ra∘ces.
pneu∘mo•hy•dro•tho•rax, *n.,*
pl. -rax∘es, -ra∘ces.
pneu∘mo•kon∘i∘o•sis
pneu•mol∘o∘gy
pneu•mol∘y•sis
pneu∘mo•me•di•as•ti•num,
n., pl. -ti∘na.
pneu∘mo•my•co•sis, *n., pl.*
-ses.
pneu∘mo•nec•to•my, *n., pl.*
-mies.
pneu∘mo•ni•a
pneumonia al∘ba
pneu•mon∘ic
pneu∘mo•ni•tis
pneu∘mo•no•co•ni•o•sis
pneu∘mo•no•ko∘ni•o•sis
pneu∘mo•nol∘y•sis
pneu∘mo•no•ul•tra•mi•cro•
scop∘ic•sil•i•co•vol•ca•no•
co•ni•o•sis
Pneu∘mo•nys•sus
pneu∘mo•per∘oi•car•di•um,,
n., pl. -di∘a.
pneu∘mo•per∘oi•to•ne•um
pneu∘mo•per∘oi•to•ni•tis
pneu∘mo•tach∘o∘gram
pneu∘mo•tach∘o∘graph
pneu∘mo•taxic
pneu∘mo•tho•rax
pneu∘mo•trop∘ic
Pneu∘mo•vax 23 *Trademark.*
Pnu-I∘mune 23 *Trademark.*
pock
pocked
pock•mark

po•dag∘ra
po•dag∘ral
po•dag•ric
po•dag•rous
po•dal∘ic
Pod-Ben-25 *Trademark.*
po•di•at•ric
po•di∘a•trist
po•di∘a•try
pod∘o•derm
pod∘o•der•ma•ti•tis
po•dol∘o∘gy
pod∘o•phyl•lic
pod∘o•phyl•lin
pod∘o•phyl•lo•tox∘in
pod∘o•phyl•lum, *n., pl.*
  -phyl∘li, -phyl•lums.
podophyllum pel•tat∘um
po•go•ni∘on
poi∘ki•lo•blast
poi∘ki•lo•blas•tic
poi∘ki•lo•cyte
poi∘ki•lo•cy•to•sis
poi∘ki•lo•der∘ma, *n., pl.* -mas,
  -ma∘ta.
poi∘ki•lo•therm
poi∘ki•lo•ther•mal
poi∘ki•lo•ther•mic
poi∘ki•lo•ther•mism
poi∘ki•lo•ther•mous
poi∘ki•lo•ther∘my, *n., pl.*
  -mies.
Point-Two *Trademark.*
poin•til•lage
poi•son, *v.,* -soned, -son•ing.
poison i∘vy
poison oak
poison su∘mac
poi•son•ing
poi•son•ous
po∘lar bod∘y
Po•lar•a•mine *Trademark.*

po•lar•im•e∘ter
po•lar∘i•met•ric
po•la•rim•e∘try
po•lar∘i•scope
po•lar∘i•scop∘ic
po•lar∘i∘ty, *n., pl.* -ties.
po•lar∘i•za•tion
po•lar•ize, *v.,* -ized, -iz•ing.
po•lar•iz∘er
po•lar∘o•gram
po•lar∘o•graph∘ic
po•la•rog•ra•phy, *n., pl.*
  -phies.
Po•len•ske num•ber
Polenske val∘ue
pol∘i•clin∘ic
po∘li∘o
po∘li∘o•en•ceph∘a•li•tis
po∘li∘o•en•ceph∘a•lo•my•
  e∘li•tis
po∘li∘o•my•e∘lit∘ic
po∘li∘o•my•e∘li•tis
po∘li∘o•sis
po∘li∘o•vi∘rus, *n., pl.* -rus∘es.
pol•it•zer bag
pol•len
pol•le•no•sis
pol•lex, *n., pl.* -li•ces.
pollex val•gus
pollex va∘rus
pol•li•cal
pol•li•no•sis
pol•lu•tion
Po•lo•caine *Trademark.*
po•lo•cyte
po•lo•ni∘um
pol∘y, *n., pl.* pol∘ys.
poly A
pol∘y•ac∘id
pol∘y•a•cryl∘a•mide
pol∘y•ad•e∘nyl∘ic ac∘id
pol∘y•al•co•hol

pol○y•am•ide
pol○y•a•mine
pol○y•an•dry
pol○y•ar•ter○i•tis
pol○y•arth•ri•tis
pol○y•ar•tic○u•lar
pol○y•ax○on
pol○y•ax○one
pol○y•ba•sic
pol○y•blast
pol○y•blas•tic
pol○y•cen○tric
pol○y•chro•ma•sia
pol○y•chro•mat○ic
pol○y•chro•mat○o•phil
pol○y•chro•mat○o•phile
pol○y•chro•mat○o•phil○i○a
pol○y•chro•mat○o•phil•lic
pol○y•chro•mi○a
Pol○y•cil•lin *Trademark.*
Polycillin-N *Trademark.*
Polycillin-PRB *Trademark.*
Pol○y•cit○ra *Trademark.*
Polycitra-K *Trademark.*
Polycitra-LC *Trademark.*
pol○y•clin○ic
Pol○y•cose *Trademark.*
pol○y•crot○ic
pol○y•cy•clic
pol○y•cy•e○sis, *n., pl.* -ses.
pol○y•cys•tic
pol○y•cy•the•mi○a
polycythemia hy○per•ton○i○ca
polycythemia ru•bra•ve○ra
polycythemia ve○ra
pol○y•cy•the•mic
pol○y•dac•tyl
pol○y•dac•tyl•ism
pol○y•dac•tyl•ous
pol○y•dac•ty○ly
pol○y•dip•si○a

pol○y•dip•sic
pol○y•dyp•si○a
pol○y•dys•pla•sia
pol○y•dys•tro•phy
pol○y•e•lec•tro•lyte
pol○y•em•bry○o○ny
pol○y•ene
pol○y•e•nic
pol○y•es•trous
pol○y•ga•lac•ti○a
pol○y•gal•ac•tu•ro•nase
pol○y•gam○ic
po•lyg○a•mist
po•lyg○a•mous
po•lyg○a○my
pol○y•gas•tric
pol○y•gene
pol○y•gen○ic
pol○y•glan•du•lar
pol○y•glob○u•li○a
pol○y•glob○u•lism
pol○y•gram
pol○y•graph
pol○y•graph○ic
po•lyg○y•nist
po•lyg○y•nous
po•lyg○y○ny
pol○y•gy•ri○a
pol○y•he•dral
pol○y•hi•dro•sis, *n., pl.* -ses.
Pol○y-His•tine CS *Trademark.*
Poly-Histine-D *Trademark.*
Poly-Histine DM *Trademark.*
pol○y•hy•brid
pol○y•i○dro•sis
pol○y•mas•ti○a
pol○y•mas•ti•gote
pol○y•me•li○a, *n., pl.* -li○as.
pol○y•men•or•rhe○a
pol○y•men•or•rhoe○a
pol○y•mer

pol○y•mer•ase

polymerase chain re•ac•tion

pol○y•me•ri○a

pol○y•mer○ic

pol○y•mer○i•cal○ly

pol○y•mer•ism

pol○y•mer○i•za•tion

po•lym○er•ize, *v.,* -ized, -iz•
ing.

pol○y•mi•cro○bial

pol○y•mi•cro○bic

pol○y•morph

pol○y•mor•phic

pol○y•mor•phism

pol○y•mor•pho•nu•cle○ar

pol○y•mor•phous

polymorphous per•verse

pol○y•mor•phous○ly

Pol○y•mox *Trademark.*

pol○y•my•al•gi○a rheu•
mat○i•ca

pol○y•my○o•si•tis

pol○y•myx○in

pol○y•neu•rit○ic

pol○y•neu•ri•tis

pol○y•neu•rop○a•thy, *n., pl.*
-thies.

pol○y•nu•cle○ar

pol○y•nu•cle○o•sis, *n., pl.*
-ses.

pol○y•nu•cle•o•tide

pol○y•o•don•tia

pol○y•o○ma

pol○y•o•pi○a

polyopia mon○oph•
thal•mi○ca

pol○y•op○ic

pol○y•or•chid•ism

pol○y•or•chis

pol○y•os•tot○ic

pol○y•ov○u•lar

pol○y•ov○u•la•tion

pol○yp

pol○y•pec•to○my, *n., pl.*
-mies.

pol○y•pep•tide

pol○y•pha•gi○a

po•lyph○a•gous

pol○y•pha•lan•gism

pol○y•phar•ma○cy

pol○y•pho•bi○a

pol○y•phy•let○ic

pol○y•phy•le•tism

pol○y•phy•le•tist

pol○y•phy○o•dont

pol○y•plas•tic

pol○y•ploid

pol○y•ploi•dic

pol○y•ploi○dy

pol•yp•ne○a

pol•yp•ne○ic

pol○y•pod

pol○y•po•di○a

pol○y•poid

pol○y•poi•dal

pol○y•po•sis

polyposis co○li

polyposis ven•tric○u•li

pol•yp•ous

pol○y•pus, *n., pl.* pol•y○pi,
pol○y•pus○es.

pol○y•ra•dic○u•li•tis

pol○y•ri•bo•nu•cle•o•tide

pol○y•ri•bo•so•mal

pol○y•ri•bo•some

pol○y•sac•cha•ride

pol○y•scope

pol○y•scop○ic

pol○y•se•ro•si•tis

pol○y•some

pol○y•so•mic

pol○y•so○my

pol○y•sor•bate

pol○y•sper•mic

pol∘y•sper∘my
Pol∘y•spo•rin *Trademark.*
pol∘y•sty•rene
pol∘y•sy•nap•tic
pol∘y•sy•nap•ti•cal∘ly
pol∘y•tene
pol∘y•the•li∘a
po•lyt∘o∘cous
pol∘y•troph∘ic
pol∘y•trop∘ic
pol∘y•un•sat∘u•rate
pol∘y•un•sat∘u•rat∘ed
pol∘y•u∘ri∘a
pol∘y•u∘ric
pol∘y•va•lence, *n., pl.* -len•
  ces.
pol∘y•va•len∘cy, *n., pl.* -cies.
pol∘y•va•lent
Pol∘y-Vi-Flor *Trademark.*
pol∘y•vi∘nyl
pol∘y•vi∘nyl•pyr•rol∘i•done
pom•ade
pom•an•der
po•ma∘tum
pom∘e•gran•ate
pom•pho∘lyx
Po•nar∘is *Trademark.*
pon•ceau dex•yl∘i•dine
pon•der•a∘ble
Pon•di•min *Trademark.*
pons, *n., pl.* pon•tes.
pons Va•ro•li∘i, *n., pl.* pontes
  Va•ro•li∘i.
Pon•stel *Trademark.*
pon•tic
pon•tic∘u•lus, *n., pl.* -tic•u∘li.
pon•tile
pon•tine
Pon•to•caine *Trademark.*
pon•to•cer∘e•bel•lar
pop•lit•e∘al
pop•lit•e∘us, *n., pl.* -lit∘e∘i.

por•ce•lain
po•ri∘on, *n., pl.* -ri∘a, -ri∘ons.
po•ro•ceph∘a•li•a•sis
Po•ro•ce•phal∘i•dae
Po•ro•ceph∘a•lus
po•ro•plastic
po•ro•sis, *n., pl.* -ses, -sis∘es.
po•ros∘i∘ty, *n., pl.* -ties.
po•rot∘ic
po•rous
por•phin
por•phine
por•pho•bi•lin∘o•gen
por•phyr∘i∘a
por•phy•rin
por•phy•ri•nu•ri∘a
por•phy•rop•sin
port-wine stain
por∘ta, *n., pl.* -tae.
porta he•pat∘is
porta ves•tib∘u•li
por•ta•ca•val
por•tal cir•cu•la•tion
portal vein
por•ti∘o, *n., pl.* -ti∘o•nes.
por•to•ca•val
po∘rus, *n., pl.* po∘ri, po•
  rus∘es.
po•si•tion
pos∘i•tive
pos∘i•tron e∘mis•sion to•
  mog•ra•phy
po•so•log∘ic
po•so•log∘i•cal
po•sol∘o•gist
po•sol∘o•gy
post•an•es•thet∘ic
post•a•nox∘ic
post•ap∘o•plec•tic
post•ar•te•ri•o•lar
post•ax•i∘al
post•ax•i•al∘ly

post•car•di•nal
post•ca○va
post•ca•val
post•cen•tral
postcentral gy○rus
post•ci•bal
post•cla•vic○u•lar
post•co○i•tal
post•com•mis•sure
post•cor○nu
post•em•bry•o•nal
post•em•bry•on○ic
post•en•ceph○a•lit○ic
post•ep○i•lep•tic
pos•te•ri○ad
pos•te•ri○or
posterior pi•tu○i•tar○y
pos•te•ri○or○ly
pos○ter○o•an•te•ri○or
pos○ter○o•ex•ter•nal
pos○ter○o•in•ter•nal
pos○ter○o•lat•er○al
pos○ter○o•me•di○al
pos○ter○o•me•di○an
pos○ter○o•su•pe•ri○or
pos○ter○o•tem•po•ral
post•feb•rile
post•gan•gli•on○ic
post•gle•noid
post•gle•noi○dal
post•hem•or•rhag○ic
pos•thi•tis
post•hu•mous
post•hu•mous○ly
post•hyp•not○ic
post•hyp•not○i•cal○ly
post•hy•poph○y•sis, *n., pl.*
  -ses.
post•ic•tal
post•ir•ra•di•a•tion
post•ma•tu•ri•ty
post•me•di○al

post•me•di○an
post•men○o•pau•sal
post•mor•tal
post•mor•tem
post•nar○is, *n., pl.* -nar○es.
post•na•sal
postnasal drip
post•na•tal
post•na•tal○ly
post•oc○u•lar
post•op•er○o•a•tive
post•op•er○o•a•tive○ly
post•o•ral
post•or•bi•tal
post•pal○a•tine
post•par•tal
post•par•tum
post•pi•tu•i•tar○y
post•pran•di○al
post•pran•di•al○ly
post•pu•ber•tal
post•py•ram○o•i•dal
post•re•duc•tion
post•scap•u○la, *n., pl.* -lae,
  -las.
post•scap○u•lar
post•sy•nap•tic
post•syn•ap•ti•cal○ly
post•trau•mat○ic
posttraumatic stress dis•or•
  der
post•treat•ment
pos•tur○al
postural hy•per•ten•sion
Pos•ture *Trademark.*
Posture-D *Trademark.*
Po•ta○ba *Trademark.*
po•tas•sic
po•tas•si○um
potassium bro•mide
Potassium Chlo•ride
potassium i○o•dide

po•ten○cy, *n.*, *pl.* -cies.
po•tent
po•ten•tia
po•ten•tial
po•ten•ti•ate, *v.*, -at○ed, -at•ing.
po•ten•ti•a•tion
po•ten•ti•a•tor
po•ten•ti•om•e○ter
po•ten•ti•o•met•ric
po○tion
po•to•ma•ni○a
Pott's dis•ease
poul•tice, *n.*, *v.*, -ticed, -tic•ing.
Pou•part's lig○a•ment
Po○van *Trademark.*
pov•er○ty
po•vi•done
pow•der
pow•der○y
pow○er
pox
pox•vi•rus, *n.* *pl.* -rus○es.
prac•ti•tion○er
Pra•me•Gel *Trademark.*
Pra•me○t FA *Trademark.*
Pram○i•let FA *Trademark.*
Pram○o•sone *Trademark.*
pran•di○al
Pran•tal *Trademark.*
pra•se•o•dym○i•um
Prav○a•chol *Trademark.*
Prav○a•sta•tin
Prax *Trademark.*
prax•e•o•log○i•cal
prax○i•ol○o○gy
prax○is, *n.*, *pl.* prax○es.
Pra•zo•sin *Trademark.*
Prazosin HCL *Trademark.*
pre-e•clamp•si○a
pre-op

pre•ad○o•les•cence
pre•ad○o•les•cent
pre•ag○o•nal
pre•a•nal
pre•an•es•thet○ic
pre•au•ric○u•lar
pre•ax○i•al
pre•can•cer•ous
pre•cap•il•lar○y
pre•car•ti•lage
pre•car•ti•lag○i•nous
pre•cau•tions
pre•ca○va, *n.*, *pl.* -vae.
pre•ca•val
pre•cen•tral
pre•chor•dal
pre•cip○i•ta•bil○i○ty
pre•cip○i•ta•ble
pre•cip○i•tant
pre•cip○i•tate, *v.*, -tat○ed, -tat•ing.
pre•cip○i•ta•tion
pre•cip○i•tin
pre•cip○i•tin○o○gen
pre•cip○i•tin○o○gen○ic
pre•clin○i•cal
pre•clin○i•cal○ly
pre•cog•ni•tion
pre•com•mis•sure
pre•con•scious
pre•con•scious○ly
pre•cop○u•la•to○ry
pre•cor•dial
pre•cor•di○um, *n.*, *pl.* -di○a.
pre•cor○nu, *n.*, *pl.* -nu○a.
pre•cos•tal
pre•crit○i•cal
pre•cu•ne○us, *n.*, *pl.* -ne○i.
pre•cur•sor
Pred Forte *Trademark.*
Pred Mild *Trademark.*
Pred•cef *Trademark.*

pre•den•tin
pre•di•a•be•tes
pre•di•a•bet•ic
pre•di•a•stol•ic
pre•di•gest
pre•di•ges•tion
pre•dis•pose, *v.*, -posed, -pos•
  ing.
pre•dis•po•si•tion
Pred•ni•cen-M *Trademark.*
pred•nis•o•lone
pred•ni•sone
pre•e•clamp•si•a
pre•e•clamp•tic
pree•mie
pre•for•ma•tion
Pre•frin *Trademark.*
pre•fron•tal
prefrontal lobe
pre•gan•gli•ar
pre•gan•gli•on•ic
pre•gen•i•tal
preg•nan•cy, *n.*, *pl.* -cies.
preg•nane
preg•nane•di•ol
preg•nant
preg•nene
preg•nen•o•i•no•lone
preg•ne•no•lone
Preg•nyl *Trademark.*
pre•hal•lux, *n.*, *pl.* -lu•ces.
pre•hen•sile
pre•hen•sil•i•ty, *n.*, *pl.* -ties.
pre•hen•sion
pre•he•pat•ic
pre•hy•poph•y•sis, *n.*, *pl.*
  -ses.
pre•in•cu•ba•tion
pre•in•duc•tion
pre•in•va•sive
pre•leu•ke•mic
pre•load•ing

Pre•lone *Trademark.*
Pre•lu-2 *Trademark.*
Pre•lu•din *Trademark.*
pre•ma•lig•nant
Prem•o•a•rin *Trademark.*
pre•mar•i•tal
pre•ma•ture
pre•ma•ture•ly
pre•ma•ture•ness
pre•ma•tur•i•ty
pre•max•il•la, *n.*, *pl.* -lae.
pre•max•il•lar•y
pre•med
pre•me•di•an
pre•med•i•cal
pre•med•i•cate, *v.*, -cat•ed,
  -cat•ing.
pre•med•i•ca•tion
pre•men•o•pau•sal
pre•men•o•pause
pre•men•stru•al
premenstrual dys•phor•ic dis•
  or•der
premenstrual syn•drome
pre•men•stru•al•ly
pre•men•stru•um, *n.*, *pl.*
  -stru•a, -stru•ums
pre•mo•lar
pre•mon•i•tar•y
pre•mon•i•to•ry
Prem•pro *Trademark.*
pre•mune
pre•mu•ni•tion, *n.*, *pl.* -tions.
pre•mu•ni•tive
pre•my•el•o•cyte
pre•na•res
pre•na•tal
pre•na•tal•ly
Prenatal/Zinc *Trademark.*
Pre•nate 90 *Trademark.*
pre•oc•cip•i•tal
pre•op

pre•op•er○a•tive
pre•op•er○a•tive○ly
pre•op•tic
pre•o•ral
pre•o•rally
pre•ov○u•la•to○ry
prep, *v.*, prepped, prep•ping.
pre•pal○a•tal
Prep○a•ra•tion H *Trademark.*
pre•par○a•tor
pre•par•tal
pre•pa•tel•lar
pre•pa•tent
Pre-Pen *Trademark.*
pre•per•cep•tion
pre•per•cep•tive
pre•phen○ic
pre•pla•cen•tal
pre•pon•tine
pre•po•ten○cy
pre•po•tent
pre•po•tent○ly
pre•psy•chot○ic
pre•pu•ber•al
pre•pu•ber•al○ly
pre•pu•ber•tal
pre•pu•ber•tal○ly
pre•pu•ber○ty
pre•pu•bes•cence
pre•pu•bes•cent
pre•pu•bi○an
pre•pu•bic
pre•puce
pre•pu•cial
pre•pu•tial
pre•pu•ti○um, *n.*, *pl.* -ti○a.
pre•py•lor○ic
pre•rec•tal
pre•re•pro•duc•tive
pre•ret○i•nal
pre•sa•cral

pres•by•a○cu•si○a
pres•by•cu•sis
pres○by•ope
pres○by○o•phre•ni○a
pres○by○o•phren○ic
pres○by○o•pi○a
pres○by•op○ic
pres•byt○ic
pre•scrib○a•ble
pre•scribe, *v.*, -scribed, -scrib•ing.
pre•scrib○er
pre•scrip•tion
pre•se•nile
pre•se•nil○i○ty
pres•en•ta•tion
pre•sent•ing symp•tom
pre•serv○a•tive
pre•so•mite
pres•phe•noid
pres•phyg•mic
pres•sor
pres•so•re•cep•tor
pres•so•sen•si•tive
pres•sure
pressure sore
pre•ster•nal
pre•ster•num, *n.*, *pl.* -ster•nums, -ster○na.
pre•su•bic○u•lum, *n.*, *pl.* -bic○u○la.
pre•sump•tive
pre•sump•tive○ly
Pre-Sun *Trademark.*
pre•sup•pu•ra•tive
pre•syl•vi○an
pre•syn•ap•tic
pre•syn•ap•ti•cal○ly
pre•sys•to○le
pre•sys•tol○ic
pre•tem•po•ral

pre∘term
pre•ter•mi•nal
pre•tib•i∘al
pre•treat•ment
pre•tu•ber•cu•lous
prev∘a•lence
Prev∘a•cid *Trademark.*
pre•ven•ta•tive
pre•ven•tive
pre•ven•to•ri∘um, *n., pl.*
-ri∘a, -ri∘ums.
pre•ves∘i•cal
Prev∘i•Dent *Trademark.*
prev∘il•lous
pre•zone
pri•ap∘ic
pri∘a•pism
pri∘a•pis•mic
pri∘a•pus, *n., pl.* pri•a∘pi,
pri•a∘pus∘es.
prick∘ly heat
Pril∘o∘sec *Trademark.*
pri•mal scream
primal ther•a∘py
pri•ma•quine
pri•ma∘ry, *adj., n., pl.* -ries.
primary sex
char•ac∘ter•is•tic
Pri•ma•tene *Trademark.*
Pri•max∘in *Trademark.*
pri•mi•grav•i∘da
pri•mip∘a∘ra
pri•mi•par∘i∘ty
pri•mip∘a•rous
pri•mite
pri•mi•ti∘ae
pri•mor•di∘al
pri•mor•di•al∘y
pri•mor•di∘um, *n., pl.* -di∘a.
pri•mus
prin•ceps
Prin•ci•pen *Trademark.*

prin•ci•ple
Prin∘i•vil *Trademark.*
Prin∘zide *Trademark.*
pri∘on
Pris•co∘line *Trademark.*
pri•vate
private-du∘ty
Pri•vine *Trademark.*
pro•ac•cel•er∘oin
pro•ac•tive
pro∘al
pro•am•ni∘on, *n., pl.* -ni•ons,
-ni∘a.
pro•am•ni•ot∘ic
pro•at•las
pro•bac•te•ri•o•phage
pro•band
pro•bang
Pro-Ban•thine *Trademark.*
probe
Pro•bec-T *Trademark.*
pro•ben∘e•cid
pro•bos•cis, *n., pl.* -cis∘es, -ci•
des.
pro•cain∘a•mide
pro•caine
procaine am•ide
Pro•can SR *Trademark.*
Pro•car•di∘a *Trademark.*
Procardia XL *Trademark.*
pro•car∘y•ote
pro•car∘y•ot∘ic
pro•cat•arc•tic
pro•ce•phal∘ic
Pro-Cep∘tion *Trademark.*
pro•cer•coid
proc•ess
pro•ces•sus, *n., pl.* -sus.
pro•chor•dal
pro•ci•den•tia
pro•con•ver•tin
proc•tal•gia

proctalgia fu∘gax
proc•tec•to∘my, *n., pl.* -mies.
proc•ti•tis
proc•toc•ly•sis
pro∘to•co•li•tis
Proc∘to•cort *Trademark.*
proc∘to•de∘um, *n., pl.* -de•
ums, -de∘a.
proc∘to•dyn∘i∘a
Proc∘to•Foam *Trademark.*
ProctoFoam-HC *Trademark.*
proc∘to•gis•moi•do•scope
proc∘to•log∘ic
proc∘to•log∘i•cal
proc•tol∘o∘gist
proc•tol∘o∘gy
Proc∘tor•Cream-HC *Trademark.*
proc∘to•scope
proc∘to•scop∘ic
proc∘to•scop∘i•cal∘ly
proc•tos•co∘py, *n., pl.* -pies.
proc∘to•sig•moid•ec•to∘my,
n., pl. -mies.
proc∘to•sig•moi•dos•co∘pis
proc∘to•sig•moi•dos•co∘py,
n., pl. -pies.
proc•tos•to∘my, *n., pl.* -mies.
pro•cum•bent
pro•dig∘i•o•sin
pro•dro∘ma, *n., pl.* -ma∘ta,
-mas.
prod•ro•mal
pro•drome
pro•dro•mic
pro•drug
pro•e•mi∘al
pro•en•zyme
pro•e•ryth•ro•blast
pro•e•ryth•ro•cyte
pro•es•trum
pro•es•trus
Pro•fas∘i *Trademark.*

pro•fi•bri•nol∘y•sin
Pro•fi•late OSD *Trademark.*
Pro•fil•nine *Trademark.*
pro•fla•vine
pro•flu•vi∘um al∘vi
profluvium lac•tis
pro•found hear•ing loss
pro•fun•dus
pro•gen∘i•tive
pro•gen∘i•tive•ness
pro•gen∘i•tor
pro•gen∘i•tor•ship
pro•ge•ri∘a
pro•ges•ta•tion∘al
pro•ges•ter•one
pro•ges•ter•on∘ic
pro•ges•tin
pro•ges•to•gen
pro•glot•tid
pro•glot•tid•e∘an
pro•glot•tis, *n., pl.* -tit∘i•des.
Pro•gly•cem *Trademark.*
prog•nath∘ic
prog•na•thism
prog•na•thous
prog•na•thy, *n., pl.* -thies.
prog•no∘sis, *n., pl.* -ses.
prog•nos•tic
prog•nos•ti•cal∘ly
prog•nos•ti•cate, *v.,* -cat∘ed,
-cat•ing.
pro•grav∘id
prog•ress
pro•gres•sive
Pro-Hep∘a•tone *Trademark.*
Pro-HI•Bit *Trademark.*
pro•jec•tive
pro•jec•tive•ly
pro•jec•tiv∘i•ty
pro•ji•cient
pro•ji•cient∘ly
pro•kar∘y•ote

pro•kar•y•ot•ic
Pro•ke•ta•zine *Trademark.*
pro•la•bi•um, *n., pl.* -bi•a.
pro•lac•tin
pro•lam•in
pro•la•mine
pro•lan
pro•lapse, *v.,* -lapsed, -laps•ing.
pro•lap•sus
prolapsus an•i
prolapsus u•ter•i
pro•lep•sis
pro•lep•tic
pro•lep•ti•cal
pro•leu•co•cyte
pro•leu•ko•cyte
pro•lif•er•ate, *v.,* -at•ed, -at•ing.
pro•lif•er•a•tion
pro•lif•er•a•tive
pro•lig•er•ous
pro•line
Pro•lix•in *Trademark.*
Pro•loid *Trademark.*
Pro•lop•rim *Trademark.*
pro•lo•ther•a•py, *n., pl.* -pies.
pro•lym•pho•cyte
Pro•ma•quid *Trademark.*
pro•ma•zine
pro•meg•a•lo•blast
pro•met•a•phase
Pro•meth•a•zine
Promethazine/Co•deine
pro•me•thi•um
Pro•Mod *Trademark.*
pro•mon•o•cyte
prom•on•to•ry, *n., pl.* -ries.
pro•mot•er
pro•mo•tor
pro•my•el•o•cyte
pro•nase

pro•nate, *v.,* -nat•ed, -nat•ing.
pro•na•tion
pro•na•tor
pronator quad•ra•tus
pronator ra•di•i•te•res
pro•na•tor•te•res
pro•neph•ron, *n., pl.* -neph•ra.
pro•neph•ros, *n., pl.* -neph•roi.
Pro•nes•tyl *Trademark.*
Pronestyl-SR *Trademark.*
pro•neth•o•a•lol
pro•no•grade
pro•nor•mo•blast
pro•nu•cle•ous, *n., pl.* -cle•i, -cle•us•es.
pro•ot•ic
Pro•pa•cet *Trademark.*
Propacet 100 *Trademark.*
pro•pa•fen•one
prop•a•gate, *v.,* -gat•ed, -gat•ing.
prop•a•ga•tion
prop•a•ga•tive
Prop•a•gest *Trademark.*
pro•pal•i•nal
pro•pam•i•dine
pro•pane
pro•pa•no•ic
pro•pa•nol
pro•pene
pro•pe•nyl
pro•per•din
pro•per•i•to•ne•al
pro•phage
pro•phase
pro•phy•lac•tic
pro•phy•lac•ti•cal•ly
pro•phy•lax•is
Pro•phyl•lin *Trademark.*

Pro•pine *Trademark.*
pro•pi•o•nate
pro•pi•on•oi•bac•te•ri•um, *n., pl.* -ri•a.
pro•pi•on•ic
propionic ac•id
Pro•plex T *Trademark.*
pro•pos•i•tus, *n., pl.* -pos• i•ti.
pro•pox•y•phene
propoxyphene hy•dro•chlo• ride
propoxyphene nap•sy•late
Propoxyphene N/APAP
pro•pran•o•lol
pro•pri•e•tar•i•ly
pro•pri•e•tar•y
pro•pri•o•cep•tion
pro•pri•o•cep•tive
pro•pri•o•cep•tor
pro•pri•o•spi•nal
prop•to•sis
Pro•pul•sid *Trademark.*
pro•pyl
pro•py•lene
pro•pyl•par•a•ben
pro•pyl•thi•ou•ra•cil
pro•scop•ic
pro•sect
pro•sec•tion
pro•sec•tor
pros•en•ce•phal•ic
pros•en•ceph•a•lon
pro•so•cele
pro•so•coel
pro•so•coele
pro•so•de•mic
pro•sop•i•cal•ly
pro•so•pla•sia
pros•o•pos•chi•sis
pros•pec•tive stud•y
pros•ta•cy•clin

pros•ta•glan•din
Pros•taph•lin *Trademark.*
pros•tate
prostate gland
prostate spe•cif•ic an•ti•gen test
pros•ta•tec•to•my, *n., pl.* -mies.
pros•tat•ic
pro•stat•o•i•co•ves•oi•cal
pros•ta•tism
pros•ta•ti•tis
pros•ta•to•cys•ti•tis
pros•ta•tog•ra•phy, *n., pl.* -phies.
pro•stat•o•lith
pro•stat•o•ves•oi•cal
pro•stat•o•ve•sic•ou•li•tis
pros•ter•na•tion
pros•the•sis, *n., pl.* -ses.
pros•thet•ic
prosthetic group
pros•thet•ics
pros•the•tist
pros•thi•on
pros•tho•don•tia
pros•tho•don•tics
pros•tho•don•tist
Pros•tho•gon•oi•mus
Pro•stig•min *Trademark.*
Pros•tin VR *Trademark.*
pros•trate, *v.,* -trat•ed, -trat• ing.
pros•tra•tion
pro•tac•tin•oi•um
pro•ta•gon
pro•tag•oo•nism
pro•tag•oo•nist
prot•a•mine
pro•ta•nom•a•ly, *n., pl.* -lies.
pro•ta•nope
pro•ta•no•pi•a

pro•ta•nop•ic
pro•te•an
pro•te•ase
pro•te•oid
pro•te•ide
pro•tein
protein coat
protein syn•the•sis
pro•tein•a•ceous
pro•tein•ase
pro•te•i•nate
pro•tein•oic
pro•te•i•noid
pro•tein•o•sis
pro•tei•nous
pro•tein•u•ri•a
pro•te•o•clas•tic
pro•te•o•lip•oid
pro•te•ol•y•sis
pro•te•o•lyt•ic
pro•te•ose
pro•te•ous, *n., pl.* **pro•te•i**
Proteus mi•rab•i•lis
Proteus mor•gan•i•i
Proteus rett•ger•i
Proteus vul•gar•is
proth•e•sis, *n., pl.* -e•ses.
pro•throm•bin
Pro•tid *Trademark.*
pro•tide
pro•tist
Pro•tis•ta
pro•tis•tan
pro•tis•tol•o•gist
pro•tis•tol•o•gy
pro•ti•um
pro•to-on•co•gene
pro•to•ac•tin•i•um
pro•to•blast
pro•to•blas•tic
pro•to•cat•e•chu•ic

pro•to•col
pro•to•cone
pro•to•co•nid
pro•to•derm
pro•to•der•mal
pro•to•gen
pro•to•heme
pro•to•me•rite
Pro•to•pam *Trademark.*
pro•to•path•ic
pro•to•pa•thy
pro•to•pec•tin
pro•to•plasm
pro•to•plas•mal
pro•to•plas•mat•ic
pro•to•plas•mic
pro•to•plast
pro•to•por•phy•rin
pro•to•pro•te•ose
pro•to•spasm
Pro•to•stat *Trademark.*
Pro•to•stron•gy•lus
pro•to•troph
pro•to•troph•ic
Pro•to•tro•pin *Trademark.*
pro•tot•ro•py
pro•to•ver•a•trine
pro•to•ver•te•bra, *n., pl.*
-brae, -bras.
pro•to•ver•te•bral
pro•tox•ide
Pro•to•zo•a
pro•to•zo•al
pro•to•zo•an, *n., pl.* -zo•ans,
-zo•a.
pro•to•zo•i•a•sis
pro•to•zo•ol•o•gist
pro•to•zo•ol•o•gy
pro•to•zo•on, *n., pl.* -zo•a.
pro•trac•tion
pro•trac•tor
pro•tu•ber•ance

pro•tu•ber•ant
pro•tu•bran•tia men•ta•lis
proud flesh
Pro•ven•til *Trademark.*
Proventil Ae•ro•sol *Trademark.*
Proventil/Ven•tol∘in *Trademark.*
pro•ven•tric∘u•lus, *n., pl.* -tric∘u∘li.
Pro•ve•ra *Trademark.*
pro•vi•ral
pro•vi•rus, *n., pl.* -rus∘es.
pro•vi•ta•min
provitamin A
prov∘o•ca•tion
pro•voc∘a•tive
Pro•vo•cho•line *Trademark.*
pro•voke, *v.,* -voked, -vok•ing.
prox∘i•mad
prox∘i•mal
prox∘i•mal∘ly
prox∘i•mate
prox∘i•mate∘ly
prox∘i∘mo•a•tax∘i∘a
prox∘i∘mo•buc•cal
prox∘i∘mo•la•bi∘al
prox∘i∘mo•lin•gual
Pro•zac *Trademark.*
pro∘zone
pru∘i•nate
Pru•let *Trademark.*
pru•rig∘i•nous
pru•ri∘go
pru•rit∘ic
pru•ri•tus
pruritus an∘i
pruritus hi•e•ma•lis
pruritus se•nil∘is
pruritus vul•vae
prus•si•ate
prus•sic
prussic ac∘id

psal•te•ri∘al
psal•te•ri∘um, *n., pl.* -ri∘a.
psam•mo∘ma, *n., pl.* -mas, -ma∘ta.
psam•mom∘a•tous
psel•lism
pseud•a•con∘i•tine
pseud•arth•ro∘sis, *n., pl.* -ses.
pseud•es•the∘sia
pseu∘do•a•con∘i•tin
pseu∘do•a•con∘i•tine
pseu∘do•ag•glu•ti•na•tion
pseu∘do•a•ne•mi∘a
pseu∘do•an•gi∘na
pseu∘do•arth•ro∘sis, *n., pl.* -ses.
pseu∘do•bul•bar
pseu∘do•cho•lin•es•ter•ase
pseu∘do•chro•mes•the∘sia
pseu∘do•cir•rho∘sis
pseu∘do•cop∘u•la•tion
pseu∘do•croup
pseu∘do•cy•e∘sis, *n., pl.* -ses.
pseu∘do•cyst
pseu∘do•diph•the•ri∘a
pseu∘do•e•phed•rine
pseu∘do•far∘cy
pseu∘do•glan•ders
pseu∘do•glob∘u•lin
pseu∘do•hal•lu•ci•na•tion
pseu∘do•he•mo•phil∘i∘a
pseu∘do•her•maph•ro•dite
pseu∘do•her•maph•ro•dit•ism
pseu∘do•hy•o•scy•a•mine
pseu∘do•hy•per•troph∘ic
pseu∘do•hy•per•tro•phy, *n., pl.* -phies.
pseu∘do•hy•po•par∘a•thy•roi•dism
pseu∘do•isoch•ro•mat∘ic
pseu∘do•ker∘a•tin

pseu○do•leu•ke•mi○a
pseu○do•ma•ni○a
pseu○do•mel○a•no•sis
pseu○do•mem•brane
pseu○do•mem•bra•nous
pseu○do•men•stru•a•tion
pseu○do•mo•nad
pseu○do•mo•nas, *n., pl.* -na•des.
Pseudomonas aer○u•gi•no○sa
Pseudomonas mal•to•phil○i○a
Pseudomonas pseu○do•mal•le○i
Pseudomonas py•o•cy•a•ne○a
pseu○do•myx○o○ma per○i•to•ne○i
pseu○do•neu•ro○ma, *n., pl.* -mas, -ma○ta.
pseu○do•pa•ral○y•sis
pseu○do•par○a•site
Pseu○do•phyl•lid○e○a
pseu○do•pod
pseu○do•po•di○um, *n., pl.* -di○a.
pseu○do•preg•nan○cy, *n., pl.* -cies.
pseu•do•preg•nant
pseu○dop•si○a
pseu○do•pto•sis
pseu○do•ra•bies
pseu○do•re•ac•tion
pseu○do•ret○i•ni•tis pig•men•to○sa
pseu○do•scle•ro•sis
pseu○do•sto○ma, *n., pl.* -ma○ta, -mas.
pseu•dot•ro•pine
pseu○do•trun•cus ar•te•ri○o•sus
pseu○do•tu•ber•cle

pseu○do•tu•ber•cu•lo•sis, *n., pl.* -ses.
pseu○do•tu•mor ce•re•bri
pseu○do•ven•tri•cle
pseu○do•vom•it•ing
pseu○do•xan•tho○ma e○las•ti•cum
psi•lo•cin
psil○o○cy•bin
psit•ta•co•sis
pso○as, *n., pl.* pso○ai, pso○ae.
pso•at○ic
pso•mo•pha•gia
pso○ra
pso•ra•len
Psor•con *Trademark.*
Psor•er•ga•tes
pso•ri•a•si•form
pso•ri•a•sis
pso•ri•at○ic
Pso•ri○on *Trademark.*
Pso•rop•tes
psy•cha•go○gy
psy•chal•gia
psych○a•nal○y•sis
psy•chan○o•a•lyst
psy•chan○o•a•lyt○ic
psy•chan○o•a•lyt○i•cal
psy•chas•the•no○ia
psy•chas•then○ic
psy•che
psych○e•del○ic
psych○e•del○i•cal○ly
psy•chi•at•ric
psy•chi•at•ri•cal
psy•chi•at•ri•cal○ly
psy•chi○a•trist
psy•chi○a•try
psy•chic
psychic blind•ness
psy•chi•cal
psy•chi•cal○ly

psy•cho, *n., pl.* -chos.
psy∘cho•a•cous•tic
psy∘cho•a•cous•tics
psy∘cho•ac•tive
psy∘cho•a∘nal∘y•sis
psy∘cho•an∘a•lyst
psy∘cho•an∘a•lyt∘ic
psy∘cho•an∘a•lyt∘ical
psy∘cho•an∘a•lyze, *v.,* -lyzed,
  -lyz•ing.
psy∘cho•bi•o•log∘ic
psy∘cho•bi•o•log∘i•cal
psy∘cho•bi•ol∘o∘gy
psy∘cho•ca•thar•sis, *n., pl.*
  -ses.
psy∘cho•chem∘i•cal
psy∘cho•cor•ti•cal
psy∘cho•di•ag•no•sis, *n., pl.*
  -ses.
psy∘cho•di•ag•nos•tic
psy∘cho•di•ag•nos•tics
Psy∘chod∘i•dae
psy∘cho•dra∘ma
psy∘cho•dra•mat∘ic
psy∘cho•dy•nam∘ic
psy∘cho•dy•nam∘i•cal∘ly
psy∘cho•dy•nam∘ics
psy∘cho•gal•van∘ic
psy∘cho•gal•va•nom•e∘ter
psy∘cho•gen•e∘sis, *n., pl.*
  -ses.
psy∘cho•ge•net∘ic
psy∘cho•gen∘ic
psy∘cho•gen∘i•cal∘ly
psy•chog•nos•tic
psy∘cho•gram
psy∘cho•graph
psy∘cho•graph∘ic
psy∘cho•graph∘i•cal∘ly
psy•chog•ra•phy, *n., pl.*
  -phies.
psy∘cho•ki•ne•sia

psy∘cho•ki•ne∘sis
psy∘cho•lep∘sy
psy∘cho•lep•tic
psy∘cho•log∘ic
psy∘cho•log∘i•cal
psy∘cho•log∘i•cal∘ly
psy•chol∘o∘gist
psy•chol∘o∘gize, *v.,* -gized,
  -giz•ing.
psy•chol∘o∘gy
psy∘cho•met∘ric
psy∘cho•met•ri•cal
psy∘cho•met•ri•cal∘ly
psy∘cho•me•tri•cian
psy∘cho•met•rics
psy•chom•e∘trist
psy•chom•e∘try
psy∘cho•mi•met∘ic
psy∘cho•mo•tor
psy∘cho•neu•ro•sis, *n., pl.*
  -ses.
psy∘cho•neu•rot∘ic
psy∘cho•nom•ics
psy∘cho•path
psy∘cho•path∘i∘a
psy∘cho•path∘ic
psy∘cho•path∘i•cal∘ly
psy∘cho•path∘o∘log∘ic
psy∘cho•path∘o∘log∘i•cal
psy∘cho•pa•thol∘o∘gist
psy∘cho•pa•thol∘o∘gy
psy•chop•a∘thy
psy∘cho•phar•ma•ceu•ti•cal
psy∘cho•phar•ma•co•log∘ic
psy∘cho•phar•ma•co•log∘i•
  cal
psy∘cho•phar•ma•col∘o∘gist
psy∘cho•phar•ma•col∘o∘gy
psy∘cho•phon•as•the•ni∘a
psy∘cho•phys∘i•cal
psy∘cho•phys∘i•cal∘ly
psy∘cho•phys∘i•cist

psy○cho•phys○ics
psy○cho•phys•i○o•log○ic
psy○cho•phys•i○o•log○i•cal
psy○cho•phys○i○ol○o○gist
psy○cho•phys○i○ol○o○gy
psy○cho•quack
psy○cho•sen•so•ri•al
psy○cho•sen•so○ry
psy○cho•sex•u○al
psy○cho•sex•u•al○i○ty
psy○cho•sex•u•al○ly
psy○cho•sis, *n., pl.* -ses.
psy○cho•so•cial
psy○cho•so•cial○ly
psy○cho•so•mat○ic
psy○cho•so•mat○i•cal○ly
psy○cho•so•mat○ics
psy○cho•sur•geon
psy○cho•sur•ger○y
psy○cho•sur•gi•cal
psy○cho•syn•the•sis, *n., pl.*
  -ses.
psy○cho•ther○a•peu•tic
psy○cho•ther○a•peu•ti•cal○ly
psy○cho•ther○a•peu•tics
psy○cho•ther○a•pist
psy○cho•ther○a○py, *n., pl.*
  -pies.
psy•chot○ic
psy•chot○i•cal○ly
psy•chot○o•gen
psy•chot○o•gen○ic
psy•chot○o•mi•met○c•al○ly
psy•chot○o•mi•met○ic
psy○cho•tox○ic
psy○cho•tro•pic
psy○chro•es•the•sia
psy•chrom•e○ter
psy•chrom•e○try
psy•chro•ther○a○py, *n., pl.*
  -pies.
psyl•li○um

ptar•mic
ptar•mus
pte•ri•on
pte•ryg○i•al
pte•ryg○i○um, *n., pl.* -ryg○i•
  ums, -ryg○i○a.
pterygium col○li
pter○y•goid
pter○y•goi•dal
pter○y•go•man•dib○u•lar
pter○y•go•pal○a•tine
pti•lo•sis
pto•maine
pto•main○ic
ptosed
pto•sis, *n., pl.* -ses.
ptosis ir○i•dis
ptosis sym•pa•thet○i○ca
pto•tic
pty•al○a•gogue
pty○a•lin
pty○a•lism
pty○a•log•ra•phy, *n., pl.*
  -phies.
pu○pil
pu•ber○al
pu•ber•tal
pu•ber•tas
pubertas ple○na
pubertas prae•cox
pubertas pre•cox
pu•ber○ty
pu•be•ru•lic
pu○bes, *n., pl.* pu○bes.
pu•bes•cence
pu•bes•cent
pu○bic
pu•bi•ot○o○my, *n.,*
  pl. -mies.
pu○bis, *n., pl.* pu○bes.
pub•lic health
pu○bo•coc•cyg○e•al

pu○bo•fem○o•ral
pu○bo•pros•tat○ic
pu•den•dal
pu•den•dum, *n.*, *pl.* -den○da.
pudendum fem○i•ni•num
pudendum mu•lie•bre
pu○dic
pu•er•il•ism
pu•er•per○o•a, *n.*, *pl.* -per○ae.
pu•er•per○al
puerperal fe○ver
pu•er•pe•ri○um, *n.*, *pl.* -ri○a.
Pu○lex
Pulex ir•ri•tans
Pu•lic○i•dae
pu•li•cid○al
pu•li•cide
pul•lo•rum dis•ease
Pul•mo•care *Trademark.*
pul•mo•gas•tric
pul•mom•e○ter
pul•mom•e○try
pul•mo•nar○y
pulmonary ar•ter○y
pulmonary cap•il•lar○y
  wedge pres•sure
pulmonary func•tion test
pulmonary in•suf•fi•cien○cy
pulmonary sten○o•sis
pulmonary valve
pulmonary vein
pul•mo•nate
pul•mo•nec•to○my, *n.*, *pl.*
  -mies.
pul•mon○ic
pul•mo•tor
pulp
pulp cav○i○ty
pul○pa co•ro•na○le
pulpa den•tis
pulpa lie•nis
pulpa ra•dic○u•la•ris

pul•pal
pul•pal○ly
pul•par
pul•pec•to○my, *n.*, *pl.* -mies.
pul•pot○o○my, *n.*, *pl.* -mies.
pulp•stone
pulque
pul•sate, *v.*, -sat○ed, -sat•ing.
pul•sa•tile
Pul•sa•til○la
pul•sa•tion
pul•sa•tor
pul•sa•to○ry
pulse, *v.*, pulsed, puls•ing.
pul•sion
pulsion di•ver•tic○u•lum
pul•sus, *n.*, *pl.* pul•sus.
pul•ta•ceous
pul•ver○i•za•tion
pul•ver•ize, *v.*, -ized, -iz•ing.
pul•ver○u•lent
pul•vi•nar
pulvinar thal○a○mi
pul•vi•nate
pul•vi•nat○ed
pul•vis an•tim○o○ni•a•lis
pum•ice
pu○na
punch bi•op○sy
punch drunk syn•drome
punc○ta do•lo•ro○sa
puncta lac•ri•ma•li○a
puncta vas•cu•lo○sa
punc•tate
punc•t•iform
punc•tum, *n.*, *pl.* punc○ta.
punctum ce○cum
punctum lac•ri•ma○le
punctum prox○i•mum
punctum re•mo•tum
punc•tu•ra ex•plo•ra•
  to•ri○a

punc•ture, *v.*, -tured, -tur•ing.
pu•pil○la, *n.*, *pl.* -lae.
pu•pil•lar○y
pu•pil•lom•e○ter
pu•pil•lom•e○try
pu•pil•lo•mo•tor
pu•pil•lo•sta•tom•e○ter
pure tone test
Pure-E *Trademark.*
pur•ga•tion
pur•ga•tive
pur•ga•tive○ly
purge, *v.*, purged, purg•ing.
Pu○ri-Clens *Trademark.*
pu•ri•form
pu•rine
Pu○ri•ne•thol *Trademark.*
Pur•kin○je af•ter•im•age
Purkinje cell
Purkinje fi○ber
Purkinje fi•bers
Purkinje fig•ure
Purkinje phe•nom○e•non
Purkinje shift
Pur•kin○je○an
Pur•kin○je's fig•ure
Purkinje's net•work
Purkinje's sys•tem
Purkinje's tis•sue
pu•ro•my•cin
Pur•pose *Trademark.*
pur•pu○ra
purpura hem•or•rhag○i○ca
pur•pu○ric
pur•pu•rin
pu•ru•lence
pu•ru•len○cy
pu•ru•lent
pu•ru•lent○ly
pu•ru•loid
pus

pus•tu•lant
pus•tu•lar
pus•tu•late, *v.*, -lat○ed, -lat•ing.
pus•tu•la•tion
pus•tule
pus•tuled
pus•tu•li•form
pus•tu•lo•sis
pu•ta•men, *n.*, *pl.* -tam○i○na.
pu•tam○i•nal
pu•tre•fa○cient
pu•tre•fac•tion
pu•tre•fac•tive
pu•tre○fy, *v.*, -fied, -fy•ing.
pu•tres•cine
py•ae•mi○a
py•ar•thro•sis, *n.*, *pl.* -ses.
pyc•nic
pyc•nom•e○ter
pyc○no•mor•phic
pyc○no•mor•phous
pyc○no•sis
pyc○not○ic
py•e•lec•ta•sis, *n.*, *pl.* -ses.
py•el○ic
py○e•lit○ic
py○e•li•tis
pyelitis cys•ti○ca
py○e•lo•cys•ti•tis
py•el○o•gram
py•el○o•graph
py○e•lo•graph○ic
py•e•lo•grra•phy, *n.*, *pl.* -phies.
py•e•lo•li•thot○o○my, *n.*, *pl.* -mies.
py○e•lo•ne•phrit○ic
py•e•lo•ne•phri•tis
py○e•lo•ne•phro•sis, *n.*, *pl.* -ses.

py•e○los•to○my, *n.*,
  pl. -mies.
py•e•lo•u•re•ter○o○gram
py•e•lo•ve•nous
py○e•mi○a
py○e•mic
py•e•sis
py○gal
py•gal•gia
pyg•ma•li•o•nism
py•gop○a•gus, *n.*, *pl.* -gop•
  a○gi.
pyk•nic
pyk•no•ep○i•lep○sy
pyk•no•lep○sy
pyk•nom•e○ter
pyk•no•sis
pyk•not○ic
py○lar
py•le○phle•bec•ta•sis, *n.*, *pl.*
  -ses.
py•le○phle•bi•tis
py•le○throm•bo•sis, *n.*, *pl.*
  -ses.
pyl○ic
py○lon
py•lor○ic
py•lo•ri•tis
py•lo•ro•gas•trec•to○my, *n.*,
  pl. -mies.
py•lo•ro•my•ot○o○my, *n.*,
  -mies.
py•lo•ro•plas○ty, *n.*, *pl.* -ties.
py•lo•ro•spasm
py•lo•rot○o○my, *n.*, *pl.* -mies.
py•lo•rus, *n.*, *pl.* -lo○ri, -lo•
  rus○es.
py○o•cele
py○o•coc•cus, *n.*, *pl.* -coc○ci.
py○o•col•pos
py○o•cy•a•nase
py○o•cy•a•nin

py○o•cy•a•nine
py○o•der○ma
pyoderma fa•ci•a○le
pyoderma gan•gre•no•sum
py○o•der•mi○a
py○o•gen
py○o•gen•e○sis
py○o•gen○ic
py○o•he•mo•tho•rax, *n.*, *pl.*
  -rax○es, -ra○ces.
py•oid
py○o•me•tra
py○o•ne○phri•tis
py○o•ne○phro•sis
py○o•ne•phrot○ic
Py○o•pen
py○o•pneu•mo•tho•rax, *n.*,
  pl. -rax○es, -ra○ces.
py○o•poi•e○sis
py•or•rhe○a
pyorrhea al•ve•o•lar○is
py•or•rhe•al
py•or•rhe○ic
py•or•rhoe○a
py○o•sal•pinx, *n.*, *pl.* -pin•
  ges.
py○o•sep•ti•ce•mi○a
py○o•sis
py○o•stat○ic
py○o•tho•rax, *n.*, *pl.* -rax○es,
  -ra○ces.
py○o•xan•those
pyr○a•mid
py•ram○i•dal
pyramidal tract
py•ram○i•da○le
py•ram○i•da•lis, *n.*, *pl.* -da•
  les, -da•lis○es.
pyr○a•mi•dot○o○my, *n.*, *pl.*
  -mies.
pyr○a•mis, *n.*, *pl.*
  py•ram○i•des.

pyramis ver•mis
pyramis ves•tib○u○li
pyr○a•nose
py•ra•zin•am•ide
py•re•thrum
py•ret○ic
py○re○to•gen○ic
py•re•tog○e○nous
pyr•e○to•ther○a○py, *n., pl.*
  -pies.
py•rex○i○a
py•rex•i○al
py•rex○ic
py•rex○in
py•rid○ic
pyr○i•dine
Py•rid○i○um *Trademark.*
py•ri•dox○al
Pyridoxal-5-Phos•phate *Trademark.*
py•ri•dox○a•mine
py•ri•dox○ic
py•ri•dox○in
py•ri•dox○ine
py•ri•form
py•ri•for•mis
py•ril○a•mine
py•ri•meth○a•mine

py•rim○i•dine
py○ro•cat○e•chin
py○ro•cat○e•chol
py○ro•gal•lol
py○ro•gen
py•ro•gen○ic
py•ro•gen○i○um
py○ro•lig•ne•ous
py•rol○y•sis
py○ro•ma•ni○a
py○ro•ma•ni○ac
py○ro•ma•ni•a•cal
py•rone
py○ro•nine
py○ro•pho•bi○a
py○ro•phos•pha•tase
py○ro•phos•phate
py○ro•phos•phor○ic
py•ro•sis
py○ro•tox○in
pyr•rol○i•done de•riv○a•
  tives
Pyr•rox•ate *Trademark.*
pyr○u•vate
py•ru○vic
pyruvic ac○id
py•tho•gen○ic
py○u•ri○a

Q

Q-wave
qat
Qi•i•namm
Quaa•lude
quack
quack•e○ry, *n., pl.* -ries.
quack•sal•ver
quad
quad•rate
qua•dra•tus

quadratus fem○o•ris
quadratus la○bi○i in•fe•ri•o•
  ris
quadratus labii su•pe•ri•o•ris
quadratus lum•bo•rum
quadratus men○ti
quad○ri•ceps, *n., pl.* -ceps○es,
  -ceps.
quadriceps ex•ten•sor
quadriceps fem○o•ris
quadriceps su○rae

quad•ori•cip•oi•tal
quad•ori•gem•oi•nal
quad•ori•gem•oi•nate
quad•ori•lat•er•al
Quad•ori•nal *Trademark.*
quad•rip•o•rous
quad•ori•ple•gi•a
quad•ori•ple•gic
quad•ori•sect
quad•roon
quad•ru•ped
quad•rup•oe•dal
quad•ru•plet
quan•ta•some
quan•tim•e•ter
quan•ti•ta•tive
in•her•oi•tance
quan•tum li•bet
quantum pla•cet
quantum sa•tis
quantum suf•fi•cit
quantum vis
quar•an•tin•o•a•ble
quar•an•tine, *n., v.,* -tined,
-tin•ing.
quar•an•tin•er
quar•tan
Quar•zan *Trademark.*
quat
quat•er•nar•y
Quel•oi•cin *Trademark.*
Quel•oi•drine *Trademark.*
quer•ce•tin
quer•ci•tin
quer•u•lant
quer•u•lent

Ques•tran *Trademark.*
Qui•bron *Trademark.*
Quibron-T *Trademark.*
Quibron-T/SR *Trademark.*
quick•en, *v.,* -ened, -en•ing.
quick•lime
quick•sil•ver
Quide *Trademark.*
qui•es•cent
qui•na
quin•a•crine
Quin•a•glute *Trademark.*
Quin•a•lan *Trademark.*
quin•al•dine
Quin•a•pril
quin•oi•cine
Quin•oi•dex *Trademark.*
quin•oi•dine
qui•nine
quin•oid
quin•oo•line
qui•nol•oo•gist
qui•nol•oo•gy, *n., pl.* -gies.
qui•none
Quin•ora *Trademark.*
qui•no•vin
qui•no•vose
quin•qui•na
quin•sied
quin•sy
quint
quin•tan
quin•tup•let
quit•tor
quo•tid•i•an

R fac•tor
rab•bet•ing
rab•bit fe∘ver
ra∘bic
rab∘id
rab•id∘i∘ty
rab•id∘ly
rab•id•ness
ra•bies
ra∘bi•form
rac∘e∘mase
rac∘e∘mate
ra•ceme
rac∘e∘mic
rac∘e∘mose
ra•chi∘al
ra•chi•cen•te•sis, *n., pl.* -ses.
ra•chid∘i∘al
ra•chid∘i∘an
ra•chi•om•e∘ter
ra•chis, *n., pl.* ra•chis∘es, rach∘i•des.
ra•chis•chi•sis, *n., pl.* -ses.
ra•chit∘ic
ra•chi•tis
rach∘i•to•gen∘ic
ra•clage
rad
ra•dec•to∘my, *n., pl.* -mies.
ra•di∘a•bil∘i∘ty, *n., pl.* -ties.
ra•di∘al
radial ker∘a•tot∘o∘my
radial sym•met∘ry
ra•di∘a•lis
ra•di∘al∘ly
ra•di∘an
ra•di∘ant
Ra•di•a∘ta
ra•di•ate, *v.,* -at∘ed, -at•ing.

ra•di•a•tio a∘cus•ti∘ca
radiatio cor•po•ris cal•los∘i
radiatio corporis stri•a∘ti
radiatio op•ti∘ca
ra•di•a•tion
radiation re•call
radiation sick•ness
rad∘i•cal
rad∘i•cle
ra•dic∘u•lar
ra•dic∘u•lec•to∘my, *n., pl.* -mies.
ra•dic∘u•li•tis
ra•dic∘u•lop∘a•thy, *n., pl.* -thies.
ra•dif•er•ous
ra•di∘i
radii len•tis
ra∘di∘o•ac•tin∘i∘um
ra∘di∘o•ac•tive
ra∘di∘o•ac•tive∘ly
ra∘di∘o•ac•tiv∘i∘ty
ra∘di∘o•au•to•gram
ra∘di∘o•au•to•graph
ra∘di∘o•au•to•graph∘ic
ra∘di∘o•au•tog•ra•phy, *n., pl.* -phies.
ra∘di∘o•bi•o•log∘ic
ra∘di∘o•bi•o•log∘i•cal∘ly
ra∘di∘o•bi•ol∘o∘gist
ra∘di∘o•bi•ol∘o∘gy, *n., pl.* -gies.
ra∘di∘o•car•bon
ra∘di∘o•chem∘i∘cal
ra∘di∘o•chemi•cal∘ly
ra∘di∘o•chem•ist
ra∘di∘o•chem•is•try
ra∘di∘o•chro•ma•to•graph∘ic

ra○di○o○chro•ma•tog•ra• phy, *n., pl.* -phies.
ra○di○o○co•balt
ra○di○o○col•loid
ra○di○o○der•ma•ti•tis
ra○di○o○don•tia
ra○di○o○don•tic
ra○di○o○don•tist
ra○di○o○e•col○o•gist
ra○di○o○e○col○o○gy, *n., pl.* -gies.
ra○di○o○el○e•ment
ra○di○o○gen○ic
ra○di○o○gram
ra○di○o○graph
ra○di○og•ra•pher
ra○di○o○graph○ic
ra○di○o○graph○i•cal○ly
ra○di○og•ra•phy, *n., pl.* -phies.
ra○di○o○hu•mer○al
ra○di○o○im•mu•no•as•say
ra○di○o○i○o•dine
ra○di○o○i•ron
ra○di○o○i•so•tope
ra○di○o○i•so•top○ic
ra○di○o○i•so•top○i•cal○ly
ra○di○o○la•bel, *n., v.,* -bel○ed, -bel○ing.
ra○di○o○lead
ra○di○o○log○ic
ra○di○o○log○i•cal
ra○di○o○log○i•cal○ly
ra○di•ol○o•gist
ra○di•ol○o○gy, *n., pl.* -gies.
ra○di○o○lu•cence or ra○di○o• lu•cen○cy
ra○di○o○lu•cent
ra○di○o○lu•mi•nes•cence
ra•di•om•e○ter
ra○di○o○met•ric
ra○di○o○met•ri•cal○ly

ra○di○om•e○try
ra○di○o○mi•crom•e○ter
ra○di○o○mi•met○ic
ra○di○o○ne•cro•sis
ra○di○o○ne•crot○ic
ra○di○o○nu•clide
ra○di○o○pac○i○ty
ra○di○o○paque
ra○di○o○phar•ma•ceu•ti•cal
ra○di○o○phos•pho•rus
ra○di○o○pro•tec•tion
ra○di○o○pro•tec•tive
ra○di○o○pro•tec•tor
ra○di○o○re•sist•ance
ra○di○o○re•sist•ant
ra○di○o○scope
ra○di○o○scop○ic
ra○di○o○scop○i•cal
ra•di•os•co○py, *n., pl.* -pies.
ra○di○o○sen•si•tive
ra○di○o○sen•si•tiv○i○ty
ra○di○o○so•di○um
ra○di○o○ster○i•li•za•tion
ra○di○o○ster○i•lized
ra○di○o○stron•ti○um
ra○di○o○sur•ger○y, *n., pl.* -ger•ies.
ra○di○o○tel○e•met•ric
ra○di○o○te•lem•e○try
ra○di○o○ther•a•peu•tic
ra○di○o○ther•a•peu•tics
ra○di○o○ther•a•pist
ra○di○o○ther•a○py, *n., pl.* -pies.
ra○di○o○ther○my
ra○di○o○tho•ri○um
ra○di○o○trans•par•en○cy
ra○di○o○trans•par•ent
ra○di○o○trop○ic
ra•di•um
ra•di•us, *n., pl.* ra•di•i, ra•di• us○es.

radius fix∘us
ra•dix, *n., pl.* ra•di•ces.
raf•fi•nose
Rail•li•e•ti∘na
Rai•ney's cor•pus•cle
rale
ra•lox∘i•fene
ra∘mal
Ra∘man effect
ram∘i•fi•ca•tion
ram•i∘fy, *v.,* -fied, -fy•ing.
Ram∘i•pril *Trademark.*
ra•mose
Rams•den eye•piece
ram∘u•lus, *n., pl.* ram•u∘li.
ra∘mus, *n., pl.* ra∘mi.
ramus com•mun∘i•cans, *n., pl.*
rami com•mun∘i•can•tes.
ran•cid∘i•fi•ca•tion
ran•cid∘i•fy, *v.,* -fied, -fy•ing.
ran•cid∘i•ty
ran•dom•ized clin∘i•cal tri∘al
range of mo•tion
ra•nine
Ra•nit∘i•dine
Ran•kine scale
ran∘u∘la, *n., pl.* -las.
ran∘u•lar
Ran•vier's node
Raoult's law
raphe
rap∘id eye move•ment
rap•ture of the deep
rap•tus
rar∘e∘fac•tion
rar•e∘fy, *v.,* -fied, -fy•ing.
ras•ce∘ta
ras•pa•to∘ry, *n., pl.* -ries.
rat-bite fe∘ver
rat•bite fe∘ver
rate
Rath•ke's pock∘et

Rathke's pouch
ra∘ti∘o, *n., pl.* -ti∘os.
ra•tion, *v.,* -tioned, -tion•ing.
ra•tion∘al
rational-e∘mo•tive ther∘a∘py
ra•tion•al∘i•ty, *n., pl.* -ties.
ra•tion•al∘i•za•tion
ra•tion•al•ize, *v.,* -ized, -iz•
ing.
rats•bane
rat•tle•snake
Rat•tus
Rau•dix∘in *Trademark.*
Rau-Sed *Trademark.*
Rau•ten•sin *Trademark.*
Rau•wi•loid *Trademark.*
rau•wolf∘i∘a
Rau•zide *Trademark.*
Ray•leigh e∘qua•tion
Ray•naud's dis•ease
Raynaud's phe•nom•e∘non
re•ab•sorb
re•ab•sorp•tion
re∘act
re•ac•tance
re•ac•tant
re•ac•tion
reaction time
re•ac•tion∘al
re•ac•ti•vate, *v.,* -vat∘ed,
-vat∘ing.
re•ac•ti•va•tion
re•ac•tive
reactive o∘be•si∘ty
re•ac•tiv∘i∘ty
re•ac•tor
re•a•gent
re•ag•gre•ga•tion
re•a•gin
re•a•gin∘ic
re•al•gar
re•al∘i∘ty, *n., pl.* -ties.

reality prin•ci•ple
ream•er
re•am•pu•ta•tion
re•at•tach•ment
Reau•mur scale
Reaumur ther•mom•e•ter
re•bel•lion
re•branch
re•cal•ci•fi•ca•tion
re•cal•ci•trant
re•can•al•i•za•tion
re•ca•pit•u•late, v., -lat∘ed,
 -lat•ing.
re•ca•pit•u•la•tion
re•ca•pit•u•la•tive
re•ca•pit•u•la•to∘ry
re•cep•tac•u•lum, n., pl. -tac•
 u∘la.
re•cep•tor
re•ces•sive
re•ces•sive•ness
re•ces•sus
re•cid•i•va•tion
re•cid∘i•vism
re•cid∘i•vist
re•cid∘i•vis•tic
rec∘i•pe
re•cip•ro•cal
re•cip•ro•ca•tion
Reck•ling•hau•sen's dis•ease
rec•og•ni•tion
rec•og•nize, v., -nized, -niz•
 ing.
re•com•bi•nant
recombinant DNA
re•com•bi•na•tion
Re•com•bi•vax HB *Trademark.*
re•com•pres•sion
re•con•di•tion
re•con•sti•tute, v., -tut∘ed,
 -tut•ing.
re•con•sti•tu•tion

re•con•struct
re•con•struc•tion
re•con•struc•tive
re•cov∘er, v., -ered, -er•ing.
re•cov•er∘y, n., pl. -er•ies.
recovery room
rec•re•ment
rec•re•men•ti•tious
re•cru•desce, v., -desced,
 -desc•ing.
re•cru•des•cence
re•cru•des•cen∘cy
re•cru•des•cent
re•cruit•ment
rec•tal
rec•tal∘y
rec•ti•fi•ca•tion
rec•ti•fi∘er
rec•ti∘fy, v., -fied, -fy•ing.
rec•to•cele
rec•toc•ly•sis, n., pl. -ses.
rec∘to•coc•cyg•e∘ous, n., pl.
 -cyg∘e∘i.
rec∘to•scope
rec∘to•sig•moid
rec∘to•sig•moi•do•scope
rec∘to•sig•moi•do•scop∘ic
rec∘to•sig•moi•dos•co∘py,
 n., pl. -pies.
rec∘to•u•ter•ine
rec∘to•ves∘i•cal
rec•tum, n., pl. rec•tums,
 rec∘ta.
rec•tus, n., pl. rec∘ti.
rectus ab•dom∘i•nis
rectus ac•ces•so•ri•ous
re•cum•ben∘cy, n., pl. -cies.
re•cum•bent
re•cu•per•ate, v., -at∘ed, -at•
 ing.
re•cu•per∘a•tion
re•cu•per∘a•tive

re•cur, *v.*, -curred, -cur•ring.
re•cur•rence
re•cur•rent
re•cur•va•tion
red
red blood cell
Red Cross
red-green blind•ness
re•di•a, *n.*, *pl.* -di•ae.
re•dial
re•dif•fer•en•ti•a•tion
red•in•te•gra•tion
red•in•te•gra•tive
Red•i•sol *Trademark.*
red•out
re•dox
re•duce, *v.*, -duced, -duc•ing.
re•duc•er
re•du•ci•bil•i•ty, *n.*, *pl.* -ties.
re•duc•i•ble
re•duc•ing a•gent
re•duc•tant
re•duc•tase
re•duc•tic
re•duc•tion
re•duc•tion•ism
re•duc•tion•ist
re•duc•tone
re•du•pli•cate, *v.*, -cat•ed,
  -cat•ing.
re•du•pli•ca•tion
Red•u•temp *Trademark.*
Re•du•vi•i•dae
Re•du•vi•ous
Reduvius per•so•na•tus
Re•dux
re•ed•u•ca•tion
re•en•force, *v.*, -forced, -forc•
  ing.
re•en•try, *n.*, *pl.* -tries.
re•fec•tion
re•fer, *v.*, -ferred, -fer•ring.

re•fer•ral
re•ferred pain
re•fill
re•flect
re•flec•tion
re•flec•tor
re•flex
reflex arc
re•flex•i•o pal•pe•brar•um
re•flex•o•gen•ic
re•flex•og•e•nous
re•flex•o•log•ic
re•flex•o•log•i•cal•ly
re•flex•ol•o•gist
re•flex•ol•o•gy, *n.*, *pl.* -gies.
re•flux
re•fract
re•frac•tile
re•frac•tion
re•frac•tion•al
re•frac•tion•ist
re•frac•tive
re•frac•tive•ly
re•frac•tive•ness
re•frac•tiv•i•ty
re•frac•tom•e•ter
re•frac•to•met•ric
re•frac•tom•e•try
re•frac•to•ri•ness
re•frac•to•ry
refractory pe•ri•od
re•frac•ture
re•fran•gi•bil•i•ty
re•fran•gi•ble
Re•fresh *Trademark.*
re•frig•er•ant
re•frig•er•ate, *v.*, -at•ed, -at•
  ing.
re•frig•er•a•tion
re•frin•gence
re•frin•gen•cy, *n.*, *pl.* -cies.
re•frin•gent

re•fu•sion
re•gen•er•a•ble
re•gen•er•ate, *v.*, -at○ed, -at•ing.
re•gen•er○a•tion
re•gime
reg○i•men
re•gion
re•gion○al
reg○is•ter, *v.*, -tered, -ter•ing.
reg○is•tered nurse
reg○is•trant
reg○is•trar
reg○is•tra•tion
reg○is•try, *n., pl.* -tries.
Reg○i•tine *Trademark.*
Reg•lan *Trademark.*
Reg○o•nol *Trademark.*
re•gress
re•gres•sion
re•gres•sive
Re•gro•ton
re•grow, *v.*, -grew, -grown, -grow•ing.
reg○u•lar
reg○u•lar○i○ty
reg○u•late, *v.*, -lat○ed, -lat•ing.
reg○u•la•tion
reg○u•la•tive
reg○u•la•tor
regulator gene
re•gur•gi•tant
re•gur•gi•tate, *v.*, -tat○ed, -tat•ing.
re•gur•gi•ta•tion
re•gur•gi•ta•tive
Reg○u•tol *Trademark.*
re•hab•doid
re•ha•bil○i•tant
re•ha•bil○i•tate, *v.*, -tat○ed, -tat•ing.

re•ha•bil○i•ta•tion
re•ha•bil○i•ta•tive
re•ha•bil○i•ta•tor
re•ha•bil○i•tee
re•ha•la•tion
Reh•fuss tube
re•hy•drate, *v.*, -drat○ed, -drat•ing.
re•hy•dra•tion
Rei•chert-Meis•sl num•ber
Reichert-Meissl val○ue
re•im•burse•ment
re•in•fec•tion
re•in•force, *v.*, -forced, -forc•ing.
re•in•force•ment
re•in•forc○er
re•in•ner•va•tion
re•in•oc○u•la•tion
re•in•te•grate, *v.*, -grat○ed, -grat•ing.
re•in•te•gra•tion
re•in•te•gra•tive
Reiss•ner's fi○ber
Rei•ter's dis•ease
Reiter's syn•drome
re•ject
re•jec•tion
re•ju•ve•nate, *v.*, -nat○ed, -nat•ing.
re•ju•ve•na•tion
re•ju•ve•nes•cence
re•ju•ve•nes•cent
Re○la *Trademark.*
Rel○a•a•fen *Trademark.*
re•lapse, *v.*, -lapsed, -laps•ing.
re•laps•ing fe○ver
re•late, *v.*, -lat○ed, -lat•ing.
re•la•tion
re•la•tion•ship
re○lax
re•lax•ant

re•lax○a•tion
re•lax○in
re•leas○er
re•leas•ing fac•tor
Rel○e•fact TRH
re•lief
re•lieve, *v.*, -lieved, -liev•ing.
re•line, *v.*, -lined, -lin•ing.
rem
REM sleep
Re•mak's fi•ber
re•me•di•a•ble
re•me•di○al
re•me•di○al○ly
rem•e○dy, *n., pl.* -e○dies.
re•mis•sion
re•mis•sive
re○mit, *v.*, -mit•ted, -mit•ting.
re•mit•tence or re•mit•ten○cy
re•mit•tent
re•mit•tent○ly
re•move, *v.*, -moved, -mov•ing.
Rem○u•lar-S *Trademark.*
ren mo•bi•lis
Ren-o○va
ren un•gui•for•mis
Re•nac○i•din
re○nal
re•na•tu•ra•tion
re•na•ture, *v.*, -tured, -tur•ing.
Re•nese *Trademark.*
Renese-R *Trademark.*
ren○i•fleur
ren○i•form
re○nin
ren○i•por•tal
ren•net
ren•nin
Re○no•graf○in *Trademark.*
re○no•gram

re○no•graph○ic
re•nog•ra•phy, *n., pl.* -phies.
Re○no-M *Trademark.*
Re○no•quid
re○no•troph○ic
re○no•trop○ic
re○no•vas•cu•lar
Re○no•vist *Trademark.*
re○o○vi•rus, *n., pl.* -rus○es.
Re○pan *Trademark.*
re•par○a•tive
re•pel•lant
re•pel•lent
re•pel•ler
re•per•co•la•tion
re•per•cus•sion
rep•e•ti•tion com•pul•sion
re•pet○i•tive mo•tion in•jur○y
re•place•ment
re•plant
re•plan•ta•tion
Re•plen○a *Trademark.*
Re•plens *Trademark.*
re•ple•tion
rep•li•ca•ble
rep•li•case
rep•li•cate, *v.*, -cat○ed, -cat•ing.
rep•li•ca•tion
rep•li•ca•tive
rep•li•con
re•po•si•tion, *v.*, -tioned, -tion•ing.
re•pos○i•to○ry, *n., pl.* -ries.
re•press
re•pressed
re•press○i•bil○i•ty
re•pres•si•ble
re•pres•sion
re•pres•sor

re•pro•duce, v., -duced, -duc•ing.
re•pro•duc•tion
re•pro•duc•tive
re•pro•duc•tive•ly
Rep•til•o•ia
re•pul•lu•la•tion
re•pul•sion
re•search
re•sect
re•sect•o•a•bil•o•i•ty, n., pl. -ties.
re•sect•o•a•ble
re•sec•tion
re•sec•tion•al
re•sec•to•scope
res•er•pine
re•ser•pin•ized
re•serve
res•er•voir
res•i•den•cy, n., pl. -cies.
res•i•dent
res•i•dent•ship
re•sid•u•al
res•i•due
re•sid•u•um, n., pl. -sid•u•a.
re•sil•ience
re•sil•ient
res•in
res•in•a
res•in•oid
res•in•ous
re•sist•ance
re•sis•tant
re•sis•tent
res•o•lu•tion
re•solve, v., -solved, -solv•ing.
re•sol•vent
res•o•nance
res•o•nant
res•o•nate, v., -nat•ed, -nat•ing.
res•o•na•tion

res•o•na•tor
re•sorb
re•sorb•ence
re•sorb•ent
re•sor•cin
re•sor•ci•nol
re•sorp•tion
re•sorp•tive
Res•paire-SR *Trademark.*
Resp•bid *Trademark.*
res•pi•ra•ble
res•pi•rat•ing
res•pi•ra•tion
res•pi•ra•tion•al
res•pi•ra•tor
res•pi•ra•to•ry
respiratory dis•tress syn•drome
respiratory quo•tient
respiratory syn•cy•tial vi•rus
respiratory sys•tem
re•spire, v., -spired, -spir•ing.
res•pi•rom•e•ter
res•pi•ro•met•ric
res•pi•rom•e•try
re•spond
re•spon•dent
re•sponse
response time
re•sponse•less
rest home
re•ste•no•sis
res•ti•form
res•ti•tu•tion
res•to•ra•tion
res•to•ra•tive
re•store, v., -stored, -stor•ing.
Res•to•ril *Trademark.*
re•strain
re•straint
Restraint Scale
re•stric•tion en•zyme

restriction frag•ment
restriction site
re•stric•tive car•di•o•my•op•a•thy
re•sul•tant
re•su•pi•nate
re•su•pi•nat•ed
re•su•pi•na•tion
res•ur•rec•tion•ism
res•ur•rec•tion•ist
re•sus•ci•ta•ble
re•sus•ci•tate, *v.*, -tat•ed, -tat•ing.
re•sus•ci•ta•tion
re•sus•ci•ta•tive
re•sus•ci•ta•tor
re•tain•er
re•tar•date
re•tar•da•tion
re•tard•ed
re•te, *n.*, *pl.* re•ti•a.
rete mi•ra•bi•le, *n.*, *pl.* retia mi•ra•bi•li•a.
re•ten•tion
re•ti•al
re•tic•u•lar
reticular for•ma•tion
re•tic•u•lar•ly
re•tic•u•late
re•tic•u•lat•ed
re•tic•u•la•tion
re•tic•u•lin
re•tic•u•lo•cyte
re•tic•u•lo•cyt•ic
re•ti•cu•lo•cy•to•sis
re•tic•u•lo•en•do•the•li•al
reticuloendothelial sys•tem
re•ti•cu•lo•en•do•the•li•o•sis
re•ti•cu•lo•en•do•the•li•um, *n.*, *pl.* -li•a.
re•tic•u•lo•sis, *n.*, *pl.* -ses.

re•tic•u•lum, *n.*, *pl.* -tic•u•la.
ret•i•form
Ret•in-A *Trademark.*
ret•i•na, *n.*, *pl.* -nas, -nae.
ret•i•nac•u•la cu•tis
retinacula un•guis
ret•i•nac•u•lum, *n.*, *pl.* -nac•u•la.
ret•i•nal
ret•i•nene
ret•i•ni•tis
retinitis pig•men•to•sa
ret•i•no•blas•to•ma, *n.*, *pl.* -mas, -ma•ta.
ret•i•no•cho•roi•di•tis
ret•i•noid
ret•i•nol
ret•i•no•pap•il•li•tis
ret•i•nop•a•thy
retinopathy of pre•ma•tu•ri•ty
ret•i•no•scope
ret•i•no•scop•ic
ret•i•nos•co•py, *n.*, *pl.* -pies.
re•tort
re•tract
re•trac•tile
re•trac•tion
re•trac•tor
re•trad
ret•ra•hent
re•trench•ment
ret•ro•ac•tion
ret•ro•bul•bar
ret•ro•cae•cal
ret•ro•ca•val
ret•ro•ce•cal
ret•ro•cede, *v.*, -ced•ed, -ced•ing.
ret•ro•ces•sion
ret•ro•dis•place•ment
ret•ro•flec•tion

ret○ro•flex
ret○ro•flexed
ret○ro•flex•ion
ret○ro•grade
retrograde e○jac○ula•tion
retrograde py○e•log•ra•phy
ret○ro•grade○ly
ret○ro•gres•sion
ret○ro•ject
ret○ro•jec○tion
ret○ro•len•tal
retrolental fi•bro•pla•sia
ret○ro•len•tic○u•lar
ret○ro•lin•gual
ret○ro•mo•lar
ret○ro•oc○u•lar
ret○ro•per○i•to•ne○al
ret○ro•per○i•to•ne•al○ly
ret○ro•posed
ret○ro•pu•bic
ret○ro•pul•sion
ret○ro•spec•tion
ret○ro•spec•tive
retrospective stud○y
ret○ro•stal•sis
ret○ro•vac•ci•na•tion
ret○ro•ver•sion
ret○ro•vert○ed
Ret○ro•vir *Trademark.*
ret○ro•vi•ral
ret○ro•vi•rus, *n., pl.* -rus○es.
re•trude, *v.,* -trud○ed, -trud•
  ing.
re•tru•sion
re•tru•sive
Ret•ziu's vein
re•vas•cu•lar○i•za•tion
re•vas•cu•lar•ize, *v.,* -ized,
  -iz•ing.
re•vel•lent
re•ver•sal
re•verse tran•scrip•tase

re•ver•si•ble
re•ver•sion
Re•ver•sol
re○vert
re○ver•tant
re•vive, *v.,* -vived, -viv•ing.
re•viv○i•fi•ca•tion
re•viv•i○fy, *v.,* -fied, -fy•ing.
rev○o•lute
re•vul•sion
re•vul•sive
Reye's syn•drome
Rh fac•tor
Rh-neg○a•tive
Rh-pos○i•tive
Rhab•di•tis
rhab•dom
rhab•dome
rhab•do•mere
rhab•do•my•ol○y•sis
rhab•do•my○o•ma, *n., pl.*
  -mas, -ma○ta.
rhabdomyoma u○ter○i
rhab•do•my○o•sar•co○ma,
  n., pl. -mas, -ma○ta.
rhab•do•vi•rus, *n., pl.* -rus○es.
rha•chi•tis
rha•ga•des
rha•ga•di•form
rham•ni•nose
rham•nose
rham•no•side
Rham•nus
rhamnus fran•gu○la
rhaphe
rhat•a○ny, *n., pl.* -nies.
rha•thy•mi○a
Rhe•a•ban *Trademark.*
rhe•a•dine
rhe•dine
rhe○in
rhe•ni•um

rhe○o•base
rhe○o•ba•sic
rhe•ol○o•gist
rhe•ol○o•gy, *n., pl.* -gies.
Rhe○o•mac•ro•dex *Trademark.*
rhe•om•e○ter
rhe○o•met•ric
rhe•om•e○try
rhe○o•stat
rhe○o•tax○is
rhe○o•trope
rhe•ot•ro•pism
rhe•sus
Rhesus fac•tor
rhesus ma•caque
rhesus mon•key
rheum
rheu•mat○ic
rheumatic fe○ver
rheumatic heart dis•ease
rheu•mat○i•cal○ly
rheu•ma•tism
rheu•ma•toid
rheumatoid arth•ri•tis
rheumatoid fac•tor
rheu•ma•toi•dal
rheu•ma•toi•dal○ly
rheu•ma•tol•o•gist
rheu•ma•tol○o•gy, *n., pl.*
   -gies.
Rheu•ma•trex *Trademark.*
rheum○ic
rheum○y, *adj.,* -i○er, -i○est.
rhex○is, *n., pl.* rhex○es.
rhi•nal
rhi•nal•gia
Rhin•de•con
rhi•nen•ce•phal○ic
rhi•nen•ceph○a•lon, *n., pl.*
   -ceph•a○la.
rhi•nen•ceph○a•lous

rhin•en•chy•sis
rhin•i○on
rhi•ni•tis
rhinitis sic•ca
rhi○no•gen○ic
rhi•nog○e•nous
rhi○no•lalia
rhinolalia a○per○ta
rhinolalia clau○sa
Rhi○no•lar *Trademark.*
Rhinolar-EX *Trademark.*
rhi○no•lar•yn•gol○o•gy, *n.,*
   pl. -gies.
rhi○no•la•ryn•go•scope
rhi○no•lith
rhi○no•lith○ic
rhi○no•log○ic
rhi○no•log○i•cal
rhi•nol○o•gist
rhi•nol○o•gy, *n., pl.* -gies.
rhi○no•phar•yn•gi•tis
rhinopharyngitis mu•ti•lans
rhi○no•phar•ynx, *n., pl.* -pha•
   ryn•ges, -phar•ynx○es.
rhi○no•pho•ni○a
rhi○no•phy○ma
rhi○no•plas•tic
rhi○no•plas○ty, *n., pl.* -ties.
rhi○nor•rha•gia
rhi○nor•rhe○a
rhi○nor•rhoe○a
rhi○no•scler○o○ma, *n., pl.*
   -ma○ta.
rhi○no•scop○ic
rhi○nos•co•pre
rhi○nos•co○py, *n., pl.* -pies.
rhi○no•spo•rid○i○o•sis
rhi○no•spo•rid○i○um, *n., pl.*
   -rid○i○a.
rhi○no•vi•rus, *n., pl.* -rus○es.
Rhi○pi•ceph○a•lus
Rhipicephalus sanguineus

rhi•zo•bi•um, *n., pl.* -bi•a.
rhi•zoid
rhi•zome
rhi•zo•pod
Rhi•zop○o•da
rhi•zop•ter○in
Rhi•zo•pus nig•ri•cans
rhi•zot○o○my, *n., pl.* -mies.
rho•da•mine
rho•da•nate
rho•da•nese
rho•dan○ic
rho•di○um
rho•dop•sin
rhoe•a•dine
Rho•GAM *Trademark.*
rhom•ben•ceph○a•lon, *n., pl.*
-ceph•a○la.
rhom•boid
rhom•boi•dal
rhom•boi•de○us, *n., pl.* -de○i.
rhomboideus oc•cip○i○talis
rhon•chal
rhon•chi○al
rhon•chus, *n., pl.* -chi.
rho•ta•cism
rho•ta•cis•mus
rhus, *n., pl.* rhus○es, rhus.
rhus•glab○ra
rhyth○m
rhythm meth○od
rhyth•mic
rhyth•mi•cal
rhyth•mi•cal○ly
rhyth•mic○i○ty
rhyt○i•do•plas○ty, *n., pl.* -ties.
ri•ba•vi•rin
rib•bon
ri•bi•tol
Ri○bo-2
ri○bo•fla•vin
ri○bo•fla•vine

ri○bo•nu•cle•ase
ri○bo•nu•cle○ic
ribonucleic ac○id
ri○bo•nu•cle○o•pro•tein
ri○bo•nu•cle○o•side
ri○bo•nu•cle○o•tide
ri•bose
ri○bo•side
ri○bo•so•mal
ribosomal RNA
ri○bo•some
ri○bo•syl
ri○bo•zy•mal
ri○bo•zyme
rib○u•lose
Ric•co's law
ri○cin
ric○i•nine
ric○i•no•le•ate
ric○i•no•le○ic
ric○i•nus
rick•ets
rick•ett•si○a, *n., pl.* -si○as,
-si○ae.
rick•ett•si○al
rick•ett•si○al•pox
rick•ett•si○o•sis
rick•ett•si○o•stat○ic
rick○e○ty
ric•tal
ric•tus, *n., pl.* -tus, -tus○es.
Ri•dau•ra
rid○er's bone
rider's strain
ridge•ling
ridg•ling
Rif○a•din *Trademark.*
Rif○a•mate *Trademark.*
rif•am•pi•cin
ri•fam•pin
rif•a•my•cin
rif•lip

Riggs' dis•ease
right-eyed
right-hand○ed
ri•gid○i•tas ar•tic○u•lo•rum
rigiditas ca•dav•er○i•ca
ri•gid○i•ty, *n., pl.* -ties.
rig○or
rigor mor•tis
ri○ma, *n., pl.* ri○mae.
rima glot•ti•dis
Ri•mac•tane *Trademark.*
ri•mose
ri•mous
Rim○so-50
rim•u○la, *n., pl.* -lae.
rin•der•pest
ring•bone
ring•boned
Ring○er so•lu•tion
Ring○er's solution
ring•worm
Ri○o•pan *Trademark.*
ri•par○i○an
risk
risk ad•just•ment
risk fac•tor
ri•so•ri○us, *n., pl.* -ri○i.
Ris•per•dal
Ris•per○i•done
ri•sus ca•ni•nus
risus sar•don○i•cus
Rit○a•lin *Trademark.*
Ritalin-SR *Trademark.*
rit○u○al
riv•er blind•ness
ri○vus lac•ri•ma•lis
riz○i•form
RNA pol○y•mer•ase
RNA syn•the•tase
RNA vi○rus
RNA•ase

R○nase
roar○er
roar•ing
Ro•bax○in *Trademark.*
Ro•bax○i•sal *Trademark.*
Ro•bi•my•cin *Trademark.*
ro•bin○i○a pseu•do•a•ca•cia
Ro•bi•nul *Trademark.*
Ro•bi•tus•sin *Trademark.*
Robitussin A-C *Trademark.*
Robitussin-CF *Trademark.*
Robitussin-DAC *Trademark.*
Robitussin-DM *Trademark.*
Robitussin-PE *Trademark.*
ro•bo•rant
Ro•cal•trol *Trademark.*
Ro•ce•phin *Trademark.*
Ro•chelle salt
Rock○y Moun•tain spot•ted
fe○ver
rod
Ro•den•tia
ro•den•ti•cide
roent•gen
roent•gen○i•za•tion
roent•gen•ize
roent•gen•ky•mo•gram
roent•gen•ky•mo•graph○ic
roent•gen•ky•mog•ra•phy,
n., pl. -phies.
roent•gen•o○gram
roent•gen•o○graph
roent•gen•o○graph○ic
roent•gen•o○graph○i•cal○ly
roent•ge•nog•ra•phy, *n., pl.*
-phies.
roent•gen•o○log○ic
roent•gen•o○log○i•cal
roent•gen•o○log○i•cal○ly
roent•gen•ol○o○gist
roent•ge•nol○o○gy, *n., pl.*
-gies.

roent•ge•nom•e•ter
roent•ge•nom•e•try
roent•gen•o•o•scope
roent•gen•o•o•scop•ic
roent•gen•o•o•scop•i•cal•ly
roent•ge•nos•co•py, *n., pl.* -pies.
roent•gen•o•other•a•py, *n., pl.* -pies.
roent•gen•ther•a•py, *n., pl.* -pies.
Ro•fe•ron-A *Trademark.*
Ro•gaine *Trademark.*
Ro•lan•dic
Rolandic ar•e•a
role mod•el
Rolf, *v.*, Rolfed, Rolf•ing.
Rolf•er
Ro•ma•now•sky stain
Rom•berg sign
Rom•berg's sign
Ron•dec *Trademark.*
Rondec-DM *Trademark.*
Rondec-TR *Trademark.*
ron•geur
ron•nel
rönt•gen
rönt•gen•i•za•tion
rönt•gen•ize
room•ing-in
root ca•nal
root canal ther•a•py
Ror•schach ink•blot test
Rorschach test
ro•sa•ce•a
ro•san•i•line
ro•sa•ry, *n., pl.* -ries.
rose ben•gal
rose ben•gale
rose fe•ver
ro•se•o•la
roseola cho•ler•i•ca

roseola in•fan•tum
roseola syph•i•lit•i•ca
roseola ty•pho•sa
roseola vac•cin•i•a
ro•se•o•lar
ro•sette
ros•in
ro•sol•ic
Ross *Trademark.*
Ross SLD *Trademark.*
ro•stel•lar
ro•stel•late
ro•stel•lum
ros•trad
ros•tral
ros•trate
ros•trum, *n., pl.* -trums, -tra.
ro•ta•cism
ro•tam•e•ter
ro•ta•ry
ro•tate, *v.*, -tat•ed, -tat•ing.
ro•ta•tion
ro•ta•tor, *n., pl.* -tors, -to•res.
rotator cuff
ro•ta•to•res spin•ae
ro•ta•to•ry
ro•ta•vi•rus, *n., pl.* -rus•es.
ro•te•none
rot•tle•ra
rot•u•lar
Rou•get cell
rough•age
rou•leau, *n., pl.* -leaux, -leaus.
round-shoul•dered
round•worm
roup
Rous sar•co•ma
Ro•wa•sa
Rox•a•nol *Trademark.*
Roxanol SR *Trademark.*
Roxanol UD *Trademark.*

Rox•i•cet *Trademark.*
Rox•i•co•done *Trademark.*
Rox•i•prin *Trademark.*
Ru-Tuss DE *Trademark.*
Ru-Tuss II *Trademark.*
Ru•barth's dis•ease
rub•ber dam
rubber room
rub•bing al•co•hol
ru•be○do
ru•be•fa•cient
ru•be•fac•tion
ru•bel○la
ru•be○o○la
ru•be○o•lar
ru•be•o•sis ir○i•dis
ru•bes•cence
ru•bes•cent
Ru•bex *Trademark.*
ru○bi○a tinc•tor○i○a
ru•bid○i•um
ru•big○i•nous
Ru○bin test
ru○bor
Ru•bra•min
ru•bro•spi•nal
Ru•bus
ruc•tus hys•ter○i•cus
ru•di•ment
ru•di•men•ta○ry
Ru○fen *Trademark.*
ru•fous
ru•ga, *n., pl.* ru○gae.
ruga vag○i•na•les
ru○gal
ru•gose
ru•gose○ly

ru•gos○i○ty, *n., pl.* -ties.
ru•gous
Rum-K
ru○men, *n., pl.* ru•mi○na, ru•
    mens.
ru•me•ni•tis
ru•men•ot○o○my, *n., pl.*
    -mies.
Ru○mex
ru•mi•nant
ru•mi•nate, *v.,* -nat○ed, -nat•
    ing.
ru•mi•na•tion
ru•mi•na•tive
run•a○round
run•ner's knee
run•ning
run•round
ru○pi○a
ru•pi○al
ru•pi•oid
rup•tur○a•ble
rup•ture, *v.,* -tured, -tur•ing.
rup•tured disk
Rus•sell's vi○per
ru•the•ni○um
ruth•er•ford
ru○tin
ru•ti•nose
Rx•o○sine *Trademark.*
Ry○na *Trademark.*
Ryna-C *Trademark.*
Ryna-CX *Trademark.*
Ry•na•tan *Trademark.*
Rynatan S *Trademark.*
Ry○na•tuss *Trademark.*
Ryth•mol *Trademark.*

Saave
sa•ba•dil∘la
Sa•bin vac•cine
sa•bi∘na
sab∘u•line
sab∘u•lose
sab∘u•lous
sa•bur∘ra
sa•bur•ral
sac•cade
sac•cad∘ic
sac•cate
sac•cha•rase
sac•cha•rate
sac•cha•rat∘ed
sac•char∘ic
sac•cha•ride
sac•cha•rif•er•ous
sac•char•i•fi•ca•tion
sac•char•i•fi∘er
sac•char•i•fy, v., -fied, -fy•
   ing.
sac•cha•rim•e∘ter
sac•cha•ri•met•ric
sac•cha•ri•met•ri•cal
sac•cha•rim•e∘try
sac•cha•rin
sac•cha•rine
sac•cha•rin∘i∘ty
sac•cha•ro•lyt∘ic
sac•cha•rom•e∘ter
sac•cha•ro•met•ric
sac•cha•rom•e∘try
Sac•cha•ro•my•ces
Sac•cha•ro•my•ce•ta•ce∘ae
sac•cha•ro•my•ce•ta•ceous
Sac•cha•ro•my•ce•ta•les
sac•cha•ro•my•cete
sac•cha•ro•my•cet∘ic

sac•cha•rose
sac•cha•rum
sac•ci•form
sac•cu•lar
saccular an•eu•rysm
sac•cu•late
sac•cu•lat∘ed
sac•cu•la•tion
sac•cule
sac•cu∘li al•ve•o•la•res
sac•cu•lus, n., pl. -cu∘li.
sacculus la•ryn•gis
sac•cus, n., pl. sac∘ci.
saccus con•junc•ti•vae
saccus en•do•lym•phat∘i•cus
saccus lac•ri•ma•lis
saccus om•pha•loen•ter∘i•
   cus
saccus vag∘i•na•lis
sac•rad
sa•cral
sa•cral∘i•za•tion
sac•rec•to•my, n., pl. -mies.
sac∘ro•coc•cyg∘e∘al
sac∘ro•coc•cyg∘e∘us, n., pl.
   -cyg∘e∘i.
sacrococcygeus dor•sa•lis
sacrococcygeus ven•tra•lis
sac∘ro•dyn∘i∘a
sac∘ro•il∘i•ac
sac∘ro•lum•ba•lis
sac∘ro•sci•at∘ic
sac∘ro•spi•na•lis
sac∘ro•spi•nous
sac∘ro•tu•ber•ous
sac•rum, n., pl. sac∘ra.
sad•dle block
sa•dism
sa•dist

sa•dis•tic
sa•dis•ti•cal•ly
sa•do•mas○o•chism
sa•do•mas○o•chist
sa•do•mas○o•chis•tic
safe sex
sag•it○ta
sag•it•tal
sag•it•tal○ly
Saint An•tho○ny's fire
Saint Lou•is en•ceph○a•li•tis
Saint Vi•tus' dance
Saint Vi•tus's dance
sal
Sal-Ac○id *Trademark.*
Sal-Plant *Trademark.*
sal vol○a•tile
Sal○Ac *Trademark.*
Sa•lac•tic Film *Trademark.*
Sal•flex *Trademark.*
sal○i•cin
sal○i•cyl•al•de•hyde
sal○i•cyl•am•ide
sal○i•cyl•an○i•lide
sa•lic○y•late
sa•lic○y•lat○ed
sal○i•cyl•a•zo○sul•fa•py○ri•
  dine
sal○i•cyl•ic
salicylic ac○id
sal○i•cyl•ism
sal○i•cyl○i•za•tion
sal○i•cy•lize, *v.,* -lized, -liz•
  ing.
sal○i•cyl•u•ric acid
sa•li•ent
sal○i•fi•a•ble
sal○i•fi•ca•tion
sal•i○fy, *v.,* -fied, -fy•ing.
sal○i•gen○in
sa•lim•e○ter
sa•line

Sal○i•nex *Trademark.*
sa•lin○i○ty
sal○i•nom•e○ter
sa•li•va
sal○i•vant
sal○i•var○y
salivary gland
sal○i•vate, *v.,* -vat○ed, -vat•
  ing.
sal○i•va•tion
Salk vac○cine
Sal•me•te•rol
sal•mine
sal•mo•nel○la, *n., pl.* -nel•lae,
  -nel•las, -nel○la.
sal•mo•nel•lo○sis
sal○ol
sal•pin•gec•to○my, *n., pl.*
  -mies.
sal•pin•gi•an
sal•pin•git○ic
sal•pin•gi•tis
sal•pin○go•o○o•pho•ri•tis
sal•pin○go•cath○e•ter•ism
sal•pin○go•cele
sal•pin○go•cy•e○sis, *n., pl.*
  -ses.
sal•pin•gog•ra•phy, *n., pl.*
  -phies.
sal•pin•go-o○o•pho•rec•
  to○my, *n., pl.* -mies.
sal•pin○go•pal○a•tine
sal•pin○go•per○i•to•ni•tis
sal•pin○go•pex○y, *n., pl.*
  -pex•ies.
sal•pin○go•pha•ryn•ge○al
sal•pin○go•plas○ty, *n.,*
  -ties.
sal•pin•gos•to○my, *n., pl.*
  -mies.
sal•pin•gy•ster○o○cy•e○sis,
  n., pl. -ses.

sal•pinx, *n., pl.* -pin•ges.
Sal•sa•late *Trademark.*
Sal•si•tab *Trademark.*
salt
sal•ta•tion
sal•ta•to•ry
salt•pe•ter
salt•pe•tre
sa•lu•bri•ous
sa•lu•bri•ous•ly
sal•u•bri•ty
sal•u•ret•ic
sal•u•ret•i•cal•ly
Sal•u•ron *Trademark.*
sal•u•tar•i•ly
sal•u•tar•y
Sal•u•ten•sin *Trademark.*
sal•vage
sal•vi•a
Sam-E.P.A. *Trademark.*
Sam•bu•cus
san•a•ta•ri•um, *n., pl.*
  -ri•ums, -ri•a.
san•a•tive
san•a•to•ri•um, *n., pl.*
  -ri•ums, -ri•a.
san•a•to•ry
sand-blind
sand crack
sand•fly fe•ver
Sand•im•mune
San•do•glob•u•lin
San•do•sta•tin
San•dril *Trademark.*
san•gui•cou•lous
san•gui•fi•ca•tion
san•gui•nar•i•a
sanguinaria can•a•den•sis
san•guin•a•rine
san•guine
san•guine•ly
san•guin•e•ous

san•guin•o•o•lent
san•gui•no•pu•ru•lent
san•gui•no•se•rous
san•gui•nous
san•guis
san•guiv•o•o•rous
san•i•cle
sa•ni•es, *n., pl.* -ni•es.
sa•ni•ous
san•i•tar•i•an
san•i•tar•i•ly
san•i•tar•i•um, *n., pl.* -ri•
  ums, -ri•a.
san•i•tar•y
sanitary nap•kin
san•i•tate, *v.,* -tat•ed, -tat•
  ing.
san•i•ta•tion
san•i•ta•tion•ist
san•i•ti•za•tion
san•i•tize, *v.,* -tized, -tiz•ing.
san•i•tiz•er
san•i•to•ri•um, *n., pl.*
  -ri•ums, -ri•a.
san•i•ty
San•o•rex *Trademark.*
San•sert *Trademark.*
san•ton•i•ca, *n., pl.* -cas.
san•to•nin
San•to•ri•ni's car•ti•lage
sa•pan•wood
sa•phe•na
sa•phe•nous
saphenous vein
sa•po, *n., pl.* sa•pos.
sap•o•gen•in
sap•o•na•ceous
sap•o•nar•i•a
sa•pon•i•fi•a•ble
sa•pon•i•fi•ca•tion
sa•pon•i•fi•er
sa•pon•i•fy, *v.,* -fied, -fy•ing.

sap○o•nin

sa•po○ta

sap○o•tox○in

sap•pan

sap•pan•wood

sap•phic

sap•phism

sa•pre•mi○a

sa•pre•mic

sap•ro•gen

sap•ro•gen○ic

sap•rog•e○nous

sap•roph○a•gous

sap•ro•phile

sap•roph○i•lous

sap•ro•phyte

sap•ro•phyt○ic

sap•ro•phyt○i•cal○ly

Sar○a•pin *Trademark.*

sar○a•pus

sar•cin○a, *n., pl.* -cin○as, -cin○ae.

sar○co•cele

sar○co•cys•tis, *n., pl.* -tis, -ti○ses.

Sarcocystis lin•de•man○ni

Sar○co•di○na

sar○co•din○i○an

sar•cog•li○a

sar•coid

sar•coi•do○sis

sar•co•lac•tic

sar•co•lac•ti○cum ac○i•dum

sar○co•lem○ma

sar○co•lem•mal

sar•col○y•sis

sar○co○ma, *n., pl.* -mas, -ma○ta.

sar○co•ma•gen○ic

sar•com○a•toid

sar○co•ma•to•sis

sar○com○a•tous

sar○co•mere

sar○co•mer○ic

sar○co•plasm

sar○co•plas○ma, *n., pl.* -ma○ta.

sar○co•plas•mat○ic

sar○co•plas•mic

sar○co•poi•et○ic

Sar•cop•tes

sar○co•sine

sar○co•so•mal

sar○co•some

sar○co•spo•rid○i•o•sis

sar○co•style

sar•cous

sar○in

sar•sa•pa•ril○la

sar•to•ri○us, *n., pl.* -ri○i.

sas•sa•fras

sa•tan○o•pho•bi○a

sat•el•lite

sat•el•li•to•sis, *n., pl.* -ses.

sa•ti•ate, *v.,* -at○ed, -at•ing.

sa•ti•a•tion

sa•ti•e○ty

sat○u•rate, *v.,* -rat○ed, -rat•ing.

sat○u•rat○ed fat

sat○u•ra•tion

sat•ur•nine

sat•ur•nism

sat○y•ri•a•sis

sau•cer○i•za•tion

sau•cer•ize, *v.,* -ized, -iz•ing.

sau•na

sau•ri•a•sis

sax○i•tox○in

scab, *v.,* scabbed, scab•bing.

scab○by, *adj.* -bi○er, -bi•est.

sca•bet○ic

scab○i•cid○al

scab○i•cide

sca•bies, *n., pl.* sca•bies.
scabies crus•to•sa
scabies pap•u•li•for•mis
scabies pap•u•lo•sa
scabies pus•tu•lo•sa
sca•bi•et•ic
sca•bi•et•i•cide
sca•bi•ous
scab•ri•ties
sca•la, *n., pl.* sca•lae.
scala me•di•a, *n., pl.* sca•lae me•di•ae.
scala tym•pa•ni, *n., pl.* scalae tym•pa•no•rum.
scala ves•tib•u•li, *n., pl.* scalae ves•tib•u•lo•rum.
sca•lene
sca•le•nec•to•my, *n., pl.* -mies.
sca•le•not•o•my, *n., pl.* -mies.
sca•le•nus, *n., pl.* -le•ni.
scalenus min•i•mus
scalenus pleu•ra•lis
scal•er
scall
scal•o•gram
scal•pel
scal•pel•lic
scal•pri•form
scal•prum, *n., pl.* -pra.
scam•mo•ny
scan, *v.,* scanned, scan•ning.
scan•di•um
scan•na•ble
scan•ner
scan•ning e•lec•tron mi•cro•scope
Scan•zo•ni's ma•neu•ver
sca•pha
scaph•o•ce•phal•ic
scaph•o•ceph•a•lism
scaph•o•ceph•a•lous

scaph•o•ceph•a•oly
scaph•oid
scap•u•la, *n., pl.* -lae, -las.
scapula a•la•ta
scap•u•lar
scap•u•lar•y, *n., pl.* -ies.
sca•pus, *n., pl.* sca•pi.
scapus pi•li
scar
scar tis•sue
scarf•skin
scar•i•fi•ca•tion
scar•i•fi•ca•tor
scar•i•fi•er
scar•i•fy, *v.,* -fied, -fy•ing.
scar•la•ti•na
scar•la•ti•nal
scar•la•ti•ni•form
scar•la•ti•no•gen•ic
scar•la•ti•noid
scar•la•ti•nous
scar•let fe•ver
Scar•pa's fas•ci•a
Scarpa's fo•ra•men
Scarpa's tri•an•gle
Scarpa's tri•gone
scar•ring
scat•o•le
scat•o•log•ic
scat•o•log•i•cal
sca•tol•o•gy
sca•to•ma, *n., pl.* -mas, -ma•ta.
sca•toph•a•gous
sca•toph•a•gy
scat•u•la, *n., pl.* -lae.
Scheib•ler's re•a•gent
Schick test
Schiff base
Schiff re•ac•tion
Schiff re•a•gent
Schil•der's dis•ease

Schil•ling in•dex

schin•dy•le○sis, *n.*, *pl.* -ses.

schir•rhus

schis○to•cyte

schis•to•cy•to•sis

schis○to•glos•si○a

schis•tom•e○lus, *n.*, *pl.* -e○li.

schis○tor•rha•chis

schis○to•so○ma

Schistosoma hae•ma•to• bi○um

Schistosoma ja•pon○i•cum

Schistosoma man•so○ni

schis•to•some

schis•to•so•mi•a•sis, *n.*, *pl.* -ses.

schistosomiasis hae•ma•to• bi○a

schistosomiasis ja•pon○i•ca

schistosomiasis man•so○ni

schiz•ax○on

schiz○o-af•fec•tive

schiz○o•cyte

schiz○o•gen•e○sis, *n.*, *pl.* -e○ses.

schiz○o•ge•net○ic

schiz○o•ge•net○i•cal○ly

schiz○o•gen○ic

schizog•e○nous

schizog•e○nous○ly

schiz○o•gon○ic

schiz•og○o○nous

schi•zog○o○ny

schiz•oid

schizoid per•son•al○i○ty dis• or•der

schiz•oid•man○ic

schiz○o•man○ic

schiz○o•my•cete

Schiz○o•my•ce•tes

schiz○o•my•cet○ic

schiz○o•my•ce•tous

schiz•ont

schiz•on•ti•cid○al

schiz•on•ti•cide

schiz○o•pha•sia

schiz○o•phre•ni○a

schiz○o•phren○ic

schiz○o•phren○i•cal○ly

schiz○o•thy•mic

schiz○o•thy•mous

Schiz○o•try•pa•num

schiz○o○typ○al per•son• al○i○ty dis•or•der

Schlemm's ca○nal

Schnei•der in○dex

Schnei•de•ri○an mem•brane

Schuff•ner's dots

Schül•ler-Chris•tian dis•ease

Schultz-Dale re•ac•tion

Schwann cell

Schwann tube

Schwan•ni○an

Schwann's sheath

sci•age

sci•at○ic

sciatic nerve

sci•at○i○ca

sci•at○i•cal○ly

scil○la

scin•ti•gram

scin•ti•graph○ic

scin•tig•ra•phy, *n.*, *pl.* -phies.

scin•til•late, *v.*, -lat○ed, -lat• ing.

scin•til•la•tion

scintillation cam•er○a

scin•till○ator

scin•til•lom•e○ter

scin•ti•scan

scin•ti•scan•ner

scin•ti•scan•ning

sci○on

scir•rhoid

scoptophilia

scir•rhos∘i∘ty
scir•rhous
scir•rhus, *n., pl.* -rhi, rhus∘es.
scis•sile
scis•sion
scis•si•par∘i∘ty
scis•su∘ra, *n., pl.* -rae.
scle∘ra, *n., pl.* -ras, -rae.
scle•ral
scler•ec•ta•sia
scler•rec•to•ir∘i•dec•to∘my, *n., pl.* -mies.
scle•rec•to∘my, *n., pl.* -mies.
scler•e∘de∘ma
scleredema ad•ul•to∘rum
scleredema ne∘o∘na•to•rum
scle•re∘ma ad∘i•po∘sum
sclerema ad•ul•to∘rum
sclerema cu∘tis
sclerema e∘de•ma•to•sum
sclerema ne∘o•na•to•rum
scle•ri•tis
scler∘o•blas•te∘ma
scler∘o•blas•te•mic
scler∘o•con•junc•ti•val
scler∘o•cor•ne∘a
scler∘o•cor•ne∘al
scle•ro•dac•tyl∘i∘a, *n., pl.* -tyl•i∘as.
scle•ro•dac•ty∘ly
scle•ro•der∘ma
scle•ro•der•ma•tous
scler∘o•gen∘ic
sclerog∘e∘nous
scle•roid
scle•ro•ker∘o•a•ti•tis
scle•ro∘ma, *n., pl.* -mas, -ma∘ta.
scle•ro•ma•la•cia
scleromalacia per•fo•rans
Scler∘o•mate

scle•ro•me•ninx, *n., pl.* -me•nin•ges.
scler∘o•mere
sclerom•e∘ter
scler∘o•nych∘i∘a
scle•ro•plas∘ty, *n., pl.* -ties.
scler∘o•pro•tein
scle•ro•sal
scle•rose, *v.,* -rosed, -ros•ing.
scle•rosed
scle•ro•sis
sclerosis co∘ri∘i
sclerosis der•ma•tis
sclerosis os∘si∘um
scle•ro•ste•no•sis
sclerostenosis cu•ta•ne∘a
scle•ros•to∘my, *n., pl.* -mies.
scle•ro•ther∘a∘py, *n., pl.* -pies.
scle•rot∘ic
scle•rot∘ica
scle•ro•ti•tis
scle•ro•ti∘um, *n., pl.* -ti∘a.
scler∘o•tome
scler∘o•tom∘ic
scle•rot∘o∘my, *pl.* -mies.
scle•rous
scol∘e•coid
sco•lex, *n., pl.* -li•ces, -le•ces, -lex∘es.
sco•li•o•sis
sco•li•ot∘ic
sco•pa•rin
sco•par•i∘us
sco•pine
sco•po∘la
sco•pol∘o•a•mine
sco•po•li∘a
sco•po•phil∘i∘a
sco•po•phil∘i∘ac
sco•po•phil∘ic
scop•to•phil∘i∘a

scop•to•phil∘i∘ac
scop•to•phil∘ic
scor•bu•tic
scor•bu•ti•cal
scor•bu•ti•cal∘ly
scor•bu•ti•gen∘ic
scor•bu•tus
scor•pi∘on
Scor•pi∘on∘i•da
sco•to•din∘i•a
sco•to•graph
sco•to∘ma, *n., pl.* -mas, -ma∘ta.
sco•tom∘a•graph
sco•tom∘a•tous
sco•tom•e∘ter
sco•to•pi∘a
sco•top∘ic
scrap∘ie
scratch test
screen
screen•ing test
screw•worm
scro•bic∘u•late
scro•bic∘u•lus cor•dis
scrof∘u∘la
scrof∘u•lo∘der∘oma
scrof∘u•lo•der•mic
scrof∘u•lo∘sis
scrof∘u•lous
scro•tal
scro•tec•to∘my, *n., pl.* -mies.
scro•to•cele
scro•tum, *n., pl.* scro∘ta, scro•tums.
scrub suit
scrub ty•phus
scru•ple
scru•pu•los∘i∘ty
scurf
scurf∘y, *adj.,* scurf∘i∘er, scurf∘i•est.

scur∘vy
scu•ti•form
Scu•tig∘er∘a
scu•tu•lum, *n., pl.* -tu∘la.
scu•tum, *n., pl.* scu∘ta.
scutum tym•pan∘icum
scyb∘a•lous
scyb∘a•lum, *n., pl.* scyb•a∘la.
sea salt
sea•sick
sea•sick•ness
sea•son∘al af•fec•tive dis•or•der
seat•worm
se•ba•ceous
sebaceous gland
se•bip∘a•rous
seb•or•rhe∘a
seb•or•rhe∘al
seb•or•rhe∘ic
seb•or•rhoe∘a
seb•or•rhoe∘ic
Seb∘u•lex
se∘bum
sebum cu•ta•ne∘um
sebum pal•pe•bra∘le
sebum prae•pu•ti•a∘le
se•cal∘e cor•nu•tum
se•cer•nent
se•clu•sion
sec∘o∘bar•bi•tal
sec∘o∘dont
Sec∘o∘nal *Trademark.*
sec•ond-de•gree burn
second im•pact syn•drome
second look lap∘a•rot∘o∘my
sec•ond•ar∘y
secondary sex char•ac•ter•is•tic
sec•ond•hand smoke
sec•on•di•nes
se•cre∘ta

se•cre•ta•gog
se•cre•ta•gogue
se•crete, *v.*, -cret○ed, -cret•
  ing.
se•cre•tin
se•cre•tion
se•cre•tion•ar○y
se•cre•to•gogue
se•cre•to•mo•tor se•cre•tor
se•cre•to○ry
sec•tar•i○an
sec•tion
sec•to•ri○al
Sec•tral *Trademark.*
se•cun•di•grav•i○da
se•cun•di•nes
se•cun•dip•a○ra
sec•un•dip○a•rous
se•cure
se•cu•ri○ty, *n.*, *pl.* -ties.
Se•da•pap *Trademark.*
se•date, *v.*, -dat○ed, -dat•ing.
se•da○tion
sed○a•tive
sed•en•tar○y
sed○i•ment
sed○i•men•ta○tion
se•do•hep•tu•lose
seg•men○ta re•na•li○a
seg•men•tal
segmental re•sec•tion
seg•men•ta○tion
seg•men•tec•to○my, *n.*, *pl.*
  -mies.
seg•ment○er
seg•re•gant
seg•re•gate, *v.*, -gat○ed, -gat•
  ing.
seg•re•ga•tion
seg•re•ga•tion○al
Seid•litz pow•ders
Sei•gnette salt

Sei•gnette's salt
sei•zure
se•junc•tion
sel○a•chyl
Sel•dane *Trademark.*
Seldane-D *Trademark.*
se•lec•tion
sel•em○i•um met•al•li•cum
se•le•nic
se•le•ni○um
se•le•no•dont
se•le•no•sis
self
self-a○buse
self-ac•cu•sa•tion
self-ac•tu•al○i•za•tion
self-ac•tu•al•ize, *v.*, -ized, -iz•
  ing.
self-a○nal○y•sis
self-an•a•lyt○ic
self-an•a•lyt○i•cal
self-an•ti•gen
self-a○ware
self-a○ware•ness
self-con•cept
self-con•cep•tion
self-dif•fer•en•ti•a•tion
self-di•ges•tion
self-ex•am○i•na•tion
self-ex•am○i•ning
self-hyp•no•sis
self-hyp•not○ic
self-hyp•no•tism
self-i○den•ti•fi•ca•tion
self-im•age
self-in•duc•tance
self-in•flict○ed
self-lim○i•tation
self-lim•it○ed
self-lim•it•ing
self-med○i•ca•tion
self-per•cep•tion

self-rep•li•cat•ing
self-rep•li•ca•tion
self-re•pres•sion
self-re•pro•duc•ing
self-stim•u•la•tion
self-treat•ment
self-a•nal•y•sis, *n., pl.* -ses.
self-hyp•no•sis
sel○la, *n., pl.* -las, -lae.
sella tur•ci○ca
sel•lar
sella tur•ci○ca, *n., pl.* sel•lae
  tur•ci•cae.
Sel•sun Blue *Trademark.*
se•mei•og•ra•phy, *n., pl.*
  -phies.
se•mei•o•log○i•cal
se•mei•ol○o○gy, *n., pl.* -gies.
se•mei•ot○ic
se•mei•ot○i•cal
se•mei•ot•ics
se○men
sem○i•car•ti•lag○i•nous
Sem○i•cid *Trademark.*
sem○i•cir•cu•lar
semicircular ca○nal
sem○i•co○ma
sem○i•co•ma•tose
sem○i•con•scious
sem○i•con•scious•ly
sem○i•con•scious•ness
sem○i•cris○ta in•ci•si○va
sem○i•dom○i•nant
Sem○i•le•note *Trademark.*
sem○i•le•thal
sem○i•lu•nar
semilunar valves
sem○i•mem•bra•no•sus, *n.,*
  pl. -no○si.
sem○i•mem•bra•nous
sem○i•nal
seminal flu○id

seminal ves○i•cle
sem○i•nal○ly
sem○i•nate, *v.,* -nat○ed, -nat•
  ing.
sem○i•na•tion
sem○i•nif•er○al
sem○i•nif•er○ous
seminiferous tu•bule
sem○i•no•ma, *n., pl.* -mas,
  -ma○ta.
sem○i•nu•ri○a
se•mi•og•ra•phy, *n., pl.*
  -phies.
se•mi•o•log○i•cal
se•mi•ol○o○gy, *n., pl.* -gies.
se•mi•ot○ic
se•mi•ot○i•cal
sem○i•per•me•a•ble
sem○i•pri○vate
sem○i•pro•na•tion
sem○i•qui•none
sem○i•spi•na•lis, *n., pl.* -na•
  les.
sem○i•syn•thet○ic
sem○i•syn•thet○i•cal○ly
se•mi•ten•di•no•sus, *n., pl.*
  -no○si.
sem○i•ten•di•nous
Sen•dai vi○rus
sen○e○ca
se•ne○ci○o, *n., pl.* -ci○os.
se•ne○ci•o•sis
sen○e○ga
sen○e•gin
se•nes•cence
se•nes•cent
se•nile
senile de•men•tia
se•nile○ly
se•nil○i○ty
Sen•iors *Trademark.*
se•ni○um

senium prae•cox
senium pre•cox
sen○na
Sen○o•kot *Trademark.*
Senokot-S *Trademark.*
Sen○o•kot•XTRA *Trademark.*
se•no•pi○a
sen•sa•tion
sen•sa•tion○al
sense
sense da○tum
sense per•cep•tion
sense-da○tum, *n., pl.* -da○ta.
sen•si•bil○i○a
sen•si•bil○i○ty, *n., pl.* -ties.
sen•si•ble
sen•si•mo•tor
sen•si•tive
sen•si•tive○ly
sen•si•tive•ness
sen•si•tiv○i○ty, *n., pl.* -ties.
sensitivity train•ing
sen•si•ti•za•tion
sen•si•tize, *v.,* -tized, -tiz•ing.
sen•so•motor
sen•sor
Sen•sor•caine *Trademark.*
sen•so•ri○al
sen•so•ri•al○ly
sen•so•ri•mo•tor
sen•so•ri•neu•ral
sen•so•ri○um, *n., pl.* -ri○ums,
  -ri○a.
sen•so○ry
sensory dep•ri•va•tion
sen•su○al
sen•su•al•ism
sen•su•al○i○ty, *n., pl.* -ties.
sen•su•al○ly
sen•sum, *n., pl.* sen○sa.
sen•tient
sep○a•ra•tion anx○i○e○ty

sep○a•ra•tor
se○pi○a
sep•sis
sep○ta
sep•tal
sep•tate
sep•tat○ed
sep•ta•tion
sep•tic
septic sore throat
sep•ti•cae•mi○a
sep•ti•cae•mic
sep•ti•cal○ly
sep•ti•ce•mi○a
sep•ti•ce•mic
sep•tic○i○ty
sep•ti•co•py•e•mi○a
sep•ti•co•py•e•mic
sep•tile
sep○to•mar•gi•nal
sep•tom•e○ter
sep○to•na•sal
sep○to•tome
Sep•tra *Trademark.*
sep•tu•lum, *n., pl.* -tu○la.
sep•tum, *n., pl.* sep○ta, sep•
  tums.
septum pel•lu•ci•dum, *n., pl.*
  sep○ta pel•lu•ci○da.
septum trans•ver•sum, *n., pl.*
  sep○ta trans•ver○sa.
sep•tup•let
se•quel○a, *n., pl.* -quel○ae.
se•quence, *n., v.,* -quenced,
  -quenc○ing.
se•quenc○er
se•ques•ter, *v.,* -tered, -ter•
  ing.
se•ques•tra•tion
se•ques•trec•to○my, *n., pl.*
  -mies.

se•ques•trum, *n., pl.* -trums, -tra.

Ser

Ser-Ap-Es *Trademark.*

se•ora

Se•rax *Trademark.*

Ser•e•no•a

Ser•en•til *Trademark.*

Ser•e•vent

se•ri•al•o•graph

ser•oi•cin

se•ries, *n., pl.* se•ries.

ser•ine

se•ro•di•ag•no•sis, *n., pl.* -ses.

se•ro•di•ag•nos•tic

se•ro•fi•brin•ous

se•ro•log•ic

se•ro•log•i•cal

se•ro•log•i•cal•ly

se•rol•o•gist

se•rol•o•gy, *n., pl.* -gies.

se•ro•mu•cous

se•ro•mus•cu•lar

Se•ro•my•cin *Trademark.*

se•ro•neg•a•tive

se•ro•neg•a•tiv•i•ty

Se•ro•phene *Trademark.*

se•ro•pos•i•tive

se•ro•pos•i•tiv•i•ty

se•ro•pu•ru•lent

se•ro•re•ac•tion

se•ro•re•sist•ance

se•ro•re•sist•ant

se•ro•sa, *n., pl.* -sas, -sae.

se•ro•sal

se•ro•san•guin•e•ous

se•ro•san•gui•nous

se•ro•si•tis

se•ros•i•ty

se•ro•syn•o•vi•tis

se•ro•ther•o•a•py, *n., pl.* -pies.

ser•o•to•nin

se•ro•type, *n., v.,* -typed, -typ•ing.

se•rous

serous mem•brane

serous o•ti•tis me•di•a

se•rous•ness

Ser•pa•sil *Trademark.*

Serpasil-A•pres•o•line *Trademark.*

Serpasil-Es•i•drix *Trademark.*

ser•pen•tar•oi•a

ser•pig•oi•onous

ser•pig•oi•onous•ly

ser•rate

ser•rat•ed

Ser•ra•tia

Serratia mar•ces•cens

ser•ra•tion

ser•ra•tus, *n., pl.* -ra•ti.

serratus mag•nus

ser•re•fine

ser•ru•late

ser•ru•lat•ed

ser•ru•la•tion

Ser•to•li cell

Ser•to•li's cell

Ser•tra•line

se•rum, *n., pl.* se•rums, se•ra.

serum al•bu•min

serum glob•u•lin

serum hep•a•ti•tis

se•rum•al

ser•vo•mech•a•nism

ses•a•me

ses•a•moid

sesamoid bone

ses•a•moi•di•tis

ses•ile

set point

se•ta, *n., pl.* se•tae.

se•ta•ceous

se•ta•ceous•ly
se○tal
Se•tar○i○a
set•fast
Seth○○•tope *Trademark.*
se•tig○er•ous
se○ton
set•up
Sev•er's dis•ease
se•vum
sex
sex change
sex chro•ma•tin
sex chro•mo•some
sex hor•mone
sex-in•ter•grade
sex-lim○i•ted
sex-link•age
sex-linked
sex ther○a○py
sex•dig○i•tal
sex•dig○i•tate
sex•dig○i•tat○ed
sex○○•log○i•cal
sex•ol○○•gist
sex•ol○○•gy, *n., pl.* -gies.
sex•tip•a○ra, *n., pl.* -ras, -rae.
sex•tu•plet
sex○u○al
sexual in•ter•course
sex○u•al○i○ty
sex○u•al○i•za•tion
sex○u•al•ize, *v.,* -ized, -iz•ing.
sex○u•al○ly
sexually trans•mit•ted dis•
    ease
Shade *Trademark.*
shad•ow-cast•ing
shak•en ba○by syn•drome
shark-liv○er oil
Shar•pey's fi○ber
sharps

shave bi○op○sy
sheath of Schwann
shell-shock
shell-shocked
shel•lac
shel•lack
shi•at○su
shi•at○zu
Shi○ga ba•cil•lus
Shiga dys•en•ter○y ba•cil•lus
shi•gel○la, *n., pl.* -lae, -las.
shig•el•lo○sis
shi•kim○ic
shin
shin splints or shin•splints
shin•bone
shin•gles
shiv○er, *v.,* -ered, -er•ing.
shock
shock ther○a○py
shock○a•bil○i○ty
shock○a•ble
Shope pap•il•lo○ma
Shope's papilloma
short sight
short-wind•ed
short•sight○ed
short•sight•ed○ly
short•sight•ed•ness
shoul•der
shoulder blade
show
Shrap•nell's mem•brane
shunt
shunt○er
si○alo•a•gog○ic
si○alo•a•gogue
si○al○ic
si○al○○•ad○e•ni•tis
si○a•lo•de•no•sis
si○al○○•do•chi•tis

si•a•log•e•nous
si•a•lo•gog•ic
si•al∘o•gogue
si•al∘o•gram
si•a•log•ra•phy, *n., pl.* -phies.
si•a•loid
si•al∘o•lith
si•a•lo•li•thi•a•sis
si•al•or•rhe•a
si•al•or•rhoe•a
Si•a•mese twin
sib∘i•lant
sib∘i•lis•mus au•ri∘um
sib•ling
sib•ship
sic•cant
sic•ca•tive
sic•cus
sick build•ing syn•drome
sick head•ache
sick si∘nus syn•drome
sick∘en, *v.,* -ened, -en•ing.
sick•lae•mi∘a
sick∘le
sickle cell
sickle-cell a•ne•mi∘a
sickle cell trait
sickle-hammed
sickle-hocked
sick•le•mi∘a
sick•le•mic
sick•ness
sick•out
sick•room
side ef•fect
sid•er•ism
sid∘er∘o•cyte
sid∘er∘o•fi•bro•sis
sid∘er∘o•pe•ni∘a
sid∘er∘o•phil
sid∘er∘o•phile

sid∘er∘o•phil∘in
sid∘er∘o•sis
siderosis bul∘bi
sid•er•ot∘ic
side•stream smoke
sig•ma•tism
sig•moid
sigmoid flex•ure
sig•moi•dal
sig•moi•dal∘ly
sig•moi•dec•to∘my, *n., pl.* -mies.
sig•moi•di•tis
sig•moid∘o•scope
sig•moid∘o•scop∘ic
sig•moid•os•co•pist
sig•moi•dos•co•py, *n., pl.* -pies.
sig•moi•dos•to∘my, *n., pl.* -mies.
sign
sig•na•ture
Sig•tab *Trademark.*
si•lent
si•lex
sil∘i•ca
sil∘i•cate
sil∘i•cea
si•li•ceous
si•lic∘ic
si•li•cious
sil∘i•co•fluor•ide
sil∘i•con
sil∘i•cone
silicone im•plant
sil∘i•co•sid∘er∘o•sis
sil∘i•co•sis
sil∘i•cot∘ic
sil∘i•co•tu•ber•cu•lo•sis
sil∘i•quose
sil∘i•quous
Sil•va•dene *Trademark.*

sil•ver ni•trate
Sil•ves•ter meth•od
Sil•ves•ter's method
si•meth•i•cone
simian vi•rus 40
Sim•i•lac *Trademark.*
Sim•monds' dis•ease
sim•ple frac•ture
simple sug•ar
Sim•plesse
sim•u•la•tion
sim•u•lator
Sim•u•li•um
Sim•va•sta•tin
si•nal
sin•a•pism
Sin•a•rest *Trademark.*
sin•cip•i•tal
sin•ci•put, *n., pl.* -ci•puts,
   -cip•i•ta.
Sine-Aid *Trademark.*
Sine-Off *Trademark.*
Sin•e•met *Trademark.*
Sin•e•quan *Trademark.*
sin•ew
sin•gle-blind
single pho•ton e•mis•sion
   com•put•ed
Sing•let *Trademark.*
sin•gul•tus
sin•i•grin
sin•is•ter
sin•is•trad
sin•is•tral
sin•is•tral•i•ty, *n., pl.* -ties.
sin•is•tral•ly
sin•is•tro•ce•re•bral
sin•is•troc•u•lar
sin•is•troc•u•lar•i•ty, *n., pl.*
   -ties.
sin•is•tro•gyra•tion

sin•is•tro•man•u•al
sin•is•trop•e•dal
sin•is•tror•sal•ly
sin•is•trorse
sin•is•trorse•ly
sin•is•tro•tor•sion
sin•is•trous
si•no•a•tri•al
sinoatrial node
si•no•au•ric•u•lar
Si•nog•ra•fin *Trademark.*
sin•se•mil•la
si•nu•a•tri•al
si•nu•au•ric•u•lar
Si•nu•fed *Trademark.*
Si•nu•lin *Trademark.*
Si•nu•mist-SR *Trademark.*
sin•u•ous
sin•u•ous•ly
si•nus, *n., pl.* -nus•es.
si•nus•i•tis
si•nus•like
si•nus•oid
si•nus•oi•dal
si•nus•oi•dal•ly
si•nus•ot•o•omy, *n., pl.* -mies.
si•phon•age
Si•phon•ap•ter•a
si•phon•ap•ter•ous
Sip•py di•et
Sippy reg•i•men
si•ren•om•e•lus, *n., pl.* -e•li.
si•ri•a•sis
sit-up
sit•fast
si•tol•o•gy, *n., pl.* -gies.
si•to•ma•ni•a
si•tos•ter•ol
si•tu
sit•u•a•tion
sit•u•a•tion•al

si∘tus, *n., pl.* si∘tus.
situs in•ver•sus
sitz bath
ska•tol
ska•tole
ska•tol∘o•gy
Ske•lax∘in *Trademark.*
skel•e∘tal
skeletal mus•cle
skel•e∘tal∘ly
skel∘e•ti•za•tion
skel∘e•tog∘e∘nous
skel∘e•to•mus•cu∘lar
skel•e∘ton
ske•ne•i•tis
Skene's gland
ske•ni•tis
ski•a•gram
ski•a•graph
ski•ag•ra•pher
ski•ag•ra•phy
ski•am•e∘try
ski•a∘scope
ski•as∘co∘py, *n., pl.* -pies.
skin fold test
skin graft
skin graft•ing
skin-pop, *v.,* -popped, -pop•ping.
Skin•ner box
Skin•ner∘i∘an
skull•cap
sleep ap∘nea
sleep•ing pill
sleeping sick•ness
sleep•walk
sleep•walk∘er
sleep•walk•ing
slim dis•ease
slime mold
slipped disk
slit lamp

sliv∘er
Slo-bid Gy•ro•caps *Trademark.*
Slo-Ni•a•cin *Trademark.*
Slo-phyl•lin *Trademark.*
slob•ber, *v.,* -bered, -ber•ing.
slough
Slow Fe *Trademark.*
Slow-K *Trademark.*
slow-re•lease
slow vi∘rus
slow-wave sleep
sluff
slur∘ry, *n., pl.* slur•ries.
small cal∘o∘rie
small in•tes•tine
small•pox
smeg∘ma
smegma cli•tor∘i•dis
smegma em•bry•o•num
smegma prae•pu•ti∘i
smi•lax
Smith-Pe•ter•son nail
smooth mus•cle
snail fe∘ver
snake•bite
snake•root
snap•ping hip syn•drome
sneeze, *v.,* sneezed, sneez•ing.
Snel•len test
snif•fle, *v.,* -fled, -fling.
snort
snort∘er
snow
snow-blind
snow-blind∘ed
snow blind•ness
snow•bird
snuf•fles
soap•stone
so∘cia pa•rot∘i•dis
socia pa•ro∘tis

so•cial
social ad•e○qua•cy in○dex
social dis•ease
social psy•chol○o○gy
so•cial○i•za•tion
so•cial•ize, *v.*, -ized, -iz•ing.
socialized med○i•cine
so•cial○ly
so○ci○o•cen•tric
so○ci○o•cen•tric○i•ty, *n., pl.*
  -ties.
so○ci○o•cen•trism
so○ci○o•cu•sis
so○ci○o•gen•e○sis, *n., pl.*
  -e○ses.
so○ci○o•ge•net○ic
so○ci○o•gen○ic
so○ci○o•gram
so○ci○o•log○ic
so○ci○o•log○i•cal
so•ci•ol○o○gist
so•ci•ol○o○gy, *n., pl.* -gies.
so○ci○o•med○i•cal
so○ci○o•met•ric
so•ci•om•e○trist
so•ci•om•e○try
so○ci○o•path
so○ci○o•path○ic
so•ci•op○a•thy
so○ci○o•sex•u○al
so○ci○o•sex•u•al○i•ty
sock○et
so•di○um
sodium ben•zo•ate
sodium bi•car•bo•nate
sodium chlo•ride
sodium ni•trite
sodium pump
so•do•ku
sod○o•mite
sod•om•ize, *v.*, -ized, -iz•ing.
sod•o○my

soft chan•cre
soft drug
soft lens
soft pal•ate
soi○a
soil•borne
so○ja
soja bean
so•journ time
So•la•na•ce○ae
so•la•na•ceous
so•lan○i•dine
so•la•nin
so•la•nine
so•la•num
So•la•quin For○te *Trademark.*
so○lar
solar plex○us
So•lar•caine *Trademark.*
so•lar○i○um, *n., pl.* -lar○i○a,
  -ums.
so•lar○i•za•tion
so•lar•ize, *v.*, -ized, -iz•ing.
So•la•tene *Trademark.*
so•la•tion
Sol•bar PF *Trademark.*
Solbar Plus *Trademark.*
So•le•nig•ly•pha
so•le•no•glyph
so•le•no•glyph○ic
so•le•no•glyph•ous
sole•plate
sole•print
so•le○us, *n., pl.* -le○i,
  -le○us○es.
soleus ac•ces•so•ri○us
Sol•fo•ton *Trademark.*
Sol•ga•nal *Trademark.*
so•li•da○go, *n., pl.* -gos.
sol•id•un•gu•late
sol○i•dus, *n., pl.* sol○i○di.
sol○i•ped

So•lu-Cor•tef *Trademark.*
Solu-Med•rol *Trademark.*
sol•u•bil•i•ty
sol•u•bil•i•za•tion
sol•u•bi•lize, *v.,* -lized, -liz•ing.
sol•u•ble
soluble fi•ber
sol•u•bly
sol•ute
so•lu•tion
sol•vate
sol•va•tion
sol•vent
sol•vol•y•sis
sol•vo•lyt•ic
So•ma *Trademark.*
so•mas•the•ni•a
so•ma•tes•the•sia
so•mat•ic
somatic cell
so•mat•i•cal•ly
so•ma•ti•co•vis•cer•al
so•ma•tist
so•ma•ti•za•tion
somatization dis•or•der
so•mat•o•chrome
so•mat•o•form dis•or•der
so•mat•o•ge•net•ic
so•mat•o•gen•ic
so•mat•o•log•i•cal
so•ma•tol•o•gy, *n., pl.* -gies.
so•mat•o•me•din
so•mat•o•met•ric
so•ma•tom•e•try
so•ma•tom•ic
so•mat•o•path•ic
so•mat•o•plasm
so•mat•o•plas•tic
so•mat•o•pleu•ral
so•mat•o•pleure
so•mat•o•pleuric

so•mat•o•psy•chic
so•mat•o•sen•so•ry
somatosensory cor•tex
so•mat•o•splanch•nic
so•mat•o•stat•in
so•mat•o•ther•a•pist
so•mat•o•ther•a•py, *n., pl.* -pies.
so•mat•o•to•ni•a
so•mat•o•top•ic
so•mat•o•top•i•cal
so•mat•o•troph•ic
so•mat•o•trop•ic
so•mat•o•tro•pin
so•mat•o•type
so•mat•o•typ•ic
so•mat•o•typ•i•cal•ly
so•ma•to•ty•pol•o•gy, *n., pl.* -gies.
so•mes•the•si•a
so•mes•the•sis, *n., pl.* -sis•es.
so•mi•tal
so•mite
so•mit•ic
som•nam•bu•lant
som•nam•bu•lar
som•nam•bu•late, *v.,* -lat•ed, -lat•ing.
som•nam•bu•la•tion
som•nam•bu•la•tor
som•nam•bu•lism
som•nam•bu•list
som•nam•bu•lis•tic
som•nam•bu•lis•ti•cal•ly
som•ni•fa•cient
som•nif•er•ous
som•nif•er•ous•ly
som•nif•ic
som•nif•u•gous
som•nil•o•quist
som•nil•o•quy, *n., pl.* -quies.
som•nip•a•thist

som•nip○a•thy
som•no•cin•e○mat○o•graph
som•no•lence
som•no•len○cy
som•no•lent
som•no•lent○ly
So•mo•phyl•lin *Trademark.*
Somophyllin-CRT *Trademark.*
Somophyllin-DF *Trademark.*
Somophyllin-T *Trademark.*
son○ic
son○i•cate, *v.,* -cat○ed, -cat•ing.
soni○c•a○tion
son○i•ca•tor
son○o•gram
so•nom•e○ter
so•no•rous
so•phis•ti•cate, *v.,* -cat○ed, -cat•ing.
so•phis•ti•ca○tion
soph○o•ra
soph○o•rine
so○por
so•po•rif•er•ous
so•po•rif•er•ous•ness
sop○o•rif○ic
sop○o•rif○i•cal○ly
so•po•rose
sor•be•fa•cient
sor•bic
sor•bi•tan
sor•bi•tol
Sor•bi•trate *Trademrak.*
sor•bose
sor•des, *n., pl.* sor•des.
sore throat
sore•head
sore•muz•zle
so•ro•ri•a•tion
sorp•tion
so•ta•lol

So•tra•de•col *Trademark.*
souf•fle
South•ern blot
sow•bread
so○ya
soy•bean
space med○i•cine
spa•cial
spal•la•tion
Span•ish fly
Spanish in•flu•en○za
spar•ga•no•sis
spar•ga•num, *n., pl.* -ga○na, -ga•nums.
spar•go•sis
Spar•ine *Trademark.*
spar•te•ine
spasm
spas•mat○ic
spas•mat○i•cal
spas•mod○ic
spas•mod○i•cal
spas•mod○i•cal○ly
spas•mo•gen○ic
spas•mol○y•sis
spas•mo•lyt○ic
spas•mo•lyt○i•cal○ly
spas•mo•phile
spas•mo•phil○i○a
spas•mo•phil○ic
spas•mus
spas•tic
spastic pa•ral○y•sis
spas•ti•cal○ly
spas•tic○i○ty, *n., pl.* -ties.
spa•tial
spatial sum•ma•tion
spa•tial○ly
spa•ti○um, *n., pl.* -ti○a.
spat○u•la
spat○u•late, *v.,* -lat○ed, -lat•ing.

spat○u•la•tion
spat•ule
spa•vin
spa•vine
spa•vined
spay, *v.*, spayed, spay•ing.
spe•cial•ism
spe•cial•ist
spe•cial○i•za•tion
spe•cial•ize -lized, -liz○ing.
spe•cial○ty, *n., pl.* -ties.
spe•cies, *n., pl.* spe•cies.
species-spe•cif○ic
species-spec○i•fic○i○ty
spe•cif○ic
specific grav○i○ty
spe•cif○i•cal○ly
spec○i•fic○i○ty
spec○i•men
spec•ta•cles
Spec•ta•zole *Trademark.*
spec•tral
spec•tral○ly
Spec•tro•bid *Trademark.*
spec○tro•chem○i•cal
spec○tro•chem•is•try
spec○tro•gram
spec○tro•graph
spec•trog•ra•pher
spec○tro•graph○ic
spec○tro•graph○i•cal○ly
spec•trog•ra•phy, *n., pl.*
 -phies.
spec•trom•e○ter
spec•trom•e○try
spec○tro•pho•tom•e○ter
spec○tro•pho•to•met•ric
spec○tro•pho•to•met•ri•cal
spec○tro•pho•to•met•ri•
 cal○ly
spec○tro•pho•tom•e○try
spec○tro•po•la•rim•e○ter

spec○tro•scope
spec○tro•scop○ic
spec○tro•scop○i•cal
spec○tro•scop○i•cal○ly
spec•tros•co•pist
spec•tros•co•py, *n., pl.* -pies.
spec•trum, *n., pl.* -tra, -trums.
spec○u•lar
spec○u•lum, *n., pl.* spec•u•ola,
 spec○u•lums.
speed
speed•ball
speed○y cut
speedy cut•ting
sperm, *n., pl.* sperm, sperms.
sperm bank
sperm cell
sper•ma•ce○ti
sper•ma○ry, *n., pl.* -ries.
sper•ma•te•li•o•sis
sper•mat○ic
spermatic cord
sper•mat○i•cal○ly
sper•ma•tid
sper•ma•tin
sper•mat○o•blast
sper•mat○o•blas•tic
sper•mat○o•cele
sper•mat○o•cid○al
sper•mat○o•cide
sper•mat○o•cyst
sper○mat○o•cys•tic
sper○mat○o•cytal
sper○mat○o•cyte
sper○ma○to•gen•e○sis, *n., pl.*
 -e○ses.
sper○ma○to•ge•net○ic
sper○mat○o•gen○ic
sper•ma•tog○e○nous
sper•ma•tog○e○ny, *n., pl.*
 -nies.
sper○mat○o•gonial

sper•mat•o•gonic
sper•ma•to•go•ni•um, *n., pl.* -ni•a.
sper•ma•toid
sper•ma•tol•y•sis
sper•mat•o•lyt•ic
sper•ma•top•a•thy
sper•mat•o•phore
sper•mat•or•rhe•a
spermatorrhea dor•mi•en•tum
sper•mat•or•rhoe•a
sper•ma•tox•in
sper•mat•o•zoal
sper•mat•o•zoan
sper•mat•o•zo•ic
sper•mat•o•zoid
sper•ma•to•zo•on, *n., pl.* -zo•a.
sper•ma•tu•ri•a
sper•mi•a•tion
sper•mi•cid•al
sper•mi•cid•al•ly
sper•mi•cide
sper•mi•dine
sper•mine
sper•mi•o•gen•e•sis, *n., pl.* -ses.
sper•mism
sper•mist
sper•mi•um, *n., pl.* -mi•a.
sper•mo•lith
sper•mol•y•sis
sper•mo•tox•in
sper•mous
spes•phthis•i•ca
sphac•e•o•late, *v.,* -lat•ed, -lat•ing.
sphac•e•o•la•tion
sphac•e•o•lo•der•ma
spha•ce•lus
sphaer•oid

Sphaer•oph•o•rus
sphen•eth•moid
sphe•ni•on
sphe•no-oc•cip•i•tal
sphe•no•bas•i•lar
sphe•no•ba•sil•ic
sphe•no•ce•phal•ic
sphe•no•ceph•a•lous
sphe•no•ceph•a•ly
sphe•no•eth•moid
sphe•no•fron•tal
sphe•noid
sphe•noi•dal
sphe•noi•di•tis
sphe•no•man•dib•u•lar
sphe•no•max•il•lar•y
sphe•no•pal•a•tine
sphe•no•pa•ri•e•tal
sphe•no•pe•tro•sal
sphe•no•sis
sphe•no•squa•mo•sal
sphe•not•ic
sphe•no•tur•bi•nal
spher•oi•cal
sphe•ro•cyte
sphe•ro•cyt•ic
sphe•ro•cy•to•sis
sphe•roid
sphe•roi•dal
sphe•rom•e•ter
Sphe•roph•o•rus
sphe•ro•plast
spher•ule
sphinc•ter
sphincter of Od•di
sphincter pu•pil•lae
sphincter va•gi•nae
sphinc•ter•al
sphinc•ter•al•gia
sphinc•ter•ec•to•my, *n., pl.* -mies.
sphinc•ter•ic

sphinc•ter•ol•y•sis
sphinc•ter•ot•o•my, *n., pl.*
  -mies.
sphin•go•lip•oid
sphin•go•lip•ide
sphin•go•my•e•lin
sphin•go•sine
sphyg•mic
sphyg•mo-os•cil•lom•e•ter
sphyg•mo•chron•o•graph
sphyg•mo•gram
sphyg•mo•graph
sphyg•mo•graph•ic
sphyg•mog•ra•phy, *n., pl.*
  -phies.
sphyg•moid
sphyg•mo•ma•nom•e•ter
sphyg•mo•man•o•met•ric
sphyg•mo•man•o•met•ri•
  cal•ly
sphyg•mo•ma•nom•e•try
sphyg•mom•e•ter
sphyg•mus
spi•ca, *n., pl.* -cae, -cas.
spic•u•lar
spic•u•late
spic•u•lated
spic•u•la•tion
spic•ule
spic•u•lum, *n., pl.* spic•u•la.
Spi•ge•li•a
spi•ge•li•an
spi•lo•ma
spi•lus
spi•na, *n., pl.* -nae.
spina bif•i•da
spin•a•cene
spi•nal
spinal an•es•the•sia
spinal ca•nal
spinal col•umn
spinal cord

spinal nerve
spinal tap
spi•na•lis
spi•nal•ly
spin•ate
spin•dle
spine
spined
spine•less
spine•like
spi•no-ol•i•var•y
spi•no•cer•e•bel•lar
spi•nose
spi•nose•ly
spi•no•tec•tal
spi•no•tha•lam•ic
spi•nous
spin•thar•o•i•scope
spin•ther•ism
spi•ny-head•ed worm
spi•ra•cle
spi•rem
spi•reme
Spir•il•la•ce•ae
spir•il•la•ceous
spir•il•li•cid•al
spi•ril•lo•sis
spi•ril•lum, *n., pl.* -ril•la.
spir•it
spir•i•tu•ous
spir•oi•tus
spiritus fru•men•ti
Spi•ro•cer•ca
spi•ro•chae•ta, *n., pl.* -tae.
Spi•ro•chae•ta•ce•ae
spi•ro•chae•tal
Spi•ro•chae•ta•les
spi•ro•chaete
spi•ro•chae•ti•cide
spi•ro•chae•to•sis
spi•ro•che•ta, *n., pl.* -tae.

spi○ro•che•tal
spi○ro•chete
spi○ro•che•te•mi○a
spi○ro•che•ti•cid○al
spi○ro•che•ti•cide
spi•ro•che•to•sis
spi○ro•gram
spi○ro•graph
spi○ro•graph○ic
spi•rom•e○ter
spi○ro•met•ric
spi○ro•met•ri•cal
spi•rom•e○try
spi○ro•no•lac•tone
spis•si•tude
spi•tal
spit•tle
splanch•nec•to•pi○a
splanch•nes•the•sia
splanch•nic
splanch•ni•cec•to○my, n., pl.
  -mies.
splanch•ni•cot○o○my, n., pl.
  -mies.
splanch○no•coel
splanch○no•coele
splanch•nol○o○gy, n., pl. -gies.
splanch•no•meg○a○ly
splanch○no•pleure
splanch○no•pleu•ric
splanch•nop•to•sis
splanch•nos•co○py, n., pl.
  -pies.
splay•foot, n., pl. -feet.
spleen
spleen○ish
sple•nal•gia
sple•nal•gic
sple•nec•to•mize, v., -mized,
  -miz•ing.
sple•nec•to○my, n., pl. -mies.
sple•ne○o•lus, n., pl. -ne○o○li.

sple•net○ic
sple•net○i•cal○ly
sple•ni○al
splen○ic
splen○i•cal
splen○i•fi•ca•tion
splen○i•form
sple•ni•tis
sple•ni○um, n., pl. -ni○a.
sple•ni○us, n., pl. -ni○i.
splen○i•za•tion
sple•nop○a•thy, n., pl. -thies.
splen○o•cyte
splen○o•dyn○i○a
splen○o•gen○ic
splen○o•hep○a•to•meg○a○ly
sple•noid
sple○no•ma•la•cia
sple○no•me•ga•li○a
sple○no•meg○a○ly
sple○no•pex○y, n., pl. -pex•
  ies.
sple•nop•to•sis
sple•not○o○my, n., pl. -mies.
splen○u•lus, n., pl. splen○u○li.
sple•nun•cu•lus, n., pl. -cu○li.
splice, v., spliced, splic•ing.
splint
splint•age
splin•ter, v., -tered, -ter•ing.
split-brain
spoke•shave
spon•dy•lit○ic
spon•dy•li•tis
spondylitis an•ky•lo•poi•
  et○i•ca
spon○dy○lo•dyn○i○a
spon•dy•lo•lis•the•sis
spon•dy•lo•lis•thet○ic
spon•dy•lol○y•sis
spon•dy•lop○a•thy, n., pl.
  -thies.

spon•dy•lo•sis

spon◦dy•lo•syn•de•sis

spon•dy•lot◦o•my, *n., pl.*
-mies.

spon•dy•lous

sponge

spon•gi•form en•ceph◦a•
lop◦a•thy

spon•gin

spon◦gi•o•blast

spon◦gi◦o•blas•to◦ma, *n., pl.*
-mas, -ma◦ta.

spongioblastoma mul•ti•
forme

spongioblastoma po•la◦re

spongioblastoma prim◦i•ti•
vum

spongioblastoma u•ni•po•
la◦re

spon◦gi◦o•cyte

spon◦gi◦o•plasm

spon◦gi◦o•plas•mic

spon◦gi◦o◦sa

spon◦gi•o•sis

spon•ta•ne•ous

spontaneous a◦bor•tion

spon•ta•ne•ous◦ly

spoon•er•ism

spo•ra•ceous

spo•ran•gi◦o•phore

spo•ran•gi◦o◦spore

spo•ran•gi◦um, *n., pl.* -gi◦a.

spore

spo◦ri•cid◦al

spo◦ri•cide

spo•rid◦i◦um, *n., pl.* -rid◦i◦a.

spo◦ro•blast

spo◦ro•cyst

spo◦ro•cys•tic

spo◦ro•cyte

spo◦ro•gen•e◦sis, *n., pl.*
-e◦ses.

spo◦ro•gen◦ic

spo•rog•e◦nous

spo•rog•e◦ny, *n., pl.* -rog•
e◦nies.

spo◦ro•gonic

spo•rog◦o•nous

spo•rog◦o◦ny

spo•ront

spo◦ro•phore

spo◦ro•phyte

spo◦ro•plasm

spo◦ro•tri•cho◦sis

spo•rot•ri•chum, *n., pl.* -cha.

Spo◦ro•zo◦a

spo◦ro•zo◦an

spo◦ro•zo◦ite

spo◦ro•zo◦on, *n., pl.* -zo◦a.

sports med◦i•cine

spor◦u•lar

spor◦u•late, *v.,* -lat◦ed, -lat•
ing.

spor◦u•la•tion

spor◦u•la•tive

spor•ule

spot re•duc•ing

spot◦ted fe◦ver

sprain

spread◦er

sprue

spur

spu•tum, *n., pl.* spu◦ta.

squa•lene

squa•ma, *n., pl.* -mae.

squama fron•ta•lis

squama oc•cip◦i•talis

squama tem•po•ralis

squa•mate

squa•mat◦ed

squame

squa◦mo-oc•cip◦i•tal

squa•mo•co•lum•nar

squa•moid

squa•mo○sa, *n., pl.* **-sas, -sae.**
squa○mo•sal
squa•mose
squa•mous
squar•rose
squar•rous
squill
squint
squint-eyed
St. John's wort sun•dew
St. Vi○tus
St. Vitus's dance
stab○i•lim•e○ter
stac•ca○to
sta•chy•drine
sta•chy•ose
stac•tom•e○ter
Sta•der splint
sta•di○um, *n., pl.* **-di○a, -di•**
ums.
Sta•dol *Trademark.*
staff of Aes•cu•la•pi○us
stage, *v.,* staged, stag•ing.
stag•gers
stag•nant bow○el syn•drome
stag•na○tion
stain
stain•a○bil○i○ty
stain○a•ble
sta•lag•mom•e○ter
stale, *v.,* staled, stal•ing.
stam•mer, *v.,* -mered, -mer•
ing.
stanch
stanch○a•ble
stanch○er
stand•still
Stan•ford-Bi○net test
stan•nate
stan•nic
stan•nous
stan•num

sta•pe•dec•to•mize, *v.,*
-mized, -miz•ing.
stapedectomized
sta•pe○dec•to○my, *n., pl.*
-mies.
sta•pe•di○al
sta•pe•di○o•ves•tib○u•lar
sta•pe○di○us, *n., pl.* -di○i.
sta•pes, *n., pl.* sta•pes, sta•
pe○des.
staph
Sta•phage Ly•sate *Trademark.*
Staph•cil•lin *Trademark.*
staph○y•lec•to○my, *n., pl.*
-mies.
staph•yl○e○de○ma, *n., pl.*
-mas, -ma○ta.
staph○y•li•nus ex•ter•nus
staphylinus in•ter•nus
staphylinus me•di○us
sta•phyl○i○on
staph○y•li•tis
staph○y•lo•coc•cal
staph○y•lo•coc•ce•mi○a
staph○y•lo•coc•ce•mic
staph○y•lo•coc•cic
staph○y•lo•coc•cus, *n., pl.*
-coc○ci.
staph○y•lo•der•ma•ti•tis
staph○y•lo○ma
staphyloma cor•ne○ae
staphyloma u•ve•a○le
staph○y•lo•plas○ty, *n., pl.*
-ties.
staph○y•lot○o○my, *n., pl.*
-mies.
staph○y•sag•ri○a
Star-Ot○ic *Trademark.*
starch
starch-block•ing
starch•block
starch○i•ness

starch•y, *adj.*, starch•i•er,
  starch•i•est.
Star•ling's law
sta•sis, *n.*, *pl.* -ses.
stasis der•ma•ti•tis
stat
stat◦ic
sta•tim
Stat◦o•bex *Trademark.*
stat◦o•cyst
stat◦o•ki•net◦ic
stat◦o•lith
stat◦o•lith◦ic
stat•ure
sta•tus
status asth•mat◦i•cus
status ep◦i•lep•ti•cus
status lym•phat◦i•cus
status thy•mi•co•lym•
  phat◦i•cus
staunch
stau•ri◦on
staves•ac◦re
stax◦is
ste•ap•sin
ste•a•rate
ste•ar◦ic
stearic ac◦id
ste•a•rin
ste◦a•rine
ste•a•rop•ten
ste•a•rop•tene
ste•a•tite
ste•a•tit◦ic
ste•a•ti•tis
ste•a•tog◦e•nous
ste◦a•tol◦y•sis, *n.*, *pl.* -ses.
ste◦a•to◦ma, *n.*, *pl.* -mas,
  -ma•ta.
ste•a•tom•a•tous
ste•a•to•py◦ga
ste•at◦o•py•gi◦a

ste•at◦o•pyg◦ic
ste•at◦o•py•gous
ste•a•tor•rhe•a
ste•a•tor•rhoe•a
ste◦a•to•sis
steg◦o•my◦ia
Stein•mann pin
Stel◦a•zine *Trademark.*
stel•late
stel•late◦ly
stel•lec•to◦my, *n.*, *pl.* -mies.
stem cell
Sten•der dish
sten•i◦on, *n.*, *pl.* -ni◦a.
sten◦o•car•di◦a
sten◦o•car•di◦ac
sten◦o•ce◦pha•li◦a
sten◦o•ce•phal◦ic
sten◦o•ceph◦a•ly
sten◦o•cho•ri◦a
sten◦o•co•ri•a•sis
sten◦o•mer◦ic
sten◦o•pae◦ic
sten◦o•pa◦ic
sten◦o•pe◦ic
Ste•no's duct
sten•ose, *v.*, -osed, -os•ing.
ste•nosed
ste•no•sis
sten◦o•therm
sten◦o•ther•mal
sten◦o•ther•mic
sten◦o•tho•rax, *n.*, *pl.*
  -rax◦es, -ra•ces.
ste•not◦ic
Sten•sen's duct
stent
ste•pha•ni◦on
Steph◦a•no•fi•lar◦i◦a
steph◦a•no•fil◦a•ri•a•sis
Steph◦a•nu•rus
step•page

ste•rad
ste•ra•di•an
Ster•ane *Trademark.*
Ster∘a•pred *Trademark.*
ster∘co•bi•lin
ster∘co•bi•lin∘o•gen
ster∘co•ra•ceous
ster•co•ral
ster•co•ro∘ma, *n., pl.* -mas,
  -ma∘ta.
ster•co•rous
ster•cu•li∘a
ster•cus, *n., pl.* ster•co∘ra.
ster∘e∘o•blas•tu∘la, *n., pl.*
  -las, -lae.
ster∘e∘o•cam•pim•e∘ter
ster∘e∘o•cil∘i∘um, *n., pl.*
  -cil∘i∘a.
ster•e•og•no•sis
ster•e•og•nos•tic
ster∘e∘o•gram
ster∘e∘o•graph
ster∘e∘o•i∘so•mer∘ic
ster∘e∘o•i∘som•er•ism
ster•e∘om•e∘ter
ster∘e∘o•met•ric
ster•e∘om•e∘try
ster•e∘op•sis
ster∘e∘o•ra•di∘o•graph
ster∘e∘o•ra•di∘o•graph∘ic
ster∘e∘o•ra•di∘og•ra•phy,
  n., pl. -phies.
ster∘e∘o•scope
ster∘e∘o•scop∘ic
ster∘e∘o•scop∘i•cal
ster∘e∘o•scop∘i•cal∘ly
ster•e∘os•co•pist
ster•e∘os•co•py, *n., pl.* -pies.
ster∘e∘o•spe•cif∘ic
ster∘e∘o•spe•cif∘i•cal∘ly
ster∘e∘o•spec∘i•fic∘i∘ty, *n.,*
  pl. -ties.

ster∘e∘o•tac•tic
stereotactic ra•di∘o•sur•
  ger∘y
ster∘e∘o•tac•ti•cal∘ly
ster∘e∘o•tax∘ic
ster∘e∘o•tax∘i•cal∘ly
ster∘e∘o•tax∘is
ster∘e∘o•tro•pism
ster∘e∘o•type
ster∘e∘o•ty∘py
ster∘oid
ster∘ide
ste•rig∘ma, *n., pl.* -ma∘ta,
  -mas.
ster•ile
ster•ile∘ly
ste•ril∘i∘ty, *n., pl.* -ties.
ster∘i•li•za∘tion
ster∘i•lize, *v.,* -lized, -liz•ing.
ster∘i•liz∘er
ster•nad
ster•nal
ster•na•lis, *n., pl.* -les.
Stern•berg cell
Sternberg-Reed cell
ster•ne•bra, *n., pl.* -brae.
ster∘no•cla•vic∘u•lar
ster∘no•clei•do•mas•toid
ster∘no•cos•tal
ster∘no•fas•ci∘a•lis, *n., pl.*
  -les.
ster∘no•hy•oid
ster∘no•mas•toid
ster∘no•thy•roid
ster•not∘o∘my, *n., pl.* -mies.
ster•num, *n., pl.* -ster•nums,
  ster∘na.
ster•nu•ta•tion
ster•nu•ta•tive
ster•nu•ta•tor
ster•nu•ta•to∘ry, *adj., n., pl.*
  -ries.

ste•ro•chem•i•cal
ste•roid
ste•roi•dal
ste•roid○o•gen•e○sis, *n., pl.*
  -e○ses.
ste•roi•do•gen○ic
ste•rol
ster•tor
ster•to•rous
ster•to•rous○ly
steth○o•graph
steth○o•graph○ic
ste•thom•e○ter
steth○o•met•ric
steth○o•scope
steth○o•scop○ic
steth○o•scop○i•cal
steth○o•scop○i•cal○ly
ste•thos•co○py, *n. pl.* -pies.
sthen○ic
sti•ba•mine
stib○i○um
sti•bo•ni○um
sti•bo•phen
stick•y end
stic○ta pul•mo•nar○i○a
stig○ma, *n., pl.* -ma○ta, -mas.
stig•mal
stig○ma•ster○ol
stig•ma○ta ni○gra
stigmata ven•tric○u•li
stig•mat○ic
stig•ma•tism
stig•ma•ti•za•tion
stig•ma•tize, *v.,* -tized, -tiz•
  ing.
stil•bam○i•dine
stil•bene
stil•bes•trol
stil•boes•trol
sti•let
sti•lette

sti•let•ted
still•birth
still•born
Still's dis•ease
Stil•phos•trol *Trademark.*
sti•lus
stim○u•lant
stim○u•late, *v.,* -lat○ed, -lat•
  ing.
stim○u•lat○er
stim○u•la•tion
stim○u•la•tive
stim○u•la•tor
stim○u•la•to○ry
stim○u•lus, *n., pl.* stim○u○li.
stip•pling
stir•rup
Stock•holm syn•drome
stock○i•net
stock○i•nette
stoi•chi○o•met•ric
stoi•chi○o•met•ri•cal
stoi•chi○o•met•ri•cal○ly
stoi•chi•om•e○try
sto○ma, *n., pl.* -ma○ta, -mas.
stom•ach
stomach hun•ger
stomach pump
stomach sta•pling
stom•ach•ache
stom•ach○al
sto•mach○ic
sto•mach○i•cal
sto•mach○i•cal○ly
sto•mal
sto•ma○ta
stom○a•tal
sto•mat○ic
sto•ma•tit○ic
sto•ma•ti•tis
stomatitis ve•ne•na○ta
sto•ma○to•gas•tric

sto•ma•to•log•ic
sto•ma•to•log•i•cal
sto•ma•tol∘o•gist
sto•ma•tol∘o•gy, *n., pl.* -gies.
sto•mat∘o•my, *n., pl.* -mies.
sto•mat∘o•plas•tic
sto•mat∘o•plas∘ty, *n., pl.*
 -ties.
sto•ma•to•sis
sto•ma•tot∘o•my, *n., pl.*
 -mies.
sto•mo•dae∘al
sto•mo•de∘al
sto•mo•de∘um, *n., pl.* -de∘a,
 -de•ums.
Sto•mox∘ys
stone
stone-blind
stone-blind•ness
stone-deaf
stone-deaf•ness
stool
stop•cock
stop•page
sto•rax
Stox∘il *Trademark.*
stra•bis•mal
stra•bis•mal∘ly
stra•bis•mic
stra•bis•mi•cal
stra•bis•mom•e∘ter
stra•bis•mom•e∘try
stra•bis•mus
straight•jack∘et
strain
strain∘er
strait•jack∘et
stra•mo•ni•um
strand∘ed
strand∘ed•ness
stran•gle, *v.,* -gled, -gling.
stran•gles

stran•gu•late, *v.,* -lat∘ed, -lat•
 ing.
stran•gu•la•tion
stran•gu∘ry
stra•tum, *n., pl.* stra∘ta, stra•
 tums.
stratum cor•ne∘um, *n., pl.*
 strata cor•ne∘a.
stratum ger•mi•na•ti•vum, *pl.*
 stra∘ta ger•mi•na•ti∘va.
stratum gran∘u•lo•sum, *n., pl.*
 strata gran∘u•lo∘sa.
stratum lu•ci•dum, *n., pl.*
 strata lu•ci∘da.
straw•ber∘ry mark
stream of con•scious•ness
strep
strep throat
streph∘o•sym•bo•li∘a
streph∘o•sym•bol∘ic
stre•pi•tus au•ri∘um
strepitus u•ter∘i
strepitus u•ter∘i•nus
strep∘o•gen∘in
Strep•tase *Trademark.*
strep•ti•dine
strep∘to•ba•cil•la∘ry
strep∘to•ba•cil•lus, *n., pl.*
 -ba•cil∘li.
Streptobacillus mon∘i•li•
 form∘is
strep∘to•bi•o•sa•mine
strep∘to•coc•cal
strep∘to•coc•ce•mi∘a
strep∘to•coc•cic
strep∘to•coc•co•sis
strep∘to•coc•cus, *n., pl.*
 -coc∘ci.
strep∘to•dor•nase
strep∘to•ki•nase
strep∘to•ly•sin

strep○to•my•ces, *n.*, *pl.* -ces,
  -ce•tes.
strep○to•my•cin
strep○to•ni•grin
strep○tose
strep○to•thri•cho•sis
strep○to•thri•cin
strep○to•thrix, *n.*, *pl.* -thri•ces.
strep○to•tri•cho•sis
stress
stress frac•ture
stress test
Stress•caps *Trademark.*
stress•ful
stress•ful○ly
stres•sor
Stress•tabs *Trademark.*
stretch mark
stretch re•cep•tor
stretch○er
stri○a, *n.*, *pl.* stri○ae.
stria lon•gi•tu•di•na•lis, *n.*,
  pl. stri○ae lon•gi•tu•di•na•
  les.
stri•a•tal
stri•ate
stri•at○ed
stri○a•tion
stri○a•tum, *n.*, *pl.* stri○a○ta.
strick○en
stric•ture
stric•tured
stri•dent
stri•dent○ly
stri•dor
stridor den•ti○um
stridor ser•rat○i•cus
strid○u•lant
strid○u•lous
string•halt
string•halt○ed
strip•per

stro•bil
stro•bi○la, *n.*, *pl.* -lae.
stro•bi•lar
stro•bi•la•tion
stro•bile
stro•bil○i•za•tion
stro•bil•oid
stro•bi•lus, *n.*, *pl.* -bi○li.
stro•bo•scope
stro•bo•scop○ic
stro•bo•scop○i•cal○ly
stroke
stroke vol•ume
stro○ma, *n.*, *pl.* -ma○ta.
stroma ir○i•dis
stroma o•var○i○i
stroma vit•re○um
stro•mal
stro•ma•tal
stro•mat○ic
stro•ma•tin
stro•muhr
stron•gyl
stron•gy•late
stron•gyle
Stron•gy•loi•de○a
Stron•gy•loi•des
Strongyloides in•tes•ti•na•lis
Strongyloides ster•co•ra•lis
stron•gy•loi•di•a○sis
stron•gy•loi•do•sis
stron•gy•lo•sis
Stron•gy•lus
stron•ti○um
stro•phan•thin
stro•phan•thus
stroph○u•lus, *n.*, *pl.* stroph•
  u○li.
strophulus pru•ri•gi•no•sus
Stro•vite Plus *Trademark.*
struc•tur○al gene
structural psy•chol○o○gy

struc•tur•al•ism
struc•tur•al∘ist
struc•tur•al∘is•tic
stru∘ma, *n., pl.* -mae, -mas.
stru•mi•form
stru•mi•tis
stru•mose
stru•mous
strych•nic
strych•nine
strych•nin•ism
strych•nin∘i•za•tion
Strych•nos
Stu•art•in∘ic *Trademark.*
Stu•art•na•tal *Trademark.*
stu•pe•fa•cient
stu•pe•fac•tion
stu•pe•fac•tive
stu•pe∘fy, *v.,* -fied, -fy•ing.
stu•por
stupor mel•an•chol∘i•cus
stupor vig∘i•lans
stup•or•ous
stur∘dy
stu•rin
stu•rine
stut•ter, *v.,* -tered, -ter•ing.
sty
stye
sty•let
sty•li•form
sty•lo•glos•sus, *n., pl.*
  -glos∘si.
sty∘lo•hy∘al
sty∘lo•hy•oid
sty•lo•hy•oi∘de∘us, *n., pl.*
  -de∘i.
sty•loid
sty•lo•man•dib•ou•lar
sty∘lo•mas•toid
sty•lo•pha•ryn•ge∘us, *n., pl.*
  -ge∘i.

sty•lus
styp•sis
styp•tic or styp•ti•cal
styptic pen•cil
styp•tic∘i∘ty
sty•ra•cin
sty•rax
sty•rene
sty•rol
sub•ab•dom∘i•nal
sub•a•cro•mi∘al
sub∘a•cute
subacute scle•ros∘ing
  pan•en•ceph•o∘a•li•tis
sub•a∘cute∘ly
sub•al∘i•men•ta•tion
sub•a•pi•cal
sub•a•pi•cal∘ly
sub•ap∘o•neu•rot∘ic
sub•a∘rach•noid
subarachnoid hem•or•rhage
sub•ar•cu•ate
sub•ar•cu•at∘ed
sub•a∘re•o•lar
sub•as•trin•gent
sub•au•ric∘u•lar
sub•ax•il•lar
sub•ax•il•lar∘y
sub•ba•sal
sub•bra•chi∘al
sub•bra•chi∘an
sub•brach∘y•ce•phal∘ic
sub•cal•ca•rine
sub•cal•lo•sal
sub•cap•su•lar
sub•car•bo•nate
sub•car•ti•lag∘i•nous
sub•cel•lu•lar
sub•chlo•ride
sub•chon•dral
sub•cho•ri•on∘ic
sub•cla•vi∘an

subclavian ar•ter•y
subclavian vein
sub•cla•vi○us, *n., pl.* -vi○i.
sub•clin○i•cal
sub•clin○i•cal○ly
sub•col•lat•er○al
sub•co○ma
sub•con•junc•ti•val
sub•con•junc•ti•val○ly
sub•con•scious
sub•con•scious○ly
sub•con•scious•ness
sub•co•ra○coid
sub•cor•tex, *n., pl.* -ti•ces,
  -tex○es.
sub•cor•ti•cal
sub•cor•ti•cal○ly
sub•cos•tal
sub•crep○i•tant
sub•crep○i•ta•tion
sub•cul•ture, *n., v.,* -tured,
  -tur•ing.
sub•cu•ra•tive
sub•cu•ta•ne•ous
sub•cu•ta•ne•ous○ly
sub•cu•tic○u•lar
sub•cu•tis, *n., pl.* -tes, -ti•ses.
sub•dam○i•nal
sub•del•toid
sub•der•mal
sub•di•a•phrag•mat○ic
sub•dol○i•cho•ce•phal○ic
sub•dol○i•cho•ceph○a•lous
sub•dor•sal
sub•dor•sal○ly
sub•duct
sub•duc•tion
sub•du○ral
subdural he•ma•to○ma
sub•du○ral○ly
sub•en•ceph○a•lon, *n., pl.*
  -ceph•a○la.

sub•en•do•car•di○al
sub•en•do•the•li○al
sub•ep○i•car•di○al
sub•ep○i•der•mal
sub•ep○i•the•li○al
su•ber○in
su•ber○i•za•tion
su•ber○ized
su•ber○y•lar•gi•nine
sub•gal•late
sub•gin•gi•val
sub•gle•noid
sub•glos•si○tis
sub•glot•tic
sub•he•pat○ic
sub•ic•ter○ic
sub•ic○u•lar
su•bic○u•lum, *n., pl.* -bic•
  u○la.
sub•in•ci•sion
sub•in•fec•tion
sub•in•gui•nal
sub•in•teg○u•men•tal
sub•in•ti•mal
sub•in•vo•lu•tion
sub•ja•cent
sub•ja•cent○ly
sub•jec•tive
sub•jec•tive○ly
sub•la•ti○o ret○i•nae
sub•la•tion
sub•le•thal
sub•le•thal○ly
sub•leu•ke•mic
sub•li•mate, *v.,* -mat○ed,
  -mat•ing.
sub•li•ma•tion
sub•li•ma•tion○al
Sub•lim•aze *Trademark.*
sub•lime, *v.,* -limed, -lim•ing.
sub•lim○i•nal
sub•lim○i•nal○ly

sub•lim○is
sub•lin•gual
sub•lin•gual○ly
sub•lob○u•lar
sub•lob○u•lar○ly
sub•lux○a•tion
sub•man•dib○u•lar
sub•mar•gi•nal
sub•max•il○la, *n., pl.* -lae, -las.
sub•max•il•lar○y
sub•me•di○al
sub•me•di•al○ly
sub•me•di○an
sub•men•tal
sub•mi•cro•scop○ic
sub•mil•i•ar○y
sub•min○i•mal
sub•mi•to•chon•dri○al
sub•mu•co○sa
sub•mu•co○sal
sub•mu•cous
sub•nar•cot○ic
sub•na•sal
sub•neu○ral
sub•nor•mal
sub•nor•mal○ly
sub•nu•cle○us, *n., pl.* -cle○i, -cle○us○es.
sub•nu•tri○tion
sub•oc•cip○i•tal
sub•oc•cip○i•tal○ly
sub•op•ti•mal
sub•op•ti•mum
sub•or•bi•tal
sub•pec•to•ral
sub•pe•dun•cu•lar
sub•per•i•o•steal
sub•phren○ic
sub•pi○al
sub•pla•cen○ta, *n., pl.* -tas, -tae.
sub•pla•cen•tal

sub•plan•ti•grade
sub•pleu•ral
sub•pleu•ral○ly
sub•po•ten○cy, *n., pl.* -cies.
sub•po•tent
sub•pu•bic
sub•ros•tral
sub•scap○u•lar
sub•scap○u•laris
sub•scle•ral
sub•scle•rot○ic
sub•scrip•tion
sub•se•ro○sa
sub•se•rous
sub•spe•cial○ty, *n., pl.* -ties.
sub•spi•nous
sub•stage
sub•stance a○buse
substance of Schwann
sub•stan•ti○a, *n., pl.* -ti○ae.
substantia nig○ra, *n., pl.* sub•stan•ti○ae nig•rae.
substantia pro•pri○a, *n., pl.* sub•stan•ti○ae pro•pri○ae.
sub•ster•nal
sub•strate
sub•stra•tum, *n., pl.* -stra○ta.
sub•struc•ture
sub•sul•fate
sub•sul•tus
subsultus clo○nus
subsultus ten•di•num
sub•ten•to•ri○al
sub•ter•mi•nal
sub•te•tan○ic
sub•tha•lam○ic
sub•thal○a•mus, *n., pl.* -thal•a○mi.
sub•thresh•old
sub•ti•lin
sub•ti•lisin
sub•tro•chan•ter○ic

sub•type
sub•un•gual
sub•un•gui•al
sub•vag•i•nal
sub•vi•ral
sub•vo•la
sub•vo•lu•tion
suc•ce•da•ne•ous
suc•ce•da•ne•um, *n., pl.* -ne•ums, ne•a.
suc•cen•tu•ri•ate
suc•ci•nate
suc•cin•chlo•ri•mide
suc•cin•ic
suc•cin•ox•i•dase
suc•ci•nyl•cho•line
succinylcholine chlo•ride
suc•ci•nyl•sul•fa•thi•a•zole
suc•co•rance
suc•co•rant
suc•cor•rhe•a
suc•cor•rhoe•a
suc•cus, *n., pl.* suc•ci.
succus en•ter•i•cus
succus gas•tri•cus
succus in•tes•ti•na•lis
succus pan•cre•at•i•cus
succus pros•tat•i•cus
suc•cus•sion
suck•le, *v.,* -led, -ling.
Su•co•strin *Trademark.*
su•crase
su•crate
su•crose
su•cro•su•ri•a
suc•to•ri•al
Su•da•fed *Trademark.*
su•da•men, *n., pl.* -dam•i•na.
su•dan•o•phil
su•dan•o•phil•i•a
su•dan•o•phil•ic
su•da•tion

su•da•to•ri•um, *n., pl.* -ri•a.
su•da•to•ry
sud•den in•fant death syn•drome
su•do•mo•tor
su•dor•if•er•ous
su•dor•if•ic
su•do•rip•a•rous
Su•fen•ta *Trademark.*
suf•fo•cate, *v.,* -cat•ed, -cat•ing.
suf•fo•ca•tion
suf•fuse, *v.,* -fused, -fus•ing.
suf•fu•sion
sug•ar
sug•gil•la•tion
su•i•cid•al
su•i•cid•al•ly
su•i•cide
su•i•ci•dol•o•gist
su•i•ci•dol•o•gy, *n., pl.* -gies.
sui•gen•der•ism
su•int
sul•cal
sul•car
sul•cate
sul•cat•ed
sul•cu•lus, *n., pl.* -cu•li.
sul•cus, *n., pl.* sul•ci.
sulcus of Ro•lan•do
sulcus lu•na•tus, *n., pl.* sul•ci lu•na•ti.
sulcus ter•mi•na•lis, *n., pl.* sul•ci ter•mi•na•les.
sul•fa
sulfa drug
Sul•fa•cet-R *Trademark.*
sul•fa•cet•o•a•mide
sul•fa•cet•o•i•mide
sul•fa•di•a•zine
sul•fa•gua•ni•dine
sul•fa•mer•a•zine

sul•fa•meth•o•a•zine
sul•fa•meth•ox•o•a•zole
sul•fa•mez•o•a•thine
Sul•fa•my•lon *Trademark.*
sul•fa•nil•o•a•mide
sul•fan•o•i•late
sul•fa•nil•o•ic
sul•fa•pyr•o•a•zine
sul•fa•pyr•o•i•dine
sul•fa•quin•ox•o•a•line
sul•far•sphen•o•a•mine
sul•fa•tase
sul•fate
sul•fa•thi•a•zole
sulf•he•mo•glo•bin
sulf•he•mo•glo•bi•ne•mi•a
sulf•hy•drate
sulf•hy•dryl
sul•fide
sul•fin•pyr•o•a•zone
sul•fi•sox•o•a•zole
sul•fite
sul•fit•o•ic
sul•fo acid
sul•fo•cy•a•nate
sul•fon•o•a•mide
sul•fo•nate
sul•fone
sul•fo•neth•yl•meth•ane
sul•fon•o•ic
sul•fon•meth•ane
sul•fo•nyl
sul•fo•nyl•o•u•re•o•a
sul•fo•sal•o•i•cyl•o•ic
Sul•fose *Trademark.*
sulf•ox•ide
sulf•ox•one
Sulf•ox•o•yl *Trademark.*
sul•fur, *v.*, -fured, -fur•ing.
sulfur bac•te•ri•o•a
sul•fu•rate

sul•fu•ret, *v.*, -ret•ed or -ret•ted, -ret•ing or -ret•ting.
sul•fu•ric
sul•fu•rize
sul•fu•rous
sul•fu•ryl
sul•fy•drate
Sul•ola *Trademark.*
sul•lage
sul•pha
sul•phate
sul•phide
sul•phite
sul•pho•nate
sul•phur
sulphur i•o•o•dat•o•um
sul•phu•rate
sul•phu•rize
sul•phu•rous
sul•phy•drate
sul•phy•dryl
Sul•trin *Trademark.*
su•ma•trip•tan
sum•mate, *v.*, -mat•o•ed, -mat•ing.
sum•ma•tion
sum•ma•tion•al
Sum•mer's Eve *Trademark.*
Su•my•cin *Trademark.*
sun
sun pro•tec•tion fac•tor
sun•block
sun•burn
sun•burnt
sun•down
Sun•kist *Trademark.*
sun•lamp
sun•screen
sun•stroke
sun•struck
Su•pac *Trademark.*
su•per•ab•duc•tion

su•per•a•cute
su•per•al•i•men•ta•tion
su•per•cen•tral
su•per•cil•i•ary
su•per•cil•i•um, *n., pl.*
-cil•i•a.
su•per•coil
su•per•coiled
su•per•e•go, *n., pl.* -gos.
Su•per•EPA *Trademark.*
su•per•ex•ci•ta•tion
su•per•ex•ten•sion
su•per•fe•cun•da•tion
su•per•fe•tate
su•per•fe•ta•tion
su•per•fi•cial
su•per•gene
su•per•hel•i•cal
su•per•he•lix, *n., pl.* -hel•i•
ces, -he•lix•es.
su•per•im•preg•nate, *v.,*
-nat•ed, -nat•ing.
su•per•im•preg•na•tion
su•per•in•duce, *v.,* -duced,
-duc•ing.
su•per•in•duc•tion
su•per•in•fect
su•per•in•fec•tion
su•per•ri•or
superior ve•na ca•va
su•pe•ri•or•i•oty com•plex
su•pe•ri•or•ly
Su•per•kids *Trademark.*
su•per•lac•ta•tion
su•per•mo•lec•u•lar
su•per•mol•e•cule
su•per•na•tant
su•per•nate
su•per•nor•mal
su•per•nu•mer•a•ry, *n., pl.*
-ries.
su•per•o•obe•si•ty

su•per•ov•o•u•late, *v.,* -lat•ed,
-lat•ing.
su•per•ov•o•u•la•tion
su•per•par•a•sit•ism
su•per•phos•phate
su•per•pig•men•ta•tion
su•per•po•ten•cy, *n., pl.* -cies.
su•per•po•tent
su•per•sat•u•rate, *v.,* -rat•ed,
-rat•ing.
su•per•sat•u•ra•tion
su•per•scrip•tion
su•per•sen•si•tive
su•per•sen•si•ti•za•tion
su•per•sep•tal
su•per•son•ic
su•per•son•i•cal•ly
su•per•struc•ture
su•per•tem•po•ral
su•per•ven•tion
su•per•vi•sor
su•per•vol•tage
su•pi•nate, *v.,* -nat•ed, -nat•
ing.
su•pi•na•tion
su•pi•na•tor
su•pine
sup•ple•ment
sup•ple•men•tal
sup•ple•men•ta•ry
sup•port group
sup•por•ter
sup•pos•i•to•ry, *n., pl.* -ries.
sup•press
sup•pres•sant
sup•pres•sion
sup•pres•sive
sup•pres•sive•ly
sup•pres•sor
suppressor T cell
sup•pu•rate, *v.,* -rat•ed, -rat•
ing.

sup•pu•ra•tion
sup•pu•ra•tive
su•pra-au•ric•u•lar
su•pra•cel•lu•lar
su•pra•cer•vi•cal
su•pra•cho•roid
su•pra•cho•roi•dal
su•pra•cho•roi•de•a
su•pra•cil•i•ar•y
su•pra•cla•vic•u•lar
su•pra•com•mis•sure
su•pra•con•dy•lar
su•pra•di•a•phrag•mat•ic
su•pra•di•a•phrag•mat•i•
    cal•ly
su•pra•gle•noid
su•pra•glot•tal
su•pra•glot•tic
su•pra•hy•oid
su•pra•lim•oi•nal
su•pra•lim•oi•nal•ly
su•pra•man•dib•u•lar
su•pra•mar•gi•nal
su•pra•mas•toid
su•pra•max•il•ola, *n., pl.* -lae,
    -las.
su•pra•max•il•lar•y
su•pra•me•a•tal
su•pra•men•tal
su•pra•mo•lec•u•lar
su•pra•na•sal
su•pra•nu•cle•ar
su•pra•oc•cip•oi•tal
su•pra•oc•clu•sion
su•pra•op•tic
su•pra•or•bit•oal
su•pra•pat•el•lar
su•pra•pu•bic
su•pra•re•nal
suprarenal gland
su•pra•re•onal•ec•to•my, *n.,*
    pl. -mies.

su•pra•scap•u•ola, *n., pl.* -lae,
    -las.
su•pra•scap•ou•lar
su•pra•sel•lar
su•pra•spi•nal
su•pra•spi•na•tus
su•pra•spi•nous
su•pra•sta•pe•di•oal
su•pra•ster•nal
su•pra•tem•po•ral
su•pra•ten•to•ri•oal
su•pra•ton•sil•lar
su•pra•troch•le•oar
su•pra•ven•tric•u•lar
supraventricular tach•y•car•
    di•a
su•pra•ver•gence
su•pra•ver•sion
su•pra•vi•tal
Sup•rax *Trademark.*
su•ora
su•oral
su•ral•oi•men•ta•tion
su•ra•min
Sur•bex *Trademark.*
Surbex-T *Trademark.*
sur•cin•gle
sur•di•tas ver•ba•lis
sur•di•oty
sur•ex•ci•ta•tion
sur•face•ac•tive
sur•fac•tant
Sur•fak *Trademark.*
sur•geon
surgeon gen•er•oal, *n., pl.* sur•
    geons gen•er•oal.
sur•geon's knot
sur•ger•y, *n., pl.* -ger•ies.
sur•gi•cal
sur•gi•cal•ly
sur•gi•cen•ter
Su•ri•tal *Trademark.*

Sur•mon•til
sur•ra
sur•rah
sur•ro•gate
surrogate moth•er
sur•sum•duc•tion
sur•sum•ver•gence
sur•sum•ver•sion
sur•veil•lance
sur•vi•val
survival curve
Sus-Phrine *Trademark.*
sus•cep•ti•bil•i•ty, *n., pl.*
 -ties.
sus•cep•ti•ble
sus•cep•ti•bly
sus•ci•tate, *v.,* -tat•ed, -tat•
 ing.
sus•ci•ta•tion
sus•pend•ed an•i•ma•tion
sus•pen•sion
sus•pen•soid
sus•pen•sor
sus•pen•so•ri•um, *n., pl.*
 -ri•a.
suspensorium he•pat•is
suspensorium tes•tis
suspensorium ves•i•cae
sus•pen•so•ry, *n., pl.* -ries.
suspensory lig•a•ment
sus•tained-re•lease
Sus•taire *Trademark.*
sus•ten•tac•u•lar
sus•ten•tac•u•lum, *n., pl.*
 -tac•u•la.
sustentaculum ta•li
su•sur•rus
susurrus su•ri•um
su•tur•al
su•ture, *v.,* -tured, -tur•ing.
sved•berg
svedberg u•nit

swab
swal•low
sway•back
sway•backed
Swed•ish mas•sage
Sween *Trademark.*
Sween-A-Peel *Trademark.*
Sween Prep *Trademark.*
swee•ney
swee•ony, *n., pl.* -nies.
sweet•bread
swell•head
swell•ing
swim•mer's ear
swimmer's itch
swim•ming pool gran•u•
 lo•ma
swin•ney
swob
sy•co•sis, *n., pl.* -ses.
sycosis bar•bae
Sy•den•ham's cho•re•a
Syl•lact *Trademark.*
syl•lep•si•ol•o•gy, *n., pl.*
 -gies.
syl•lep•sis
Syl•vian aq•ue•duct
Sylvian fis•sure
sym•bal•lo•phone
sym•bi•on
sym•bi•ont
sym•bi•o•sis, *n., pl.* -ses.
sym•bi•ote
sym•bi•ot•ic
sym•bi•ot•i•cal
sym•bi•ot•i•cal•ly
sym•bleph•a•ron
sym•bol•ism
sym•bol•i•za•tion
sym•bol•o•pho•bi•a
sym•me•olus, *n., pl.* -me•li.
Sym•met•rel *Trademark.*

sym•met•ric
sym•met•ri•cal
sym•me∘try, *n., pl.* **-tries.**
sym•pa•thec•to∘my, *n., pl.*
  -mies.
sym•pa•thet∘ic
sym•pa•thet∘i•cal∘ly
sym•pa•thet∘i•co•mi•met∘ic
sym•pa•thet∘i•co•to•ni∘a
sym•pa•thet∘i•co•ton∘ic
sym•pa•thet∘o•blast
sym•path∘i•co•blast
sym•path∘i•co•blas•to∘ma,
  n., pl. **-mas, -ma∘ta.**
sym•path∘i•co•go•ni∘o∘ma,
  n., pl. **-mas, -ma∘ta.**
sym•path∘i•co•lyt∘ic
sym•path∘i•co•mi•met∘ic
sym•path∘i•co•to•ni∘a
sym•path∘i•co•ton∘ic
sym•path∘i•co•trop∘ic
sym•pa•thin
sym•pa•thism
sym•pa•thiz∘er
sym•path∘o•blast
sym•path∘o•go•ni∘a
sym•pa•tho•go•ni∘o∘ma, *n.,*
  pl. **-mas, -ma∘ta.**
sym•pa•tho•lyt∘ic
sym•pa•tho•mi•met∘ic
sym•pa•thy, *n., pl.* **-thies.**
sym•pha•lan•gism
sym•phys∘e∘al
sym•phys•i∘al
sym•phys•i∘on
sym•phys∘i•ot∘o∘my, *n., pl.*
  -mies.
sym•phy•sis, *n., pl.* **-ses.**
symphysis pu∘bis
sym•phy•so•dac•tyl∘i∘a
sym•plasm
sym•plast

sym•po•si∘um, *n., pl.* **-si∘a,**
  -si•ums.
symp•tom
symp•to•mat∘ic
symp•to•mat∘i•cal
symp•to•mat∘i•cal∘ly
symp•to•mat∘o•log∘ic
symp•to•mat∘o•log∘i•cal
symp•to•mat∘o•log∘i•cal∘ly
symp•to•ma•tol∘o∘gy, *n., pl.*
  -gies.
symp•tom•less
sym•pus
sympus di∘pus
sympus mon∘o∘pus
Sy•na•cort *Trademark.*
syn•ae•re•sis
syn•aes•the•sia
syn•aes•thet∘ic
Syn∘a•lar *Trademark.*
Synalar-HP *Trademark.*
Syn•al•gos-DC *Trademark.*
syn∘a•nas•to•mo•sis
syn•anche
syn•an•the∘ma, *n., pl.*
  -ma∘ta, -mas.
syn•an•throp∘ic
syn•an•thro∘py, *n., pl.* **-pies.**
syn•apse, *n., v.,* **-apsed, -aps•**
  ing.
syn•ap•sis, *n., pl.* **-ses.**
syn•ap•tic
syn•ap•ti•cal
syn•ap•ti•cal∘ly
syn•ap•ti•ne•mal com•plex
syn•ap•tol∘o∘gy, *n., pl.* **-gies.**
syn•ap•to•ne•mal com•plex
syn•ap•to•so•mal
syn•ap•to•some
Syn∘a•rel *Trademark.*
syn•ar•thro•di∘a
syn•ar•thro•di∘al

syn•ar•thro•di•al•ly
syn•arth•ro•phy•sis, *n., pl.*
 -ses.
syn•arth•ro•sis, *n., pl.* -ses.
syn•car•oy•oon
syn•ceph•o•a•lus
syn•chon•dro•ses cra•ni•oi
synchondroses ster•na•les
syn•chon•dro•sis, *n., pl.* -ses.
syn•chon•drot•o•o•my, *n., pl.*
 -mies.
syn•chro•nic•oi•o•ty
syn•chro•nism
syn•chro•nous
syn•chro•ny, *n., pl.* -nies.
syn•chro•tron
syn•chy•sis
synchysis scin•til•lans
syn•cli•nal
syn•clit•oic
syn•clo•nus
synclonus bal•lis•mus
synclonus tre•mens
syn•co•pal
syn•co•ope
syncope an•gi•no•sa
syn•cop•ic
syn•cy•tial
syn•cy•ti•o•troph•o•blast
syn•cy•ti•oum, *n., pl.* -ti•oa.
syn•dac•tyl
syn•dac•tyle
syn•dac•tyl•oi•oa
syn•dac•tyl•oic
syn•dac•tyl•ism
syn•dac•tyl•ous
syn•dac•ty•oly, *n., pl.* -lies.
syn•de•sis
syn•des•mi•tis
syn•des•mo•cho•ri•al
syn•des•mo•sis, *n., pl.* -ses.

syndesmosis tib•i•o•fib•ou•
 lar•ois
syndesmosis tym•pa•no•sta•
 pe•di•oa
syn•des•mot•oic
syn•des•mot•o•o•my, *n., pl.*
 -mies.
syn•drome
syndrome X
syn•drom•oic
syn•ech•oi•oa, *n., pl.* -ech•i•oae.
synechia vul•vae
Syn•e•mol *Trademark.*
sy•neph•rine
syn•er•e•osis
syn•er•get•oic
syn•er•gi•oa
syn•er•gic
syn•er•gi•cal
syn•er•gi•cal•oly
syn•er•gism
syn•er•gist
syn•er•gis•tic
syn•er•gis•ti•cal
syn•er•gis•ti•cal•oly
syn•er•o•gy, *n., pl.* -gies.
syn•es•the•sia
syn•es•thete
syn•es•thet•oic
syn•e•oze•sis
Syn•ga•mus
syn•ga•omy
syn•ge•ne•oic
syn•ge•ne•si•o•trans•plan•
 ta•tion
syn•gen•e•osis, *n., pl.* -e•oses.
syn•ge•net•oic
syn•gig•nos•cism
syn•i•ze•sis
synizesis pu•pil•lae
syn•kar•oi•oon
syn•kar•oy•oon, *n., pl.* -kar•oy•oa.

Syn•kay•vite *Trademark.*
syn•ki•ne○sis
syn•ki•net○ic
syn○o•phrys
Syn○o•phy•late *Trademark.*
syn•op•to•phore
syn•or•chid•ism
syn•or•chism
syn•os•te○o○sis, *n., pl.* -ses.
syn•os•tose, *v.,* -tosed, -tos•
  ing.
syn•os•to○sis, *n., pl.* -ses.
syn•os•tot○ic
syn•os•tot○i•cal○ly
syn○o○tia
syn○o○tus
syn○o•vec•to○my, *n., pl.*
  -mies.
syn○o○vi○a
syn○o○vi○al
syn○o○vi○al○ly
syn○o○vi○o○ma, *n., pl.* -mas,
  -ma○ta.
syn○o○vit○ic
syn○o○vi•tis
synovitis hy•per•plas•ti○ca
syn•tac•tic
syn•tac•ti•cal
syn•tac•tics
syn•tal○i○ty
syn•tax○is
syn•tec•tic
syn•tec•ti•cal
syn•thase
syn•ther•mal
syn•the○sis, *n., pl.* -ses.
syn•the○size, *v.,* -sized, -siz•
  ing.
syn•the•tase
syn•thet○ic
syn•thet○ical
syn•thet○i•cal○ly

Syn•throid *Trademark.*
Syn•to•ci•non *Trademark.*
syn•ton○ic
syn•tro•phism
syn•troph○o•blast
syn•troph○o•blas•tic
syn•trop○ic
syn•tro○py
Sy•pha•cia
syph○i•le•mi○a
syph○i•lid
syph○i•lis
syphilis he•red○i•tar○i○a
syphilis in•son•ti○um
syphilis tech•ni○ca
syph○i•lit○ic
syph○i•lit○i•cal○ly
syph○i•li•za•tion
syph○i•lize, *v.,* -lized, -liz•ing.
syph○i•lo•derm, *n., pl.* -derms.
syph○i•lo•der○ma, *n., pl.*
  -ma○ta.
syph○i•log•ra•pher
syph○i•log•ra•phy, *n., pl.*
  -phies.
syph○i•loid
syph○i•lol○o○gist
syph○i•lol○o○gy, *n., pl.* -gies.
syph○i•lo○ma, *n., pl.* -mas,
  -ma○ta.
syph○i•lom○a•tous
syph○i•lo•nych○i○a ex•ul•
  cer•ans
syphilonychia sic○ca
syph○i•lo•phobe
syph○i•lo•pho•bi○a
syph○i•lo•psy•cho○sis, *n., pl.*
  -ses.
syph○i•lo•ther○a○py, *n., pl.*
  -pies.
Syp•rine *Trademark.*
syr○ing•ad••e○nous

sy•ringe, *n.*, *v.*, -ringed,
-ring•ing.
sy•rin•go•bul•bi•a
syr•in•go•ma, *n.*, *pl.* -mas,
-ma•ta.
sy•rin•go•my•e•li•a
sy•rin•go•my•el•ic
sy•rin•go•my•e•lo•cele
syr•inx, *n.*, *pl.* sy•rin•ges, syr•
inx•es.
sys•sar•co•sis
sys•tal•tic
sys•tem
sys•te•oma
sys•te•mat•ic

sys•te•mat•i•cal
sys•te•mat•i•cal•ly
sys•te•mat•i•za•tion
sys•tem•a•tize, *v.*, -tized,
-tiz•ing.
sys•tem•ic
systemic lu•pus er•y•the•
ma•to•sus
sys•tem•i•cal•ly
sys•to•le
sys•tol•ic
syst•rem•ma
Sy•to•bex *Trademark.*
sy•zyg•i•al
sy•zy•gy

T

T
T cell
T-group
T help•er cell
T lymph•o•cyte
TA
tab
ta•bac•um
Ta•ban•i•dae
Ta•ba•nus
tab•ar•dil•lo
ta•bel•la, *n.*, *pl.* -lae.
ta•bes
tabes cox•ar•i•a
tabes do•lo•ro•sa
tabes dor•sal•is
tabes er•got•i•ca
tabes mes•en•ter•i•ca
ta•bes•cent
ta•bet•ic
ta•bet•i•form
tab•id
ta•ble•spoon

ta•ble•spoon•ful, *n.*, *pl.* -fuls.
tab•let
ta•boo, *n.*, *pl.* ta•boos.
ta•bo•pa•ral•y•sis, *n.*, *pl.*
-ses.
ta•bo•pa•re•sis
ta•bu, *n.*, *pl.* ta•bus.
tab•u•lar
Tac•a•ryl *Trademark.*
TACE *Trademark.*
tache noire, *n.*, *pl.* taches
noires.
ta•chet•ic
ta•chis•to•scope
ta•chis•to•scop•ic
ta•chis•to•scop•i•cal•ly
tach•o•gram
ta•chog•ra•phy, *n.*, *pl.* -phies.
ta•chom•e•ter
tach•y•ar•rhyth•mi•a
tach•y•aux•e•sis, *n.*, *pl.* -ses.
tach•y•car•di•a
tach•y•car•di•ac
tach•y•lo•gia

ta•chym•e∘ter
tach∘y•pha•gia
tach∘y•phy•lax∘is
tach•yp•ne∘a
tach•yp•ne∘ic
tach•yp•noe∘a
tach∘y•rhyth•mi∘a
ta•chys•ter∘ol
tach∘y•sys•to∘le
tac•tic
tac•tile
tactile cor•pus•cle
tac•til∘i∘ty
tac•tion
tac•toid
tac•tom•e∘ter
tac•tu∘al
tac•tu•al∘ly
tae•di∘um vi•tae
tae•ni∘a
Taenia e∘chi•no•coc•cus
Taenia na∘na
Taenia sag∘i•na∘ta
Taenia so•li∘um
tae•ni∘a•cide
tae•ni∘ae a∘cus•ti•cae
taeniae co∘li
taeniae py•lo∘ri
taeniae te•la•rum
tae•ni•a•fuge
Tae•n•i•a•rhyn•chus
tae•ni•a•sis
Tag∘a•met *Trademark.*
tag∘a•tose
tail•bone
ta•ko•sis
Tal∘a•cen *Trademark.*
ta•lal•gia
tal•cum
tal∘i•ped
tal∘i•pes

tal∘i•pom•o•a•nus
ta•lo•cal•ca•ne∘al
ta•lo•na•vic∘u•lar
ta•lo•nid
ta•lo•tib•i∘al
talotibial ex•os•to•ses
ta∘lus, *n., pl.* ta∘li.
Tal•win *Trademark.*
Talwin Nx *Trademark.*
Tam•bo•cor *Trademark.*
tam•bour
ta•mox∘i•fen
tam•pon, *n., pl.* -pons.
tam•po∘nade
tam•pon•age
Tan•de•a•ril *Trademark.*
tan•nase
tan•nate
tan•nic
tan•nin
tan•ta•lum
tan•trum
Tao *Trademark.*
tap
Ta•pa•zole *Trademark.*
ta•pe•tal
ta•pe•to•ret∘i•nal
ta•pe∘tum, *n., pl.* -pe∘ta.
tapetum al•ve∘o∘li
tapetum lu•ci•dum
tape•worm
taph•e∘pho•bi∘a
tap∘i•no•ceph∘a∘ly
tap∘i•o∘ca
tap∘i•roid
ta•pote•ment
Ta•rac•tan *Trademark.*
tar•an•tism
ta•ran•tu∘la, *n., pl.* -las, -lae.
tar•ax∘a•cum
tar•dive

tardive dys•ki•ne•sia
tare, *v.*, tared, tar•ing.
tar•get
target or•gan
ta○ro, *n., pl.* ta○ros.
tar○ry, *adj.*, -ri○er, -ri○est.
tar•sa•de•ni•tis
tar•sal
tar•sa○le, *n., pl.* -li○a.
tar•sal•gia
tar•sec•to○my, *n., pl.* -mies.
tar•si•tis
tar○so•ma•la•cia
tar○so•met○a•tar○sal
tar○so•pha•lan•ge○al
tar○so•phy○ma, *n., pl.* -mas,
  -ma○ta.
tar○so•plas○ty, *n., pl.* -ties.
tar•sor•rha•phy, *n., pl.* -phies.
tar•sot○o○my, *n., pl.* -mies.
tar•sus, *n., pl.* tar○si.
tar•tar
tartar e○met○ic
tar•tar•at○ed
tar•tar○ic
tar•trate
tar•trat○ed
tat•ra•vac•cine
tat•too, *n., pl.* tat•toos.
tau•rine
tau•ro•cho•late
tau•ro•chol○ic
tau•to•me•ni○al
tau•to•mer○ic
tau•tom•er•ism
Tav•ist *Trademark.*
Tavist-D *Trademark.*
tax○is, *n., pl.* tax○es.
tax○ol
tax○o•nom○ic
tax○o•nom○i•cal
tax○o•nom○i•cal○ly

tax•on○o•mist
tax•on○o•omy, *n., pl.* -mies.
Tay-Sachs dis•ease
Ta•zi•cef *Trademark.*
Ta•zi•dime *Trademark.*
teach•ing hos•pi•tal
tear gas, *n.*
tear-gas, *v.*, -gassed, -gas•sing.
Tears Nat○u•ra○le II *Trademark.*
Tears Plus *Trademark.*
te•art
tea•spoon
tea•spoon•ful, *n., pl.* -fuls,
  -spoons•ful.
tech•ne•ti○um
technetium-99m
tech•ne•tron○ic
tech•nic
tech•ni•cal
tech•ni•cian
tech•nique
tech•nol○o•gist
tech•nol○o○gy, *n., pl.* -gies.
tec•ti•form
tec•to•ceph○a•ly
tec•ton○ic
tec•to•ri○al
tec•to•ri○um, *n., pl.* -ri○a.
tec•to•spi•nal
tec•tum, *n., pl.* tec○ta.
tectum mes•en•ceph○a•li
Te•dral SA *Trademark.*
teeth
teethe, *v.*, teethed, teeth•ing.
teeth•ridge
Teg○oi•son *Trademark.*
teg•men, *n., pl.* -mi○na.
tegmen mas•to•ide○um
tegmen tym•pa○ni
teg•men•tal
teg•men•tum, *n., pl.* -men○ta.

temple

tegmentum rhom•ben•ceph•a•li

Te•go•pen *Trademark.*

Teg•re•tol *Trademark.*

teg•u•ment

teg•u•men•tal

teg•u•men•ta•ry

teg•u•men•tum, *n., pl.* -men•ta.

tei•chop•si•a

Tel-E-Dose *Trademark.*

te•la, *n., pl.* te•lae.

tel•aes•the•sia

tel•aes•thet•ic

tel•al•gia

tel•an•gi•ec•ta•si•a, *n., pl.* -si•as.

tel•an•gi•ec•ta•sis, *n., pl.* -ses.

telangiectasis fa•cie•i

telangiectasis lym•phat•i•ca

tel•an•gi•ec•tat•ic

tel•an•gi•o•ma, *n., pl.* -mas, -ma•ta.

tel•an•gi•o•sis

Tel•drin *Trademark.*

tel∘e•car•di•o•gram

tel∘e•car•di•o•phone

tel∘e•den•dron

tel∘e•di•a•stol∘ic

te•leg∘o•ny

tel∘e•ki•ne∘sis

tel∘e•lec•tro•car•di•o•gram

te•lem•e•ter

tel∘e•met•ric

tel∘e•met•ri•cal∘ly

te•lem•e•try

tel•en•ce•phal∘ic

tel•en•ceph∘a•lon, *n., pl.* -ceph∘a•la.

te•le•o•log∘ic

te•le•o•log∘i•cal

te•le•ol∘o∘gy, *n., pl.* -gies.

te•le•op•si∘a

te•le•o•roent•gen∘o•gram

Tel∘e•paque *Trademark.*

tel∘e•path∘ic

tel∘e•path∘i•cal∘ly

te•lep∘a•thist

te•lep∘a•thy

tel∘e•ra•di•og•ra•phy, *n., pl.* -phies.

tel•er∘gy

tel∘e•roent•gen∘o•gram

tel∘e•roent•gen•og•ra•phy, *n., pl.* -phies.

tel•es•the•sia

tel•es•thet∘ic

tel∘e•sys•tol∘ic

tel∘e•ther∘a•py, *n., pl.* -pies.

tel•lu•rate

tel•lu•ric

tel•lu•ri•um

tel∘o•cen•tric

tel∘o•den•dri∘on, *n., pl.* -dri∘a.

tel∘o•lec∘i•thal

tel∘o•mere

tel∘o•phase

tel∘o•pha•sic

tel∘o•phrag∘ma, *n., pl.* -ma∘ta.

Te•lo•spo•rid∘i∘a

te•lo•spo•rid•i∘an

Tem∘a•ril *Trademark.*

Te•maz•e•pam

Te•mo•vate *Trademark.*

tem•per∘a•ment

tem•per•ate

tem•per•ate∘ly

tem•per•ate•ness

tem•per∘a•ture

tem•plate

tem•ple

tem•plet
tem•po•ral
temporal bone
temporal lobe
tem•po•rar○y
tem•po•ro-oc•cip○i•tal
tem•po•ro•man•dib○u•lar
temporomandibular joint syn•
 drome
tem•po○ro•max•il•lar○y
tem•po○ro•pa•ri•e•tal
Ten-K *Trademark.*
te•na•cious
te•nac○i○ty
te•nac○u•lum, *n., pl.* -nac•
 u○la, -lums.
Ten•cet *Trademark.*
Ten•con *Trademark.*
ten•den○cy, *n., pl.* -cies.
ten•der
ten•der•ness
ten•di•ni•tis
ten•di•no•plas○ty, *n., pl.*
 -ties.
ten•di•no•sis
ten•di•nous
ten•do, *n., pl.* -di•nes.
tendo A○chil•lis
tendo cal•ca•ne○us
tendo con•junc•ti•vus
tendo cri•co•e•so•pha•ge○us
ten•dol○y•sis, *n., pl.* -ses.
ten•do•mu•cin
ten•don, *n., pl.* -dons.
ten•do•ni•tis
ten•do•plas○ty, *n., pl.* -ties.
ten•do•vag○i•nal
ten•do•vag○i•ni•tis
tendovaginitis crep○i•tans
tendovaginitis gran○u•lo○sa
tendovaginitis sten○o•sans
te•nec•to○my, *n., pl.* -mies.

te•nes•mus
Ten○ex *Trademark.*
te•ni○a
te•ni•a•cide
te•ni•a•fuge
te•ni•a•sis
te•ni○o○la ci•ne•re○a
ten•nis el•bow
tennis leg
tennis toe
ten○o•de○sis, *n., pl.* -ses.
ten○o•dyn○i○a
te•nol○y•sis, *n., pl.* -ses.
ten○o•my○o•plas○ty, *n., pl.*
 -ties.
ten○o•my•ot○o•my, *n., pl.*
 -mies.
ten○o•nec•to○my, *n., pl.*
 -mies.
ten○o•nitis
Ten•on's capsule
te•non•to•my○o•plas○ty, *n.,*
 pl. -ties.
te•non•to•my•ot○o•my, *n.,*
 pl. -mies.
ten○o•per○i•os•ti•tis
ten○o•phyte
ten○o•plast○ic
ten○o•plas○ty, *n., pl.* -ties.
Ten○o•ret○ic *Trademark.*
Te•nor•min *Trademark.*
te•nor•rha•phy, *n., pl.* -phies.
ten•os•to•sis
ten○o•syn○o•vec•to○my, *n.,*
 pl. -mies.
ten○o•syn○o•vi•tis
tenosynovitis crep○i•tans
ten○o•tome
te•not○o•mist
te•not○o•mize, *v.,* -mized,
 -miz•ing.
te•not○o•o○my, *n., pl.* -mies.

ten∘o•vag∘i•ni•tis
Ten•si•lon *Trademark.*
ten•si∘om•e∘ter
ten•sion
ten•sor
tent
ten•ta•cle
ten•ti∘go ve•ne•re∘a
ten•to•ri∘al
ten•to•rim cer∘e•bel∘li
ten•to•ri∘um, *n., pl.* -ri∘a.
tentorium cer∘e•bel∘li
Ten•u•ate *Trademark.*
te∘pa
Te•pa•nil *Trademark.*
ter∘as, *n., pl.* ter∘a∘ta.
te•rat∘ic
ter∘a•tism
ter∘a∘to•blas•to∘ma, *n., pl.*
  -mas, -ma∘ta.
ter∘a∘to•car•ci•no∘ma, *n., pl.*
  -mas, -ma∘ta.
te∘rat∘o∘gen
ter∘a∘to•gen•e∘sis, *n., pl.*
  -e∘ses.
te∘rat∘o∘ge•net∘ic
te∘rat∘o∘gen∘ic
te∘rat∘o∘ge•nic∘i∘ty
ter∘a•tog∘e∘ny
ter∘a•toid
ter∘a∘to•log∘ic
ter∘a∘to•log∘i•cal
ter∘a•tol∘o∘gist
ter∘a•tol∘o∘gy, *n., pl.* -gies.
ter∘a•to∘ma, *n., pl.* -mas,
  -ma∘ta.
ter∘a∘to•pho•bi∘a
ter∘a∘to•sis
ter∘a∘to•sper•mi∘a
Ter∘a•zol *Trademark.*
Terazol 7 *Trademark.*
Ter∘a•zo•sin

ter•bi∘um
Ter•con∘a•zole
ter•e∘bene
ter•e∘bin•thi•nate
ter•e∘bin•thine
ter•e∘bra•che•sis, *n., pl.* -ses.
te∘res, *n., pl.* ter∘e∘es.
Ter•fen∘a•dine
Terfenadine/Pseu∘do•e•
  phed•rine
ter•mi•nal
ter•mi•nal∘ly
ter•mi•na•tion
ter•mi•nol∘o∘gy, *n., pl.* -gies.
ter•mi•nus, *n., pl.* -mi∘ni, -mi•
  nus∘es.
ter•na∘ry
ter•pene
ter•pen∘ic
ter•pin
ter•pin•e∘ol
ter•pi•nol
ter∘ra alba
Terra-Cor•tril *Trademark.*
terra sig∘il•la∘ta
Ter•ra•my•cin *Trademark.*
ter•tian
ter•ti•ar∘y
ter•tip•a∘ra
Tes-Tape *Trademark.*
Tes•lac *Trademark.*
Tes•sa•lon *Trademark.*
test-cross
test-tube ba∘by
test•cross
tes•ti•cle
tes•tic∘u•lar
tes•tis, *n., pl.* -tes.
tes•toid
tes•tos•ter•one
Tes•tred *Trademark.*
test tube or test-tube

tet○a•nal
te•tan○ic
te•tan○i•cal
te•tan○i•cal○ly
te•tan○i•form
tet○a•nig○e○nous
tet○a•nil○la
tet○a•nism
tet○a•ni•za•tion
tet○a•nize, *v.*, -nized, -niz•ing.
tet○a•node
tet○a•noid
tet○a•nol○y•sin
tet○a•nom•e○ter
tet○a•no•spas•min
tet○a•nus
tetanus in•fan•tum
tetanus ne•o•na•to•rum
tet•a○ny
tet•ar•cone
tet•ar•co○nid
tet•ar•ta•no•pi○a
tet•ar•to•cone
tet•ar•to•co○nid
tet○ra•ba•sic
tet○ra•ba•sic○i○ty, *n.*, *pl.* -ties.
tet○ra•ben○a•zine
tet○ra•bra○chi•us
tet○ra•bro•mo•phe•nol•
  phtha•le○in
tet○ra•caine
tet○ra•chlor•eth•ane
tet○ra•chlo•ride
tet○ra•chlo•ro•e•thane
tet○ra•chlo•ro•eth○y•lene
tet○ra•cy•cline
tet•rad
tet○ra•dac•ty○ly
tet•rad○ic
tet○ra•eth○yl
tet○ra•eth•yl•am•mo•ni○um
tet○ra•eth•yl•thi•u•ram

tet•rag○e○nous
tet•ra•hy•dric
tet•ra•hy•dro•can•nab○i•nol
tet•ra•hy•me○na
te•tral○o○gy, *n.*, *pl.* -gies.
tetralogy of Fal•lot
tet○ra•mas•ti○a
Tet○ra•me•res
tet○ra•meth•yl•am•mo•
  ni○um
tet○ra•meth•yl•e•ne•di○a•
  mine
tet○ra•nop•si○a
tet○ra•o•don•tox○in
tet○ra•pep•tide
tet○ra•ple•gia
tet•ra•ploid
tet•ra•ploi•dy
tet○ra•pod
tet○ra•pus
tet○ra•pyr•role
tet○ra•sac•ca•ride
tet○ras•ce•lus
tet○ra•som○ic
tet○ra•sti•chi•a•sis
tet○ra•tom○ic
tet○ra•va•lent
Tet•rex *Trademark.*
te•tro•do•tox○in
tet•rose
tet•rox•ide
tet•ter
Tex○as fe○ver
tex○is
tex•ti•form
tex•tu•ral
tex•ture
thal○a•men•ce•phal○ic
thal○a•men•ceph○a•lon, *n.*,
  pl. -ceph•a○la.
tha•lam○ic
tha•lam○i•cal○ly

thal○a○mo•cele
thal○a○mo•coele
thal○a○mo•cor•ti•cal
thal○a○mo•len•tic○u•lar
thal○a○mo•teg•men•tal
thal•a•mot○o○my, *n., pl.*
  -mies.
thal○a•mus, *n., pl.* thal•a○mi.
tha•las•sa•ne•mi○a
thal•as•se•mi○a
thal•as•se•mic
tha•las•so•pho•bi○a
thal•as•so•ther○a•py, *n., pl.*
  -pies.
tha•lid○o•mide
Thal○i•tone *Trademark.*
thal•li○um
thallium stress test
Thal•loph○y○ta
thal•lo•phyte
thal•lo•phyt○ic
tha•llo•spore
thal•lo•tox○i○co•sis
thal•lus, *n., pl.* thal○li.
Tham *Trademark.*
Tham-E *Trademark.*
tha•mu○ria
than○a○to•bi•o•log○ic
than○a•tog•no•mon○ic
than○a•toid
than○a•to•log○i•cal
than○a•tol○o•gist
than○a•tol○o○gy, *n., pl.* -gies.
than○a•to•ma•ni○a
than○a•to•phid○i○a
than○a•to•pho•bi○a
than○a•top○sy, *n., pl.* -sies.
Than○a•tos
Than○a•tot○ic
the•ba○ic
the•baine
the•be•si○an chan•nel

thebesian vein
thebesian ves•sel
the○ca, *n., pl.* the•cae.
theca ex•ter○na
theca fol•lic○u•li
theca in•ter○na
the○cal
the•cate
the•ci•tis
the•co•dont
the•co○ma, *n., pl.* -mas,
  -ma○ta.
the•co•steg•no•sis
Thee•lin *Trademark.*
thee•lol
thei•le○ri○a, *n., pl.* -ri○ae,
  -ri○as.
thei•le•ri•a•sis
thei•le•ri○o•sis
the•ine
the•lal•gia
the•larche
The•la○zia
the•la○zi•a•sis
the•le○plas○ty, *n., pl.* -ties.
the•ler○e•thism
the•li•tis
the•li○um, *n., pl.* -li○a.
the•lon•cus
the•lor•rha•gia
the•lo•thism
thel○y•gen○ic
thel○y•to•cia
The•mat○ic Ap•per•cep•tion
  Test
the•nar
Theo○o-24 *Trademark.*
Theo-Dur *Trademark.*
Theo-Or•gan○i•din *Trademark.*
the○o•bro○ma oil
the○o•bro•mine
The○o•chron *Trademark.*

The○o•clear *Trademark.*
The○o•lair *Trademark.*
Theolair-SR *Trademark.*
The○o•lix○ir *Trademark.*
the○o•ma•ni○a
the○o•pho•bi○a
The○o•phyl *Trademark.*
the○o•phyl•line
the○o•ret○ic
the○o•ret○i•cal
the○o•ret○i•cal○ly
the○o•ry, *n., pl.* -ries.
The○o•stat 80 *Trademark.*
Ther○a-Flur *Trademark.*
Thera-Flur-N *Trademark.*
Thera-Ge○sic *Trademark.*
Ther○a•bid *Trademark.*
Ther○a•Cys BCG *Trademark.*
Ther○a•Flu *Trademark.*
Ther○a•gran *Trademark.*
Theragran-M *Trademark.*
ther○a•peu•sis, *n., pl.* -ses.
ther○a•peu•tic
therapeutic in•dex
therapeutic vac•cine
therapeutic win•dow
ther○a•peu•ti•cal
ther○a•peu•ti•cal○ly
ther○a•peu•tics
ther○a•peu•tist
the•ra•pi○a
ther○a•pist
ther○a•py, *n., pl.* -pies.
ther•en•ceph○a•lous
Ther○e•vac *Trademark.*
the•ri○ac
the•ri•a○ca
theriaca an•drom•a○chi
the•ri•at•rics
The•ri•di•i•i•dae
the•ri•o○ma, *n., pl.* -mas,
  -ma○ta.

ther•mae
ther•mal
ther•mal•ge•sia
ther•ma•tol○o○gy, *n., pl.*
  -gies.
ther•mes•the•sia
ther•mes•the•si•om•e○ter
ther•mic
ther•mis•tor
ther○mo•an•al•ge•sia
ther○mo•an•es•the•sia
ther○mo•cau•ter○y, *n., pl.*
  -ter•ies.
ther○mo•chem•is•try
ther•moch○ro•ism
ther○mo•co•ag○u•la•tion
ther○mo•cou•ple
ther○mo•cur•rent
ther○mo•dif•fu•sion
ther○mo•di•lu•tion
ther○mo•dur○ic
ther○mo•dy•nam•ics
ther○mo•ex•ci•to○ry
ther○mo•gen•e○sis, *n., pl.*
  -e○ses.
ther○mo•ge•net○ic
ther○mo•gen○ic
ther○mo•gram
ther○mo•graph
ther•mog•ra•pher
ther○mo•graph○ic
ther○mo•graph○i•cal○ly
ther•mog•ra•phy, *n., pl.*
  -phies.
ther○mo•hy•per•al•ge•sia
ther○mo•hy•per•es•the•sia
ther○mo•hyp○es•the•sia
ther○mo•in•hib○i•to○ry
ther○mo•la•bile
ther○mo•la•bil○i○ty
ther•mol○y•sis, *n., pl.* -ses.
ther○mo•lyt○ic

ther•mo•mas•sage
ther•mom•e•ter
ther•mo•met•ric
ther•mom•e•try
ther∘mo•neu•ro•sis
ther•moph•a∘gy
ther∘mo•phil
ther∘mo•phile
ther∘mo•phil∘ic
ther•moph∘i•lous
ther∘mo•pho•bi•a
ther∘mo•phore
ther∘mo•phyl∘ic
ther∘mo•pile
ther∘mo•plas•tic
ther∘mo•ple•gia
ther∘mo•po•lyp•ne∘a
ther∘mo•re•cep•tor
ther∘mo•reg∘u•late, *v.*,
   -lat∘ed, -lat•ing.
ther∘mo•reg∘u•la•tion
ther∘mo•reg∘u•la•tor
ther∘mo•reg∘u•la•to∘ry
ther∘mo•scope
ther∘mo•set
ther∘mo•sta•bil∘i∘ty
ther∘mo•sta•ble
ther∘mo•stat
ther∘mo•stat∘i•cal∘ly
ther∘mo•ster•e∘osis
ther∘mo•stro•muhr
ther∘mo•sys•tal•tic
ther∘mo•tac•tic
ther∘mo•tax∘ic
ther∘mo•tax∘is
ther∘mo•ther∘a∘py, *n., pl.*
   -pies.
ther∘mo•to•nom•e∘ter
ther∘mo•tra•che•ot∘o∘my,
   n., pl. -mies.
ther∘mo•trop∘ic
ther∘mo•tro•pism

the•sau•ro•sis
the•sis, *n., pl.* -ses.
the∘ta rhythm
thi•a•ben•da•zole
thi•a•ce•ta•zone
Thi•a•cide *Trademark.*
Thi•am∘i•late *Trademark.*
thi•a•min
thi•a•mi•nase
thi•a•mine
thi•a•zide
thi•a•zol•sul•fone
thick-wind∘ed
thigh
thigh•bone
thig•mes•the•sia
thig•mo•tax∘is
thig•mot•ro•pism
thi•mer∘o•sal
thin-lay∘er chro•ma•tog•ra•
   phy
thi•o•ba•cil•lus, *n., pl.* -cil∘li.
thi•o•bac•ter∘i∘um, *n., pl.*
   -ter•i∘a.
thi•o•car•bam•ide
thi•o•chrome
thi•o•cy•a•nate
thi•o•di•phen•yl•a•mine
Thi•o•gua•nine *Trademark.*
Thi•o•la *Trademark.*
thi•o•ne•ine
thi•on∘ic
thi•o•pen•tal
thiopental so•di•um
thi•o•pen•tone
thi•o•phene
Thi•o•ri•daz•ine
thi•o•sin•a•mine
thi•o•sul•fate
Thi•o•sul•fil *Trademark.*
Thi•ot∘e•pa *Trademark.*
thi•o•u•ra•cil

thi•o•u•re•a
third-de•gree burn
third-par•ty
thix•o•trop•ic
thix•ot•ro•py
Thom•as splint
Thom•sen's dis••ease
thon•zyl•a•mine
tho•ra•cec•to•my, *n., pl.*
-mies.
tho•ra•cen•te•sis, *n., pl.* -ses.
tho•rac•ic
thoracic duct
tho•ra•co•ce•los•chi•sis
tho•ra•co•cen•te•sis, *n., pl.*
-ses.
tho•ra•co•cyl•lo•sis
tho•ra•co•dyn•i•a
tho•ra•co•gas•tros•chi•sis
tho•ra•co•lap•a•rot•o•my,
n., pl. -mies.
tho•ra•co•lum•bar
tho•ra•col•y•sis, *n., pl.* -ses.
tho•ra•com•e•olus, *n., pl.* -e•oli.
tho•ra•cop•a•gus, *n., pl.*
-cop•a•gus•es, -cop•a•gi.
thoracopagus par•a•sit•i•cus
thoracopagus tribra•chi•us
thoracopagus trip•us
tho•ra•co•par•a•ceph•a•lus,
n., pl. -ceph•a•li.
tho•ra•co•plas•ty, *n., pl.* -ties.
tho•ra•cos•chi•sis
tho•ra•co•scope
tho•ra•co•scop•ic
tho•ra•cos•co•py, *n., pl.*
-pies.
tho•ra•cos•to•my, *n., pl.*
-mies.
tho•ra•cot•o•my, *n., pl.*
-mies.

tho•rax, *n., pl.* -rax•es, -ra•
ces.
Tho•ra•zine *Trademark.*
tho•ri•um
tho•rough•pin
thought dis•or•der
thread•worm
threat•en
thre•o•nine
thre•ose
Thre•o•stat *Trademark.*
threp•sol•o•o•gy, *n., pl.* -gies.
thresh•old
throb, *v.,* throbbed, throb•
bing.
throm•base
throm•bas•the•ni•a
throm•bec•to•my, *n., pl.*
-mies.
throm•bi
throm•bin
Throm•bi•nar *Trademark.*
throm•bo•an•gi•i•tis
thromboangiitis ob•lit•er•ans
throm•bo•ar•ter•i•tis
throm•bo•blast
throm•boc•la•sis
throm•bo•clastic
throm•bo•cyte
throm•bo•cy•the•mi•a
throm•bo•cyt•ic
throm•bo•cy•to•pe•ni•a
throm•bo•cy•to•pe•nic
thrombocytopenic pur•pu•ra
throm•bo•cy•to•poi•e•sis
throm•bo•cy•to•sis
throm•bo•em•bo•lec•to•my,
n., pl. -mies.
throm•bo•em•bol•ic
throm•bo•em•bo•lism
rom•bo•en•dar•ter•ec•
to•my, *n., pl.* -mies.

throm○bo•en•do•car•di•tis

throm○bo•gen

throm○bo•gen○ic

throm○bo•ki•nase

throm○bo•lym•phan•gi•tis

throm•bol○y•sis

throm○bo•lyt○ic

throm•bon

throm•bop○a•thy

throm○bo•pe•ni○a

throm○bo•phil○i○a

throm○bo•phle•bi•tis

throm○bo•plas•tic

throm○bo•plas•ti•cal○ly

throm○bo•plas•tin

throm○bo•plas•tin○o○gen

throm○bo•poi•e○sis

throm•bose, *v.*, -bosed, -bos•ing.

throm○bo•sis

throm○bo•sta•sis, *n.*, *pl.* -ses.

Throm○bo•stat *Trademark.*

throm•bot○ic

throm•box•ane

throm•bus, *n.*, *pl.* throm○bi.

thrombus ne•o•na•to•rum

thrombus vul•vae

throt•tle, *v.*, -tled, -tling.

thrush

thu○ja oc•ci•den•ta•lis

thu•li○um

thumb

thumb•nail

thy•mec•to•mize, *v.*, -mized, -miz•ing.

thy•mec•to○my, *n.*, *pl.* -mies.

thy•mer•ga•sia

thym○ic

thy•mi•co•lym•phat○ic

thy•mi•dine

thy•mine

thy•mi•tis

thy•mo•cyte

thy•mol

thy•mo•lep•tic

thy•mo○ma, *n.*, *pl.* -mas, -ma○ta.

thy•mop○a•thy, *n.*, *pl.* -thies.

thy•mo•sin

thy•mus, *n.*, *pl.* -mus○es, thy•mi.

Thy•rar *Trademark.*

thy○ro•ar○y•te•noid

thy○ro•cal•ci•to•nin

thy○ro•car•di○ac

thy○ro•cele

thy○ro•cer•vi•cal

thy○ro•chon•drot○o○my, *n.*, *pl.* -mies.

thy○ro•cri•cot○o○my, *n.*, *pl.* -mies.

thy○ro•ep○i•glot•tic

thy○ro•gen○ic

thy•rog○e○nous

thy○ro•glob○u•lin

thy○ro•glos•sal

thy○ro•hy○al

thy○ro•hy○oid

thy○ro•hy•oi•de•an

thy•roid

thyroid gland

thyroid-stim○u•lat○ing hor•mone

thy•roi•dal

thy•roi•dec•to•mize, *v.*, -mized, -miz•ing.

thy•roi•dec•to○my, *n.*, *pl.* -mies.

thy•roi•din○i○um

thy•roid○i•tis

thy•roid•less

thy•roid•ot○o○my, *n.*, *pl.* -mies.

thy•roid•stim•u•lat•ing hor•mone

Thy○ro•lar *Trademark.*

thy○ro•nine

thy○ro•par○a•thy•roi•dec•to○my, *n., pl.* -mies.

thy○ro•pri•val

thy○ro•pro•tein

thy•rop•to•sis

thy•rot○o○my, *n., pl.* -mies.

thy○ro•tox○ic

thy○ro•tox•ic○i○ty, *n., pl.* -ties.

thy○ro•tox•i○co•sis

thy○ro•tox•in

thy○ro•troph○ic

thy○ro•troph○i•cal○ly

thy○rot•ro•phin

thy○ro•trop○ic

thy○ro•tro•pin

thyrotropin-re•leas•ing hor•mone

thy•rox○in

thy•rox•ine

Thy•tro•par *Trademark.*

tib○i○a, *n., pl.* tib•i○ae, tib•i○as.

tib○i○al

tib•i•a○le ex•ter•num

tibiale pos•ti•cum

tib○i•a•lis, *n., pl.* -les.

tibialis se•cun•dus

tib○i○o•fib•u○la, *n., pl.* -lae, -las.

tib○i○o•fib○u•lar

tib○i○o•tar•sal

tic

tic dou•lou•reux

Ti•car *Trademark.*

tick-borne

tick fe○ver

ti•dal

Ti•gan *Trademark.*

tight•ness

tig•roid

ti•grol○y•sis

tim•ber

tim•bre

timed-re•lease

Tim•en•tin *Trademark.*

Tim○o•lide *Trademark.*

tim○o•lol

Ti•mop•tic *Trademark.*

Ti•nac•tin *Trademark.*

tinc•tion

tinc•to•ri○al

tinc•to•ri•al○ly

tinc•ture, *n., v.,* -tured, -tur•ing.

Tin•dal *Trademark.*

tin○e○a

tinea bar•bae

tinea cap○i•tis

tinea cor•po○ris

tinea cru•ris

tinea pe○dis

tinea ver•si•col○or

tin○e○al

tin•gle, *v.,* -gled, -gling.

tin•ni•tus

tinnitus au•ri○um

tinnitus cra•ni○i

tin•to•met•ric

tin•tom•e○try

Tin•ver *Trademark.*

ti•queur

ti•sane

Ti•se•li○us apparatus

Tiselius cell

tis•sue

tissue cul•ture

tissue plas•min○o•gen ac•ti•va•tor

tis•su•lar

ti•ta•ni•um
ti•ter
tit•il•la•tion
ti•trant
ti•trate, *v.*, -trat∘ed, -trat•ing.
ti•tra•tion
ti∘tre
tit∘u•bant
tit∘u•ba•tion
to•bac∘co, *n.*, *pl.* -cos, -coes.
To•brex *Trademark.*
to•cai∘nide
to∘c•o•dy•na•mom•e∘ter
to•col∘o∘gy, *n.*, *pl.* -gies.
to•coph•er∘ol
toe
toe•drop
toe•nail
Tof•ra•nil *Trademark.*
Tofranil-PM *Trademark.*
to•ga•vi•rus, *n.*, *pl.* -rus∘es.
toi•let
to•ko•dy•na•mom•e∘ter
to•kol∘o∘gy, *n.*, *pl.* -gies.
tol•bu•ta•mide
To•lec•tin
tol•er•ance
tol•er•ant
tol•er•ate, *v.*, -at∘ed, -at•ing.
tol•er∘a•tion
To•le•rex *Trademark.*
Tol•frin∘ic *Trademark.*
Tol∘i•nase *Trademark.*
Tol•me•tin *Trademark.*
tol•naf•tate
to•lo•ni•um
tol∘u•ene
tol∘u•i•dine
tol∘u∘ol
to•ma•tine
to•men•tum, *n.*, *pl.* -men∘ta.

Tom•es's fi∘ber
Tomes's fi•bril
to•mo•gram
to•mo•graph
to•mo•graph∘ic
to•mo•graph∘i•cal∘ly
to•mog•ra∘phy, *n.*, *pl.* -phies.
to•mo•ma•ni∘a
tone, *n.*, *v.*, toned, ton•ing.
tone-deaf
tone-deaf•ness
tongue
tongue•less
tongue-tie, *v.*, -tied, -ty•ing.
ton∘ic
ton∘i•cal∘ly
to•nic∘i∘ty
Ton∘o•card *Trademark.*
ton∘o•clonic
to•no•fi•bril, *n.*, *pl.* -brils.
to•no•fi•bril∘la, *n.*, *pl.* -lae.
ton∘o•gram
ton∘o•graph
to•nog•ra•phy, *n.*, *pl.* -phies.
to•nom•e∘ter
ton∘o•met•ric
to•nom•e∘try
ton∘o•plast
ton∘o•scope
ton•sil
ton•sil∘la cer∘e∘bel∘li
tonsilla lin•gua•lis
tonsilla pal∘a•ti∘na
tonsilla pha•ryn•ge∘a
tonsilla tu•bar∘i∘a
ton•sil•lar
ton•sil•lary
ton•sil•lec•to∘my, *n.*, *pl.*
  -mies.
ton•sil•lit∘ic
ton•sil•li•tis
ton•sil•lo•lith

ton•sil•lo•tome
ton•sil•lot•o•my, *n., pl.* -mies.
to•nus
tooth, *n., pl.* teeth.
tooth•ache
top•ag•no•sis
to•pal•gia
to•pec•to•my, *n., pl.* -mies.
top•es•the•sia
to•pha•ceous
to•phus, *n., pl.* to•phi.
top•i•cal
top•i•cal•ly
Top•i•cort *Trademark.*
top•og•no•si•a, *n., pl.* -si•as.
top•og•no•sis
top•o•graph•ic
to•pog•ra•phy, *n., pl.* -phies.
to•pol•o•gy, *n., pl.* -gies.
top•o•nar•co•sis
top•o•neu•ro•sis
top•o•nym
top•o•pho•bi•a
Topp Trims *Trademark.*
Top•rol-XL *Trademark.*
To•ra•dol IM *Trademark.*
tor•cu•lar
torcular He•ro•phil•i
To•re•can *Trademark.*
tor•mi•na al•vi
Tor•na•late *Trademark.*
to•rose
tor•por
torpor in•tes•ti•no•rum
torque, *v.,* torqued, torqu•ing.
tor•re•fac•tion
tor•re•fy, *v.,* -fied, -fy•ing.
tor•ri•fy, *v.,* -fied, -fy•ing.
tor•sion
tor•so, *n., pl.* tor•sos, tor•si, tor•soes.
tor•ti•col•lis

torticollis spas•ti•ca
tor•u•la, *n., pl.* -lae, -las.
tor•u•lop•sis, *n., pl.* -ses.
to•ru•lo•sis
tor•u•lus, *n., pl.* tor•u•li.
to•rus, *n., pl.* to•ri.
To•ta•cil•lin-N *Trademark.*
to•tal bod•y fail•ure
total par•en•ter•al nu•tri•tion
to•ti•po•ten•cy, *n., pl.* -cies.
to•tip•o•tent
to•ti•po•ten•tial
to•ti•po•ten•ti•al•i•ty, *n., pl.* -ties.
Tou•rette's syn•drome
tour•is•ta
tour•ni•quet
tox•ae•mi•a
tox•ae•mic
tox•a•phene
tox•a•phor•ic
Tox•as•ca•ris
tox•e•mi•a
tox•e•mic
tox•ic
toxic shock syn•drome
tox•i•cal•ly
tox•i•cant
tox•ic•i•ty, *n., pl.* -ties.
Tox•i•co•den•dron
tox•i•co•der•o•ma, *n., pl.* -mas, -ma•ta.
tox•i•co•der•ma•ti•tis
tox•i•co•gen•ic
tox•i•coid
tox•i•co•log•ic
tox•i•co•log•i•cal
tox•i•co•log•i•cal•ly
tox•i•col•o•gist
tox•i•col•o•gy, *n., pl.* -gies.
tox•i•co•ma•ni•a

tox∘i∘co∘path∘ic
tox∘i∘co∘pho∘bi∘a
tox∘i∘co∘sis, *n.*, *pl.* -ses.
tox∘i∘der∘mi∘tis
tox∘if∘er∘ine
tox∘if∘er∘ous
tox∘i∘gen∘ic
tox∘i∘ge∘nic∘i∘ty, *n.*, *pl.* -ties.
tox∘in
toxin-an∘ti∘tox∘in
Tox∘o∘ca∘ra
tox∘oid
tox∘oph∘o∘rous
tox∘o∘plas∘ma, *n.*, *pl.* -plas∘mas, -plas∘ma∘ta, -plas∘ma.
tox∘o∘plas∘mic
tox∘o∘plas∘mo∘sis
tra∘bec∘u∘la, *n.*, *pl.* -lae, -las.
trabecula sep∘to∘mar∘gi∘na∘lis
tra∘bec∘u∘lae car∘ne∘ae
trabeculae cor∘dis
trabeculae li∘e∘nis
tra∘bec∘u∘lar
tra∘bec∘u∘late
tra∘bec∘u∘lat∘ed
tra∘bec∘u∘la∘tion
trace el∘e∘ment
trac∘er
tra∘che∘a, *n.*, *pl.* -che∘ae, -che∘as.
tra∘che∘al
trach∘e∘al∘gia
tra∘che∘i∘tis
tra∘che∘lec∘to∘my, *n.*, *pl.* -mies.
trach∘e∘lis∘mus
trach∘e∘li∘tis
trach∘e∘lo∘dyn∘i∘a
trach∘e∘lo∘mas∘toid
tra∘che∘lo∘plas∘ty, *n.*, *pl.* -ties.

tra∘che∘lor∘rha∘phy, *n.*, *pl.* -phies.
tra∘che∘lot∘o∘my, *n.*, *pl.* -mies.
tra∘che∘o∘bron∘chi∘al
tra∘che∘o∘bron∘chi∘tis
tra∘che∘o∘bron∘chos∘co∘py, *n.*, *pl.* -pies.
tra∘che∘o∘esophageal
tra∘che∘oph∘o∘ny, *pl.* -nies.
tra∘che∘o∘plas∘ty, *n.*, *pl.* -ties.
tra∘che∘o∘py∘o∘sis
tra∘che∘or∘rhagia
tra∘che∘os∘chi∘sis, *n.*, *pl.* -ses.
tra∘che∘os∘co∘py, *n.*, *pl.* -pies.
tra∘che∘o∘ste∘no∘sis
tra∘che∘os∘to∘my, *n.*, *pl.* -mies.
tra∘che∘ot∘o∘mist
tra∘che∘ot∘o∘mize, *v.*, -mized, -miz∘ing.
tra∘che∘ot∘o∘my, *n.*, *pl.* -mies.
tra∘cho∘ma
tra∘chom∘a∘tous
tra∘chy∘chro∘mat∘ic
tra∘chy∘pho∘ni∘a
Tra∘cri∘um *Trademark.*
trac∘tion
trac∘tion∘al
trac∘tor
trac∘tot∘o∘my, *n.*, *pl.* -mies.
trac∘tus, *n.*, *pl.* trac∘tus.
trag∘a∘canth
tra∘gal
trag∘o∘mas∘cha∘li∘a
tra∘gus, *n.*, *pl.* tra∘gi.
train∘sick
train∘sick∘ness
Tral *Trademark.*
Tram∘a∘dol
Tran∘co∘pal *Trademark.*

Tran•date HCT *Trademark.*
tran•quil•ize, *v.,* -ized, -iz•ing.
tran•quil•iz∘er
tran•quil•liz∘er
Trans-Plan•tar *Trademark.*
Trans-Ver-Sal *Trademark.*
trans•ab•dom∘i•nal
trans•a•ce•tyl•ase
trans•ac•tion
trans•ac•tion∘al
transactional a∘nal∘y•sis
trans•ac•tion•al∘ly
trans•am∘i•nase
trans•am∘i•nate, *v.,* -nat∘ed,
   -nat•ing.
trans•am∘i•na•tion
trans•an∘i•ma•tion
trans•au•di•ent
trans•ca•lent
trans•cal•lo•sal
trans•con•dy•lar
trans•cor•ti•cal
tran•scribe, *v.,* -scribed, -scrib•
   ing.
tran•scrib∘er
tran•scrip•tase
tran•scrip•tion
trans•cu•ta•ne∘al
trans•cu•ta•ne•ous
Trans•derm *Trademark.*
Transderm-Ni∘tro *Trademark.*
Transderm-Scop *Trademark.*
trans•der•mal
trans•duce, *v.,* -duced,
   -duc∘ing.
trans•duc•tant
trans•duc•tion
trans•duc•tion∘al
tran•sect
tran•sec•tion
trans fat∘ty ac∘ids
trans•fect

trans•fec•tion
trans•fer RNA
trans•fer•ase
trans•fer•ence
trans•fer•en•tial
trans•fer•rin
trans•fix
trans•fix•ion
trans•fo•ra•tion
trans•form
trans•for•ma•tion
trans•for•ma•tion∘al
trans•fus•a•ble
trans•fuse, *v.,* -fused, -fus•ing.
trans•fus∘i•ble
trans•fu•sion
trans•fu•sion∘al
trans•fu•sive
trans•gene
trans•gen∘ic
transgenic mouse
tran•sient
transient is•che•mic at•tack
tran•sil•i∘ac
trans•il•lu•mi•nate, *v.,*
   -nat∘ed, -nat•ing.
trans•il•lu•mi•na•tion
trans•il•lu•mi•na•tor
tran•sisth•mi∘an
tran•sis•tor
trans•late, *v.,* -lat∘ed, -lat•ing.
trans•la•tion
trans•la•tion∘al
trans•lo•ca•tion
trans•lu•cen∘cy, *n., pl.* -cies.
trans•lu•cent
trans•mem•brane
trans•meth•yl•a•tion
trans•mi•gra•tion
trans•mis•si•bil∘i∘ty, *n., pl.*
   -ties.
trans•mis•si•ble

trans•mis•sion
trans•mit, *v.*, -mit•ted, -mit•ting.
trans•mit•ta•ble
trans•mit•tal
trans•mit•tance
trans•mit•ter
trans•mu•ral
trans•or•bi•tal
trans•pep•ti•da•tion
trans•per•son•al
trans•per•son•al•ly
trans•phos•pho•ryl•a•tion
trans•pir•a•ble
trans•pi•ra•tion
tran•spire, *v.*, -spired, -spir•ing.
trans•pla•cen•tal
trans•plant
trans•plant•a•ble
trans•plan•ta•tion
trans•port
trans•pose, *v.*, -posed, -pos•ing.
trans•po•si•tion
trans•po•si•tion•al
trans•pos•i•tive
trans•po•son
trans•seg•men•tal
trans•sex•u•al
trans•sex•u•al•ism
trans•sex•u•al•i•ty
trans•tho•rac•ic
trans•tho•rac•i•cal•ly
trans•tra•che•al
tran•sub•stan•ti•ate, *v.*, -at•ed, -at•ing.
tran•sub•stan•ti•a•tion
tran•su•date
tran•su•da•tion
tran•sude, *v.*, -sud•ed, -sud•ing.

trans•u•re•thral
trans•vag•i•nal
trans•ver•sa•lis
trans•verse
transverse co•lon
transverse proc•ess
trans•ver•sec•to•my, *n.*, *pl.* -mies.
trans•ver•sion
trans•ver•sus, *n.*, *pl.* -ver•si.
transversus nu•chae
trans•vest•ism
trans•ves•tite
trans•ves•ti•tism
Tranx•ene-SD *Trademark.*
Tranxene T-TAB *Trademark.*
tran•yl•cyp•ro•mine
tra•pe•zi•al
tra•pe•zi•form
tra•pe•zi•um, *n.*, *pl.* -zi•ums, -zi•a.
tra•pe•zi•us, *n.*, *pl.* -zi•us•es.
trap•e•zoid
trau•ma, *n.*, *pl.* -ma•ta, -mas.
trau•mat•ic
trau•mat•i•cal•ly
trau•ma•tism
trau•ma•ti•za•tion
trau•ma•tize, *v.*, -tized, -tiz•ing.
trau•ma•tol•o•gist
trau•ma•tol•o•gy, *n.*, *pl.* -gies.
trau•ma•top•ne•a
tra•vail
Trav•ase *Trademark.*
trav•el•ers' di•ar•rhe•a
Trav•ert *Trademark.*
trea•cle
treat•a•bil•i•ty, *n.*, *pl.* -ties.
treat•a•ble
treat•ment

Tre•ca•tor-SC *Trademark.*
tree of life
tre•ha•lase
tre•ha•lose
Treitz's lig•a•ment
Treitz's mus•cle
Trem○a•to○da
trem○a•tode
trem•ble, *v.,* -bled, -bling.
trem•el•loid
trem•el•lose
trem○o•pho•bi○a
trem○or
trem•or•ous
trem•u•lous
trem•u•lous•ly
trem•u•lous•ness
trench fe○ver
trench foot
trench mouth
Tren•del•en•burg po•si•tion
Tren•tal *Trademark.*
tre•pan, *v.,* -panned, -pan•ning.
trep○a•na•tion
tre•pan•ner
treph○i•na•tion
tre•phine, *v.,* -phined, -phin•ing.
treph○o•cyte
treph•one
trep○i•dant
trep○i•da•tion
trep○o•ne○ma, *n., pl.* -ma○ta, -mas.
trep○o•ne•mal
trep○o•ne•ma•to•sis
trep○o•nem○a•tous
trep○o•neme
trep○o•ne•mi•cid○al
tre•pop•ne○a
trep○ope

Trest *Trademark.*
tre•tin○o•in
Trex○an
Tri-Im•mu•nol *Trademark.*
Tri-Le•ven
Tri-Lev•len
Tri-No•ri•nyl *Trademark.*
Tri-Vi-Flor *Trademark.*
tr•iac○e○tin
tri○ad
triad of Whip•ple
tri•age, *n., adj., v.,* -aged, -ag•ing.
tri○al
tri•am•cin○o•lone
Triamcinolone aer○o•sol
Tri•a•min○ic *Trademark.*
Tri•a•min•i•cin *Trademark.*
Tri•a•min•i•col *Trademark.*
tri•am•ter•ene
Triamterene/HCTZ
tri•an•gle
tri•an•gu•lar○is, *n., pl.* -lar○es.
tri•at○o•ma
tri•a•tom○ic
Tri•a•vil *Trademark.*
tri•a•zine
tri•bade
tri•bad○ic
tri•ba•dism
trib•a○dy
tri•ba•sic
tri•bo•lu•mi•nes•cence
trib•ro•mo•eth○a•nol
tri•bu○ty•rin
tri•car•box•yl○ic
tricarboxylic ac○id cy•cle
tri•ceps, *n., pl.* -ceps○es, -ceps.
tri•chi•a•sis
tri•chi○na, *n., pl.* -nae, -nas.
trich○i•nel○la, *n., pl.* -lae.

Trichinella spi•ra•lis
trich•i•nel•li•a•sis
trich•i•ni•a•sis
trich•i•ni•za•tion
trich•i•nize, *v.*, -nized, -niz•ing.
trich•i•no•scope
trich•i•no•sis
trich•i•nous
trich•i•on
tri•chlo•ra•ce•tic
tri•chlor•eth•yl•ene
tri•chlor•fon
tri•chlo•ride
tri•chlo•ro•a•ce•tic
tri•chlo•ro•eth•yl•ene
tri•chlo•ro•meth•ane
trich∘o•bac•te•ri∘a
trich∘o•be•zoar
trich∘o•ceph∘a•li•a•sis
Trich∘o•ceph∘a•lus
trich∘o•cyst
Trich∘o•dec•tes
Trich∘o•der•ma
trich∘o•ep•oi•the•li∘o•ma, *n.*, *pl.* -mas, -ma•ta.
trich∘o•es•the•sia
trich∘o•gen
trich∘o•gen∘ic
tri•chog∘e∘nous
trich∘o•glos•si∘a
tri•choid
tri•chol∘o∘gy, *n.*, *pl.* -gies.
tri•cho•ma
tri•cho•ma•to•sis
tri•chom∘a•tous
trich•ome
tri•chom∘ic
trich∘o•mon•a•cid•al
trich∘o•mon•a•cide
trich∘o•mon•ad
trich∘o•mo•nad∘al

trich∘o•mo•nal
Trich∘o•mo•nas
trich∘o•mo•ni•a•sis
trich∘o•my•co•sis
trich∘o•no•do•sis
tri•chop∘a•thy, *n.*, *pl.* -thies.
trich∘o•pha•gi∘a
trich∘o•pho•bi∘a
trich∘o•phy•tid
trich∘o•phy•to•be•zoar
trich∘o•phy•ton, *n.*, *pl.* -phy•ta, -phy•tons.
trich∘o•phy•to•sis
trich∘o•pti•lo•sis
trich•or•rhex∘is, *n.*, *pl.* -rhex∘es.
trich∘o•san•thin
tri•cho•sis, *n.*, *pl.* -ses.
Trich∘o•spo•ron
trich∘o•spo•ro•sis, *n.*, *pl.* -ses.
trich∘o•sta•sis, *n.*, *pl.* -ses.
trich∘o•stron•gy•lo•sis
Trich∘o•stron•gy•lus
trich∘o•til•lo•ma•ni∘a
trich∘o•til•lo•man∘ic
tri•chot∘o•my, *n.*, *pl.* -mies.
tri•chro∘ic
trich•ro•ism
trich•ro•mat
tri•chro•mat∘ic
tri•chro•ma•tism
tri•chro•ma•top•si∘a
tri•chrome
tri•chro•mic
trich∘o•u•ri•a•sis
Trich•u•ris
tri•cip∘i•tal
Tri•clos
tri•corn
tri•cor∘nute
tri•cre•sol
tri•crot∘ic

tri•cro•tism

tri•cus•pid

tricuspid in•suf•fi•cien•cy

tricuspid valve

tri•cus•pi•date

tri•cus•pi•dat○ed

tri•cy•clic

tri•dac•tyl

tri•dac•tyle

tri•dac•tylous

tri•dent

tri•den•tate

tri•der•mic

Tri•des○i•lon *Trademark.*

Tri•dil *Trademark.*

Tri•di•one *Trademark.*

tri•eth○a•nol•a•mine

tri•ethi○o•dide

tri•eth•yl•a•mine

tri•eth○y•lene•mel○a•mine

tri•fa•cial

tri•fid

tri•flu○o•per○a•zine

tri•fo•cal

tri•fo•li○o•sis

tri•fo•li○um

tri•fur•cate, *v.,* -cat○ed, -cat•
ing.

tri•fur•ca•tion

tri•gem○i•nal

trigeminal nerve

trigeminal neu•ral•gia

tri•gem○i•nus, *n., pl.* -gem•
i○ni.

tri•gem•i○ny, *n., pl.* -nies.

tri•glyc•er•ide

tri•gon

tri•go•nal

tri•go•nal○ly

tri•gone

tri•go•nel•line

tri•go•nid

tri•go•ni•tis

tri•gon○o•ce•phal○ic

tri•gon○o•ceph○a•lous

trig○o•no•ceph○a○ly

tri•go•num, *n., pl.* -go•nums,
-go○na.

trigonum ha•ben○u•lae

tri•hy•brid

tri•i•o•do•thy•ro•nine

Tril○a•fon *Trademark.*

tri•lam○i•nar

tri•lam○i•nate

Tri•lis•ate *Trademark.*

tri•lo•bate

tri•lo•bat○ed

tri•lobed

tri•loc○u•lar

tri•loc○u•late

tril○o•gy, *n., pl.* -gies.

tri•man•u○al

tri•mes•ter

tri•meth○o•a•di•one

tri•meth○o•prim

Tri•meth/Sul•fa•meth

tri•meth•yl○a•mine

tri•meth•y•lene

tri•morph○ic

tri•mor•phous

Tri•mox *Trademark.*

Trim•pex *Trademark.*

Trin○a•lin *Trademark.*

trin○i•tro•glyc•er○in

trin○i•tro•phe•nol

trin○i•tro•tol•u○ene

Trin•si•con *Trademark.*

tri•nu•cle•ate

tri•nu•cle○o•tide

tri•o•le○in

tri•ose

tri•ox•ide

tri•pal•mi•tin

trip○a○ra

Tronolane

tri•par•tite
tri•pe•len•na•mine
tri•pep•tide
tri•pha•sic
Tri•pha•sil *Trademark.*
tri•phen•yl•meth•ane
tri•phos•pha•tase
tri•phos•phate
tri•phos•pho•py•ri•dine
  nu•cle•o•tide
tri•ple•gia
tri•plet
Tri•ple•vite/Fluor•ide *Trade-mark.*
tri•plex
trip•lo•blas•tic
trip•loid
trip•loi•dy
tri•plo•pi•a
tri•pod
trip•sis
tri•que•trous
tri•que•trum
tri•ra•di•al
tri•ra•di•al•ly
tri•ra•di•ous, *n., pl.* -di•i.
tri•sac•ca•ride
tris•kai•dek•a•pho•bi•a
tris•kai•dek•a•pho•bic
tris•mic
tris•mus, *n., pl.* -mus•es.
tri•so•mic
tri•so•my, *n., pl.* -mies.
trisomy 21
Tri•so•ra•len *Trademark.*
tri•splanch•nic
tri•ste•a•rin
Tri•sul•fam *Trademark.*
trit•an•o•ope
trit•an•o•pi•a
tri•ti•at•ed
trit•oi•ca•le

tri•ti•ceous
tri•ti•ce•um, *n., pl.* -ce•i.
trit•oi•cum
tri•ti•um
trit•o•cone
trit•o•co•nid
tri•tu•ra•ble
trit•u•rate, *v.,* -rat•ed, -rat•ing.
trit•u•ra•tion
tri•va•lence
tri•va•len•cy, *n., pl.* -cies.
tri•va•lent
tri•valve
tri•val•vu•lar
tRNA syn•the•tase
Tro•bi•cin *Trademark.*
tro•car
tro•chant•er
tro•chan•ter•ic
tro•chan•tin
tro•chan•tine
tro•chan•tin•i•an
tro•char
tro•che, *n., pl.* -ches.
troch•le•a, *n., pl.* -le•ae, -le•as.
troch•le•ar
tro•chle•ar•oi•form
tro•chle•ar•ois
tro•cho•ce•pha•li•a
tro•choid
tro•choi•des, *n., pl.* -choi•des.
Trog•lo•tre•ma sal•min•co•la
tro•land
Trom•bic•u•la
Trombicula al•fred•du•ge•si
Trombicula ir•ri•tans
Trom•bic•u•li•dae
trom•bi•di•a•sis
Tron•o•lane *Trademark.*

tro•pa•co•caine

Tro•pa•mine *Trademark.*

tro•pane

tro•pate

tro•pe•ine

Troph-Ioron *Trademark.*

tro•phec•to•derm

troph•e•o•de∘ma, *n., pl.* -mas,
-ma∘ta.

troph•e•o•ma

troph•e•o•sy

troph∘ic

troph∘i•cal∘ly

tro•phism

Tro•phite *Trademark.*

troph∘o•blast

troph∘o•blas•tic

troph∘o•cyte

troph∘o•derm

troph∘o•dy•nam•ics

tro•phol∘o∘gy, *n., pl.* -gies.

troph∘o•neu•ro•sis

troph∘o•neu•rot∘ic

troph∘o•nu•cle∘us, *n., pl.*
-cle∘i.

tro•phop∘a•thy, *n., pl.* -thies.

troph∘o•plast

troph∘o•spon•gi∘a

troph∘o•spon•gi∘um

troph∘o•tax∘is

troph∘o•trop∘ic

tro•phot∘ro•pism

troph∘o•zo∘ite

tro•pi∘a

trop∘ic ac∘id

trop∘i•cal

tro•pine

tro•pism

tro•po•col•la•gen

tro•pom•e∘ter

tro•po•my•o•sin

tro•po•nin

trun•cal

trun•cate, *v.,* -cat∘ed, -cat•
ing.

trun∘ci in•tes•ti•na•les

trunci lum•ba•les

trun•cus, *n., pl.* trun∘ci.

truncus ar•te•ri•o•sus

Tru•sopt *Trademark.*

truss

truth se∘rum

Try•mex *Trademark.*

try•pan blue

trypan red

try•pan∘o•cid∘al

try•pan∘o•cide

try•pan∘o•so∘ma, *n., pl.* -mas,
-ma∘ta.

try•pan∘o•so•mal

try•pan∘o•some

try•pan∘o•so•mi•a•sis

try•pan∘o•som∘ic

try•par•sam•ide

tryp•sin

tryp•sin∘i•za•tion

tryp•sin∘o•gen

tryp•ta•mine

tryp•tic

Tryp∘to-Som *Trademark.*

tryp∘to•phan

tryp∘to•pha•nase

tryp∘to•phane

Tryp∘to•plex *Trademark.*

Try•sul *Trademark.*

tset∘se, *n., pl.* tset∘se, tset•
ses.

tsu•tsu•ga•mu•shi

tu∘ba

tu•bage

tu∘bal

tubal li•ga•tion

Tu•ba•sal *Trademark.*

tube

tu•bec•to•my, *n., pl.* -mies.

tube•like

tu•ber

tuber ci•ne•re•um

tu•ber•cle

tubercle ba•cil•lus

tu•ber•cled

tu•ber•cu•lar

tu•ber•cu•lar∘ly

tu•ber•cu•late

tu•ber•cu•lat∘ed

tu•ber•cu•la•tion

tu•ber•cu•lid

tu•ber•cu•lide

tu•ber•cu•lin

tu•ber•cu•lo•cid∘al

tu•ber•cu•lo•derm

tu•ber•cu•lo•der∘ma

tu•ber•cu•lo•fi•broid

tu•ber•cu•loid

tu•ber•cu•lo∘ma, *n., pl.* -mas, -ma∘ta.

tuberculoma en•plaque

tu•ber•cu•lo•pho•bi∘a

tu•ber•cu•lo•sis

tu•ber•cu•lo•stat∘ic

tu•ber•cu•lous

tu•ber•cu•lous∘ly

tu•ber•cu•lum, *n., pl.* -cu∘la.

tuberculum cin•re•um

tube•rose

tu•ber•os∘i•tas, *n., pl.* -os∘i• ta•tes.

tu•ber•os∘i∘ty, *n., pl.* -ties.

tu•ber•ous

Tu•bex *Trademark.*

Tu•bi•zid *Trademark.*

tu∘bo-o•var•i∘an

tu∘bo-cu•ra•rine

tu∘bo•lig∘a•men•tous

tu∘bo•per∘i•to•ne∘al

tu∘bo•u•ter•ine

tu∘bo•vag∘i•nal

tu•bu•lar

tub•ule

tu•bu•lus, *n., pl.* -bu•li.

tu•bus di•ges•to•ri∘us

tubus med•ul•lar∘is

tubus ver•te•bralis

tu•la•rae•mi∘a

tu•la•re•mi∘a

tu•la•re•mic

tulle gras

tu•me•fa•ci•ent

tu•me•fac•tion

tu•me∘fy, *v.,* -fied, -fy∘ing.

tu•mer∘ic

tu•mes•cence

tu•mes•cent

tu∘mid

tu•mid∘i•ty

tum∘my, *n., pl.* -mies.

tummy tuck

tu∘mor

tumor mark∘er

tumor ne•cro•sis fac•tor

tu•mo•ral

tu•mor∘i•gen•e∘sis, *n., pl.* -e∘ses.

tu•mor∘i•gen∘ic

tu•mor∘i•ge•nic∘i∘ty, *n., pl.* -ties.

tu•mor•like

tu•mo•rous

tu•mour

Tums *Trademark.*

tu•mul•tus

tumultus cor•dis

tumultus ser•mo•nis

Tun∘ga

Tunga pen∘e•trans

tung•sten

tu∘nic

tu•ni∘ca, *n., pl.* -cae.

tunica al•bu•gin∘e∘a, *n., pl.*
tu•ni•cae al•bu•gin•e∘ae.
tun•nel
tunnel vi•sion
tunnel-vi•sioned
tu•ra•cin
tur•bid
tur•bi•dim•e∘ter
tur•bi•di•met•ric
tur•bi•di•met•ri•cal∘ly
tur•bi•dim•e∘try
tur•bid∘i∘ty
tur•bi•nal
tur•bi•nate
tur•bi•nat∘ed
tur•bi•nec•to∘my, *n., pl.*
-mies.
tur•bi•not∘o∘my, *n., pl.* -mies.
tur•ges•cence
tur•es•cent
tur•gid
tur•gid∘i∘ty
tur•gid•ness
tur•gor
tu•ris∘ta
Türk cell
Türk's cell
tur•mer∘ic
Tur•ner's syn•drome
tur•pen•tine
tur•ri•ceph∘a∘ly
Tuss-Or•nade *Trademark.*
Tus•sa•fed *Trademark.*
tus•sal
Tus•sar *Trademark.*
Tussar DM *Trademark.*
Tussar SF *Trademark.*
Tus∘si-Or•gan∘i•din *Trademark.*
Tus•si•o•nex *Trademark.*
tus•sis
tussis con•vul•si∘va

tus•sive
tween-brain
tweez•ers
Twelve Step
twen∘ty-twen∘ty
twin, *n., v.,* twinned, twin•
ning.
twin stud∘y
twin•born
twinge, *v.,* twinged, twing•
ing.
Two•Cal HN *Trademark.*
Ty•le•nol *Trademark.*
ty•lo∘ma, *n., pl.* -mas, -ma∘ta.
ty•lo•sin
ty•lo•sis
ty•lot∘ic
Ty•lox *Trademark.*
tym•pa•nal
tym•pan∘ic
tympanic bone
tympanic mem•brane
tym•pa•nism
tym•pa•ni•tes
tym•pa•nit∘ic
tym•pa•ni•tis
tym•pa•no•mas•toid
tym•pa•no•mas•toi•di•tis
tym•pa•no•plas∘ty, *n., pl.*
-ties.
tym•pa•no•sta•pe•di∘al
tym•pa•not∘o∘my, *n., pl.*
-mies.
tym•pa•nous
tym•pa•num, *n., pl.* -pa∘na,
-pa∘nums.
tym•pa∘ny, *n., pl.* -nies.
Type A
Type B
typh•lec•to∘my, *n., pl.* -mies.
typh•li•tis
typh•lo•dic•li•di•tis

typh•lo•em•py•e•ma
typh•lo•li•thi•a•sis
typh•lo•meg•a•ly
typh•lop•to•sis
typh•lo•sis
typh•los•to•my, *n., pl.* -mies.
ty•phoid
Typhoid Mar•y
ty•phoi•dal
ty•pho•pneu•mo•ni•a
ty•phous
ty•phus
typhus ex•an•the•ma•tique
typ•i•cal
Tyr

ty•ra•mine
ty•ro•ci•din
ty•ro•ci•dine
Ty•rode so•lu•tion
Ty•rode's so•lu•tion
ty•rog•e•nous
ty•roid
ty•ro•si•nase
ty•ro•sine
ty•ro•si•ne•mi•a
ty•ro•si•no•sis
ty•ro•si•nu•ri•a
ty•ro•thric•in
Ty•zine *Trademark.*

U

u•ber•ty
u•bi•qui•none
u•biq•ui•tin
ud•der
ug•ly par•ent syn•drome
ul•ber•ous
ul•cer, *v.,* -cered, -cer•ing.
ul•cer•ate, *v.,* -at•ed, -at•ing.
ul•cer•o•a•tion
ul•cer•o•a•tive
ul•cer•o•gen•ic
ul•cer•o•mem•bra•nous
ul•cer•ous
ul•cus, *n., pl.* ul•cus.
u•le•gyr•i•a
u•le•ry•the•ma
ulerythema cen•trif•u•gum
ulerythema o•ophry•og•o•e•nes
ulerythema sy•co•si•forme
u•let•ic
ul•na, *n., pl.* ul•nae, ul•nas.
ul•nad
ul•nar
u•loid

u•lo•sis
u•lot•ic
u•lot•o•my, *n., pl.* -mies.
u•lot•ri•chous
ul•ti•mo•gen•i•ture
ul•ti•mum mo•ri•tens
ul•tra•brach•y•ce•phal•ic
Ul•tra•cef *Trademark.*
ul•tra•cen•tri•fu•ga•tion
ul•tra•cen•tri•fuge
Ul•tra•cho•line *Trademark.*
ul•tra•fil•ter
ul•tra•fil•tra•tion
Ul•tra•len•te *Trademark.*
Ul•tram *Trademark.*
ul•tra•mi•cro•scope
ul•tra•mi•cro•scop•ic
ul•tra•mi•cro•scop•i•cal•ly
ul•tra•mi•cros•co•py, *n., pl.*
   -pies.
ul•tra•mi•cro•tome
ul•tra•son•ic
ul•tra•son•i•cal•ly
ul•tra•son•o•gram

ul○tra•so•nog•ra•phy, *n., pl.*
  -phies.
ul○tra•sound
ul○tra•struc•tu•ral
ul○tra•struc•tu•ral○ly
ul○tra•struc•ture
ul○tra•thin
ul○tra•vi•o•let
ul○tra•vi•rus, *n., pl.* -rus○es.
um•bil○i•cal
umbilical cord
um•bil○i•cate
um•bil○i•cat○ed
um•bil○i•ca•tion
um•bil○i•cus, *n., pl.* -bil•i○ci,
  -bil○i•cus○es.
um•bil○i•form
um○bo, *n., pl.* -um•bo○nes,
  um○bos.
um•bo•nate
un•an•es•the•tized
U○na•syn *Trademark.*
un•bal•ance, *v.,* -anced, -anc•
  ing.
un○cal
un○ci○a, *n., pl.* -un○ci○ae.
un•ci•form
un•ci•nal
un•ci•nar○i○a
un•ci•na•ri•a•sis
un•ci•nate
un•ci•na•tum, *n., pl.* -na○ta,
  -na•tums.
un•cir•cum•cised
un•com•pli•cat○ed
un•con•di•tion○al
un•con•di•tioned
un•con•scious
un•con•scious○ly
un•con•scious•ness
un•co○or•di•nat○ed
unc•tion

unc•tu•ous
unc•tu•ous○ly
un○cus, *n., pl.* un○ci.
un•de•cyl○e•nate
un•de•cy•len○ic
un○der•a•chiev○er
un○der•arm
un○der•cook
un○der•cut
un○der•de•vel•oped
un○der•de•vel•op•ment
un○der•lip
un○der•nour○ished
un○der•nour○ish•ment
un○der•nu•tri•tion
un○der•sexed
un○der•shot
un○der•slung
un○der•toe
un○der•weight
un•de•scend○ed
un•di•ag•nosed
un•dif•fer•en•ti•at○ed
un•di•gest○ed
un•dine
un•du•lant
undulant fe○ver
un•du•late
un•du•lat○ed
un•du•la•tion
un•en•cap•su•lat○ed
un•e○rupt○ed
un•gu○al
un•guent
un•guen•tar○y
Un•guic○u•la○ta
un•guic○u•late
un•guic○u•lat○ed
un•gui○nal
un•guis, *n., pl.* -gues.
unguis in•car•na•tus

un•gu○la, *n., pl.* -lae.
Un•gu•la○ta
un•gu•late
un•gu•li•grade
un•health○y, *adj.* -heal•thi○er, -thi○est.
u○ni•al•gal
u○ni•ar•tic○u•lar
u○ni•ax•i○al
u○ni•ax•i•al○ly
u○ni•ba•sal
u○ni•cam•er○al
u○ni•cam•er•al○ly
u○ni•cel•lu•lar
u○ni•cel•lu•lar○i○ty
u○ni•cen•tral
u○ni•cen•tric
u○ni•cor•nous
u○ni•cus•pid
u○ni•cus•pi•date
u○ni•di•rec•tion○al
u○ni•fac•to•ri○al
U○ni•fi•ber *Trademark.*
u○ni•fi•lar
u○ni•flag○el•late
u○ni•glan•du•lar
u○ni•grav•i○da
u○ni•lat•er○al
u○ni•lat•er•al○ly
U○ni•lax *Trademark.*
u○ni•lo•bar
u○ni•loc○u•lar
un•im•paired
un•in•hib•it○ed
u○ni•nu•cle○ar
u○ni•nu•cle•ate
u○ni•oc○u•lar
u○ni•o○val
u○ni•ov○u•lar
u○nip•a○ra
u○ni•pa•ren•tal
u○nip○a•rous

U○ni•pen *Trademark.*
U○ni•phyl *Trademark.*
u○ni•po•lar
u○ni•po•lar○i○ty
u○nip○o○tent
u○ni•po•ten•tial
U○ni•pres *Trademark.*
u○ni•sep•tate
u○ni•sex•u○al
U○ni•som *Trademark.*
u○ni•tar○y
u○ni•va•lent
u○ni•ver•sal do○nor
un•linked
un•me•dul•lat○ed
un•my○e•lin•at○ed
un•of•fi•cial
un•or•gan•ized
un•paired
un•pas•teur•ized
un•phys•i○o•log○ic
un•phys•i○o•log○i•cal
un•pig•ment○ed
un•re•ac•tive
un•re•duced
un•re•spon•sive
un•rest
un•sat○u•rat○ed
un•sex
un•sound
un•spec○i•fied
un•sta•ble
un•stained
un•stri•ated
un•vac•ci•nat○ed
un•well
up○per
up○set, *v.*, up○set, up○set• ting.
up•stream
up•take
u○ra•chal

u○ra•chus
u○ra•cil
u○ra•cra•sia
u○rae•mi○a
u○rae•mic
u○ra•gogue
u○ra•mil
u○ra•nin
u○ra•ni○um
u○ra•no•plas○ty, *n.*, *pl.* -ties.
u○ra•no•ple•gia
u○ra•nos•chi•sis, *n.*, *pl.* -ses.
u○ra•no•staph○y•lo•plas○ty,
 n., *pl.* -ties.
u○ra•no•staph○y•lor•rha•
 phy, *n.*, *pl.* -phies.
u○ra•ro○ma
u○rate
u○ra•te•mi○a
u○rat○ic
u○ra•tu•ri○a
ur•ce•i•form
ur•ce•o•late
u○re○a
urea cy○cle
U○re•a•cin *Trademark.*
u○re○al
u○re•am•e○ter
u○re•am•e○try
u○re•ase
U○re•choline *Trademark.*
u○re•de○ma, *n.*, *pl.* -mas,
 -ma○ta.
u○re○do
u○re•ide
u○re•mi○a
u○re•mic
u○re•mi•gen○ic
u○re•om•e○ter
u○re○o•tel○ic
u○re○o•te•lism
u○re•si•es•the•sia

u○re•sis
u○re•ter
u○re•ter○al
u○re•ter•ec•ta•sia
u○re•ter•ec•ta•sis
u○re•ter•ec•to○my, *n.*, *pl.*
 -mies.
u○re•ter○ic
u○re•ter•oi•tis
ureteritis cys•ti○ca
u○re•ter○o•cele
u○re•ter○o•co•los•to○my, *n.*,
 pl. -mies.
u○re•ter○o•cys•tos•to○my,
 n., *pl.* -mies.
u○re•ter○o•en•ter○ic
u○re•ter○o•en•ter•os•to○my,
 n., *pl.* -mies.
u○re•ter•og•ra•phy, *n.*, *pl.*
 -phies.
u○re•ter○o•hy•dro•ne•phro•
 sis
u○re•ter○o•il○e•os•to○my,
 n., *pl.* -mies.
u○re•ter○o•in•tes•ti•nal
u○re•ter○o•lith
u○re•ter○o•lith○i•a•sis, *n.*, *pl.*
 -ses.
u○re•ter○o•li•thot○o○my, *n.*,
 pl. -mies.
u○re•ter•ol○y•sis, *n.*, *pl.* -ses.
u○re•ter○o•ne○o•cys•tos•
 to○my, *n.*, *pl.* -mies.
u○re•ter○o•ne○o•py•e○los•
 to○my, *n.*, *pl.* -mies.
u○re•ter○o•neph•rec•to○my,
 n., *pl.* -mies.
u○re•ter•op○a•thy, *n.*, *pl.*
 -thies.
u○re•ter○o•pel•vic
u○re•ter○o•plas○ty, *n.*, *pl.*
 -ties.

u∘re∘ter∘o•py•e•li•tis
u∘re•ter∘o•py•e∘log•ra•phy, *n., pl.* -phies.
u∘re•ter∘o•py•e∘lo•ne∘os•to∘my, *n., pl.* -mies.
u∘re∘ter∘o•py•e∘lo•neph•ri•tis
u∘re•ter∘o•py•e∘lo•neph•ros•to∘my, *n., pl.* -mies.
u∘re•ter∘o•py•e∘lo•plas∘ty, *n., pl.* -ties.
u∘re•ter∘o•py•e∘los•to∘my, *n., pl.* -mies.
u∘re•ter•or•rha•gia
u∘re•ter•or•rha•phy, *n., pl.* -phies.
u∘re•ter∘o•sig•moid•os•to∘my, *n., pl.* -mies.
u∘re•ter•os•to∘my, *n., pl.* -mies.
u∘re•ter•ot∘o∘my, *n., pl.* -mies.
u∘re∘ter∘o•vag∘i•nal
u∘re∘ter∘o•ves∘i•cal
u∘re•than
u∘re•thane
u∘re•thra, *n., pl.* -thras, -thrae.
urethra fem∘i•ni•na
urethra mas•cu•li∘na
urethra mu•lie•bris
urethra vir∘i•lis
u∘re•thral
u∘re•threc•to∘my, *n., pl.* -mies.
u∘re•thrit∘ic
u∘re•thri•tis
urethritis cys•ti∘ca
urethritis ve•ne•re∘a
u∘reth∘ro•bul•bar
u∘reth∘ro•cele
u∘re•thro•cys•ti•tis
u∘reth∘ro•gram

u∘reth∘ro•graph
u∘re•throm•e∘ter
u∘reth∘ro•per∘i•ne∘al
u∘re•thro•plas∘ty, *n., pl.* -ties.
u∘reth∘ro•pros•tat∘ic
u∘reth∘ro•rec•tal
u∘re•thror•rha•phy, *n., pl.* -phies.
u∘reth•ror•rhe ex•lib∘i•dine
u∘reth•ror•rhe∘a
u∘re•thro•scope
u∘re•thro•scop∘ic
u∘re•thros•co∘py, *n., pl.* -pies.
u∘reth∘ro•spasm
u∘re•thro•ste∘no•sis
u∘re•thros•to∘my, *n., pl.* -mies.
u∘reth∘ro•tome
u∘re•throt∘o∘my, *n., pl.* -mies.
u∘reth∘ro•vag∘i•nal
U∘rex *Trademark.*
ur•gen∘cy
ur•gi•cen•ter
ur•hi•dro•sis
u∘ric
uric ac∘id
u∘ric•ac∘i•de•mi∘a
u∘ric•ac∘i•du•ri∘a
u∘ri•case
u∘ri•ce•mi∘a
u∘ri•col∘y•sis
u∘ri∘co•lyt∘ic
u∘ri∘co•su•ri∘a
u∘ri∘co•su•ric
u∘ri∘co•tel∘ic
u∘ri∘co•tel•ism
u∘ri•dine
u∘ri∘na chy∘li
urina ju•men•to∘sa
urina po∘tus
urina san•gui•nis

u○ri•nal
u○ri•nal○y•sis, *n., pl.* -ses.
u○ri•nar○y
urinary blad•der
urinary cal•cu•lus
u○ri•nate, *v.,* -nat○ed, -nat• ing.
u○ri•na•tion
u○rine
u○ri•nif•er•ous
u○ri•nip○a•rous
u○ri•no•gen○i•tal
u○ri•no○ma, *n., pl.* -mas, -ma○ta.
u○ri•nom•e○ter
u○ri•nom•e○try
u○ri•nous
U○rised *Trademark.*
U○ris•pas *Trademark.*
U○ro-KP-Neu•tral *Trademark.*
Uro-Mag *Trademark.*
Uro-Phos•phate *Trademark.*
u○ro•bi•lin
u○ro•bi•li•ne•mi○a
u○ro•bi•lin○o○gen
u○ro•bi•lin○o○ge•nu•ri○a
U○ro•bi•ot○ic-250 *Trademark.*
u○ro•chrome
u○ro•chro•mo○gen
U○ro•cit-K *Trademark.*
u○ro•cor•tin
u○ro•cri○sia
u○ro•cy•an○o•gen
u○ro•cy○a•no•sis
u○ro•e•ryth•rin
u○ro•gas•trone
u○ro•gen○i•tal
u○rog○e•nous
u○ro•glau•cin
u○ro•gram
u○rog•ra•phy, *n., pl.* -phies.
u○ro•he•ma•tin

u○ro•ki•nase
U○ro•lene Blue *Trademark.*
u○ro•lith
u○ro•lith○i•a•sis
u○ro•lith○ic
u○ro•log○ic
u○ro•log○i•cal
u○rol○o○gist
u○rol○o○gy
u○ro•lu•te○in
u○rom•e○ter
u○ron○ic ac○id
u○ro•nos•co○py, *n., pl.* -pies.
u○rop○a•thy, *n., pl.* -thies.
u○ro•pep•sin
u○ro•phe○in
u○ro•poi•e○sis
u○ro•poi•et○ic
u○ro•por•phy•rin
U○ro•quid-Acid *Trademark.*
u○ro•ru•bin
u○ros•che•sis
u○ro•scop○ic
u○ros•co○py, *n., pl.* -pies.
u○ro•sep•sis, *n., pl.* -ses.
u○ro•tox○ic
u○ro•tox•ic○i○ty, *n., pl.* -ties.
u○rox•an•thin
ur•ti•cant
ur•ti•car○i○a
ur•ti•car○i○al
ur•ti•car•i○o•gen○ic
ur•ti•cate, *v.,* -cat○ed, -cat• ing.
ur•ti•ca•tion
u○ru•shi○ol
us•tu•la•tion
u○ta
u○ter•al•gia
u○ter•ine
u○ter•i•tis
u○ter○o-o•var•i○an

u•ter•o•ab•dom•i•nal
u•ter•o•cer•vi•cal
u•ter•o•ges•ta•tion
u•ter•og•ra•phy, *n., pl.* -phies.
u•ter•om•e•ter
u•ter•o•pelvic
u•ter•o•pex•y, *n., pl.* -ies.
u•ter•o•plas•ty, *n., pl.* -ties.
u•ter•o•sa•cral
u•ter•o•sal•pin•gog•ra•phy, *n., pl.* -phies.
u•ter•ot•o•omy, *n., pl.* -mies.
u•ter•o•ton•ic
u•ter•o•tu•bal
u•ter•o•vag•i•nal
u•ter•o•ves•i•cal
u•ter•us, *n., pl.* u•ter•i.
u•tic
U•ti•cil•lin VK *Trademark.*
U•ti•cort *Trademark.*
u•tri•cle
u•tric•u•lar
u•tric•u•li•tis
u•tric•u•lo•sac•cu•lar

u•tric•u•lus, *n., pl.* u•tric•u•li.
utriculus mas•cu•li•nus
utriculus pros•tat•i•cus
u•ve•a, *n., pl.* u•ve•as.
u•ve•al
u•ve•it•ic
u•ve•i•tis
u•ve•o•pa•rot•oid
u•ve•o•par•o•ti•tis
u•ve•o•scle•ri•tis
u•vi•o•re•sis•tant
u•vu•la, *n., pl.* -las, -lae.
uvula cer•e•bel•li
uvula fis•sa
uvula pal•a•ti•na
uvula ver•mis
uvula ves•i•cae
u•vu•lar
u•vu•lar•ly
u•vu•lec•to•my, *n., pl.* -mies.
u•vu•li•tis
u•vu•lop•to•sis
u•vu•lo•tome
u•vu•lot•o•omy, *n., pl.* -mies.

V

V-Cil•lin *Trademark.*
V-Cillin K *Trademark.*
vac•ci•na•ble
vac•ci•nal
vac•ci•nate, *v.,* -nat•ed, -nat•ing.
vac•ci•na•tion
vac•ci•na•tor
vac•cine
vac•ci•nee
vac•cin•oi•a, *n., pl.* -cin•oi•as.
vaccinia gan•gre•no•sa
vaccinia ne•cro•sum

vac•cin•oi•al
vac•cin•oi•form
vac•ci•noid
vac•ci•no•ther•a•py, *n., pl.* -pies.
vac•u•o•lar
vac•u•o•late, *v.,* -lat•ed, -lat•ing.
vac•u•o•la•tion
vac•u•ole
vac•u•o•li•za•tion
vac•u•um, *n., pl.* vac•u•ums, vac•u•o•a.
vacuum as•pir•a•tion

va°gal
vagal block
va•gi°na, *n.*, *pl.* -nae, -nas.
vagina ten•di•nis
vag°i•nal
vag°i•na•li•tis
vag°i•nal°ly
va•gi•na•pex°y, *n.*, *pl.* -ies.
vag°i•nate
vag°i•nat°ed
va•gi•nec•to•my, *n.*, *pl.* -mies.
vag°i•nis•mus
vag°i•ni•tis
vag°i•no•cele
vag°i•no•dyn°i°a
vag°i•no•fix•a•tion
vag°i•no•la•bi°al
va°gi°no•my•co•sis
va•gi•no•per°i•ne°ot•o•my, *n.*, *pl.* -mies.
va•gi•no•plas°ty, *n.*, *pl.* -ties.
vag°i•no•scope
va•gi•nos•co•py, *n.*, *pl.* -pies.
va•gi•not•o•my, *n.*, *pl.* -mies.
Vag°i•sec *Trademark.*
Vagisec Plus *Trademark.*
Vag°i•stat *Trademark.*
Vag°i•trol *Trademark.*
va•gi°tus
vagitus u°ter°i•nus
vagitus vag°i•na•lis
va•got°o•mize, *v.*, -mized, -miz•ing.
va•got°o•my, *n.*, *pl.* -mies.
va•go•to•ni°a, *n.*, *pl.* -ni°as.
va•go•ton°ic
va•got•o°ny
va•go•trop°ic
va•go•va•gal
va•grant
va°gus, *n.*, *pl.* va°gi.

va•lence
va•len°cy, *n.*, *pl.* -cies.
va•lent
val•er•ate
va•le•ri°an
val•er•i°a°na of•fic°i•na•lis
va•le•ri•an°ic ac°id
va•ler°ic ac°id
val°e•tu•di•nar•i°an
val°e•tu•di•nar°i•a•nism
val•gus, *n.*, *pl.* -gus°es.
val•ine
val°i•no•my•cin
Val°i•sone *Trademark.*
Val°i•um *Trademark.*
val•late
val•lec•u°la, *n.*, *pl.* -lae.
vallecula cer°e•bel•li
vallecula ep°i•glot•ti°ca
vallecula lin•guae
vallecula un•guis
val•lum un•guis
Val•mid *Trademark.*
Val•pin 50 *Trademark.*
val•pro°ic ac°id
Val•re•lease *Trademark.*
Val•sal°va ma•neu•ver
val°va, *n.*, *pl.* -vae.
valve
valve of Bau•hin
valve of Ger•lach
valve of Has°ne
valve of Heis•ter
valve of Hous•ton
valve of Kerck•ring
valve of The•be•si°us
valve of Vieus•sens
val•vi•form
val•vot•o•my, *n.*, *pl.* -mies.
val•vu°la, *n.*, *pl.* -lae.
valvula co°li

valvula con•ni•vens, *n., pl.*
  valvulae con•ni•ven•tes.
valvula spi•ra•lis, *n., pl.* valvulae spi•ra•les.
valvulae a•na•les
valvulae con•ni•ven•tes
val•vu•lar
val•vu•li•tis
val•vu•lo•plas•ty, *n., pl.* -ties.
val•vu•lo•tome
val•vu•lot•o•my, *n., pl.* -mies.
vam•pire
vam•pir•ism
van den Bergh test
van den Bergh's test
van Hoorne's ca•nal
Van Slyke meth•od
van•o•a•date
va•na•di•um
va•na•di•um•ism
Van•ce•nase *Trademark.*
Vancenase AQ *Trademark.*
Van•ce•ril *Trademark.*
Van•co•cin HCL *Trademark.*
Van•co•led *Trademark.*
van•co•my•cin
Van•cor *Trademark.*
va•nil•la
va•nil•late
va•nil•lic
va•nil•lin
va•nil•lism
Va•no•bid *Trademark.*
Va•nox•ide-HC *Trademark.*
Van•seb
Vanseb-T
va•por
va•por•i•za•tion
va•po•rize, *v.,* -rized, -riz•ing.
va•por•iz•er
va•po•ther•a•py, *n., pl.* -pies.
Va•quez's dis•ease

Var•i-Fla•vors *Trademark.*
var•i•a•bil•i•ty, *n., pl.* -ties.
var•i•a•ble
var•i•ance
var•i•ant
var•i•a•tion
var•i•ca•tion
var•i•ce•al
var•i•cel•la
varicella gan•gre•no•sa
varicella in•oc•u•la•ta
varicella zos•ter vi•rus
var•i•cel•lar
var•i•cel•li•form
var•i•ces
var•i•co•bleph•a•ron
var•i•co•cele
var•i•co•ce•lec•to•my, *n., pl.*
  -mies.
var•i•coele
var•i•cog•ra•phy, *n., pl.*
  -phies.
var•i•coid
var•i•com•phal•lus
var•i•co•phle•bi•tis
var•i•cose
var•i•cosed
var•i•co•sis, *n., pl.* -ses.
var•i•cos•i•ty, *n., pl.* -ties.
var•i•cot•o•my, *n., pl.* -mies.
va•ric•u•la
va•ri•o•la
variola vac•cin•o•ia
variola ve•ra
va•ri•o•lar
var•i•o•late, *v.,* -lat•ed, -lat•
  ing.
var•i•o•loid
var•i•o•lous
var•i•o•lo•vac•cine
var•ix, *n., pl.* var•i•ces.
varix lym•phat•oi•cus

Va•ro•li•an

var•ru•ca se•nil•is

var•us

vas, *n.*, *pl.* va•sa.

vas def•er•ens, *n.*, *pl.* vasa def•er•en•ti•a.

vasa bre•vi•a

vasa ef•fer•en•tia

vasa va•so•rum

vas a•ber•rans, *n.*, *pl.* vasa a•ber•ran•tes.

va•sal

Vas•cor *Trademark.*

Vas•co•ray *Trademark.*

vas•cu•lar

vas•cu•lar•i•ty

vas•cu•lar•i•za•tion

vas•cu•lar•ize, *v.*, -ized, -iz•ing.

vas•cu•la•ture

vas•cu•li•tis, *n.*, *pl.* -lit•i•des.

va•sec•to•mize, *v.*, -mized, -miz•ing.

va•sec•to•my, *n.*, *pl.* -mies.

Vas•e•ret•ic *Trademark.*

vas•o•i•fac•tion

vas•o•i•fac•tive

vas•o•i•form

va•si•tis

vas•o•o•ac•tive

vas•o•o•ac•tiv•i•ty, *n.*, *pl.* -ties.

vas•o•o•ci•din *Trademark.*

vas•o•o•con *Trademark.*

vas•o•o•con•stric•tion

vas•o•o•con•stric•tive

vas•o•o•con•stric•tor

vas•o•o•de•pres•sor

vas•o•o•dil•o•a•ta•tion

vas•o•o•di•la•tion

vas•o•o•di•la•tive

vas•o•o•di•la•tor

vas•o•o•fac•tive

vas•o•o•for•ma•tive

vas•o•o•gan•gli•on, *n.*, *pl.* -gli•a, -gli•ons.

vas•og•ra•phy, *n.*, *pl.* -phies.

vas•o•o•in•hib•i•tor

vas•o•o•in•hib•i•to•ry

vas•o•o•liga•tion

vas•o•o•mo•tion

vas•o•o•mo•tor

vas•o•o•neu•ro•sis

vas•o•o•pres•sin

vas•o•o•pres•sor

vas•o•o•re•flex

vas•o•o•sec•tion

vas•o•o•spasm

vas•o•o•spas•tic

Vas•o•o•tec *Trademark.*

vas•o•o•to•cin

vas•ot•o•o•my, *n.*, *pl.* -mies.

vas•o•o•ton•ic

vas•o•o•va•gal

vasovagal re•sponse

vas•o•o•vas•os•to•my, *n.*, *pl.* -mies.

Va•sox•yl *Trademark.*

vas•tus ex•ter•nus

vastus in•ter•me•di•us

vastus in•ter•nus

vastus lat•er•a•lis

vastus me•di•a•lis

Va•ter's am•pul•la

Vater's cor•pus•cle

vec•tor

vec•tor•car•di•o•gram

vec•tor•car•di•og•ra•phy, *n.*, *pl.* -phies.

vec•to•ri•al

vec•to•ri•al•ly

Vee•tids *Trademark.*

ve•gan

ve•gan•ism

veg•e•ta•ble

veg•e•tal
vegetal pole
veg•e•tar•i•an
veg•e•tar•i•an•ism
veg•e•ta•tion
veg•e•ta•tive
ve•hi•cle
Veil•lo•nel•la al•ca•les•cens
Veillonella dis•coi•des
Veillonella or•bic•u•lus
Veillonella par•vu•la
Veillonella ren•i•for•mis
vein
ve•la•men, *n., pl.* -lam•i•na.
velamen vul•vae
vel•a•men•tous
vel•a•men•tum, *n., pl.*
  -men•ta.
ve•lar
Vel•ban *Trademark.*
ve•li•form
vel•li•cate, *v.,* -cat•ed, -cat•
  ing.
vel•li•ca•tion
ve•loc•i•ty, *n., pl.* -ties.
Ve•lo•sef *Trademark.*
Ve•lo•su•lin *Trademark.*
Vel•peau's ban•dage
ve•lum, *n., pl.* ve•la.
ve•na, *n., pl.* ve•nae.
vena ca•va, *n., pl.* venae ca•
  vae.
vena ca•val
ve•na•ca•vog•ra•phy, *n., pl.*
  -phies.
vena co•mes, *n., pl.* venae co•
  mi•tes.
venae vor•ti•co•sae
ve•na•tion
ve•nec•to•my, *n., pl.* -mies.
ve•ne•nate, *v.,* -nat•ed, -nat•
  ing.

ven•e•na•tion
ven•e•nif•er•ous
ven•e•punc•ture
ve•ne•re•al
venereal dis•ease
venereal wart
ve•ne•re•o•log•i•cal
ve•ne•re•ol•o•gist
ve•ne•re•ol•o•gy, *n., pl.*
  -gies.
ven•er•ol•o•gy, *n., pl.* -gies.
ven•e•ry
ven•e•sec•tion
ven•e•su•ture
ven•in
ven•i•punc•ture
ven•i•sec•tion
Ven•la•fax•ine
ve•noc•ly•sis, *n., pl.* -ses.
ve•no•fi•bro•sis
ve•no•gram
ve•no•graph•ic
ve•nog•ra•phy, *n., pl.* -phies.
ve•nol•o•gy
ven•om
ve•no•mo•sal•i•var•y
ve•no•mo•tor
ven•o•mous
ve•no•per•i•to•ne•os•
  to•my, *n., pl.* -mies.
ve•no•pres•sor
ve•no•scle•ro•sis
ve•nose
ve•nos•i•ty
ve•nos•ta•sis, *n., pl.* -ses.
ven•ot•o•my, *n., pl.* -mies.
ve•nous
ve•nous•ly
ve•nous•ness or ve•nos•i•ty
ve•no•ve•nos•to•my, *n., pl.*
  -mies.
ven•ter

ven•ti•late, *v.*, -lat○ed, -lat•
  ing.
ven•ti•la•tion
Ven•to•lin *Trademark*
ven•trad
ven•tral
ven•tra•lis
ven•tri•cle
ven•tri•co•lum○na, *n., pl.*
  -nae.
ven•tri•cor○nu, *n., pl.*
  -cor○nu○a.
ven•tri•cose
ven•tric○u•lar
ventricular fib•ril•la•tion
ven•tric○u•laris
ven•tric○u•li•tis
ven•tric○u•lo•cis•ter•nos•
  to○my, *n., pl.* -mies.
ven•tric○u•lo•gram
ven•tric○u•log•ra•phy, *n., pl.*
  -phies.
ven•tric○u•lo•punc•ture
ven•tric○u•los•co○py, *n., pl.*
  -pies.
ven•tric○u•los•to○my, *n., pl.*
  -mies.
ven•tric○u•lo•sub•a•rach•
  noid
ven•tric○u•lot○o•o•my, *n., pl.*
  -mies.
ven○tric○u•lus, *n., pl.* ven•
  tric•u○li.
ven•tri•duc•tion
ven•tri•me•sal
ven○tro•fix•a•tion
ven•tro•hys•ter○o•pex○y, *n.,*
  pl. -ies.
ven•tro•lat•er•al
ven•tro•lat•er•al○ly
ven○tro•me•di○al
ven•tro•me•di○al○ly

ven○tro•me•di○an
ven•tros•co○py, *n., pl.* -pies.
ven•tro•sus•pen•sion
ven•tro•ves○i•co•fix•a•tion
ven○u•la
ven○u•lae rec•tae
venulae stel•la•tae
ven○u•lar
ven•ule
Ve•Pes○id *Trademark.*
ve•rap○a•mil
Verapamil SR
ver○a•trine
ver○a•trum
ver•bal
ver•bal○ly
ver•big•er○a•tion
ver•bile
ver•bo•ma•ni○a
ver•di•gris
ver•do•pe•rox○i•dase
Ver○e•lan *Trademark.*
ver•gence
ver○mi•cid○al
ver○mi•cide
ver•mic○u•lar
ver•mic○u•la•tion
ver○mi•cule
ver•mic○u•lose
ver○mi•form
vermiform ap•pen•dix
ver•mif○u•gal
ver○mi•fuge
ver•mil•ion
ver•mil•ion•ec•to○my, *n., pl.*
  -mies.
ver•mil•lion
ver•min, *n., pl.* ver•min.
ver○mi•na•tion
ver○min○o•sis
ver○mi•nous
ver○mi•nous○ly

ver•mis, *n., pl.* ver•mes.
ver•mix
Ver•mox *Trademark.*
ver•nal
ver•nier
ver•nix
vernix ca•se•o•sa
ver•no•ni•a
Verr-Canth *Trademark.*
Ver•rex *Trademark.*
ver•ru•ca, *n., pl.* -cae.
verruca ac•u•mi•na•ta
verruca plan•tar•is
verruca vul•gar•is
ver•ru•ci•form
ver•ru•cose
ver•ru•cose•ness
ver•ru•co•sis
ver•ru•cos•i•ty
ver•ru•cous
ver•ru•ga
verruga per•u•a•na
verruga pe•ru•vi•a•na
Ver•ru•sol *Trademark.*
Ver•sa•pen *Trademark.*
Versapen-K *Trademark.*
Versed *Trademark.*
ver•si•col•or
ver•si•col•ored
ver•sion
ver•sion•al
ver•te•bra, *n., pl.* -brae, -bras.
vertebra den•ta•ta
vertebra mag•na
vertebra pla•na
vertebra prom•i•nens
ver•te•bral
ver•te•bral•ly
Ver•te•bra•ta
ver•te•brate
ver•te•brat•ed

ver•te•brec•to•my, *n., pl.* -mies.
ver•te•bro•chon•dral
ver•te•bro•cos•tal
ver•te•bro•sa•cral
ver•tex, *n., pl.* -tex•es, -ti•ces.
vertex cor•ne•ae
vertex ves•i•cae
ver•ti•cal
ver•ti•cal•ly
ver•ti•cil
ver•ti•cil•late
ver•tig•i•nous
ver•tig•i•nous•ly
ver•tig•i•nous•ness
ver•ti•go, *n., pl.* -ti•goes, -ti•gos, -tig•i•nes.
ver•u•mon•ta•ni•tis
ver•u•mon•ta•num
ver•y low cal•o•rie di•et
ve•si•ca, *n., pl.* -cae.
vesica bi•par•ta
vesica du•plex
vesica fel•le•a
vesica um•bil•i•ca•lis
vesica u•ri•nar•i•a
ves•i•cal
ves•i•cant
ves•i•cate, *v.,* -cat•ed, -cat•ing.
ves•i•ca•tion
ves•i•ca•to•ry, *n., pl.* -ries.
ves•i•cle
ves•i•co•cele
ves•i•co•cer•vi•cal
ves•i•co•pros•tat•ic
ves•i•cot•o•my, *n., pl.* -mies.
ves•i•co•u•ter•ine
ves•i•co•vag•i•nal
ve•sic•u•la, *n., pl.* -lae, -las.
vesicula fel•le•a
vesicula oph•thal•mi•ca

vesicula pros•tat∘i∘ca
vesicula sem∘i∘na•lis
ve•sic∘u•lar
ve•sic∘u•late
ve•sic∘u•la•tion
ve•sic∘u•lec•to∘my, *n., pl.*
  -mies.
ve•sic∘u•li•tis
ve∘sic∘u∘lo•cav∘er•nous
ve•sic∘u•log•ra•phy, *n., pl.*
  -phies.
ve∘sic∘u∘lo•pap∘u•lar
ve∘sic∘u∘lo•pus•tu•lar
ve•sic∘u•lot∘o∘my, *n., pl.*
  -mies.
Ves•prin *Trademark.*
ves•sel
ves•tib∘u•lar
ves•ti•bule
ves∘tib∘u∘lo•spi•nal
ves•tib∘u•lot∘o∘my, *n., pl.*
  -mies.
ves∘tib∘u∘lo∘u∘reth•ral
ves•tib∘u•lum, *n., pl.* -tib•
  u∘la.
ves•tige
ves•tig∘i∘al
ves•tig∘i∘al∘ly
ves•tig∘i∘um, *n., pl.* -tig∘i∘a.
ve∘ta
vet•er•i•nar∘i∘an
vet•er∘i•nar∘y, *n., pl.* -nar•
  ies.
ve•tre•bro•ster•nal
Vi-Day•lin *Trademark.*
Vi-Daylin/F *Trademark.*
vi∘a, *n., pl.* vi∘ae.
vi∘a•bil∘i∘ty, *n., pl.* -ties.
vi∘a•ble
vi∘a•bly
vi∘al
vi∘bex, *n., pl.* -vi∘bi•ces.

Vi•bra-Tabs *Trademark.*
Vi•bra•my•cin *Trademark.*
vi•brate, *v.,* -brat∘ed, -brat•
  ing.
vi•bra∘tion
vi•bra•tor
vi•bra•to∘ry
vib•ri∘o, *n., pl.* -ri∘os.
vib•ri∘oid
vib•ri∘on
vib•ri•o•sis
vi•bris∘sa, *n., pl.* -sae.
vi•bur•num
vi∘car∘i∘ous
vi∘car∘i∘ous∘ly
vi∘car∘i∘ous•ness
vi∘ci•a•nose
vi∘cious
Vicks *Trademark.*
Vi•co∘din *Trademark.*
Vicodin ES *Trademark.*
Vi•con Forte *Trademark.*
Vid∘i∘an ar•ter∘y
Vidian nerve
vig∘il
vig∘il•am•bu•lism
vig∘i•lance
vig∘i•nal
vig∘or
vil∘li in•tes•ti•na•les
villi pleu•ra•les
villi syn∘o•vi•a•les
vil•lose
vil•lo•si•tis
vil•los∘i∘ty, *n., pl.* -ties.
vil•lous
vil•lous∘ly
vil•lus, *n., pl.* vil∘li.
vil•lus•ec•to∘my, *n., pl.* -mies.
vin•blas•tine
Vin∘ca
vin•ca•leu•ko•blas•tine

Vin•cent's an•gi•na
Vincent's in•fec•tion
Vincent's sto•ma•ti•tis
vin•cris•tine
vin•cu•lum, *n.*, *pl.* -cu•lums,
  -cu•la.
vin•e•gar
vin•ic
vi•nous
vi•nyl e•ther
vi•nyl•ben•zene
Vi•o•form *Trademark.*
Vi•o•kase *Trademark.*
vi•o•la tri•col•or
vi•o•la•ceous
vi•o•my•cin
vi•o•ste•rol
vi•per
Vi•per•oi•dae
Vi•ora-A *Trademark.*
vi•rae•mi•a
vi•ral
Vi•ra•nol *Trademark.*
Vi•ra•zole *Trademark.*
Vir•chow's node
vi•re•mi•a
vi•re•mic
vi•res
vir•gin
vir•gi•nal
vir•gin•i•ty
vir•gin•i•um
vi•ri•cid•al
vi•ri•cide
vir•ile
vir•i•les•cence
vir•il•ism
vi•ril•i•ty, *n.*, *pl.* -ties.
vi•ril•i•za•tion
vir•i•lize, *v.*, -lized, -liz•ing.
Vir•i•lon *Trademark.*
vi•ri•on

vir•i•po•tent
vi•ro•log•ic
vi•ro•log•i•cal
vi•ro•log•i•cal•ly
vi•rol•o•gist
vi•rol•o•gy, *n.*, *pl.* -gies.
Vi•rop•tic *Trademark.*
vi•ro•sis, *n.*, *pl.* -ses.
vir•tu•al
vi•ru•cid•al
vi•ru•cide
vir•u•lence
vir•u•len•cy
vir•u•lent
vir•u•lent•ly
vi•ru•lif•er•ous
vi•rus, *n.*, *pl.* vi•rus•es.
vi•rus•like
vi•ru•stat•ic
vis, *n.*, *pl.* vi•res.
vis a ter•go, *n.*, *pl.* vires a
  ter•go.
vis•cer•a, *n.pl.*, *sing.* vis•cus.
vis•cer•al
vis•cer•al•gia
vis•cer•al•ly
vis•cer•o•gen•ic
vis•cer•o•in•hib•i•tor•y
vis•cer•o•meg•a•ly
vis•cer•o•mo•tor
vis•cer•o•parietal
vis•cer•op•to•sis
vis•cer•op•tot•ic
vis•cer•o•sen•so•ry
vis•cer•o•tome
vis•cer•o•to•ni•a
vis•cer•o•ton•ic
vis•cer•o•trop•ic
vis•cer•ot•ro•pism
vis•cid
vis•cid•i•ty
vis•cid•ly

vis•com•e•ter
vis•com•e•try
vis•co•sim•e•ter
vis•co•sim•e•try
vis•cos•i•ty, *n. pl.* -ties.
vis•cous
vis•cum al•bum
vis•cus, *n., pl.* -cer•a.
Vi•sine *Trademark.*
vi•sion
Vis•ken *Trademark.*
Vis•ta•ril *Trademark.*
vis•u•al
visual a•cu•i•ty
visual field
vis•u•al•i•za•tion
visualization ther•a•py
vis•u•al•ize, *v.*, -ized, -iz•ing.
vis•u•al•iz•er
vis•u•o•au•di•to•ry
vis•u•og•no•sis
vis•u•o•psy•chic
vis•u•o•sen•so•ry
vis•u•o•spa•tial
Vi•ta-Kid *Trademark.*
Vita-Min *Trademark.*
Vi•ta•fol *Trademark.*
vi•tal
vital ca•pac•i•ty
vital signs
vi•tal•ism
vi•tal•ist
vi•tal•is•tic
vi•tal•i•ty, *n., pl.* -ties.
vi•tals
vi•ta•mer
vi•ta•min
vi•ta•min•ic
vi•ta•min•i•za•tion
vi•ta•min•ize, *v.*, -ized, -iz•ing.
vi•tel•lin

vi•tel•line
vi•tel•lo•gen•e•sis, *n., pl.* -e•ses.
vi•tel•lo•lu•te•in
vi•tel•lo•ru•bin
vi•tel•lus
vi•ti•a•tion
vi•ti•lig•oi•nous
vit•i•li•go
vitiligo cap•i•tis
vitiligo ir•i•dis
vit•i•li•goid
vit•rec•to•my, *n., pl.* -mies.
vit•re•o•den•tine
vit•re•ous
vitreous hu•mor
vit•re•um
vi•tri•na
vitrina au•di•to•ri•a
vitrina au•ris
vitrina oc•u•laris
vit•ri•ol
vit•ri•ol•ic
Vi•va•cil *Trademark.*
vi•var•i•um, *n., pl.* -var•i•a,
   -var•i•ums.
vi•vax ma•lar•i•a
viv•i•dif•fu•sion
viv•i•fi•ca•tion
viv•i•par•i•ty
vi•vip•a•rous
viv•i•sec•tion•ist
Vi•vo•nex *Trademark.*
Vle•minckx' lo•tion
Vleminckx' so•lu•tion
vo•cal
vocal cords
vocal folds
vo•ces
Vo•ges-Pros•kau•er re•ac•
   tion
Voges-Proskauer test

vo○la
vola ma•nus
vo○lar
vol○a•tile
vol○a•til○i•za•tion
vol○a•til•ize, *v.*, -ized, -iz•ing.
vo•le•mic
vo•li•tion
vo•li•tion•al
Volk•mann's ca○nal
vol•ley, *n., pl.* -leys, -lies.
vol•sel•lum, *n., pl.* -sel•la.
volt-am•me•ter
volt-am•pere
vol•tage
vol•ta○ic
vol•ta•ism
vol•tam•e○ter
Vol•ta•ren *Trademark.*
volt•me•ter
vo•lu•me•nom•e○ter
vol•un•tar○y
voluntary mus•cle
vo•lute
vol○u•tin
vol•vox
vol•vu•lus, *n., pl.* -lus○es.
vo○mer
vo•mer•ine
vom•er○o•bas○i•lar
vom•er○o•na•sal
vom•i○ca
vom○it
vom○i•tive
vom○i•to○ry
vom○i•tu•ri•tion
vom○i•tus
vomitus cru•en•tes

vomitus ma•ri•nus
vomitus ma•tu•ti•nus
Von•trol *Trademark.*
vor•tex, *n., pl.* -ti•ces, -tex○es.
vortex coc•cyg○e○us
vortex cor•dis
vortex len•tis
vor•ti•cel○la, *n., pl.* -lae, -las.
vor•ti•cose
Vo○Sol *Trademark.*
vox, *n., pl.* vo○ces.
vo•yeur
vo•yeur•ism
voy•eur○is•tic
voy•eur○is•ti•cal○ly
vul•ca•ni•za•tion
vul•can•ize, *v.*, -ized, -iz•ing.
vul•ga•ris
vul•ner○o•a•bil○i○ty, *n., pl.* -ties.
vul•ner○o•a•b•le
vul•ner•ar○y, *n., pl.* -ar•ies.
vul•sel○la
vul•sel•lum, *n., pl.* -sel○la.
vul○va, *n., pl.* -vae.
vulva con•ni•vens
vulva hi○ans
vul•val
vul•var
vul•vate
vul•vec•to○my, *n.. pl.* -mies.
vul•vi•form
vul•vi•tis
vul•vo•cru•ral
vul•vo•vag○i•nal
vul•vo•vag○i•ni•tis
Vy•tone *Trademark.*

wad•ding
wad•dle, *v.*, -dled, -dling.
wa∘fer
waist•line
wake•ful•ness
Wal•dey•er's ton•sil•lar ring
Walldeyer's zo∘nal lay∘er
Wal•le•ri∘an de•gen•er∘a•tion
wall•eye, *n.*, *pl.* -eyes.
wall•eyed
wap•per-jawed
war•ble
War•burg ap•pa•rat∘us
ward
war•fa∘rin
warm-blood∘ed
warm•blood∘ed
wart
Wart-Off *Trademark.*
wart∘ed
wart∘y, *adj.* -wart∘i∘er, -i•est.
wash
Was•ser•mann re•ac•tion
Wassermann test
waste
wast∘er
watch•ful wait•ing
Wa•ter Ba•bies *Trademark.*
water blis•ter
water cure
water on the brain
water pick
water pill
water-sol∘u•ble
water tooth•pick
wa•ter•borne

Wa•ter•house-Fri•der•ich•sen syn•drome
wa•ter•shed
Wat•son-Crick mod∘el
Wat•so∘ni∘ous
wat•tage
wat•tle
watt•me•ter
wave•length
weal
wean•ling
wea•sand
Web∘er-Fech•ner law
Web•er's cor•pus•cle
Weber's law
Weber's pouch
Wechs•ler-Belle•vue test
Wechs•ler Scales
Weh•less-105
Wei•gert's meth∘od
weight•less•ness
Weil-Fe•lix re•ac•tion
Weil-Felix test
Weil's dis•ease
Weis•man•ni∘an
Welch ba•cil•lus
Well•bu•trin *Trademark.*
well•ness
wen
Werl•hor's dis•ease
Wer•nick∘e-Kor•sa•koff syn•drome
Wer•ni•cke's cen•ter
Wert•heim's op•er∘a•tion
West•cort *Trademark.*
Wes•ter•gren meth∘od
West•ern blot
wet dream
wet pack

weth○er
Whar•ton's duct
Wharton's jel○ly
wheal
wheal and flare re•sponse
wheel•chair
wheeze, *v.*, wheezed, wheez•
   ing.
whelk
whelp
whip•lash
whip•worm
whirl•pool
whirlpool bath
whis•per, *v.*, -pered, -per•
   ing.
white blood cell
white mat•ter
white•comb
white•head
Whit•field's oint•ment
whit•low
whole blood
who•lism
who•lis•tic
whoop
whoop•ing cough
Wi○dal re•ac•tion
Widal's re•ac•tion
wide-an○gle glau•co○ma
wig•gler
Wi•graine *Trademark.*
wild type
Wil•der•muth's au•ri•cle
Wildermuth's ear
Wil•lis's ar•ter○y
Willis's cir•cle
Willis's cords
Willis's tra•bec○u•lae
Wilms's tu○mor
Wil•son's dis•ease
wind-puff

wind suck•ing
wind•age
wind•bro•ken
wind•burn
wind•burned
wind•chill
wind•gall
wind•pipe
wind•puff
Wins•low's fo•ra•men
Win•strol
win•ter•green
wis•dom tooth
wish-ful•fill•ing
wish-ful•fill•ment
with•draw○al
with•ers
wit•zel•sucht
wob•bles
wohlf•ahr•ti○a
Wohlfahrtia mag•nif○i•ca
Wohlfahrtia o•pa○ca
Wohlfahrtia vig○il
Wolff-Par•kin•son-White syn•
   drome
Wolff○i○an bod○y
Wolffian duct
wolf•ram
wolfs•bane
Wol•las•ton dou•blet
womb
won•der drug
Wool•ner's point
Woolner's tip
Woolner's tu•ber•cle
wool•sort•er's dis•ease
word-as•so•ci•a•tion
   test
word-blind
word blind•ness
word-deaf
word deaf•ness

word sal∘ad
work-up
work∘up
worm
Wor•mi∘an bone
worm•seed
worm•wood
wor•ried well
wort
Woulff bot•tle
wound
Wright's stain
wrin•kle
Wris•berg's car•ti•lage
Wrisberg's gan•gli∘on
Wrisberg's nerve

wrist
wrist•drop
wri•ter's cramp
wry•neck
Wu•che•re•ri∘a
wu•che•re•ri•a•sis
Wy•a•mine *Trademark.*
Wy•a•my•cin E *Trademark.*
Wyamycin S *Trademark.*
Wy•a•noids *Trademark.*
Wy•cil•lin *Trademark.*
Wy•dase *Trademark.*
Wy•ge•sic *Trademark.*
Wy∘mox *Trademark.*
Wy•ten•sin *Trademark.*

X Y Z

X chro•mo•some
X-dis•ease
X-ir•ra•di•ate
X-ir•ra•di•a•tion
X-linked
X-ra•di•a•tion
x-ray, *n., v.,* x-rayed, x-ray•ing
x-ray ther∘a∘py
Xan∘ax *Trademark.*
xan•than
xan•thate
xan•the•las•ma
xan•thene
xan•thic
xan•thin
xan•thine
xan∘tho•chro•mat∘ic
xan∘tho•chro•mi∘a
xan∘tho•chro•mic
xan∘tho•cy•a•nop•si∘a
xan∘tho•gran∘u•lo∘ma, *n., pl.* -mas, -ma∘ta.

xan∘tho∘ma, *n., pl.* -mas, -ma∘ta.
xan∘tho•ma•to•sis
xan•thom∘a•tous
xan•thone
xan∘tho•phyll
xan∘tho•pro•te∘ic
xan∘tho•pro•tein
xan•thop•si∘a
xan•thop•sin
xan•thop•ter∘in
xan∘tho•sine
xan∘tho•sis
xan•thous
xan•thu•re•nic
xe∘nic
xe•ni•cal∘ly
xen∘o•bi•ol∘o∘gy, *n., pl.* -gies.
xen∘o•bi•ot∘ic
xen∘o•di•ag•no•sis
xen∘o•di•ag•nos•tic
xen∘o•ge•ne∘ic

xen○o•graft
xen○o•me•ni○a
xen○on
xen○o•par○a•site
xen○o•pho•bi○a
xen•oph•thal•mi○a
Xen•op•syl○la
Xenopsylla che○o•pis
Xen○o•pus
Xe○rac *Trademark.*
xe•ran•tic
xe○ro•der○ma
xeroderma pig•men•
  to•sum
xe○ro•me•ni○a
xe○ro•myc•te•ri○a
xe○ro•pha•gi○a
xe•roph•a○gy
xe•roph•thal•mi○a
xe•roph•thal•mic
xe○ro•ra•di○og•ra•phy, *n.,*
  pl. -phies.
xe○ro•sis
xerosis con•junc•ti•vae
xerosis in•fan•ti•lis
xe○ro•sto•mi○a
xe○ro•tes
xe•rot○ic
xiph○i•ster•nal
xiph○i•ster•num, *n., pl.*
  -ster○na.
xiph○o•cos•tal
xiph○o•dyn○i○a
xiph•oid
xi•phoi•dal
xiph•oi•di•tis
xi•phop○a•gus
X ray or x-ray
Xue
xy•lene
xy•li•tol
Xy•lo•caine *Trademark.*

xy•lo•ke•tose
xy○lol
xy•lose
xy•lu•lose
xys•ma
xys•ter
Y chro•mo•some
yaw
yaw○ey
yaws
yeast
yel•low fe○ver
yellow jack○et
yellow spot
yellow lo•cust
yer○ba ma○té
yer•sin○i○a pes•tis
yilt
yo-yo di•et•ing
Yo•con *Trademark.*
Yo•dox○in *Trademark.*
yo○ga
yo•ghurt
yo•gurt
yo•him•bine
Yo•hi•mex *Trademark.*
yoke, *v.,* yoked, yok•ing.
yolk
yolk sac
yolk stalk
y○per•ite
yp•sil○i•form
yt•ter•bi○um
yt•tri○um
yup•pie flu
Yu•to•par *Trademark.*
Z-plas○ty
Za•no•sar *Trademark.*
Zan•tac *Trademark.*
Zan•thox○y•lum
Za•ron•tin *Trademark.*

Za•rox○o•lyn *Trademark.*
ze•a•tin
ze•ax•an•thin
Zee•man ef•fect
Zef○a•zone *Trademark.*
ze○in
Ze•nate *Trademark.*
ze•o•lite
Zeph○i•ran *Trademark.*
Zeph•rex *Trademark.*
ze○ro, *n., pl.* ze○ros, ze○roes.
Zes•to•ret○ic *Trademark.*
Zes•tril *Trademark.*
Ze○tar *Trademark.*
Zi○ac
zi•do•vu•dine
Zim•mer•mann re•ac•tion
Zimmermann test
Zi•na•cef *Trademark.*
zinc
zinc oint•ment
zinc ox○ide
zin•cif•er•ous
zinc•oid
Zinc○on *Trademark.*
Zin•ker's flu○id
Zinn's lig○a•ment
zir•co•ni○um
Zith•ro•max *Trademark.*
zo○a
zo○a•can•tho•sis, *n.,*
  pl. -ses.
zo•an•thro○py, *n., pl.*
  -pies.
Zo○cor *Trademark.*
zo•et○ic
zo•e•trope
zo○ic
Zo•la•dex *Trademark.*
Zo•li•cef *Trademark.*
Zöl•lner's lines
Zo•loft

Zol•pi•dem
Zo•lyse *Trademark.*
zo○na, *n., pl.* zo○nae, zo○nas.
zona pel•lu•ci○da, *n., pl.*
  zonae pel•lu•ci•dae.
zona in•ter•me•di○a
zo○nal
zo•nal○ly
zona pel•lu•ci○da
zona re•tic○u•lar○is
zo•na○ry
zo•nate
zo•nat○ed
Zone-A *Trademark.*
zo•nes•the•sia
zo•nif○u•gal
zo•nip○e•tal
zo•nu○la, *n., pl.* -lae, -las.
zonula ad•hae•rens
zonula cil•i•a•ris
zonula oc•clu•dens
zon○u•lar
zon•ule
zonule of Zinn
zo•nu•li•tis
zo•nu•ly•sis
zo○o•der•mic
zo○o•e•ras•ti○a
zo○o•ge•ne•ous
zo○o•gen○ic
zo•og○e•nous
zo○o•ge•o•graph○ic
zo○o•ge•o•graph○ical
zo○o•ge•o•graph○i•
  cal○ly
zo•o○ge•og•ra•phy, *n., pl.*
  -phies.
zo○o•gle○a
zo○o•gle○al
zo○o•gloe○a, *n., pl.* -gle○as,
  -gloe•as, -gle○ae, -gloe○ae.
zo•og•o•ny

zo○o•graft
zo•oid
zo○o•lag•ni○a
Zo○o•mas•tig○i○na
zo○o•on, n., pl. zo○o•a.
zo○o•no•sis, n., pl. -ses.
zo○o•not○ic
zo○o•par○a•site
zo○o•par○a•sit○ic
zo○o•pa•thol○o○gy, n., pl.
  -gies.
zo○o•oph○a•gous
zo○o•phile
zo○o•phil○i○a
zo•oph○i•lism
zo•oph○i•list
zo○o•phil•lic
zo•oph○i•lous
zo○o•pho•bi○a
zo○o•plas•tic
zo○o•plas○ty, n., pl. -ties.
zo○o•pro•phy•lax○is
zo•op•si○a
zo○o•spore
zo○o•ste•rol
zo○o•tech•nics
zo○o•ther○a○py, n., pl. -pies.
zo○o•trope
zo○o•troph○ic
Zor•prin Trademark.
zos•ter
zoster au•ric○u•laris
zoster bra•chi•a•lis
zoster fa•ci•a•lis
zoster fem○o•ra•lis
zoster oph•thal•mi•cus
zos•ter bra•chi○a•lis
zos•ter fa•ci○a•lis
zos•ter○i•form
zos•ter•oid
Zos•trix Trademark.
Zo•vi•rax Trademark.

Zy•done Trademark.
zy•ga•poph○y•sis, n.,
  pl. -ses.
zyg•i○on, n., pl. -gi○a,
  -gi•ons.
zy○go•dac•ty○ly
zy○go•gen•e○sis
zy○go•ge•net○ic
zy○go○ma, n., pl. -ma○ta,
  -mas.
zy○go•mat○ic
zygomatic arch
zygomatic bone
zygomatic proc•ess
zy○go•mat○i•co•au•ric○u•
  lar○is, n., pl. -lar○es.
zy○go○mat○i○co•facial
zy○go○mat○i○co•max•il•
  lar○y
zy○go○mat○i○co•or•bi•tal
zy○go○mat○i○co•tem•
  po•ral
zy○go•mat○i•cus
zy○go•max•il•lar○y
zy○go•mor•phic
zy○go•mor•phism
zy○go•mor•phous
zy○go•mor•phy
Zy○go•my•ce•tes
zy○go•my•ce•tous
zy○go•sis, n., pl. -ses.
zy○gos○i○ty
zy○go•sperm
zy○go•spore
zy○go•style
zy•gote
zy•go•tene
zy•got○ic
zy•got○i•cal○ly
Zy•lo•prim Trademark.
zy•mase
zy○mo•gen

zy○mo•gen○ic
zy•mog○e○nous
zy○mo•hy•drol○y•sis, *n., pl.*
  -ses.
zy•moid
zy○mo•log○ic
zy•mol○o•gist
zy•mol○o○gy, *n., pl.* -gies.
zy•mol○y•sis
Zy•mon○e•ma

zy○mo•plas•tic
zy○mo•pro•tein
zy○mo•san
zy○mo•scope
zy•mo•sis, *n., pl.* -ses.
zy•mos•then○ic
zy•mot○ic
zy•mot○i•cal○ly
Zyr•tec *Trademark.*

MEDICAL
WEB SITES

MEDICAL WEB SITES

http://www.amhrt.org/

The official site of the American Heart Foundation provides information to health care professionals and the public about heart disease and stroke.

http://www.fda.gov/fdahomepage.html

The home page of the U.S. Food and Drug Adminstration provides links to information for consumers, industry, and health professionals.

http://www.healthfinder.gov/

Healthfinder is a service of the U.S. Department of Health and Human Services. It links visitors to information on all types of health issues.

http://www.hhs.gov/

The home page of the Department of Health and Human Services acts as a gateway to its many offices.

http://www.cdc.gov/

The Web site of the Centers for Disease Control and Prevention provide information and statistics on infectious diseases in the United States.

http://www.hcfa.gov/

The latest information on Medicare and Medicaid is available at the site of the Health Care Financing Administration.

http://www.samhsa.gov/

The Substance Abuse and Mental Health Services Administration's Web site provides practical information and statistics on drug and alcohol abuse and mental health.

http://www.nih.gov/

The site of the National Institutes of Health provides information on the workings of the NIH plus updates on all conditions and diseases being studied at the institutes.

http://www.nci.nih.gov/

The National Cancer Institute site provides up-to-date information on the diagnosis and treatment of all kinds of cancer to patients and physicians.

http://www.nhgri.nih.gov/

The National Human Genome Research Institute site keeps us up-to-date with the latest findings of the Human Genome Project.

http://www.cidr.jhmi.edu/

The Center for Inherited Disease Research coordinates research of investigators seeking to find the causes for inherited diseases.

http://www.cdc.gov/nchstp/hiv_aids/hiv info.htm

This division of the Centers for Disease Control and Prevention provides the latest information on AIDS prevention and treatment.

http://www.cdc.gov/travel/travel.html

This site provides information on outbreaks of disease around the world and the precautions and requirements necessary for travelers.

http://www.nimh.nih.gov/publicat/index.htm

The National Institute of Mental Health site offers information for the public on specific mental disorders, their diagnosis and treatment. Eating disorders, depression, panic attacks, and Alzhiemers disease are a few of the topics covered.

http://www.nih.gov/news/infoline.htm

The Information Line page of the National Institutes of Health lists phone numbers through which one can get information on a variety of health issues.

http://altmed.od.nih.gov/

The federal government's Office of Alternative Medicine maintains this site, which offers the latest scientific information on a variety of alternative treatments including acupuncture, homeopathic medicine, and medicinal herbs.

http://www.cancer.org/frames.html

The site of the American Cancer Society offers information on preventing and coping with cancer.

http://www.who.org/

The site of the World Health Organization offers statistics, publications, travel information, and information on the organization's programs.